GET ONLINE.

trpress.cengage.com/comp

T he easy-to-navigate website for **COMP: Write** offers guidance on key topics in writing, proofreading, research, and grammar in a variety of engaging formats, including tutorials and podcasts. You also have the opportunity to ne and check your understanding via interactive quizzes and hcards. Videos of professional writers discussing their proaches and experiences provide inspiration for your own ting. And, in order to make **COMP: Write** an even better rning tool, we invite you to speak up about your experience n **COMP: Write** by completing a survey form and sending our comments.

Get online and discover the following resources:

Writing Tutorials
Online Handbook
Documentation Guidance
Interactive Grammar Quizzes
Videos
Grammar Podcasts
Flashcards
Speak Up!

Number of hours the average student spends online every day.

At **4ltrpress.cengage.com/comp**, you'll find tools that foster an exciting learning environment.

71

The percentage of students who go online to study for a class.

With **COMP: Write**, you have even more reasons to study online! Each new book comes with free access to **4ltrpress.cengage.com/comp**, where you will find a variety of ways to practice and refine your understanding of key concepts.

COMP
Are you in?

an innovative concept in teaching and learning solutions designed to best reach today's students

COMP: Write
Randall VanderMey, Verne Meyer, John Van Rys, Pat Sebranek

Senior Publisher: Lyn Uhl

Executive Editor: Monica Eckman

Acquisitions Editor: Margaret Leslie

Assistant Editor: Amy Haines

Editorial Assistant: Elizabeth Ramsey

Media Editor: Amy Gibbons

Marketing Manager: Jennifer Zourdos

Senior Marketing Communications Manager: Stacey Purviance

Senior Content Project Manager, Editorial Production: Margaret Park Bridges

Art Directors: Jill Haber, Jill Ort

Print Buyer: Sue Spencer

Text Permissions Account Manager: Margaret Chamberlain-Gaston

Production Service: Sebranek, Inc.

Senior Photo Permissions Account Manager: Deanna Ettinger

Design Assistant: Hannah Wellman

Cover Image: © Getty Images

Compositor: Sebranek, Inc.

Sebranek, Inc.: Steven J. Augustyn, April Lindau, Colleen Belmont, Chris Erickson, Mariellen Hanrahan, Dave Kemper, Tim Kemper, Rob King, Chris Krenzke, Lois Krenzke, Mark Lalumondier, Jason C. Reynolds, Janae Sebranek, Lester Smith, Jean Varley

For product information and technology assistance, contact us at
Cengage Learning Customer & Sales Support, 1-800-354-9706
For permission to use material from this text or product,
submit all requests online at **www.cengage.com/permissions**
Further permissions questions can be emailed to
permissionrequest@cengage.com

Library of Congress Control Number: 2009932833

ISBN-13: 978-1-4390-8439-7
ISBN-10: 1-4390-8439-4

Wadsworth
20 Channel Center Street
Boston, MA 02210-1202
USA

Cengage Learning is a leading provider of customized learning solutions with office locations around the globe, including Singapore, the United Kingdom, Australia, Mexico, Brazil, and Japan. Locate your local office at:
international.cengage.com/region

Cengage Learning products are represented in Canada by Nelson Education, Ltd.

For your course and learning solutions, visit **academic.cengage.com**

Purchase any of our products at your local college store or at our preferred online store **www.ichapters.com**.

Printed in the United States of America
1 2 3 4 5 6 7 13 12 11 10 09

BRIEF CONTENTS

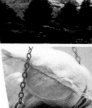

CONTENTS

PART ONE PROCESS

> ### What are LOs?
>
> LOs are Learning Outcomes—what students will gain as they work through each chapter.

© Reuters/CORBIS

© Todd Taulman, 2009 / Used under license from Shutterstock.com

© Supri Suharjoto, 2009 / Used under license from Shutterstock.com

PART TWO FORMS

Personal

Analytical

Persuasive

12 Argumentation 131

13 Persuasion 145

Literary Analysis

14 Analyzing the Arts 159

Practical

Research

© HomeStudio, 2009/ Used under license from Shutterstock.com

19 Researching 223

20 Research Paper 241

21 MLA and APA Styles 251

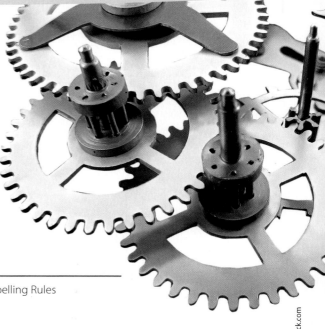

PART THREE HANDBOOK

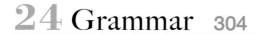
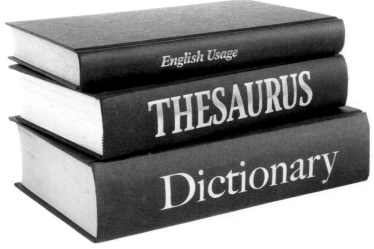

THEMATIC CONTENTS

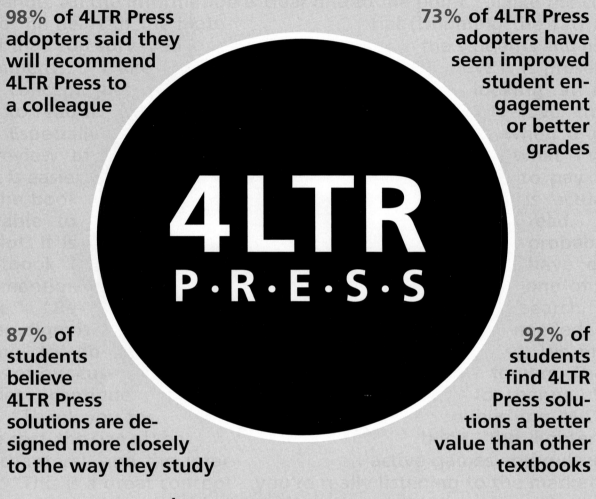
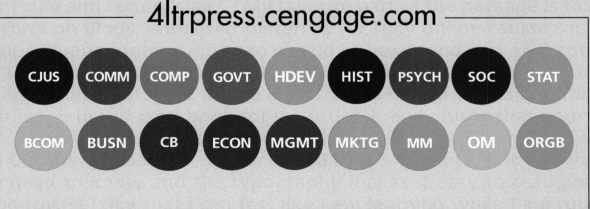

"I am an obsessive rewriter,
doing one draft and then another and another, usually five.
In a way, I have nothing to say but a great deal to add."

—Gore Vidal

1

One Writer's Process

How do you move from a writing assignment to a finished, polished essay? The best strategy is to take matters one step at a time, from your initial planning to your final proofreading, or stated in another way, to approach writing as a process rather than as an end product. Using the **writing process** helps you stay with a piece of writing longer and develop it more thoroughly and thoughtfully. If you, on the other hand, think "end product" right from the start, you will try to do everything all at once and end up with a weak, poorly formed paper.

Accomplished writers know that they can't rush their writing. They do as much planning, drafting, and revising as needed to develop their work. In the quotation on the previous page, author Gore Vidal says that it usually takes five rewrites before he has a worthy piece of writing. You shouldn't rush your writing either—not if you expect to develop strong essays and papers. So promise yourself never again to try to churn out an essay at the last minute. That just doesn't work. Instead, give yourself enough time and space to use the writing process effectively for each new project.

This chapter shows you how student writer Angela Franco followed the process step-by-step to develop an essay for her Environmental Policies class. As you will see, her writing goes through many significant changes before it is ready to publish. After you complete this chapter, you can learn more about each step in the writing process— *getting started*, *planning*, *writing*, *revising*, *editing*, and *publishing*—in the six chapters that follow.

Learning Outcomes

LO1 Initiate the process.

LO2 Plan the writing.

LO3 Write the first draft.

LO4 & **LO5** Complete first and second revisions.

LO6 & **LO7** Edit the writing for style and correctness.

LO8 Complete the final copy.

What do you think?

I focus more on process than on end product when I write.

1	2	3	4	5
strongly agree				strongly disagree

writing process
the steps that a writer should follow to develop a thoughtful and thorough piece of writing

L○1 Initiate the process.

To get started, Angela had to do three things: (1) clearly understand the assignment, (2) select a suitable writing topic, and (3) collect information about it. Without completing these three tasks, she would not be able to do any planning or writing. As author Tom Wolfe says, "There's no use getting into a writing schedule until you've done the reporting [selecting and collecting], and you have the material." Note below how Angela thoughtfully approached her first step in the process.

STUDY THE ASSIGNMENT.

Angela first reviewed the assignment's subject, purpose, audience, form, and **method of assessment**—and responded with notes. In doing so, she established the basics for the work that would follow.

The Assignment

The instructor had given an explicit assignment: Explain in a two- or three-page essay how a recent environmental issue is relevant to the world community. Using *Write* as your guide, format the paper and document sources in APA style.

The project was straightforward, but Angela took time to think about it and take some initial notes. She noted the general subject: "I will write about a recent environmental issue." She considered the purpose: "I need to explain how the issue is relevant to all people. That means I must show how this issue affects my audience—both positively and negatively."

Next, Angela thought about her audience: "Who will read my essay? Probably people like me—neighbors, classmates, and community members. I'll need to keep in mind what they already know and what they need to know." Then she took note of the form: "I'm supposed to write a two- or three-page essay—that sounds formal. I'll need to write a thesis statement, support it, and cite my sources using APA style."

Finally, Angela considered assessment—how she would evaluate her writing throughout

method of assessment
the way in which a piece of writing is evaluated, with a rubric, by peer review, or so on

clustering
a form of brainstorming by freely recording words and phrases around a nucleus word

nucleus word
the central term in a cluster, connecting all other ideas

the process: "I'll use the guidelines and checklists in my book to review and revise my writing. I'll also get feedback from Jeanie and from the writing center."

fyi For each step in the writing process, choose strategies that fit your writing situation. For example, a personal essay in a sociology class may require a great deal of initial reflecting and exploring, while a lab report in a chemistry class may require little or none.

SEARCH FOR A TOPIC.

To begin searching for a specific topic, Angela first considered different types of environmental issues: renewable sources of energy, recycling, air pollution, water pollution, and so on. She decided to consider "water pollution" more closely.

Exploring

Angela explored the issue of water pollution in more detail by **clustering**. Using "water pollution" as her **nucleus word**, she drew from memories, experiences, readings, and class discussions to record related ideas.

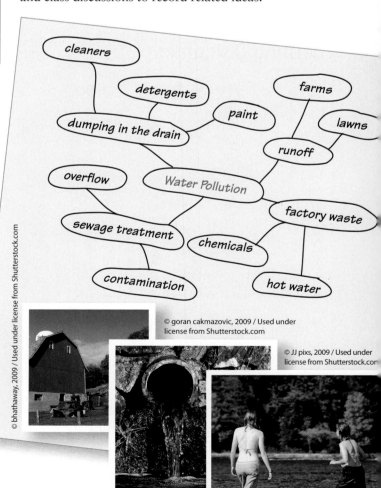

cleaners — detergents — farms — paint — lawns — dumping in the drain — runoff — overflow — Water Pollution — factory waste — sewage treatment — chemicals — contamination — hot water

© goran cakmazovic, 2009 / Used under license from Shutterstock.com

© JJ pixs, 2009 / Used under license from Shutterstock.com

© bhathaway, 2009 / Used under license from Shutterstock.com

The cluster brought to mind an incident that Angela had read about in an article. Improper sewage treatment in a small Canadian community had dangerously polluted the drinking water. To gather her thoughts about this incident, she decided to complete a **freewriting** to get her ideas on paper.

I remember reading an article about problems in a small Canadian town. People actually died. The water they drank was contaminated. This is becoming a problem in developed countries like ours. I thought for a long time this was a problem only in developing countries. So who is responsible for sewage treatment? Who guarantees the safety of our drinking water? How does water get contaminated? Are there solutions for contamination: mercury problems . . .

Angela's Topic

After clustering and freewriting, Angela was ready to choose her topic. Based on her work so far, Angela decided that writing about this specific incident could serve as a worthy topic. It seemed to have the right depth and breadth for a two- or three-page essay. She then rephrased her assignment so that it included her topic: "Explain in a two- or three-page essay how a recent water pollution problem in a small Canadian town is relevant to the world community."

COLLECT INFORMATION.

Once Angela had a suitable topic in mind, she set out to learn more about it. At this point, all she had was her brief freewriting. To get the basic facts straight, she re-read the article in *Maclean's*, a Canadian weekly newsmagazine. After the reading, she answered the journalistic questions (5 W's and H) about the incident.

Angela found out **who** had been involved in the incident—the farm operators, wastewater officials, and the Walkerton residents. She established **what** the real problem was—the clean, fresh water supply depleted,

replaced with a contaminated supply that spread *E. coli* bacteria and caused disease. She knew **where** this had happened (Walkerton, Ontario), **when** (May 2000), and **why** (improper regulation and human error). Angela's answer to **how** the pollution occurred involved groundwater from irrigation, untreated sewage, and runoff.

Researching

Angela continued her research by taking more notes from the article. She also consulted additional sources of information, including other periodicals and an environmental group. She recorded all of the essential data on each source and then listed the specific details related to her topic. Here are some of her additional notes from the *Maclean's* article.

Nikiforuk, Andrew. (2000, June 12). "When water kills." <u>Maclean's</u>. 18–21.

- Factory farms hold as many as 25,000 cattle

- Manure contains things like heavy metals (from mineral-rich feed), nutrients, and pathogens (E. coli)

- 8,000 hogs can produce as much waste as 240,000 people

- Six rural Ontario counties had high E. coli 0157 levels in 1990 and 1995

fyi During your own research, you may want to create or copy visuals (charts, graphs, or photos) that clarify details about your topic. If you copy an item, be sure to record the source as well. To create a graphic, gather the data that you want to present, and then choose the type of graphic (table, pie graph, bar graph) that best displays your point.

freewriting
a form of nonstop writing used during the early stages of the writing process to collect thoughts and ideas

L○2 Plan the writing.

During her **planning**, the next main step in the process, Angela first made sure that she still had a strong interest in her topic and that she had gathered enough solid information to write about it. Since she still felt strongly about her topic, she was ready to complete these planning tasks: (1) form a thesis, (2) select an appropriate method of organization for her essay, and (3) outline or organize her research. Completing each one of these tasks helped her focus her efforts for writing.

Planning is at the core of great writing.

FORM A THESIS STATEMENT.

A **thesis statement** expresses what a writer wants to say about a topic. It makes a specific claim about the topic or highlights a particular part of it. Angela wrote three versions of a statement before it expressed her claim: "The water pollution incident in Walkerton, Ontario *(topic)*, had a devastating effect that every town should learn from *(claim)*." (See page 31 for more information.)

SELECT AN ORGANIZATION PATTERN.

Once Angela formed her thesis statement, she was ready to think about the structure of her essay. Very often, a thesis statement will suggest a particular type of organization. (See pages 32-33 for more information.) Through freewriting Angela was able to sort through her options and decide on one method: "I see that I can use a cause-effect or a problem-solution pattern. But after making two quick lists of the main points, using both patterns, I've decided to use the problem-solution approach. I'll still talk about causes and effects in my essay—they just won't be front and center.

"With the problem-solution approach, I need to first present the problem clearly so that the reader can fully understand it and see why it's important. Then I need to explore solutions to the problem—maybe what they did in Walkerton, and what we all need to do, to make water safe."

planning
the thinking and organizing that go into establishing a direction and structure for writing

thesis statement
a sentence or set of sentences that sums up the central idea of a piece of writing

ORGANIZE THE RESEARCH.

With her method of organization in place, Angela could go about putting her research in order.

A writer can organize the ideas that support or explain the thesis in several ways—either by listing the ideas, outlining the information, or by using a graphic organizer. (See pages 34-37 for examples.) Angela chose the graphic organizer below. Note how it groups supporting information around the core element of the problem-solution structure.

Problem/Solution

Parts of the Problem — **Problem** — Future Implications

Causes of the Problem

Possible Solutions

fyi Many of your essays will be organized according to one basic method or approach. However, within that basic structure, you may want to include other methods. For example, while developing a comparison essay, you may do some describing or classifying. In other words, you should choose methods of development that (1) help you understand the topic and (2) help the reader understand your message.

L○3 Write the first draft.

Writing a **first draft** gave Angela an opportunity to connect the facts and details about her topic. She understood that this draft was a first look at a developing writing idea, and that the draft would go through a series of changes before it said what she wanted it to say. In the beginning paragraph, she introduces her topic in an interesting way and states her thesis. In the middle paragraphs, she develops or explains her thesis using her planning (graphic organizer) as a general guide. In the closing paragraph, see links her topic to the world community.

Running Head: WATER WOES   3

Water Woes

The writer uses a series of images to get the reader's attention.

It's a hot day. Several people just finished mowing their lawns. A group of bicyclists—more than 3,000—have been passing through your picturesque town all afternoon. Dozens of Little Leaguers are batting, running, and sweating. What do all these people have in common? They all drink lots of tap water, especially on hot summer days. They also take for granted that the water is clean and safe. But in reality, the water they drink could be contaminated and pose a serious health risk.

The thesis statement introduces the subject.

That's just what happened in Walkerton, Ontario, where a water pollution incident had a devastating effect that every town can learn from.

The writer describes the cause of the problem.

What happened in Walkerton, Ontario? Heavy rains fell on May 12. It wasn't until May 21 that the townspeople were advised to boil their drinking water. The rains washed cattle manure into the town well. The manure contained E coli, a type of bacteria. E coli is harmless to cattle. It can make people sick. Seven days after the heavy rains, people began calling public health officials. The warning came too late. Two people had already died (Wickens, 2000).

The writer cites the source of facts and details.

Once Walkerton's problem was identified, the solutions were known. The government acted quickly to help the community and to clean the water supply. One Canadian newspaper reported that a $100,000 emergency fund was set up to help families with expenses. Bottled water for drinking and containers of bleach for sanitizing and cleaning were donated by local businesses.

So what messed up Walkerton? Basically, people screwed up! According to one news story, a flaw in the water treatment system allowed the bacteria-infested water to enter the well. The manure washed into the well, but the chlorine should have killed the deadly bacteria. In Walkerton, the PUC group fell asleep at the wheel.

(continued on page 8)

first draft
the initial writing in which the writer connects facts and details about the topic

At last, the Provincial Clean Water Agency restored the main water and sewage systems by flushing out all of the town's pipes and wells. The ban on drinking Walkerton's water was finally lifted seven months after the water became contaminated.

Could any good come from Walkerton's tragedy? Does it have a silver lining? It is possible that more people are aware that water may be contaminated. Today people are beginning to take responsibility for the purity of the water they and their families drink. In the end, more and more people will know about the dangers of contaminated water—without learning it the hard way.

The writer covers the solutions that resolved the problem.

The concluding paragraph stresses the importance of public awareness.

A Working Bibliography

As she researched her topic, Angela kept a working bibliography—a list of resources that she could use to find information for her essay. During the writing process, she deleted some resources, added others, and edited her final reference list (page 17) according to APA style.

Working Bibliography

Wickens, Barbara. (2000, June 5). Tragedy in Walkerton. Maclean's 113 (23): 34-36.
Phone interview with Alex Johnson, Walkerton Police Department
Department, 23 September 2007.
Blackwell, Thomas. (2001, January 9). Walkerton doctor defends response. The Edmonton Journal. http://edmontonjournal.com.
Nikiforuk, Andrew. (2000, June 12). When water kills. Maclean's 18-21.

L◯4 Complete a first revision.

After finishing her first draft, Angela set it aside for a while. The time away helped her "see" her writing more clearly when she did review it. During her **revising**, she concentrated on three key traits: ideas (content), organization, and **voice**. Angela knew that these traits are especially important because they comprise the core substance of the message. She wrote notes to herself to keep her revising on track.

Angela's Comments

I need to give my opening more energy.

Does my thesis still fit the paper?— Yes.

Using time sequence, put sentences in better order.

Move this paragraph—it interrupts the discussion of causes.

Running Head: WATER WOES   3

Water Woes

an unusually   Saturday afternoon ⊙

It's ˄ a hot ~~day.~~ Several people just finished mowing their lawns. A group of bicyclists, ~~more than 3,000 have been passing through your picturesque town all afternoon.~~ ˄ *pedal up the street* ⊙ Dozens of Little Leaguers are batting, running, and sweating. What do all these people have in common? They all drink lots of tap water, especially on hot summer days. They also take for granted that the water is clean and safe. But in reality, the water they drink could be contaminated and pose a serious health risk. That's just what happened in Walkerton, Ontario, where a water pollution incident had a devastating effect that every town can learn from.

What happened in Walkerton, Ontario? Heavy rains fell on May 12. ⌈It wasn't until May 21 that the townspeople were advised to boil their drinking water.⌉ The rains washed cattle manure into the town well. The manure contained E coli, a type of bacteria. E coli is harmless to cattle. It can make people sick. Seven days after the heavy rains, people began calling public health officials. The warning came too late. Two people had already died (Wickens, 2000).

Once Walkerton's problem was identified, the solutions were known. The government acted quickly to help the community and to clean the water supply. One Canadian newspaper reported that a $100,000 emergency fund was set up to help families with expenses. Bottled water for drinking and containers of bleach for basic sanitizing and cleaning were donated by local businesses.

(continued on page 10)

revising
improving a draft through large-scale changes such as adding, deleting, rearranging, and reworking

voice
the tone of the writing, often affected by the personality of the writer

My voice here is too informal. Also need transitions.

So what *went wrong in* ~~messed up~~ Walkerton? *Human error was a critical factor. First,* ~~Basically, people screwed up!~~ According to one news story, a flaw in the water treatment system allowed the bacteria-infested water to enter the well. *Even after* The manure washed into the well, ~~the~~ chlorine should have killed the deadly bacteria. In Walkerton, the ~~PUC group fell asleep at the wheel.~~

Explain "fell asleep." Move paragraph three here and combine.

~~At last,~~ *In addition,* the Provincial Clean Water Agency restored the main water and sewage systems by flushing out all of the town's pipes and wells. The ban on drinking Walkerton's water was finally lifted seven months after the water became contaminated.

Cut the cliches.

Could any good come from Walkerton's tragedy? ~~Does it have a silver lining?~~ It is possible that more people are aware that water may be contaminated. Today people are beginning to take responsibility for the purity of the water they and their families drink. In the end, more and more people will know about the dangers of contaminated water—without learning it the hard way.

Public Utilities Commission was responsible for overseeing the testing and treating of the town's water, but they failed to monitor it properly. Apparently, shortcuts were taken when tracking the water's chlorine level, and as a result, some of the water samples were mislabeled. There was also a significant delay between the time that the contamination was identified and the time it was reported.

L◯5 Complete a second revision.

Angela also asked a writing peer to review her work. The comments in the margin indicate that this person gave Angela's work a great deal of thought and provided excellent advice. His first comment, for example, offers a specific suggestion rather than a quick observation like, "Your opening needs work." Angela carefully considered all of the reviewer's comments before making changes. Most significantly, she wrote a new opening and a new closing.

Angela's Changes

Reviewer's Comments

Running Head: WATER WOES   3

Water Woes

WARNING: City tap water is polluted with animal waste. Using the water for drink-ing, cooking, or bathing could cause sickness or death.

According to the Seirra Club, run-off pollutants from farm cites are steadily seeping into our streams, lakes, reservoirs and wells. Because much of our drinking water comes from these resources warnings like the one above are already posted in a number of U.S. and Canadian communities, and many more postings will be needed (Sierra Club, n.d.). As the Seirra Club argues, the pollution and related warnings are serious, and failure to take them seriously could be deadly. For example, a few years ago the citizens of Walkerton Ontario learned that the water that they believed to be clean was actually poisoned.

The events
~~What happened~~ in Walkerton, ~~Ontario? Heavy rains fell~~ on May 12. ~~The~~ *began*
~~rains~~ *, 2000, when heavy rains* washed cattle manure into the town well. The manure contained E coli, a type of bacteria. E coli is harmless to cattle. It can make people sick. Seven
to complain of nausea and diarrhea⊙
days after the heavy rains, people began calling public health officials. It wasn't until May 21 that the townspeople were advised to boil their drinking water. The
, and more than 2,000 were ill
warning came too late. Two people had already died (Wickens, 2000).
Several factors contributed to the terrible tragedy in Walkerton, including human error.
~~So what went wrong in Walkerton? Human error was a critical factor.~~ First,
The Edmonton Journal
according to ~~one news story,~~ a flaw in the water treatment system allowed the
(Blackwell 2001)⊙
bacteria-infested water to enter the well. Even after the manure washed into the well, the chlorine should have killed the deadly bacteria. In Walkerton, the Public Utilities Commission was responsible for overseeing the testing and treating of the town's water, but they failed to monitor it properly. Apparently, shortcuts were

(continued on page 12)

Reviewer's Comments

Could you make the opening more relevant and urgent?

Could you clarify your focus on the topic?

Add the year and other specific details.

Make sure you document all source material—you have just one citation in your draft.

Use active voice.

taken when tracking the water's chlorine level, and as a result, some of the water samples were mislabeled. There was also a significant delay between the time that the contamination was identified and the time it was reported.

Once Walkerton's problem was identified, ~~the solutions were known.~~ The government acted quickly to help the community ~~and to clean the water supply.~~ *The Edmonton Journal* ~~One Canadian newspaper~~ reported that a $100,000 emergency fund was set up to help families with expenses. *Local businesses donated* Bottled water for drinking and containers of bleach for basic sanitizing and cleaning ~~were donated by local businesses~~. In addition, the Provincial Clean Water Agency restored the main water and sewage systems by flushing out all of the town's pipes and wells. The ban on drinking Walkerton's water was finally lifted (2001) seven months after the water became contaminated.

As the Sierra Club warned and the citizens of Walkerton learned, water purity is a life-and-death issue. Fortunately, both the United States and Canada have been addressing the problem. For example, since 2001, more states and provinces are tightening their clean-water standards, more communities have begun monitoring their water quality, and more individuals have been using water-filtration systems, bottled water, or boiled tap water. However, a tragedy like that in Walkerton could happen again. To avoid such horror, all of us must get involved by demanding clean tap water in our communities and by promoting the policies and procedures needed to achieve that goal.

Consider adding details—calling readers to action and restating your thesis.

fyi Ask at least one or two trusted peers to review your work early in the writing process to make sure that you're heading in the right direction. And if necessary, ask the staff in your school's writing center to help you. *Note:* Treat each reviewer's comments as suggestions; after carefully considering them, act on those that you truly agree with.

© Focon, 2009 / Used under license from Shutterstock.com

LO6 Edit the writing for style.

Once Angela had made all of the necessary revisions, she was ready to **edit** a clean copy of her writing for style and readability. To do so, she focused on these two traits: word choice and sentence fluency. Her goal was to make her writing as clear and engaging as possible. **The first page of Angela's edited copy is shown below.**

Running Head: WATER WOES   3

in Walkerton
Water Woes

> Warning: City tap water is polluted with animal waste. Using the water for drinking, cooking, or bathing could cause sickness or death.

The writer changes the title.

According to the Seirra Club, run-off pollutants from farm cites are steadily seeping into our streams, lakes, reservoirs and wells. Because much of our drinking water comes from these resources warnings like the one above are already posted in a number of U.S. and Canadian communities, and many more postings ~~will~~ *might* be needed *in the future* (n.d.). As the Seirra Club argues, the pollution and related warnings are serious, and failure to take them seriously could be deadly. For example, a few years ago the citizens of Walkerton Ontario learned that the water that they believed to be clean was *tragically* ~~actually~~ poisoned.

She qualifies her statement, replacing "will" with "might."

The events in Walkerton began on May 12, 2000, when heavy rains washed cattle manure into the town well. The manure contained ~~E coli. a~~ *commonly called* bacteria. *While E Coli* E coli is harmless to cattle. It can make people sick. Seven days after the heavy rains, people began calling public health officials to complain of nausea and diarrhea. It wasn't until May 21 that the townspeople were advised to boil their drinking water. The warning came too late. Two people had already died, and more than 2,000 were ill (Wickens, 2000).

She rewrites and combines several choppy sentences.

Several factors contributed to the ~~terrible~~ tragedy in Walkerton, including human error. First, according to *The Edmonton Journal*, a flaw in the water treatment system allowed the ~~bacteria~~-infested water to enter the well (Blackwell 2001). Even after the manure washed into ~~the~~ *Walkerton's* well, the chlorine should have killed the deadly bacteria. In Walkerton, the Public . . .

Angela deletes unnecessary words and adds one for clarity.

editing
refining a draft in terms of word choice and sentence style and checking it for conventions

LO7 Edit the writing for correctness.

Next, Angela edited her writing for correctness. To be as thorough as possible, she focused on one **convention** at a time: spelling, grammar, mechanics, and so on. She referred to *Write* when she had any questions about grammar or mechanics, and she used the spell-checker and grammar-checker on her word-processing program. In addition, she asked a tutor in the writing center to help her refine the essay. The tutor explained a few correctness issues and pointed out weaknesses in her documentation. **The first page of Angela's corrected copy is shown below.**

The writer corrects errors that the spell-checker did not pick up.

She adds a comma after the city and after the province.

She adds periods and italicizes "E. coli" to show that it is a scientific term.

She adds a comma to the citation.

Running Head: WATER WOES   3

Water Woes in Walkerton

> *Warning: City tap water is polluted with animal waste. Using the water for drinking, cooking, or bathing could cause sickness or death.*

According to the Sierra Club, run-off pollutants from farm sites are steadily seeping into our streams, lakes, reservoirs, and wells. Because much of our drinking water comes from these resources, warnings like the one above are already posted in a number of U.S. and Canadian communities, and many more postings might be needed in the future (n.d.). As the Sierra Club argues, the pollution and related warnings are serious, and failure to take them seriously could be deadly. For example, a few years ago the citizens of Walkerton, Ontario, learned that the water that they believed to be clean was tragically poisoned.

The events in Walkerton began on May 12, 2000, when heavy rains washed cattle manure into the town well. The manure contained bacteria commonly called E. coli. While E. coli is harmless to cattle, it can make people sick. Seven days after the heavy rains, people began calling public health officials to complain of nausea and diarrhea. It wasn't until May 21 that the townspeople were advised to boil their drinking water. The warning came too late. Two people had already died, and more than 2,000 were ill (Wickens, 2000).

Several factors contributed to the tragedy in Walkerton, including human error. First, according to *The Edmonton Journal*, a flaw in the water treatment system allowed the infested water to enter the well (Blackwell, 2001). Even after the manure washed into Walkerton's well, the chlorine should have . . .

---

conventions
the standard rules for spelling, punctuation, mechanics, usage, and grammar

L○8 Complete the final copy.

While formatting her edited essay, Angela added a heading and page numbers. She also added more documentation and a ref-erence list at the end, following APA documentation style. She then **proofread** her final copy before submitting it. (Because her instructor said that no title page or abstract was required, Angela did not produce them.)

Complete details are supplied in the heading.

The title is finalized. The warning is emphasized in red.

An appropriate typeface and size are used.

Running Head: CLEAN WATER   3

Angela Franco

Professor Kim Van Es

Environmental Policies

October 19, 2009

Clean Water Is Everyone's Business

Warning: City tap water is polluted with animal waste. Using the water for drinking, cooking, or bathing could cause sickness or death.

According to the Sierra Club, runoff pollutants from farm sites are steadily seeping into our streams, lakes, reservoirs, and wells. Because much of our drinking water comes from these resources, warnings like the one above are already posted in a number of U.S. and Canadian communities, and many more postings might be needed in the future (n.d.). As the Sierra Club argues, the pollution and related warnings are serious, and failure to take them seriously could be deadly. For example, a few years ago the citizens of Walkerton, Ontario, learned that the water that they believed to be clean was tragically poisoned.

The events in Walkerton began on May 12, 2000, when heavy rains washed cattle manure into the town well. The manure contained bacteria commonly called *E. coli*. While *E. coli* is harmless to cattle, it can make people sick. Seven days after the heavy rains, people began calling public health officials to complain of nausea and diarrhea. It wasn't until May 21 that the townspeople were advised to boil their drinking water. The warning came too late. Two people had already died, and more than 2,000 were ill (Wickens, 2000).

(continued on page 16)

proofread
check a final copy for errors before submitting it

A shortened title and page number are used on each page.

Each claim is supported with clear reasons and solid evidence.

The writer continues to cite her sources throughout the essay.

The writer restates her thesis and calls the reader to action.

Several factors contributed to the tragedy in Walkerton, including human error. First, according to *The Edmonton Journal*, a flaw in the water treatment system allowed the infested water to enter the well (Blackwell, 2001). Even after the manure washed into Walkerton's well, the chlorine should have killed the deadly bacteria. In Walkerton, the Public Utilities Commission was responsible for overseeing the testing and treating of the town's water, but it failed to monitor the procedure properly ("Walkerton's water-safety," 2000). Apparently, shortcuts were taken when tracking the water's chlorine level, and as a result, some of the water samples were mislabeled. There was also a significant delay between the time that the contamination was identified and the time it was reported.

Once Walkerton's problem was identified, the government acted quickly to help the community. In its December 7, 2000, edition, *The Edmonton Journal* reported that a $100,000 emergency fund was set up to help families with expenses. Local businesses donated bottled water for drinking and containers of bleach for basic sanitizing and cleaning. In addition, the Provincial Clean Water Agency restored the main water and sewage systems by flushing out all of the town's pipes and wells. Seven months after the water became contaminated, the ban on drinking Walkerton's water was finally lifted (2001).

As the Sierra Club warns and the citizens of Walkerton learned, water purity is a life-and-death issue. Fortunately, both the United States and Canada have been addressing the problem. For example, since 2001, more states and provinces have been tightening their clean-water standards, more communities have been monitoring their water quality, and more individuals have been using water-filtration systems, bottled water, or boiled tap water. However, a tragedy like that in Walkerton could happen again. To avoid such horror, all of us must get involved by demanding clean tap water in our communities and by promoting the policies and procedures needed to achieve that goal.

(continued on page 17)

Sources used are listed correctly, in alphabetical order.

Each entry follows APA rules for content, format, and punctuation.

References

Blackwell, T. (2001, January 9). Walkerton doctor defends response. *The Edmonton Journal*. Retrieved from <http://edmontonjournal.com>.

Sierra Club. (n.d.). Water sentinels: Keeping it clean around the U.S.A. Retrieved September 24, 2009, from <http://sierraclub.org/watersentinels/>.

Walkerton's water-safety tests falsified regularly, utility official admits. (2000, December 7). *The Edmonton Journal*. Retrieved from <http://edmontonjournal.com>.

Wickens, B. (2000, June 5). Tragedy in Walkerton. *Maclean's, 113*(23), 34–36.

Reading for Better Writing

Complete these activities by yourself or with classmates.

1. Review Angela's writing process. How does it compare with your own writing process on a recent assignment?

2. Review the changes that Angela made in her first revision (pages 9-10) and those she made in her second revision (pages 11-12). What is the most important change that happened at each stage? Why do you think that Angela changes more the second time around?

3. Review Angela's editing for style (page 13) and her editing for correctness (page 14). What types of changes does she make at each stage? Do you focus on stylistic issues and correctness separately? Why or why not?

"**I think I did pretty well,**
considering I started out with nothing but a bunch
of blank paper."

—Steve Martin

2

Starting

LO1 Discover your process.

You've probably heard about the writing process—prewriting, writing, revising, editing, and publishing. And yet, you may know excellent writers who do not follow that progression at all. Some tend to jump right into writing, only to go back and gather more details later on. Others are in the midst of revising when they throw the whole thing away. There's no point talking about a single writing process when writers work differently. Here is Kurt Vonnegut's take on different processes, from his novel *Timequake*:

"Tellers of stories with ink on paper, not that they matter any more, have been either swoopers or bashers. Swoopers write a story quickly, higgledy-piggledy, crinkum-crankum, any which way. Then they go over it again painstakingly, fixing everything that is just plain awful or doesn't work. Bashers go one sentence at a time, getting it exactly right before they go on to the next one. When they're done they're done."

Are you a swooper or a basher—or some other kind of writer? There's no right way to do it; what matters is the end result.

What is your writing process? This chapter will help you discover it . . . and help you do your best writing.

Learning Outcomes

LO1 Discover your process.

LO2 Analyze the situation.

LO3 Understand the assignment.

LO4 Select a topic.

LO5 Gather details.

What do you think?

I am a swooper.

1	2	3	4	5
strongly agree				strongly disagree

© Outline./Corbis

Kurt Vonnegut

THE WRITING PROCESS

The flowchart to the right maps out the basic steps in the writing process. As you work on your writing project, review this diagram as needed to keep yourself on task.

To get started with an assignment, you need to understand it, decide on a topic, and collect information. Once you have enough information, you can begin **planning** your writing. You'll form a **thesis statement** and determine how to organize your ideas.

Having planned your work, you'll begin **drafting** it—creating an opening, a middle, and a closing—simply getting your ideas on paper. After you complete a first draft, you'll make large-scale changes, adding, deleting, rearranging, and reworking parts. This step is called **revising.** Getting opinions from other students can help. After making these changes, you'll begin **editing** for style and for the conventions of language.

In the end, of course, you'll submit your work, either to your professor or to a publication. When you do so, it's important to make sure that your writing fits the specific design and documentation requirements.

planning
the thinking and organizing that go into establishing a direction and structure for writing

thesis statement
a sentence or set of sentences that sums up the central idea of a piece of writing

drafting
writing sentences and paragraphs to create an initial draft with an opening, a middle, and a closing

revising
improving a draft through large-scale changes such as adding, deleting, rearranging, and reworking

editing
refining a draft in terms of word choice and sentence style and checking it for conventions

THE PROCESS AND YOU

The writing process shown above is fluid, not rigid. As a writer, you must work through the process, adapting it to your situation and assignment. To do so, consider the idea that writing does not follow a straight path. While it may begin with an assignment and end with a reader, the journey in between is often indirect. The steps in the flowchart overlap to show that when you write, you may move back and forth between steps, meaning that the process is recursive. For example, while revising, you may discover that you need to draft a new paragraph or do more research.

Modifying the Process

Each assignment calls for its own process. A personal essay may develop best through clustering or freewriting; a literary analysis through close reading of a story; a lab report through the experimental method; and a position paper through informed, balanced reasoning.

Writers also work differently. Some writers do extensive research and planning before drafting, while others do not. Some develop detailed outlines, while others draft brief lists of ideas. Experiment with the strategies introduced in this and the following five chapters, adopting those that help you.

Writing can involve collaboration. From discussing topic choices with your roommate to working on a major report with a group, college writing is not solitary writing. In fact, many colleges have writing centers to help students refine their assignments. (See pages 64-65.)

Finally, good writing can't be rushed. Although some students regard pulling an all-nighter as a badge of honor, good writing takes time. A steady, disciplined approach will generally produce the best results. For example, brainstorming or reading early in a project stimulates your subconscious mind to mull over issues, identify problems, and project solutions—even while your conscious mind is working on other things. Similarly, completing a first draft early enough gives you time to revise objectively.

The Focused Effort

The different steps of the process focus on different writing issues. As you use the writing process, keep your focus where it belongs: (1) When you plan and draft, focus on global issues: ideas, structure, and voice. (2) When you revise, fix big content problems by cutting, adding, and thoroughly reworking material. (Students benefit the most from revising—but often spend the least time doing it.) (3) When you edit and proofread, pay attention to small, local issues: word choice, sentence smoothness, and grammatical correctness. (Worrying about these issues too early can interrupt the flow of drafting.) (4) Before submitting, check for appropriate format and design and complete a clean final copy.

L○2 Analyze the situation.

Rhetoric is the art of using language effectively. As Aristotle, Quintilian, and others have explained, your language is effective when all aspects of your message (including content and style) fit your **subject**, address the needs of your **audience**, and fulfill your **purpose**.

THE RHETORICAL SITUATION

Before you put fingers to the keyboard, you must carefully think about your subject, audience, and purpose. By doing so, you are analyzing your **rhetorical situation**—the conditions or issues that will affect your writing decisions, including choosing the best **form** (such as an essay or a report), the best **medium** (such as paper or electronic), and the best **organizing pattern** (such as cause/effect or chronological order).

Subject

Audience

Purpose

Your Subject

Ideas—and the information that relates to them—are the substance of all good writing. Without informative ideas, your writing cannot fulfill the needs of your audience and will not achieve your purpose. Understanding your subject involves gathering and assimilating all relevant details, including its history, makeup, function, and impact on people and culture. Knowing these details will help you decide what to include in your writing and how to organize it.

Your Audience

For any writing task, you must understand your audience in order to develop writing that meets their needs. To assess your audience, answer questions like these: Who are my readers: Instructor? Classmates? Web surfers? What do they know about my topic, and what do they need to know? How well do they understand the terminology, procedures, and technology? What are their attitudes toward the topic and toward me? How well do they read written English—or visuals such as graphs and charts? How will they use my writing: To be informed? Entertained? Persuaded?

Note: Answers to such questions will help you develop meaningful sentences (pages 70–74), choose appropriate words (pages 74–77), and select relevant visuals.

Your Purpose

Knowing your purpose—why you are writing—will help you make decisions, such as choosing an organizational strategy. In assignments, key words (especially verbs) either hint at or specify your purpose. For example, an assignment asking you to analyze a topic requires that you break the subject into subparts and then explain the relationships between those subparts. Organizational patterns useful for analyzing a topic include classification, definition, and process (page 22).

rhetoric
the art of using language effectively

subject
the general area covered by a writing assignment

audience
the intended reader or readers for your writing

purpose
the goal of a piece of writing; for example, to inform, analyze, or persuade

rhetorical situation
the dynamics—subject, audience, and purpose—that affect a writer's decisions about the initial selecting and research

form
the type of writing; for example, report, letter, proposal, editorial, essay, story, or poem

medium
the way that writing is delivered; for example, in a printed publication or online

organizing pattern
the way that details are arranged in writing; for example, chronological order or cause/effect order

LO3 Understand the assignment.

Each college instructor has a way of personalizing a writing assignment, but most assignments will spell out (1) the objective, (2) the task, (3) the formal requirements, and (4) suggested approaches and topics. Your first step, therefore, is to read the assignment carefully, noting all of its aspects.

READ THE ASSIGNMENT.

By taking time to read the assignment carefully, you'll discover its main objective, figure out exactly what you need to do, and avoid the backtracking that consumes valuable hours. Your instructor will likely use key words to indicate the particular task of the assignment, so understanding these words is important. Refer to the following guide.

Quick Guide — Key Words

Analyze: Break down a topic into subparts, showing how those parts relate.

Apply: Use knowledge in a practical way or in a new context.

Argue: Defend a claim with logical arguments.

Classify: Divide a large group into well-defined subgroups.

Compare/contrast: Point out similarities and/or differences.

Define: Give a clear, thoughtful definition or meaning of something.

Describe: Show in detail what something is like.

Evaluate: Weigh the truth, quality, or usefulness of something.

options
choices provided within an assignment

restrictions
limitations of choice within an assignment

assessment
the way that writing will be evaluated

Key Words (cont.)

Explain: Give reasons, list steps, or discuss the causes of something.

Interpret: Tell in your own words what something means.

Reflect: Share your well-considered thoughts about a subject.

Summarize: Restate someone else's ideas very briefly in your own words.

Synthesize: Connect facts or ideas to create something new.

Options and Restrictions

Often an assignment will provide **options**, allowing you to choose your own topic or a unique approach to a topic. But the assignment may also present **restrictions**. Consider the following example.

> **Reflect on the way a natural disaster or major historical event has altered your understanding of the past, the present, or the future.**
>
> **Options:** The assignment allows you to (1) choose any natural disaster or major historical event, (2) focus on the past, present, or future, and (3) examine any kind of alteration.
>
> **Restrictions:** The assignment requires you to (1) reflect on a change in your understanding and (2) address only a *natural* disaster or only a *major* historical event.

THINK IT THROUGH.

Think about what you are supposed to get out of this assignment: Knowledge? Research experience? Improved writing skills? Polished style? Creativity? Make sure your goals for the assignment match the instructor's goals.

Also consider how the assignment contributes to the goals of the course. One way to connect the assignment to course goals is to note how much weight it carries for your overall grade, which indicates how important the assignment is to your instructor. **Assessment**, then, is also important. Be certain you understand the criteria (such as this book's instructions and checklists) used to grade your completed assignment.

Think next about how this assignment fits with others. Does it lead up to a more difficult task, or is this assignment the "big one"? Put it in perspective. Also think about the typical approach to your assignment. Are you going to follow the well-beaten path or forge your own trail?

Remember, too, that you'll do your best writing if your subject interests you. Can you connect a personal interest to this assignment, perhaps an idea from another course or an activity outside of school? Success with an assignment is often linked to this personal connection.

LO4 Select a topic.

For some assignments, finding a suitable topic (or subject) may require little thinking on your part. If an instructor asks you to summarize an article in a professional journal, you will write about the article in question. But suppose the instructor asks you to analyze how a feature of popular culture impacts society. What will you do then?

LIMIT THE SUBJECT AREA.

Many of your writing assignments will relate to general subject areas you are currently studying. Your task, then, will be to derive a specific topic from the general area of study—a limited topic that can be adequately addressed within the assignment's parameters.

Your topic must . . .
— meet the requirements of the assignment.
— be limited in scope (specific).
— seem reasonable (either familiar or within your means to research).
— genuinely interest you.

© Used under license from Shutterstock.com

Note: A general subject like *energy sources* is broad. It comprises many related topics. The limited topic *wind power* is one of the related topics. It is narrower and represents a more manageable writing idea.

EXPLORE POSSIBLE TOPICS.

Finding a writing idea that meets the requirements of the assignment should not be difficult if you know how and where to look. Start by checking your class notes and handouts for ideas related to the assignment. Also bounce ideas off your instructor, who may know other information specialists you could consult.

Of course, you may search the Internet. Use either a keyword search or, for a narrower subject, a subject-tree search. (See pages 212-213, 236-239.)

And don't forget about the library. In addition to traditional print materials, libraries offer many online aids such as EBSCOhost subscriptions, giving you free access to millions of articles on specialized topics. Remember that librarians are experts in tracking down information, and most are glad to help.

You can also discover a writing topic by using one of the following strategies:

Journal Writing

Write in a **journal** on a regular basis. Reflect on your personal feelings, develop your thoughts, and record the happenings of each day. Periodically go back and underline ideas that you would like to explore in writing assignments. In the following journal-writing sample, the writer found an idea for a writing assignment about how popular culture impacts society.

I read a really disturbing news story this morning. I've been thinking about it all day. In California a little girl was killed when she was struck by a car driven by a man distracted by a billboard ad for lingerie featuring a scantily clothed woman. Not only is it a horrifying thing to happen, but it also seems to me all too symbolic of the way that sexually charged images in the media are putting children, and especially girls, in danger. That reminds me of another news story I read this week about preteen girls wanting to wear the kinds of revealing outfits that they see in music videos, TV shows, and magazines aimed at teenagers. Too many of today's media images give young people the impression that sexuality should begin at an early age. This is definitely a dangerous message.

journal
a notebook used regularly for personal writing

Freewriting

Freewriting is the writing you do without having a specific outcome in mind. You simply write down whatever pops into your head as you explore your topic. Write nonstop for 10 minutes or longer to discover possible writing ideas. As a starting point, use a key concept related to the assignment. You'll soon discover potential writing ideas that might otherwise have never entered your mind. Note in the following example that the writer keeps writing even when he runs out of ideas. The writer also ignores mistakes. He just keeps writing.

> Popular culture. What does that include? Television obviously but that's a pretty boring subject. What else? Movies, pop music, video games. Is there a connection between playing violent video games and acting out violent behavior? Most video game players I know would say no but sometimes news reports suggest a connection. Is this something I'd want to write about? Not really. What then? Don't know. Not sure. Keep writing. Oh. Maybe I could think about this a different way and focus on the positive effects of playing video games. They release tension for one thing and they can really be challenging. Other benefits? They help to kill time, that's for sure, but maybe that's not such a good thing. I would definitely read more if it weren't for video games, tv, etc. Maybe I could write about how all the electronic entertainment that surrounds us today is creating a generation of nonreaders or maybe I could focus on whether people aren't getting much physical exercise because of the time they spend with electronic media. Maybe both. At least I have some possibilities to work with.

freewriting
a form of nonstop writing used during the early stages of the writing process to collect thoughts and ideas

clustering
a form of brainstorming by freely recording words and phrases around a nucleus word

Quick Guide — Freewriting

1. Use your particular topic or assignment as a starting point.

2. Write nonstop and record whatever comes to mind (for at least 10 minutes).

3. Write without judging, editing, or correcting your writing.

4. Continue to write even when you think you have exhausted all of your ideas.

5. Watch for promising ideas as you write.

6. Review your freewriting and underline the ideas you like.

7. If possible, listen to and read the freewriting of others.

Clustering

Clustering is a matter of grouping related ideas around one central idea. To begin **clustering**, write a nucleus word or phrase related to the assignment in the center of your paper. Circle it, and then cluster ideas around it. Circle each idea as you record it, and draw a line connecting it to the closest related idea. Keep going until you run out of ideas and connections. The photo shows a student's cluster on the subject of sports.

Listing

Listing is simply that, making a list. Beginning with a key concept related to the assignment, freely list ideas as they come to mind. When a group of people compiles a list, the process is called *brainstorming*. The following is an example of a student's list of possible topics related to the subject of news reporting:

Feature of popular culture: News reporting
- Sensationalism
- Sound bites rather than in-depth analysis
- Focus on the negative
- Shock radio
- Shouting matches pretending to be debates
- Press leaks that damage national security, hurt individuals, etc.
- Lack of observation of people's privacy
- Bias
- Contradictory health news confusing to readers
- Little focus on "unappealing" issues like poverty
- Celebration of "celebrity"

TIP

After 4 or 5 minutes of listing or clustering, scan your work for an idea to explore in a freewriting. A writing idea should begin to emerge during this freewriting session.

Moving On

You can use the strategies discussed on the previous pages—journal writing, freewriting, clustering, and listing—to find appropriate topics for your assignments. But these writing tools can help you do more than get started. They are valuable for gathering details, organizing ideas, exploring new directions, and taking whatever steps you must to keep going with an assignment.

LO5 Gather details.

Writer and instructor Donald Murray said that "writers write with information. If there is no information, there will be no effective writing." How true! Before you can develop a thoughtful piece of writing, you must gain a thorough understanding of your topic; to do so, you must carry out the necessary reading, reflecting, and researching.

Writing becomes a satisfying experience once you can speak with authority about your topic. Use the guidelines listed here when you start collecting information.

Gathering Guidelines

_____ Determine what you already know about your topic. (Use the ideas discussed on the next page.)

_____ Consider listing questions you would like to answer during your research.

_____ Identify and explore possible sources of information.

_____ Carry out your research following a logical plan.

DISCOVER WHAT YOU KNOW.

Uncover what you already know about a topic by using the strategies listed on pages 23–25. You can also use a technique called **focused freewriting**. With this technique, you either freewrite from a specific angle or simply write a quick draft of the paper.

One other effective strategy is to answer the **5 W** questions about the topic—*who? what? when? where?* and *why?* Add *how?* to the list for better coverage.

Another effective strategy is **directed writing.** Write whatever comes to mind about your topic, using one of the thinking moves listed here:

Directed Writing Strategies

- **Describe it:** What do you see, hear, feel, smell, and taste?
- **Compare it:** What is it similar to? What is it different from?
- **Associate it:** What connections between this topic and others come to mind?
- **Analyze it:** What parts does it have? How do they work together?
- **Argue it:** What do you like about the topic? What do you not like about it? What are its strengths and weaknesses?
- **Apply it:** What can you do with it? How can you use it?

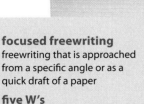

focused freewriting
freewriting that is approached from a specific angle or as a quick draft of a paper

five W's
the questions *who? what? when? where?* and *why?* (and sometimes *how?*)

directed writing
an exploration tactic using one of a set of thinking moves: describe, compare, associate, analyze, argue, or apply

ASK QUESTIONS.

To expand on what you already know, you'll need to do more collecting and researching about your topic. It may be helpful to list questions that you want answered. Alternatively, you can use the questions below. These questions address problems, policies, and concepts, and most topics fall under one of these categories. Use those questions that seem helpful for your particular assignment.

	PROBLEMS	POLICIES	CONCEPTS
DESCRIPTION	What is the problem? What type of problem is it? What are its parts? What are the signs of the problem?	What is the policy? How broad is it? What are its parts? What are its important features?	What is the concept? What are its parts? What is its main feature? Whom or what is it related to?
FUNCTION	Who or what is affected by it? What new problems might it cause in the future?	What is the policy designed to do? What is needed to make it work? What are or will be its effects?	Who has been influenced by this concept? Why is it important? How does it work?
HISTORY	What is the current status of the problem? What or who caused it? What or who contributed to it?	What brought about this policy? What are the alternatives?	When did it originate? How has it changed over the years? How might it change in the future?
VALUE	What is its significance? Why? Why is it more (or less) important than other problems? What does it symbolize or illustrate?	Is the policy workable? What are its advantages and disadvantages? Is it practical? Is it a good policy? Why or why not?	What practical value does it have? Why is it superior (or inferior) to similar concepts? What is its social worth?

IDENTIFY POSSIBLE SOURCES.

Finding meaningful sources of information is crucial as you get started. Allow yourself time. You don't want to discover at the last minute that the book you need is checked out or that a key online service isn't available. And don't feel that you have to "go it alone." The specialists in your school library are trained to find reliable, relevant information.

Remember that not all sources are created equal. For example, while immediately accessible, Web sites can also be out of date, biased, unreliable, or just plain wrong. So can print materials. Learn to evaluate sources to determine their worth. (See pages 214–215.)

Once you've found some solid sources, use them to find others. Follow links from helpful Web sites and track down materials listed in bibliographies. Tracking down sources can actually be an adventure—if you've planned enough time for searching.

Primary and Secondary Sources

Of course, books and Web sites are not the only possible sources of information. Primary sources such as interviews, observations, and surveys may lead you to a more thorough and meaningful understanding of a topic. (See pages 225–228.)

Primary sources are original sources. They inform directly, not through another person's explanation or interpretation. Such sources include albums, artifacts, cartoons, censuses, e-mails, equations, experiments, films (fiction), interviews, lab results, lectures, letters, journals, live performances, maps, novels, observations, paintings, protests, rallies, sculptures, source material, and surveys.

Secondary sources are not original sources. They contain information that other people have gathered and interpreted. Such sources include abstracts, articles, blogs, books (nonfiction), brochures, documentaries, editorials, encyclopedias, essays, forewords/afterwords, government publications, letters to the editor, monographs, pamphlets, posters, proposals, research reports, reference books, reviews, summaries, and textbooks.

CARRY OUT YOUR RESEARCH.

As you conduct your research, try to use a variety of reliable sources. It's also a good idea to choose an efficient note-taking method before you start. You will want to take good notes on the information you find and record all the publishing information necessary for documenting your sources. (See pages 217–218.)

Reserve a special part of a notebook to question, evaluate, and reflect on your research as it develops. The record of your thoughts and actions created during this process will mean a great deal to you—as much as or more than the actual information you uncover. Reflection helps you make sense of new ideas, refocus your thinking, and evaluate your progress.

"**Have a vision.**
Be demanding."

—Colin Powell

3

Planning

As you learned in the last chapter, no two people develop their writing in quite the same way. Some people are free spirits ("swoopers"), ready to write on just about any topic at any time. Others are more systematic ("bashers"), interested in keeping things under control as they go along. No matter how you approach writing, you must, sooner or later, do some **planning** to make sure that what you have to say is focused and coherent.

When you plan an essay, you have two main objectives: (1) establishing a thesis or focus for your writing and (2) organizing the supporting information to develop that focus. For a **personal narrative**, very little organizing may be required since you're sharing a memorable experience. For an **academic essay**, however, you will need to identify a method of development—comparison, cause/effect, classification—that best supports your thesis, and then organize your details accordingly.

The first part of this chapter provides an inventory that will help you assess your prewriting progress. The second part addresses a critical point in the process, forming a thesis statement, and the third part shows you how a thesis statement can suggest a method of organization for your writing. The final part of the chapter addresses outlining or using a graphic organizer to arrange your supporting details. Once you do all of these things, you will be more than ready to write a first draft.

Learning Outcomes

LO1 Take inventory of your thoughts.

LO2 Form your thesis statement.

LO3 Select a method of development.

LO4 Develop a plan or an outline.

What do you think?

I carefully plan my writing before starting my first draft.

1	2	3	4	5
strongly agree				strongly disagree

IN PERSPECTIVE

Writer and instructor Ken Macrorie offers this insight about planning: "Good writing is formed partly through plan and partly through accident." In other words, too much early planning can get in the way. Writing at its best is a process of discovery. You never know what new insights or ideas will spring to mind until you put pen to paper or fingers to the keyboard.

planning
the thinking and organizing that go into establishing a direction and structure for writing

personal narrative
writing about a memorable experience; may include personal reflections and thoughts

academic essay
carefully planned writing in which the writer analyzes, explains, interprets, or argues for or against a topic

LO1 Take inventory of your thoughts.

You should always assess and evaluate your progress (or lack of it) at key points during the writing process. One of those key points is right after you have done your initial searching and collecting. Let's suppose you're at that point, and you've succeeded in discovering some interesting information and perspectives about your subject. To assess the quality of your work so far, reflect on the **rhetorical situation** of your assignment.

REFLECT ON THE RHETORICAL SITUATION.

After considering the following questions about your subject, audience, and purpose, you should know if you are ready to move ahead with your planning, or if you should reconsider your topic.

Subject

Start your inventory by considering your understanding of the topic. *Do you know enough about the topic after your initial research, or do you need to know more? If more research is in order, do you know where to find additional information?* Then, of course, there is the essential question: *Do you still have a strong interest in writing about this topic?* Until you answer these questions, you really can't plan any further.

Audience

Consider how well your topic matches up with your readers. *Will the readers be interested in the topic, at least from what you know about it so far? What do they already know about it, and what new information can you offer? And how can you get them interested in what you have to say?* There's little reason to write about something that won't spark a response from your readers. More than anything, academic writing is a way to prompt or further the conversation about an important idea or issue.

---

rhetorical situation
the dynamics—subject, audience, and purpose—that affect a writer's decisions about the initial selecting and research

level of language
the level of formality that a writer uses—informal, semiformal, or formal

---

Purpose

Consider again your reason for writing. *What are the specifics of the assignment? Are you writing to entertain, to inform, to explain, to analyze, or to persuade? Do you have enough time to do a good job with this topic? How important is this writing, and how will it be assessed?* Writing with purpose is much like following an exercise routine; it keeps you focused and on track.

fyi The form of your writing is usually stated in the assignment: "Write an *essay,* in which you . . ." However, if the assignment is more open-ended, that decision may be up to you, as may other decisions, such as choosing an appropriate **level of language**. Considering the rhetorical situation will help you make these decisions.

KEEP GOING.

Writing, like establishing a strong relationship, often involves taking a few steps back before you can move forward. That is the recursive nature of writing (and dating). As was stated in the previous chapter (see page 20), the writing journey is often indirect. So once you assess your rhetorical situation, you may decide that you need to learn more about your topic before you consider anything else.

Research more deeply.

If you need to know more about your topic, continue collecting your own thoughts and/or investigating other sources of information. Without a solid knowledge base, you can't write effectively about any topic. In James Thurber's wise words, "To write about . . . bloodhounds, you have to know bloodhounds; to write about the Loch Ness monster, you have to find out about it." Remember that it is important to investigate both primary and secondary sources. (See page 224.)

Review your material.

When you are ready to move ahead, carefully review your notes. As you read through this material, circle or underline ideas that seem important enough to include in your writing. Then look for ways in which these ideas connect or relate. What you're doing, essentially, is beginning to focus your thinking about your topic by establishing some very general parameters for your writing. The activities that follow will help you to further focus your thoughts.

LO2 Form your thesis statement.

As you gain knowledge about your topic, you should concurrently develop a more focused interest in it. If all goes well, this narrowed focus will bring to mind a thesis. A **thesis statement** identifies the central idea for your writing. It usually highlights a special condition or feature of the topic, expresses a specific claim about it, or takes a stand. Artists go through a similar process, sorting through untold numbers of thoughts, experiences, and images until a controlling vision comes into focus.

State your thesis in a sentence that effectively expresses what you want to explore or explain in your essay. Sometimes a thesis statement develops early and easily; at other times, the true focus of your writing will emerge only after you've done some initial writing. Eventually, you must establish a thesis that truly reflects your idea about the topic. How else will you be able to approach your writing with the proper care and concern?

fyi Why is a thesis statement so important? An effective thesis statement gives you control and direction, helping you know what to say first, second, and so on. Trying to write without an effective thesis in place would be like trying to maneuver a rudderless sailboat; you would have no control.

FIND A FOCUS.

A general subject area is typically built into your writing assignments. Your task, then, is (1) to select a limited writing topic (covered in the previous chapter) and (2) to identify a special part of it to focus on in your writing. (You will use this focus to form the thesis statement.) This graphic shows how the process usually works.

GENERAL SUBJECT (Alternative energy sources)

LIMITED TOPIC (Wind power)

SPECIFIC FOCUS

(Wind power is a viable energy source in the plains states.)

STATE YOUR THESIS.

If needed, use the following formula to write a thesis statement for your essay. Keep in mind that at this point you're writing a working thesis—a statement-in-progress, so to speak. You may change it as your thinking on the topic evolves. *Remember:* A thesis statement sets the **tone** and direction for your writing.

a manageable or limited topic	wind power
a specific claim or focus	provides a viable energy source in the plains states

+

an effective thesis statement	Wind power provides a viable energy source in the plains states.

If the thesis had said, "Wind power provides a viable energy source," the claim would not be specific enough for an essay. Where would the writer begin and end the discussion? Limiting the discussion to the viability of wind power in the plains states makes the statement workable. A thesis statement can also be too specific. For example, "Wind power in the plains states has one drawback" would be too limiting for an essay. There's not much that a writer can do with that idea, other than point out the one drawback. Use the following checklist as a guide to assess the effectiveness of your thesis statements:

Thesis Statement Checklist

_____ Does the thesis statement reflect a limited topic?

_____ Does it clearly state the specific idea you plan to develop?

_____ Is the thesis supported by the information you have gathered?

_____ Does the thesis suggest a pattern of organization for your essay?

thesis statement
a sentence or set of sentences that sums up the central idea of a piece of writing

tone
the overall feeling or effect created by a writer's thoughts and use of words

LO3 Select a method of development.

In his classic book *On Writing Well*, William Zinsser identifies "striving for order" as one of the keys to effective writing. For some assignments, this is not a problem because an **organizing pattern** is built right into the assignment. For example, you might be asked to develop a process paper, which you would organize chronologically. When a pattern is not apparent, one might still evolve naturally as you gather information. If this doesn't happen, examine your thesis statement to see what method of development it suggests.

LET YOUR THESIS GUIDE YOU.

Notice how the thesis statements below provide direction and shape for the essays they generate. Each one addresses a different form of academic writing. Each one can also serve as a model to help you with the wording of your own thesis statements.

Personal Narrative Thesis

Thesis: What began as a simple prank ended up being something far more serious.

This statement identifies the focus of a personal narrative. It suggests that the essay will recount a personal experience and will most likely be arranged chronologically, beginning with the planning and execution of the prank and then examining the consequences that followed. The writer could also begin the essay by revealing the serious result of the prank, and then sharing the details that lead up to it. (In some situations, even without a directly stated thesis, an underlying theme or focus can guide your narrative writing.)

organizing pattern
the way that details are arranged in writing; for example, chronological order or cause/effect order

spatial organization
a pattern of organization in which you logically order descriptive details from far to near, from left to right, from top to bottom, and so on

> Examine your thesis statement to see what method of development it suggests.

Descriptive Essay Thesis

Thesis: As children we imagined the overgrown lot next to my boyhood home to be a forest full of danger and adventure.

This statement indicates that the writer will describe a special place from his childhood. The description could follow **spatial organization**, moving, perhaps, from the edges of the lot to its interior. The description may also be organized thematically, focusing on specific features of the lot as the children's adventures unfold. Remember, too, that using one organizing pattern does not exclude using others within an essay. This is often the case with descriptions. For example, the sample thesis statement about an overgrown lot and its possibility for adventure predicts some chronological narration as well as description.

Cause-and-Effect Essay Thesis

Thesis: For their own health and the well-being of others, people must understand what stress is—both its causes and its effects. In addition, to avoid its negative effects, people must learn to manage the stress in their lives.

This two-sentence thesis indicates that the writer is developing a cause-and-effect essay. Essays following this pattern usually explore one or more causes and then examine the effects, or they discuss a primary effect and then explain the causes. To develop this thesis, the writer will explore the causes of stress before examining its effects. When you develop a cause-and-effect essay, you are essentially analyzing an issue in a way that makes it clear to the reader.

Essay of Comparison Thesis

Thesis: As they both enter adulthood, Bigger in *Native Son* and Alan in *Equus* come to realize that they are controlled by work, religion, and the media.

This thesis clearly indicates that the writer is developing a comparison essay. Comparisons are usually patterned in one of two ways: Either you discuss one of the subjects completely and then the other (whole versus whole), or you discuss both subjects at the same time (point by point). The writer of this thesis compares the two literary characters point by point. (See pages 112–113 for this essay.) Generally speaking, a point-by-

point comparison helps the reader see more clearly the similarities and differences between the two topics.

Essay of Classification Thesis

Thesis: There are four main perspectives, or approaches, that readers can use to converse about literature.

The writer is developing an essay of classification. Essays following this pattern identify the main parts or categories of a topic and then examine each one. (*Classify* means "to arrange in classes or categories.") In this thesis, the writer identifies four ways to discuss literature and then examines each one in detail. (See pages 100–102 for this essay.)

Process Essay Thesis

Thesis: When a cell begins to function abnormally, it can initiate a process that results in cancer.

As indicated in the thesis, the writer will explain how cancer cells manifest themselves, multiply, and affect the body. Process essays such as this one are organized chronologically. Each step is carefully examined to help the reader understand the complete process. (See pages 104-105 for this essay.) A process essay can tell how something works or how to do or make something.

Essay of Definition Thesis

Thesis: The word *gullible* connects people and birds, relating them to each other by their willingness to "swallow."

This essay explores the root meaning of the word *gullible*. To do so, the writer analyzes the word's **etymology** (history) and identifies its lingual association. An extended-definition essay examines a word in additional ways, perhaps by including quotations that contain the word, personal definitions, negative definitions (what it is not), anecdotes, and so on.

Essay Proposing a Solution Thesis

Thesis: The best way to control deer populations is to stay as close to nature's ways as possible, and game management by hunting meets this criterion.

The writer of this thesis is developing a problem-solution essay. Essays following this pattern usually be-

gin with a discussion of the problem and its causes and then examine possible solutions. In this essay, the writer presents background information to put the problem in perspective. He then dismisses various solutions before promoting the one identified in the thesis.

Persuasive Essay Thesis

Thesis: Environmentalists say that "just as there is no way to be half-pregnant, there is no 'sensitive' way to drill in a wilderness" (McCarthy). They are right.

This is a persuasive thesis because the writer is taking a stand or expressing an opinion against drilling for oil in wilderness areas. Persuasive writing is often organized by **order of importance**, which means you either (1) start with your most compelling argument and work your way down or (2) do just the opposite—work your way up to the strongest argument in favor of your opinion. If the audience may be resistant to an argument, the first approach will probably work best. If, on the other hand, you have a receptive audience, consider the second approach. Finally, your audience and the strength of any opposing points of view should dictate where you address the opposition in your essay. (See pages 151–153 for this essay.)

© Alfred Bondarenko, 2009 / Used under license from Shutterstock.com

etymology
the origin of a word

order of importance
a pattern of organization often used in persuasive writing in which the writer begins or ends with the most convincing argument

LO4 Develop a plan or an outline.

After writing a thesis and reviewing the methods of development (see pages 32-33), you should be ready to organize the information you have collected. A **basic listing** of main points, an outline, or an appropriate graphic organizer will help you arrange your information.

fyi You don't have to include every last detail in your plan or outline. Simply provide an overall structure for your essay by placing the key or essential details in the order that you want to discuss them. You can work in other details during the drafting process.

CHOOSE A METHOD OF ORGANIZATION.

If you have a lot of information to arrange, you might want to use a topic or sentence outline for your planning. For research papers and other extended essays, your instructor might require you to submit an outline with the final copy of your writing. If that is the case, think of your outline at this stage in the process as a working outline.

basic listing
a brief, somewhat informal itemizing of main points

topic outline
a less formal method of arrangement in which you state each main point and essential detail as a word or a phrase

Topic Outline

A **topic outline** is a method of arrangement in which you state each main point and key detail as a word or phrase. Before you start constructing your outline, write your thesis statement at the top of your paper to keep you focused on the topic. (Do not attempt to outline your opening or closing paragraphs unless you are specifically asked to do so.)

Try to keep items parallel in your outline. In other words, state the main points (I, II, III) in the same way and the essential details (A, B, C) in the same way. In the sample outline below, the items are parallel in structure.

Topic Outline

Thesis: There are four main perspectives, or approaches, that readers can use to converse about literature.

   I. Text-centered approaches
      A. Also called formalist criticism
      B. Emphasis on structure of text and rules of genre
      C. Importance placed on key literary elements

  II. Audience-centered approaches
      A. Also called rhetorical or reader-response criticism
      B. Emphasis on interaction between reader and text

 III. Author-centered approaches
      A. Emphasis on writer's life
      B. Importance placed on historical perspective
      C. Connections made between texts

 IV. Ideological approaches
      A. Psychological analysis of text
      B. Myth or archetype criticism
      C. Moral criticism
      D. Sociological analysis

> **Note:** An outline is a very effective way to arrange large chunks of information.

Sentence Outline

A **sentence outline** is a more formal method of arrangement in which you state each main point and essential detail as a sentence. Writing a sentence outline helps you determine how you will express your ideas in the actual writing. Here is an example.

Sentence Outline

Thesis: There are four main perspectives, or approaches, that readers can use to converse about literature.

   I. A text-centered approach focuses on the literary piece itself.
      A. This approach is often called formalist criticism.
      B. This method of criticism examines text structure and the genre's rules.
      C. A formalist critic determines how key literary elements reinforce meaning.

  II. An audience-centered approach focuses on the "transaction" between text and reader.
      A. This approach is often called rhetorical or reader-response criticism.
      B. Each reader's interaction with a text is unique.

 III. An author-centered approach focuses on the origin of a text.
      A. An author-centered critic examines the writer's life.
      B. This method of criticism may include a historical look at a text.
      C. Connections may be made between the text and related works.

 IV. The ideological approach applies ideas outside of literature.
      A. Some critics apply psychological theories to a literary work.
      B. Myth or archetype criticism applies anthropology and classical studies to a text.
      C. Moral criticism explores the moral dilemmas in literature.
      D. Sociological approaches include Marxist, feminist, and minority criticism.

Graphic Organizers

If you are a visual learner, you may prefer using a graphic organizer to arrange your ideas for writing. A **graphic organizer** allows you to arrange main points and essential details in an appropriate chart or diagram. Graphic organizers can help you map out your ideas and illustrate relationships between them. Here is a **line diagram** that was used to organize some of the same ideas that were outlined previously.

Line Diagram

Thesis: There are four main perspectives, or approaches, that readers can use to converse about literature.

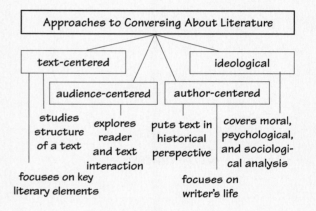

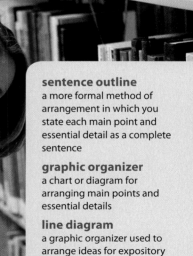

sentence outline
a more formal method of arrangement in which you state each main point and essential detail as a complete sentence

graphic organizer
a chart or diagram for arranging main points and essential details

line diagram
a graphic organizer used to arrange ideas for expository writing

TYPES OF GRAPHIC ORGANIZERS

The following graphic organizers relate to the methods of development discussed on pages 32-33. Each one will help you collect and organize information for expository or persuasive writing. Adapt the organizers as necessary to fit your particular needs or personal style.

Comparison

Qualities	Subject A	Subject B

Comparison/Contrast

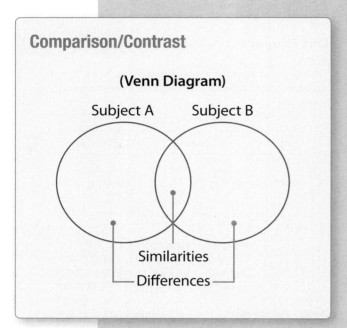

(Venn Diagram)

Subject A   Subject B

Similarities
Differences

Cause-Effect

Subject: _____

Causes	Effects
(Because of . . .)	(. . . these conditions resulted)
•	•
•	•
•	•

Problem/Solution

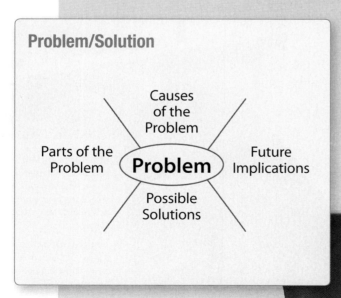

Causes of the Problem

Parts of the Problem — **Problem** — Future Implications

Possible Solutions

SMART IDEAS
FUTURE IDEAS
GREAT IDEAS
WONDERFUL
SUCCESSFUL IDEAS
ORIGINAL IDEAS
FABULOUS IDEAS

IDEA

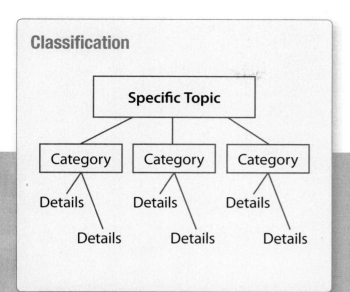

Classification

Specific Topic

Category | Category | Category

Details | Details | Details

Details | Details | Details

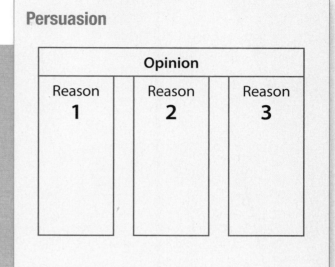

Persuasion

Opinion		
Reason **1**	Reason **2**	Reason **3**

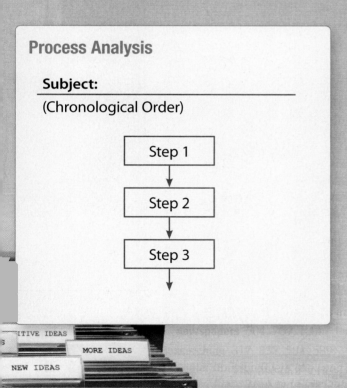

Process Analysis

Subject: _____

(Chronological Order)

Step 1

↓

Step 2

↓

Step 3

↓

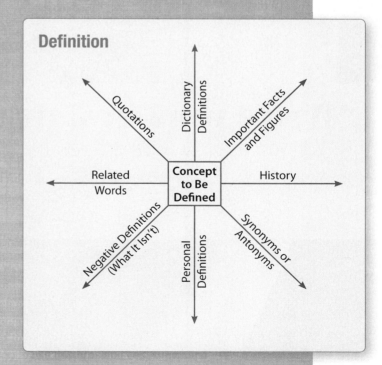

Definition

Quotations

Dictionary Definitions

Important Facts and Figures

Related Words

Concept to Be Defined

History

Negative Definitions (What It Isn't)

Personal Definitions

Synonyms or Antonyms

"**Write your first draft**
with your heart. Re-write with your head."
—from the movie *Finding Forrester*

4

Drafting

LO1 Review the writing situation.

The early twentieth-century French novelist Anatole France is reported to have said that one of his first drafts could have been written by any schoolboy, his next draft by a bright upper-level student, his third draft by a superior graduate, his fourth draft by a seasoned professional, and his final draft "only by Anatole France."

Even if that report is exaggerated, the point is well taken: The first draft is not the one that will distinguish you as a writer. It's a way of getting material together, of starting out, of connecting your ideas. A first draft gives you something to work with—a verbal sketch—that will later, through revising and editing, result in a polished piece of writing.

This chapter will introduce you to strategies for drafting that first "sketch"—your earliest vision of writing that is taking shape.

Learning Outcomes

LO1 Review the writing situation.

LO2 Open with interest.

LO3 Develop the middle.

LO4 End with purpose.

LO5 Use sources effectively.

What do you think?

My first drafts are like rough sketches.

1	2	3	4	5
strongly agree			strongly disagree	

RECONSIDER THE RHETORICAL SITUATION.

Driving-safety schools teach that before turning the key to start your car, it's smart to take a few moments to think about where you're going, what the weather is like, and what driving conditions you're likely to face. Similarly, just before starting to write your first draft, it's a good idea to mentally prepare for the journey by reviewing your **audience**, **purpose**, and subject.

Subject, Audience, and Purpose

Review who your readers are, including their knowledge of and attitude toward your topic. Then get ready to talk with them, person to person, in your writing.

Reconsider your purpose by briefly reviewing (1) what you want your writing to do (your task), (2) what you want it to say (your thesis), and (3) how you want to say it (your list of ideas or outline).

Finally, focus on your subject as you begin to write freely. Don't be too concerned about neatness and correctness; concentrate on developing your ideas, not on producing a final copy. In this draft, use the most natural voice you can so that the writing will flow smoothly. If your voice is too formal during drafting, you'll be tempted to stop and edit your words.

While using your writing plan or any charts, lists, or diagrams you've produced, don't feel absolutely bound by them. Those tools will help you focus on developing your main points, but you should allow new ideas to emerge naturally as well. Include as much detail as possible, and quote sources accurately by using your word-processing program's copy-and-paste features or by handwriting or typing quotations carefully.

audience
the intended reader or readers for your writing

purpose
the goal of a piece of writing; for example, to inform, analyze, or persuade

Continue drafting until you reach a logical stopping point. If at all possible, complete your first draft in one or two sittings. The longer you take to complete it, the more difficult it will be to maintain your focus.

BUILD THE BASIC STRUCTURE.

The following chart lists the main writing moves that occur during the development of a piece of writing. Use it as a general guide for all of your drafting. Remember to keep your purpose and audience in mind throughout the drafting process.

Opening

Engage your reader.
Stimulate and direct the reader's attention.

Establish your direction.
Identify the topic and put it in perspective.

Get to the point.
Narrow your focus and state your thesis.

Middle

Advance your thesis.
Provide background information and cover your main points.

Test your ideas.
Raise questions and consider alternatives.

Support your main points.
Add substance and build interest.

Build a coherent structure.
Start new paragraphs and arrange the support.

Use different levels of detail.
Clarify and complete each main point.

Ending

Reassert the main point.
Remind the reader of the purpose and rephrase the thesis.

Urge the reader.
Gain the reader's acceptance and look ahead.

LO2 Open with interest.

The opening paragraph is one of the most important elements in any composition. It is the writer's opportunity to get the reader's attention and encourage her or him to read on.

The conventional way of approaching this paragraph is to view it as a "funnel" that draws the reader in and narrows to the main point or **thesis statement**. Whether you use this conventional approach or some other pattern, it is important to simply relax and start writing. You can always come back and change the opening once you have written the rest of the essay (in fact, many professional writers do this).

ENGAGE YOUR READER.

Any reader will be preoccupied with other thoughts until you seize, stimulate, and direct his or her attention. To "hook" the reader, mention little-known facts about the topic, pose a challenging question, or offer a thought-provoking quotation. You might also tell a brief, illuminating story. Sometimes introducing your angle or **focus** on the topic will be enough to capture the reader, if that angle or focus is sufficiently unusual.

Establish your direction.

The direction of your line of thought should become clear in your opening. To set the right course, you must (1) identify your topic and (2) put it in perspective. For example, your topic (issue) may be a problem, a need, or an opportunity. Deepen this issue by connecting it to others and showing its importance. You may also ac-

If you have trouble getting started on your first draft, imagine your writing as half a conversation with a friend or with a reader you invent. Talk to your silent partner. As you write, think about what you've already said and let that help you decide what you should say next.

knowledge other points of views by telling what others are saying or thinking about the topic.

Introduce your main point.

You may choose to state your main point up front, or you may wait until later to introduce your thesis. For example, you could work inductively by asking a question in your opening and then building toward the answer, your thesis, in the conclusion. You may also simply imply your thesis, as long as the reader can discern the central issue of your paper. Here are three ways to get to the point: (1) explain what interests you about the topic; (2) raise a question and answer it in the rest of the essay; or (3) craft a sentence that boils down your thinking to a central claim. Your thesis sentence can also direct the organization of the rest of your essay. (See pages 32-33.)

OPENINGS: WEAK AND STRONG

Weak Opening

Although the opening below introduces the topic, the writing lacks interesting details and establishes no clear focus for the essay.

> I would like to tell you about the TV show *The Simpsons*. It's about this weird family of five people who look kind of strange and act even stranger. In fact, the characters aren't even real—they're just cartoons.

Strong Opening

The essay opener on the next page gets the reader's attention and identifies the subject in the first paragraph. In the second paragraph, a question leads the reader to the thesis statement (underlined).

thesis statement
a sentence or set of sentences that sums up the central idea of a piece of writing

focus
the specific part of a subject to be covered in your writing

The Simpsons, stars of the TV show by the same name, are a typical American family, or at least a parody of one. Homer, Marge, Bart, Lisa, and Maggie Simpson live in Springfield, U.S.A. Homer, the father, is a boorish, obese oaf who works in a nuclear power plant. Marge is an overprotective, nagging mother with an outrageous blue hairdo. Ten-year-old Bart is an obnoxious, "spiky-haired demon." Lisa is eight and a prodigy on the tenor saxophone and in class. The infant Maggie never speaks but only sucks on her pacifier.

What is the attraction of this yellow-skinned family that stars on a show in which all of the characters have pronounced overbites and only four fingers on each hand? Viewers see a little bit of themselves in everything the Simpsons do. The world of Springfield is a parody of the viewer's world, and Americans can't get enough of it. Viewers experience this parody in the show's explanations of family, education, workplace, and politics.

Note how the writer, after stating the thesis, forecasts the support he will present in the rest of the essay, encouraging the reader to read on.

LO3
Develop the middle.

The middle of an essay is where you do the "heavy lifting." In this part you develop the main points that support your thesis statement. As you write, you will likely make choices that you could not have predicted when you began. Use "scratch outlines" (temporary jottings) along the way to show where your new ideas may take you, but always keep your thesis in mind; writing that wanders from its purpose loses its hold on the reader. Finally, be sure to include effective details; without them, the reader will see only a vague image of your intent.

ADVANCE YOUR THESIS.

If you stated a thesis in the opening, you can advance it in the middle paragraphs by covering your main points and

Quick Guide | **Advancing Your Thesis**

You can support your main points with . . .

_____ an **explanation** that provides important facts, details, and examples.

_____ **narration** that shares a brief story or re-creates an experience to illustrate an idea.

_____ a **description** that tells in detail how someone or something looks or works.

_____ a **definition** that identifies or clarifies the meaning of a term or an idea.

_____ an **analysis** that examines the parts of something to better understand the whole.

_____ a **comparison** that provides examples to show how two things are alike or different.

_____ an **argument** that uses logic or evidence to prove that something is true.

_____ a **reflection** that expresses your thoughts or feelings about something.

_____ **expert evidence** that adds the analysis or commentary of an authority.

supporting them in one or more of the following ways: explanation, narration, description, definition, analysis, comparison, argument, reflection, and expert evidence.

Test your ideas.

When you write a first draft, you're testing your initial thinking about your topic. You're determining whether your thesis is valid and whether you have enough compelling information to support it. Here are ways to test your line of thinking as you write: (1) **raise questions,** trying to anticipate the questions your reader may have; (2) **consider alternatives,** looking at your ideas from different angles, weighing various options, and reevaluating your thesis; and (3) **answer objections,** dealing directly or indirectly with possible problems that a skeptical reader may point out.

Build a coherent structure.

Design paragraphs as units of thought that develop and advance your thesis clearly and logically. For example, look at the brief essay below, noting how each body paragraph presents ideas with supporting details that build on and deepen the main idea.

The opening below introduces the topic (incandescent versus fluorescent bulbs), suggests the comparison/contrast organizational pattern, and states the thesis (underlined). Then, in the first body paragraph, the writer offers a basic explanation of how the two lightbulbs function, including details that show their differences. Next, he shifts his attention to the fluorescent bulb, admitting its weaknesses in one paragraph and applauding its strengths in another. Within the final body paragraph, he acknowledges and justifies the higher cost of the fluorescent bulb. The closing rephrases the thesis as a challenge to the reader.

Seeing the Light

All lightbulbs make light, so they're all the same, right? Not quite. You have many choices regarding how to light up your life. Two types of bulbs are the traditional incandescent and the newer, more compact fluorescent. <u>By checking out how they're different, you can better choose which one to buy.</u>

While either incandescent or compact fluorescent bulbs can help you read or find the bathroom at night, each bulb makes light differently. In an incandescent bulb, electricity heats up a tungsten filament (thin wire) to 450 degrees, causing it to glow with a warm, yellow light. A compact fluorescent is a glass tube filled with mercury vapor and argon gas. Electricity causes the mercury to give off ultraviolet radiation. That radiation then causes phosphors coating the inside of the tube to give off light.

Both types of bulbs come in many shapes, sizes, and brightnesses, but compacts have some restrictions. Because of their odd shape, compacts may not fit in a lamp well. Compacts also may not work well in very cold temperatures, and they can't be used with a dimmer switch.

On the other hand, while compact fluorescents are less flexible than incandescents, compacts are four times more efficient. For example, a 15-watt compact produces as many lumens of light as a 60-watt incandescent! Why? Incandescents turn only about 5 percent of electricity into light and give off the other 95 percent as heat.

But are compacts less expensive than incandescents? In the short run, no. A compact costs about $15 while an incandescent costs only a dollar. However, because compacts burn less electricity—and last 7 to 10 times longer—in the long run, compacts are less expensive.

Now that you're no longer in the dark about lightbulbs, take a look at the lamp you're using to read this essay. Think about the watts (electricity used), lumens (light produced), efficiency, purchase price, and lamp life. Then decide how to light up your life in the future.

ORGANIZATIONAL PATTERNS

Organization is vital to a clear message. When details and ideas are included haphazardly, their collective meaning is lost. However, presenting information in a logical pattern within a paragraph and throughout an essay will strengthen the writing's coherence. The following pages explain and illustrate 10 organizational strategies.

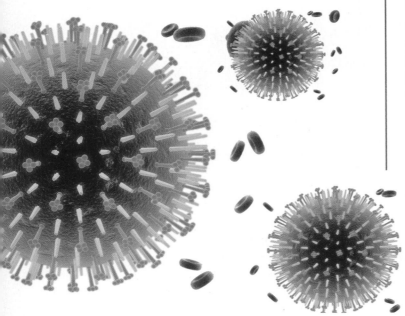

Analogy

An analogy is a comparison that a writer uses to explain a complex or unfamiliar phenomenon (how the immune system works) in terms of a familiar one (how mall security works).

> The human body is like a mall, and the immune system is like mall security. Because the mall has hundreds of employees and thousands of customers, security guards must rely on photo IDs, name tags, and uniforms to decide who should be allowed to open cash registers and who should have access to the vault. In the same way, white blood cells and antibodies need to use DNA cues to recognize which cells belong in a body and which do not. Occasionally security guards make mistakes, wrestling Kookie the Klown to the ground while DVD players "walk" out of the service entrance, but these problems amount only to allergic reactions or little infections. If security guards become hypervigilant, detaining every customer and employee, the situation is akin to leukemia, in which white blood cells attack healthy cells. If security guards become corrupt, letting thieves take a "five-finger discount," the situation is akin to AIDS. Both systems—mall security and human immunity—work by correctly differentiating friend from foe.

—Rob King

Chronological Order

Chronological (time) order helps you tell a story or present steps in a process. For example, the following paragraph describes how cement is made. Notice how the writer explains every step and uses transitional words to lead readers through the process.

> The production of cement is a complicated process. The raw materials that go into cement consist of about 60 percent lime, 25 percent silica, and 5 percent alumina. The remaining 10 percent is a varying combination of gypsum and iron oxide (because the amount of gypsum determines the drying time of the cement). First, this mixture is ground up into very fine particles and fed into a kiln. Cement kilns, the largest pieces of moving machinery used by any industry, are colossal steel cylinders lined with firebricks. They can be 25 feet in diameter and up to 750 feet long. The kiln is built at a slant and turns slowly as the cement mix makes its way down from the top end. A flame at the bottom heats the kiln to temperatures of up to 3,000 degrees Fahrenheit. When the melted cement compound emerges from the kiln, it cools into little marble-like balls called clinker. Finally, the clinker is ground to a consistency finer than flour and packaged as cement.

—Kevin Maas

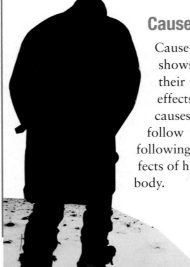

Cause and Effect

Cause-and-effect organization shows how events are linked to their results. If you start with effects, follow with specific causes; if you begin with causes, follow with specific effects. The following example discusses the effects of hypothermia on the human body.

Even a slight drop in the normal human body temperature of 98.6 degrees Fahrenheit causes hypothermia. Often produced by accidental or prolonged exposure to cold, the condition forces all bodily functions to slow down. The heart rate and blood pressure decrease. Breathing becomes slower and shallower. As the body temperature drops, these effects become even more dramatic until it reaches somewhere between 86 and 82 degrees Fahrenheit and the person lapses into unconsciousness. When the temperature reaches between 65 and 59 degrees Fahrenheit, heart action, blood flow, and electrical brain activity stop. Normally such a condition would be fatal. However, as the body cools down, the need for oxygen also slows down. A person can survive in a deep hypothermic state for an hour or longer and be revived without serious complications.

—Laura Black

Classification

When classifying a subject, place it in its appropriate category and then show how it is different from other subjects in the same category. In the following paragraph, a student writer uses classification to describe the theory of temperament.

Medieval doctors believed that "four temperaments rule mankind wholly." According to this theory, each person has a distinctive temperament or personality (sanguine, phlegmatic, melancholy, or choleric) based on the balance of four elements in the body, a balance peculiar to the individual. The theory was built on Galen's and Hippocrates' notion of "humors," which stated that the body contains blood, phlegm, black bile, and yellow bile—four fluids that maintain the balance within the body. The sanguine person was dominated by blood, associated with fire: Blood was hot and moist, and the person was fat and prone to laughter. The phlegmatic person was dominated by phlegm (associated with earth) and was squarish and slothful—a sleepy type. The

© Eugene Ivanov, 2009 / Used under license from Shutterstock.com

melancholy person was dominated by cold, black bile (connected with the element of water) and, as a result, was pensive, peevish, and solitary. The choleric person was dominated by hot, yellow bile (air) and thus was inclined to anger.

—Jessica Radsma

Compare and Contrast

To compare and contrast, show how two or more subjects are similar and different. See models on pages 112–115.

Climax

Organizing according to climax involves presenting the details first, and then drawing from them a general climactic statement or conclusion.

Reading is, for most people, a passive act. Words move from the page into the readers' minds almost of their own accord, building their argument. The reader who struggles, whether to understand or to resist, typically quits reading. Those people who do not quit reading become converts to the message. This is how the writer rules the world.

—Lester Smith

Definition

A definition provides the denotation (dictionary meaning) and connotation (feeling) of a given term. It may also offer examples, anecdotes, and negative definitions—what the thing is not. In the paragraph below, the writer begins his definition by posing a question.

First of all, what is the grotesque—in visual art and in literature? A term originally applied to Roman cave art that distorted the normal, the grotesque presents the body and mind so that they appear abnormal—different from the bodies and minds that we think belong in our world. Both spiritual and physical, bizarre and familiar, ugly and alluring, the grotesque shocks us, and we respond with laughter and fear. We laugh because the grotesque seems bizarre enough to belong only outside our world; we fear because it feels familiar enough to be part of it. Seeing the grotesque version of life as it is portrayed in art stretches our vision of reality. As Bernard McElroy argues, "The grotesque transforms the world from what we 'know' it to be to what we fear it might be. It distorts and exaggerates the surface of reality in order to tell a qualitative truth about it."

—John Van Rys

Illustration

An illustration supports a general idea with specific reasons, facts, and details.

As the years passed, my obsession grew. Every fiber and cell of my body was obsessed with the number on the scale and how much fat I could pinch on my thigh. No matter how thin I was, I thought I could never be thin enough. I fought my sisters for control of the TV and VCR to do my exercise programs and videos. The cupboards were stacked with cans of diet mixes, the refrigerator full of diet drinks. Hidden in my underwear drawer were stacks of diet pills that I popped along with my vitamins. At my worst, I would quietly excuse myself from family activities to turn on the bathroom faucet full blast and vomit into the toilet. Every day I stood in front of the mirror, a ritual not unlike brushing my teeth, and scrutinized my body. My face, arms, stomach, buttocks, hips, and thighs could never be small enough.

—Paula Treick

Narration

In the paragraph below, the writer uses narration and chronological order to relate an anecdote—a short, illustrative story.

Philip walked along Parliament Street. It was a fine day, and there was a bright, frosty sun which made the light dance in the street. It was crowded. There was a tenuous mist in the distance, and it softened exquisitely the noble lines of the buildings. He crossed Trafalgar Square. Suddenly his heart gave a sort of twist in his body; he saw a woman in front of him who he thought was Mildred. She had the same figure, and she walked with that slight dragging of the feet which was so characteristic of her. Without thinking, but with a beating heart, he hurried till he came alongside, and then, when the woman turned, he saw it was someone unknown to him. It was the face of a much older person, with a lined, yellow skin. He slackened his pace. He was infinitely relieved, but it was not only relief that he felt; it was disappointment too; he was seized with horror of himself. Would he never be free from that passion? At the bottom of his heart, notwithstanding everything, he felt that a strange, desperate thirst for that vile woman would always linger. That love had caused him so much suffering that he knew he would never, never quite be free of it. Only death could finally assuage his desire.

—W. Somerset Maugham, *Of Human Bondage*

Process

In the paragraph that follows, a student writer describes the process of entering the "tube," or "green room," while surfing.

At this point you are slightly ahead of the barreling part of the wave, and you need to "stall," or slow yourself, to get into the tube. There are three methods of stalling used in different situations. If you are slightly ahead of the tube, you can drag your inside hand along the water to stall. If you are a couple of feet in front of the barrel, apply all your weight onto your back foot and sink the tail of the board into the water. This is known as a "tail stall" for obvious reasons, and its purpose is to decrease your board speed. If you are moving faster than the wave is breaking, you need to do what is called a "wraparound." To accomplish this maneuver, lean back away from the wave while applying pressure on the tail. This shifts your forward momentum away from the wave and slows you down. When the wave comes, turn toward the wave and place yourself in the barrel.

—Luke Sunukjian, "Entering the Green Room"

LO4 End with purpose.

Closing paragraphs are important for tying up loose ends, clarifying key points, or signing off with the reader. In a sense, the entire essay is a preparation for an effective ending; the ending helps the reader look back to the essay with new understanding and appreciation. Many endings leave the reader with fresh food for thought.

FINISHING WELL

You may have heard this formula for writing an essay: "Tell what you're going to say, say it, and then tell what you've just said." Remember, though, if you follow this pattern, to "tell what you've just said" in a fresh way, with new words. The ending is important, so draft a number of them. Then choose the one that flows best and captures a sense of the whole.

Tell what you'll say.

Say it.

Tell what you said.

Reassert the main point.

If an essay is complicated, the reader may need reclarification at the end. Show that you are fulfilling the promises you made in the beginning. Remind the reader of what you first set out to do, check off the key points you've covered, or answer any questions left unanswered. *Finally, rephrase the thesis, restating it in light of the most important support you've given.* Take this opportunity to deepen and expand your original thesis, now that your reader has the background to better understand your purpose.

Urge the reader.

Your reader may still be reluctant to accept your ideas or argument. The ending is your last chance to gain the reader's acceptance. Be convincing by delivering reasonable final comments. Depending on your topic, you might (1) talk about the **implications** of a certain action or inaction, (2) predict future problems or solutions, or (3) list the **benefits** of accepting or applying your ideas.

ENDINGS: WEAK AND STRONG

The final paragraphs of an essay are your last opportunity to refocus, unify, and otherwise reinforce your message. Draft the closing carefully, not merely to finish the essay but to further advance your purpose and thesis.

Weak Ending

The ending below does not focus on or show commitment to the essay's main idea. Rather than reinforcing this idea, the writing takes an entirely new direction.

> So the bottom line is that Mom's photo showed how much I liked my little stream. Of course, I have lots of other good childhood memories as well, like the times Dad would read to me before bedtime. I loved those books. How about you? Do you have good childhood memories?

Think about your document's opening and closing as a type of contract that you make with your reader. Whereas the opening explains what you intend to do, the closing reviews and confirms what you have done.

implications
natural results, direct and indirect, whether good or bad

benefits
positive or helpful results

Strong Endings

The following ending is a revised version of the closing on the previous page. Listen to its sincere tone, and note how the writer has invested personal feeling and insight for the reader's benefit.

> Sometimes, I want to go back there, back into that photo. I want to step into a time when life seemed safe, and a tiny stream gave us all that we needed. In that picture, our smiles last, our hearts are calm, and we hear only quiet voices, forest sounds, and my bubbling stream. Bitter words are silenced and tears held back by the click and whir of a camera.
>
> I've been thinking about making the journey again, past the hunter's fort, under the stand of cedars, through the muck and mire, and over the rocky rise. But it's been a long summer, and the small seasonal stream running out of the overflow of the pond has probably dried up. (See the full essay on pages 92–93.)

LO5 Use sources effectively.

Writing a first draft often involves exploring your own thinking in relation to the ideas and information you have discovered through research. Use creativity and care—the creativity to see connections and to trace lines of thinking, and the care to respect ideas and information from other sources. (See pages 248–249 for drafting strategies for research papers.)

THINK RHETORICALLY.

Decide which sources aid your purpose (to entertain, to inform, to persuade) and help you connect with your audience. Also focus on your role as the writer. In a research paper, you are not only using sources to support your own ideas, but you are also conversing with those sources. While showing respect for your sources, you want to avoid being intimidated by them.

summary
a shortened version of a piece of writing, giving all the main points but no supporting details

paraphrase
to put a whole passage in your own words

quotation
a word-for-word statement or passage from an original source

PRACTICE DRAFTING STRATEGIES.

To work with sources during your drafting, try these strategies:

Drafting Strategies

• **Keep your sources handy.** While drafting, keep source material at your fingertips, whether in paper or electronic form, so that you can integrate **summaries**, **paraphrases**, and **quotations** without disrupting the flow of your drafting.

• **Start your draft with a strong source reference.** Could something from a source get your paper off to an engaging start? Consider these powerful beginnings: A pithy, thought-provoking, or startling quotation; a problematic or controversial statement or fact from a source; or an anecdote (a brief example, story, or case study) that makes the issue concrete.

• **Take care not to overwhelm your draft with source material.** As you draft, keep the focus on your own ideas. Avoid strings of references and chunks of source material with no personal discussion, explanation, or interpretation in between. Don't offer entire paragraphs of material from a source (whether paraphrased or quoted) with a single in-text citation at the end. When you do so, your thinking disappears. Be careful not to overload your draft with complex information and dense data lacking explanation. Resist the urge to simply copy and paste big chunks from sources. Even if you document the sources, your paper will quickly become a patchwork of source material with a few weak stitches (your contribution) holding it together.

• **Advance and deepen your thesis with reliable reasons and evidence.** A typical supporting paragraph starts with a topic sentence and elaborates it with detailed evidence and careful reasoning. Note this pattern in the paragraph that follows:

Sample Supporting Paragraph

The topic sentence supports the thesis of the greater essay.

Careful reasoning develops the main idea.

Evidence from source material further develops the idea.

A concluding statement revisits the main idea.

Antibiotics are effective only against infections caused by bacteria and should never be used against infections caused by viruses. Using an antibiotic against a viral infection is like throwing water on a grease fire—water may normally put out fires but will only worsen the situation for a grease fire. In the same way, antibiotics fight infections, but they harm the body when they are used to fight infections caused by viruses. Viruses cause the common cold, the flu, and most sore throats, sinus infections, coughs, and bronchitis. Yet antibiotics are commonly prescribed for these viral infections. The *New England Journal of Medicine* reports that 22.7 million kilograms (25,000 tons) of antibiotics are prescribed each year in the United States alone (Wenzel and Edmond, 1962). Meanwhile, the CDC reports that approximately 50 percent of those prescriptions are completely unnecessary ("Antibiotic Overuse" 25). "Every year, tens of millions of prescriptions for antibiotics are written to treat viral illnesses for which these antibiotics offer no benefits," says the CDC's antimicrobial resistance director David Bell, M.D. (qtd. in Bren 30). Such mis-prescribing is simply bad medical practice that contributes to the problem of growing bacterial infection.

• **Save the best for last.** Consider using an especially thought-provoking statement, quotation, or detail in your conclusion. Doing so clinches your point and leaves the reader with something to think about. Also track the borrowed material you use in your draft. As you include those summaries, paraphrases, or quotations, mark them clearly with codes, highlighting, brackets, or other symbols that will allow you to identify the material during the revising and editing steps.

"**The great thing about revision**
is that it's your opportunity to fake being brilliant."

—Will Shetterly

5

Revising

Admit it. Sometimes when it comes to revising, you rely too much (or exclusively!) on your word processor's handy "checkers." However, while the checkers are useful for editing and proofreading, they simply cannot do the analysis and rewriting needed for revision.

Revising and editing are two different steps in the writing process. Revising means reviewing "big picture" issues such as a paper's ideas, organization, and voice and making the necessary changes—adding details, rearranging ideas, rewriting different parts, and so on. Editing deals with line-by-line issues of style and correctness and becomes important after revising. So be sure to address each step at the proper time—first revising and then editing.

This chapter focuses on **revising**. Good writing almost always requires substantial revising. This means you will need to set aside plenty of time for it. *Remember:* When it comes to college writing, pulling an all-nighter the night before a paper is due will rarely produce a quality paper.

In this chapter, you will find valuable revising guidelines and strategies to use in all of your writing. You will learn how to energize your writing voice, unify your paragraphs, and strengthen your ideas and supporting details. All of these strategies will help you produce meaningful documents and make you a more thoughtful writer.

Learning Outcomes

LO1 Address whole-paper issues.

LO2 Revise your first draft.

LO3 Revise for ideas and organization.

LO4 Revise for voice.

LO5 Address paragraph issues.

LO6 Revise collaboratively.

LO7 Use the writing center.

What do you think?

I leave enough time
to revise my first draft.

1   **2**   **3**   **4**   **5**
strongly agree   strongly disagree

revising
improving a draft through large-scale changes such as adding, deleting, rearranging, and reworking

LO1 Address whole-paper issues.

When revising, first look at the big picture. Take it all in. Determine whether the content is interesting, informative, and worth sharing. Note any gaps or soft spots in your line of thinking. And ask yourself how you can improve what you have done so far. The information that follows will help you address big-picture issues in your work.

THE BIG THREE

The whole-paper issues will be adequately addressed in three steps. Reconsider the rhetorical situation dictated by the assignment, examine your general approach to the topic, and find ways to refresh any stale sections of writing.

Revisit your rhetorical situation.

Remember why you are writing—your *purpose*. Are you entertaining the reader, sharing information, recalling an experience, explaining a process, or arguing a point? Does your writing achieve that purpose? Also consider your *audience*. How much do they know about the subject? What else do they need to know? Finally, revisit the *subject*. Has your draft addressed the topic fully and clearly?

> Effective writing prompts the reader to think carefully about the topic.

Consider your overall approach.

Sometimes it's better to start fresh if your writing seems uninspired in stretches. A number of different circumstances may require such an action. For example, a dull title like "Lead Poisoning" may mark a **worn-out topic** . . . or at least a topic addressed in an uninteresting way. Think about approaching it with a new twist ("Get the Lead Out!") or find a new topic. A second signal that a fresh start is in order is a predictable or **fake writing voice**. If your writing sounds bland or is overly academic, consider a more vibrant approach. Similarly, an overall **uninspiring draft,** one in which you pay an equal amount of attention to everything and stress nothing, calls for substantial revision. Strengthen such a draft by condensing less important material and expanding what is important. Finally, if your writing sounds **formulaic,** try something creative. A draft bogged down by rigid adherence to a formula, such as the five-paragraph format, might need a more original approach.

Energize your writing.

So how can you energize stale writing? One approach is to freewrite about your topic. Ten minutes of non-stop freewriting might help you discover a new angle or point of view for your essay. A second approach is to review your notes for additional details of interest. If you can't find any, do some more research. A third approach is to list and respond to the opposing arguments to your thesis. This strategy will give you a better understanding of your topic and revitalize your message.

LO2 Revise your first draft.

Revising helps you turn your first draft into a complete, thoughtful piece of writing. But before you jump into making changes, take some time to get organized. Ideally, you should set your draft aside for a few days before you look at it. The time away will help you assess your writing more objectively. If you've drafted on paper, photocopy the writing. If you've drafted on a computer, print out a copy of your paper (double-spaced). In either case, save the original first draft for reference. Then make changes with a good colored pencil or pen.

worn-out topic
an essay topic that is dull or unoriginal

fake writing voice
a writing voice that sounds overly academic, bland, or unnatural

uninspiring draft
a draft in which a writer fails to engage the reader and make a lasting impression

formulaic writing
writing that stiffly adheres to a traditional format and fails to make a strong impact

THINK GLOBALLY.

When you are ready to revise, don't pay undue attention to spelling, grammar, and punctuation. Doing so may distract you from the task at hand: improving the content of your writing. At this point, you should attend to the overall strength of your ideas, organization, and voice. (The conventions come later.)

Ideas: Check the thesis or focus of your writing. Has your thinking about this topic changed? Also consider your reader's most pressing questions concerning this topic. Have you answered these questions? Finally, consider your reasoning and support. Are both complete and sound?

Organization: Check the **overall design** of your writing, making sure the reader can move smoothly and logically from one point to the next. Is your essay built effectively, well ordered with main points and supporting details in place? Do you shift directions cleanly? Fix structural problems in one of these ways:

Reorder material to improve the sequence.

Cut information that doesn't support the thesis.

Add details where the draft is thin.

Rewrite parts that seem unclear.

Improve links between points by using transitions.

Voice: Voice is your personal presence on the page, the tone and attitude that others hear when reading your work. In other words, voice is the between-the-lines message your audience gets (whether you want them to or not). When revising, make sure that the tone of your message matches your purpose, whether it is serious, playful, or satiric.

LO3 Revise for ideas and organization.

As you review your draft for content, make sure the ideas are fully developed and the organization is clear. The ideas should be thoroughly elaborated and hold the reader's attention from start to finish, while the organization should unify the ideas and make them easy to follow. Use the following information to strengthen your thinking and sequencing.

EXAMINE YOUR IDEAS.

Review the ideas in your writing, making sure that each point is logical, complete, and clear. Be aware of **logical fallacies** or fuzzy thinking in your essay. Logical problems in your thinking will weaken your paper. To test the logic in your writing, see pages 138–141.

Complete Thinking

Complete writing effectively answers the reader's questions about the topic. It includes ideas about the topic that go beyond what the audience already knows and expects. Incomplete writing leaves the reader asking for more, as in the original passage that follows. The revised version is clearly more complete.

Original Passage (Too general):

As soon as you receive a minor cut, the body's healing process begins. Blood from tiny vessels fills the wound and begins to clot. In less than 24 hours, a scab forms.

Revised Version (More specific):

As soon as you receive a minor cut, the body's healing process begins. Within the wounded layers of skin are tiny blood vessels called capillaries. Severed, these vessels bleed into the wound, releasing minute structures called platelets, which help stop the bleeding. The platelets stick to the edges of the cut and to one another, forming a plug. Then they release chemicals that react with certain proteins in the blood to form a clot. Finally, the fiber network of the clot begins to join the edges of the wound together, and as the clot dries, a scab forms—usually in less than 24 hours.

Clear Thesis

Make sure that your writing centers on one main issue or thesis. The thesis should be stated in a way that effectively expresses a special condition or feature of the topic that you want to explore or explain in your essay. The original passage on the next page lacks a thesis; the revision has one.

overall design
the pattern the writing takes to move the ideas along—time order, compare-contrast, and so on

logical fallacies
false arguments based on bits of fuzzy, dishonest, or incomplete thinking

Original Passage (Lacks a thesis):

Teen magazines are popular with young girls. These magazines contain a lot of how-to articles about self-image, fashion, and boy-girl relationships. Girls read them to get advice on how to act and how to look. The most eager readers seem to be girls who are unsure of themselves.

Revised Version (Contains a **thesis statement**):

Adolescent girls often see teen magazines as handbooks on how to be teenagers. These magazines influence how young girls act and look, and for girls who are unsure of themselves, the pressure to conform can be enormous. **Unfortunately, the advice these magazines give about self-image, fashion, and boys may do more harm than good.**

EXAMINE YOUR ORGANIZATION.

Good writing has structure. It leads the reader logically and clearly from one point to the next. When revising for organization, consider four areas: the overall plan, the opening, the flow of ideas, and the closing. Pay special attention to the sequence of ideas or events that you share. Does that sequence advance your thesis? Do the points build effectively to a clear idea? Are there gaps or weak spots in the overall organization? If you find such problems, address them during revising. For example, refine the focus or emphasis by rearranging material within the text. Fill in gaps with new details from your planning notes, and delete any ideas that wander from your purpose. Rework or rearrange parts that need more structure.

As you reexamine your essay, remember that the best organizational choice is dictated by the kind of writing you are doing. For example, personal narratives and process essays are usually organized chronologically. Expository essays may be organized according to cause and effect or classification; descriptions according to spatial order or comparison/contrast; persuasive essays by opinion and reasons; and so on.

Typically, however, a combination of organizational methods is needed to develop a writing idea. If you are comparing two subjects, for example, you can add depth to your analysis by contrasting them as well. If you are describing a complex subject, you can examine the subject more closely by distinguishing and classifying its parts. If you are telling a story in time order, you can enhance the narration with a description at some point, perhaps according to spatial order. Strive to share your ideas in a logical, careful order for the reader's comprehension and enjoyment. (See pages 32–33 for more on the common methods of development.)

Opening Ideas

Review your opening paragraph(s). Is the information organized effectively? Does it engage the reader, establish a direction for your writing, and express your thesis or focus? The original opening below does not accomplish these goals, but the revised version engages the reader and builds to a compelling thesis.

Original Opening (Lacks interest and direction):

The lack of student motivation is a common subject in the news. Educators want to know how to get students to learn. Today's higher standards mean that students will be expected to learn even more. Another problem in urban areas is that large numbers of students are dropping out. How to interest students is a challenge.

Revised Version (Effectively leads the reader):

How can we motivate students to learn? How can we help them meet today's rising standards of excellence? How can we, in fact, keep students in school long enough for them to learn? The answer to these questions is quite simple. Give them money. Pay students to study, to learn, and to stay in school.

Flow of Ideas

Look closely at the beginning and ending of each of your paragraphs. Have you connected your thoughts clearly? (See page 61 for a list of transition words.) The beginning phrases below are taken from a sequence of four paragraphs in an essay of description. They do not connect the ideas for the reader. Note, though, how the revised versions order the ideas by location, connecting the paragraphs and leading the reader.

Original Phrases (No links):

There was a huge, steep hill …

Buffalo Creek ran …

A dense "jungle" covering …

Within walking distance from my house …

Revised Versions (Strong transitions):

Behind the house, there was a huge, steep hill …

Across the road from the house, Buffalo Creek ran …

On the far side of the creek bank was a dense "jungle" covering …

Up the road, within walking distance from my house …

Within your paragraphs, be certain that you have provided evidence to support your ideas. Whether it is statistics and expert testimony in a press release or test results and experimental data in a science journal, evidence strengthens ideas and improves a paper's credibility. Review the types of evidence on pages 136-138 to bolster weak or unconvincing passages.

Closing Ideas

Reread your closing paragraph(s). Do you offer an effective summary, reassert your main point in a fresh way, and provide the reader with food for thought? Or is your ending abrupt, repetitive, directionless? The original ending below is uninspiring; it gives the reader little to consider. The revision, however, summarizes the main points in the essay and urges the reader to think again about the overall point of the writing.

Original Ending (Sketchy and flat):

Native Son deals with a young man's struggle against racism. It shows the effects of prejudice. Everyone should read this book.

Revised Version (Effective and thought provoking):

Native Son deals not only with a young man's struggle in a racist society, but also with so much more. It shows how prejudice affects people, how it closes in on them, and how it drives them to find a way out. Anyone who wants to better understand racism in the United States should read this book.

TIP

To generate fresh ideas for your closing, freewrite answers to questions like these: Why is the topic important to me? What should my reader have learned? Why should this issue matter to the reader? What evidence or appeal (page 142) will help the reader remember my message and act on it? How does the topic relate to broader issues in society, history, or life?

appeal
an argument that connects to the reader's needs, such as achievement, belonging, or survival

LO4 Revise for voice.

Generally, readers trust writing that speaks in an informed voice, a voice that is clear and natural in style. To develop an informed voice, be sure that your details are correct and complete; to develop a clear and natural style, make sure that your writing is well organized and unpretentious. Also check for the following issues. (For a definition of *voice*, see page 53.)

CHECK THE LEVEL OF COMMITMENT.

Consider how and to what degree your writing shows that you care about the topic and the reader. For example, note how the original passage below reveals nothing about the writer's connection to—or interest in—the topic. In contrast, the revision shows that the writer cares about the topic.

Original Passage   (Lacks voice):

Cemeteries can teach us a lot about history. They make history seem more real. There is an old grave of a Revolutionary War veteran in the Union Grove Cemetery....

Revised Version   (Personal, sincere voice):

I've always had a special feeling for cemeteries. It's hard to explain any further than that, except to say history never seems quite as real as it does when I walk among old gravestones. One day I discovered the grave of a Revolutionary War veteran....

CHECK THE INTENSITY OF YOUR WRITING.

All writing—including academic writing—is enriched by an appropriate level of **intensity** or passion. In the original passage that follows, the writer's concern for the topic is unclear because she sounds neutral. In contrast, the revised version exudes energy.

intensity
a writer's level of concern for the topic, as indicated by the writing voice

Original Passage   (Lacks feeling and energy):

Motz blames Barbie dolls for all the problems that women face today. Instead, one should look to romance novels, fashion magazines, and parental training for causes of these societal problems.

Revised Version   (Expresses real feelings):

In other words, Motz uses Barbie as a scapegoat for problems that have complex causes. However, a girl's interest in romance is no more Barbie's fault than the fault of books like *On the Shores of Silver Lake*. Fashion magazines targeted at adolescents are the cause of far more anorexia than is Barbie. And mothers who encourage daughters to find security in men teach female dependency, but Barbie doesn't.

To enhance your essay's voice, freely record your thoughts and feelings about the topic. Then revitalize your writing with any fresh ideas and directions that occur to you.

DEVELOP AN ACADEMIC STYLE.

Most college writing requires an academic style, but *academic* doesn't have to mean "stuffy." You're not trying to impress readers with ten-dollar words. Rather, you are using language that facilitates a thoughtful, engaged discussion of the topic. To choose the best words for such a conversation, consider the issues that follow.

Personal Pronouns

In some academic writing, personal pronouns are acceptable. This is the case with informal writing such as journaling and in personal essays involving narration, description, and reflection. In addition, *I* is correctly used in academic writing rooted in personal research, sometimes called an I-search paper.

Generally, however, avoid using *I*, *we*, and *you* in traditional academic writing. The concept, instead, is to focus on the topic itself and let your attitude be

> **TIP**
>
> In academic prose, use the pronoun *one*, meaning "a person," sparingly. It can easily result in a stilted style: *One never knows what one's future holds.*

revealed indirectly. As E. B. White puts it, "To achieve style, begin by affecting none—that is, begin by placing yourself in the background."

> **No:** I really think that the problem of the homeless in Chicago is serious. Many of the homeless there die, as I know from my experience where I grew up.

> **Yes:** Homelessness in Chicago often leads to death. This fact demands the attention of more than lawmakers and social workers; all citizens must address the problems of their suffering neighbors.

Technical Terms and Jargon

Technical terms and jargon—"insider" words—are the specialized vocabulary of a subject, a discipline, a profession, or a social group. As such, jargon can be difficult for "outsiders" to understand.

You may use technical terms to communicate with people within the profession or discipline. But be careful; jargon can devolve into meaningless buzzwords and catchphrases.

Avoid jargon when writing for readers outside the profession or discipline. Use simpler terms and define technical terms that must be used.

> **Technical:** Bin's Douser power washer delivers 2200 psi p.r., runs off standard a.c. lines, comes with 100 ft. h.d. synthetic-rubber tubing, and features variable pulsation options through three adjustable s.s. tips.

> **Simple:** Bin's Douser power washer has a pressure rating of 2200 psi (pounds per square inch), runs off a common 200-volt electrical circuit, comes with 100 feet of hose, and includes three nozzles.

Level of Formality

Most academic writing (especially research papers, literary analyses, lab reports, and argumentative essays) should meet the standards of formal English. **Formal English** is characterized by a serious tone; careful attention to word choice; longer sentences that reflect complex thinking; strict adherence to traditional conventions of grammar, mechanics, and punctuation; and avoidance of contractions and **slang**.

> Formal English, modeled in this sentence, is worded correctly and carefully so that it can withstand repeated readings without seeming tiresome, sloppy, or cute.

Other types of writing, such as personal essays, commentaries, and journals may employ informal English. **Informal English** is characterized by a personal tone, the occasional use of popular expressions, shorter sentences with slightly looser syntax, contractions, and personal pronouns (*I, we, you*); but it still adheres to basic conventions.

> Informal English sounds like one person talking to another person. It's the type of language you are reading now—comfortable and real, not affected or breezy.

Unnecessary Qualifiers

Using **qualifiers** (such as *mostly, often, likely,* or *tends to*) is an appropriate strategy for developing defendable claims in argumentative writing. (See pages 135–136.) However, overqualifying your ideas or adding intensifiers (*really, truly*) can result in an insecure voice and give the impression that you lack confidence in your ideas. The cure? Say what you mean, and mean what you say.

> **Insecure:** I totally and completely agree with the new security measures at sporting events, but that's only my opinion.

> **Secure:** I agree with the new security measures at sporting events.

fyi Each academic discipline has its own vocabulary and its own vocabulary resources. Such resources include dictionaries, glossaries, and handbooks. Check your library for the vocabulary resources in your discipline. Use them regularly to deepen your grasp of that vocabulary.

> **formal English**
> carefully worded language suitable for most academic writing
>
> **slang**
> words considered outside standard English because they are faddish, familiar to few people, and sometimes insulting
>
> **informal English**
> language characterized by a more relaxed, personal tone suitable for personal writing
>
> **qualifiers**
> words or phrases that limit or refine a claim, making it more reasonable

KNOW WHEN TO USE PASSIVE VOICE.

Most verbs can be active or passive. When a verb is active, the sentence's subject performs the action. When the verb is passive, the subject is acted upon. A common mistake is to avoid the **passive voice** at all costs. It is true that the **active voice** is usually the best choice because it is direct and energetic. However, the passive voice is more effective when the writer wants to stress the receiver rather than the doer. Use the information that follows to guide your use of the active or passive voice.

> **Active:** If you *can't attend* the meeting, *notify* Richard by Thursday.
>
> **Passive:** If a meeting *can't be attended* by you, Richard *must be notified* by Thursday.

Weaknesses of Passive Voice: The passive voice tends to be wordy and sluggish because the verb's action is directed backward, not ahead. In addition, passive constructions tend to be impersonal, making people disappear.

> **Passive:** The sound system *can* now *be used* by parents to listen in on sessions in the therapy room. Constructive one-on-one communication methods with children *will be modeled* by therapists.
>
> **Active:** Parents *can* now *use* the sound system to listen in on sessions in the therapy room. Therapists *will model* constructive one-on-one communication methods with children.

Strengths of Passive Voice: Using the passive voice isn't wrong. In fact, the passive voice has some important uses: (1) when you need to be tactful (say, in a bad-news letter), (2) if you wish to stress the object or person acted upon, and (3) if the actual actor is understood, unknown, or unimportant.

> **Active:** Our engineers determined that you *bent* the bar at the midpoint.
>
> **Passive:** Our engineers determined that the bar *had been bent* at the midpoint. (tactful)
>
> **Active:** Congratulations! We *have approved* your scholarship for $2,500.
>
> **Passive:** Congratulations! Your scholarship for $2,500 *has been approved*. (emphasis on receiver; actor understood)

LO5 Address paragraph issues.

While drafting, you may have constructed paragraphs that are loosely held together, poorly developed, or unclear. So when you revise, pay special attention to paragraph issues such as **unity, coherence**, and completeness (pages 59-62). A unified paragraph focuses on one concise idea; a coherent paragraph flows smoothly from one idea to the next; a complete paragraph thoroughly develops one main idea. The information that follows will further address important paragraph issues.

CHECK THE BASICS.

A paragraph should be a concise unit of thought. When you revise a paragraph, ask yourself the following questions: Is the paragraph organized around a controlling idea? Is the idea stated in a topic sentence? Do the supporting sentences develop the controlling idea? Does the paragraph conclude with a sentence that summarizes the main point and prepares the reader for the next paragraph or main point? Does the paragraph serve a specific function in a piece of writing—opening, supporting, developing, illustrating, countering, describing, or closing?

---

passive voice
a subject-verb construction in which the subject is acted upon

active voice
a subject-verb construction in which the subject performs the action

unity
oneness in a paragraph achieved through focus on a single idea

coherence
strong connection between sentences in a paragraph, achieved through transition and repetition

TIP

Avoid using the passive voice unethically to hide responsibility. For example, an instructor who says, "Your assignments could not be graded because of scheduling difficulties," may be evading the truth: "I did not finish grading your assignments because I was watching *CSI*."

Sample Paragraph

Topic Sentence

Supporting Sentences

Closing Sentence

Tumor cells can hurt the body in a number of ways. First, a tumor can grow so big that it takes up space needed by other organs. Second, some cells may detach from the original tumor and spread throughout the body, creating new tumors elsewhere. This happens with lymphatic cancer—a cancer that's hard to control because it spreads so quickly. A third way that tumor cells can hurt the body is by doing work not called for in their DNA. For example, a gland cell's DNA code may tell the cell to produce a necessary hormone in the endocrine system. However, if cancer damages or distorts that code, sick cells may produce more of the hormone than the body can use—or even tolerate (Braun 4). Cancer cells seem to have minds of their own, and this is why cancer is such a serious disease.

KEEP THE PURPOSE IN MIND.

Use these questions to evaluate the purpose of each paragraph: What function does the paragraph fulfill? How does it add to your line of reasoning or the development of your thesis? Would the paragraph work better if it were divided in two—or combined with another paragraph? Does the paragraph flow smoothly from the previous paragraph, and does it lead effectively into the next one?

CHECK FOR UNITY.

A unified paragraph is one in which all the details help to develop a single main topic or achieve a single main effect. Test for unity by following these guidelines.

Topic Sentence

Very often the topic of a paragraph is stated in a single sentence called a "topic sentence." Check whether your paragraph needs a topic sentence. If the paragraph has a topic sentence, determine whether it is clear, specific, and well focused. Following is a formula for writing good topic sentences, along with an example:

Formula:

A limited topic + a specific feeling or thought about it = an effective topic sentence.

Example:

The fear that Americans feel (limited topic) comes partly from the uncertainty related to this attack (a specific thought).

Placement of the Topic Sentence

Normally the topic sentence is the first sentence in the paragraph. However, it can appear elsewhere in a paragraph.

Middle Placement: Place a topic sentence in the middle when you want to build up to and then lead away from the key idea.

During the making of *Apocalypse Now*, Eleanor Coppola created a documentary about the filming called *Hearts of Darkness: A Filmmaker's Apocalypse*. In the first film, the insane Colonel Kurtz has disappeared into the Cambodian jungle. As Captain Willard searches for Kurtz, the screen fills with horror. However, as *Hearts of Darkness* relates, the horror portrayed in the fictional movie was being lived out by the production company. For example, in the documentary, actor Larry Fishburne shockingly says, "War is fun. . . . Vietnam must have been so much fun." Then toward the end of the filming, actor Martin Sheen suffered a heart attack. When an assistant informed investors, the director exploded, "He's not dead unless I say he's dead."

End Placement: Place a topic sentence at the end when you want to build to a climax, as in a passage of narration or persuasion.

When sportsmen stop to reflect on why they find fishing so enjoyable, most realize that what they love is the feel of a fish on the end of the line, not necessarily the weight of the fillets in their coolers. Fishing has undergone a slow evolution over the last century. While fishing used to be a way of putting food on the table, most of today's fishermen do so only for the relaxation that it provides. The barbed hook was invented to increase the quantity of fish a man could land so that he could better feed his family. This need no longer exists, so barbed hooks are no longer necessary.

Supporting Sentences

All the sentences in the body of a paragraph should support the topic sentence. The closing sentence, for instance, will often summarize the paragraph's main point or emphasize a key detail. If any sentences shift the focus away from the topic, revise the paragraph so all the sentences support the topic sentence.

If a paragraph lacks unity, try one of these strategies to solve the problem: (1) Delete any material that doesn't relate to the topic sentence. (2) Rewrite the material so that it clearly supports the topic sentence. (3) Create a separate paragraph based on relevant deleted material. (4) Revise the topic sentence so that it relates more closely to the support.

Consistent Focus

Examine the following paragraph about fishing hooks. The original topic sentence focuses on the point that some anglers prefer smooth hooks. However, the writer leaves this initial idea unfinished and turns to the issue of the cost of new hooks. In the revised version, unity is restored: The first paragraph completes the point about anglers who prefer smooth hooks; the second paragraph addresses the issue of replacement costs.

Original Paragraph (Lacks unity):

According to some anglers who do use smooth hooks, their lures perform better than barbed lures as long as they maintain a constant tension on the line. Smooth hooks can bite deeper than barbed hooks, actually providing a stronger hold on the fish. Some people have argued that replacing all of the barbed hooks in their tackle would be a costly operation.

Revised Version (Unified):

According to some anglers who do use smooth hooks, their lures perform better than barbed lures as long as the anglers maintain a constant tension on the line. Smooth hooks can bite deeper than barbed hooks, actually providing a stronger hold on the fish. These anglers testify that switching from barbed hooks has not noticeably reduced the number of fish that they are able to land. In

repetition
repeating words or synonyms where necessary to remind the reader of what has already been said

parallelism
repeating phrases or sentence structures to show the relationship between ideas

(cont.)

their experience, and in my own, enjoyment of the sport is actually heightened by adding another challenge to playing the fish (maintaining line tension).

Some people have argued that replacing all of the barbed hooks in their tackle would be a costly operation. While this is certainly a concern, barbed hooks do not necessarily require replacement. With a simple set of pliers, the barbs on most conventional hooks can be bent down, providing a cost-free method of modifying one's existing tackle....

fyi Paragraphs that contain unrelated ideas lack unity and are hard to follow. As you review each paragraph for unity, ask yourself these questions: Is the topic of the paragraph clear? Does each sentence relate to the topic? Are the sentences organized in the best possible order?

CHECK FOR COHERENCE.

When a paragraph is coherent, the parts stay together. A coherent paragraph flows smoothly because each sentence connects to the others. To strengthen the coherence in your paragraphs, consider using repetition or transitions.

Effective Repetition

To achieve coherence in your paragraphs, consider using **repetition**—repeating words or synonyms where necessary to remind the reader of what you have already said. You can also use **parallelism**—repeating phrase or sentence structures to show the relationship between ideas. At the same time, you will add a unifying rhythm to your writing.

Original (Nonparallel phrases used):

The floor was littered with discarded soda cans, newspapers that were crumpled, and wrinkled clothes.

Revised (Parallel phrases used):

The floor was littered with discarded soda cans, crumpled newspapers, and wrinkled clothes.

Original (Dissimilar structures):

Reading the book was enjoyable; to write the critique was difficult.

Revised (Similar structures repeated):

Reading the book was enjoyable; writing the critique was difficult.

Clear Transitions

Transitions or linking words and phrases such as "next," "on the other hand," and "in addition" connect ideas by showing the relationships between them. There are transitions that show location and time, compare and contrast things, emphasize a point, conclude or summarize, and add or clarify information. Note the use of transitions in the following examples:

In fact (Used to emphasize a point):

The paradox of Scotland is that violence was once the norm in this now-peaceful land. **In fact,** the country was born and bred in war.

First (Used to show time or order):

The production of cement is a complicated process. **First,** the mixture of lime, silica, alumina, and gypsum is ground into very fine particles.

Yet another way to achieve coherence in your paragraphs is to use pronouns effectively. A pronoun forms a link to the noun it replaces and ties that noun (idea) to the ideas that follow. As always, don't overuse or rely too heavily on pronouns to establish coherence in your paragraphs.

Transitions and Linking Words

If your writing at any point causes you to stumble, consider using transitions to tie ideas together. The word bank that follows lists common transitions and linking words and is organized according to how these words are used.

© Ljupco Smokovski , 2009 / Used under license from Shutterstock.com

Quick Guide — Transitions

Show location: above, behind, down, on top of, across, below, in back of, onto, against, beneath, in front of, outside, along, beside, inside, over, among, between, into, throughout, around, beyond, near, to the right, away from, by, off, under

Show time: about, during, next, today, after, finally, next week, tomorrow, afterward, first, second, until, as soon as, immediately, soon, when, at, later, then, yesterday, before, meanwhile, third

Show similarities: also, in the same way, likewise, as, like, similarly

Show differences: although, even though, on the other hand, still, but, however, otherwise, yet

Emphasize a point: again, for this reason, particularly, to repeat, even, in fact, to emphasize, truly

Conclude or summarize: all in all, finally, in summary, therefore, as a result, in conclusion, last, to sum up

Add information: additionally, and, equally important, in addition, again, another, finally, likewise, along with, as well, for example, next, also, besides, for instance, second

Clarify: for instance, in other words, put another way, that is

transitions
words and phrases that help tie ideas together

CHECK FOR COMPLETENESS.

The sentences in a paragraph should support and expand on the main point or topic sentence. If your paragraph does not provide enough supporting information, you will need to add details. There are many types of details, including the following:

facts	anecdotes	analyses	sensations
statistics	quotations	explanations	comparisons
examples	definitions	summaries	analogies

The type of details you add depends on the type of writing you are doing. If you are sharing a personal experience or describing something, you might need to add **sensory details** to create more effective images. (Sensory details help the reader to see, hear, feel, taste, and so on.) If you are sharing information or writing persuasively, you might need to include additional facts, examples, explanations, or analyses to strengthen your thesis.

Specific Details

The original paragraph that follows fails to answer fully the question posed by the topic sentence. In the revised paragraph, the writer uses an **anecdote** to answer the question.

Original Paragraph (Lacks completeness):

So what is stress? Actually, the physiological characteristics of stress are some of the body's potentially good self-defense mechanisms. People experience stress when they are in danger. In fact, stress can be healthy.

Revised Version (Full development):

So what is stress? Actually, the physiological characteristics of stress are some of the body's potentially good self-defense mechanisms. Take, for example, a man who is crossing a busy intersection when he spots an oncoming car. Immediately his brain releases a flood of adrenaline into his bloodstream. As a result, his muscles contract, his eyes dilate, his heart pounds faster, his breathing quickens, and his blood clots more readily. Each one of these responses

sensory details
sights, sounds, smells, tastes, textures, temperatures, and other details connected to the five senses—showing rather than telling about the subject

anecdotes
brief stories or "slices of life" that help make a point

(cont.)

helps the man leap out of the car's path. His muscles contract to give him exceptional strength. His eyes dilate so that he can see more clearly. His heart pumps more blood and his lungs exchange more air—both to increase his metabolism. If the man were injured, his blood would clot faster, ensuring a smaller amount of blood loss. In this situation and many more like it, stress symptoms are good (Curtis 25–26).

If, when revising for completeness, a paragraph gets too long, consider dividing it at a natural stopping point. You might also need to add a topic sentence to the new paragraph.

LO6 Revise collaboratively.

Every writer can benefit from feedback from an interested audience, especially one that offers constructive and honest advice during a writing project. Members of an existing writing group already know how valuable it is for writers to share their work. Others might want to start a writing group to experience the benefits. Your group might collaborate online or in person. In either case, the information below and on the next page will help you get started.

KNOW YOUR ROLE.

Writers and reviewers should know their roles and fulfill their responsibilities during revising sessions. Essentially, the writer should briefly introduce the draft and solicit honest responses. Reviewers should make constructive comments in response to the writing.

Feedback can take many forms, including the three approaches that follow.

Basic Description: In this simple response, the reviewer listens or reads attentively and then simply describes what she or he hears or sees happening in the piece. The reviewer offers no criticism of the writing.

> **Ineffective:** "That was interesting. The piece was informative."
>
> **Effective:** "First, the essay introduced the challenge of your birth defect and how you have had to cope with it. Then, in the next part, you . . ."

Summary Evaluation: Here the reviewer reads or listens to the piece and then provides a specific evaluation of the draft.

> **Ineffective:** "Gee, I really liked it!" or "It was boring."
>
> **Effective:** "Your story, at the beginning, really pulled me in, and the middle explained the issue strongly, but the ending was a bit flat."

Thorough Critique: The reviewer assesses the ideas, organization, and voice in the writing. Feedback should be detailed and constructive. Such a critique may also be completed with the aid of a review sheet or checklist. As a reviewer, be prepared to share specific responses, suggestions, and questions. But also be sure to courteously focus your comments on the writing, not on the writer.

> **Inappropriate:** "You really need to fix that opening! What were you thinking?"
>
> **Appropriate:** "Let's look closely at the opening. Could you rewrite the first sentence so it grabs the reader's attention? Also, I'm somewhat confused about the thesis statement. Could you rephrase it so it states your position more clearly?"

ASK THE "WRITE" QUESTIONS.

As a reviewer, you have the opportunity to ask questions that will help a fellow writer improve his or her writing. To help writers reflect on their purpose and audience, ask, *Why are you writing this? Who will read this, and what do you they need to know?* To help writers focus their thoughts, ask, *What message are you trying to get across? Do you have more than one main point? What*

are the most important examples? To help writers think about their information, ask, *What do you know about the subject? Does this part say enough? Does your writing cover the basics—who? what? where? when? why? and how?* And finally, to help writers with their openings and closings, ask, *What are you trying to say in the opening? How else could you start your writing? What thoughts or ideas do you want to share with the reader in the ending?*

Respond using the OAQS method.

The OAQS method uses a simple four-step scheme—**observe, appreciate, question, suggest**—to respond to a peer's work. Using this method ensures that you will give the writer a balanced response—one that both supports the writer's effort and offers constructive criticism.

Response Strategies

- **Observe** Take notice of what another person's essay is designed to do and say something about its purpose. For example, you might say, "Even though you are writing about your boyfriend, it appears that you are trying to get a message across to your parents."

- **Appreciate** Praise something in the writing that impresses or pleases you. You can find something to appreciate in any piece of writing. For example, you might say, "You make a very convincing point" or "With your description, I can actually see his broken tooth."

- **Question** Ask whatever you want to know after you've read the essay. You might ask for background information, a definition, an interpretation, or an explanation. For example, you might ask, "Can you tell us what happened when you got to the emergency room?"

- **Suggest** Give helpful advice about possible changes. For example, you might say, "With a little more physical detail—especially more sounds and smells—your third paragraph could be the highlight of the whole essay. What do you think?"

LO7 Use the writing center.

A college writing center or lab is a place where a trained adviser will help you develop and strengthen a piece of writing. You can expect this person to assist you, but certain things only you can do. (For a quick reference concerning the adviser's role versus your own, refer to the quick guide on this page.)

BE PREPARED.

To get the most out of the writing center, visit it several days before your paper is due, and take your assignment sheet with you to each advising session. When you are revising, read your work aloud, slowly, to "hear" clearly what you have written. You may have to rethink your writing from scratch. Do not defend your wording—if it needs defense, it needs revision. And always ask questions. (No question is "too dumb.") Request clarification of anything you don't understand, and ask for examples or illustrations of important points. Write down all practical suggestions, and, if necessary, ask the adviser to summarize or restate his or her remarks. Rewrite your paper as soon as possible after the advising session. Then return to the writing center for a response to your revision.

TIP

To take advantage of the counsel you receive in the writing center, review your revisions. The checklist on the next page will help you do that.

Quick Guide | **Writing Center**

Your Job	Adviser's Job
Be respectful	Make you feel at home
Be ready to work	Discuss your needs
Decide on a topic	Help you choose a topic
Know your purpose and audience	Discuss your purpose and audience
Embrace the best ideas	Help you generate ideas
Consider other points of view; stretch your own perspective	Help you develop your logic
Do the research	Help you understand how to research your material
Share your writing	Read your draft
Recognize and fix problems	Identify problems in organization, logic, expression, and format
Learn important principles	Teach ways to correct weaknesses
Correct all errors	Help you with grammar, usage, diction, vocabulary, and mechanics

Revising Checklist

Ideas

_____ My thesis statement reflects a limited topic.

_____ The thesis clearly states the specific idea I plan to develop.

_____ The thesis is supported by the information I have gathered.

_____ The thesis suggests a pattern of organization for my essay.

_____ My writing focuses on the thesis from beginning to end.

_____ I have fully developed and supported my thesis with relevant, accurate, well-researched details.

Organization

_____ My writing follows a clear pattern of organization that advances the main idea.

_____ I have added, cut, reordered, and rewritten material as needed.

_____ All of the paragraphs are unified, coherent, and complete.

Voice

_____ The tone is matched to the assignment, the reader, and the purpose.

_____ The style is clear, genuine, and appropriately academic.

_____ My voice sounds energetic and interested.

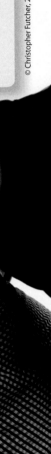

"**Mistakes are a fact of life.**
It is the response to the error that counts."

—Nikki Giovanni

6

Editing

In any writing project, there comes a point (like a fast-approaching due date) when you must stop "futzing" with the content and prepare your writing for publishing by editing and proofreading it. Editing and proofreading deal with the line-by-line changes you make to improve the readability and accuracy of your writing. More specifically, when **editing**, you make sure that your words, phrases, and sentences are clear and correct. When **proofreading**, you check your final copy for errors.

Before you begin, make sure you have the proper tools at hand: *Write,* a dictionary, a computer spell-checker and grammar-checker, and so on. As you work, focus on one element at a time (sentence variety, strong verbs, spelling). This will help you edit more thoroughly. To track editing changes, make your changes on a printed copy of your writing; or use your computer's program to track changes. Also ask at least one writing peer (or a tutor from the writing center) to check your work. You're too close to your writing to catch everything on your own. Prepare your final draft, following the guidelines established by your instructor, and proofread it for errors.

The guidelines and strategies in this chapter will help you edit your writing for style, clarity, and correctness. Pay special attention to the information on sentence style (pages 68–74) and word choice (pages 74–77). Developing an effective writing style is a lifetime challenge, and each writing project is another chance to work on it. So set high standards for yourself, and reach for the best words, phrases, and sentences to convey your thoughts.

Learning Outcomes

LO1 Review the overall style of your writing.

LO2 Write effective sentences.

LO3 Check your sentences for style and correctness.

LO4 Replace imprecise, misleading, and biased words.

LO5 Edit and proofread for conventions.

What do you think?

I always ask one of my peers to help me with my editing.

1	2	3	4	5
strongly agree				strongly disagree

editing
refining a draft in terms of word choice and sentence style and checking it for conventions

proofreading
checking a final copy for errors before submitting it

LO1 Review the overall style of your writing.

Editing only becomes important after you have checked the big-ticket items in your writing—the ideas, organization, and voice. Once your writing says what you want it to say, then, and only then, should you focus on editing. Think of revising as the process of making deep changes in your writing, and editing as the process of making **surface changes**. Both are important, but only in their proper turn.

DOING THE WORK

Use the following information as a general editing plan.

Read your revised writing aloud. Do this only after having set it aside for a day or two. You might also have a writing peer read it aloud to you. Highlight any words, phrases, or sentences that don't seem to work. Keep writer Michael Kaplan's thought in mind during your review: "Any words that aren't working for you are working against you."

Reconcile your style with your rhetorical situation: Does your writing sound as if you have a clear aim or goal in mind? Is the tone honest and sincere? Do all of the words and phrases sound like you? Does your style suit the topic in terms of seriousness or playfulness, complexity or simplicity? Your answers to questions like these will help you plan your editing.

Study your sentences. Henry David Thoreau may have the best advice when checking your sentences for **style** and clarity. He said, "A sentence should read as if its author, had he held a plough instead of a pen, could have drawn a furrow deep and straight to the end." In other words, a sentence works if it communicates a clear unit of thought. To that end, do the following: Replace sentences that are wordy or rambling; combine or expand sentences that are short and choppy. Also vary the beginnings of your sentences and avoid sentence patterns that are too predictable. (See pages 69–74.)

Consider your word choice. The best words are the ones that effectively communicate the meaning, feeling, and voice in your writing. Pay special attention to the nouns and verbs that you use. Are they specific and strong—*Godzilla* instead of *creature*, *lunged* instead of *moved*? (See page 74.) Writing with general nouns (*woman, book, idea*) and weak verbs (*is, are, was, were*) forces you to use a lot of **modifiers**. For this reason, the French writer Voltaire called the adjective "the enemy of the noun." This is not to say that you shouldn't use modifiers. Just use them sparingly, when they truly add to your writing: "Rosie slid *gracefully* to the end of the *park* bench" creates a more effective image than "Rosie slid to the end of the bench."

Here are some additional considerations for word choice: Avoid **redundancy**, words used together that mean nearly the same thing: *repeat again, refer back*. Watch for repetition that detracts from the writing. Starting three sentences in a row with *The man . . .* would be an example of distracting repetition. Avoid **jargon**, or highly technical terms, that may confuse your reader. (See page 75.) Also watch for words or phrases that are biased or demeaning. (See pages 75–76.)

LO2 Write effective sentences.

In Roy Peter Clark's latest book, *Writing Tools*, he says, "Fear not the long sentence." He adds that using long sentences is a sign that a writer is mastering the craft. Of course, a piece of writing shouldn't contain all long sentences. The goal is to use a variety of sentence lengths to emphasize certain ideas, to create a particular rhythm, to speed things up or slow them down.

What you will find if you study the writing of your favorite authors may surprise you—sentences that seem

---

surface changes
the edited (corrected) words, phrases, and sentences in your writing

style
the personal variety, originality, and clarity of your writing

modifiers
words that limit or describe other words or groups of words; adjectives and adverbs

redundancy
words used together that mean nearly the same thing

jargon
highly technical terms not familiar to the general reader

to flow on forever, sentences that sneak up on you, sentences that are so direct that they hit you right between the eyes, and sentences that aren't by definition complete thoughts. Some of these sentences you may want to try in your own writing because you like the way they sound or the way they make a point.

EXPANDING SENTENCES

Professional writers don't write sentences that are easy to classify because they don't write with sentence types in minds. They don't say, for example, "It's time that I use a compound sentence" or "A simple sentence would be good here." They write to make meaning and share this meaning in the most effective way. (Of course, when they edit, they pay special attention to sentences that don't work.) Sentence length in and of itself really has no value to writers. Whether long or short, their best sentences say exactly what they want them to say. But professional writers also know that expanded sentences can say more—and say it more expressively.

Expanding the Structure

Expanding sentences is the process of extending basic ideas with different types of phrases and clauses. Two types of expanded sentences that writers use are **loose sentences** and **cumulative sentences**. Some people consider these types to be synonymous. Others make this distinction: A loose sentence usually provides a base clause at the beginning followed by explanatory phrases and clauses. A cumulative sentence can have modifying details before, after, and in the middle of the base clause. Both types carry a lot of meaning and can add style to writing. Here is an example of each type:

> **Loose sentence:** Julie was studying **at the kitchen table, completely focused, memorizing a list of vocabulary words.**
>
> *Analysis:* Notice how each new detail adds to the richness of the final sentence. Also notice how the modifying phrases are set off by commas.
>
> **Cumulative sentence: With his hands on his face,** Tony was laughing **half-heartedly, looking puzzled and embarrassed.**
>
> *Analysis:* Notice that this cumulative sentence contains modifiers both before and after the base clause, creating a natural flow or rhythm.

fyi In your writing notebook, record well-made sentences (loose, cumulative, or otherwise) that you come across. Then try writing your own versions of these sentence patterns. (You do not have to follow the pattern exactly.) Keep practicing, just as you would a musical instrument or an athletic skill. Over time, you will internalize these structures and begin to use them naturally in your own writing.

Expanding with Details

The key to writing expanded sentences that flow smoothly and carry your intended meaning is to know when to stop, the point at which you have said enough. Obviously, the more you use the expanded sentence, the better feel you will have for it. What follows are seven ways to expand the main idea, the base clause, in a loose or cumulative sentence: (Refer to the index for more information about each one of these words, phrases, or clauses.)

Detail Devices	Examples
Adjective / Adverb:	embarrassed, half-heartedly
Prepositional Phrase:	with his hands on his face
Absolute Phrase:	his head titled to one side
Participial Phrase:	looking puzzled
Infinitive Phrase:	to hide his embarrassment
Subordinate Clause:	while his friends talked
Relative Clause:	who isn't laughing at all

© Simone van den Berg, 2009 / Used under license from Shutterstock.com

sentence expanding
extending basic ideas with different types of phrases and clauses

loose sentence
a sentence that provides a base clause near the beginning, followed by explanatory phrases and clauses

cumulative sentence
a sentence that has modifying phrases and clauses before, after, or in the middle of the base clause

COMBINING SENTENCES

When editing, always look for series of shorter sentences that you could combine to improve the readability of your writing. By combining sentences you can show relationships and make connections between ideas.

Combining Techniques

The five sentences that follow contain five basic ideas. The **sentence combining** techniques listed below have been used to form longer, more effective sentences.

> The longest and largest construction project in history was the Great Wall of China. The project took 1,700 years to complete. The Great Wall of China is 1,400 miles long. It is between 18 and 30 feet high. It is up to 32 feet wide.

Use a series to combine three or more similar ideas.

> The Great Wall of China is **1,400 miles long, between 18 and 30 feet high**, and **up to 32 feet wide**.

Use a relative pronoun (*who, which, that,* and so on) to introduce subordinate (less important) ideas.

> The Great Wall of China, **which is 1,400 miles long and between 18 and 30 feet high,** took 1,700 years to complete.

Use an introductory phrase or clause.

> **Having taken 1,700 years to complete,** the Great Wall of China was the longest construction project in history.

Use a semicolon and a conjunctive adverb (*however, instead,* and so on) if appropriate.

> The Great Wall took 1,700 years to complete; it is 1,400 miles long and up to 30 feet high and 32 feet wide.

Repeat a key word or phrase to emphasize an idea.

> The Great Wall of China was the longest construction **project** in history, a **project** that took 1,700 years to complete.

sentence combining
combining ideas in sentences to show relationships and make connections

Use correlative conjunctions (*either, or; not only, but also*) to compare or contrast two ideas in a sentence.

> The Great Wall of China is **not only** up to 30 feet high and 32 feet wide, **but also** 1,400 miles long.

Use an appositive to emphasize an idea.

> The Great Wall of China—**the largest construction project in history**—is 1,400 miles long, 32 feet wide, and up to 30 feet high.

fyi You quite naturally combine ideas when you use compound and complex sentences in your writing. Writing loose and cumulative sentences is another, more stylistic way to do so. But also remember that short sentences can be very effective, even in a series. They are used to draw special attention to a particular idea.

LO3 Check your sentences for style and correctness.

Writer E. B. White advised emerging writers to "approach sentence style by way of simplicity, plainness, orderliness, and sincerity." That's good advice from a writer steeped in style. Perhaps the best sentences are the ones that do not draw undue attention to themselves. They are smooth reading and engaging, effectively carrying the reader along from one main point to the next. They don't confuse the reader, sound too choppy, or ramble on and on. They just work.

LOOKING FOR TROUBLE

Looking for and correcting sentence problems can imbue your writing with clarity, authority, and a natural style. As you learn to deal successfully with trouble spots in your sentences, as well as with issues of variety, parallelism, and voice covered on the following pages, you will see the improvement in your writing. Also turn to pages 318–333 for more about making your sentences correct, clear, and acceptable.

Sentence Problems	Solutions
Short, Choppy	Combine or expand any short, choppy sentences; use the examples and guidelines on pages 69–70.
Flat, Predictable	Rewrite any sentences that sound predictable and uninteresting by varying their structure and expanding them with modifying words, phrases, and clauses.
Incorrect	Look carefully for fragments, run-ons, and comma splices and correct them.
Unclear	Edit any sentences that contain unclear wording, misplaced modifiers, dangling modifiers, or incomplete comparisons.
Unacceptable	Change sentences that include nonstandard language, double negatives, or unparallel construction.
Unnatural	Rewrite sentences that contain jargon, cliches, or flowery language.

BUILDING SENTENCE VARIETY

If the sentences in your writing seem too predictable or sound too much alike, edit them for **sentence variety**. You can vary your sentences by combining or expanding some of the shorter ones, by using different types of sentences, by varying your sentence beginnings, and so on. Use the following strategy to analyze your sentence beginnings, lengths, and types.

Sentence Variety Strategy

• **In one column** on a piece of paper, list the opening words in each of your sentences. Then decide if you need to vary some of your sentence beginnings.

• **In another column,** identify the number of words in each sentence. Then decide if you need to change the lengths of some of your sentences.

• **In a third column,** list the kinds of sentences used (exclamatory, declarative, interrogative, and so on). Then, based on your analysis, use the instructions on the next two pages to edit your sentences as needed.

Vary sentence structure.

Depending on your analysis using the sentence variety strategy, you have many options when it comes to varying your sentences. The next section covers the key ones. *Remember:* Do not rework sentences simply for the sake of making changes. Instead, base each change on a genuine concern for clarity and fluency in your writing. Part of becoming an effective editor is acquiring a writer's sixth sense—the ability to know what in your writing needs work, and what does not.

Vary sentence openings. Move a modifying word, phrase, or clause to the beginning of a sentence to change the emphasis. However, avoid creating dangling or misplaced modifiers. (See page 331–332.)

The norm: We apologize for the inconvenience this may have caused you.

Variation: For the inconvenience this may have caused you, we apologize.

Vary sentence length. Short sentences (10 words or fewer) are ideal for making points crisply. Medium sentences (10 to 20 words) should carry the bulk of your information. When well crafted, occasional long sentences (more than 20 words) can develop and expand your ideas.

Short: Welcome back to Magnolia Suites!

Medium: Unfortunately, your confirmed room was unavailable last night when you arrived. For the inconvenience this may have caused you, we apologize.

Long: Because several guests did not depart as scheduled, we were forced to provide you with accommodations elsewhere; however, for your trouble, we are happy to cover the cost of last night's lodging.

Vary sentence kinds. The most common sentence is declarative—it states a point. For variety, try exclamatory, imperative, interrogative, and conditional sentences.

Exclamatory: Our goal is providing you with outstanding service!

Declarative: To that end, we have upgraded your room at no additional expense.

Imperative: Please accept, as well, this box of chocolates as a gift to sweeten your stay.

Interrogative: Do you need further assistance?

Conditional: If you do, we are ready to fulfill your requests.

Vary sentence arrangement. Where do you want to place the main point of your sentence? You make that choice by arranging sentence parts into loose, periodic, balanced, or cumulative patterns. Each pattern creates a specific effect.

Loose sentence: The Travel Center offers an attractive flight-reservation plan for students, one that allows you to collect bonus miles and receive $150,000 in life insurance per flight.

Analysis: This pattern is direct. It states the main point immediately and then tacks on extra information.

Periodic sentence: Although this plan requires that you join the Travel Center's Student-Flight Club and pay the $10 admission fee, **in the long run, you will save money!**

Analysis: This pattern postpones the main point until the end. The sentence builds to the point, creating an indirect, dramatic effect.

Balanced sentence: Joining the club in your freshman year will save you money over your entire college career; in addition, **accruing bonus miles over four years will earn you a free trip to Europe!**

Analysis: This pattern gives equal weight to complementary or contrasting points; the balance is often signaled by a comma and a conjunction (*and, but*) or by a semicolon. Often a conjunctive adverb (*however, nevertheless*) or a transitional phrase (*in addition, even so*) will follow the semicolon to further clarify the relationship.

Cumulative sentence: Because the club membership is in your name, **you can retain its benefits** as long as you are a student, even if you transfer to a different college or go on to graduate school.

Analysis: This pattern puts the main idea (boldfaced) in the middle of the sentence, surrounding it with modifying words, phrases, and clauses.

Use positive repetition. Although you should avoid needless repetition, occasional repetition to emphasize a key word or point is acceptable.

Repetitive sentence: Each year more than a million young people leave high school **reading poorly**—reading newspapers **poorly, reading** job ads **poorly,** and **reading** safety instructions **poorly**—with no understanding.

Emphatic sentence: Each year, more than a million young people leave high school **reading poorly**—so **poorly** that they cannot read and understand newspapers, job ads, or safety instructions.

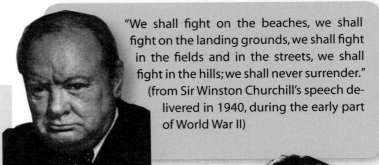

"We shall fight on the beaches, we shall fight on the landing grounds, we shall fight in the fields and in the streets, we shall fight in the hills; we shall never surrender." (from Sir Winston Churchill's speech delivered in 1940, during the early part of World War II)

"Ask not what your country can do for you—ask what you can do for your country." (from John F. Kennedy's inaugural address in 1961)

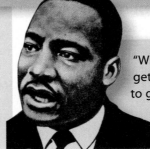

"With this faith we will be able to work together, to play together, to struggle together, to go to jail together. . . ." (from Martin Luther King's "I Have a Dream" speech in 1963)

BUILDING PARALLEL STRUCTURE

Parallelism refers to repeating phrases or sentence structures to show the relationship between ideas. However, in order for structures to be parallel, they must be stated in the same grammatical terms. (See page 329.) Some of the most memorable quotations in contemporary history are parallel in structure.

Keep elements in a series consistent (words, phrases, or clauses).

Not parallel: I have tutored students in Biology 101, also Chemistry 102, not to mention my familiarity with Physics 200.

Parallel: I have tutored students in *Biology 101, Chemistry 102,* and *Physics 200.*

Not parallel: I have worked as a hospital receptionist, have been a hospice counselor, and as an emergency medical technician.

Parallel: I have worked as *a hospital receptionist, a hospice counselor, and an emergency medical technician.*

Use both parts of correlative conjunctions (*either, or; neither, nor; not only, but also; as, so; whether, so; both, and*) so that both segments of the sentence are balanced.

> **Not parallel:** Not only did Blake College turn 20 this year, enrollment also grew by 16 percent.
>
> **Parallel:** *Not only* did Blake College turn 20 this year, *but* its enrollment *also* grew by 16 percent.

Keep compound elements parallel (compound subjects, compound predicates, compound objects).

> **Not parallel:** MADD wants drunk driving stopped because this offense leads to *a great number* of deaths and sorrow.
>
> **Parallel:** MADD wants drunk driving stopped because this offense leads to *many* deaths and *much* sorrow.

Express details in a parallel way (words, phrases, clauses) to emphasize a comparison/contrast.

> **Unparallel contrast:** In a week, the average child watches 24 hours of television but reads for only 36 minutes.
>
> **Parallel contrast:** In a week, the average child *watches television for 24 hours* but *reads for only about a half hour*.

BUILDING BETTER CONSTRUCTIONS

Energize your statements by using verbs in **active voice**: *Children* <u>must consume</u> *plenty of calories*. Because the subject (*children*) does something, it is active. This sentence is more energetic than the following one in which the verb is in **passive voice** and the subject (*plenty*) is being acted upon. *Plenty of calories* <u>must be consumed</u> *by children*. Active sentences are easy to follow and effectively move your writing forward from one idea to the next. (For more on active and passive voice, see page 312). Also watch out for nominal constructions, expletives, and negative constructions.

Nominal Constructions

The **nominal construction** is both sluggish and wordy. Avoid it by changing the noun form of a verb (*description or instructions*) to a verb (*describe or instruct*). At the same time, delete the weak verb that preceded the noun.

Noun form of verb	Verb
Tim gave a **description** ...	Tim **described** ..
Lydia provided **instructions** ...	Lydia **instructed** ...

Notice how the adjustment demonstrated below moves the writing from sluggish to energetic.

> **Sluggish:** John had a *discussion* with the tutors regarding the incident. They gave him their *confirmation* that similar problems had occurred before, but they had not provided *submissions* of their reports.
>
> **Energetic:** John *discussed* the incident with the tutors. They *confirmed* that similar problems had occurred before, but they had not *submitted* their reports.

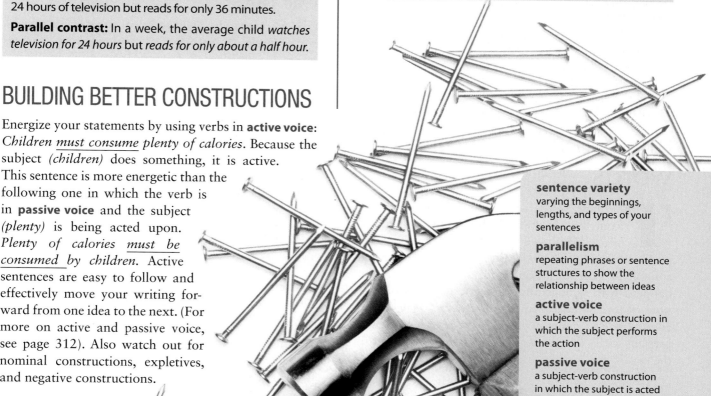

© David Fischer/Stockbyte/Getty Images

sentence variety
varying the beginnings, lengths, and types of your sentences

parallelism
repeating phrases or sentence structures to show the relationship between ideas

active voice
a subject-verb construction in which the subject performs the action

passive voice
a subject-verb construction in which the subject is acted upon

nominal constructions
noun forms of verbs such as *description, instructions, confirmation*

Expletives

Expletives such as "it is" and "there is" are fillers that serve no purpose in most sentences—except to make them wordy and unnatural.

> **Sluggish:** *It is* likely that Nathan will attend the Communication Honors Banquet since *there is* a journalism scholarship he hopes to win.
>
> **Energetic:** Nathan will likely attend the Communication Honors Banquet since he hopes to win a journalism scholarship.

Negative Constructions

Sentences including the negatives *no, not, neither/nor* can be wordy and difficult to understand. It's clearer and more direct to state ideas positively.

> **Negative:** During my four years on the newspaper staff, I *have not failed* to make significant contributions. My editorial skills *have* certainly *not deteriorated,* as I *have never been adverse* to tackling challenging assignments.
>
> **Positive:** During my four years on the newspaper staff, I *have made* significant contributions. My editorial skills *have steadily developed* as I *have tackled* difficult assignments.

LO4 Replace imprecise, misleading, and biased words.

The best words are the ones that effectively contribute to the overall meaning, feeling, and sound in a piece of writing. A sentence such as *The football player made an interception in the end zone* gives general, lackluster details. But look what happens with stronger, more precise words: *Crusader safety Ross Hilman leaped over three receivers in the end zone to make a game-saving interception.* This sentence presents a clear image that captures the excitement of the moment.

specific nouns
nouns, such as *Meryl Streep,* that are clear, exact, and strong

vivid verbs
specific action verbs, such as *lunge,* that create clear images

fyi Always keep your writing situation (*subject, audience, purpose*) in mind when you make decisions about word choice. The words you use to report on a football game would probably be inappropriate for a literary analysis or a research paper.

REPLACE NONSPECIFIC WORDS.

When editing, reconsider both your noun and your verb choices. Adjustments may be necessary to clarify and enhance your message.

Specific Nouns

Make it a habit to use **specific nouns** for subjects. General nouns give the reader a vague, uninteresting picture. More-specific nouns give the reader a better picture. And, finally, very specific nouns offer a clear, colorful image.

General		Specific
Person	woman | actress | Meryl Streep	
Place	school | university | Notre Dame	
Thing	book | novel | *Pride and Prejudice*	
Idea	theory | scientific theory | relativity	

Vivid Verbs

Like specific nouns, **vivid verbs** can create clear images. For example, the verb *looked* says one thing, whereas *stared, glared, glanced,* or *peeked* says quite another.

Use a verb that is strong enough to stand alone without the help of an adverb.

> **Verb/Adverb:** John **fell down** in the student lounge.
>
> **Vivid verb:** John **collapsed** in the student lounge.

Limit your use of the "be" verbs (*is, are, was, were*) and helping verbs. Often a main verb can be made from another word in the same sentence.

> **"Be" verb:** Cole **is** someone who follows international news.
>
> **Stronger verb:** Cole **follows** international news.

Use active rather than passive verbs. (Use passive verbs only if you want to downplay the performer of the action in a sentence. See page 312.)

> **Passive verb:** Another provocative essay **was submitted** by Kim.
>
> **Active verb:** Kim **submitted** another provocative essay.

Use verbs that show rather than tell.

> **Verb that tells:** Dr. Lewis **is** very thorough in his lectures.
>
> **Verb that shows:** Dr. Lewis **prepares** very thorough lectures.

REPLACE JARGON AND CLICHES.

Jargon and cliches may be easy to use, but they can make your writing hard to read. Replace them with words that are plain, fresh, and clear.

Jargon

Jargon is language used in a certain profession or by a particular group of people. Whereas jargon may be acceptable for a specific audience, to most ears, these words sound technical, unnatural, or pretentious.

> **Jargon:** The bottom line is that our output is not within our game plan.
> **Clear:** Production is not on schedule.
>
> **Jargon:** I'm having conceptual difficulty with these academic queries.
> **Clear:** I don't understand these review questions.
>
> **Jargon:** Pursuant to our conversation, I have forwarded you a remittance attached herewith.
> **Clear:** As we discussed, I am mailing you the check.

Cliches

Cliches are overused words or phrases. They give the reader a stale thought instead of a fresh idea. Because cliches spring quickly to mind, they can easily find their way into your writing. Always replace them with original phrases.

Also be alert to cliches of purpose or voice in your writing, and correct them. For example, vague, overused purpose statements like these become cliches: *It is my purpose to . . .* or *The purpose of this paper is to . . .* Similarly, words conveying a false sense of authority (*I have determined that there are three basic types of newspapers. My preference is for the third.*) or no sense of authority (*I flipped when I saw* Viewpoints!) create an inauthentic or cliched voice.

Common Cliches to Avoid

an axe to grind | as good as dead |
beat around the bush | burning bridges |
easy as pie | between a rock and a hard place |
piece of cake | planting the seed |
rearing its ugly head | stick your neck out |
up a creek | throwing your weight around

CAUTION

REPLACE BIASED WORDS.

Avoid **biased words** when depicting individuals or groups according to their differences. Instead, use language that implies equal value and respect for all people.

Disabilities and Conditions

Regarding **disabilities**, for example, it was common for a while to use alternatives to the term *disabled*, including *physically challenged, exceptional,* or *special.* Today these terms have fallen out of favor. They are not precise enough to serve those who live with disabilities. Of course, it is always wise to avoid degrading labels such as *crippled, maimed, invalid,* and so on.

Also avoid terms that make people synonymous with various disabilities and **conditions** (*quadriplegics, depressives, epileptics*). In reality, these are people who simply happen to have a particular disability. As much as possible, remember to refer to the person first, the disability second.

Gender

Then there are **gender** issues to consider. Use parallel language for both sexes: *women* and *men, Hank* and *Marie, Mrs. Joy Gumble* and *Mr. Bob Gumble.* The courtesy titles *Mr., Mrs., Ms.,* and *Miss* ought to be used according to the person's preference.

Use nonsexist alternatives to words with masculine connotations: *humankind,* not mankind; *synthetic,* not man-made; *artisan,* not craftsman. And don't use masculine-only or feminine-only pronouns (*he, she, his, her*) when referring to a human being in general. Instead, use *he or she,* use a plural construction, or eliminate the pronoun by recasting. Here are correct examples: *A politician can kiss privacy good-bye when she or he runs for office. / Politicians can kiss privacy good-bye when they run for office. / A politician can kiss privacy good-bye when running for office.*

Finally, do not use gender-specific references in the salutation of a business letter when you don't know the person's name. Instead, address the position you are contacting: *Dear Personnel Officer,* not Dear Sir; *Dear Members of the Steering Committee,* not Dear Gentlemen. (See the following pages for a quick guide that addresses non-biased language.)

> **cliches**
> overused words and phrases such as *piece of cake*
>
> **biased words**
> words that unfairly or disrespectfully depict individuals or groups

Nonbiased Language

When Referring to Ethnicity . . .

GENERAL TERMS	SPECIFIC TERMS
American Indians, Native Americans	Cherokee people, Inuit people, and so forth
Asian Americans (not Orientals)	Chinese Americans, Japanese Americans, and so forth
Latinos, Latinas, Hispanics	Mexican Americans, Cuban Americans, and so forth

Note:

African Americans, blacks: "African American" is widely accepted, though the term "black" is preferred by some individuals.

Anglo Americans (English ancestry), **European Americans:** Use these terms to avoid the notion that "American," used alone, means "white."

NOT RECOMMENDED	PREFERRED
Eurasion, mulatto	**person of mixed ancestry**
nonwhite	**person of color**
Caucasian	**white**
American (to mean U.S. citizen)	**U.S. citizen**

When Referring to Occupations . . .

NOT RECOMMENDED	PREFERRED
chairman	**chair, presiding officer, moderator**
salesman	**sales representative, salesperson**
mailman	**mail carrier, postal worker, letter carrier**
fireman	**firefighter**
businessman	**executive, manager, businessperson**
congressman	**member of Congress, representative, senator**
steward, stewardess	**flight attendant**
policeman, policewoman	**police officer**

When Referring to Disabilities or Impairments . . .

NOT RECOMMENDED	PREFERRED
handicapped	**disabled**
birth defect	**congenital disability**
stutter, stammer, lisp	**speech impairment**
mechanical foot	**prosthetic foot**
false teeth	**dentures**

When Referring to People with Conditions . . .

NOT RECOMMENDED	PREFERRED
an AIDS victim	**person with AIDS**
the disabled	**people with disabilities**
the crippled	**people who have difficulty walking**
the retarded	**people with a developmental disability**
dyslexics	**students with dyslexia**
neurotics	**patients with neuroses**
subjects, cases	**participants, patients**
suffering from cancer	**has cancer**
quadriplegics	**people who are quadriplegic**
wheelchair users	**people who use wheelchairs**

Note:

hearing impairment = partial hearing loss, hard of hearing (not *deaf*, which is total loss of hearing)

visual impairment = partially sighted (not *blind*, which is total loss of vision)

communicative disorder = speech, hearing, and learning disabilities affecting communication

When Referring to Age . . .

AGE GROUP	ACCEPTABLE TERMS
up to age 13 or 14	**boys, girls**
between 13 and 19	**youth, young people, young men, young women**
late teens and 20s	**young adults, young women, young men**
30s to age 60	**adults, men, women**
60s and older	**older adults, older people (not elderly)**
65 and older	**seniors, senior citizens**

LO5 Edit and proofread for conventions.

To complete your editing, check your writing to be sure that it follows **conventions**—the standard rules for spelling, punctuation, mechanics, usage, and grammar. Refer to the following guidelines to make sure that you don't miss anything. And remember to ask a trusted peer (or tutor in the writing center) to check your writing for errors as well.

Correcting Your Writing

Punctuation and Mechanics

1. Check for proper use of commas before coordinating conjunctions in compound sentences, after introductory clauses and long introductory phrases, between items in a series, and so on.

2. Look for apostrophes in contractions, some plurals, and possessive nouns.

3. Examine quotation marks in quoted information, titles, or dialogue.

4. Watch for proper use of capital letters for first words in written conversation and for proper names of people, places, and things.

Usage and Grammar

1. Look for misuse of any commonly mixed-up words: *there/their/they're; accept/except.*

2. Check for verb use. Subjects and verbs should agree in number: Singular subjects go with singular verbs; plural subjects go with plural verbs. Verb tenses should be consistent throughout.

3. Review for pronoun-antecedent agreement problems. A pronoun and its antecedent must agree in number, person, and gender.

Spelling

1. Use a spell-checker. Your spell-checker will catch most errors.

2. Check each spelling you are unsure of. Especially check those proper nouns and other special words that your spell-checker cannot correct.

3. Consult an up-to-date dictionary when double-checking your spelling.

Form and Presentation

1. Note the title. A title should be appropriate and predict the theme or content of the writing.

2. Examine any quoted or cited material. Are all sources of information properly presented and documented? (See pages 251–271.)

3. Look over the finished copy of your writing. Does it meet the requirements for a final manuscript?

punctuation, mechanics, usage, and grammar

"**Start with something interesting**
and promising; wind up with something the reader will remember."

—Rudolf Flesch

7

Publishing

Publishing a final paper (sharing it with others) is the driving force behind writing, the reason why you may have spent so much time planning, drafting, revising, and editing in the first place—to produce a piece of writing that effectively expresses your thoughts and feelings. Of course, the most immediate form of submitting writing is sharing a completed paper with your instructor and writing peers. This form may also prove to be the most helpful because, as writer Tom Liner states, "You learn ways to improve your writing by seeing its effect on others." You can, in addition, submit your writing to different print and online sources, including newspapers and magazines, or include it in your writing portfolio. Self-publishing is another option if you have a personal blog site, or if you want to post your work on one of the social media sites.

Submitting your academic or personal writing to a publication may never have occurred to you before. Yet you should certainly consider publishing any strong piece of writing. There are publishers for all types of writing—essays, articles, reviews, stories, scripts, and poems—if you know where to look. To find them, refer to resources like *Writer's Market* or *Writer's Market: The Electronic Edition*. Also refer to such resources to find specific guidelines for making a submission, or contact the publisher for this information. Consider the submission process a learning experience. You may or may not get published, but as you walk through the steps, you will become more familiar with this aspect of writing. And of course, the more submissions you make, the better chance you will have of someday getting published.

This chapter addresses two topics related to publishing (1) formatting your writing for in-class publishing and (2) developing a writing portfolio.

Learning Outcomes

LO1 Format your writing.

LO2 Create a writing portfolio.

What do you think?

I am the most demanding audience for my writing.

1	**2**	**3**	**4**	**5**
strongly agree				strongly disagree

publishing
sharing your finished writing with your instructor and peers, and/or sending it out to a print or online publication

L**O**1 Format your writing.

Effective **page design** makes your writing clear and easy to follow. Keep that in mind when you format final copies for your instructor and writing peers. Each design element should add to the readability of your writing. Articles published in contemporary magazines may have flashy design elements, whereas academic documents should be formatted according to your instructor's (or department's) guidelines.

DESIGN FOR CLARITY.

Review the following design guidelines and apply them to your academic writing. Also make sure that you understand any formatting guidelines established by your instructor. In addition, study the models in *Write* for examples of effective design in action. Remember that the best design has a sense of transparency about it, facilitating the reader without drawing attention to itself.

page design
the elements (typography, spacing, graphics) that create the look of a paper; readability is the focus of design for academic writing

typography
the size and style of type that is used

serif type
type that has tails at the top and the bottom of the letters; works best for text copy

sans serif type
type that does not have tails; may work well for headings and subheadings

widow
a single word or a short line carried over to the top of a page

orphan
a single line of a new paragraph at the bottom of a page

tombstone
a heading or a subheading sitting alone at the bottom of a page

Formatting

Keep the design clear and uncluttered, aiming for a sharp, polished look. And be sure to follow the designated documentation form, observing all the requirements outlined in the MLA (pages 267-268) or APA (pages 269-271) style guides.

Typography

Use an easy-to-read serif font for the main text. **Serif type,** like this, has "tails" at the tops and bottoms of the letters. For most types of writing, use 10- or 12-point type size. Then consider using a sans serif font for the titles and headings. **Sans serif type,** like this, does not have "tails." Use larger type, perhaps 18-point, for your title and 14-point type for any headings. You may also use boldface for headings if they seem to get lost on the page.

fyi Because most people find a sans serif font easier to read on-screen, consider a sans serif font for the body and a serif font for the titles and headings in any writing that you publish online or display in a multimedia presentation.

Spacing

Follow all the requirements for indents and margins. This usually means indenting the first line of each paragraph five spaces, maintaining a one-inch margin around each page, and double-spacing throughout the paper. In addition, avoid widows, orphans, and tombstones. A **widow** is a single word or short line carried over to the top of the next page. An **orphan** is a single line of a new paragraph at the bottom of a page. A **tombstone** is a heading or subheading that sits alone at the bottom of a page.

Graphic Devices

Create bulleted or numbered lists to highlight important points, but be selective. Your writing should not include too many lists. Include charts or other graphics if applicable. Graphics should neither be so small that they get lost on the page, nor so large that they overpower the page.

LO2 Create a writing portfolio.

A **writing portfolio** is a collection of your work, usually showing your skills as a writer. People in many lines of work compile portfolios to show prospective employers or clients the type of work they can do. Architects, graphic designers, interior designers, and illustrators generally keep well-maintained, up-to-date portfolios. Of course, at this point you're compiling a portfolio as a course requirement, but a portfolio is also useful when you apply for a scholarship, seek admission into graduate school, or pursue a job.

There are two basic types of writing portfolios: (1) a **working portfolio** in which you store documents at various stages of development and (2) a **showcase portfolio** in which you compile appropriate finished pieces of writing for evaluation. Most instructors will expect you to turn in a printed version of a showcase portfolio, but some may want you to submit it electronically.

COMPILING A SHOWCASE PORTFOLIO

Think of compiling a showcase portfolio as a long-term project. Make sure that you understand the requirements for your portfolio: How many pieces should you include? What else should your portfolio contain (see the next column), and so on? Keep track of all your work (notes, drafts, and such) for each writing project. Then, when it is time to create your portfolio, you will have everything to work with. Also keep your papers in a safe environment, such as an expandable folder or a dependable online file. In addition, be sure to maintain a regular writing schedule. Then you won't have to do everything at the last minute. And most importantly, take pride in your work. Your portfolio will showcase your writing skills.

What You Should Include

Compiling a portfolio allows you to participate in the evaluation process. You decide, after all, which pieces to include, you reflect upon your writing progress, and you make sure the complete package presents you at your best. Showcase portfolios commonly contain the following documents, but be sure to check with your instructor for specific requirements.

Showcase Portfolio

- **A table of contents** listing the pieces included in your portfolio

- **An opening essay** or letter detailing the story behind your portfolio (how you compiled it, why it contains this collection of writing, what you have learned about writing, and so on)

- **A specified number** of finished pieces representing different types of writing

- **A cover sheet** attached to each piece of writing, discussing the reason for its selection, the amount of work that went into it, and so on

- **Evaluation sheets** or checklists charting your writing progress and skills mastery

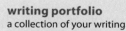

writing portfolio
a collection of your writing

working portfolio
a collection of documents at various stages of development

showcase portfolio
a collection of appropriate finished pieces of writing for evaluation

"By three methods
we may learn wisdom: first, by reflection, which is noblest; second, by imitation, which is easiest; and third, by experience, which is the most bitter."

—Confucius

8

Personal Writing

In his book *On Writing*, Stephen King makes the argument that descriptive writing is a form of **telepathy**. As evidence, he describes a table with a red tablecloth. On it sits a small cage containing a white bunny nibbling a carrot. The bunny's back is marked with a number 8. Do you see the image?

In his office in Maine in 1997, Stephen King described that **tableau**, in words that help you, wherever and whenever you are, see the same table, cage, bunny, carrot, and number 8. That's the power of description.

When you write a description, your job is to take what is in your mind and put it into the mind of another person—possibly across miles and years. When you write narration, your job is to have your reader feel as if he or she is living the experience firsthand. And when you write a reflection, your job is to return to a past experience and consider what it meant to you then and what it means to you now.

Writing is serious stuff. It connects people. As Stephen King says in *On Writing*, "If you can take it seriously, we can do business. If you can't or won't, it's time for you to close the book and do something else." Please don't close the book. Instead, turn the page, and learn the power of writing description, narration, and reflection.

Learning Outcomes

LO1 Describe a person, place, or thing.

LO2 Narrate an event.

LO3 Reflect on life.

What do you think?

I can see Bunny Number 8.

1	**2**	**3**	**4**	**5**
strongly agree			strongly disagree	

telepathy
communicating thoughts over distance

tableau
a dramatic scene or setting; a striking picture

LO1 Describe a person, place, or thing.

Your goal is to write a vivid description that uses **sensory** and **thought details** to clearly portray a person, place, or thing. Write in a way that allows the reader to picture, hear, and touch what you describe.

1. Select a topic. Think of people, places, or things that you know well and can describe in numerous ways. Besides familiarity, consider subjects that have an emotional connection or attachment for you, especially one that you can convey to the reader. Here are possible topics:

People with amazing personalities, appearances, minds, experiences, or accomplishments

Places that inspire you, comfort you, frighten you, amaze you, or confuse you

sensory details
sights, sounds, smells, tastes, textures, temperatures, and other details connected to the five senses—showing rather than telling about the subject

thought details
impressions, emotions, predictions, and reflections; details that reveal perceptions rather than sensations

camera-eye approach
sharing details as though through a camera lens moving across a subject

order of location
organizing details according to their position; progressing from near to far, inside to outside, and so on

Things you use daily, desire, prize, fear, or wish for

2. Gather details. If you can personally interact with the subject, do so. Otherwise, gather photos, videos, audios, or other items that will help you describe your subject. Draw a picture and label it. Also collect details by thinking about your subject. You can use the following graphic organizers to record your information.

Sensory Details

See	Hear	Smell	Taste	Touch

Thought Details

Impressions	Emotions	Predictions	Reflections

3. Write your first draft. Create a description with an effective opening, middle, and closing.

Start strong. Capture your reader's attention in the opening paragraph. Focus on what makes the subject interesting, offer a powerful sensory or thought detail, identify something amazing or surprising about the subject, and so on.

Organize the middle. Provide sensory and thought details in an organized way. Imagine that you are a filmmaker revealing your subject for the first time to the audience. Would you begin far away and zoom in, or start with a tight shot and zoom out? Would you begin at the subject's foot and move to its head, or vice versa? Providing details using this **camera-eye approach** is one way to create effective **order of location**. Consider the following options for ordering details.

From	To
Near	Far
Inside	Outside
Front	Back
Left	Right
Top	Bottom

Transition Words and Phrases

The following transition words and phrases can help you show order of location.

above	across	against
along	among	around
behind	below	beneath
beside	between	by
down	in back of	in front of
inside	into	near
next to	on top of	outside
over	throughout	to the right
	under	

End well. Wrap up your description with an especially memorable image. Reflect on the importance of your topic and leave the reader with a final strong impression.

4. Share your description. Have someone read your draft and then describe the subject to you. Have you included all the details you intended to include? Ask which parts contain the clearest images. Ask which parts could be clearer.

5. Revise your description. Carefully review and revise your writing. Remember that your goal is to create a description that transfers the vision in your own mind to the mind of the reader. Ask yourself the following questions:

Ask?

- Does the writing focus on a specific person, place, or thing?
- Does the description contain effective sensory and thought details?
- Does the description use words that capture the subject?
- Is the importance of the topic clear?

6. Edit and proofread. Check your writing for punctuation, capitalization, spelling, and grammar errors.

7. Prepare your final copy. Use an appropriate type font and size. Leave the right margin ragged (uneven). Place photographs or drawings close to the text they illustrate. Print your final copy on quality paper.

A MAYAN SOJOURN

Student writer David Bani wrote the following essay about his trip to the Mayan village of Yaxhachen.

SQ3R
Survey Question Read Recite Review

Beyond the End of the Road

Our van moves slowly down the narrow, winding roads that lead to Yaxhachen. Like a carnival ride, these roads swing from side to side and up and down. We drive through fields of *henequen*, and under the red *flamboyan* and gold *lluvia de oro* trees. We pass through small villages, ride over *topes* (speed bumps), dodge tricycle taxis, and bounce through potholes. Field workers are making their way home on bicycles, their *coas* or machetes strapped to their backs. **1 (A)**

Our van, carrying only my dad, mom, two sisters, and me, passes through Oxkubskab, a center where orchard owners take their produce. All types of fruit grown in Yucatan can be found here, and the smells are powerful variations of sweet ripeness. On the way back, we'll pick up some bags of oranges and mandarins, one or two papayas, plus anything else that looks good. But right now we're getting near our destination. **2**

Next, we enter Xul, the end of the road. It's the end of the road both in name (*xul* is Maya for the end of the road) and in reality—the pavement ends here. Beyond this point, only a serpentine, dirt trail leads on, and its boulders and rocks make traveling even slower. Though we must drive only about 12 miles, the journey takes over half an hour. **3 (B)**

Finally, we arrive at Yaxhachen. The first one to welcome us to this Mayan village is a pig, but once we reach the center of town, people begin to gather. We get out of the van, stretch, and then walk around the town square and down side streets. While some streets were paved at one time, the pavement has long since crumbled. We explore the area with no fear of getting lost. All streets eventually meander back to the center of town. **4**

While walking through town, I feel a little self-conscious because we are the only white people here. For most residents, whites are a rare sight, but for some small children at least, we are a novelty. Yet everyone, **5**

(A) The writer describes the sights he sees outside the van.
(B) He inserts a definition of a Spanish word in parentheses.

(C) young and old, treats us kindly. Some children shyly peek at us from over stone walls and giggle, while others follow us at a distance. Old men and women, sitting on logs in front of their houses, nod pleasantly.

6   Everything in the village smells earthy and sweaty, including us. In this climate you can't help sweating, and you don't mind it because it feels right.

7   Why are we here? One of Dad's hobbies is helping
(D) people in outlying villages find sources for clean water. He already has some pump equipment out and is looking at the control box for the submersible pump. A few years ago, he installed this pump, and another one on the edge of town.

8   Dusk starts to settle in, and the air begins to cool.
(E) Dad is just finishing his repairs when one of the church elders invites us to have supper at his house—a cluster of stick and thatch huts. We sit down on anything our
(F) host can find, like some wooden folding chairs from the church. We eat by ourselves—partly because there isn't enough room around the tables for both his family and us, but mostly because serving us separately is the Mayan way of showing respect. As we eat, our host sits nearby to make pleasant talk and to order one of his children to get us more tortillas, or whatever else he sees we need. To honor us, he serves us "city food," which is Spam, scrambled eggs, and soft drinks. But the better food is the handmade tortillas and refried beans.

© James Steidl , 2009 / Used under license from Shutterstock.com

When it's dark enough, we walk to the church and   9
set up the projector outside in the cool night air. A large crowd gathers because any film is a rare event, and because this film (which tells the story of Jesus) is one of the few movies in the Mayan language. In fact, the first time that Dad showed the film to a Mayan audience, he didn't explain that it was in Maya, and the people were both surprised and pleased. They marveled that the voices in the film spoke their language, even though   (G) they shyly tried to hide their amazement. Tonight, some people are not dressed for the cold, and many cannot find a place to sit, but still they come. The young men sit on the stone wall in the back so that they can talk as they watch the movie.

By the time the film is finished, it's too late for us to   10
leave Yaxhachen, so we set up hammocks in the church. We take everything off the floor, and we secure the door to prevent small animals from entering the building. Then, feeling well fed, welcome, and tired, we sleep soundly in this village beyond the end of the road.   (H)

Reading for Better Writing

1. In a sentence, state the dominant impression this essay creates of Yaxhachen.

2. Review the descriptive details in the first six paragraphs. To what senses do these details appeal? Do the details help you imagine the sites? Give examples of strong or weak word choices.

3. The writer uses verbs in the present tense. Is this a good choice? Why or why not? Choose a paragraph and explain how its impact would be different if the verbs were in the past tense.

4. Cite words and phrases that communicate the writer's attitude toward the people and scenes that he describes. Why is this place meaningful to the writer?

5. The writer does not comment on his reasons for describing these scenes. Is he contented simply to remember details, or does he seem to have an unexpressed purpose?

(C) The writer gives details about the village and its people.
(D) A question signals a shift in focus.
(E) The words "dusk" and "cool" suggest a shift in time.
(F) The description moves inside.
(G) The writer uses details to describe the Mayan people.
(H) He concludes by repeating the title.

LO2 Narrate an event.

Your goal is to write a personal narrative about something significant that has happened to you. Write in a way that allows your readers to vividly relive the experience and to learn something about you and about themselves.

1. Select a topic. Think about your own experiences. Sort through the stories you recall and choose one that is important enough to share with others. Think of a way to approach this experience in a personal narrative.

TIP
If you can't think of an interesting story, try writing in response to the following statement: *Remember a time when you first discovered that the world was (a) stranger, (b) more wonderful, or (c) more complex than you had thought as a child.* **Think about how that experience prepared you to be who you are today.**

2. Narrow your focus. Once you have chosen an experience to write about, begin to narrow your topic by focusing on a specific moment or outcome. The following questions can help you find a clear focus:

Ask ?
- What is the key moment—the significant point or **climax**—in the story?
- What led up to this key moment? What resulted from it?
- What was really going on?
- How did others experience the event?
- What has time taught you about this experience?
- What would you have changed?

3. Determine your purpose and audience. After you have a specific focus, decide why you are telling your story and who might read the story. Personal narratives can serve one of many purposes and appeal to many audiences. Consider these purposes:

To entertain	To warn	To challenge
To celebrate	To illustrate	To persuade
To remind	To gain sympathy	To encourage

4. Gather details. Gather material that will serve your purpose. Try sorting through photo albums, home videos, and letters. Interview someone who shared your experience or saw you through it. Consult your journal or diary.

5. Collaborate. Tell someone your story; then ask for comments and questions. Based on the feedback you receive, create a basic writing plan. Your plan can be anything from a simple list to a detailed outline.

6. Write your first draft. As you write, keep in mind your specific focus and your overall purpose for telling this story. Use the following strategies as you create your first draft:

Set the stage. Show where things happened. Describe the atmosphere, the people, and the events by using precise details that appeal to the five senses. If appropriate, use comparisons and **metaphors** to make the descriptions vivid.

Include dialogue. To infuse your narrative with a sense of reality, recall and create conversations between the people in your story. These conversations should enhance a scene or explain the relationship between people. Never let **dialogue** dribble on for its own sake.

climax
the most exciting moment in a narrative; the moment at which the person succeeds, fails, or learns something

metaphor
a comparison that equates two dissimilar things without using *like* or *as;* saying that one thing is another

dialogue
the words spoken by people and set apart with quotation marks

Build the plot. Arouse and sustain interest by establishing **conflict**, building suspense, highlighting the main point, and showing the outcome.

Express your feelings. It may help to include both past and present thoughts and feelings—those you had during the experience and those you have now, looking back on the past.

Use transitions. Words like *as, before, meanwhile,* and *later* show where your story is leading. (See page 61.)

Select verbs carefully. Verbs affect the movement and voice of your story. Choose strong, active verbs, and make sure tenses accurately reflect time sequences and relationships.

7. Share your story. Show your draft to someone. What main point does this reader see in your story? What suggestions or questions does the reader have?

8. Revise your writing. Carefully review and revise your writing. Remember that your goal is to recreate an interesting incident or event for your readers. Ask yourself the following questions:

Ask?

- Does the writing focus on a specific incident or event?
- Does the writing contain effective details, descriptions, and dialogue?
- Does the narrative effectively state or imply a theme, thesis, or point of significance?
- Does the writing sound sincere and natural?
- Will readers appreciate the way the story is told?

9. Edit and proofread. Check your revised writing for errors in punctuation, capitalization, spelling, and grammar.

10. Prepare your final copy. Use an appropriate type font and size. Leave the right margin ragged (uneven). Place photographs or drawings close to the text they illustrate. Print your final copy on quality paper.

conflict
the obstacles or adversaries confronted by people in narratives; person vs. person, person vs. society, person vs. the supernatural, person vs. nature, person vs. self, person vs. technology

A JOURNEY INTO GRIEVING

In this essay, student writer Jacqui Nyangi Owitti recalls an important personal experience in her life that taught her the pain of loss.

SQ3R
Survey Question Read Recite Review

Mzee Owitti

I am about 12 years old. We are en route from Nairobi, the capital city, to the rural area of Kisumu on the eastern shores of Lake Victoria in western Kenya, where my grandparents live. My five brothers and I are traveling with Mum on the overnight train. I am not particularly sad, though I know what has happened. I base my reactions on my mother's, and since she appears to be handling the whole thing well, I am determined to do the same. You see, my grandfather has died. My dad's dad. *(1) (A)*

We reach the town of my ancestry just as dawn lazily turns into early morning. We buy snacks and hire a car for the last leg of the journey. We then meander through a bewildering maze of mud huts, sisal scrub, and sandy clay grassland, until we come within sight of my grandfather's land, the place where my father grew up. *(2)*

The first thing I notice is a crude "tent" made by sticking four poles in the ground, crisscrossing the top with long branches, and covering that with thatch. Despite the early hour, the place is filled with dignitaries, guests, and people like my mother's parents, who have traveled far to honor our family. I am struck by the stillness and all-pervading silence. Everything seems frozen. Time itself seems to mourn, and even the wind is still. The car stops a short distance from the property, and we sit motionless and quiet. *(3) (B)*

I turn to my mother, questioning. But she has drawn a handkerchief from somewhere and is climbing out of the car. Almost as an actor on the stage, she releases a sound I have never heard before. It is a moan, a scream, and a sob that is deep-throated, guttural, and high-pitched all at the same time. This sudden transformation from a calm, chipper person to a stricken stranger strikes in me a fear that I will long remember. Holding *(4) (C)*

(A) The opening sets the scene and gives background information.

(B) The narrator describes what she sees and how she feels.

(C) Verbs in present tense describe the action.

her handkerchief to her face, she breaks into a shuffling run. I sit in the car petrified, watching the drama unfold.

5   Out of seemingly nowhere, wailing answers my mother's cry. Other women appear at a run, heading for my mother, hands fluttering from the tops of their heads, to their waists, to their feet. Their heads are thrown back and from side to side in restless anguish. Their bodies are half-bent forward, and their feet are in constant motion even though no distance is covered. My aunts and close female relatives weep, letting loose high-pitched, ululating moaning in support of my (D) mother. As the wife of the first child and only son, she commands a high place, and she must not grieve alone.

6   In the confusion, one lady is knocked down, and she seems to rock with her legs separated in a way that in other circumstances would be inappropriate and humiliating. Oddly, the people in the tent, mostly male, appear to have seen and heard nothing. They continue silent and still. The whole scene seems unreal. Seeing my fear and confusion, the driver talks soothingly, explaining what is going on.

7   The wailing and mourning continue intermittently (E) for a couple of days. Then the time comes for my grandfather to be taken from the mortuary in Kisumu to his final resting place. We all travel to the mortuary. He is dressed in his best suit and then taken to church, where his soul is committed to God. Afterward, the procession starts for home. On the way we are met by the other mourners, who, according to tradition, will accompany the hearse on foot, driving along the cows that are a symbol of wealth in life and a testament to a good life, respectability, and honor in death. Being city kids unable to jog for an hour with the mourners and cows, we ride in a car.

8   Finally, we are back at the homestead. My grand- (F) father is put in the house where he spent the latter part of his life. The crying and mourning are now nearly at a feverish pitch, and the sense of loss is palpable. However, before people may enter the house to pay their last respects, one—they call him "Ratego"—must lead the way to say his good-byes. Suddenly, there is a commotion, and I stare in disbelief as a big bull, taller than my tall-for-my-age twelve-year-old height and wider than the doorway, is led toward my grandfather's house.

Long, thick horns stick out of the colossal head. The (G) body, pungent with an ammonia-laced, grassy smell, is a mosaic of black and brown—an odorous, pulsing mountain.

9   The bull's wild, staring eyes seem fixed on me. An old, barefoot man, dressed in a worn, too-short jacket and dusty black pants, leads this bull with a frayed rope. He waves his rod, yelling and leaping in syncopation with the bull's snorting and pawing. Dust puffs dance around their feet. The bull is a symbol of high honor for my grandfather, and only the largest bull in the land can embody this deep respect. Although I do not fully comprehend its significance, I know that it is the biggest animal I have ever seen. I step back as people try to get the bull into the house to pay its respects to my grandfather. After much yelling, shoving, and cries of pain from those whose feet the bull steps on, the effort is abandoned. Ratego is much too big.

10   As the bull is led away into the boma, people enter (H) the room that has been emptied of furniture. I squeeze through the heaving, weeping mass, almost suffocating in the process. The room is surprisingly cool and dim, unlike the hot and bright sun outside. I approach curiously and cautiously, not knowing what to expect. At last I stand before the casket and look at my grandfather. He does not look dead. In fact, he is smiling! He looks like the person I remember, who always had a smile and an unshared secret lurking in the depths of his eyes.

11   I peer into his face, recalling a time when I was four (I) and he caught me doing something that deserved a reprimand. I had thought no one had seen me. However, my grandfather, on one of his rare visits to the city, had seen. Standing in front of his casket, I again hear him laugh. I remember how his kind, brown eyes had twinkled, and his white mustache, white teeth, and rich bitter-chocolate face had broken into an all-knowing, but-you-can-trust-me smile. I remember how the deep love that radiated from him assured me that I was his no matter what. And I remember how I had responded to his

(D) The last sentence explains the women's actions.
(E) A paragraph describes one segment of the ceremony.
(F) A transition word indicates a shift.

(G) Precise words tell what the narrator sees and smells.
(H) The narrative approaches its climax.
(I) A flashback adds depth to the present.

love by laughing happily and then skipping away, his answering laugh reverberating in my ears.

12 That is my grandfather. Death cannot possibly touch him! Then I look closer and realize that the white streak breaking up his face is not the white teeth I remember. It is, instead, cotton stuffed into his mouth, as white as his teeth had been, making a mockery of my memories. At that moment, my granddaddy dies.

(J)

13 Until this point, the whole has been a drama played out before my stunned, wide-eyed gaze. Rich in ancestry and tradition, its very nature and continuity are a celebration of life rather than death, fostering in me a keen sense of identity and a strong desire to keep the an-

cestral torch burning brightly, fiercely, and with pride. Now, however, Grandpa is dead. It is now that I cry. I am grieving. My granddaddy is gone, and the weighted arrow of sorrow pierces home. The pain is personal, unrelenting, and merciless. I stare at him and cannot tear myself away. I weep, saying over and over that he is smiling, he is smiling. My heartbreak and tears echo the refrain. He is smiling—a radiant, unforgettable smile. (K)

(J) The narrator describes a pivotal point in the story.
(K) The last sentence offers a powerful image.

Reading for Better Writing

Working by yourself or with a group, answer these questions:

1. The writer uses verbs in the present tense to tell her story. How does this choice affect (a) the clarity of the plot, (b) the tension in the episode about the bull, and (c) your empathy with the narrator in the closing?

2. Choose a paragraph containing a particularly vivid description. How do the word choice, sentence structure, and punctuation affect your ability to sense the action?

3. In a conversation with an editor of this book, Jacqui Nyangi Owitti described her love for her grandfather and her pride in her heritage. Does the story reflect that love and pride? Explain.

L03 Reflect on life.

Your goal is to write an essay in which you carefully describe one or more past experiences and reflect on their importance in your life.

1. Select a topic. Choose an experience or experiences that influenced you in some key way—either confirming what you were thinking or planning at that time, or changing those thoughts or plans.

2. Get the big picture. Once you have chosen one or more experiences to write about, gather your thoughts. Review photo albums and home videos to trigger memories; talk to someone who shared your experiences or saw you through them; or consult your journal, diary, old letters, and saved e-mail. Next, reflect on the following questions through brainstorming or by freewriting.

Ask

- What are the key moments—the **pivotal points**—in your experiences?
- What led to those key moments? Why? What resulted from them?
- What was going on from your perspective?
- How did others experience the events?
- What did you learn from these experiences?
- Did these experiences end as you had hoped? Why or why not?
- What themes, conflicts, and insights arose from these experiences?
- How do your feelings now differ from your feelings then?

3. Get organized. First, review your brainstorming or freewriting and highlight key details, quotations, or episodes that you want to include in your writing. Next, draft a brief outline that shows where key information fits into the big picture. List the main events in **chronological order**. You may also use a cluster to gather and order the details related to your experiences.

4. Write the first draft. Review your outline and rough out the first draft in one sitting. As you decide which details to include and how to organize your information, consider what your audience needs to know to understand and appreciate your story. Then test your reflection for its significance by noting whether it answers these questions: What happened? How did the experience affect you? How do you feel about it now?

5. Review and revise. After drafting the essay, take a break. Then read your paper again for accuracy and completeness. Look first at the entire piece. Does it say what you want to say? Does it include any gaps or weak spots? Check your outline to make sure all key details are covered in the right sequence.

6. Test your reflection. Consider the voice and point of view of your writing by answering these questions:

Ask

- Does the tone—whether sarcastic, humorous, regretful, or meditative—fit the content of the reflection?
- Have you established a viewpoint, and is the reflection built on this **point of view**?
- Will the intended readers appreciate the treatment of the subject?

pivotal points
moments in which an important change occurs; literally, a point at which a person changes direction

chronological order
time order; relating details in the order that they occurred

point of view
the perspective from which the writer approaches the writing, including first-person, second-person, or third-person point of view

7. Get feedback. Ask a classmate or someone in the writing center to read your paper, looking for the following elements:

8. Edit and proofread your essay. Once you have revised the content, organization, and voice of your personal reflection, polish it. Carefully check your choice of words; the clarity of your sentences; and your grammar, usage, and mechanics.

9. Publish your writing. It's time to share your writing in one or more of the following ways. You may make copies and give them to friends and family members, publish your reflection in a journal or on a Web site, read and discuss it in a small group or in class. Also consider placing the piece in your portfolio, and, of course, submit a copy to your instructor.

© Jupiterimages

LAKESIDE REFLECTIONS

Nicole Suurdt is a student from Ontario, Canada. In this essay, she describes a time and place that she loved as a child, and yearns for as an adult.

SQ3R
Survey Question Read Recite Review

The Stream in the Ravine

Behind my childhood home is a small ravine, and through it runs the seasonal overflow of a little pond deep within the woods. It's a noisy stream, just narrow enough for an eight-year-old to take one stretching step across and reach the other side with dry shoes. And when I was eight, this stream was everything to me. *1 (A)*

You see, for most of my childhood, I lived on a small hobby farm in Ontario, Canada, where rolling pasture and croplands surrounded my home. The pasture fenced in Scottish Highland cattle with terrifying horns, unbroken horses with skittish hooves, and one half-blind, unpredictable donkey. These creatures separated me from the woods just beyond the pasture. But when I was little, it wasn't simply my fear of these fitful animals that penned me in on my side of the fence—it was a fear of what lay beyond the shadowy barrier of maples and pines. *2*

It's not that I'd never been to the woods before. I had, twice. The first time, my brother took me in search of the tallest tree in the forest and got us lost for a couple of hours. My second visit was a dark winter journey. Dad dragged the family into the woods late one night in search of a missing cow. We found her half-devoured body lying in bloodstained snow, packed down by wolves' paws. *3 (B)*

But eventually, curiosity overpowered my fears. One spring day when I was eight, armed with a staff, I skirted the pasture and headed for the forest. I approached the fence that my dad had put up to ward off the woods. Quickly I scaled the fence, but then stood some time holding on to its boards, figuring that if a wolf came along, I could scramble back to the other side. However, after five minutes passed and no wolf appeared, I calmed down, let go of the fence, and stepped *4 (C)*

(A) The writer introduces the topic and then gives background information.

(B) Descriptions of the visits build tension.

(C) A transition signals a shift in the action.

into the forest—lured on by the sound of chipmunks, birds, wind through trees, and snapping twigs.

5   Drawn forward, I discovered rocky burrows of unknown creatures. I chased chipmunks. I sang. I passed a hunter's fort perched high in a pine, deserted after last fall's deer-hunting season. I passed under an archway of tall cedars. I waded through the muck and mire surrounding a small swamp and plodded my mud-caked shoes up a small rise, thick with the faded, crumbled leaves of last year's fall. One particular sound kept pulling me forward—the gurgle of running water.

6   Standing at the peak of the rise, with brown leaves
(D) stuck to my muddy sneakers, I found the source. Below me, within its shallow bed, ran a tiny stream, little more than a trickle, really. But to me it was a beautiful, rushing brook, my own source of clear, cold water protected by oak, maple, and pine sentries. That day I spent hours scooping decaying leaves out of my stream's bed and sitting by her side to watch the water spill over the rocks and roots. She was my own discovery, my own territory, my own secret place. From that day on, the little stream past the hunter's fort, under the cedar archway, through the muck and the mire, and over the rocky rise became my quiet, private place.

7   But I never could keep a secret for long. During
(E) dinner one Sunday, I told my parents about my stream. I figured that it needed a bridge, something only Dad could help me build. And so, that afternoon, I led Mom and Dad over the fence, into the woods, and up to my secret stream. Together, we built a bridge using the fallen branches lying about. Mom took a picture of Dad and me sitting on our homemade, lopsided bridge, the water washing over the toes of the big rubber boots that she had insisted we wear.

8   My parents separated eight years after that picture was taken, and I haven't gone back to my stream since, though I think of it often. Somewhere, tucked away in Mom's photo albums, is the picture of a little girl in her dreamland, her dad beside her, his big feet hanging near her small ones. Her mom stands in the water just a few feet away behind the camera lens.

9   Sometimes, I want to go back there, back into that
(F) photo. I want to step into a time when life seemed safe, and a tiny stream gave us all that we needed. In that picture, our smiles last, our hearts are calm, and we hear only quiet voices, forest sounds, and my bubbling stream. Bitter words are silenced and tears held back by the click and whir of a camera.

10   I've been thinking about making the journey again past the hunter's fort, under the stand of cedars, through the muck and mire, and over the rocky rise. But it's been a long summer, and the small, seasonal stream running out of the overflow of the pond has probably dried up.

(F) The writer yearns for life as shown in the photo.

(D) The writer describes the stream and shares its personal importance.

(E) The picture shows the father, the daughter, and their bridge.

© Robert Hackett, 2009 / Used under license from Shutterstock.com

Reading for Better Writing

Working by yourself or with a group, answer these questions:

1. Three times in the essay, the writer mentions four sites (hunter's fort, cedar archway, muck and mire, rocky rise) along her route. What do the references to these sites contribute to the description?

2. How does the writer organize her description? Identify the strategies used and discuss their effectiveness.

3. Review the references to the photograph taken by the mother, and describe what the photo shows. What does the writer mean when she says, "Sometimes, I want to go back there, back into that photo"?

4. Reread the opening and closing paragraphs, comparing how the writer describes the stream in each paragraph. Are the details and voices of the two passages different? Give examples.

"**Are we to paint what's**
on the face, what's inside the face, or
what's behind it?"

—Pablo Picasso

9 Analysis

Pablo Picasso was a master of observation. He looked closely at things, studied them from every angle, and reproduced them in his art. Early on, his work was photo-realistic, but he soon became impatient with that approach. It showed its subject from only one perspective. Picasso wanted to go a step further: to depict a subject from multiple perspectives at once. So he invented cubism.

When you analyze a subject in writing, you also need to show your subject from multiple perspectives. Start with careful observation. Circle around your topic, looking at it from all angles. Hoist it in your hands and feel its heft, its smoothness or grit, its heat or chill. Carry the topic around with you and set it next to other things and toss it to your friends and drop it to see if it bounces or breaks. Once you understand the topic, you can write about it from multiple perspectives. You can show it in a way that makes readers feel that they are seeing it for the first time.

In this chapter, you'll explore three types of analyses. An extended definition goes far beyond **denotation** into **connotation** and correlation and context. A classification essay groups ideas and connects them in new ways—creating a **taxonomy** of thought. And a process essay explores the temporal connections between stages and phases.

Learning Outcomes

LO1 Create an extended definition.

LO2 Write a classification essay.

LO3 Explain a process.

What do you think?

When I look at a Picasso painting, I feel as though I am seeing a subject from many angles.

1	2	3	4	5
strongly agree				strongly disagree

denotation
the dictionary definition of a word; a word's literal meaning

connotation
the suggestion made by a word; a word's implied meaning

taxonomy
a system of classification of items—plants, animals, ideas, movements, and so on

LO1 Create an extended definition.

Your goal is to choose a word or phrase that interests you, explore what it means (and doesn't mean), and write an **extended definition** that helps the reader better understand, appreciate, and use that term.

1. Select a topic. The best topics for extended definitions are abstract nouns (*totalitarianism*, *individualism*, or *terrorism*), complex terms (*dementia*, *spousal abuse*, or *Italian opera*), or adjectives connected to a personal experience. Use the list below as a beginning point for selecting your topic.

Words that . . .
– are related to an art or a sport.
– are in the news (or should be).
– are overused, underused, or abused.
– make you chuckle, frown, or fret.
– do or do not describe you.

2. Identify what you know about the topic. Write freely about the word, letting your writing go where it chooses. Explore both your personal connections and your academic connections with the word.

3. Gather information about the word's history, usage, and grammatical form. Use the following strategies as a starting point.

• **Consult a general dictionary** that lists both denotative (literal) and connotative (associated) meanings for the word. • **Consult specialized dictionaries** that define words from specific disciplines or occupations: music, literature, law, medicine, and so on. • **Interview experts** or students, when appropriate, on your topic. • **Check reference books** such

extended definition
a type of analytical writing that explores the meaning of a specific term, providing denotation, connotation, and a variety of perspectives on the term

as *Bartlett's Famous Quotations* to see how famous speakers and writers have used the word. • **Research the word's etymology** and usage by consulting appropriate Web sources such as dictionary.com, m-w.com, or xrefer.com. • **Do a general search on the Web** to see where the word pops up in titles of songs, books, or films; company names, products, and ads; nonprofit organizations; and news topics. • **List synonyms** (words with the same—or nearly the same—meaning) and antonyms (words with opposite meanings).

4. Compress what you know. Based on your freewriting and research, try writing a one-sentence formal definition that satisfies the following equation:

Term = general class + specific characteristics

Swedish pimple = fishing lure + silver surface, tubular body, three hooks
melodrama = stage play + flat characters, contrived plot, moralistic theme
Alzheimer's = dementia + increasing loss of memory, hygiene, social skills

5. Organize the information that you have and identify details that you may want to add. Fill out a definition diagram like the one on page 37.

TIP
Although you can draft your essay directly from the organizer, you may save time by writing a traditional outline that lists your main points, subpoints, and supporting details.

6. Draft the essay. Review your outline as needed to write the first draft of your essay. Include an opening, a middle, and a closing, as described here.

Opening: Get the reader's attention and introduce the term. If you are organizing the essay from general to specific, consider using an anecdote, an illustration, or a quotation to set the context for what follows. If you are organizing it from specific to general, consider including an interesting detail from the word's history or usage. Wherever you use a dictionary definition, do so with a new slant and avoid the dusty phrase "According to *Webster's*. . . ."

Middle: Show your reader precisely what the

word does or does not mean. Build the definition in unified paragraphs, each of which addresses distinct aspects of the word: common definitions, etymology, usage by professional writers, and so on. Link paragraphs so that the essay unfolds the word's meaning one layer after another.

Closing: Review your main point and close your essay. (You might, for example, conclude by encouraging the reader to use—or not use—the word.)

7. Get feedback. Ask a classmate or someone from the college's writing center to read your essay for the following:

Engaging opening—Does the introduction identify the word and set the context for what follows?

Clarity—Is each facet of the definition clear, showing precisely what the word does and does not mean?

Continuity—Is each paragraph unified, and is each one linked to the paragraphs that precede and follow it? Is the essay focused and unified?

Completeness—Is the definition complete, telling the reader all that she or he needs to know to understand and use the word?

Fitting closing—Does the conclusion wrap up the message and refocus on the word's core meaning?

8. Revise and edit the essay. Use the feedback to revise the essay. If necessary, do additional research to find information to answer your reader's questions. Edit the essay to ensure clear sentences; correct quotations; specific, appropriate words; and correct grammar, spelling, usage, and punctuation.

9. Publish the essay. Share your writing with interested readers, including friends, family, and classmates. Submit the essay to your instructor.

© Tomasz Trojanowski, 2009 / Used under license from Shutterstock.com

A MODERN SCOURGE DEFINED

The excerpt below comes from a research paper by student writer Shon Bogar. The paper focuses on the problems of human trafficking and slavery as phenomena associated with current trends in globalization. After reviewing global economic trends since the end of the cold war, Bogar defines the key terms that readers must understand if they are to appreciate the problem. (For more on research writing, see chapters 18–21.)

SQ3R
Survey Question Read Recite Review

Economic Disparities Fuel Human Trafficking

. . . . These great economic disparities, from extreme poverty to fabulous wealth, have helped fuel the international trade in human cargo, as those people with nothing seek a better life serving those with excess.   *1* (A)

The buying, selling, and forced exploitation of people—slavery—is not a new phenomenon. Most nations and most cultures have, at one time or another, enslaved others and been themselves enslaved in turn. The pattern continues today; in fact, slavery exists far beyond the developing world and reaches into the comfortable first world of the United States, Europe, Japan, and Australia. However, examining current trends in the trade of human cargo shows that trafficking and slavery are extremely difficult to define and understand, and that they coexist with and are codependent upon each other. These problems, moreover, have a variety of complex causes and too few solutions that offer a realistic possibility of ending this global abomination.   *2* (B)

Human trafficking, in particular, is a term that is difficult to define properly, but it must first be clarified if the problem itself is to be addressed. To begin, migration, human smuggling, and human trafficking are distinct but related phenomena, and incorrect definitions would put different groups of people in the wrong category, with potentially dire consequences. For example, the Trafficking Victims Prevention Act (TVPA), which came into law in 2000, requires the U.S. government to ensure that victims of trafficking are not jailed or   *3* (C)

(A) The final sentence of the introduction transitions to the extended definition.

(B) An informal definition of the broader concept of slavery prefaces the extended definition.

(C) The main term is distinguished from related terms using reliable source material.

"otherwise penalized solely for unlawful acts as a direct result of being trafficked" (U.S. Department of State, 2004), whereas illegal immigrants are still subject to deportation and criminal proceedings. The U.S. State Department recognizes the potentially "confusing" difference between smuggling and human trafficking, so it defines human smuggling as "the procurement or transport for profit of a person for illegal entry in a country" (2004). However, even if the smuggling involves "dangerous or degrading conditions," the act is still considered smuggling, not human trafficking, and so smuggling is considered an immigration matter, not necessarily a human rights issue (2004).

4   What distinguishes trafficking from smuggling is
(D) the element of exploitation, including but not limited to "fraud, force, or coercion" (U.S. Department of State, 2004). With this distinction in mind, the United Nations Convention Against Transnational Organized Crime has developed this standard definition of human trafficking: "the recruitment, transportation, transfer, harbouring or receipt of persons, by means of the threat or use of force or other forms of coercion, of abduction, of fraud, of deception, of the abuse of power, or of a position of vulnerability or of the giving or receiving of payments or benefits to achieve the consent of a person having control over another person, for the pur-
(E) pose of exploitation" (U.N. Resolution 25, 2001). To unravel the U.N. legalese, human trafficking involves any use of force, coercion, fraud, or deception by those with power so as to exploit people, primarily by moving them into some form of slavery. Under this definition, smuggling can become trafficking if the smugglers have used any means of deception. Unfortunately, the requirement that the smuggler/trafficker be aware of the "victim's final circumstances" makes distinguishing between smuggling and trafficking an inexact science (U.S. Department of State, 2004), and it creates a new set of problems in combating trafficking apart from smuggling. Nevertheless, this definition of human trafficking is a helpful starting point from which the

United Nations and governments around the globe can start to fight the trafficking and eventual enslavement of people.

    All difficulties of definition aside, human trafficking   5 and slavery are real problems—historical problems that (F) have taken new shapes due to globalization. In fact, today human trafficking is linked to millions of people experiencing multiple forms of slavery, from traditional "chattel slavery" to sexual slavery to debt bondage. . . .

Reading for Better Writing

Working by yourself or with a group, answer these questions:

1. Without looking back at the model, define "human trafficking" in a sentence or two.

2. Examine each of the three main paragraphs of Bogar's extended definition. What does each paragraph accomplish? How do the paragraphs build on each other?

3. Identify the strategies that the author uses to argue that the definition is necessary. Is the reasoning compelling? Why or why not?

4. Look again at the sources that the writer uses to develop the necessary definitions. Why are these sources appropriate for the terms in question? Which other types of sources might be useful?

5. Examine how the writer transitions into and out of the extended definition. Are these transitions effective? Why or why not?

(D) The writer offers a formal definition of the key term "human trafficking" by going to official sources.

(E) The writer restates a complex legal definition in a reader-friendly style.

(F) The writer stresses the definition's usefulness in the fight against a real problem.

© Chee-Onn Leong, 2009 / Used under license from Shutterstock.com

LO2 Write a classification essay.

Your goal is to divide a group of people, places, things, or concepts into subgroups and then to write an essay that helps the reader understand each subgroup, the relationships between subgroups, and the topic as a whole. You will sort items into subgroups that are consistent (meaning that all items have the same trait or feature), exclusive (meaning that items do not appear in more than one subgroup), and complete (meaning all items are included in a subgroup).

1. Select a topic. Start by writing five or six general headings, such as *engineering, biology, social work,* or *education;* then list two or three related topics under each heading. (See the examples below.) Finally, pick a topic that can best be explained by breaking it into subgroups.

- **Engineering:** machines | bridges | buildings | tools
- **Biology:** whales | fruits | biomes | systems
- **Social Work:** child welfare | organizations | interventions
- **Education:** learning styles | testing methods | approaches

2. Look at the big picture. Conduct preliminary research to get an overview of your topic. Review your purpose (to explain, persuade, inform, and so on) and consider which classification criteria will help you divide the subject into distinct, understandable subgroups.

3. Choose and test your criteria for creating subgroups. These criteria should produce subgroups that are consistent (all members fit the criterion), exclusive (subgroups are distinct—no member of the group fits into more than one subgroup), and complete (each member fits into a subgroup with no member left over).

> ### TIP
> To better visualize how you are dividing your topic and classifying its members, take a few minutes to fill out a graphic organizer like the one shown below.

4. Gather and organize information from library and Web resources as well as interviews. To take notes and organize your information, consider using a classification grid like the one shown below. Set up the grid by listing the subgroups down the left column and listing the classification criteria in the middle column. Then fill in the grid with appropriate details. (The following grid lists the classification criteria and subgroups used in "Four Ways to Talk About Literature," pages 100–102.)

Classification Grid

	Classification criteria	Details of each approach
Subgroup 1	Text-centered approach	Trait 1 Trait 2 Trait 3
Subgroup 2	Audience-centered approach	Trait 1 Trait 2 Trait 3
Subgroup 3	Author-centered approach	Trait 1 Trait 2 Trait 3
Subgroup 4	Ideas outside literature	Trait 1 Trait 2 Trait 3

Note: If you do not use a grid similar to this one, construct an outline to help organize your thoughts.

5. Draft a working thesis (one you revise later as needed) that states your **topic** and **main point**. Include language introducing your criteria for classifying subgroups.

6. Draft the essay. Write your first draft, using either the organizational pattern in the classification grid or an outline. Include an opening, a middle, and a closing as described here.

Opening: Get the reader's attention, introduce the subject and thesis, and give your criteria for dividing the subject into subgroups.

Middle: Develop the thesis by discussing each subgroup, explaining its traits, and showing how it is distinct from the other subgroups. For example, in the middle section of "Four Ways to Talk About Literature," the writer first shows the unique focus of each of the four approaches to literary criticism, and then illustrates each approach by applying it to the same poem, "My Last Duchess."

Closing: While the opening and the middle of the essay separate the subject into components and subgroups, the closing brings the components and subgroups back together. For example, in "Four Ways to Talk About Literature," the writer closes by identifying three characteristics that the four subgroups have in common (see pages 100–102).

7. Get feedback. Ask a classmate or someone from the writing center to read your essay, looking for the following:

- An engaging opening that introduces the subject, thesis, and criteria for classification
- A well-organized middle that distinguishes subgroups, shows why each subgroup is unique, and includes adequate details
- A clear closing that reaches some sort of conclusion

8. Revise and edit your draft, checking for the items in this list:

Revising and Editing Checklist

The writing has . . .

_____ Subgroups that are consistent, exclusive, and complete
_____ Organization that helps the reader understand the subject
_____ Appropriate examples that clarify the nature and function of each subgroup
_____ A unifying conclusion
_____ An informed, reader-friendly voice
_____ Clear, complete sentences
_____ Unified paragraphs linked with appropriate transitions
_____ Correct usage, grammar, punctuation, and spelling

9. Publish your essay. Share your writing by offering copies to classmates and friends, publishing it in a journal or on a Web site, or placing a copy in your professional portfolio.

A LITERARY CLASSIFICATION

In this essay, John Van Rys, a college professor, classifies four basic approaches to literary criticism. His essay is intended to help college freshmen interpret literature.

SQ3R
Survey Question Read Recite Review

Four Ways to Talk About Literature

Have you ever been in a conversation in which you suddenly felt lost—out of the loop? Perhaps you feel that way in your literature class. You may think a poem or short story means one thing, and then your instructor suddenly pulls out the "hidden meaning." Joining the conversation about literature—in class or in an essay—may indeed seem daunting, but you can do it if you

1
(A)

know what to look for and what to talk about. There are four main perspectives, or approaches, that you can use to converse about literature.

2
(B) Text-centered approaches focus on the literary piece itself. Often called *formalist criticism,* such approaches claim that the structure of a work and the rules of its genre are crucial to its meaning. The formalist critic determines how various elements (plot, character, language, and so on) reinforce the meaning and unify the work. For example, the formalist may ask the following questions concerning Robert Browning's poem "My Last Duchess": How do the main elements in the poem—irony, symbolism, and verse form—help develop the main theme (deception)? How does Browning use the dramatic monologue genre in this poem?

3
(C) Audience-centered approaches focus on the "transaction" between text and reader—the dynamic way the reader interacts with the text. Often called *rhetorical* or *reader-response criticism,* these approaches see the text not as an object to be analyzed, but as an activity that is different for each reader. A reader-response critic might ask these questions of "My Last Duchess": How does the reader become aware of the duke's true nature if it's never actually stated? Do men and women read the poem differently? Who were Browning's original readers?

4
(D) An author-centered approach focuses on the origins of a text (the writer and the historical background). For example, an author-centered study examines the writer's life—showing connections, contrasts, and conflicts between his or her life and the writing. Broader historical studies explore social and intellectual currents, showing links between an author's work and the ideas, events, and institutions of that period. Finally, the literary historian may make connections between the text in question and earlier and later literary works. The author-centered critic might ask these questions of "My Last Duchess": What were Browning's views of marriage, men and women, art, class, and wealth? As an in-

© krechet , 2009 / Used under license from Shutterstock.com

stitution, what was marriage like in Victorian England (Browning's era) or Renaissance Italy (the duke's era)? Who was the historical Duke of Ferrara?

The fourth approach to criticism applies ideas outside of literature to literary works. Because literature mirrors life, argue these critics, disciplines that explore human life can help us understand literature. Some critics, for example, apply psychological theories to literary works by exploring dreams, symbolic meanings, and motivation. Myth or archetype criticism uses insights from psychology, cultural anthropology, and classical studies to explore a text's universal appeal. Moral criticism, rooted in religious studies and ethics, explores the moral dilemmas literary works raise. Marxist, feminist, and minority criticism are, broadly speaking, sociological approaches to interpretation. While the Marxist examines the themes of class struggle, economic power, and social justice in texts, the feminist critic explores the just and unjust treatment of women as well as the effect of gender on language, reading, and the literary canon. The critic interested in race and ethnic identity explores similar issues, with the focus shifted to a specific cultural group. 5 (E)

Such ideological criticism might ask a wide variety of questions about "My Last Duchess": What does the poem reveal about the duke's psychological state and his personality? How does the reference to Neptune deepen the poem? What does the poem suggest about the nature of evil and injustice? In what ways are the 6 (F)

(A) The writer introduces the topic and criteria for creating four subgroups.

(B) He describes the first subgroup and gives an example.

(C) He describes the second subgroup and gives an example.

(D) He describes the third subgroup and gives examples.

(E) He describes the fourth subgroup along with several of its divisions and examples of each.

(F) The writer cites sample questions.

duke's motives class based and economic? How does the poem present the duke's power and the duchess's weakness? What is the status of women in this society?

7 If you look at the variety of questions critics might (G) ask about "My Last Duchess," you see both the diversity of critical approaches and the common ground between them. In fact, interpretive methods actually share important characteristics: (1) a close attention to literary elements such as character, plot, symbolism, and metaphor; (2) a desire not to distort the work; and (3) a sincere concern for increasing interest in and understanding of a text. In actual practice, critics may develop a hybrid approach to criticism, one that matches their individual questions and concerns about a text. Now that you're familiar with some of the questions defining literary criticism, exercise your own curiosity (and join the ongoing literary dialogue) by discussing a text that genuinely interests you.

(G) The closing presents qualities shared by all four approaches.

Reading for Better Writing

Working by yourself or with a group, answer these questions:

1. Explain how the writer introduces the subject and attempts to engage the reader. Is this strategy effective? Why or why not?

2. The writer uses one poem to illustrate how each of the four critical approaches works. Explain why this strategy is or is not effective.

3. Review the last paragraph and explain why it does or does not unify the essay.

© spaxiax, 2009 / Used under license from Shutterstock.com

LO3 Explain a process.

Your goal is to analyze a process, break it into specific steps, and write about it using one of the following forms: a *description* of a process, an *explanation* of the process, or *instructions* on how to carry out the process. You will need to understand the process well and show how each step logically leads to the next. Write to your least-knowledgeable reader and include necessary information in language that she or he can understand.

1. Select a topic. Think about processes that involve multiple steps carried out over time. Also consider whether you will describe the process, explain it, or give instructions for carrying it out.

Consider a process that . . .
– is related to your course work.
– keeps you healthy.
– you have mastered.
– is in the news.
– helps you get a job.
– is part of your planned occupation.

Process Organizer

Subject
• Step 1
• Step 2
• Step 3
Outcome

2. Review the process. Use your knowledge of the topic to fill out a process organizer like the one on the left. List the subject at the top, each of the steps in chronological order, and the outcome at the bottom. Review the organizer to find gaps or issues you may need to research.

3. Research to find information that spells out the process: what it is, what steps are required, what order the steps should follow, how to do the steps, what outcome the process should produce, and what safety precautions are needed. If pos-

© Cameramannz, 2009 / Used under license from Shutterstock.com

sible, observe the process in action or perform it yourself. Carefully record correct names, materials, tools, and safety or legal issues.

4. Organize the information. After conducting your research, revise the organizer by adding or re-ordering steps as needed. Then develop an outline, including steps listed in the organizer as well as supporting details from your research.

5. Draft the document using the guidelines below.

Describing a Process

Opening: Introduce the topic, stating its importance and giving an overview of the steps.

Middle: Describe each step clearly (usually in separate paragraphs), and link steps with transitions like *first, second, next, finally,* and *while.* Describe the outcome and its importance.

Closing: Describe the process as a whole and re-state key points.

Writing Instructions

Opening: Name the process in the title; summarize the process and list any materials and tools needed.

Middle: Present each step in a separate—usually one- or two-sentence—paragraph. Number the steps and state them as commands in parallel form (see page 105).

Closing: In a short paragraph, explain any follow-up action.

Explaining a Process

Opening: Introduce the topic and give an overview of the process.

Middle: Explain what each step involves and how to do it (typically using a separate paragraph for each). Use transitions such as *first, second,* and *next* to link the steps. Explain the outcome.

Closing: Explain follow-up activity and restate key points.

6. Revise the writing. Check your document for a clear opening that identifies the process and for steps that are stated plainly and in the correct order.

In explanations and instructions, check for specific details explaining how to perform each step and for a closing that includes necessary follow-up activity. Instructions also require exact and correct safety precautions.

7. Test the writing. Read the writing for organization and completeness. For explanations and instructions, perform the process yourself using the writing as a guide. For each step, do only what you're told to do. Note where the writing is incomplete, out of order, and/or lacking adequate safety precautions. Revise as needed.

8. Get feedback. Ask a classmate who is unfamiliar with the process to read the writing for clarity, completeness, and correctness. For instructions, have the person use the writing as a guide to perform the process, noting where details are incomplete or unclear and where word choice is either imprecise or too technical. Use the feedback to revise further.

9. Edit your draft, checking for the items in this list:

Editing Checklist

_____ Word choice appropriate for your least-informed reader

_____ Clear transitions between steps

_____ Consistent verb tense in all steps

_____ For *instructions*—verbs that give clear commands (imperative mood)

_____ Correct, consistent terminology

_____ Informed, respectful voice

_____ Proper format (particularly for *instructions*—adequate white space)

10. Publish the essay. Share your writing with instructors or students working with the process, offer explanations and instructions to people who can use them to do their work on campus or at non-profit agencies, or post the writing on a suitable Web site.

A DEGENERATIVE PROCESS

Student writer Kerri Mertz wrote this essay to help non-scientists understand how cancer cells multiply and affect the body.

SQ3R
Survey Question Read Recite Review

Wayward Cells

1
(A) Imagine a room containing a large group of people all working hard toward the same goal. Each person knows his or her job, does it carefully, and cooperates with other group members. Together, they function efficiently and smoothly—like a well-oiled machine.

2 Then something goes wrong. One guy suddenly drops his task, steps into another person's workstation, grabs the material that she's working with, and begins something very different—he uses the material to make little reproductions of himself, thousands of them. These look-alikes imitate him—grabbing material and making reproductions of themselves. Soon the bunch gets so big that they spill into other people's workstations, getting in their way, and interrupting their work. As the number of look-alikes grows, the work group's activity slows, stutters, and finally stops.

3
(B) A human body is like this room, and the body's cells are like these workers. If the body is healthy, each cell has a necessary job and does it correctly. For example, right now red blood cells are running throughout your body carrying oxygen to each body part. Other cells are digesting that steak sandwich that you had for lunch, and others are patching up that cut on your left hand. Each cell knows what to do because its genetic code—or DNA—tells it what to do. When a cell begins to function abnormally, it can initiate a process that results in cancer.

4
(C) The problem starts when one cell "forgets" what it should do. Scientists call this "undifferentiating"—meaning that the cell loses its identity within the body (Pierce 75). Just like the guy in the group who decided to do his own thing, the cell forgets its job. Why this happens is somewhat unclear. The problem could be caused by a defect in the cell's DNA code or by some-thing in the environment, such as cigarette smoke or asbestos (German 21). Causes from inside the body are called genetic, whereas causes from outside the body are called carcinogens, meaning "any substance that causes cancer" (Neufeldt and Sparks 90). In either case, an undifferentiated cell can disrupt the function of healthy cells in two ways: by not doing its job as specified in its DNA and by not reproducing at the rate noted in its DNA.

5
(D) Most healthy cells reproduce rather quickly, but their reproduction rate is controlled. For example, your blood cells completely die off and replace themselves within a matter of weeks, but existing cells make only as many new cells as the body needs. The DNA codes in healthy cells tell them how many new cells to produce. However, cancer cells don't have this control, so they reproduce quickly with no stopping point, a characteristic called "autonomy" (Braun 3). What's more, all their "offspring" have the same qualities as their messed-up parent, and the resulting overpopulation produces growths called tumors.

6
(E) Tumor cells can hurt the body in a number of ways. First, a tumor can grow so big that it takes up space needed by other organs. Second, some cells may detach from the original tumor and spread throughout the body, creating new tumors elsewhere. This happens with lymphatic cancer—a cancer that's hard to control because it spreads so quickly. A third way that tumor cells can hurt the body is by doing work not called for in their DNA. For example, a gland cell's DNA code may tell the cell to produce a necessary hormone in the endocrine system. However, if cancer damages or distorts that code, sick cells may produce more of the hormone than the body can use—or even tolerate (Braun 4). Cancer cells seem to have minds of their own, and this is why cancer is such a serious disease.

7
(F) Fortunately, there is hope. Scientific research is already helping doctors do amazing things for people with cancer. One treatment that has been used for some time is chemotherapy, or the use of chemicals to kill off all fast-growing cells, including cancer cells. (Unfortunately, chemotherapy can't distinguish between healthy and unhealthy cells, so it may cause negative side effects such as damaging fast-growing hair follicles, resulting in hair loss.) Another common treatment is radiation,

---

(A) The writer uses the title and an analogy to introduce the topic.

(B) She uses a simile to complete the analogy.

(C) She describes the first step in the process and cites a potential cause.

(D) She describes the next step and its result.

(E) She describes the third step—how tumors damage the body.

(F) A transition signals a shift from the illness to treatments.

or the use of light rays to kill cancer cells. One of the newest and most promising treatments is gene therapy—an effort to identify and treat chromosomes that carry a "wrong code" in their DNA. A treatment like gene therapy is promising because it treats the cause of cancer, not just the effect. Year by year, research is helping doctors better understand what cancer is and how to treat it.

8 Much of life involves dealing with problems like wayward workers, broken machines, or dysfunctional organizations. Dealing with wayward cells is just another problem. While the problem is painful and deadly, there is hope. Medical specialists and other scientists are making progress, and someday they will help win the battle against wayward cells.

Note: The works-cited page is not shown.

(G) The writer reconsiders her analogy and reviews main points.

Reading for Better Writing

Working by yourself or with a group, answer these questions:

1. Review the opening three-paragraph analogy used to introduce and describe the process. Explain why the analogy is or is not effective.

2. Review the three steps cited by the writer and note the transitions that lead into and out of each step. Are the transitions effective?

3. Review the guidelines on pages 102–103 to introduce a topic, describe each step, and, finally, recap the process as a whole. Explain how this essay does or does not follow these guidelines.

INSTRUCTIONS FOR A PROCESS

These instructions, like those for many technical devices, include both written and visual elements. The writer lists the necessary materials and states the steps in chronological order and parallel form. Boldfaced words call special attention to key information, and the closing notes a common problem.

Downloading Photographs from the MC-150 Digital Camera

Note: MC-150 software must be loaded on your computer to download photographs from the camera.

1. Turn your computer on.

2. Plug the camera's USB cable into your computer.

3. Turn the camera's mode dial to the **data transfer setting.** (See Figure 1.)

4. Open the camera's flash-card door and plug the other end of the USB cable into the **camera port.** (See Figure 2.)

5. Select USB transfer from the camera screen menu. The MC-150 software will then launch on your computer.

6. Follow the instructions on the computer screen to download all of your photos or specific photos.

7. When your download is complete, turn the camera off and unplug the USB cable from the camera and the computer.

Note: If the MC-150 software doesn't launch, disconnect the camera (step 7); then restart the computer and continue from step 2.

Figure 1: Data Transfer Setting

Figure 2: Camera Port

"**Shall I compare**
thee to a summer's day? Thou art more lovely and
more temperate."

—William Shakespeare

10

Analytical Strategies

LO1 Understand special strategies.

The Matterhorn in the Alps is one of the most iconic mountains in the world, with its hooked top and steep-sloping sides. It's one thing to marvel at its grandeur. It's another to understand how the Matterhorn and the Alps came to be. They rose when the African plate crashed into the European plate, thrusting up the seafloor and piling much older African gneiss atop much younger limestone. That's why fossilized seashells are embedded in the side of the Matterhorn.

Clearly, to understand the causes behind the formation of the Matterhorn is to better understand this great peak.

The Matterhorn is also one of the deadliest mountains in the world. At 14,691 feet, it may be only half the height of Everest (at 29,029 feet), but the Matterhorn claims more lives per year. This fact may be because the Matterhorn attracts many more climbers. Clearly, to compare and contrast the Matterhorn to Everest is to understand both mountains better.

Cause-effect and **comparison-contrast analyses** provide in-depth insight into a topic. This chapter will teach you how to write such analyses.

Learning Outcomes

LO1 Understand special strategies.

LO2 Create a cause-effect essay.

LO3 Write a comparison-contrast essay.

What do you think?

I'd rather climb the lower, deadlier Matterhorn than the higher, safer Everest.

1   2   3   4   5

strongly agree   strongly disagree

---

cause-effect analysis
a paper that examines the conditions or actions that lead to specific outcomes

comparison-contrast analysis
a paper that shows the similarities and differences between two topics

LO2 Create a cause-effect essay.

Your goal is to analyze and explain the causes, the effects, or both the causes and the effects of some phenomenon (fact, occurrence, or circumstance).

1. Select a topic. Begin by thinking about categories such as those listed below. Then brainstorm a list of phenomena related to each category. From this list, choose a topic and prove its causes, its effects, or both.

- **Family life:** adult children living with parents, increasing number of stay-at-home dads, families choosing to simplify their lifestyles, more people squeezed by needs of children and parents, older women having babies

- **Politics:** decreasing number of student voters, increasing support for oil exploration, increased interest in third-party politics, tension between political action groups

- **Society:** nursing shortage, security concerns, nursing-care facilities, immigrant-advocacy groups, shifting ethnic balances

- **Environment:** common water pollutants, new water-purification technology, effects of a community's recycling program

- **Workplace:** decreasing power of unions, more businesses providing child-care services, need for on-the-job training in technology

2. Narrow and research the topic. Write down or type your topic. Below it, brainstorm a list of related causes and effects in two columns. Next, do preliminary research to expand the list and distinguish primary causes and effects from secondary ones. Revise your topic as needed to address only primary causes and/or effects that research links to a specific phenomenon.

Topic: Cause/Effect	
1. Cause	1. Effect
2. Cause	2. Effect
3. Cause	3. Effect

3. Draft and test your thesis. Based on your preliminary research, draft a working thesis (you may revise it later) that introduces the topic, along with the causes and/or effects you intend to discuss. Limit your argument to only those points you can prove.

4. Gather and analyze information. Research your topic, looking for clear evidence that links specific causes to specific effects. At the same time, avoid arguments mistaking a coincidence for a cause-effect relationship. Use the list of logical fallacies (see pages 138–141) to weed out common errors in logic. For example, finding chemical pollutants in a stream running beside a chemical plant does not "prove" that the plant caused the pollutants.

5. Get organized. Develop an outline that lays out your thesis and argument in a clear pattern. Under each main point asserting a cause-effect connection, list details from your research that support the connection.

Thesis:
Main Point
Supporting Detail
Supporting Detail

6. Use your outline to draft the essay. Try to rough out the essay's overall argument before you attempt to revise it. As you write, show how each specific cause led to each specific effect, citing examples as needed. To show those cause-effect relationships, use transitional words like the following:

accordingly	hence	therefore
as a result	just as	thus
because	since	to illustrate
consequently	so	whereas
for this purpose	such as	while
for this reason	thereby	

7. Revise the essay. Whether your essay presents causes, effects, or both, use the checklist below to trace and refine your argument.

Revising Checklist

____ The thesis and introduction clearly identify the causes and/or effects.

____ All major causes and/or effects are addressed.

____ Statements regarding the causes and/or effects are sufficiently limited and focused.

____ Supporting details are researched, relevant, and strong.

____ Links between causes and effects are clear and logical.

____ The conclusion restates the main argument and unifies the essay.

8. Get feedback. Ask a peer reviewer or someone from the college's writing center to read your essay for the following:

Ask ?

Does the writing have …

• an engaging opening?

• a clear and logical thesis?

• clear and convincing reasoning that links specific causes to specific effects?

• a closing that wraps up the argument, leaving no loose ends?

9. Edit the essay for clarity and correctness. When editing your essay, check for and correct the following: Does the essay use precise, appropriate word choice? Are the sentences complete and smooth? Are transitions between paragraphs clear? Have names, dates, and supporting details been checked for correctness? Have I corrected mechanics, usage, and grammar as needed?

10. Publish your essay. Share your writing with others. Consider submitting it to your instructor or posting it on the class's or department's Web site. Submit the essay for presentation at an appropriate conference, or send it as a service to relevant non-profit agencies.

CAUSES OF ADRENALINE HIGHS

When she wrote this essay, Sarah Hanley was a college student living on a U.S. military base in Germany. In this essay, she uses both research and her military experience to identify the causes and effects of adrenaline highs.

SQ3R
Survey Question Read Recite Review

Adrenaline Junkies

Who are "adrenaline junkies"? Bungee jumpers hurling themselves from bridges? Mythbusters blowing up anything they can get hold of? Retirees excitedly stuffing quarters in slot machines? Actually, all three qualify as adrenaline junkies if they do the activities to get their adrenaline highs. But what, exactly, is an adrenaline high, what causes it, what are its effects, and are the effects positive? **1 (A)**

Adrenaline (also called epinephrine) is a hormone linked to the two adrenal glands located on top of the kidneys. Each gland has two parts: the outer portion called the cortex, and the inner portion called the medulla. When a person experiences an unusual exertion or a crisis situation, his or her brain triggers the medullas, which release little packets of adrenaline into the bloodstream (Nathan). The rush of adrenaline in the blood leads to increased blood pressure, heart rate, sugar metabolism, oxygen intake, and muscle strength. All these phenomena cause an adrenaline high: feeling highly alert and very energetic (Scheuller 2). **2 (B)**

However, while all healthy people experience adrenaline highs, different people need different levels of stimuli to trigger the highs. The level of stimulus that a person needs depends on the amount of protein in his or her medullas. In other words, the medullas release adrenaline through channels containing a certain protein. If the channels contain a large amount of the protein, they release adrenaline more easily than channels containing less protein. Therefore, a person with a higher level of protein in the channels of his or her medullas experiences an adrenaline release more easily than someone with a lower level of the protein (Scheuller 4). **3**

(A) The writer introduces the topic by asking a series of questions.

(B) She describes the causes and effects of an adrenaline high.

4
(C) To illustrate this difference, we'll call the people with a higher level of protein (and a more easily stimulated output of adrenaline) Type N, for nervous; the others we'll call Type C, for calm. Because Type N people release adrenaline more easily than Type C people do, Type Ns require a lesser stimulus to trigger an adrenaline release. For example, a Type N person may get an adrenaline high from finishing his research paper on time, whereas a Type C person will get a similar buzz only when she parachutes from a plane at 10,000 feet!

5
While different people get their adrenaline highs differently, any person's highs can be channeled for healthy or harmful effects. For example, the Type N person who gets a rush from finishing the research project could do good work as a research technician in a science lab. As long as he avoids becoming a workaholic, seeking the highs won't threaten his health, and the work may contribute to the overall welfare of society. Similarly, the Type C person who gets her highs by jumping out of airplanes could do good work as a firefighter or a brain surgeon. As long as she gets periodic relief from the tension, the highs won't hurt her health, and the work could help her community.

6
(D) On the other hand, pursuing the wrong type of adrenaline high, or seeking too many highs, can be destructive. Examples of this kind of behavior include compulsive gambling, drug use, careless risk taking in sports, and win-at-all-cost business practices. Destructive pursuits have many high-cost results including bankruptcy, broken relationships, physical injury, drug addiction, and death (Lyons 3).

7
(E) Because adrenaline highs can lead to positive results, maybe people shouldn't worry about becoming adrenaline junkies. Instead, they should ask how to pursue those highs positively. In other words, the proteins, hormones, and chemical processes that produce adrenaline highs are, themselves, very good—and they can be used for good. In fact, someone may figure out how to bottle the stuff and put it on the market!

Note: The works-cited page is not shown.

(C) She uses an illustration to clarify a point.
(D) An introductory phrase signals a shift in focus.
(E) The writer concludes by reviewing her main points.

Reading for Better Writing

1. Name two or more ways that the opening paragraph engages you and effectively introduces the topic and thesis.
2. Paragraphs three and four explain how different people need different levels of stimulus to trigger adrenaline highs. Is this explanation clear and believable? Why or why not?
3. In one sentence, summarize the writer's explanation of the causes and effects of an adrenaline high. Explain why you do or do not find this interpretation convincing.
4. The writer concludes the essay with a playful sentence suggesting that someday adrenaline may be bottled and sold. Explain why you think the sentence is or is not an effective closing.

LO3 Write a comparison-contrast essay.

Your goal is to write an essay that (1) sets two or more subjects side by side, (2) shows the reader how they are similar and/or different, and (3) draws conclusions or makes some point based on what you have shown.

1. Select a topic. List subjects that are similar and/or different in ways that you find interesting, perplexing, disgusting, infuriating, charming, or informing. To get started, think about pairs of objects, events, places, processes, people, ideas, beliefs, and so on. Choose two subjects whose comparison and/or contrast gives the reader some insight into who or what they are.

2. Get the big picture. Using a computer or a paper and pen, create three columns as shown below. Brainstorm a list of traits under each heading. (Also see the Venn diagram on page 36.)

Subject 1 Traits • *Shared Traits* • *Subject 2 Traits*

3. Gather information. Review your list of traits, highlighting those that could provide insight into one or both subjects. Research the subjects, using hands-on analysis when possible. Consider writing your research notes in the three-column format shown above.

4. Draft a working thesis. Review your expanded list of traits and eliminate those that now seem unimportant. Write a sentence stating the core of what you learned about the subjects and whether you are comparing, contrasting, or both. If you're stuck, try completing the sentence below. (Switch around the terms "similar" and "different" if you wish to stress similarities.)

While _____ and _____ seem similar, they are different in several ways, and the differences are important because _____.

5. Get organized. Decide how to organize your essay. Generally, subject by subject works best for short, simple comparisons. Trait by trait works best for longer, more complex comparisons.

6. Draft the essay. Review your outline and write your first draft in one sitting if possible. Check your outline for details and integrate them into the text. Employ one of the two patterns listed.

Subject-by-subject pattern:

Subject-by-subject organization is a pattern of essay organization that first deals with one subject and then deals with the next; a simple pattern to write but a more difficult one to read

> **Opening**—get readers' attention and introduce the subjects and thesis.
> **Middle**—describe one "package" of traits representing the first subject and a parallel set of traits representing the second subject.
> **Conclusion**—point out similarities and differences, note their significance, and restate your main point.

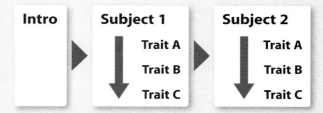

Trait-by-trait pattern:

Trait-by-trait organization is a pattern of essay organization that compares and contrasts two subjects one trait at a time; a more complex pattern to write but a simpler pattern to read

> **Opening**—get readers' attention and introduce the subjects and thesis.
> **Middle**—compare and/or contrast the two subjects trait by trait (include transitions that help readers look back and forth between the two subjects).
> **Conclusion**—summarize the key relationships, note their significance, and restate your main point.

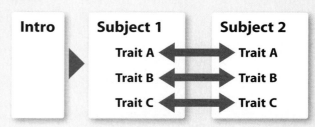

7. Revise the essay. Check the essay for the following:

Revising Checklist

____ Balanced comparisons and contrasts of comparable traits

____ Complete and thoughtful treatment of each subject

____ Genuine and objective voice

____ Clear, smooth sentences with varied structure

____ Title and introduction that spark interest

____ Thoughtful, unifying conclusion

8. Get feedback. Ask a classmate or someone in the writing center to read your paper, looking for the following:

 Ask

Does the writing have ...

• a clear, interesting thesis?

• an engaging and informative introduction?

• a middle that compares and/or contrasts significant, parallel traits?

• ideas that offer insight into the subject?

• a conclusion that restates the main point and unifies the essay?

9. Edit your essay. Look for transitions that signal comparisons and link paragraphs: *on the other hand, in contrast, similarly, also, both, even though, in the same way.* Check and correct quotations and documentation. And finally, correct spelling, punctuation, usage, and grammar

10. Publish your essay. Share your writing with others by submitting it to your instructor, sharing it with other students, or publishing it on a Web site.

TWO TRAGIC FIGURES

In this essay, Janae Sebranek compares the fate of two tragic literary characters, Bigger in *Native Son* and Alan in *Equus*. The student writer makes a trait-by-trait comparison, exploring how work, religion, and the media affect the characters.

SQ₃R
Survey Question Read Recite Review

Beyond Control

Most children, no matter what their personal or family situation, lead more or less controlled lives. As they grow, they begin to sense the pressure of controlling factors in their lives, and start struggling to take control themselves. This can be a difficult process. In the works *Native Son* and *Equus,* Richard Wright and Peter Shaffer, respectively, create two characters who must deal with this struggle. Bigger in *Native Son* and Alan in *Equus* are both entering adulthood and have come to realize that they are controlled by work, religion, and the media. In the midst of these characters' efforts to gain control, each character falls into a tragic situation. **1 (A)**

We find Alan experiencing the pressure of working as a clerk at Bryson's appliance store. The customers are demanding, and the many products and brand names are confusing. He finds that he cannot function in this work environment. Later, under hypnosis, he admits to Dr. Dysart that his "foes" are the myriad of brand names he is challenged to locate and explain to the customers—"The Hosts of Hoover. The Hosts of Philco. Those Hosts of Pifco. The House of Remington and all its tribe!" (73). However, by recognizing the demands of this job, Alan attempts to take some control over his life. **2 (B)**

Alan exercises further control when he decides to look for another job. He likes being around horses, so he pursues and lands a job with Mr. Dalton, a stable owner. He enjoys his job and begins to deal more effectively with the whole concept of work. **3**

Bigger must also struggle with the pressure and anxiety of his first job. Because of his family's desperate **4 (C)**

(A) The writer introduces her topic, main points of comparison, and thesis.

(B) She describes one of the traits of the first character.

(C) She describes a parallel trait of the second character and then contrasts the traits.

financial situation, he is forced to take the one job he is offered, coincidentally, by a Mr. Dalton. He works as a chauffeur for Mr. Dalton's wealthy suburban family. Bigger cannot relate to them. He sees himself as a foreigner, forced to live and work among the privileged. The Daltons tell him where, when, and even how to drive. Bigger struggles; but, like Alan, he cannot deal with the extreme discomfort he is feeling. He quits after only two days on the job. Unlike Alan, however, he does not have the option of getting a job that interests him.

5   Alan and Bigger also find religion to be a controlling factor in their lives. Alan's mother, Dora, "doses [religion] down the boy's throat" as she whispers "that Bible to him hour after hour, up there in his room" (33). Obviously, Alan's mother believes that he needs the controlling force of religion in his life, so she preaches to him every night. For a time, he is fascinated by the Bible's imagery and ideas. Eventually, though, this fascination begins to fade.

6   Bigger's mother does not push the issue of religion
(D) to the extreme that Alan's mother does. Instead, she tries to make her son see its value with daily comments such as "You'll regret how you living someday" (13). She offers her advice by singing religious songs from behind a curtain in their one-room apartment. She tries to show Bigger that religion is a valid way of dealing with a world out of control. But Bigger refuses to accept her religion, and he is left with no spiritual footing or direction.

7   Finally, we find the media playing a tormenting,
(E) controlling role in both Alan's and Bigger's lives. Alan's father calls television a "dangerous drug" (27) that can control the mind. Alan still manages to watch television, but only because his mother "used to let him slip off in the afternoons to a friend next door" (31) to watch. Later, while he is under psychiatric care, he watches television every night and eventually finds himself becoming controlled by the medium.

8   Bigger, in a more tragic way, is also controlled by the media. He reads about himself in the newspapers and begins to believe certain things that have no valid basis. He is referred to as a "Negro killer" who looks "as if about to spring upon you at any moment" (260). The papers remark that Bigger "seems a beast utterly untouched" (260) by and out of place in the white man's world. Unfortunately, Bigger has no control over what is printed or over what other people believe about him.

9   Bigger's ultimate fate is clearly beyond his control.
(F) He is falsely accused of raping and killing a woman, and he cannot convince anyone of the truth. Bigger's identity is too closely linked with the descriptions given in the newspapers. And this identity tragically leads to his death. Alan's fate is different, although tragic in its own right. While in the psychiatric ward, he gains a certain control with the help of therapy and medication. However, he loses his passion for life: "Passion, you see, can be destroyed by a doctor. It cannot be created" (108). This is Alan's personal tragedy.

10   Ultimately, both Alan and Bigger fail to gain real control over the outside forces in their lives. Alan forfeits his interest in life, and Bigger forfeits life itself. They, like so many people, become victims of the world in which they live.

Note: The works-cited page is not shown.

(F) She summarizes her argument and restates the thesis.

(D) She notes a contrast.
(E) She introduces her last point of comparison.

Reading for Better Writing

1. Do the opening paragraphs adequately introduce the topic and the thesis? Why or why not?

2. This essay is organized trait by trait. Is this strategy used effectively?

3. Does the writer focus on similarities, differences, or both? Is her choice effective?

LOOKING WITH TWO MINDS

Mark Twain is best known for his novels *The Adventures of Tom Sawyer* and *The Adventures of Huckleberry Finn.* In this excerpt from his 1883 memoir, *Life on the Mississippi,* Twain contrasts his mindset as an apprentice with his perspective as a steamboat pilot.

SQ3R
Survey Question Read Recite Review

Two Views of the River

1   Now when I had mastered the language of this water, and had come to know every trifling feature that bordered the great river as familiarly as I knew the letters of the alphabet, I had made a valuable acquisition. But I had (A) lost something, too. I had lost something which could never be restored to me while I lived. All the grace, the beauty, the poetry, had gone out of the majestic river! I still keep in mind a certain wonderful sunset which I witnessed when steamboating was new to me. A broad expanse of the river was turned to blood; in the middle distance the red hue brightened into gold, through which a solitary log came floating black and conspicuous; in one place a long, slanting mark lay sparkling upon the water; in another the surface was broken by boiling, tumbling rings that were as many-tinted as an opal; where the ruddy flush was faintest, was a smooth (B) spot that was covered with graceful circles and radi-

ating lines, ever so delicately traced; the shore on our left was densely wooded, and the somber shadow that fell from this forest was broken in one place by a long, ruffled trail that shone like silver; and high above the forest wall a clean-stemmed dead tree waved a single leafy bough that glowed like a flame in the unobstructed splendor that was flowing from the sun. There were graceful curves, reflected images, woody heights, soft distances; and over the whole scene, far and near, the dissolving lights drifted steadily, enriching it every passing moment with new marvels of coloring.

2   I stood like one bewitched. I drank it in, in a speechless rapture. The world was new to me, and I had never seen anything like this at home. But as I have said, a day (C) came when I began to cease from noting the glories and the charms which the moon and the sun and the twilight wrought upon the river's face; another day came when I ceased altogether to note them. Then, if that sunset scene had been repeated, I should have looked upon it without rapture, and should have commented upon it, inwardly, after this fashion: "This sun means that we are going to have wind tomorrow; that floating log means that the river is rising, small thanks to it; that slanting mark on the water refers to a bluff reef which is going (D) to kill somebody's steamboat one of these nights, if it keeps on stretching out like that; those tumbling 'boils' show a dissolving bar and a changing channel there; the lines and circles in the slick water over yonder are a warning that that troublesome place is shoaling up dangerously; that silver streak in the shadow of the for-

(A) The writer starts the sentence with the contrasting conjunction *but.*

(B) The sunset is described in a long, one-sentence list of sensory details.

(C) Again a sentence begins with *but.*

(D) Another long, one-sentence list counters the earlier description of the river.

est is the 'break' from a new snag, and he has located himself in the very best place he could have found to fish for steamboats; that tall dead tree, with a single living branch, is not going to last long, and then how is a body ever going to get through this blind place at night without the friendly old landmark?"

3   No, the romance and beauty were all gone from the river. All the value any feature of it had for me now was the amount of usefulness it could furnish toward compassing the safe piloting of a steamboat. Since those days, I have pitied doctors from my heart. (E) What does the lovely flush in a beauty's cheek mean to a doctor but a "break" that ripples above some deadly disease? Are not all her visible charms sown thick with what are to him the signs and symbols of hidden decay? Does he ever see her beauty at all, or doesn't he simply view her professionally, and comment upon her unwholesome condition all to himself? And doesn't he sometimes wonder whether he has gained most or lost most by learning his trade?

> (E) The paragraph ends with a series of interrelated questions.

Reading for Better Writing

Working by yourself or with a group, answer these questions:

1. The purpose for comparing and contrasting two things is to make a point. What two specific things is Twain comparing and contrasting, and what is the point he is making? How do you know?

2. Twain first describes one way of looking at the river, then another. How else might he have organized the ideas in this passage? Make an argument for the organizational pattern that you think is most effective.

3. At two points in the passage, Twain begins sentences with the conjunction *but*. Why doesn't he simply combine these sentences with those that precede them?

4. Find examples of short, average, and long sentences in this passage. Where are they located, and why does Twain vary his sentence length in this way?

5. This passage ends with a series of rhetorical questions—questions that are intended to provoke thought but not an expressed answer. What clues suggest that Twain is expecting thought rather than actual answers? Why might he use this strategy?

"**Don't compromise yourself.**
You're all you've got."
—Janis Joplin

11

Reports

LO1 Understand report writing

In 1970, Dick Cavett conducted a famous interview of the legendary rocker Janis Joplin, in which she spoke about a very private part of her life:

> **Cavett:** Do you ever get back to Port Arthur, Texas?
>
> **Joplin:** No, but I'm going back in August, man, and guess what I'm doing....
>
> **Cavett:** I don't know—
>
> **Joplin:** I'm going to my tenth annual high-school reunion....Would you like to go, man?
>
> **Cavett:** Well, I don't remember—I don't have that many friends in your high school class.
>
> **Joplin:** I don't either....That's why I'm going....
>
> **Cavett:** Were you not surrounded by friends in high school?
>
> **Joplin:** They laughed me out of class, out of town, and out of the state.
>
> **Cavett:** Hm.
>
> **Joplin:** So I'm going home.

Some interview reports, like this one, explore a person's life and mind in surprising ways. Others present the person as an expert about a topic. And still other reports—lab, experiment, or field reports—share new discoveries and findings about important subjects.

In this chapter, you will learn about writing interview, lab, experiment, and field reports. Discover something new, document it, and share what you've found.

Learning Outcomes

LO1 Understand report writing.

LO2 Write an interview report.

LO3 Write a lab, experiment, or field report.

What do you think?

I would love to interview a legendary rocker.

1 2 3 4 5
strongly agree   strongly disagree

LO2 Write an interview report.

Your goal is to gain insights by interviewing someone and then sharing the revelations you discover with readers. Aim to ask the right questions, record answers accurately, and report results clearly.

1. Choose a person to interview. Select an **interviewee** from one of the following categories:

• **The expert:** Who is an authority on your topic? Could you find such an expert in your college or community, through local organizations or businesses, or on the Internet?

• **The experienced:** Who has had unique, direct experiences with the topic? Who has participated in, witnessed, or been affected by the situation?

• **The unique:** When your purpose is to focus on a person rather than on a topic, choose someone intriguing—someone from a particular background, generation, ethnicity, nationality, or occupation.

2. Plan the interview. First, address certain key issues. Determine your **goal**—what you want your interview to accomplish and what information and insights you want to gather and discover. Next, choose a sensible **recording method** (pen and paper, recorder) and a **medium** (face-to-face, telephone, e-mail). Then consider what you already know about the topic and the interviewee, and figure out what you must know in order to ask meaningful questions. If necessary, do some **research** on the interview subject. After this, **contact** the interviewee and politely request an interview. Explain who you are, why you need the interview, and how you will use it. **Schedule** a time and a place convenient for the interviewee. If you wish to record the interview, ask permission. Finish your plan by gathering and testing the **tools and equipment** you will use: a notebook, pens, and, perhaps, recording equipment (tape, video, digital camera).

3. Prepare questions. Building questions in advance will help you structure the interview. Use the following checklist as you prepare your questions.

Interview Questions Checklist

5 W's + H

_____ Consider using some or all of the journalistic questions (*who, what, when, where, why,* and *how*).

Dynamics

_____ Understand the difference between open and closed questions. **Closed questions** ask for simple, factual answers; **open-ended questions** ask for detailed explanations.

    Closed: How many months did you spend in Vietnam?

      Open: Can you describe your most vivid memory of Vietnam?

Cautions

_____ Avoid **slanted questions**. Such questions pressure a person to give specific answers, providing biased rather than honest information.

interviewee
the person who is the focus of the interview and answers the interviewer's questions

closed questions
questions that can be answered with a simple fact or with a *yes* or a *no*

open-ended questions
questions that require elaborate answers

slanted questions
questions that presuppose a specific answer

Slanted: Aren't you really angry that draft dodgers didn't do their duty?

Neutral: How do you feel about those who avoided the draft?

Focus

_____ Think about specific topics to cover and write questions for each one. Start with a simple question to lay the groundwork and establish a **rapport**. Plan target questions—ones that you must ask to get the information you need.

Preparedness

_____ As a practical matter, put questions on the left side of the page with room for notes on the right. Rehearse your questions, visualizing how the interview should go.

4. Conduct the interview. Arrive on time and be professional. Introduce yourself, reminding the interviewee why you've come. With permission, set up any equipment off to the side so that it doesn't interfere with the conversation. Even if you're recording, take notes on key facts and quotations. Listen actively and respond with nods and eye contact. Pay attention to the interviewee's **body language**. Also be flexible. If the person looks puzzled by a question, rephrase it or ask another. And if an answer needs amplification, respond with another question:

Need	Response Questions
Clarification	"Do you mean this or that?"
Explanation	"What do you mean by that?"
Details	"What happened exactly? Can you describe that?"
Analysis	"What were the causes? The outcomes?"
Implicit Meaning	"What do you think that meant?"
Comparison	"Did that remind you of anything?"
Context	"What else was going on then? Who else was involved?"
Summary	"Overall, what was your response? What was the net effect?"

Finally, be **tactful**. If the person avoids a question, politely rephrase it. Don't react negatively or forcefully invade the interviewee's private territory. Listen "between the lines" for what the interviewee seems to want to say. Expect important points to come up late in the interview, and give the interviewee a chance to add any final thoughts.

5. Follow up. As soon as possible, review your notes and fill in the blanks. By phone or in writing, clarify points and thank the interviewee.

6. Organize and draft the report. Shape the opening to seize interest, the middle to sustain interest, and the closing to reward interest. Plan first by analyzing and interpreting the interview results. Locate the heart or theme of your report, and develop an outline supporting the theme. Then begin your report with background and a point that grabs the reader's interest. Summarize and paraphrase material from the interview. (See pages 219–221.) Use quotations selectively to give insight or to stress a point. If appropriate, you may weave your thoughts and reflections into the report.

7. Get feedback and revise the report. Ask someone to answer these questions: Does the report supply complete, satisfying insights? Is the organization effective, with an engaging opening and closing? Is the writing lively, fair, and respectful?

8. Edit and proofread. Review your report for precise word choice, smooth sentences, and correct grammar. In particular, make sure that quotations are integrated smoothly. (See pages 246-247.)

9. Prepare a final copy. Submit a clean copy to your instructor (and perhaps the interviewee), but also look for ways to publish your report—as a Web page with digital photos and sound clips, or as a presentation for classmates.

© R. Gino Santa Maria , 2009 / Used under license from Shutterstock.com

rapport
personal connection, trust, and teamwork

body language
the physical cues that indicate a person's level of comfort, interest, engagement, and so forth

tactful
being sensitive to the feelings of others; avoiding unnecessary offense

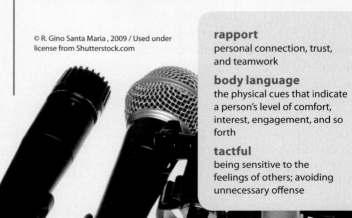

AN INTERVIEW REPORT

Because of a disturbing childhood experience, college student Benjamin Meyer toured a funeral home and interviewed the director. In the following essay, Benjamin reports on what he learned.

SQ3R
Survey Question Read Recite Review

The Dead Business

1 "You're going to tour a what?"

(A)   "A funeral home."

3   My friends were shocked. They laughed while describing scenes from *Night of the Living Dead* and *The Shining*.

4   But their stories didn't frighten me—I feared something else. When I was ten, my grandmother died, and my family drove to the funeral home to view the body. As we entered the place, I noticed the funeral director standing in the corner, looking like a too-eager-to-please salesman who'd made a deal he didn't deserve. The guy's thin-lipped smile seemed unnatural—almost glib. Like a ghoul in a business suit, he didn't seem to care that a stroke had stopped my grandmother's beating heart midway through the doxology that concluded the Sunday-evening church service. He didn't seem to care that she and I would share no more cookies, no more coloring books, no more Rook games, no more laughing, no more. I was ten, very sad, and he didn't seem to care.

5   Now a college student, I wanted to tour a different funeral home to work through my earlier experience. While I no longer feared ghouls, I was still nervous while driving to the Vander Ploeg Furniture Store/Funeral Home. I remembered the thin-lipped smile.

6   I walked inside not knowing what to expect. Sud-
(B) denly, a man from behind a desk hopped out of his chair and said, "Hi, I'm Howard Beernink."

7   I looked at the tall, smiling guy, paused a moment, and glanced back at the door. His partner had stepped in front of the exit while scribbling on tags that dangled from Lazy Boy rockers. I realized that this interview was something I had to do . . . like getting a tetanus shot.

8   Howard led me into a room full of furniture where
(C) he found a soft, purple couch. We sat down, and he described how the business started.

9   In 1892, pioneers established the town of Sioux
(D) Center, Iowa. Winter storms and disease pummeled the tiny community, and soon residents needed someone to bury the dead. A funeral director wasn't available, but a furniture maker was. The furniture maker was the only person with the tools, hardwood, and knowledge to build coffins. As a result, the Vander Ploeg Furniture Store/Funeral Home was born.

10   Today, starting a funeral home isn't that easy. For
(E) example, a funeral home requires the services of an embalmer, and an embalmer must be certified by the state. To get a certificate, the person must complete two years of college, one year of embalming school, and one year of apprentice work. After that, the individual must pass a state exam every year to retain certification.

11   "But why a funeral home director?" I was baffled. Why would anyone embalm dead bodies for a living?

12   "Because it's a family business." Howard smiled as if he expected my question. "Vander Ploegs and Beerninks have run this place for generations. Today it's difficult to start a funeral home because there are so many of them with long histories and good reputations."

13   After he answered the rest of my questions, Howard asked if I wanted to see the embalming room.

14   "Okay," I said, tentatively.

15   He led me through doors, down hallways, up a
(F) staircase, and into a well-lighted display room containing several coffins. Finally, we entered a small, cold room containing a row of cupboards, a large ceramic table, and a small machine that resembled a bottled-water cooler.

16   "We like to keep the room cold when we're not using it," Howard said.

17   "What is all this stuff?" I asked.

18   Howard described why embalming is done and what it involves. The purpose of embalming is to extend the period for viewing the body, and the process includes replacing body fluids with embalming fluid. He opened a cupboard, pulled out a bottle of fluid and
(G) said, "Here . . . smell."

19   "Smells like Pepto-Bismol," I replied.

(A) The writer starts with background information that creates a personal theme.

(B) Freely using "I," the writer tells the story of his visit and interview.

(C) He describes the setting.

(D) He relates the early history of the business.

(E) The writer summarizes, paraphrases, and quotes from the interview.

(F) He narrates what happened during the interview.

(G) The writer shares surprises and what he learned.

20   After he embalms the body, Howard applies make-up so the face appears "more natural." He gets his cosmetics (common powders and tints) from the local Avon lady.

21   "But sometimes we also have to use this," Howard said, pulling out another bottle.

22   "Tissue builder?" I asked, squinting at the label.

23   "It's like silicon implants," he answered. "We inject it into sunken cheeks, like the cheeks of cancer victims."

24   When the body is ready for burial, the funeral director must show a price list to the family of the deceased. The Funeral Rule, adopted in 1984 by the Federal Trade Commission, requires that a price list be shown to the family before they see caskets, cement boxes, and vaults. The purpose of the Funeral Rule is to prevent unethical funeral directors from manipulating customers with comments like, "But that's a pauper's casket; you don't want to bury your mother in that. Bury her in this beauty over here." Unfortunately, only a third of the country's 22,000 funeral homes abide by the Funeral Rule.

25   "After showing customers where the caskets are, I step away so they can talk among themselves," said Howard. "It's unethical to bother the family at this difficult time."

26   Before burying a casket, Howard and his partner place it in either a cement box or a vault. A cement box is a container that's neither sealed nor waterproofed, whereas a vault is both sealed and waterproofed. Howard explained, "Years ago, cemeteries began to sink and cave in on spots, so state authorities demanded containers. Containers make the cemetery look nicer."

27   After the tour, I asked Howard, "How has this job affected your life?"

28   He glanced at the ceiling, smiled,
(H) and said, "It's very fulfilling. My partner and I comfort people during a stressful time in their lives, and it strengthens our bond with them."

29   As I drove back to the college, I thought again about Howard's comment, and about my childhood fear. Howard was right. He doesn't exploit people. Instead, he comforts them and helps them move on. And while I still fear the pain of saying good-bye to someone I love, I don't fear funeral directors anymore. They're just people who provide services that a community needs.

> (H) He ends the report with a strong quotation and personal reflection.

Reading for Better Writing

Working by yourself or with a group, answer these questions:

1. This report centers on the writer's own story, reflections, and needs. Discuss how these elements are woven into the report. Are they effective? Why or why not?

2. Examine the opening and the closing of the essay. Do they work well together? Do they effectively share the theme of the report? Explain.

3. Describe how the writer organizes the interview's results. Is the organization effective? Explain.

4. Look carefully at the writer's use of summary and paraphrase on the one hand and at his use of quotations on the other. Are the strategies effective? Explain.

© istock.com

LO3 Write a lab, experiment, or field report.

Your goal is to accurately record and thoughtfully interpret the results of a scientific study or experiment so clearly that others could repeat the work themselves.

1. Review the assignment. Begin by reviewing the lab manual and any handouts. In most science courses, studies and experiments are assigned through textbooks, manuals, and handouts. Study those materials to understand what you must do and why. Read background information on the topic in textbooks and other sources.

2. Establish a field or lab notebook. Accurate, complete record keeping is crucial to doing good scientific research. Use the notebook to plan research, record what you do, collect data, make drawings, and reflect on results. For each notebook entry, record the date and your goal.

3. Plan and complete your study or experiment. For a productive study, develop key research questions. If you are conducting an experiment (not just a study), state your hypotheses and design procedures for testing them. Gather the proper tools, equipment, and materials required to conduct your work. Then carefully conduct your tests and perform your observations. Take copious notes, being especially careful to record data accurately, clearly, and completely. If helpful, use a data-collection sheet.

4. Draft the report. Relying on your notebook, wrestle with your data. What do they mean? Were results expected or unexpected? Which factors could explain those results? What further research might be necessary? Once you have conducted this analysis, draft parts of the report in the sequence outlined below:

Drafting Strategy

• **Methods:** Start by explaining what you did to study the topic or test the hypothesis. Supply essential details, factors, and explanations. Be so clear that someone else could repeat the steps you took.

• **Results:** Using two strategies, present the data you collected. First, share data in graphical forms—as tables, line charts, bar graphs, photographs, and so on. While the correct design of graphics and the proper presentation of statistical data are beyond the scope of this book, follow this basic rule: Separate your graphics from the written text by giving them descriptive titles, clear headings and labels, units of measurement, and footnotes. A reader should be able to study your graphics and see the "story" of your study. Second, draw attention to the major observations and key trends available in the data. However, do not interpret the data or give your reactions to them in this part of the report.

• **Discussion:** Interpret the results by relating the data to your original questions and hypotheses, offering conclusions and supporting each conclusion with details. Essentially, answer the question "What does it all mean?" Explain which hypotheses were supported, and why. Also explore unexpected results, and suggest possible explanations. Conclude by re-emphasizing the value of what you learned.

• **Introduction:** Once you have mapped out the methods, results, and discussion, write an introduction that creates a framework for the report. Explain why you undertook the study, provide background information and any needed definitions, and raise your key questions and/or hypotheses.

• **Summary or abstract:** If required, write a summary of your study's purpose, methods, results, and conclusions. An abstract is a one-paragraph summary that allows the reader to (1) get the report in a nutshell and (2) determine whether or not to read the study.

• **Title:** Develop a precise title that captures the "story" of your study. Worry less about the length of the title and more about its clarity.

• **Front and end matter:** If so required, add a title page, reference page, and appendixes.

5. Share and revise the draft. Once you have roughed out the report, show it to a peer or a tutor in the writing center. Ask these questions:

Ask❓

• Are the report's purpose, hypotheses, conclusions, and support clear and complete?

• Is the traditional structure of a lab or field report followed effectively?

• Is the voice objective, curious, and informed?

6. Edit and proofread. Carefully examine the style of your report, checking for the conventions of science writing in this checklist:

Conventions Checklist

_____ **Measured use of passive voice:** Generally, use the passive voice only when needed—usually to keep the focus on the action and the receiver, not the actor. (See page 58.)

_____ **Past and present tenses of verbs:** Generally, use the past tense in your report. However, present tense may be appropriate when discussing published work, established theories, and your conclusions.

_____ **Objectivity:** Make sure that your writing is precise (not ambiguous), specific (not vague), and concise (not wordy).

_____ **Mechanics:** Follow the conventions in the discipline with respect to capitalization, abbreviations, numbers, and symbols.

7. Prepare and share your report. Following the format and documentation conventions of the discipline, submit a polished report to your instructor. Also find ways to share your study with the scientific community.

A LAB REPORT

Student Coby Williams wrote the basic lab report below to describe a chemical compound and inform readers about its nature.

SQ3R
Survey Question Read Recite Review

Working with Hydrochloric Acid

Overview and Purpose

The goal in writing this report is to educate others on the dangers of using and storing hydrochloric acid in the lab (HCl) and in the home (muriatic acid). In addition, this report will list appropriate ways to protect against burns when using HCl as well as ways to dispose of it properly.   *1*

Characteristics   *2*

Hydrochloric acid (HCl), which is made from hydrogen gas and chlorine gas, is a clear, colorless to slightly yellow, fuming liquid with a sharp, irritating odor. HCl is a strong, highly corrosive acid, soluble in water and alcohol. Other characteristics include the following: *(A)*

✔ The chemical reaction is $H_2 + Cl_2 = 2HCl$.
✔ Its molecular weight is 36.45.
✔ Its boiling point is 85°C.
✔ Its specific gravity is 1.16.

Hydrochloric acid is commercially known as muriatic acid, a substance used to manufacture dyes and plastics or to acidize (activate) petroleum wells. It is also used in the food processing of corn syrup and sodium glutamate and is an ingredient in many household and industrial cleaners.   *3*

Safety Procedures   *4*

Hydrochloric acid is highly corrosive and can severely burn skin. Whenever HCl is used, it must be handled according to the following precautions:

Storage   *5*
• Keep hydrochloric acid in tightly capped bottles back from the edge of the shelf or table.
• Keep bottles away from metals. Contact will corrode metals and could release hydrogen gas, which is highly explosive.

(A) The writer identifies the chemical compound and states its nature.

(B) *Protection*

6
- Always wear safety glasses to protect your eyes.
- Wear latex gloves and old clothes when using concentrated HCl—not short-sleeved shirts, shorts, or sandals.
- Do not breathe the fumes, which can cause fainting.
- If acid spills on skin or splashes in someone's eyes, rinse the area with water for five minutes. Treat burns appropriately. In each case, get medical help immediately.

7 **Usage**

(C) In the lab, hydrochloric acid is either diluted or titrated.
- When diluting, always pour the acid into the water. Doing the reverse can cause boiling, splashing, and burning.
- When titrating, carefully measure the HCl needed. Then react the HCl with a sample that has a base such as sodium hydroxide to get an accurate measurement of the base in the sample.

8 **Disposal**
- To dispose of HCl, neutralize it by mixing the acid with a sodium-hydroxide solution. Flush the neutralized solution down the drain.
- If you spill HCl, cover the spill with baking soda. After the fizzing stops, sweep up the soda and flush it down the drain.

(B) He organizes details in distinct categories.
(C) Information is accurate and terms are precise.

Reading for Better Writing

Working by yourself or with a group, answer these questions:

1. Who would be the main audience for this type of report? What evidence can you point to that supports your answer?
2. List the strategies used to organize the report. Are these strategies effective? Explain.
3. How does this report demonstrate scientific thinking?

AN EXPERIMENT REPORT

In this report, student writer Andrea Pizano shares the results of a lab experiment she completed to explore how different factors affect fermentation.

SQ3R
Survey Question Read Recite Review

The Effects of Temperature and Inhibitors on the Fermentation Process for Ethanol

Andrea Pizano
January 29, 2008

Introduction

1
(A)
Alcoholic liquids were made and used for centuries before scientists fully understood the process by which alcohol developed. An Egyptian papyrus dated 3500 B.C.E. mentions wine making, although production of alcoholic spirits like gin and brandy started only about a thousand years ago. From beverages such as beer and wine to fuel additives such as ethanol, alcohol has been used by people for recreation, religious rites, medical purposes, energy, and industry. Even today people are surprised to learn that it is ethanol—a by-product of yeast growth—that makes bread smell good. Studying the process by which alcohol is made can help make the process more efficient and successful.

2
Generally, alcohol can be made by fermenting different types of sugars, including sucrose, glucose, and fructose. Fermentation is a process that creates heat and changes the properties of a substance through a leavening or fermenting agent. For the fermentation process to succeed, certain enzymes must function as catalysts. These enzymes are present in yeast, the fermenting agent. While useful as catalysts, these enzymes are sensitive to temperature changes and inhibitors.

3
(B)
In this experiment, ethanol—a specific type of alcohol—was synthesized from sucrose in the presence of yeast. The effects of extreme temperatures and of inhibitors on the rate of fermentation were tested quantitatively. The factors below were tested, and the outcomes below were anticipated. First, extremely high temperatures denature enzymes. Therefore, fermentation in the

(A) The opening creates context and explains concepts.
(B) The writer describes the experiment and states her hypotheses.

sample was expected to stop. Second, extremely cool temperatures reduce the kinetic energy of molecules. Therefore, the reaction rate in the sample was expected to drastically slow. Third, sodium fluoride can inhibit one of the enzymes needed in the fermentation process. Therefore, the presence of sodium fluoride was expected to effectively stop the reaction. Fourth, normal fermentation usually delivers a maximum of up to 15% ethanol. Through distillation, a 95% concentration of ethanol can be obtained. However, the presence of concentrated ethanol kills the yeast cells and also acts as a negative feedback mechanism to the enzymes necessary for the fermentation process. Therefore, concentrated ethanol was expected to effectively stop the reaction.

4 **Method**

(C)   To test each of these hypotheses, the following procedure was followed in this experiment:

1. 200 mg of yeast were mixed with 1.25 mL of warm water in a 5-mL round-bottomed, long-necked flask. The mixture was shaken until the yeast was well distributed.

2. 9 mg of disodium hydrogen phosphate, 1.30 g sucrose, and 3.75 mL warm water were added to the flask. This mixture was left for 15 minutes—until the fermentation was proceeding at a vigorous rate.

3. The fermentation mixture was then divided equally into 5 reaction tubes.
   - To tube 1, 1.0 mL of water was added.
   - To tube 2, 1.0 mL of 95% ethanol was added.
   - To tube 3, 1.0 mL of 0.5 M sodium fluoride solution was added.
   - To each of tubes 4 and 5, 1.0 mL of water was added.

(D) 4. The bubbles produced in a reaction tube filled with water were counted. A septum was first fit over the neck of each reaction tube. Then some polyethylene tubing was connected from the septum to the water-filled reaction tube. In this way, the reaction rate could be quantitatively measured by counting the number of gas bubbles that were released into the water each minute for 5 minutes.

5. Test tube 4 was heated for 5 minutes in boiling water. Then it was cooled to room temperature, and the

fermentation rate was measured as explained in step 4.

6. Test tube 5 was put on ice for 5 minutes, and then the fermentation rate was measured as explained in step 4, while the reaction tube was kept on ice to maintain the low temperature.

7. After the experiment was completed, the solutions were washed down the drain as waste.

Results   5

    The reaction rates of the 5 reaction conditions are plotted on Figure 1 below.

                    Figure 1   6

    With the sample containing water at room temperature, the fermentation rate peaked at 13 bubbles/ (E) minute at minute 4. The fermentation rate of the sample with 95% ethanol started at 17 bubbles/minute, but within 2 minutes the rate quickly slowed to 5 bubbles/minute. By 3 minutes, the rate was 0 bubbles/minute. In the sample with sodium fluoride, the fermentation increased to 20 bubbles/minute after 3 minutes, but then quickly reached 0 bubbles/minute after 5 minutes. In the sample that was boiled, the fermentation rate was consistently 0 bubbles/minute. In the sample placed on ice, the fermentation rate increased to 17 bubbles/minute after 2 minutes, but then gradually slowed to 4 bubbles/minute after 5 minutes.

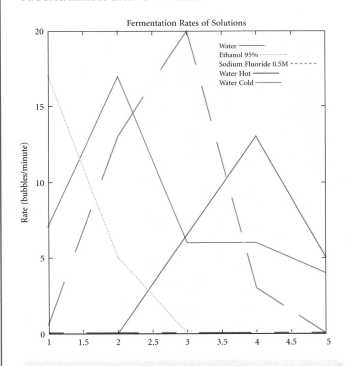

Fermentation Rates of Solutions

Water ———
Ethanol 95% ·············
Sodium Fluoride 0.5M – – – –
Water Hot ———
Water Cold ———

Rate (bubbles/minute)

7 **Discussion**

(F)   Many different factors affect fermentation rates. For example, when ethanol concentration is very high, yeast usually dies. So when 95% ethanol is added to a fermenting sugar and yeast mixture, one would expect the fermentation rate to decline sharply. The experiment's data support this hypothesis. After 3 minutes, the fermentation had completely stopped.

8   In addition, sodium fluoride inhibits the action of a specific enzyme in yeast, an enzyme needed for the fermentation process. Therefore, when sodium fluoride is added to a fermenting mixture, one would expect a halted fermentation rate. However, the reaction rate initially increased to 20 bubbles/minute when sodium fluoride was added. This increase may have occurred because not all of the enzymes were inhibited at first. Perhaps the fermentation rate declined to 0 bubbles/minute only when the sodium fluoride became evenly distributed. This measurement occurred after 5 minutes.

9   Temperature is a third factor affecting fermentation. On the one hand, high temperatures denature many enzymes; therefore, when a fermenting mixture is placed in boiling water for 5 minutes, one would expect the fermentation rate to stop because no enzymes are present at that point to carry out the fermentation process. This hypothesis is supported by the data, as no fermentation occurred in the hot mixture. On the other hand, cold temperatures reduce the kinetic energy of molecules. As a result, the speed decreases, and the likelihood of the enzymes making contact with the substrate decreases exponentially in relation to the temperature. One would expect that the reaction rate would slow down drastically after the mixture has been cooled. This (G) hypothesis is somewhat supported by the data. After an initial increase in the reaction rate to 17 bubbles/minute, the reaction rate slowed to 4 bubbles/minute after 5 minutes. A repeat of the experiment would be needed to clarify this result. Moreover, because the measuring method was somewhat unsophisticated (as indicated by the spikes in the line graph), perhaps a new experiment could be designed to measure fermentation-rate changes more sensitively.

10   This experiment helped quantify the effects that various factors such as temperature, inhibitors, and (H) high ethanol concentration have on fermentation rates. Even though the measuring apparatus was fairly basic, the experiment largely supported the hypotheses. Such data are helpful for determining methods of efficient and successful fermentation. Further research testing other factors and other inhibitors would add to this knowledge.

(F) The writer interprets the results for each hypothesis.

(G) She explores possible explanations for unexpected results and suggests further research.

(H) The closing summarizes the experiment's value.

Reading for Better Writing

Working by yourself or with a group, answer these questions:

1. Where does the writer discuss the experiment's purpose and value? Are her efforts convincing?

2. In the "Method" section, which strategies does the writer use to ensure that the experiment can be repeated?

3. In the "Results" section, what is the relationship between the line graph and the paragraph?

4. In the "Discussion" section, the writer addresses results that did and did not support the hypotheses. Are her interpretations and conclusions sound? Explain your answer.

A FIELD REPORT

In the following workplace report, a team of writers investigates the causes and effects of cockroach infestation in an apartment complex. In the study, they use their findings to recommend solutions.

SQ3R
Survey Question Read Recite Review

Sommerville Development Corporation

Date: September 20, 2008

To: Bert Richardson, VP of Tenant Relations

From: Hue Nguyen, Cherryhill Complex Manager
Sandra Kao, Building Superintendent
Roger Primgarr, Tenant Relations
Juan Alexander, Tenant Representative

(A) **Subject: Investigation of Cockroach Infestation at 5690 Cherryhill**

1 During the month of July 2008, 26 tenants of the 400-
(B) unit building at 5690 Cherryhill informed the building superintendent that they had found cockroaches in their units. On August 8, the management-tenant committee authorized us to investigate these questions:

1. How extensive is the cockroach infestation?
2. How can the cockroach population best be controlled?

2 We monitored this problem from August 9 to September 8, 2008. This report contains a summary, an overview of our research methods and findings, conclusions, and recommendations.

SUMMARY

3 The 5690 Cherryhill building has a moderate infesta-
(C) tion of German cockroaches. Only an integrated control program can manage this infestation. Pesticide fumigations address only the symptoms, not the causes. We recommend that Sommerville adopt a comprehensive program that includes (1) education, (2) cooperation, (3) habitat modification, (4) treatment, and (5) ongoing monitoring.

RESEARCH METHODS AND FINDINGS

Overview of Research

We researched the problem in the following ways: *4*
1. Contacted the Department of Agriculture, the   (D) Ecology Action Center, and Ecological Agriculture Projects.
2. Consulted three exterminators.
3. Inspected the 5690 Cherryhill building, from ground to roof.
4. Placed pheromone traps in all units to monitor the cockroach population.

The Cockroach Population

Pheromone traps revealed German cockroaches, a com-   *5*
mon variety. Of the 400 units, 112 units (28 percent)   (E) showed roaches. Based on the numbers, the infestation is rated as moderate.

The German Cockroach

Research shows that these roaches thrive in apartment   *6* buildings.
- Populations thrive when food, water, shelter, and migration routes are available. They prefer dark, humid conditions near food sources.
- The cockroach seeks shelter in spaces that allow its back and underside to remain in constant contact with a solid surface.

Methods of Control

Sources we consulted stressed the need for an integrat-   *7*
ed program of cockroach control involving sanitation,   (F) habitat modification, and nontoxic treatments that attack causes. Here are the facts:
- The German cockroach is immune to many chemicals.
- Roaches detect most pesticides before direct contact.
- Spot-spraying simply causes roaches to move to unsprayed units.

(A) The subject line functions as a title.
(B) The opening clarifies the study's purpose and goals.
(C) The summary focuses on outcomes.

(D) Research methods are described.
(E) Results are categorized logically.
(F) Findings are presented clearly and concisely.

- Habitat modification through (1) eliminating food and water sources, (2) caulking cracks and crevices, (3) lowering humidity, and (4) increasing light and airflow makes life difficult for cockroaches.

CONCLUSIONS

8 Based on our findings, we conclude the following:

(G) 1. A single method of treatment, especially chemical, will be ineffective.
2. A comprehensive program of sanitation, habitat modification, and nontoxic treatments will eliminate the German cockroach.

RECOMMENDATIONS

9 We recommend that Sommerville Development adopt

(H) an Integrated Program of Cockroach Prevention and Control for its 5690 Cherryhill building. Management would assign the following tasks to appropriate personnel:

10 **Education:** (1) Give tenants information on sanitation, prevention, and home remedies; and (2) hold tenant meetings to answer questions.

11 **Habitat Modification:** Revise the maintenance program and renovation schedule to give priority to the following:

- Apply residual insecticides before sealing cracks.
- Caulk cracks and crevices (baseboards, cupboards, pipes, sinks). Insert steel wool in large cavities (plumbing, electrical columns).
- Repair leaking pipes and faucets. Insulate pipes to eliminate condensation.
- Schedule weekly cleaning of common garbage areas.

12 **Treatment:** In addition to improving sanitation and prevention through education, attack the roach population through these methods:

- Use home remedies, traps, and hotels.
- Use borax or boric acid powder formulations as residual, relatively nontoxic pesticides.
- Use chemical controls on an emergency basis.

(G) Conclusions follow logically from the findings.
(H) Recommendations apply what was learned in the study.

- Ensure safety by arranging for a Health Department representative to make unannounced visits to the building.

Monitoring: Monitor the cockroach population in the 13 following ways:
1. Every six months, use traps to check on activity in all units.
2. Keep good records on the degree of occurrence, population density, and control methods used.

We believe that this comprehensive program will solve 14 the cockroach problem. We recommend that Sommer- (I) ville adopt this program for 5690 Cherryhill and consider implementing it in all its buildings.

(I) The closing stresses the value and benefits of the study.

Reading for Better Writing

Working by yourself or with a group, answer these questions:

1. Examine the report's format and organizational strategies. How is this workplace report similar to and different from the other lab and experiment reports in this chapter?

2. Describe the tone of the report. What does this tone accomplish?

3. This report depends extensively on cause/effect thinking. Where do the writers use cause/effect thinking, and how effective is it?

{ Paper due? Now what? }

With **COMP: Write,** *you have a multitude of writing tools at your fingertips.*

After reading the chapters, check out these ideas for further help organizing, drafting, revising, and editing your paper:

Chapter review cards include all learning outcomes, definitions, and visual summaries for each chapter.

Online, printable flashcards give you additional ways to check your comprehension of key writing concepts.

Videos of professional writers discussing their approaches and experiences are sure to provide inspiration for your own writing.

Other great resources to help you with the writing process include **interactive writing tutorials, online grammar quizzes, an online handbook, documentation guidance,** and more!

You can find it all at **4ltrpress.cengage.com/comp**.

"**Put the argument in concrete shape** . . .
and the cause is half won."

—Ralph Waldo Emerson

12

Argumentation

Early in his inaugural address, Barack Obama established his thesis, or main claim (underlined). Next, he put his thesis in historical context by providing background information. Then he expanded on the challenges, the first of which being the economy.

> Today I say to you that the challenges we face are real. They are serious and they are many. . . . <u>But know this, America: They will be met.</u>

> The time has come to reaffirm our enduring spirit, to choose our better history; to carry forward . . .

> This is the journey we continue today. The state of our economy calls for action, bold and swift, and we will act. . . .

Learning Outcomes

LO1 Understand an argument.

LO2 Recognize an argument's organization.

LO3 Understand what makes a strong claim.

LO4 Identify claims of truth, value, and policy.

LO5 Assess the quality of the support.

LO6 Recognize logical fallacies.

LO7 Learn about additional strategies.

It is one thing to appreciate this eloquent address when it was delivered on January 21, 2009. President Obama captivated this country and the world with his historic remarks. It is quite another thing to enjoy it as a skillfully constructed **argumentative essay**, which it is. (The excerpts above note key features in the first part.)

This chapter will help you analyze and appreciate all types of argumentative writing, from inaugural addresses to literary essays, from personal commentaries to editorials. It explains the foundations of argumentation and persuasion and helps you assess the value of an argument.

What do you think?

I understand the working parts of arguments.

1   2   3   4   5

strongly agree   strongly disagree

argumentative essay
writing that presents an argument about a timely, debatable topic

LO1 Understand an argument.

An **argument** is a course of logical thinking intended to convince you, the reader, to accept an idea or to take action. Knowing this helps you identify, understand, and evaluate arguments.

An argument at its most basic level consists of one point of view or claim supported by a single reason. Of course, more complex arguments like those in your academic reading consist of a main argument or claim plus additional supporting arguments, all connected by solid reasoning.

AN AWARD-WINNING COLUMNIST ON THE DRAFT

The essay that follows, "Uncle Sam and Aunt Samantha," was written by Pulitzer Prize-winning writer Anna Quindlen and was first published in 2001 in *Newsweek*. Because the essay is a complex argument, you should expect to find a main argument plus related claims supported by compelling evidence, all intended to convince you to accept a position or take action.

argument
a course of logical thinking intended to convince the reader to accept an idea or to take action

SQ₃R
Survey Question Read Recite Review

Uncle Sam and Aunt Samantha

One out of every five new recruits in the United States military is female.   1   (A)

The Marines gave the Combat Action Ribbon for service in the Persian Gulf to 23 women.   2

Two female soldiers were killed in the bombing of the USS *Cole*.   3

The Selective Service registers for the draft all male citizens between the ages of 18 and 25.   4

What's wrong with this picture?   5

As Americans read and realize that the lives of most women in this country are as different from those of Afghan women as a Cunard cruise is from maximum-security lockdown, there has nonetheless been little attention paid to one persistent gender inequity in U.S. public policy. An astonishing anachronism, really: While women are represented today in virtually all fields, including the armed forces, only men are required to register for the military draft that would be used in the event of a national-security crisis.   6   (B)

Since the nation is as close to such a crisis as it has been in more than sixty years, it's a good moment to consider how the draft wound up in this particular time warp. It's not the time warp of the Taliban, certainly,   7

(A) Each of the first five paragraphs is one sentence long.
(B) The writer identifies the problem that she wants solved.

(C) stuck in the worst part of the 13th century, forbidding women to attend school or hold jobs or even reveal their arms, forcing them into sex and marriage. Our own time warp is several decades old. The last time the draft was considered seriously was twenty years ago, when registration with the Selective Service was restored by Jimmy Carter after the Soviet invasion of, yep, Afghanistan. The president, as well as the Army chief of staff, asked at the time for the registration of women as well as men.

8   Amid a welter of arguments—women interfere with esprit de corps, women don't have the physical strength, women prisoners could be sexually assaulted, women soldiers would distract male soldiers from their mission—Congress shot down the notion of gender-blind registration. So did the Supreme Court, ruling that since women were forbidden to serve in combat positions and the purpose of the draft was to create a combat-ready force, it made sense not to register them.

9   But that was then, and this is now. Women have indeed served in combat positions, in the Balkans and the Middle East. More than 40,000 managed to serve in the Persian Gulf without destroying unit cohesion or failing because of upper-body strength. Some are even now taking out targets in Afghanistan from fighter jets, and apparently without any male soldier's falling prey to some predicted excess of chivalry or lust.

10   Talk about cognitive dissonance. All these military personnel, male and female alike, have come of age at a time when a significant level of parity was taken for granted. Yet they are supposed to accept that only males will be required to defend their country in a time of national emergency. This is insulting to men. And it is insulting to women. Caroline Forell, an expert on
(D) women's legal rights and a professor at the University of Oregon School of Law, puts it bluntly: "Failing to require this of women makes us lesser citizens."

11   Neither the left nor the right has been particularly inclined to consider this issue judiciously. Many feminists came from the antiwar movement and have let their dis-
(E) taste for the military in general and the draft in particular mute their response. In 1980 NOW [National Organization for Women] released a resolution that buried support for the registration of women beneath opposition to the draft, despite the fact that the draft had been redesigned to eliminate the vexing inequities of Vietnam, when the sons of the working class served and the sons of the Ivy League did not. Conservatives, meanwhile, used an equal-opportunity draft as the linchpin of opposition to the Equal Rights Amendment, along with the terrifying specter of unisex bathrooms. (I have seen the urinal, and it is benign.) The legislative director of the right-wing group Concerned Women for America once defended the existing regulations by saying that most women "don't want to be included in the draft." All those young men who went to Canada during Vietnam and those who today register with fear and trembling in the face of the Trade Center devastation might be amazed to discover that lack of desire is an affirmative defense.

12   Parents face a series of unique new challenges in this more egalitarian world, not the least of which would be sending a daughter off to war. But parents all over this country are doing that right now, with daughters who enlisted; some have even expressed surprise that young women, in this day and age, are not required to register alongside their brothers and friends. While all involved in (F) this debate over the years have invoked the assumed opposition of the people, even ten years ago more than half of all Americans polled believed women should be made eligible for the draft. Besides, this is not about comfort but about fairness. My son has to register with the Selective Service this year, and if his sister does not when she turns 18, it makes a mockery not only of the standards of this household but of the standards of this nation.

13   It is possible in Afghanistan for women to be treated like little more than fecund pack animals precisely because gender fear and ignorance and hatred have been codified and permitted to hold sway. In this country, largely because of the concerted efforts of those allied with the women's movement over a century of struggle, much of that bigotry has been beaten back, even buried. Yet in improbable places the creaky old ways surface, the ways suggesting that we women were made of finer stuff. The finer stuff was usually porcelain, decorative and on the shelf, suitable for meals and show. Happily, the finer stuff has been transmuted into the right stuff. But with rights come responsibilities, as teachers like to tell their students. This is a responsibility that should fall equally upon all, male and female alike. If the empirical evidence is considered rationally, if the decision is divested of outmoded stereotypes, that's the only possible conclusion to be reached.

(C) She provides background about the source and history of the problem.

(D) A quotation helps explain why the writer understands the situation to be a problem.

(E) The writer anticipates and addresses counterarguments to her position.

(F) She supports her position with statistics as well as personal anecdotes and comparisons to other situations.

LO2 Recognize an argument's organization.

To identify an argument's organization, (1) determine whether the overall line of reasoning is inductive or deductive and (2) clarify how supporting points are arranged.

HOW IT WORKS

Identifying the type of organization and the pattern of supporting points is critical to your understanding of the writer's line of reasoning. With this information, you can adequately evaluate the argument.

Inductive and Deductive Reasoning

Depending on his or her purpose for writing, a writer may use inductive or deductive reasoning.

Inductive reasoning works from the particular toward general conclusions. When reading an essay organized inductively, look at facts first to find a pattern leading to the writer's conclusion. For example, in "To Drill or Not to Drill," Rebecca Pasok first details specific threats to the environment before arriving at her claim that drilling for oil in an Alaskan wilderness refuge is not America's best option. (See pages 151–153.)

Deductive reasoning—the opposite of inductive reasoning—starts with general principles and follows with specific applications, support, and/or examples to reach a conclusion. When reading an essay organized deductively, be sure that the general principles or facts are true and that the application is logical. For example, Martin Luther King opened his 1963 "I Have a Dream" speech by noting that more than one hundred

years earlier the "Emancipation Proclamation" promised African Americans justice and freedom. He then described the continuing unjust treatment of African Americans, deducing that the promises in the Proclamation remained unfulfilled.

Patterns of Support

© gary718 , 2009 / Used under license from Shutterstock.com

Argumentation requires a clear line of reasoning, and each point made should support or develop the thesis. Below are two common patterns of support for an argument.

In the first pattern, the writer presents her or his supporting arguments, then addresses counterarguments, and concludes with the strongest argument.

> **Pattern 1**
>
> **Introduction:** Question, concern, or claim
> 1. Strong argument-supporting claim
>   • Discussion and support
> 2. Other argument-supporting claims
>   • Discussion and support for each
> 3. Objections, concerns, and counterarguments
>   • Discussion, concessions, answers, and/or rebuttals
> 4. Strongest argument-supporting claim
>   • Discussion and support
>
> **Conclusion:** Argument consolidated—claim reinforced

© George Spade , 2009 / Used under license from Shutterstock.com

inductive reasoning
reasoning that works from the particular details toward general conclusions

deductive reasoning
reasoning that works from general principles or ideas; through specific applications, support, and/or examples; to a conclusion

In the second pattern, the writer addresses the arguments and counterarguments point by point.

Pattern 2

Introduction: Question, concern, or claim

1. Strong argument-supporting claim
   - Discussion and support
   - Counterarguments, concessions, and/or rebuttals
2. Other argument-supporting claims
   - Discussion and support for each
   - Counterarguments, concessions, and/or rebuttals for each
3. Strongest argument-supporting claim
   - Discussion and support
   - Counterarguments, concessions, and/or rebuttals

Conclusion: Argument consolidated—claim reinforced

nyt Now it's your turn to identify the organization and pattern of support in the essay by Anna Quindlen (pages 132–133). First review the reading and then answer these questions: How does Quindlen organize her argument? Outline her argument, using one of the above patterns as a guide. Is the organization effective? Why or why not?

LO3 Understand what makes a strong claim.

An argument centers on a **main claim**, which is a debatable statement and is the thesis or key point developed throughout such an essay. Strong claims are reasonable, logical, and supportable. They are also ethically sound and worthy of debate. To evaluate the strength of an argument, you must evaluate the strength of its claims.

THINGS TO CONSIDER

Strong claims reveal strong, complex thinking. They are not simple facts, opinions, or beliefs; and an effective evaluation requires an understanding of how the claim is formed.

Claims vs. Facts and Opinions

Meaningful claims evolve from logical thought and reliable evidence. **Facts**, an important element in a body of evidence, are statements that can be checked for accuracy. **Opinions**, in contrast, are personally held attitudes or feelings. While claims can be debated, facts and opinions cannot.

Fact: *The Fellowship of the Ring* is the first book in *The Lord of the Rings Trilogy.*

Opinion: I liked the movie as much as the book.

Claim: *The Fellowship of the Ring* film does not completely follow the novel's plot but faithfully captures its spirit.

A fact's accuracy can be easily checked, and an opinion statement offers a personal assessment; but a claim states an idea that can be supported with reasoning and evidence.

Avoiding Extremes

Skilled writers avoid **extreme claims**, which often include words that are overly positive or negative, such as *all, best, never,* and *worst.* Such claims leave no room for exceptions and are easy to attack. Here is an example of an extreme claim: *All people charged even once for DUI should never be allowed to drive again.* In addition to the extreme claim, obvious or trivial claims are shallow and not worth debating. The following claims, for example, provide little if any depth for a meaningful argument: *College athletes sometimes receive special treatment. The Rec Center is a good place to get fit.*

UNDERSTANDING QUALIFIERS

Qualifiers are words or phrases that limit or restrict claims, making them more reasonable. Notice the difference between these two claims:

Unqualified claim: Star athletes take many academic shortcuts.

Qualified claim: Some star athletes take academic shortcuts.

main claim
a debatable statement, the thesis or key point in an argument

facts
statements that can be checked for accuracy

opinions
personally held attitudes or beliefs

extreme claims
claims that include words *(all, best, never, worst)* that are overly positive or negative

qualifiers
words or phrases that limit or restrict a claim, making it more reasonable

Qualified claims narrow the focus and leave room for exceptions. Words like the following are often used to limit or qualify a claim.

almost	many	often	tends to
frequently	maybe	probably	typically
likely	might	some	usually

LO4 Identify claims of truth, value, and policy.

Claims of truth, value, and policy are all made in arguments. The effectiveness of an argument depends on the strength of each claim. Use the information that follows to help you evaluate the claims that you come across in your reading.

KNOWING THE DIFFERENCE

Knowing the difference between these claims will enable you to evaluate them more effectively.

Claims of truth state that something is or is not the case. Writers want the reader to accept their claims as trustworthy. "An Apology for the Life of Ms. Barbie D. Doll" on pages 148–149 makes a truth claim in paragraph 1. Here are some other examples.

> The Arctic ice cap will begin to disappear as early as 2050.
>
> The cholesterol in eggs is not as dangerous as previously feared.
>
> *Caution:* If a writer's claim is (1) obviously true or (2) impossible to prove, the argument will likely lack substance and credibility.

Claims of value state that something does or does not have worth. Writers want the reader to accept their judgment. Here are some examples of value claims:

> Volunteer reading tutors provide a valuable service.
>
> Many music videos fail to present positive images of women.

authoritative
backed by research and expert analysis

> *Caution:* Claims of value must be supported by references to a known or agreed-upon standard. Be wary of value claims lacking such support.

Claims of policy state that something ought or ought not to be done. Writers want the reader to approve their proposed courses of action. "Preparing for Agroterror" on pages 155–157 makes a policy claim in paragraph 15. Here are some other examples:

> Special taxes should be placed on gas-guzzling SUVs.
>
> The developer should not be allowed to fill in the pond where the endangered tiger salamander lives.
>
> *Caution:* Policy claims focus on action. To arrive at them, writers must often first establish certain truths and values. When reading such arguments, remember that if the truth and value claims are not sound, the policy claim is unwarranted.

nyt Now it's your turn to identify and evaluate some claims. Highlight or underline two or three claims in Anna Quindlen's essay (pages 132–133). What types of claims does Quindlen assert? Are these claims effectively stated and supported? Explain.

LO5 Assess the quality of the support.

A claim succeeds or fails on its support. In other words, a claim is only as good as the reasoning and evidence that accompanies it. And evidence is only good if it is accurate, relevant, and **authoritative**.

WHAT EVIDENCE DO YOU HAVE?

The following quick guide explains the different types of evidence a writer may use. It also discusses the strengths and weaknesses of each type.

Quick Guide | **Types of Evidence**

Observations and anecdotes share what people have seen, heard, smelled, touched, tasted, and experienced. Such evidence offers an "eyewitness" perspective shaped by the observer's viewpoint:

Most of us have closets full of clothes: jeans, sweaters, khakis, T-shirts, and shoes for every occasion.

Caution: At times, observations or anecdotes may prove to be narrow or subjective.

Statistics offer concrete numbers about a topic:

Pennsylvania spends $30 million annually in deer-related costs.

Wisconsin has an estimated annual loss of $37 million for crop damage alone.

Caution: Numbers don't "speak for themselves," however. They need to be interpreted and compared properly—not slanted or taken out of context. Statistics also need to be up-to-date, relevant, and accurate.

Tests and experiments provide hard data developed through the scientific method:

According to the two scientists, the rats with unlimited access to the functional running wheel ran each day and gradually increased the amount of running; in addition, they started to eat less.

Caution: Be sure, however, to study and properly interpret experimental data.

Graphics provide information in visual form—from simple tables to more complex charts, maps, drawings, and photographs. See the line graph in the experiment report on page 125 and the photographs in "Downloading Photographs . . ." on page 105.

Caution: When poorly done, however, graphics can distort the truth.

Analogies compare two things, creating clarity by drawing parallels.

It is obvious today that America has defaulted on this promissory note insofar as her citizens of color are concerned. Instead of honoring this sacred obligation, America has given the Negro people a bad check; a check which has come back marked "insufficient funds." But we refuse to believe that the bank of justice is bankrupt.

—Martin Luther King, Jr.

Caution: Analogies will weaken and break down a claim if pushed too far.

Expert testimony offers insight from an authority on the topic:

One specialist opposed to drilling is David Klein, a professor at the Institute of Arctic Biology at the University of Alaska–Fairbanks. Klein argues that if the oil industry opens up the ANWR for drilling, the number of caribou will likely decrease because the calving locations will change.

Caution: Such testimony always has limits: Experts don't know it all, and they work from distinct perspectives, which means that they can disagree.

Illustrations, examples, and demonstrations support general claims with specific instances, making such statements more concrete and observable:

Think about how differently one can frame Rosa Parks' historic action. In prevailing myth, Parks—a holy innocent—acts almost on whim. . . . The real story is more empowering: It suggests that change is the product of deliberate, incremental action.

Caution: An example may not be your best support if it isn't familiar.

Analyses examine parts of a topic through thought patterns—cause/effect, compare/contrast, classification, process, or definition:

A girl's interest in romance is no more Barbie's fault than the fault of books like *On the Shores of Silver Lake*. Fashion magazines targeted at adolescents are the cause of far more anorexia cases than is Barbie.

Caution: Such analysis can make sense of a topic's complexity, but it can muddle the topic when poorly done.

Predictions offer insights into possible outcomes or consequences by forecasting what might happen under certain conditions:

While agroterrorist diseases would have little direct effect on people's health, they would be devastating to the agricultural economy, in part because of the many different diseases that could be used in an attack.

Caution: Like weather forecasting, predicting can be tricky. To be plausible, a prediction must be rooted in a logical analysis of present facts.

fyi Finding evidence is one thing; using it well is quite another. So as you read argumentative pieces, ask yourself these three questions: (1) Did the writer go for quality, not just quantity? More evidence is not necessarily better. (2) Is the argument organized inductively or deductively? The pattern of organization should make sense in terms of the main claims and supporting evidence. (3) Do the claims and supporting evidence have a logical connection? This connection is called the *warrant*.

Consider the warrants.

For an argument to be compelling, all of the elements must logically work together. Each claim must be logically linked to its supporting evidence; multiple claims must be logically linked to each other; and all claims must be logically linked by reason. These links or connections are called **warrants**—the unspoken thinking used to build a coherent argument. If the warrants are valid, the elements of the argument will hold together.

Read the brief argument below, built with a policy claim, supporting evidence, and an understood warrant connecting the claim and the evidence.

Policy claim: Emeryville should immediately shut down its public swimming pools.

Evidence: The reservoir is 34 feet below its normal depth, and DNR officer Ted Kicken said that if current trends continue, the reservoir will be empty in two years.

Warrant: The swimming pools draw significant amounts of water from the reservoir.

nyt Now it's your turn to assess the quality of evidence used in Anna Quindlen's essay (pages 132–133). What is the main claim in Anna Quindlen's article? What types of supporting evidence does she use? Could she have used other types of evidence? Is the evidence logically connected or properly warranted to the claim? Explain.

LO6 Recognize logical fallacies.

Logical fallacies are false assertions that weaken an argument by distorting the issue, sabotaging the argument, drawing faulty conclusions, misusing evidence, or misusing language.

FINDING FALLACIES

In order to evaluate the strength of an argument, you must recognize whether it contains logical fallacies. Review the following quick guide for explanations and examples of these flaws in logic.

Quick Guide | **Logical Fallacies**

Distorting the Issue

Bare Assertion A basic way to distort an issue is to deny that it exists. This fallacy claims, "That's just how it is."

The private ownership of handguns is a constitutional right. (*The claim shuts off discussion of the U.S. Constitution or the reasons for regulation.*)

Begging the Question Also known as circular reasoning, this fallacy arises from assuming the very point you need to prove.

We don't need a useless film series when every third student owns a DVD player or VCR. (*There may be uses for a public film series that private video viewing can't provide. The word "useless" begs the question.*)

Oversimplification This fallacy reduces complexity to simplicity. Beware of phrases like "It's a simple question of." Serious issues are rarely simple.

Capital punishment is a simple question of protecting society.

Either/Or Thinking Also known as black-and-white thinking, this fallacy reduces all options to two extremes. Frequently, it derives from a clear bias.

Either this community develops light-rail transportation or the community will not grow in the future. (*The claim ignores the possibility that growth may occur through other means.*)

Complex Question Sometimes by phrasing a question a certain way, a person ignores or covers up a more basic question.

Why can't we bring down the prices that corrupt gas stations are charging? (*This question ignores a more basic question—"Are gas stations really corrupt?"*)

Straw Man In this fallacy, the writer argues against a claim that is easily refuted. Typically, such a claim exaggerates or misrepresents the opponents' position.

Those who oppose euthanasia must believe that the terminally ill deserve to suffer.

Sabotaging the Argument

Red Herring This strange term comes from the practice of dragging a stinky fish across a trail to throw tracking dogs off the scent. When a person puts forth a volatile idea that supersedes the real issue, the reader becomes distracted. Suppose the argument addresses drilling for oil in the Arctic National Wildlife Refuge (ANWR) of Alaska, and the writer begins with this statement:

In 1989, the infamous oil spill of the *Exxon Valdez* led to massive animal deaths and enormous environmental degradation of the coastline. (*Introducing this notorious oil spill distracts from the real issue—how oil drilling will affect the ANWR.*)

Misuse of Humor Jokes, satire, and irony can lighten the mood and highlight a truth; when humor distracts or mocks, however, it undercuts the argument. What effect would the mocking tone of this statement have in an argument about tanning beds in health clubs?

People who use tanning beds will just turn into wrinkled old prunes or leathery sun-dried tomatoes!

Appeal to Pity This fallacy engages in a misleading tug on the heartstrings. Instead of using a measured emotional appeal, an appeal to pity seeks to manipulate the audience into agreement.

Affirmative-action policies ruined this young man's life. Because of them, he was denied admission to Centerville College.

Use of Threats A simple but unethical way of sabotaging an argument is to threaten opponents. More often than not, a threat is merely implied: "If you don't accept my argument, you'll regret it."

If we don't immediately start drilling for oil in the ANWR, we will soon face hour-long lines at gas stations from New York to California.

Bandwagon Mentality Someone implies that a claim cannot be true because a majority of people are opposed to it, or it must be true because a majority support it. (History shows that people in the minority have often had the better argument.) At its worst, such an appeal manipulates people's desire to belong or be accepted.

It's obvious to intelligent people that cockroaches live only in the apartments of dirty people. (*Based on popular opinion, the claim appeals to a kind of prejudice and ignores scientific evidence about cockroaches.*)

Appeal to Popular Sentiment This fallacy consists of associating your position with something popularly loved: the American flag, baseball, apple pie. Appeals to popular sentiment sidestep thought to play on feelings.

Anyone who has seen the movie *Bambi* could never condone hunting deer.

Drawing Faulty Conclusions from the Evidence

Appeal to Ignorance This fallacy suggests that because no one has proven a particular claim, it must be false; or, because no one has disproven a claim, it must be true. Appeals to ignorance unfairly shift the burden of proof onto someone else.

Flying saucers are real. No scientific explanation has ruled them out.

Hasty or Broad Generalization Such a claim is based on too little evidence or allows no exceptions. In jumping to a conclusion, the writer may use intensifiers such as *all*, *every*, or *never*.

Today's voters spend too little time reading and too much time being taken in by 30-second sound bites. (*Quite a few voters may, in fact, spend too little time reading about the issues, but it is unfair to suggest that this is true of everyone.*)

False Cause This well-known fallacy confuses sequence with causation: If A comes before B, A must have caused B. However, A may be one of several causes, or A and B may be only loosely related, or the connection between A and B may be entirely coincidental.

> Since that new school opened, drug use among young people has skyrocketed. Better that the school had never been built.

Slippery Slope This fallacy argues that a single step will start an unstoppable chain of events. While such a slide may occur, the prediction lacks evidence.

> If we legalize marijuana, it's only a matter of time before hard drugs follow and America becomes a nation of junkies and addicts.

Misusing Evidence

Impressing with Numbers In this case, the writer coerces the reader into agreement with an overwhelming deluge of statistics and numbers. In addition, the numbers haven't been properly interpreted.

> At 35 ppm, CO levels factory-wide are only 10 ppm above the OSHA recommendation, which is 25 ppm. Clearly, that 10 ppm is insignificant in the big picture, and the occasional readings in some areas of between 40 and 80 ppm are aberrations that can safely be ignored. (*The 10 ppm may be significant, and higher readings may indicate real danger.*)

Half-Truths A half-truth contains part of but not the whole truth. Because it leaves out "the rest of the story," it is both true and false simultaneously.

> The new welfare bill is good because it will get people off the public dole. (*This may be true, but the bill may also cause undue suffering for some truly needy individuals.*)

Unreliable Testimonial An appeal to authority has force only if the authority is qualified in the proper field. If he or she is not, the testimony is irrelevant. Note that fame is not the same thing as authority.

> On her talk show, Alberta Magnus recently claimed that most pork sold in the United States is tainted. (*Although Magnus may be an articulate talk show host, she is not an expert on food safety.*)

Attack Against the Person This fallacy directs attention to a person's character, lifestyle, or beliefs rather than to the issue.

> Would you accept the opinion of a candidate who experimented with drugs in college?

Hypothesis Contrary to Fact This fallacy relies on "if only" thinking. It bases the claim on an assumption of what would have happened if something else had, or had not, happened. Being pure speculation, such a claim cannot be tested.

> If only multiculturalists hadn't pushed through affirmative action, the United States would be a united nation.

False Analogy Sometimes a person will argue that X is good (or bad) because it is like Y. Such an analogy may be valid, but it weakens the argument if the grounds for the comparison are vague or unrelated.

> Don't bother voting in this election; it's a stinking quagmire. (*Comparing the election to a "stinking quagmire" is unclear and exaggerated.*)

Misusing Language

Obfuscation This fallacy involves using fuzzy terms like *throughput* and *downlink* to muddy the issue. These words may make simple ideas sound more profound than they really are, or they may make false ideas sound true.

> Through the fully functional developmental process of a streamlined target-refractory system, the U.S. military will successfully reprioritize its data throughputs. (*What does this sentence mean?*)

Ambiguity Ambiguous statements can be interpreted in two or more opposite ways.

Although ambiguity can result from unintentional careless thinking, writers sometimes use ambiguity to obscure a position.

> Many women need to work to support their children through school, but they would be better off at home. (Does they refer to children or women? What does better off mean? These words and phrases can be interpreted in opposite ways.)

Slanted Language By choosing words with strong positive or negative connotations, a writer can draw the reader away from the true logic of the argument. Here is an example of three synonyms for the word *stubborn* that the philosopher Bertrand Russell once used to illustrate the bias in slanted language:

> I am firm. You are obstinate. He is pigheaded.

LO7 Learn about additional strategies.

Think of an argument as an intelligent, lively dialogue between the writer and you, the reader. To participate effectively in this dialogue, you need to understand certain strategies that writers use in argumentative writing.

GOING THE NEXT MILE

Writers employ the following strategies to finalize and strengthen their arguments. They make concessions; address counterarguments; consolidate claims; and appeal to credibility, logic, and the reader's needs.

Making Concessions

By offering **concessions**, writers acknowledge the limits of their arguments and the truth of other positions. Such concessions actually strengthen their own arguments by making them seem more credible. When you see words like those in the next column, look for the concession that will likely follow.

> Granted, Barbie's physical appearance isn't realistic. As Motz explains . . .

Words of Concession		
Admittedly	Granted	I agree that
I cannot argue with	It is true that	You're right
I accept	No doubt	Of course
I concede that	Perhaps	Certainly it's true

Developing Rebuttals

Even when they concede a point, writers often answer that objection by rebutting it. A good rebuttal is a small, tactful argument aimed at a weak spot in the opposing argument. The following types of **rebuttals** are common:

1. **Pointing out the opposing argument's** limits by showing how it omits important evidence or doesn't address all of the writer's claims.
2. **Telling the other side of the story** by reinterpreting the opposing argument's evidence, or offering stronger, more reliable, and more convincing evidence.
3. **Addressing logical fallacies** in the opposing argument. When you see this strategy, be alert! The writer may be using either/or logic: "Either accept that weak argument or my strong one."

> Granted, Barbie's physical appearance isn't realistic. As Motz explains . . . I say, so what? While the only "real" version of Barbie's body would be a long-limbed 13-year-old with breast implants, who cares? Arguing that Barbie's bod isn't realistic and that the lack of realism hurts girls' self-esteem is weak logic. Children have had dolls for ages. For example . . .

Restating Claims

After making concessions and rebutting objections, a writer may need to **redirect** the argument by restating her or his main claim.

> Playing with Barbies need not be an unimaginative, antisocial activity that promotes conformity, materialism, and superficial ideals.

Always look carefully at restated claims to make sure that the writer isn't changing the argument.

concessions
recognizing valid arguments on the other side

rebuttal
a tactful argument aimed at weakening the opposing point of view

redirect
restate the main claim or argument

BEING CREDIBLE, LOGICAL, AND CARING

To persuade the reader, an argument must be logical, but it also must seem honest, realistic, and sincere. To achieve these qualities, writers include in their arguments appeals to credibility, logic, and the reader's needs. When reading an argument, look for these appeals and assess how they affect the argument.

Appeal to credibility.

To build credibility, good writers begin with **being thoroughly honest**. They treat the topic with integrity—not falsifying data, spinning evidence, ignoring facts, or incorrectly documenting sources. Credible writing **makes realistic claims**; it avoids emotionally charged statements, pie-in-the-sky forecasts, and undeliverable deals. Finally, credible writers **develop and maintain trust** by treating the topic, the reader, and opposing viewpoints respectfully.

Appeal to logic.

To develop arguments based on logic, good writers avoid overly emotional appeals. Instead, they **engage the reader positively** by appealing to his or her sense of honor, justice, social commitment, and enlightened self-interest. They will **use a fitting tone** appropriate for the topic, purpose, situation, and audience. Logical writing will **aim to motivate** (not manipulate) the reader and avoid bullying, guilt-tripping, and tugging on heartstrings. The writing will **honor the opposition** by showing tact, respect, and understanding. Finally, the writing will employ arguments and evidence that the reader can **understand and appreciate**.

Appeal to the reader's needs.

To build honest, transparent arguments, good writers must show that they are mindful of the reader's needs and are prepared to address them. They **know their reader** (identity, allegiances, worries, and dreams). They **accept their reader**, including the one who needs convincing. And they use appeals that **match their reader's needs** and values.

fyi When reading an argument, you can use psychologist Abraham Maslov's hierarchy of human needs to assess how effectively the writer knows and addresses the reader. The hierarchy that is shown below is based loosely on Maslov's writing, and it ranks people's needs from the most basic (bottom of table) to the most complex (top of table). For example, the bottom line addresses *having necessities* (a basic need) and the top line addresses *helping others* (a more complex need).

Need	Topic/Action	Appeal
to improve the world	helping others	to values and social obligation
to achieve	being good at something	to self-fulfillment, status
to achieve	getting recognition	to appreciation
to belong	being part of a group	to group identity, acceptance
to survive	avoiding threats	to safety, security
to survive	having necessities	to physical needs

When assessing the quality of an argument's appeals, ask whether the appeals used (1) fit the topic, (2) match the reader's values, and (3) address real needs.

nyt Now it's your turn to examine how Anna Quindlen uses these final strategies in her article (pages 132–133). Does Quindlen show attention to opposing perspectives in her article? Does she offer concessions and/or rebuttals? With respect to appeals, identify three strategies that Quindlen uses to engage her *Newsweek* audience in terms of credibility, logic, and/or needs. Are these appeals fair, appropriate, and effective? Explain.

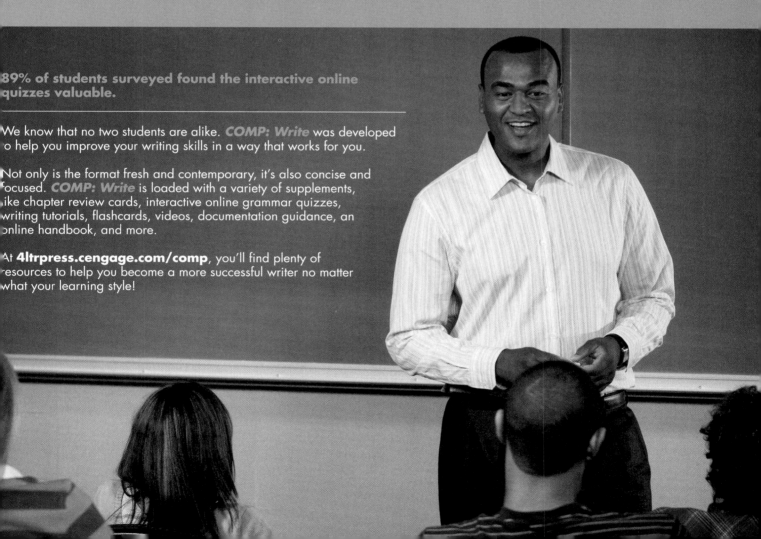

{ Learning Your Way }

89% of students surveyed found the interactive online quizzes valuable.

We know that no two students are alike. *COMP: Write* was developed to help you improve your writing skills in a way that works for you.

Not only is the format fresh and contemporary, it's also concise and focused. *COMP: Write* is loaded with a variety of supplements, like chapter review cards, interactive online grammar quizzes, writing tutorials, flashcards, videos, documentation guidance, an online handbook, and more.

At **4ltrpress.cengage.com/comp**, you'll find plenty of resources to help you become a more successful writer no matter what your learning style!

"**I would rather try to** persuade a man to go along, because once I have persuaded him he will stick. If I scare him, he will stay just as long as he is scared, and then he is gone."
——Dwight D. Eisenhower

13

Persuasion

LO1 Understand persuasion.

Persuasion is a challenging task, requiring that you convince readers to believe you, rethink their own perspectives, and take a concrete step. In the end, you want them to change their minds and their actions.

Consider the quotation from Dwight D. Eisenhower on the facing page. This general and president understood that persuasion is not the same as coercion. Scaring people into compliance does not change their "hearts and minds."

So, how can you persuade? Instead of browbeating your reader, appeal to the person's values, wants, and needs. Most people desire security, justice, acceptance, health, wealth, peace, and so on. Demonstrate how accepting and acting on your position will improve the life of the reader in one or more of these ways. Then you are truly persuading.

In an essay persuading readers to act, you seek to change readers' opinions on a debatable, complex, and timely issue about which you care deeply, such as wise energy policies or the problem of racism. In addition, your essay presses for the next logical step—motivating readers to act. You achieve that goal with sound logic, reliable support, and fitting appeals. In a sense, you say to readers, "Come, let us reason together."

What do you feel strongly about, and which actions do you want to influence? This chapter will help you write in a way that stirs people to action.

Learning Outcomes

LO1 Understand persuasion.

LO2 Take a position.

LO3 Persuade readers to act.

LO4 Propose a solution.

What do you think?

I could persuade a reluctant friend to go to a concert with me.

1   2   3   4   5

strongly agree   strongly disagree

LO2 Take a position.

Your goal is to take a stand on a controversial issue. Aim to explain what you believe and why you believe it. Be thoughtful but bold, encouraging readers to respect and even adopt your position.

1. Select a topic. Through reading, viewing, or surfing the Internet, explore current issues (like those listed below) that reasonable people disagree upon. Select an issue that you care about, and identify one facet of the issue that you could address in an essay:

- **Dividing-line issues:** Which issues in your community set people against one another? Religion, gender, money, class, sports? Think about these broad subjects, and then identify a focused issue in one of them.

- **Fresh-fare issues:** What unexpected topics, such as barbed versus barbless fishing hooks, would make for an interesting essay? Sometimes such topics offer the most potential. Avoid tired issues unless you can revive them with a fresh perspective.

- **Burning issues:** Which issues related to family, work, education, recreation, technology, the environment, or popular culture do you care about? Which issues do you want to confront?

- **Current-affairs issues:** What recent trends, new laws, major changes, or **controversies** are being discussed in the news media, journals, or on-line discussion groups?

2. Take stock. Before you dig into your topic, assess your starting point. What is your current position on the topic? Why? What evidence do you have?

3. Get inside the issue. To take a **defensible position**, study the issue carefully. Develop and measure your position using the following strategies.

Position Strategies

- **Investigate** all possible positions on the issue. Through brainstorming and research, think through all arguments and issues on all sides.

- **Gather** information by doing firsthand research. It will help you speak with authority and passion.

- **Write** your position at the top of a page. Below it, set up "Pro" and "Con" columns. List arguments in each column.

- **Develop** a line of reasoning to support your position. Test that reasoning for two things:

  1. Avoid logical fallacies, such as broad generalization, either/or thinking, oversimplification, or slanted language. (See pages 138–141.)

  2. Provide an effective range of support: statistics, observations, expert testimony, comparisons, experiences, and analysis. (See pages 136–137.)

4. Refine your position. By now, you may have sharpened or radically changed your starting position. Before you organize and draft your essay, clarify your position. To do that, consider completing the following sentence starter.

I believe this to be true about …: _____.

controversies
issues about which there are two or more strongly opposing sides; highly debatable issues

defensible position
a claim that is debatable but can be strongly supported by evidence; a claim that is neither a fact nor an unsupportable opinion

5. Organize your development and support. Now you've committed yourself to a position. Before drafting, review these organizational options:

• **Traditional pattern:** Introduce the issue, state your position, support it, address and **refute** opposition, and restate your position.

• **Blatant confession:** Place your position statement in the first sentence—boldly displayed for your reader to chew on.

• **Delayed gratification:** In the first part of your essay, explore the various positions available on the topic; compare and contrast them, and then state and defend your position.

• **Changed mind:** If your research changed your mind on the topic, build that shift into the essay itself. Your reader may respond well to such honesty.

• **Winning over:** If the reader may strongly oppose your position, then focus on that opposition. Defend your position by anticipating and answering each question, concern, and objection.

6. Write your first draft. If helpful, set aside your notes and get your position and support down on paper. Or, if you prefer, work closely from your outline. Here are some possible strategies:

Drafting Strategies

Opening: Seize the reader's imagination. Raise concern for the issue with a dramatic story, a pointed example, a vivid picture, a thought-provoking question, or a personal confession. Supply background information that the reader needs to understand the issue.

Development: Deepen, clarify, and support your position statement, using solid logic and reliable support. A clear, well-reasoned defense will help the reader accept your position.

Closing: End on a lively, thoughtful note that stresses your commitment. If appropriate, make a direct or indirect plea to the reader to adopt your position.

Title: Build a bold title that offers a choice or emphasizes a stand.

7. Share your position. At this point, feedback from a peer or a tutor in the writing center might help. Does your reviewer accept your position? Why or why not?

8. Revise your writing. Consider your reviewer's comments and review the draft yourself. Cut, change, and/or add material with the following questions in mind:

Ask ?

• Is the position clearly stated? Is it effectively qualified and refined?
• Have you shown how your stand affects yourself and others?
• Are the reasoning and support sound and complete?
• Does the essay show awareness of questions, concerns, and other positions?
• Do the ideas flow smoothly?
• Is the tone confident and sincere, not bullying, cocky, or apologetic?

9. Edit and proofread. See pages 67-77 for guidelines, but check especially that your writing is free of slogans, **cliches,** platitudes, insults, and mystifying jargon. Make your language lively, concrete, and energetic.

10. Prepare and publish your final essay. Submit your position paper according to your instructor's requirements. In addition, seek a forum for your position—with peers in a discussion group, with relatives, or online.

refute
prove false, illogical, or undesirable

cliches
overused words and phrases such as *piece of cake*

A DOLL'S EYE VIEW

Rita Isakson was asked to use logic and her personal experience to critique an article in which the writer asserted that Barbie dolls harm young girls' development. In her essay below, Isakson analyzes the article and builds a counterargument.

SQ3R
Survey Question Read Recite Review

An Apology for the Life of Ms. Barbie D. Doll

1
(A) Barbie's boobs and spacious mansion helped cause the decay of today's youth, supposed experts say. For example, in her article, "'I Want to Be a Barbie Doll When I Grow Up': The Cultural Significance of the Barbie Doll," Marilyn Ferris Motz argues the following: Barbie dolls encourage young girls to be conformists focused on "leisure activities, personal appearance, popularity, and the consumption of materials" (125). Barbie's skinny waist, huge bosom, and narrow hips entice girls into poor diets and eating disorders. Barbie-play trains girls to depend on Ken-figures (or other males) to achieve self-worth. Barbie's all-American-girl values teach con-
(B) formity; and Barbie's racy cars, plush houses, and chic outfits cause materialism (128–132). But I don't buy Motz's "reasons." They sound fake—like the theories of somebody who lacks firsthand experience. I had Barbie dolls—twelve of them, in fact, and the Barbie Mansion and Soda Shop to boot—but I don't consider myself an anorexic, dependent, conforming, materialistic girl, at least no more than I would be had I foregone the Barbie experience.

2
(C) Granted, Barbie's physical appearance isn't realistic. As Motz explains, "If Barbie stood five feet nine inches tall, her bust measurement would be 33 inches, her waist a meager 18 inches, and her hips only 28 1/2 inches" (128). In addition, Motz says, "Barbie's arms are extremely thin and her hands disproportionately small. Her legs are much too long . . ." (128–129). I say, so what? While the only "real" version of Barbie's body would be a long-limbed 13-year-old with breast implants, who cares? Arguing that Barbie's unrealistic body hurts girls' self-esteem is weak logic. Children have had dolls for ages. For example, in Pompeii, the preserved remains of a 3,000-year-old doll are displayed. That doll has an egghead, and a body that looks like a thick, shapeless rock. If Barbie's proportions hurt modern girls' self-esteem, I pity antiquity's girls, who had these lumps for models!

3
(D) Motz says that the average age of girls who play with Barbie is six, and that girls this age imitate the doll's values, like her preoccupation with appearance (127). However, while I was about six when I played with Barbie, I didn't imitate her. At age seven, I had a bowl haircut that was constantly snarled because I wouldn't take time to brush it. I didn't care about my own appearance, while fixing Barbie's was fun. I didn't fuss over my own hair and weight until I was in high school, and fashion mags were scripture. In other words, Motz's theory—that girls' preoccupation with Barbie's appearance leads to later preoccupation with their own—simply doesn't reflect my experience. Nor does her theory reflect the experiences of many other girls, including my two roommates.

4
(E) In response to Motz's idea that Barbies make girls dependent on males, I say, "Phooey." I played with Barbies until every last cow came home, and I am now a happy single girl. In fact, I have often been single, free from all romantic attachments. True, I've had boyfriends, but I never felt compelled to sacrifice my needs or identity to keep a boyfriend. And I am not an exception to Motz's rule! I know many girls whose primary concerns are their friends, family, and/or schoolwork. Admittedly, there is probably an equal number of girls who live only for their beaus; however, their behavior doesn't prove that Barbie causes female dependency. For example, my own interest in boys was prompted most by "good" TV shows and books—like Laura Ingalls Wilder's *On the Shores of Silver Lake*. It was stories like these—about teenage girls in love—that encouraged me to crave romance.

5
(F) In other words, Motz uses Barbie as a scapegoat for problems that have complex causes. For example, a girl's interest in romance is no more Barbie's fault than the fault of books like *On the Shores of Silver Lake*. Fashion magazines targeted at adolescents are the cause of far more anorexia cases than is Barbie. Mothers who

---

(A) The writer states her opponent's arguments and disagrees with them.

(B) Her tone is forceful and playful, but thoughtful.

(C) She concedes a point but rebuts the argument.

(D) Her own experience adds support.

(E) The writer rebuts each point in turn, often quoting directly from the article.

(F) She summarizes her disagreement and offers alternative explanations.

encourage daughters to find security in men teach female dependency, but Barbie doesn't. In fact, Motz herself points out that when "the Barbie doll was created, many parents hailed the doll as a model of wholesome teenage behavior and appearance" (130). I would add that today many parents still hail Barbie as a model for wholesome behavior. But it is more the manner in which parents give toys to their children—the parents' ideas and instructions about how to play—that determine whether Barbie-play is good or bad.

6   To Motz and similar "experts," I say this: Some of
(G) my finest childhood memories are of my best friend, Solara, coming over to my house with her pink carry-on suitcase stuffed with Barbies and their accoutrements. For hours we would play with them, giving haircuts, filling mixing bowls to make swimming pools, and creating small "campfires" so Barbie could make s'mores. Sometimes we dressed her in store-bought clothes, and sometimes we designed clothing for her. Other times we turned Barbie into the heroines in our books, and she helped us act out the plots. Playing with Barbies need not be an unimaginative, antisocial activity that promotes conformity, materialism, and superficial ideals. I played with Barbies and I'm fine. Take that, Motz!

(G) Speaking directly to the opposition, the writer shares an anecdote and restates her counterclaim.

© Graham Mitchel/iStockphoto.com

Reading for Better Writing

Working by yourself or with a group, answer these questions:

1. The word *apology* can mean *defense*, as well as a statement of regret for wrongdoing. Is the use of the word fitting in the title? Why or why not?

2. This essay is a counterargument that relies heavily on logic and personal experience for support. How does the writer treat the original source? How do concessions and rebuttals function in the argument?

LO3 Persuade readers to act.

Your goal is to urge individual readers to change their behavior or to take action on an issue. To accomplish this goal, you need to change the minds of those who disagree with you, and give encouragement to those who do agree with you.

1. Select a topic. List issues about which you feel passionate, issues in which you see a need for change. Here are some starter ideas:

• **Personal experiences:** What personal experiences have raised questions or concerns for you?

• **Personal ideas:** What issues often occupy your mind? What do you stew about or fear? What makes you say, "Something should be done"?

• **Community concerns:** What issues affect the various communities to which you belong—family, college, race, ethnic group, or gender?

• **National or international affairs:** Which national or global issues are discussed in your circle of friends, your college community, or the news?

• **"No comment" topics:** What issues are new to you? What issues would you like to develop a strong stance on?

Then choose a topic that meets these criteria: The **topic is debatable**, significant, current, and manageable.

2. Choose and analyze your audience. Think about who your readers are. Make a list of words and phrases describing their perspectives on the issue.

debatable topic
a topic that is not a mere fact but can be argued from at least two different angles

3. Narrow your focus and determine your purpose. Consider what you can achieve within the assignment's constraints. Should you focus on one aspect of the issue or all of it? Which patterns of thinking and behavior can you try to change? Considering your particular audience, which actions can you call for?

4. Generate ideas and support. Use prewriting strategies like those below to develop your thinking and gather support:

- Set up "opposing viewpoints" columns. In one column, take one side; in the other column, take the other side.
- Construct a dialogue between two people—yourself and someone who doesn't support your position.
- Talk to others about the issue. How do peers, friends, coworkers, and relatives respond to your ideas?
- Research the issue to find current, reliable sources from a variety of perspectives. Consider interviewing an expert.
- Consider what outcome or results you want.

5. Organize your thinking. Get your thoughts organized so that you can step confidently into your first draft. The two following strategies will help you:

> **1. Make** a sharp claim about the issue, a claim that points toward action. Try this pattern:
>
> On the issue of ——→ , I believe ——→ .
> Therefore, we must change ——————→ .
>
> **2. Review** the evidence, and develop your line of reasoning by generating an outline or using a graphic organizer. (See pages 36–37.)
>
> Simple Outline
> Introduction: claim
> | Support: point 1
> | Support: point 2
>   ▼ Support: point 3
> Conclusion: call to action

tone
the overall feeling or effect created by the writer's thoughts and use of words

jargon
highly technical terms not familiar to the general reader

6. Write your first draft. As you write, remember your goal to persuade, and keep your audience in mind. Use the following points to help you write your first draft.

Opening: Gain the reader's attention, raise the issue, help the reader to care about it, and state your claim.

Development: Follow your outline but feel free to explore new ideas that arise. Decide where to place your most persuasive supporting argument: first or last. Anticipate the reader's questions and objections, and use appropriate logical and emotional appeals to overcome any resistance.

Closing: Do one or more of the following: Restate your claim, summarize your support, and encourage the reader to take the action you want.

Title: Develop a thoughtful, energetic working title that stresses a vision or change. (For ideas, scan the titles of the sample essays in this chapter.)

7. Share your essay. Try out your thinking and persuasive appeals with a reader. Does he or she find your argument convincing? Why or why not?

8. Revise your writing. Think about your reviewer's comments and consider the following questions before changing your draft:

Ask

- Does your argument flow effectively? Consider shuffling points to make the sequence more persuasive. Add transitions if necessary.
- Is the evidence credible and persuasive? Does your logic have gaps? Do you need to qualify some points and strengthen others?
- Do images, examples, and analogies help the reader understand and identify with your cause? Do these elements urge the reader to act?
- Is the voice fitting—energetic but controlled, confident but reasonable? Will your **tone** persuade the reader, or start a quarrel?

9. Edit and proofread. See pages 67–77 for guidelines, but check especially for appropriate word choice and clear sentences. Avoid cliches and **jargon**.

10. Prepare and publish your final essay. Submit your essay according to your instructor's format and documentation requirements. If appropriate, "publish" your essay and solicit feedback from your audience—perhaps on a Web site, in the school newspaper, or with an appropriate discussion group.

TIP
Consider how one or more well-placed visuals (graph, photograph, and so on) might strengthen your argument.

OF OIL AND WILDERNESS

Rebecca Pasok is an environmental studies major who wrote this ecological essay to persuade readers to support lifestyle choices and energy policies that do not require drilling for oil in the Arctic National Wildlife Refuge.

SQ3R
Survey Question Read Recite Review

To Drill or Not to Drill

1 Known as "America's Last Frontier," the Arctic National Wildlife Refuge (ANWR) is located in the northeast corner of Alaska, right along the Beaufort Sea. President Dwight D. Eisenhower established the refuge in 1960, and today its 19 million acres make it one of the biggest refuges in the United States and home to a wide variety of wildlife such as eagles, wolves, moose, grizzly bears, polar bears, and caribou. During the last few years, however, the security of that home has been threatened by those who want to use one section of the ANWR to drill for oil. That section—named Area 1002—encompasses 1.5 million acres of pristine land near the coast.

2 One of the strongest arguments against oil drilling anywhere in the refuge is that the environmental impact of drilling conflicts with the very purpose of the ANWR. The primary mandate for the ANWR, as laid out by the U.S. Fish and Wildlife Service that administers the ref-

(A)

(B)

uge, is "to protect the wildlife and habitats of the area for the benefit of people now and in the future." The question then is whether drilling for oil supports, or is in conflict with, this mandate. President George W. Bush and others argue that oil drilling does not conflict with the mandate because new oil-drilling techniques cause only minimal damage to the environment. These techniques include drilling fewer wells, placing wells closer together, and building pipelines above ground so as not to disturb the animals (McCarthy).

3 Some environmental experts support the argument that the new techniques will not hurt wildlife. While these individuals acknowledge that some land disturbance will result, they argue that animals such as caribou will not suffer. One expert taking this position is Pat Valkenberg, a research coordinator with the Alaska Department of Fish and Game; he maintains that the caribou population is thriving and should continue to thrive. To support this point, Valkenberg notes that between 1997 and 2000, the caribou population actually grew from 19,700 to 27,128 (Petroleum News).

4 Other experts challenge those statistics with information about the caribou's birthing patterns. These experts point to herds like the porcupine caribou that live in the ANWR and move along the coast of the Beaufort Sea in the United States and also into Canada. A majority of the females in this herd wear radio collars that have been tracked to Area 1002 during calving season. Experts who argue against drilling note that the calves born on ANWR's coastal plain have a greater chance of surviving than those that are born in the foothills, where many of their predators live (*U.S. Fish and Wildlife*). This difference in survival ratios, argue antidrilling experts, may not be accounted for in the statistics used by prodrilling advocates like Valkenberg.

(C)

5 One specialist opposed to drilling is David Klein, a professor at the Institute of Arctic Biology at the University of Alaska–Fairbanks. Klein argues that if the oil industry opens up the ANWR for drilling, the number of caribou will likely decrease because the calving locations would change. He points out that oil-industry work in the Prudhoe oil field (also in Alaska) has already split up the Central Arctic herd of caribou, so it is likely that drilling in Area 1002 will similarly affect the porcupine herd (McCarthy).

(A) The opening provides background information before raising the controversial position.
(B) The writer starts with a strong argument against drilling but then maps out why others support it.

(C) She counters the position with expert testimony for the other side.

6   But caribou are not the only wildlife that would be affected by drilling in Area 1002. Musk oxen, polar bears, and grizzly bears could be driven out of the refuge and possibly into regions where people live, thereby threatening both the animals' and people's safety. Clearly, the bottom line in this debate is that drilling in Area 1002 will destroy at least some of the ecological integrity that makes ANWR a natural treasure. Environmentalists say that "just as there is no way to be half-pregnant, there is no 'sensitive' way to drill in a wilderness" (McCarthy). They are right.

(D)

7   However, oil drilling in ANWR will hurt more than the environment and wildlife; the drilling also will hurt at least one of the two Inuit tribes living in Alaska—the Inupiat Eskimos and the Gwich'in Indians. The Inupiat is the larger group, and they favor drilling. Money generated by the oil industry, say the Inupiat, will help them improve a variety of tribal services such as education and health care. On the other hand, the Gwich'in tribe depends on the porcupine caribou for food. As a result, if oil drilling displaces such animals, the people will suffer. Not only do they need the caribou to survive, but they also need them to retain the tribe's dignity and way of life. In other words, while oil drilling in ANWR may give some residents more money, others clearly will pay a price.

(E)

8   So if oil drilling in ANWR would have so many negative effects, what is driving the argument for drilling? Unfortunately, nothing more than a shortsighted, ill-informed effort to satisfy America's excessive appetite for oil: To continue using too much, we want to produce more. But is drilling in the ANWR the answer to our consumption problem?

(F)

9   At best, getting more oil from Alaska is a shortsighted solution: ANWR's reserves are simply too small to provide a long-term solution. A 1998 study by the U.S. Geological Survey concluded that the total amount of accessible oil in the ANWR is 5.7 to 16 billion barrels, with an expected amount of 10.4 billion barrels

(Arctic Power). While these figures are considered the official estimate, the National Resources Defense Council (a group of lawyers, scientists, and environmentalists) disagrees. It estimates the accessible amount to be 3.2 billion barrels—a resource the United States would use up in just six months! In the meantime, using the ANWR oil would do nothing to ease our dependence on Middle Eastern countries for oil. There has to be a better choice.

10   And there is. The question is not whether drilling should take place in the ANWR, but how to provide energy for everyone, now and in the future. A poll taken by the *Christian Science Monitor* shows that voters believe that the best option for Americans is to develop new technologies (Dillan). Finding new energy sources, they say, is more important than finding new oil reserves.

(G)

11   There are two main problems with relying primarily on oil for our energy: Oil supplies are limited, and oil use pollutes. Democratic Representative Rosa DeLauro of Connecticut made this point well when she said the following:

12   "We need a serious energy policy in the United States. Drilling in the Arctic National Wildlife Refuge is not the solution. We should look to increase domestic production while balancing our desire for a cleaner environment. We must also look at ways to reduce our dependency on fossil fuels themselves, a smart and necessary step that will lead to a cleaner environment" (qtd. in Urban).

(H)

(G) The writer redirects the discussion to the root of the problem.

(H) A closing quotation focuses and supports the writer's objections.

(D) The writer strongly states her thesis—that she agrees with opponents of drilling.

(E) By looking at effects on people, the writer expands her opposition.

(F) A question serves as a transition to a key counterargument.

13   While reducing our use of fossil fuels will not be easy, it is possible if we do two things: (1) develop energy-saving technologies and (2) make lifestyle choices that conserve energy. Unlike the short-term (and short-sighted) solution of drilling in the ANWR, these strategies will help save the environment. In addition, the strategies will help people both now and in the future.

    Note: The works-cited page is not shown.

Reading for Better Writing

Working by yourself or with a group, answer these questions:

1. The writer describes both positions on drilling before stating her opposition explicitly. Is this strategy effective?

2. The writer uses the testimony of experts extensively. Why?

3. What does the writer do to acknowledge, concede points to, and refute support for drilling?

4. Review pages 136–137 about types of support. Then trace the types of evidence provided in this essay. Evaluate the quality and completeness of the evidence.

5. Does the last paragraph offer an effective closing to the writer's argument? Why or why not?

GUIDELINES

LO4 Propose a solution.

Your goal is to argue for a positive change, convincing the reader to accept and contribute to that change. To accomplish this goal, aim to describe a problem, analyze its causes and effects, argue for one solution among several options, defend that solution against objections, and prove that the solution is both **feasible** and desirable.

1. Select a topic. In today's world, one might argue, there are plenty of problems to go around. Finding one to analyze and solve effectively in a problem-solution essay, however, requires forethought. Consider the following starting points for your topic search.

- **People problems:** What problems are faced by different generations— your own or another's?

- **College problems:** What top ten problems are faced by college students? In your major, which problems are experts trying to solve?

- **Social problems:** Which problems do your community or country face? Where do you see suffering, injustice, waste, or harm?

- **Workplace problems:** What challenges do you encounter at work?

> **feasible**
> doable; reasonable—given time, budgets, resources, and consequences

Before settling on a topic, you must test it to see if you can address it adequately in an essay. To do this, ask yourself the questions below. If you can answer yes to every point, you've likely found a workable topic.

 Ask

- Is the problem real, serious, and fairly complex? Does it show brokenness, danger, or disadvantage? Does it predict future harm?
- Do you care about this problem and believe that it must be solved?
- Can you offer a workable solution?
- Considering the limitations on an essay, have you adequately narrowed the focus of your topic (perhaps by dealing with part of the greater problem, or by looking at a local angle)?

2. Identify and analyze your audience. Potentially, you could have three audiences: decision makers with the power to deliver change, people affected by the problem, and a public that needs to learn about the problem and get behind a solution. Once you've determined your audience, study them:

 Ask

- What do they know about the problem? What are their attitudes toward it, their likely questions, and their potential concerns?
- Why might they accept or resist change? Would they prefer a specific solution?
- Does the problem affect them directly or indirectly? What can and can't they do about the problem?
- What arguments and evidence would convince them to agree that the problem exists, to care about it, and to take action?
- What common ground do you and your readers share?

3. Probe the problem. Next, consider your topic in depth, using the following strategies.

- **Define the problem.** What is it, exactly? What are its parts or dimensions?

- **Determine the problem's seriousness.** Why should it be fixed? Who is affected and how? What are its immediate, long-term, and potential effects?

- **Analyze causes.** What are its root causes and contributing factors?

- **Explore context.** What is the problem's background, history, and connection to other problems? What solutions have been tried in the past? Who, if anyone, benefits from the problem's existence?

- **Think creatively.** Take a look at the problem from other perspectives—other states and countries, both genders, different races and ethnic groups, and other generations.

4. Brainstorm possible solutions. List all imaginable solutions—both modest and radical fixes. Then list and evaluate the alternatives. To do this, list criteria that any solution should meet. (These measurements indicate a solution's effectiveness at resolving the problem: The solution must . . .) Then compare and contrast alternatives by examining strengths, weaknesses, and workability.

5. Choose the best solution and map out support. In a sentence, state the solution that best solves the problem—a workable plan that attacks causes and treats effects. Try this pattern for your thesis: "Given [the problem—its seriousness, effects, or causes], we must [the solution]." Next, identify support for your solution. Compared with alternatives, why is it preferable? Is it more thorough, beneficial, or practical?

6. Outline your proposal and complete a first draft. A proposal's structure is quite simple: Describe the problem, offer a solution, and defend the solution. However, developing each section of this structure can be complicated. Choose strategies that fit your purpose and audience.

The problem: Consider whether readers understand the problem and accept its seriousness. Inform and/or persuade them about the problem by using appropriate background information, cause/effect analysis, examples, analogies, parallel cases, visuals, and expert testimony.

The solution: If necessary, first argue against alternative solutions. Then present your solution. State clearly what should happen, who should be involved, and why. For a complex solution, lay out the different stages.

The support: Show how the solution solves the problem. Use facts and analysis to argue that your solution is feasible. Also address objections. You may choose to accept some objections while refuting others.

7. Get feedback and revise the draft. Share your draft with a peer or a tutor in the writing center, getting answers to the following questions:

Ask ?

- Does the solution fit the problem? Is the proposal precise, well reasoned, realistic, and complete? Does it address all objections?
- Is the evidence credible, compelling, clear, and well documented?
- Does the voice fit the problem and treat the opposition tactfully?
- Is the opening engaging? Is the closing thoughtful, forceful, and clear?

8. Edit and proofread. Check for accurate word choice and helpful definitions; smooth, energetic sentences; and correct grammar, spelling, and format.

9. Prepare and share your final essay. Submit your proposal to your instructor, but also consider posting it on the Web.

A DINNER TABLE THREAT

In this essay, student writer Brian Ley defines agroterrorism, predicts that it could become a serious problem, and proposes a multifaceted solution.

SQ3R
Survey Question Read Recite Review

Preparing for Agroterror

An al-Qaeda terrorist in Africa obtains a sample of fluid from a cow infected with foot-and-mouth disease, and he sends the fluid to an accomplice in a small, rural American town. This terrorist takes the sample around the country, stopping at several points to place small amounts of the fluid on objects that animals are likely to touch. When he is finished, he drives to the nearest airport and leaves the country unnoticed. **1 (A)**

Cows, pigs, and sheep then come into contact with this highly contagious disease. Over the next few days, farmers see blisters on the feet and mouths of their animals. Thinking that the animals have a bacterial infection, the farmers administer antibiotics and wait for improvement. However, because antibiotics can't kill a virus, the animals get sicker. Meanwhile, the virus is spreading by means of wind and the movement of animals and humans. Within a few weeks, the virus is out of control. **2**

While the story above is hypothetical, it is also very possible. People used to think of terrorists as men in ski masks blowing up embassies and taking hostages. But after the events of September 11, 2001, and the subsequent anthrax scares, it is clear that more kinds of terrorism are possible. **3**

(A) The writer opens by illustrating the problem.

4
One type rarely considered is agroterrorism, which involves using diseases as weapons to attack a country's agriculture industry in order to attack the country itself. The agroterrorist's weapons of choice are those diseases that affect plants, animals, and even humans. Professor Peter Chalk of the RAND Corporation, an expert on transnational terrorism, believes that agroterrorism should be a huge concern for Americans because it has many advantages from a terrorist's point of view (37).

5
First of all, an attack on the agricultural sector of the United States would be quite easy. The diseases needed to kill large populations of animals can be obtained with little difficulty; the most devastating ones are ready for use in their natural form. These samples pose little risk to the terrorist because many of the diseases are harmless to humans.

6
In addition, doing agroterrorism is less risky in terms of getting caught and getting punished. Agroterrorism is hard to trace, especially because Americans have assumed that all animal epidemics are natural in origin and that American livestock contract such diseases only by accident. Consequences for those caught inflicting a disease on animals are also less severe than for terrorists who harm humans. In fact, because agroterrorism first affects the health of plants and animals rather than humans, terrorists using this strategy can even escape some guilt for their actions.

7
However, while agroterrorist diseases would have little direct effect on people's health, they would be devastating to the agricultural economy, in part because of the many different diseases that could be used in an attack. One of the most devastating is foot-and-mouth disease. This illness hurts all infected animals by impeding their weight gain, and it hurts dairy cows in particular by decreasing their milk production. Because the disease is highly contagious, all infected animals, along with any cloven-hoofed animals within about 50 miles of the infection site, must be killed. *(D)*

8
While foot-and-mouth disease is not dangerous to humans, other animal diseases are. One of these is bovine spongiform encephalopathy, better known as mad-cow disease ("Mad Cow"). This illness is not easily spread, but a few cases in the United States would send people into a panic. Meat consumption would drop sharply, and the agricultural economy would be deeply shaken.

9
Another disease that could be used as a weapon is West Nile encephalitis. This virus can be spread by insects and can even cross species, affecting horses, birds, pigs, and humans. It is a fatal illness without a vaccination or a cure. These diseases are likely candidates for use in an agroterrorist attack (Smith 249).

10
The agricultural community is particularly susceptible to a terrorist attack. Unlike "typical" terrorist targets in metropolitan areas, farms do not have sophisticated security systems to protect against intruders. The average farmer's security system includes a mean dog and a shotgun: the dog for humans and the gun for animal pests. If terrorists wanted to infect a dairy, swine operation, or even a large-scale cattle-finishing

> (B) The writer defines the problem and presents expert testimony.
> (C) He analyzes why the problem could become serious.

> (D) Using specific details, he outlines the problem's potential effects.

operation, they would encounter few obstacles. The terrorists merely have to place a piece of infected food in an area with livestock. This single action could start an epidemic.

11   Agroterrorism is a threat that demands a response. Several actions can be taken to discourage terrorism as well as to deal with its consequences. One of the first steps is convincing all citizens—farmers and nonfarmers alike—that agroterrorism could happen, and that it could cause horrific consequences. Farmers must realize that they are susceptible to an attack, even though they may live far from large metropolitan areas. Nonfarmers must realize how an attack could affect them. If nonfarmers know that an attack could create panic, drive up food prices, and possibly eliminate food sources, they will look out for suspicious activity and report it.

12   Preventive action on farms is needed to ensure the
(E) safety of the food supply. For example, the South Dakota Animal Industry Board recently published a newsletter outlining several precautions that farmers can take. Farms should have better security, especially in areas where animals are kept. These security measures include allowing only authorized persons to have access to farm buildings and animals and keeping all key farm buildings locked ("Precautions").

13   Farmers also need training to detect the diseases that terrorists might use and to know what actions can contain and decontaminate an infected area. For example, if a farmer discovers that cows have blisters on their tongues and noses, and that they are behaving abnormally, the owner should immediately call a veterinarian to assess the situation. Because the disease might be foot-and-mouth, no cattle should leave the farm until a diagnosis has been made.

In addition, public authorities need a plan for re- 14
sponding to an identified agroterrorism attack. For example, thousands of animals may have to be killed and disposed of—an action with significant environmental concerns. Moreover, public money should be used for continued research of the diseases that may be spread by agroterrorists. Vaccines and treatments may be produced that would stop diseases or limit them from becoming epidemic.

Agroterrorism has not yet been used on a large scale 15
anywhere on the globe. However, its use seems inevi- (F)
table. The United States is a prime target for terrorism of this sort because the country has the largest, most efficiently raised food supply in the world. Destroying part of this supply would affect not only the United States but also all those countries with whom it trades. Because the United States is a prime target, it must act now to develop its defenses against agroterrorism. If the country waits until an attack happens, people may become ill, the overall economy could be damaged, and the agricultural economy may never recover.

Note: The works-cited page is not shown.

(F) The closing stresses the problem's seriousness and calls for action.

(E) The writer proposes a multifaceted solution.

Reading for Better Writing

Working by yourself or with a group, answer these questions:

1. This essay predicts that a problem might develop. Is the writer's prediction persuasive? Why or why not?

2. What tactics does the writer use to convince the reader to be concerned about the problem? Are these strategies successful?

3. The solution proposed is multifaceted. Briefly list who must do what. Is this solution persuasive? Is it workable? Does it get at root causes?

4. A strong proposal provides convincing evidence about both the problem and the solution. Trace the evidence used in this essay. Are the types of evidence convincing? Do any gaps need to be filled?

"**Books are the carriers of** civilization. Without books, history is silent, literature dumb, science crippled, thought and speculation at a standstill."
—Barbara W. Tuchman

14

Analyzing the Arts

LO1 Understand the arts.

The Story of Edgar Sawtelle by David Wroblewski tells of a young mute boy who is part of a mysterious family of dog breeders and trainers. When Edgar discovers his father dying in the kennel barn, he suspects that his uncle committed the murder. The suspicion deepens when Edgar learns that his uncle and mother are having an affair. Edgar sees the ghost of his father and searches for answers about his family's past, his father's death, and his family's future. Since Edgar is able to hear but not speak, his isolation in this quest is intense.

Edgar Sawtelle is a 20th-century tragedy with strong links to *Hamlet,* the famous Shakespearean tragedy written 400 years ago. Even so, the novel can surely be enjoyed without recognizing the *Hamlet* parallels. The information about dog breeding, the Sawtelle way, is extremely fascinating; Edgar is a truly memorable character on his own; and the story turns into a multiple-murder thriller. But making the *Hamlet* connection adds another level of appreciation and another way to analyze the novel.

Of course, the more exposure you have to the arts—literature, music, art, film, and architecture—the more connections you can make between novels and plays, music and poetry, art and architecture, and so on. Traditionally, a goal of a liberal arts education has been to immerse students in all aspects of the arts to help them appreciate the culture and the arts of different times and places. Whether or not that tradition is still strong depends on your university and your particular course of study.

This chapter provides guidelines and models to help you create in-depth and thoughtful analyses of the arts.

Learning Outcomes

LO1 Understand the arts.

LO2 Write about the arts.

LO3 Understand literary terms.

LO4 Understand poetic terms.

What do you think?

I would rather analyze a short story than a painting.

1	2	3	4	5
strongly agree				strongly disagree

LO2 Write about the arts.

Your goal is to experience an artwork or a performance, understand its elements, and then write an essay analyzing and perhaps evaluating the work.

1. Select a topic. Choose an art form or a type of performance with which you are familiar or are willing to learn about. Consider the ideas below.

- **Poems:** There are thousands of great poems to choose from in literature or poetry anthologies and in literary magazines.

- **Short stories:** Like poems, you'll find many short stories in literature anthologies, literary or popular magazines, and on Web sites.

- **Novels:** Though novels require significant time to read, analyzing a novel can be very rewarding.

- **Paintings:** Analyzing a painting or other artwork requires careful attention to its appearance and also encourages interesting research into its history and creator.

- **Films:** While you could write about a current big-name film, consider analyzing a classic film or one not shown in area theaters. Choosing a film on video enables you to replay the entire film or specific scenes.

- **Concerts:** Analyze major concerts in your city or on campus, or consider performances by lesser-known artists at student recitals or in backstreet theaters.

- **Plays:** Choices include big-name touring shows, campus productions, plays staged in your community, or plays you read.

2. Understand the work. Experience it thoughtfully (two or three times, if possible), looking carefully at its content, form, and overall effect.

Review Strategies

- **Plays/Films:** For plays and films, examine the plot, setting, characters, dialogue, lighting, costumes, sound effects, music, acting, and directing.

- **Novels/Short stories:** For novels and short stories, focus on point of view, plot, setting, characters, style, diction, and theme. (See pages 167–169.)

- **Poems:** For poems, examine diction, tone, sound, figures of speech, symbolism, irony, form, and theme. (See page 170.)

- **Music:** For music, focus on harmonic and rhythmic qualities, dynamics, melodic lines, lyrics, and interpretation.

3. Gather information. Take notes on what you experience, using the list above to guide your thoughts. Seek to understand the whole work before you analyze the parts. Consider freewriting briefly on one or more aspects of the work to explore your response and to dig more deeply into the work. If you are analyzing a written text, annotate it.

4. Organize your thoughts. Review the notes you've taken so far. What key insight about the work have you discovered? Make that insight or judgment your thesis, and then organize supporting points logically in a list or an outline.

5. Write the first draft.

Opening: The ideas that follow can help you create an effective opening. You must gain the reader's attention, identify your topic, narrow the focus, and state your thesis.

- **Summarize** your subject briefly. Include the title, the author, and the literary form or performance.

In her poem "Let Evening Come," Jane Kenyon points to hope in the face of death.

- **Start** with a quotation from the film, story, or poem and then comment on its importance.

- **Explain** the artist's purpose and how well she or he achieves it.

- **Open** with a general statement about the artist's style or aesthetic process.

> The work of American poet Jane Kenyon is influenced primarily by the circumstances and experiences of her own life.

- **Begin** with a general statement about the plot or performance.

> In Stephen Spielberg's movie *War of the Worlds,* Ray Ferrier and his two children flee from their New Jersey home in a stolen minivan.

- **Assert** your thesis. State your key insight about the work—the focus that you will seek to support in your essay.

Middle: Develop or support your focus by following this pattern:

- **State** the main points, relating them clearly to the focus of your essay.

- **Support** each main point with specific details or direct quotations.

- **Explain** how these details prove your point.

Conclusion: Tie key points together to clarify your analysis. Assert your thesis or evaluation in a fresh way, leaving the reader with a sense of the larger significance of your subject.

6. Review and revise. Once you have a first draft written, relax for a time, and then reread your essay for its logic and completeness. Check whether you have supported each of your observations with evidence from the poem, story, film, or other artwork. Test your analysis with questions like these:

Ask❓

- Do you fully understand the performance, the reasons for the acting style or costuming, the lyrics of the song, or whatever is central to the work?
- Have you explored the ironies, if present, or any important images, vocal nuances, dramatic action, shifts in setting, or symbolism?
- Have you brought your analysis to a clear conclusion?

7. Get feedback. Ask a knowledgeable classmate, friend, or tutor to read your essay, using the following checklist:

Feedback Checklist

Does the writing have . . .

____ an analytical thesis statement supported by evidence?

____ key insights into both content or meaning on the one hand and form or style on the other hand?

____ clear transitions between sentences and paragraphs?

____ a tone that is respectful and honest?

8. Edit and proofread. Once you have revised your essay, clarified your transitions, and checked your evidence, polish the phrasing and diction. Make certain your paper is free of awkward syntax or errors in usage, punctuation, spelling, or grammar. In particular, check that you have used the special terms of the literary genre or art form correctly.

9. Publish your essay. There are numerous ways to publish your work. For example, you may share your essay with friends or family, publish it in a journal or on a Web site, or place a copy in your portfolio.

A GOOD COUNTRY SHORT STORY

In the essay below, student writer Anya Terekhina analyzes the characters and ideas in Flannery O'Connor's short story "Good Country People."

SQ3R
Survey Question Read Recite Review

"Good Country People": Broken Body, Broken Soul

Flannery O'Connor's short stories are filled with char- [1] acters who are bizarre, freakish, devious, and some- [A] times even murderous. Every short story, according to O'Connor in *Mystery and Manners: Occasional Prose,* should be "long in depth" and meaning (94). To achieve this, O'Connor develops characters with heavily symbolic attributes and flaws, and "it is clearly evident that boldly outlined inner compulsions are reinforced dramatically by a mutilated exterior self" (Muller 22).

(A) The writer provides background for understanding the characters in O'Connor's stories.

In "Good Country People," Joy-Hulga is a typical O'Connor character—grotesque yet real. Her realness comes from her many flaws and, ironically, her flaws are a self-constructed set of illusions. Throughout the story, O'Connor carefully links Joy-Hulga's physical impairments with deeper handicaps of the soul; then, at the closing, she strips Hulga of these physical flaws while helping her realize that her corresponding beliefs are flawed as well.

2   O'Connor first introduces her character as Joy Hopewell, a name of optimism. However, we soon understand that her chosen name, Hulga, is more fitting. The new name distresses her mother, Mrs. Hopewell, who is "certain that she [Joy] had thought and thought until she had hit upon the ugliest name in any language" (O'Connor 1943). Hulga has connotations of "hull = hulk = huge = ugly" (Grimshaw 51), and all of these are accurate descriptions of her. Far from having a sweet temperament, Hulga stomps and sulks around the farm, "constant outrage . . . [purging] every expression from her face" (1942).

3   Although Hulga's demeanor could be blamed on
(B) her physical impairments, she devises her own rationalizations for behaving as she does. Ironically, each rationale is symbolized by one of her physical disabilities, yet she doesn't recognize the handicaps for what they imply.

4   One of Hulga's many ailments is her weak heart, which will likely limit her life span. Hulga blames this affliction for keeping her on the Hopewell farm, making it plain that "if it had not been for this condition, she would be far from these red hills and good country people" (1944). Having a Ph.D. in philosophy, Hulga claims to want work as a university professor, lecturing to people at her intellectual level. Hulga's weak heart functions as more than a dream-crusher; it "symbolizes her emotional detachment—and inability to love anyone or anything" (Oliver 233). She exhibits no compassion or love for anything, not even "dogs or cats or birds or flowers or nature or nice young men" (1944–45).

5   Hulga also suffers from poor vision. Without her eyeglasses, she is helpless. Strangely though, her icy blue eyes have a "look of someone who has achieved blindness by an act of will and means to keep it" (1942). Her self-induced blindness symbolizes her blindness to

reality. She is indeed intelligent, but she has packed her brain full of ideas and thoughts that only obscure common sense, let alone truth. Because of Hulga's extensive education and her focus on philosophical reasoning, she considers herself superior to everyone around her. For example, she yells at her mother, "Woman! . . . Do you ever look inside and see what you are not? God!" (1944).

6   Hulga's last and most noticeable physical impairment is her missing leg, which was "literally blasted off" (1944) in a hunting accident when she was ten years old. In *Mystery and Manners,* O'Connor stresses that the wooden leg operates interdependently at a literal and a symbolic level, which means "the wooden leg continues to accumulate meaning" throughout the story (99). Hulga's biggest physical handicap symbolizes her deepest affliction: her belief in nothing.

7   Hulga's philosophical studies did focus on the
(C) study of nothing, particularly on the arguments of the French philosopher Nicolas Malebranche. O'Connor describes Hulga as believing "in nothing but her own belief in nothing" (Mystery 99). Over time, Hulga's belief in nothing develops into more than just academic study. Her nihilism becomes her religion—suitable for a woman who considers herself superior and despises platitudes. As she explains to Manley Pointer, "We are all damned . . . but some of us have taken off our blindfolds and see that there's nothing to see. It's a kind of salvation" (1952). Hulga's religious terms suggest that she uses faith in nothingness to find the meaning that she can't find elsewhere.

8   Hulga's nihilism is symbolized by her wooden leg,
(D) which is the only thing she tends to with care: "She took care of it as someone else would his soul, in private and almost with her own eyes turned away" (1953). This limb is wooden and corresponds to Hulga's wooden soul. Whereas she believes she worships Nothing, what she actually worships is an "artificial leg and an artificial belief" (Oliver 235).

9   Not realizing that her false leg and false religion cripple her both physically and spiritually, Hulga considers seducing Manley Pointer, the Bible salesman. She delightfully imagines that she will have to help him deal with his subsequent remorse, and then she will instruct him into a "deeper understanding of life" (1950). Of

(B) The writer begins listing the protagonist's physical disabilities and explains how each one symbolizes a deeper problem in her soul.

(C) She points out the root of the protagonist's problems: her lack of belief in anything.

(D) The writer demonstrates how the protagonist's flaws lead her to make distorted judgments.

course, her intellectual blindness keeps her from realizing that her superiority is only an illusion. Instead, she views Manley as "a vulnerable innocent, a naïve Fundamentalist, and she wishes to seduce him to prove that her sophisticated textbook nihilism is superior to his simpleminded faith" (Di Renzo 76).

10 In classic O'Connor fashion, the characters and situation reverse dramatically at the end of the story. Hulga and Manley are alone in a hayloft and begin embracing. At first, Hulga is pleased with her reaction to kissing as it aligns well with Malebranche's teachings: "it was an unexceptional experience and all a matter of the mind's control" (1951). Soon, however, she realizes that she is enjoying the first human connection of her life. At this point, the *innocent* Bible salesman has already stripped Hulga of her first physical impairment: her weak heart.

11 Hulga hardly notices when Manley takes advantage
(E) of her next impairment: "when her glasses got in his way, he took them off of her and slipped them into his pocket" (1952). With her heart opened and her intellectual perspective fuzzy, Hulga swiftly descends into what she despises—platitudes. Hulga and Manley exchange clichéd mumblings of love, and this leads Manley to ask if he can remove her artificial leg. After brief hesitation, Hulga agrees because she feels he has touched and understood a central truth inside her. She considers it a complete surrender, "like losing her own life and finding it again, miraculously, in his" (1953).

12 As soon as the artificial leg is off, Manley whips out one of his Bibles, which is hollow. Inside are whiskey, obscene playing cards, and contraceptives. In only moments, Hulga loses control: As each of her physical handicaps is exploited, pieces of her worldview crumble, leaving her confused and weak.

13 In an ironic reversal, Hulga becomes the naïf and Manley becomes the cynic. Hulga pleads in disbelief, "Aren't you . . . just good country people?" (1954). She knows that she has reverted to her mother's platitudes: "If the language is more sophisticated than any at Mrs. Hopewell's command, it is no less trite, and the smug self-deception underlying it . . . is, if anything, greater" (Asals 105). Manley assumes a startling, haughty air,
(F) exclaiming, "'I hope you don't think . . . that I believe in that crap! I may sell Bibles but I know which end is up and I wasn't born yesterday and I know where I'm going!'" (1954). Although they exchange roles, both

characters use clichés to express their immature, yet authentic, worldviews.

14 Manley runs off with Hulga's wooden leg, leaving her vulnerable and dependent, two things she previously despised. But "Hulga's artificial self—her mental fantasy of her own perfection—has gone out the door with her artificial limb. She is stuck in the hayloft with her actual self, her body, her physical and emotional incompleteness" (Di Renzo 79).

15 In one brief morning of delusional seduction, Hul-
(G) ga learns more about herself and her world than she learned in all her years of university. Forced to acknowledge her physical, emotional, and spiritual disabilities, Hulga begins to realize what she is not—neither a wise intellectual for whom there is *hope*, nor "good country people" who merely *hope well*.

Note: The works-cited page is not shown.

> (G) The closing explains how Hulga finally acknowledges the truth about herself.

Reading for Better Writing

Working by yourself or with a group, answer these questions:

1. In her opening, Terekhina cites O'Connor's view that short stories should be "long in depth" and meaning. Does Terekhina ably explore that depth and meaning? Why?

2. In her second paragraph, Terekhina analyzes Hulga Hopewell's first name; in the last paragraph, she comments on the last name. Does Terekhina's attention to names help you understand Hulga's character and the story's themes? How?

3. A writer's thesis is a type of "contract" that she or he makes with readers, spelling out what the essay will do. Review Terekhina's thesis (last sentence, first paragraph) and assess how effectively she fulfills that contract. Cite supporting details.

4. Flannery O'Connor is praised for her clearly developed, complex characters. Does Terekhina adequately explore that complexity? How?

5. Many laud O'Connor for the tough philosophical or ethical questions she raises. What questions does Terekhina identify in "Good Country People"? Does she effectively discuss them?

6. What does Terekhina say about the story's plot, symbols, and diction? Does she effectively analyze these elements? Why?

> (E) She revisits the protagonist's physical disabilities, showing how the Bible salesman exploits each one.
> (F) The writer reflects on the change in both characters.

AN EVENING POEM

In the essay on the following two pages, student writer Sherry Van Egdom analyzes the form and meaning of the poem below, "Let Evening Come," by American poet Jane Kenyon. Born in 1947 and raised on a farm near Ann Arbor, Michigan, Kenyon settled in New Hampshire at Eagle Pond Farm after she married fellow poet Donald Hall. During her life, Kenyon struggled with her faith, with depression, and with cancer. At the time of her death in 1995 from leukemia, she was the poet laureate of New Hampshire.

Before you read the student writer's analysis, read the poem aloud to enjoy its sounds, rhythm, images, diction, and comparisons. Then read the piece again to grasp more fully how the poem is structured, what it expresses, and how its ideas might relate to your life. Finally, read Van Egdom's analysis and answer the questions that follow it.

Let Evening Come
by Jane Kenyon

Let the light of late afternoon
shine through chinks in the barn, moving
up the bales as the sun moves down.

Let the crickets take up chafing
as a woman takes up her needles
and her yarn. Let evening come.

Let dew collect on the hoe abandoned
in long grass. Let the stars appear
and the moon disclose her silver horn.

Let the fox go back to its sandy den.
Let the wind die down. Let the shed
go black inside. Let evening come.

To the bottle in the ditch, to the scoop
in the oats, to air in the lung
let evening come.

Let it come, as it will, and don't
be afraid. God does not leave us
comfortless, so let evening come.

© Marina Krasnorutskaya , 2009 / Used under license from Shutterstock.com

SQ3R
Survey Question Read Recite Review

"Let Evening Come": An Invitation to the Inevitable

The work of American poet Jane Kenyon is influenced primarily by the circumstances and experiences of her own life. She writes carefully crafted, deceptively simple poems that connect both to her own life and to the lives of her readers. Growing out of her rural roots and her struggles with illness, Kenyon's poetry speaks in a still voice of the ordinary things in life in order to wrestle with issues of faith and mortality (Timmerman 163). One of these poems is "Let Evening Come." In this poem, the poet takes the reader on a journey into the night, but she points to hope in the face of that darkness. **1** (A) (B)

That movement toward darkness is captured in the stanza form and in the progression of stanzas. Each three-line stanza offers a self-contained moment in the progress of transition from day to night. The first stanza positions the reader in a simple farm setting. Late afternoon fades into evening without the rumble of highways or the gleam of city lights to distract one's senses from nature, the peace emphasized by the alliteration of "l" in "Let the light of late afternoon." As the sun sinks lower on the horizon, light seeps through cracks in the barn wall, moving up the bales of hay. In the second stanza, the crickets get busy with their nighttime noises. Next, a forgotten farm hoe becomes covered with dew drops, and the silvery stars and moon appear in the sky. **2** (C) (D)

(A) The writer introduces the poet and her poetry.

(B) Narrowing her focus to the specific poem, the writer states her thesis.

(C) She begins her analysis by explaining the stanza structure and progression.

(D) The writer shows attention to the poem's fine details and to secondary sources on the poem.

In the fourth stanza, complete blackness arrives as a fox returns to its empty den and the silent wind rests at close of day. The alliteration of "d" in "den" and "die down" gives a sinking, settling feeling (Timmerman 176). In the fifth stanza, a bottle and scoop keep still, untouched in their respective places, while sleep comes upon the human body. In the final stanza, Kenyon encourages readers to meet this emerging world of darkness without fear.

3
(E) Within this stanza progression, the journey into the night is intensified by strong images, figures of speech, and symbols. The natural rhythm of work and rest on the farm is symbolized by the light that rises and falls in the first stanza (Timmerman 175). The simile comparing the crickets taking up their song to a woman picking up her knitting suggests a homespun energy and conviction. The moon revealing her "silver horn" implies that the moon does not instantly appear with brightness and beauty but rather reveals her majesty slowly as the night comes on. The den, the wind, and the shed in stanza four stress a kind of internal, hidden darkness. Then stanza five focuses on connected objects: the thoughtlessly discarded bottle resting in the ditch, oats and the scoop for feeding, human lungs and the air that fills them. Kenyon mentions the air in the lung after the bottle, ditch, scoop, and oats in order to picture humanity taking its position among the established natural rhythm of the farm (Harris 31).

4
(F) The refrain, "let evening come," is a powerful part of the poem's journey toward darkness, though critics interpret the line differently. Judith Harris suggests that it symbolizes an acceptance of the inevitable: Darkness will envelop the world, and night will surely come, just as mortality will certainly take its toll in time. This acceptance, in turn, acts as a release from the confinement of one's pain and trials in life. Rather than wrestle with something that cannot be beaten or worry about things that must be left undone, Kenyon advises herself and her readers to let go (31). Night intrudes upon the work and events of the day, perhaps leaving them undone just as death might cut a life short and leave it seemingly unfinished.

5
By contrast, John Timmerman argues that "let" is used twelve times in a supplicatory, prayer-like manner (176). The final two lines, in turn, act as a benediction upon the supplications. The comfort of God is as inevitable as the evening, so cling to faith and hope and let evening come. Although the Comforter is mentioned only in the last two lines, that statement of faith encourages readers to find a spiritual comfort in spite of the coming of the night.

6
(G) When asked how she came to write "Let Evening Come," Jane Kenyon replied that it was a redemptive poem given to her by the Holy Ghost. When there could be nothing—a great darkness and despair—there is a great mystery of love, kindness, and beauty (Moyers 238). In the poem's calm journey into the night, Kenyon confronts darkness and suffering with a certain enduring beauty and hope (Timmerman 161). Death will come, but there remains divine comfort. "Let Evening Come" encourages readers to release their grip on the temporary and pay attention to the Comforter who reveals Himself both day and night.

Note: The works-cited page is not shown.

(G) In her conclusion, the writer offers the poet's explanation of the poem's origin and then expands on the thesis.

(E) She advances her reading of the poem by exploring images, comparisons, and symbols: the poem's "imaginative logic."

(F) The writer compares possible interpretations of a central, repeated statement in the poem.

Reading for Better Writing

Working by yourself or with a group, answer these questions:

1. Review the opening and closing paragraphs of the essay. How do they create a framework for the writer's analysis of the poem?

2. On which elements of the poem does the writer focus? Does this approach make sense for her analysis? Explain.

3. In her essay, the writer refers to the poet's life and to ideas from secondary sources. Do these references work well with her analysis? Why or why not?

4. Read the essay "Four Ways to Talk About Literature" on pages 100–101. Which approach does the student writer use to analyze Kenyon's poem? Does this approach make sense? How might another approach interpret the poem differently?

AN ALIENATING FILM

In the film review below, David Schaap analyzes Stephen Spielberg's film *War of the Worlds* by asking key questions about the filmmaker's strategies and their effects.

SQ3R
Survey Question Read Recite Review

Terror on the Silver Screen: Who Are the Aliens?

1
(A) In Steven Spielberg's 2005 movie *War of the Worlds*, Ray Ferrier and his two children flee their New Jersey home in a stolen minivan. To escape outer-space aliens who are destroying houses and killing people from their enormous three-legged machines, this father, son, and daughter lurch through scene after scene of 9/11-type destruction. At one point, the daughter surveys the violence, panics, and shrieks, "Is it the terrorists?"

2
(B) The girl's question nudges the audience to ask the same question, "Are the aliens terrorists?" That would make sense. Often filmmakers will play off members of the audience's real-life emotions to give them a sensational imaginary experience as well as a glimpse at their real world. In this case, by suggesting that the aliens' imaginary attack resembles Al Qaeda's 9/11 attack, Spielberg could be doing two things: (1) heightening fear of the alien characters and (2) suggesting a political theme.

3
(C) But is Spielberg's *War of the Worlds* this type of film? First, does the film inspire fear by suggesting that the aliens' attack is similar to Al Qaeda's attack? And second, does the film's alien attack represent a future terrorist invasion of the United States?

4
(D) The answer to the first question is yes. Spielberg inspires fear of his outer-space aliens by emphasizing their resemblance to 9/11 terrorists. In a series of scenes, he shows a crashed airliner like the ones used on 9/11, a wall covered with posters of missing loved ones, and mobs of ash- and dust-covered characters like those escaping the collapsing World Trade Center. Because the film takes place in the United States, viewers subconsciously further fear the aliens' violence.

5
(E) However, do the aliens invading the United States represent Al Qaeda fighters? Not really. The aliens are Spielberg's universal stand-in for whatever strikes fear into viewers' hearts. This film does not examine the political, psychological, or cultural roots of any problem. The film's focus is on the effect of violence, not the identity of the perpetrators. *War of the Worlds* is about terror, not terrorists.

> (A) The writer introduces the filmmaker and film; he then describes a pivotal scene.
>
> (B) He cites an important quotation and explores its significance.
>
> (C) Two questions focus the writer's analysis.
>
> (D) He answers the first question and offers supporting details.

> (E) He answers the second question by explaining the film's focus.

Reading for Better Writing

Working by yourself or with a group, answer these questions:

1. Where in this analysis does the writer share his thesis?
2. Explain how the writer prepares the reader for his focus. In your explanation, include details or quotations from the analysis.
3. Is the writer's method of development effective? Explain.

AN ICELANDIC PERFORMANCE

In the essay below, student writer Annie Moore reviews the performance of a rock music group, Sigur Ros. She praises several qualities of their experimental music.

SQ3R
Survey Question Read Recite Review

Sigur Ros, *Agaetis Byrjun*

1
(A) Sigur Ros, an experimental noise quartet hailing from Reykjavik, is the biggest thing since Bjork. Those Icelandic folk must know something we don't. Never before has a rock/pop album captured the beauty and

> (A) The writer states the accomplishments of the group.

quiet strength that pervades *Agaetis Byrjun*, the band's sophomore release.

2
(B) The album flows seamlessly as a single stream of consciousness. Jonsi Birgisson's ethereal vocals are divine as his falsetto effortlessly rides the sweeping melodies. Tension builds from the delicate intros, gathers fury, and then explodes in a burst of percussion and crashing guitars hammered by violin bow. The storm ends, a quiet lull follows, and then the cycle begins again. Added pianos, muted horns, and the strings of the Icelandic Symphony Orchestra give the songs of *Agaetis Byrjun* the essence of a twentieth-century classic.

3
(C) Although the lyrics are impossibly cryptic, written entirely in Icelandic, they are sung with an emotion and urgency so intense they are not merely perceived, but felt. The full force of the music resonates deep in the souls of listeners. It is exactly this "inarticulate speech of the heart," of which Van Morrison once spoke, that gives *Agaetis Byrjun* its heart-wrenching sense of sincerity.

4
With impeccable musicianship and a skillful mix of the traditional and innovative, Sigur Ros will change the world of music. Or perhaps they already have.

> **(B)** She describes the quality of their sound.
> **(C)** She describes the music's effect on the audience.

Reading for Better Writing

Working by yourself or with a group, answer these questions:

1. Which characteristics of the vocalists does the writer cite? Why?

2. Which other instrumental sounds does she cite?

3. Why does she tell us of the effect on the audience?

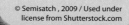

LO3 Understand literary terms.

Your analysis of novels, poems, plays, and films will be deeper and more sophisticated if you understand the most common literary terms. Review the quick guide that follows. Then employ it as a reference as you write your own analyzes.

| **Quick Guide** | **Literary Terms** |

Allusion is a reference to a person, a place, or an event in history or literature.

Analogy is a comparison of two or more similar objects, suggesting that if they are alike in certain respects, they will probably be alike in other ways, too.

Anecdote is a short summary of an interesting or humorous, often biographical incident or event.

Antagonist is the person or thing actively working against the protagonist, or hero, of the work.

Climax is the turning point, an intense moment characterized by a key event.

Conflict is the problem or struggle in a story that triggers the action. There are five basic types of conflict:

Person versus person: One character in a story is in conflict with one or more of the other characters.

Person versus society: A character is in conflict with some element of society: the school, the law, the accepted way of doing things, and so on.

Person versus self: A character faces conflicting inner choices.

Person versus nature: A character is in conflict with some natural happening: a snowstorm, an avalanche, the bitter cold, or any other element of nature.

Person versus fate: A character must battle what seems to be an uncontrollable problem. Whenever the conflict is a strange or unbelievable coincidence, it can be attributed to fate.

Denouement is the outcome of a play or story. See *resolution*.

Diction is an author's choice of words based on their correctness or effectiveness.

Archaic words are old-fashioned and no longer sound natural when used, such as "I believe thee not" for "I don't believe you."

Colloquialism is an expression that is usually accepted in informal situations and certain locations, as in "He really grinds my beans."

Heightened language uses vocabulary and sentence constructions that produce a stylized effect unlike that of standard speech or writing, as in much poetry and poetic prose.

Profanity is language that shows disrespect for someone or something regarded as holy or sacred.

Slang is the everyday language used by group members amongst themselves.

Trite expressions lack depth or originality, or are overworked or not worth mentioning in the first place.

Vulgarity is language that is generally considered common, crude, gross, and, at times, offensive. It is sometimes used in fiction, plays, and films to add realism.

Exposition is the introductory section of a story or play. Typically, the setting, main characters, and themes are introduced, and the action is initiated.

Falling action is the action of a play or story that follows the climax and shows the characters dealing with the climactic event or decision.

Figure of speech is a literary device used to create a special effect or to describe something in a fresh way. The most common types are *antithesis, hyperbole, metaphor, metonymy, personification, simile,* and *understatement.*

Antithesis is an opposition, or contrast, of ideas.

"It was the best of times, it was the worst of times, it was the age of wisdom, it was the age of foolishness ..."

— Charles Dickens, *A Tale of Two Cities*

Hyperbole (hi-pur´ ba-lee) is an extreme exaggeration or overstatement.

"I have seen this river so wide it had only one bank."

—Mark Twain, *Life on the Mississippi*

Metaphor is a comparison of two unlike things in which no word of comparison (*as* or *like*) is used: "Life is a banquet."

Metonymy (ma-ton´a-mee) is the substituting of one term for another that is closely related to it, but not a literal restatement.

"Friends, Romans, countrymen, lend me your ears." (The request is for the *attention* of those assembled, not literally their *ears*.)

Personification is a device in which the author speaks of or describes an animal, object, or idea as if it were a person: "The rock stubbornly refused to move."

Simile is a comparison of two unlike things in which *like* or *as* is used.

"She stood in front of the altar, shaking like a freshly caught trout."

—Maya Angelou, *I Know Why the Caged Bird Sings*

Understatement is stating an idea with restraint, often for humorous effect. Mark Twain described Aunt Polly as being "prejudiced against snakes." (Because she hated snakes, this way of saying so is *understatement*.)

Genre refers to a category or type of literature based on its style, form, and content. The mystery novel is a literary genre.

Imagery refers to words or phrases that a writer uses to appeal to the reader's senses.

"The sky was dark and gloomy, the air was damp and raw, the streets were wet and sloppy."

—Charles Dickens, *The Pickwick Papers*

Irony is a deliberate discrepancy in meaning or in the way something is understood. There are three kinds of irony:

Dramatic irony, in which the reader or the audience sees a character's mistakes or misunderstandings, but the character does not.

Verbal irony, in which the writer says one thing and means another ("The best substitute for experience is being sixteen").

Irony of situation, in which there is a great difference between the purpose of a particular action and the result.

Mood is the feeling that a piece of literature arouses in the reader: happiness, sadness, peacefulness, anxiety, and so forth.

Paradox is a statement that seems contrary to common sense yet may, in fact, be true: "The coach considered this a good loss."

Plot is the action or sequence of events in a story. It is usually a series of related incidents that build upon one another as the story develops. There are five basic elements in a plot line: *exposition, rising action, climax, falling action,* and *resolution.*

Point of view is the vantage point from which the story unfolds.

In the **first-person** point of view, the story is told by one of the characters: "I stepped into the darkened room and felt myself go cold."

In the **third-person** point of view, the story is told by someone outside the story: "He stepped into the darkened room and felt himself go cold."

Third-person narrations can be *omniscient,* meaning that the narrator has access to the thoughts of all the characters, or *limited,* meaning that the narrator focuses on the inner life of one central character.

Protagonist is the main character or hero of the story.

Resolution (or denouement) is the portion of the play or story in which the problem is solved. The resolution comes after the climax and falling action and is intended to bring the story to a satisfactory end.

Rising action is the series of conflicts or struggles that build a story or play toward a fulfilling climax.

Satire is a literary tone used to ridicule or make fun of human vice or weakness, often with the intent of correcting or changing the subject of the satiric attack.

Setting is the time and place in which the action of a literary work occurs.

Structure is the form or organization a writer uses for her or his literary work. A great number of possible forms are used regularly in literature: parable, fable, romance, satire, farce, slapstick, and so on.

Style refers to how the author uses words, phrases, and sentences to form his or her ideas. Style is also thought of as the qualities and characteristics that distinguish one writer's work from the work of others.

Symbol is a person, a place, a thing, or an event used to represent something else. For example, the dove is a symbol of peace.

Theme is the statement about life that a particular work shares with readers. In stories written for children, the theme is often spelled out clearly at the end. In more complex literature, the theme will often be more complicated and will be implied, not stated.

Tone is the overall feeling, or effect, created by a writer's use of words. This feeling may be serious, mock-serious, humorous, satiric, and so on.

LO4 Understand poetic terms.

Your analysis of poems will be more effective if you understand and use the terminology that is specific to creating poetry. Review the quick guide that follows. Then employ it as a reference as you analyze the poetry of others or generate your own.

Quick Guide   Poetic Terms

Alliteration is the repetition of initial consonant sounds in words such as "rough and ready." An example of alliteration is underlined below:

> "Our gang paces the pier like an old myth …"
> —Anne-Marie Oomen, "Runaway Warning"

Assonance is the repetition of vowel sounds without the repetition of consonants.

> "My words like silent rain drops fell …"
> —Paul Simon, "Sounds of Silence"

Blank verse is an unrhymed form of poetry. Each line normally consists of ten syllables in which every other syllable, beginning with the second, is stressed. As blank verse is often used in very long poems, it may depart from the strict pattern from time to time.

Consonance is the repetition of consonant sounds. Although it is very similar to alliteration, consonance is not limited to the first letters of words:

> " …and high school girls with clear-skin smiles …"
> —Janis Ian, "At Seventeen"

Foot is the smallest repeated pattern of stressed and unstressed syllables in a poetic line. (See *verse*.)

  Iambic: an unstressed followed by a stressed syllable (re-peat´)

  Anapestic: two unstressed followed by a stressed syllable (in-ter-rupt´)

  Trochaic: a stressed followed by an unstressed syllable (old´-er)

  Dactylic: a stressed followed by two unstressed syllables (o´-pen-ly)

  Spondaic: two stressed syllables (heart´-break´)

  Pyrrhic: two unstressed syllables (Pyrrhic seldom appears by itself.)

Onomatopoeia is the use of a word whose sound suggests its meaning, as in *clang, buzz,* and *twang*.

Refrain is the repetition of a line or phrase of a poem at regular intervals, especially at the end of each stanza. A song's refrain may be called the *chorus*.

Rhythm is the ordered or free occurrence of sound in poetry. Ordered or regular rhythm is called *meter*. Free occurrence of sound is called *free verse*.

Stanza is a division of poetry named for the number of lines it contains:

  Couplet: two-line stanza
  Triplet: three-line stanza
  Quatrain: four-line stanza
  Quintet: five-line stanza
  Sestet: six-line stanza
  Septet: seven-line stanza
  Octave: eight-line stanza

Verse is a metric line of poetry. It is named according to the kind and number of feet composing it: *iambic pentameter, anapestic tetrameter,* and so on. (See *foot.*)

  Monometer: one foot
  Dimeter: two feet
  Trimeter: three feet
  Tetrameter: four feet
  Pentameter: five feet
  Hexameter: six feet
  Heptameter: seven feet
  Octometer: eight feet

{ Speak Up! }

COMP: Write was built on a simple principle: to create new teaching and learning solution that reflects the way today's faculty teach and the way you learn.

Through conversations, focus groups, surveys, and interviews, we collected data that drove the creation of the current version of **COMP: Write** that you are using today. But it doesn't stop there. In order to make **COMP: Write** an even better learning experience, we'd like you to **SPEAK UP** and tell us how **COMP: Write** worked for you. What did you like about it? What would you change? Are there additional ideas you have that would help us build a better product for next semester's freshman composition students?

At **4ltrpress.cengage.com/comp,** you'll find a survey form to send us your comments—in addition to all of the resources you need to become a confident and effective writer.

Speak Up! Go to **4ltrpress.cengage.com/comp** today.

"Writing is not only alive
and well in the business world, but writing whose style reflects flair,
eloquence, and a confident sense of self can springboard employees
forward in their careers."

—Christine Mowat

15

Workplace

Imagine you are applying for a position as a writer, and the interviewer says, "Please rewire this wall outlet," or "Please play **'La Marseillaise'** on this accordion," or "Please check my blood pressure." You would probably object. After all, why does a writer need to know how to rewire an outlet, play an accordion, or check blood pressure?

Now imagine you are applying for a job as an electrician, an accordion player, or a nurse, and the interviewer says, "Please fill out this application and provide a résumé showing your past experience." You would do it. That's because just about every job requires you to write well.

Why is that? It's because writing is the lifeblood of business. When you apply for a job, you write a résumé and cover letter. When you get a job, you record your daily activities and write e-mails to colleagues and clients. When you come up with an idea for improving a process, system, product, or service, you write up the idea. When you vie for a promotion, you write to convince your boss that you deserve it.

In business, writing always serves two functions: it communicates your ideas to a reader and it also represents you when you are absent. That's why businesspeople who can express themselves well in writing have an easier time landing jobs, doing their jobs, and rising through the corporate structure.

This chapter provides guidelines and models for creating the basic forms of workplace writing such as e-mails, memos, and letters. You'll also find help with formal business documents such as application essays and résumés.

Learning Outcomes

LO1 Create correspondence.

LO2 Correctly format a letter.

LO3 Write an application essay.

LO4 Prepare a résumé.

What do you think?

Electricians, accordion players, and nurses need to be able to write.

1	2	3	4	5
strongly agree				strongly disagree

"La Marseillaise"
the song of Marseille; the national anthem of France

LO1 Create correspondence.

Your goal is to effectively and appropriately communicate an idea through business correspondence, whether via text message, e-mail, memo, or letter.

1. Understand the writing situation. Think about your subject, purpose, and audience:

Subject: What are you writing about? Is the message public or private? Does it need an immediate response? Should it be documented?

Purpose: Why you are writing? What do you want the writing to accomplish? What do you want the reader to do?

Audience: Who is your reader? Will there be multiple readers? What does your reader know and need to know? How will the reader feel about the message?

2. Select an appropriate form. Consider the **continuum of communication** and choose the form that best fits the writing situation.

Continuum of Communication

Informal (Quick)

Continuum of Forms	Online Chat
	Text Message
	E-Mail
	Memo
	Letter

Formal (Deliberate)

continuum of communication
a list of written communication options from informal to formal

3. Write your main point. In one or two sentences, write the main thing you want your reader to know. For more informal types of communication, this may be the totality of your message—but make sure to reread it before pressing "Send."

4. Gather details. For more formal and complex messages, gather details that support your main point. Think about what the reader knows and needs to know.

5. Write a first draft. Follow the format of the medium you have chosen—e-mail, memo, or letter. (For specific formats, see pages 175–180.) Organize your details based on the reader's likely response.

Good/Neutral News: After politely greeting your reader, state your main point and provide supporting details. This approach also works for complaint letters, in which it is important to state the problem directly.

Bad News: Politely greet your reader and provide a buffer statement that emphasizes something neutral or positive in the business relationship. Give an explanation that leads to the bad news, and then exit gracefully.

Persuasion: Politely greet the reader and capture her or his attention. Then build interest and desire and lead to your main point—a call to action.

6. Revise and edit your writing. For any business correspondence as formal as an e-mail message, be sure to read over what you have written to decide whether it clearly communicates your message. Add, delete, rearrange, and rewrite as needed. Also carefully check punctuation, capitalization, spelling, and grammar. Remember that a business message represents you when you are not there. Sending an error-filled message reflects poorly on you.

AN E-MAIL OUTREACH

The following e-mail message from Sherry West is addressed to the members of the student outreach committee at St. George's University. Note the use of a salutation and closing, the short paragraphs, and the position of the main point in the first sentence.

SQ3R
Survey Question Read Recite Review

From: "Sherry West" SWEST@stgeorge.edu
Subject: Agenda for Student Outreach Committee Meeting
Date: Mon, 21 Sept 2009 14:13:06 CST
To: outreach@stgeorge.edu

Hi, everybody:

Please remember that our next meeting is this Wednesday, Sept. 24, at 8:00 p.m. in SUB Room 201. We'll discuss the following agenda items:

1. The minutes of our Sept. 10 meeting
2. A proposal from SADD about Alcohol Awareness Week
3. A progress report on the Habitat for Humanity project

Before the meeting, please review the minutes and the SADD proposal attached to this message.

Thanks,
Sherry

EFFECTIVE E-MAIL CREATION

An e-mail message allows instant communication through computer networks across the globe. E-mail messages have increasingly replaced formal business letters as the workhorses of business, and since they are permanent and can be subpoenaed, they require more care than most people give them. Use the following tips to get the most out of e-mail.

TIP

Stick to facts. Use e-mail to provide specific facts such as meeting times and locations, the results of surveys, or changes in procedures. Avoid e-mail in emotionally charged or sensitive situations, in which the context cues of tone of voice and facial expression are vital to clear communication.

Provide a clear subject line. Capitalize the first word and the first letter in each important word thereafter (not articles or short prepositions). Include key words so readers can search for e-mail messages.

Select readers carefully. Address e-mails only to those who need to be in on the conversation. Very rarely (such as alerting readers to your address change) should you send e-mails to your whole address book. For large mailings, consider sending

the message to yourself and placing all other receivers in the BCC (blind carbon copy) line, to protect their e-mail addresses.

Use short paragraphs and lists. E-mails are meant to be scanned. Keep them succinct, and use bulleted or numbered lists for important details.

Carefully revise and edit your message before clicking "send." A carefully revised e-mail provides a permanent record of clear communication. A poorly revised e-mail provides a permanent record of miscommunication.

Err on the side of caution. Remember that an e-mail can immediately go to hundreds or thousands of other recipients. Do not write something that you would be embarrassed to see on a billboard, because it could well end up there.

Provide appropriate attachments. Place long, complex information in an attachment rather than in the e-mail itself. Use widely accepted file formats and avoid e-mailing files that are gigantic.

A WRITING LAB MEMO

The following memo from Kerri Kelley was posted at the front entrance to the Bascom Hill Writing Lab, announcing changes to hours, new computers, and upcoming holidays.

SQ3R
Survey Question Read Recite Review

Date: September 25, 2009

To: All Users of the Bascom Hill Writing Lab

From: Kerri Kelley, Coordinator

(A) Subject: New Hours/New Equipment

(B) Beginning October 3, the Bascom Hill Writing Lab will expand its weekend hours as follows: Fridays, 7:00 A.M.–11:00 P.M.; Saturdays, 8:00 A.M.–11:00 P.M.

Also, six additional computers will be installed next week, making it easier to get computer time. We hope these changes will help meet the increased demand for time and assistance we've experienced this fall. Remember, it's still a good idea to sign up in advance. To reserve time, call the lab at 462–7722 or leave your request at bhill@madwis.edu.

(C) Finally, long-range planners, mark your calendars. The lab will be closed on Thanksgiving Day morning and open from 1:00 P.M. to 11:00 P.M. We will also be closed on Christmas and New Year's Day. We will post our semester-break hours sometime next month.

(A) The subject line clarifies the memo's purpose.
(B) The main point is stated immediately.
(C) Readers are asked to take note of a few final facts.

EFFECTIVE MEMO CREATION

A memorandum is a written message sent from one person to one or more other people within the same organization. It can vary in length from a sentence or two to a four- or five-page report. As such, it is more formal than an e-mail message but may be less formal than a business letter. A memo can be delivered in person, dropped in a mailbox, or sent via e-mail.

When to Use Memos

Use memos when e-mail won't serve. For longer, more complex issues, use a memo and attach it to an e-mail. For messages to people for whom you do not have e-mail addresses (as in the example), create a memo. For confidential information, create a memo, mark it "CONFIDENTIAL," and distribute it on paper only to those who need to see it.

Remember:
Use clear organization. Create a concise subject line so that the topic is clear and the memo is easy to file. Write short paragraphs and use lists when helpful.

LO2 Correctly format a letter.

Your goal is to create a business letter that gets your message across and follows correct business letter format. Letters are more formal than e-mail messages.

1. Heading The heading gives the writer's complete address, either in the letterhead (company stationery) or typed out, followed by the date.

2. Inside Address The **inside address** gives the reader's name and address.

• If you're not sure which person to address or how to spell someone's name, you could call the company or check its Web site for the information.

• If the person's title is a single word, place it after the name, separated by a comma (Mary Johnson, President). Place a longer title on a separate line.

3. Salutation The **salutation** begins with *Dear* and ends with a colon, not a comma.

• Use *Mr.* or *Ms.* plus the person's last name, unless you are well acquainted. Do not guess at *Miss* or *Mrs.*

• If you can't get the person's name, replace the salutation with *Dear* or *Attention* followed by the title of an appropriate reader (*Dear Dean of Students:* or *Attention: Personnel Manager*).

Note: See pages 75–77 for a complete list of "unbiased" ways to refer to an individual or a particular group.

4. Body The body should consist of single-spaced paragraphs with double-spacing between paragraphs. (Do not indent the paragraphs.)

• If the body goes to a second page, put the reader's name at the top left, the number 2 in the center, and the date at the right margin.

5. Complimentary Closing For the **complimentary closing**, use *Sincerely, Yours sincerely,* or *Yours truly* followed by a comma; use *Best wishes* if you know the person well.

6. Signature The signature includes the writer's name, both handwritten and keyed.

7. Initials When someone keys the letter for the writer, that person's initials appear (in lowercase) after the writer's initials (in capitals), separated by a colon.

8. Enclosure If a document (brochure, form, copy, or other form) is enclosed with the letter, the word *Enclosure* or *Encl.* appears below the initials.

9. Copies If a copy of the letter is sent elsewhere, type *cc:* beneath the enclosure line, followed by the person's or department's name.

inside address
the reader's name and address

salutation
the greeting in a letter; the line that begins *Dear*

complimentary closing
the polite sign-off line of a letter, following the body and preceding the signature

A LETTER OF INVITATION

The following letter was written by Dave Vetter, president of the Earth Care Club on Balliole College Campus.

SQ3R
Survey Question Read Recite Review

Heading

Box 143
Balliole College
Eugene, OR 97440–5125
August 28, 2009

Four to Seven Spaces

Note:
This letter's purpose is to persuade the reader to join a club. The writer captures the reader's attention, builds interest, and calls for a response or an action.

Inside Address

Ms. Ada Overlie
Ogg Hall, Room 222
Balliole College
Eugene, OR 97440–0222

Double Space

Salutation

Dear Ms. Overlie:

Double Space

As the president of the Earth Care Club, I welcome you to Balliole Community College. I hope the year will be a great learning experience both inside and outside the classroom.

Double Space

Body

That learning experience is the reason I'm writing—to encourage you to join the Earth Care Club. As a member, you could participate in the educational and action-oriented mission of the club. The club has most recently been involved in the following:

- Organizing a reduce, reuse, recycle program on campus

- Promoting cloth rather than plastic bag use among students

- Giving input to the college administration on landscaping, renovating, and building for energy efficiency

- Putting together the annual Earth Day celebration

Double Space

Which environmental concerns and activities would you like to focus on? Bring them with you to the Earth Care Club. Simply complete the enclosed form and return it by September 8. Then watch the campus news for details on our first meeting.

Double Space

Complimentary Closing and Signature

Yours sincerely,

Dave Vetter **Four Spaces**

Dave Vetter
President

Double Space

Initials Enclosures Copies

DW:kr
Encl. membership form
cc: Esther du Toit, membership committee

A LETTER OF APPLICATION

Your letter of application (or cover letter) introduces you to an employer and often highlights information on an accompanying résumé.

© Used under license from Shutterstock.com

Ogg Hall, Room 222
Balliole College
Eugene, OR 97440–0222
April 17, 2009

Address a specific person, if possible.

Professor Edward Mahaffy
Greenhouse Coordinator
Balliole College
Eugene, OR 97440–0316

Note:
Your goal in writing this type of letter is to convince an employer to invite you for an interview.

© Used under license from Shutterstock.com

Dear Professor Mahaffy:

State the desired position and your chief qualification.

I recently talked with Ms. Sierra Benning in the Financial Aid Office about work-study jobs for 2009–2010. She told me about the Greenhouse Assistant position and gave me a job description. As a full-time Balliole student, I'm writing to apply for this position. I believe that my experience qualifies me for the job.

Focus on how your skills meet the reader's needs.

As you can see from my résumé, I spent two summers working in a raspberry operation, doing basic plant care and carrying out quality-control lab tests on the fruit. Also, as I was growing up, I learned a great deal by helping with a large farm garden. In high school and college, I studied botany. Because of my interest in this field, I'm enrolled in the Environmental Studies program at Balliole.

Request an interview and thank the reader.

I am available for an interview. You may phone me any time at 341–3611 (and leave a message on my machine) or e-mail me at dvrl@balliole.edu. Thank you for considering my application.

Yours sincerely,

Ada Overlie

Ada Overlie

Encl. résumé

© Used under license from Shutterstock.com

A RECOMMENDATION REQUEST

When you apply for a job or program, present references or recommendations to show your fitness for the position.

SQ3R
Survey Question Read Recite Review

Note:

To get support from people familiar with your work (instructors and employers), you need to ask for it. You can do so in person or by phone, but a courteous and clear letter or e-mail message makes your request official and helps the person complete the recommendation effectively.

2456 Charles Street
Lexington, KY 40588–8321
March 21, 2009

Dr. Rosa Perez
271 University Boulevard
University of Kentucky
Lexington, KY 40506–1440

Dear Dr. Perez:

Present your request.

As we discussed on the phone, I would appreciate your writing a recommendation letter for me. You know the quality of my academic work, my qualities as a person, and my potential for working in the medical field.

Explain the situation.

As my professor for Biology 201 and 202, you are familiar with my grades and work habits. As my adviser, you know my career plans and should have a good sense of whether I have the qualities needed to succeed in the medical profession. I am asking you for your recommendation because I am applying for summer employment with the Lexington Ambulance Service. I recently received my Emergency Medical Technician (Basic) license to prepare for such work.

Provide necessary details.

Please send your letter to Rick Falk, EMT Coordinator, at the University Placement Office by April 8. Thank you for your help. Let me know if you need any other information (phone 231–6700; e-mail jnwllms@ukentucky.edu).

Yours sincerely,

Jon Williams

Jon Williams

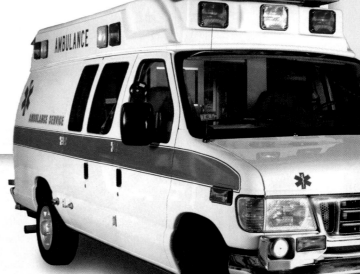

LO3 Write an application essay.

Your goal in writing an **application essay** is, of course, to convince the reader to accept your application. You may be applying for admission to an academic program (social work, engineering, optometry school) or for an internship, a scholarship, or a research grant. Whatever the situation, what you write and how well you write it will be important factors in the success of your application.

1. Analyze the situation. Carefully read any instructions for writing the essay. Then think about your subject, purpose, and audience.

Subject: What topics are you asked to write about? What position are you applying for? What qualities suit you for the position?

Purpose: How can you convince the reader that your application should be accepted?

Audience: Who will read your application essay? What does the person know about you (from other documents included)? What does the person want in an applicant?

2. Gather details. To gather the details for your essay, answer the questions below:

Ask

- What **topic** should I focus on in my essay?
- What is the **position** I am applying for?
- What **qualities** would an ideal candidate have?
- What **qualities** do I have?
- What **education** prepares me for the position?
- What **experiences** prepare me for it?
- What **special skills** do I have?
- What **factors** set me apart from other applicants?

3. Write your first draft. Carefully reread the instructions for writing the essay, making sure you are on topic. Also note any directions about organization, emphasis, style, length, and method of submission. Then create a three-part structure:

An **opening** with a fresh, interesting starting statement and a clear focus or theme

A **middle** that develops the focus or theme clearly and concisely—with some details and examples—in a way appropriate to the instructions

A **closing** that stresses a positive point and looks forward to participating in the program, internship, organization, or position

4. Revise your essay. Once again, reread the instructions for writing the essay, and then review your essay. If possible, ask a peer or an adviser to read the instructions and essay and provide revision suggestions. Answer the questions below:

Ask

- Does my essay match the instructions?
- Are my topic and focus clear and effective?
- Have I created an effective three-part structure?
- Is my voice personal but professional?
- Does my word choice fit the writing situation, and have I avoided cliches?
- Do my sentences read smoothly?

5. Edit and submit your essay. Check your essay for errors in punctuation, capitalization, spelling, and grammar. Also make sure the essay follows any presentation suggestions made in the directions—margins, font, spacing, and so forth. Follow the instructions about submitting the essay, whether on paper or online.

application essay
a reflective essay that focuses on experiences and qualities that suit the writer for a specific position or program

AN APPLICATION ESSAY

In the application essay below, Jessy Jezowski demonstrates the qualities and experiences that have prepared and encouraged her to study social work.

SQ3R
Survey Question Read Recite Review

February 27, 2009
Jessy Jezowski

Personal Statement

> The opening provides a clear focus for the essay.

While growing up in Chicago, I would see people hanging out on street corners, by grocery stores, and in parks—with no home and barely any belongings. Poverty and its related problems are all around us, and yet most people walk by them with blinders on. I have found myself quick to assume that someone else will help the poor man on the corner, the woman trapped in an abusive relationship, or the teenager struggling with an eating disorder. But I know in my heart that all members of society are responsible to and for each other. Social welfare issues affect every member of society—including me.

> The writer demonstrates knowledge of the field and explains what she hopes to learn.

Because these issues are serious and difficult to solve, I wish to major in social work and eventually become a social worker. In the major, I want to gain the knowledge, skills, and attitudes that will make me part of the solution, not part of the problem. By studying social work institutions, the practices of social work, and the theory and history behind social work, I hope to learn how to help people help themselves. When that pregnant teenager comes to me, I want to have strong, practical advice—and be part of an effective social work agency that can help that teen implement the advice.

> Two concrete examples help back up her general statements.

I am especially interested at this point in working with families and teenagers, in either a community counseling or school setting. Two experiences have created this interest. First, a woman in my church who works for an adoption agency, Ms. Lesage, has modeled for me what it means to care for individuals and families within a community and around the world. Second, I was involved in a peer counseling program in high school. As counselors, we received training in interpersonal relationships and the nature of helping. In a concrete way, I experienced the complex challenges of helping others.

> The conclusion summarizes her goals for the future.

I believe strongly in the value of all people and am interested in the well-being of others. As a social worker, I would strive to make society better (for individuals, families, and communities) by serving those in need, whatever their problems.

LO4 Prepare a résumé.

Your goal is to create a **résumé** that presents a vivid word picture of your skills, knowledge, and past responsibilities. The résumé should say exactly who you are. Though most people start with a general résumé filled with all their vital information, you should also customize this résumé to target each specific job application.

1. Consider the writing situation. What job are you applying for? What company or organization are you seeking to join? Who will be reading your résumé? What qualities will the person want to see in a strong candidate? What qualities best suit you for the position?

2. Gather details. Study any job announcements you can find for the position. Then write down specific information—numbers, dates, and names—about your qualifications. Also make sure to note awards, honors, licenses, certifications, and extracurricular involvement. Then summarize skills that you have that relate to the job you are applying for.

3. Create a first draft. Supply information for each of the categories below. Reorder the "Skills Summary," "Experience," and "Education" sections as needed to place the most impressive or important information first.

Personal Data: name, address, phone number, e-mail address (enough for the reader to identify you and reach you easily)

Job Objective: the type of position you want and the type of organization for which you want to work

Skills Summary: the key qualities and skills you bring to a position, listed with supporting details

Skill Areas to Consider

- Communication
- Management (people, money, other resources)
- Organization
- Working with people, counseling, training
- Problem solving
- Sales, marketing, public relations
- Computer
- Languages

Experience: positions you've held (where and when), your specific duties, and your accomplishments

Education: degrees, courses, and special projects

Other Experiences: volunteer work, awards, achievements, tutoring jobs, extracurricular activities (related to your job objective), licenses, and certifications

4. Revise your first draft. Reread the job announcement and your résumé. If possible, ask a peer or an adviser to review the announcement and résumé and offer suggestions for revision. Ask the following questions:

Ask

- Does my résumé paint a vivid word picture of my skills, knowledge, and past responsibilities?
- Does the résumé target the specific job I am applying for?
- Have I used everyday language and short, concise phrases?
- Are my lists parallel (similar items have similar structures)?
- Have I used boldface type, underlining, white space, and indentations for readability?

5. Edit and submit your résumé. Carefully edit your résumé, correcting any factual errors as well as errors in punctuation, capitalization, spelling, and grammar. Also carefully proofread your writing. Follow any formatting instructions in the original job announcement and submit your résumé in the way indicated in the announcement.

fyi Often, résumés are submitted electronically. For a résumé attached to an e-mail, provide the document in an easy-to-read format, such as **RTF** (rich text file) or **PDF** (portable document file). For a résumé pasted into a job-search engine, remove special coding and make sure the résumé features search terms drawn from the job announcement (position title, skill requirements, educational requirements, and so forth). See page 185 for a sample digital résumé.

résumé
a document that outlines a person's job objective, skills, experience, and education; a curriculum vitae (cv)

RTF
rich text file; a file format that preserves basic formatting such as bolds, italics, and tabs but is readable by most word processors

PDF
portable document file; a file format that preserves a document according to its exact appearance and is readable using Adobe Reader software

A PRINT RÉSUMÉ

In the following résumé, the writer itemizes the skills, experience, and education that qualify her for a job.

Ada Overlie

Present contact information and employment objectives.

Home	**School**
451 Wiser Lake Road	Ogg Hall, Room 222
Ferndale, WA 98248–8941	Balliole College
(360) 354–5916	Eugene, OR 97440–0222
	Phone: (503) 341–3611
	E-mail: dvrl@balliole.edu

Job Objective: Part-time assistant in a nursery or greenhouse.

Feature skills with appropriate headings and lists.

Skills Summary:

Horticultural Skills: Familiar with garden planting, care, and harvesting practices—planning, timing, companion planting, fertilizing.

Lab Skills: Familiar with procedures for taking fruit samples, pureeing them, checking for foreign objects, and testing sugar content.

List work and education chronologically, from most to least current.

Experience:

Summers 2008 and 2009: Lab Technician.
   Mayberry Farms and Processing Plant, Ferndale, WA.
   Worked in Quality Control testing raspberries to make sure they met company standards.

Summers 2006 and 2007: Camp Counselor.
   Emerald Lake Summer Camp, Hillsboro, WA.
   Supervised 12–year-olds in many camp activities, including nature hikes in which we identified plants and trees.

Education:

August 2008 to present: Balliole College, Eugene, OR.
   Environmental Studies and Communication major.
   Courses completed and in progress include environmental studies and general botany. First semester GPA 3.7.

Format:
Use boldface, underlining, bulleted or indented lists, and two-column structure only in a printed résumé.

August 2004 to June 2008: Ferndale High School, Ferndale, WA.
   Courses included biology, agriculture, U.S. government, and economics.
   Special Projects: Completed research papers on clean-water legislation and organic-farming practices.

Offer references.

References available upon request.

A DIGITAL RÉSUMÉ

To find employees, companies often use computer programs to search electronic résumés for keywords (especially nouns) found in job descriptions or ads.

SQ3R
Survey Question Read Recite Review

Note:
Anticipating an electronic search, the writer identifies key words in the job description and inserts them into his résumé.

Present contact information and employment objective.

Jonathan L. Greenlind
806 5th Avenue
Waterloo, Iowa 50701
Telephone: 319.268.6955
E-Mail: grnlnd@aol.com

OBJECTIVE
Position as hydraulics supervisor that calls for hydraulics expertise, technical skills, mechanical knowledge, reliability, and enthusiasm

List skills, experiences, and education using many keywords.

SKILLS
Operation and repair specialist in main and auxiliary power systems, subsystems, landing gears, brakes and pneumatic systems, hydraulic motors, reservoirs, actuators, pumps and cylinders from six types of hydraulic systems
Dependable, resourceful, strong leader, team worker

E-mail format:
- one column
- asterisks as bullets
- simple sans serif typeface
- flush-left margin
- no italics, boldface, or underlining
- ASCII or RTF text (readable by all computers)

EXPERIENCE
Aviation Hydraulics Technician
United States Navy (2003–present)
* Repair, test, and maintain basic hydraulics, distribution systems, and aircraft structural hydraulics systems
* Manufacture low-, medium-, and high-pressure rubber and Teflon hydraulic hoses and aluminum stainless-steel tubing
* Perform preflight, postflight, and other periodic aircraft inspections
* Operate ground-support equipment
* Supervise personnel
Aircraft Mechanic
Sioux Falls International Airport (2001–2003)
Sioux Falls, South Dakota
* Performed fueling, engine overhauls, minor repairs, and tire and oil changes of various aircraft

EDUCATION
* United States Navy (2003–2007)
* Certificate in Hydraulic Technical School "A", GPA 3.8/4.0
* Certificate in Hydraulic, Pneumatic Test Stand School, GPA 3.9/4.0
* Courses in Corrosion Control, Hydraulic Tube Bender, Aviation Structural Mechanics
* Equivalent of 10 semester hours in Hydraulic Systems Maintenance and Structural Repair

Offer references.

References available upon request.

"**When I took office,**
only high-energy physicists had ever heard of what is
called the Worldwide Web. . . . Now even my cat has its
own page."
—Bill Clinton

16

Web

You probably don't remember a world without the Web. It was a very different world. Before the Web, few people had access to cat videos. People had no way to find out if Abe Vigoda was alive or dead. And the only people who knew what Ashton Kutcher had for breakfast were Ashton and his mom.

Yes, the Web has changed life in many ways—trivial and profound. Google and Wikipedia changed the way the world finds answers, YouTube and iTunes changed the way the world entertains itself, Amazon and E-Bay changed the way the world buys and sells, and Facebook and Twitter changed the way the world connects.

Over the course of two centuries, the Industrial Revolution transformed our country from an agrarian society to a society of factories and stores. Over the course of just two decades, the Information Revolution is transforming our country from a society of factories and stores to a society of online goods and services. The world will never be the same, and you are a product of that world.

The letters www in many Web addresses stand for "World Wide Web," but perhaps they should stand for "Web-Wide World"—the only world you'll ever know. Since this is your world, it's crucial that you understand how to write and design for the Web. This chapter will show you how.

Learning Outcomes

LO1 Understand page elements.

LO2 Develop a Web site.

LO3 Consider sample sites.

LO4 Understand other writing venues.

What do you think?

I remember a world
without the Web.

1   2   3   4   5

strongly agree   strongly disagree

LO1 Understand page elements.

To design an effective Web site and develop dynamic Web pages, you need to start with a basic understanding of page elements and functions. Because Web pages use the same elements as printed pages, many of the same design principles apply. However, unlike printed pages, Web pages are fluid (flowing their contents to match screen and browser settings), and they can include both elements and functions, as shown and discussed below and on the pages that follow.

PAGE ELEMENTS

On the Web, page elements are defined primarily by purpose—headings, body text, image, and so forth. Before designing a Web page, it helps to understand the purpose of those elements.

Because readers can scan them quickly, lists are an efficient way to present information.

- **Images** Images can include photographs, clip art, graphs, line drawings, cartoon figures, icons, and animations. These can make a page much slower to display, so use them judiciously. Always be sure you have the legal right to use any images that you include in your pages. (See "Avoiding Copyright Violations Strategy," page 244.)

- **Background** Background color for a Web page is white by default (medium gray in older browsers), but, as shown below, dark backgrounds also can work.

- **Tables** Tables are a common tool for Web page layout. Simply put, tables are grids made up of rows and columns. By creating a table with no visible borders, a Web designer can gain some control over where elements appear on a page.

- **Headings** Headings (also called headers) come in six levels and are used to separate different sections and subsections of Web documents. Heading 1 is the largest; heading 6 is the smallest.

- **Body text** Body text is organized into chunks, called paragraphs, which are separated by white space. Unlike printed text, paragraphs on the Web do not generally have a first-line indentation. By default, body text is a black serif font roughly the same size as a heading level 4 (though not bold).

- **Preformatted** Preformatted text is "monospaced"; it displays all characters at the same width, like typewriter font. It is used primarily to show mathematical formulas, computer code, and the like.

- **Lists** Lists can be formatted in three types: Ordered lists are numbered, unordered lists are bulleted, and definition lists present pairs of information—usually terms alongside their definitions, which are indented.

Sample Web Page

Images courtesy of The Museum of Flight and Heath Moffett, photographer.

(A) Clear title
(B) Major sections
(C) Concise text
(D) Feature graphic
(E) Topic heading
(F) Feature heading
(G) Concise text
(H) Plain background for legibility

Remember that . . .

It's not always black and white. Not all Web pages have black serif font on a white background. However, because Web browsers are designed to flow content to suit each computer screen, changing the default styles can be problematic.

Simple is best. Simple pages display the fastest and have the least chance of breaking. The more graphics you add, the longer a page takes to load. The more you change the default font settings, the more complicated the code becomes and the greater the chance of computer error.

Different computers display things differently. Not every computer has the same font styles installed, and colors look different on different monitors. Always check your work on many different systems.

The user is king (or queen). No matter which font style and size you choose, the reader can change how things display on her or his machine. So focus on useful content and clear organization instead of struggling to control graphic design.

PAGE FUNCTIONS

Web-page functions set electronic pages apart from printed pages. On the Web, readers can browse pages in almost any order, send and receive e-mail, send messages and files, post messages, and join live "chat" sessions. In short, readers can interact with Web pages in ways they cannot with printed pages. Like Web-page elements, Web-page functions should serve your site's purpose.

• **Hyperlinks** Hyperlinks are strings of specially formatted text that enable readers to jump to another spot on the Web. Internal hyperlinks (links for short) take you to another section of the same Web page or to another page on the same site. External links lead to pages on other Web sites. "Mail to" links allow readers to address e-mail to recipients, such as a professor or a classmate.

• **Menus** Menus offer structured lists of links that operate like a Web site's table of contents. Menus are typically presented in a column or row at the edge of a Web page. Good Web sites include a standard site menu on every page so readers don't get lost.

• **Forms** Forms enable the host of a Web site to interact with the site's readers. Web forms can be used for questionnaires, surveys, complaints and service requests, job applications, or suggestion boxes.

LO2 Develop a Web site.

Regardless of the subject, purpose, or audience, you can develop an effective and attractive Web site.

MANAGING THE SITE ZONES

When you write an essay, you make a plan, usually during the prewriting step. Developing a Web site requires that you make a plan as well. The following pages will take you through six planning steps, from creating an overview for your Web site to thinking about which support materials to include.

Create an overview.

Create an overview of the project—the subject, the purpose, and the audience. The questions below will help you get focused and develop fitting content for the site.

What is the site's central subject? What do I already know about the subject? What do I need to learn, and where can I find the information? How will I demonstrate that the information is credible and reliable? What will my audience want to know about the subject? How can I divide the information into brief segments? What visual elements would help present my message? Which other Web sites address this subject? Should my Web site link to them?

What is the primary purpose of the site? Am I creating a library of documents that my audience will reference? Am I going to present information and announcements about myself or my organization? Am I trying to promote a specific product or service?

hyperlinks
specially formatted text that enables readers to click to another spot on the Web

menus
structured lists of links that operate like a Web site's table of contents

forms
questionnaires, surveys, suggestion boxes, and other features that allow visitors to Web sites to interact with the host

Who is the site's audience? Which people will seek out this site? Why? What do they need? How often will they visit the site, and how often should it be updated? How comfortable is my audience with using computers and Web sites? What level of language—formal or informal—is appropriate? Which graphics, colors, and design will appeal to my audience?

Establish your central message.

After you've made decisions about your subject, purpose, and audience, write out the main idea you want to communicate. You might call this the theme or "mission statement" of your Web site.

> The purpose of this Web site is to inform fellow students and the general public about current research into hybrid-vehicle transportation.

To help you stay on target with your project, post this mission statement in plain sight. Note, too, that you might modify your goal as the site develops, or add secondary goals for the site.

Create a site map.

As you gather content for your site, create a site map. Web sites can be as simple as an elementary school bulletin board or as complex as a United States federal government site. Here are four principles to keep in mind:

No one will read your entire site. People curl up with books, not Web sites. If your audience is not asking for content, don't provide it.

Your site will have many small audiences—not one big audience. A site's audience may include anyone with a computer, an Internet connection, and an interest in your site's subject. Keep all potential readers in mind.

Web sites are not linear. A single "home page" or "splash page" introduces the site, which branches out like tree limbs into pages with varied content. Web sites "conclude" whenever the reader quits reading.

You may need to build the site in phases. You can add pages to a Web site after it has been published, so be careful that your site's organization does not limit future additions.

Sample Site Map

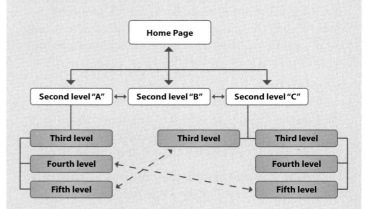

A map for a simple site might include only four items—a home page, page "A," page "B," and page "C" (as shown in white on the diagram). Users can "jump" between any of the secondary-level pages or back to the home page.

A more complex Web site typically needs more levels (as shown in green on the diagram). Likewise, its menu will offer more navigation choices. Related pages might be connected with links (as represented by the dotted lines).

Study similar sites.

Learn from successful sites, especially sites that serve a similar purpose—a campus club site, a department site, a personal job-search site. How do similar sites use elements: headings, body text, preformatted text, background color, lists, images, and tables? How do the sites use functions—links, menus, and forms? The seven traits can also supply helpful benchmarks for evaluating sites.

1. **Ideas:** Does the site present clear ideas and information?

2. **Organization:** Is the content carefully and clearly structured?

3. **Voice:** Is the tone fitting for the subject and audience?

4. **Words:** Is the language understandable? Is the wording concise?

5. **Sentences:** Are the sentences easy to read and generally short?

6. **Correctness:** Does the site avoid distracting errors?

7. **Design:** Are the pages user friendly? Is the site easy to navigate?

Gather and prioritize content.

Brainstorm and research the actual content, with the goal of creating an outline for your site. How many topics will the site address? How wide will your coverage of a topic be? How deep? Your outline can also be used to create the Web site's table of contents. Based on your research, discussions with others, and the deadlines for the project, select the content, features, and functions your site will offer.

Think about support materials.

List the documents (brochures, artwork, instructions, poems, reports) that will be presented on your site and note whether they will be displayed as Web pages, made available for readers to download, or both. Construct a grid to keep track of how documents will be used.

List graphics that could make your pages more visual and informative and could help readers grasp the meaning of complex data or processes. Photographs may help "put a face" on your organization. Logos and icons will help brand your pages. Review the list below for electronic files that may be appropriate to your topic, audience, and purpose. (Remember: Use only graphics that are legally available. See the discussion of copyright on page 244.)

Images	Audio	Video
charts	music	animations
drawings	sound effects	film clips
graphs	spoken text	presentations
photographs		webcasts

DESIGN AND DRAFT PAGES.

When you actually create individual pages for your site, consider both the design and the content—specifically, how to make the two work well together.

Design

As you design your Web pages, consider certain design principles. Most Web pages—and the pages of most other publications—are designed on grids. Look at any newspaper or magazine page, and you should be able to draw horizontal and vertical lines denoting columns and rows of content. Some rows may span multiple columns, and some columns may overrun several rows.

Another fundamental design concept is balance. You might balance light elements with dark ones, text with images, and so forth. The balance of your page design should be driven by the purpose of your Web site, its audience, and its topic.

Web sites may contain a variety of pages—each one tailored to different purposes, audiences, and topics—to present some combination of informational and promotional content. Use each page's purpose to guide decisions about which elements and functions to include.

Drafting

Keep the following principles in mind as you go about the business of drafting the content for your Web site.

Identify the site. Working from your mission statement, write a brief introduction informing visitors about the site's purpose.

Provide clear links. Create links for your pages, using clear descriptors such as "Original Poetry." (Avoid phrases such as "Click here for poetry.") If necessary, add a descriptive sentence to further identify the link. Let visitors know precisely where each link will take them.

Introduce each page. Search sites may deliver some visitors to a page on your site other than the home page. Give each page a brief introduction that clearly identifies it. Also, remember to provide a link back to your home page.

Title each page. Atop the browser window is a title bar where the current page should be identified. This title is used in browser bookmarks, search engine listings, and the like, so be sure to give every page on your Web site a descriptive title.

Keep pages uncluttered. Dense text is even more difficult to read on screen than on paper, so use short paragraphs when you can. Add headings to identify sections, and include visuals to help break up the text.

Save the page as HTML. To be viewed in a Web browser, your pages must be formatted in hypertext markup language (HTML). Your word processor may have a "Save as HTML" or "Save as Web page" option. Many HTML editing programs are also available on the Web.

TEST, REFINE, AND POST YOUR SITE.

Most Web sites are developed through the combined efforts of writers, graphic designers, and programmers. In such an environment, many content and layout ideas might be considered, rejected, and reformulated to produce and launch the site. Of course, the audience ultimately decides a Web site's success or failure. For that reason, test and refine your site before posting it.

Check the site yourself. Open your home page from your Web browser. Does the site make sense? Can you navigate it easily?

Get peer review. Ask classmates—both experienced and inexperienced with the Web site's topic and with Internet searching—to use your site. Watch them navigate it, and take notes about any confusion they have.

Check the text. Reread all the text on your site. Trim wherever possible (the shorter, the better online), and check all spelling and punctuation.

Check the graphics. Do images load properly? Do they load quickly? Are menus and page headings in the same place on every page?

Provide a feedback link. Provide your e-mail address on the site, inviting visitors to contact you with any comments after the site goes "live."

Post the site. Upload the site to your hosting space. (Check your host's instructions for doing so.) Add the posting date to each page and update it each time you change a page.

Check for universality. View the site on several different types of computers, using different browsers. Does the layout display well on all of them? Make any needed changes.

Announce the site. Advertise your site in e-mails. Submit it to search sites. Consider joining a "Web ring" of similar sites to draw more traffic. Let your professors, classmates, friends, and family know about your site.

Monitor the site. After a site has been launched, its success may be measured by the amount of traffic it receives, feedback submitted by users, and any use of resources or services. (Check with your host for ways to measure traffic.)

Make adjustments and updates. A Web site should be a living thing. Update the content when possible to keep it fresh, and make any adjustments needed to adapt to changing technologies.

INSIGHT Avoid using any features and functions that do not support your overall purpose for writing. If you find yourself distracted by the many bells and whistles of the Web, remember that it's better to have a simple Web site that presents information clearly and effectively than a complex site that does not.

LO3 Consider sample sites.

As said earlier in this chapter, reviewing other sites can be helpful. Look for what works and for what doesn't work, for what enhances understanding and for what confuses, as you gather ideas for your own site.

SITE SURVEYS

On the next two pages, you'll find sample pages from student and academic Web sites. Study each model for insights about what makes for strong Web content and design.

Student-Designed Web Site

The following Web site was developed by undergraduate students from a southwestern U.S. university who were studying abroad. Southwest Sojourners is a multiuser site with blogs and chat rooms that allow students to keep in touch with one another and with friends and family back home.

© MANDY GODBEHEAR, 2009 / Used under license from Shutterstock.com

Design Strategy:

Purpose: This site is a gathering place for undergraduate students studying abroad. It describes itself as a "home away from home" for such students. The tone is light, conversational, and inviting, as befitting the purpose of connecting these students to one another and to the important people in their lives.

Audience: The site is meant for students, friends, and family members. By providing straight news, individualized blogs, and chat rooms and e-mail options, the site allows users to be as passive or as active as they wish. Membership is required for active participation, and members must "sign" a user's agreement before posting material.

Format: The golden bands and cactus icon visually convey the Southwest theme, while the minimalist format makes the site easy to navigate. A large four-item toolbar on the left directs users to the linked pages, and brief text on the right gives a clear indication of what lies at the end of each link.

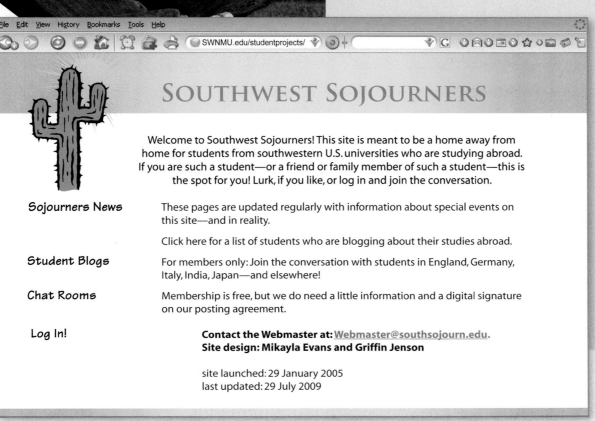

File Edit View History Bookmarks Tools Help

SWNMU.edu/studentprojects/

SOUTHWEST SOJOURNERS

Welcome to Southwest Sojourners! This site is meant to be a home away from home for students from southwestern U.S. universities who are studying abroad. If you are such a student—or a friend or family member of such a student—this is the spot for you! Lurk, if you like, or log in and join the conversation.

Sojourners News These pages are updated regularly with information about special events on this site—and in reality.

Click here for a list of students who are blogging about their studies abroad.

Student Blogs For members only: Join the conversation with students in England, Germany, Italy, India, Japan—and elsewhere!

Chat Rooms Membership is free, but we do need a little information and a digital signature on our posting agreement.

Log In!

Contact the Webmaster at: Webmaster@southsojourn.edu.
Site design: Mikayla Evans and Griffin Jenson

site launched: 29 January 2005
last updated: 29 July 2009

Academic Web Site

The Massachusetts Institute of Technology's Space Nanotechnology Laboratory Web site is an academic research site. It contains information about a specialized laboratory in the MIT Kavli Institute for Astrophysics and Space Research.

Design Strategy:

Purpose: This site aims to inform a very specific audience about a team of professors, graduate research assistants, and staff and their work to develop nanotechnology for space exploration. The site features the laboratory's creation of the "MIT Nanoruler," a device capable of measuring to the billionth of a meter. The site also provides pages that outline the laboratory's mission, history, people, projects, and facilities.

Audience: This Web site addresses "a consortium of microfabrication facilities with shared interests." In addition to providing articles of interest to this group, the site includes a list of available positions for professionals and students who may wish to join the laboratory. A sponsors' page shows that the audience also includes funding agencies such as NASA and the National Science Foundation.

Format: The top of the home page announces the site and the university, using iconic images of waveforms and a satellite to convey its central focus. Beneath this masthead, the page features the laboratory's current great achievement: "Home of the MIT Nanoruler" and "Read more about the Nanoruler." A selection of photos highlights work in the lab, and to the left, a list of pages makes navigation transparent.

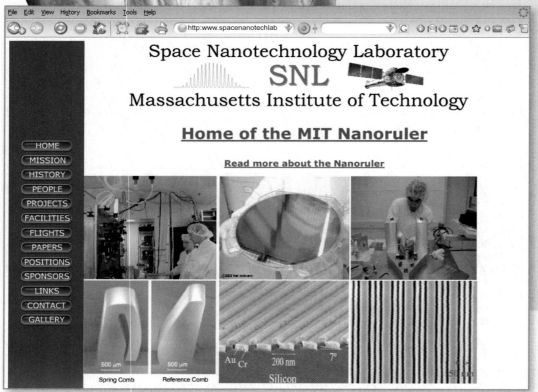

Courtesy of Space Nanotechnology Laboratory, Massachusetts Institute of Technology.

LO4 Understand other writing venues.

The Internet is a complex construct made up of much more than Web pages. Other writing venues on the Net are described below, with writing tips for each.

OWLs Your university or college probably has a writing lab where you can seek help with your writing assignments. It might also have a Web-based OWL (online writing lab) where you can access help. OWLs post answers to questions you may have about writing, and they often allow you to e-mail or send an instant message (see below) to a writing tutor. Before contacting an OWL tutor, carefully read any instructions posted on the site.

Example: Purdue University OWL, owl.english. purdue.edu

MUDs, MOOs, and MUSHes Some instructors hold classes or deliver lectures online in a MUD (multiuser dimension), a text-based "world" that people can share. (MOOs and MUSHes are variants of MUDs.) MUDs have virtual rooms to explore and virtual objects to examine and handle. To use a MUD, you must learn the text commands for interacting with it. Most MUDs require software for a telnet connection, but some are accessible via telnet-enabled Web pages.

Example: Diversity University MOO, www. marshall.edu/commdis/moo

Message Boards Many Web sites have forms that allow visitors to post messages for public display. The messages and any replies are usually listed together so that readers can follow the message "thread."

Mailing Lists Mailing lists allow users to send and receive text messages within a specific group of people interested in a particular subject. The software that maintains a mailing list is called a "list server." Some mailing lists are excellent resources of specialized information.

Example: QUANTUMTEACHING-NMC <MTEACHING-NMC@LISTS.MAINE.EDU>

Chat Servers A chat server provides a place on the Net where you can type a message that other people will see instantly. Those people can then respond with text messages of their own. Some teachers and tutors may use a chat room to confer with students or to hold a class discussion online. Although some chat servers require special software, many are available as Web pages.

Example: Yahoo! Chat, chat.yahoo.com

Blogs A blog (short for "Weblog") is basically just an online journal posted to a Web page. In effect, it is a one-person message board. For many people, blogging is more convenient than creating a Web page of their own, because it involves no design issues and requires no uploading of files.

Instant Messaging Instant messaging (IM) services allow you to send a text message instantaneously to friends and colleagues who use the same software. Most IMs also allow users to send computer files to one another. (Just be careful not to pass on a computer virus this way.)

Example:

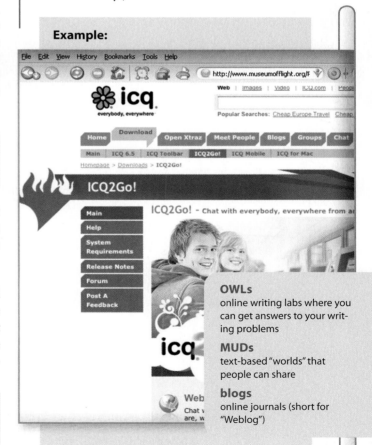

OWLs
online writing labs where you can get answers to your writing problems

MUDs
text-based "worlds" that people can share

blogs
online journals (short for "Weblog")

"Nothing in life is to be feared. It is only to be understood."

—Madame Curie

17

Assessment

You may have had at least one exam-panic dream by now. In this dream, you find yourself in a lather because you're late for an exam or you can't find the room where it will be administered or you show up in one of your classes with an exam in progress, and you know nothing about it! If you haven't had one of these dreams yet, you will, probably sooner than you think. And here's a sad fact: Exam-panic dreams can reoccur many times, even after you've completed your schooling.

Experts say that these dreams often happen when you're very busy or on stress overload—such as, during final-exam week. No surprise there. The deep-seated cause is quite simple. You want to do well on your exams (or in other endeavors), but you worry about your preparation or you wonder if you're up to the challenge. If you consider yourself a high achiever, you may be a prime candidate for many exam-panic dreams.

This chapter is designed to reduce your exam anxieties, and perhaps limit the number of panic dreams you have. It offers (1) strategies for preparing for tests, (2) guidelines for taking essay exams, (3) suggestions for answering objective-test questions, and (4) tips for coping with exams. It doesn't, however, offer any additional dream analysis.

Learning Outcomes

LO1 Prepare for exams.

LO2 Respond to essay questions.

LO3 Understand objective questions.

What do you think?

I prefer essay questions to objective questions.

1	2	3	4	5
strongly agree				strongly disagree

LO1 Prepare for exams.

Proper preparation is the key to doing well on exams, and your preparation should begin with a review of your notes after each class, starting with the very first session. Reviewing material while it is still fresh in your mind helps move it from your short-term memory into your long-term memory. Spending as little as 5 or 10 minutes reviewing can make a significant difference in the amount of information you'll remember.

You should also consider weekly reviews of course material. Spend about one hour reviewing the material for each week; work on your own, with a partner, or with a study group (see below). In weekly reviews, make flash cards of important information, answer review questions, explain what you know to a partner, and so on. *Remember:* Repetition is the single most important factor in learning anything.

© Monkey Business Images, 2009 / Used under license from Shutterstock.com

FORM A STUDY GROUP.

A **study group** can keep you interested in a subject, impel you to keep up with class work, and increase your retention of important material. Group energy, as you may know, can be more powerful than individual energy. In a study group, for instance, you hear other points of view and other ways to approach a subject. If you use a chat room, you can meet via a computer. However the group meets, its success will require patience and cooperation among its members.

study group
a group of classmates working together to understand course material

Handle with Care

Use the following strategies to bring interested individuals into a viable study group.

Group Strategy

• **Members:** Find five to six people who seem to be highly motivated and collaborative. Ask your instructor to inform the class about the opportunity.

• **Meeting:** Decide whether you will meet in person or online. Check with your instructor and student services about the availability of chat rooms on your campus network. Go to any search engine (Yahoo!, Google, Excite, and so on) and enter the term "chat room." For example, Yahoo! provides both private and public chat rooms ("clubs") free.

• **Schedule:** Arrange a time and a place for one session. (It may become obvious at the first meeting that your group won't work out.) Agree on a time limit for the initial session. Choose somebody in the group to keep everyone on task (or rotate this duty), and agree to accept any prodding and nudging with good humor.

• **Plan:** Set realistic goals and decide on a plan of action. Discuss what the group needs to accomplish during this particular session. Agree to practice "people skills" (listening, observing, cooperating, responding, and clarifying). Decide which parts of the course work you will review (lectures? labs? texts? exam questions?).

• **Review:** Evaluate the group's performance at the end of the first session. Honestly and tactfully discuss any problems that arose. Ask who wants to continue. Choose a time (and place) for your next session and determine an agenda for your time together. Exchange necessary information such as phone numbers, e-mail addresses, chatroom passwords, and so forth.

USE MNEMONICS AND OTHER MEMORY GUIDES.

While our brains retain everything, we recall only what is important to us or what we train ourselves to remember. Dividing information into smaller, more manageable units makes the information easier to remember.

Mnemonics is a time-tested memory technique in which you associate new ideas with more recognizable or memorable words, images, or ideas. The ancient Greeks classified two types of memory: natural and artificial. Natural memory is what you use automatically in daily life; artificial memory is learned and practiced using mnemonics and other devices. Mnemonics help you remember things that your natural memory cannot grasp. Here are a few common mnemonics.

Acronyms Use the first letter in each word to form a new word. Everyone learns a few acronyms during their school years, but feel free to make up your own.

> HOMES (the Great Lakes—**H**uron, **O**ntario, **M**ichigan, **E**rie, **S**uperior)

Acrostics Form a phrase or silly sentence in which the first letter of each word helps you remember the items in a series.

> **Z**oe **C**ooks **C**howder **I**n **P**ink **P**ots **I**n **M**iami. (essential minerals—**z**inc, **c**alcium, **c**hromium, **i**ron, **p**otassium, **p**hosphorus, **i**odine, **m**agnesium)

Categories Organize your information into categories for easier recall.

> **Types of joints in body**
> **immovable:** skull sutures, teeth in sockets …
> **slightly movable:** between vertebrae, junction at front of pelvis …
> **freely movable:** shoulder, elbow, hip, knee, ankle …

Peg words Create a chain of associations with objects in a room, a sequence of events, or a pattern with which you are familiar (such as the player positions on a baseball diamond).

> To remember a sequence of Civil War battles, you might "peg" them to the positions on a baseball field. For example, you might peg Shiloh to home plate (think of the "high" and "low" balls); the Battle of Bull Run to the pitcher's mound (think of the pitcher's battle for no runs); and so on.

Rhymes Make up rhymes or puns.

> *Brown v. Board of Education* / ended public-school segregation.

Images What images come to mind when you consider a new concept? Use them to recall material.

> To remember the freedoms established by the first amendment to the Constitution, you might think of colonial figures or events: pilgrims *(religion)*, Benjamin Franklin *(printing press)*, Patrick Henry *(speech)*, and the Boston Tea Party *(protest or petition)*.

LO2 Respond to essay questions.

There's a right way and a wrong way to approach essay questions. Here's the wrong way: Responder A quickly skims the question and then writes down everything and anything about the topic as fast as he can. His pen is flying across the paper in a frenzied attempt to fill in as many blue books as possible. He takes no time to think about the question or to plan an appropriate response.

Here's the right way: Responder B reads the question several times until she is sure she understands what it is asking. She pays special attention to the key word(s) found in every essay-test question. After thinking about the question, she turns it into a topic sentence or thesis statement. Then after quickly planning what main points to include, she crafts her response. The information in this section will help you follow Responder B's lead and respond to essay-test questions with as much care and deliberation as time permits.

UNDERSTAND KEY WORDS.

The key word or words in each essay-test question help to define your task, so be sure to pay special attention to them. These words tell you what type of information to include and how to present it. The quick guide on the next page lists, defines, and demonstrates key words you will likely find on your essay tests.

> **mnemonics**
> memory techniques in which you associate new ideas with more recognizable or memorable words, images, or ideas

Analyze To analyze is to break down a larger problem or situation into separate parts of relationships.

> Analyze the major difficulties found at urban housing projects.

Classify To classify is to place persons or things (especially animals and plants) together in a group because they share similar characteristics. Science uses a special classification or group order: phylum, class, order, family, genus, species, and variety.

> Classify three kinds of trees found in the rainforests of Costa Rica.

Compare To compare is to use examples to show how things are similar and different, placing the greater emphasis on similarities.

> Compare the vegetation in the rainforests of Puerto Rico with the vegetation in the rainforests of Costa Rica.

Contrast To contrast is to use examples to show how things are different in one or more important ways.

> Contrast the views of George Washington and Harry S Truman regarding the involvement of the United States in world affairs.

Compare and contrast To compare and contrast is to use examples that show the major similarities and differences between two things (or people, events, ideas, and so forth). In other words, two things are used to clarify each other.

> Compare and contrast people-centered leadership with task-centered leadership.

Define To define is to give the meaning for a term. Generally, defining involves identifying the class to which a term belongs and explaining how it differs from other things in that class.

> Define the term "emotional intelligence" as it pertains to humans.

Describe To describe is to give a detailed sketch or impression of a topic.

> Describe how the Euro tunnel (the Chunnel) was built.

Diagram To diagram is to explain with lines or pictures—a flowchart, map, or other graphic device. Generally, a diagram will label the important points or parts.

> Diagram the parts of a DNA molecule.

Discuss To discuss is to review an issue from all sides. A discussion answer must be carefully organized to stay on track.

> Discuss how Rosa Parks's refusal to move to the back of the bus affected the civil rights movement.

Evaluate To evaluate is to make a value judgment by giving the pluses and minuses along with supporting evidence.

> Evaluate the efforts of midsized cities to improve public transportation services.

Explain To explain is to bring out into the open, to make clear, and to analyze. This term is similar to *discuss* but places more emphasis on cause/effect relationships or step-by-step sequences.

> Explain the effects of global warming on a coastal city like New Orleans.

Justify To justify is to tell why a position or point of view is good or right. A justification should be mostly positive—that is, the advantages are stressed over the disadvantages.

> Justify the use of antilock brakes in automobiles.

Outline To outline is to organize a set of facts or ideas by listing main points and subpoints. A good outline shows at a glance how topics or ideas fit together or relate to one another.

> Outline the events that caused the United States to enter World War II.

Prove To prove is to bring out the truth by giving evidence to back up a point.

> Prove that Atticus Finch in *To Kill a Mockingbird* provided an adequate defense for his client.

Review To review is to reexamine or to summarize the key characteristics or major points of the topic. Generally speaking, a review presents material in the order in which it happened or in decreasing order of importance.

> Review the events since 1976 that have led to the current hip-hop culture.

State To state is to present a concise statement of a position, fact, or point of view.

State your reasons for voting in the last national election.

Summarize To summarize is to present the main points of an issue in a shortened form. Details, illustrations, and examples are usually omitted.

Summarize the primary responsibilities of a school in a democracy.

Trace To trace is to present—in a step-by-step sequence—a series of facts that are related. Usually the facts are presented in chronological order.

Trace the events that led to the fall of the Union of Soviet Socialist Republics.

© Kuzma , 2009 / Used under license from Shutterstock.com

PLAN AND WRITE YOUR RESPONSE.

Yes, the clock is running, but before you do anything else, be sure to review the essay exam, question by question. Ask your instructor for clarification if you don't understand something. You'll also want to know if each question counts equally; if you can use any aids, such as a dictionary or handbook; and if there are any corrections or changes to the exam.

When planning and writing a response to a specific question, time is the primary controlling element. You're working against the clock, so to speak, so you must use your time wisely. It might help you to portion your time in the following way: Let's say you have 45 minutes to plan and write a response. Reserve the first 5 to 10 minutes for planning (reading the question, forming a thesis, and so on). Then use the next 30 minutes for the actual writing, and the final 5 minutes for reviewing your response. (If you have more or less time for each question, adjust this schedule accordingly.)

Here are the basic steps to follow:

1. **Reread the question several times.** Pay special attention to any key words used in the question.

2. **Rephrase the question** into a topic sentence/thesis statement with a clear point.

> **Question:** Explain why public housing was built in Chicago in the 1960s.
>
> **Thesis statement:** Public housing was built in Chicago because of the Great Migration, the name given to the movement of African Americans from the South to the North.

3. **Outline the main points you plan to cover in your answer.** Time will probably not allow you to include many supporting details in your outline.

> ___ no need for cotton pickers
> ___ factories/stockyards hiring
> ___ Jim Crow laws contrib.
> ___ relatives already in Chicago
> ___ population + speculators …

4. **Write your essay (or paragraph).** Begin with your thesis statement (or topic sentence). Add whatever background information may be needed, and then follow your outline, writing as clearly as possible.

5. **Review your response** for missing information or words, wrong words, confusing phrases, spelling, punctuation, and so on.

TIP

On most essay tests, you won't have time for significant revising or rewriting, so resist the temptation to make major changes when you review your response. Instead look for and correct obvious omissions and errors.

One-Paragraph Answer

If you feel that only one paragraph is needed to answer the question, use the main points of your outline as supporting details for your topic sentence.

Exam Question:

> Explain why public housing was built in Chicago in the 1960s.

Response:

(A)　　Public housing was built in Chicago because of the Great Migration, the name given to the movement of African Americans from the South to the North. The mechanical cotton picker, introduced in the 1920s, replaced field hands in the cotton fields of the South. At that time Chicago's factories and stockyards were hiring workers. In addition, Jim Crow laws caused hardships and provided reasons for African Americans to move north. Finally, some African Americans had family and relatives in Chicago who had migrated earlier and who,

(B)　it was thought, could provide a home base for the new migrants until they could get work and housing. According to the U.S. Census Reports, there were 109,000 African Americans in Chicago in 1920. By 1960, there were more than 800,000. However, this increase in population could have been handled except that the public wanted to keep the African Americans in the Black Belt, an area in South Chicago. Reluctant lending agencies and realtors made it possible for speculators to operate.

(C)　Speculators increased the cost of houses by 75 percent. All of these factors led to a housing shortage for African Americans, which public housing filled.

> (A) Topic sentence
> (B) Supporting details
> (C) Conclusion

Multiparagraph Answer

If the question is too complex to be handled in one paragraph, your opening paragraph should include your thesis statement and any essential background information. Begin your second paragraph by rephrasing one of the main points from your outline into a suitable topic sentence. Support this topic sentence with examples, reasons, or other appropriate details. Handle additional paragraphs in the same manner. If time permits, add a summary or concluding paragraph to bring all of your thoughts to a logical close.

Exam Question:

> Explain the advantages and disadvantages of wind energy.

Outline:

> Thesis: Wind energy has an equal number of advantages and disadvantages.
>
> Outline
> I. Advantages of wind energy
> 　A. Renewable
> 　B. Economical
> 　C. Nonpolluting
> II. Disadvantages of wind energy
> 　A. Intermittent
> 　B. Unsightly
> 　C. A danger to some wildlife

Response:

　　Wind energy has an equal number of advantages and disadvantages. It is renewable, economical, and nonpolluting; but it is also intermittent, unsightly, and a danger to the bird population. 　1 (A)

　　Wind energy is renewable. No matter how much wind energy is used today, there will still be a supply tomorrow. As evidence indicates that wind energy was used to propel boats along the Nile River about 5000 B.C.E., it can be said that wind is an eternal, renewable resource. 　2

　　Wind energy is economical. The fuel (wind) is free, but the initial cost for wind turbines is higher than for fossil-fueled generators. However, wind energy costs do not include fuel purchases and involve only minimal operating expenses. Wind power reduces the amount of foreign oil the United States imports and reduces health and environmental costs caused by pollution. Is it possible to sell excess power? The Public Utilities Regulatory Policy Act of 1978 (PURPA) states that a local electric company must buy any excess power produced by a qualifying individual. This act encourages the use of wind power. 　3 (B)

　　Wind energy does not pollute. Whether one wind turbine is used by an individual or a wind farm supplies energy to many people, no air pollutants or green- 　4 house gases are emitted. California reports that 2.5 billion pounds of carbon dioxide and 15 million pounds of other pollutants have *not* entered the air thanks to wind energy.

5 How unfortunate is it that wind energy is intermittent? If a wind does not blow, there is little or no electrical power. One way to resolve this dilemma is to store the energy that wind produces in batteries. The word *intermittent* also refers to the fact that wind power is not always available at the places where it is most needed. Often the sites that offer the greatest winds are located in remote locations far from the cities that demand great electrical power.

6 (C) Are wind turbines unsightly? A home-sized wind machine rises about 30 feet with rotors between 8 and 25 feet in diameter. The largest machine in Hawaii stands about 20 stories high with rotors a little longer than the length of a football field. This machine supplies electricity to 1,400 homes. Does a single wind turbine upset the aesthetics of a community as much as a wind farm? The old adage "Beauty is in the eye of the beholder" holds up wherever wind turbines rotate. If ongoing electrical costs are almost nil, that wind turbine may look beautiful.

7 (D) How serious is the issue of bird safety? The main questions are these: (1) Why do birds come near wind turbines? (2) What, if any, are the effects of wind development on bird populations? (3) What can be done to lessen the problem? If even one bird of a protected species is killed, the Endangered Species Act has been violated. If wind turbines kill migratory birds, the Migratory Bird Treaty Act has been violated. As a result, many countries and agencies are studying the problem carefully.

© Rafa Irusta , 2009 / Used under license from Shutterstock.com

The advantages of wind energy seem to outweigh the disadvantages. The wind-energy industry has been growing steadily in the United States and around the world. The new wind turbines are reliable and efficient. People's attitudes toward wind energy are mostly positive. Many manufacturers and government agencies are now cooperating to expand wind energy, making it the fastest-growing source of electricity in the world. 8 (E)

(A) The introductory paragraph sets up the essay's organization.
(B) Each paragraph follows a point in the outline.
(C) Specific details explain the main point.
(D) Questions help the reader understand the issue.
(E) The ending shares a final opinion about the topic.

Reading for Better Writing

Working by yourself or with a group, answer these questions:

1. What is the thesis of this response?

2. How is the response organized? What benefits does this method of organization offer the writer? The reader?

3. How do the sentences used to introduce the advantages differ from those used to introduce the disadvantages?

4. Does the writing effectively support each main point (topic sentence)? If so, give two or three strong supporting details.

5. How does the writer conclude the response?

LO3 Understand objective questions.

Objective questions—multiple-choice, true-false, matching, fill-in-the-blank, and so on—have a correct answer. They are not subjective. Even so, objective questions commonly require analysis, judgment, and selection of the best answer, not just the right one. The following strategies will help you avoid some common pitfalls.

Test Strategies

True/False Test

- **Read:** Read the entire question before answering. Often the first half of a statement will be true or false, while the second half is just the opposite. For an answer to be true, the entire statement must be true.

- **Pay Attention:** Read each word and number. Pay special attention to names, dates, and numbers that are similar and could be easily confused.

- **Beware:** Look out for true/false statements that contain words such as *all, every, always,* and *never.* Often these statements will be false.

- **Watch:** Take note of statements that contain more than one negative word. *Remember:* Two negatives make a positive.

  Example: It is <u>unlikely</u> ice will <u>not</u> melt when the temperature rises above 32 degrees F.

Matching Test

- **Take Note:** Read through both lists quickly before you begin answering. Note any descriptions that are similar and pay special attention to the differences.

- **Match Words to Words:** When matching a word to a word, determine the part of speech of each word. If the word is a verb, for example, match it with another verb.

- **Match Words to Phrases:** When matching a word to a phrase, read the phrase first and look for the word it describes.

- **Cross Out:** When you find an answer, cross it out—unless you are told that answers can be used more than once.

- **Capitalize:** Use capital letters rather than lowercase letters because they are less likely to be misread by the person correcting the test.

Multiple-Choice Test

- **Read:** Review the directions to determine whether you need to choose the correct answer, the best answer, or multiple correct answers. Some questions can have two (or more) correct answers.

- **Check:** Read the first part of the question, checking for qualifying words such as *not, never, except,* and *unless.*

- **Think:** Answer the question in your mind before looking at the choices.

- **Choose:** Read all the choices before selecting your answer. This step is important on tests that direct you to select the best answer, or on tests in which one of your choices is a combination of two or more answers.

  Example:
  d. Both a and b
  e. All of the above
  f. None of the above)

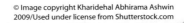

Coping with Test Anxiety

Study smart. Use a variety of study techniques.

Join a study group. Prepare with the members.

Prepare physically and mentally. Get a good night's sleep and eat a light meal before the exam.

Get some exercise. Aerobic exercise (running, swimming, walking) relieves stress and makes you more alert.

Get to class early . . . but not too early! Hurrying increases anxiety, but so does waiting.

Relax. Take a few deep breaths and think positively. The more relaxed you are, the better your memory will serve you.

Scan the entire test. Then plan your time, and pace yourself accordingly.

Answer the questions that you know. This process relieves anxiety and may trigger answers to other questions.

Don't panic. Keep focused on the exam, and do the best that you can.

"**Life is either**
a daring adventure or nothing at all."
—Helen Keller

18

Getting Started

I n 1978, Ben Cohen and Jerry Greenfield pooled $8,000 of their own money and borrowed another $4,000 to open a small ice-cream shop in Burlington, Vermont. From that insignificant start, Ben and Jerry's Ice Cream has grown into a highly profitable multinational business known for its innovations and social conscience. (In 2000, Unilever, an Anglo-Dutch corporation, bought Ben and Jerry's for $326 million dollars.)

From a distance, it would seem that Cohen and Greenfield have approached this "project" with a *joie de vivre* that should be the envy of everyone. They've developed an irresistible line of ice cream, created a wonderful work environment, committed millions to good causes, and on and on. What's not to like about Ben and Jerry's?

So what does this story have to tell you about your own research projects? (1) Start with topics that truly interest you; this is the only way you can do meaningful work. (2) Learn as much as you can about each one. You can't guess in a research paper; you have to know what you're talking about. (3) Take a few risks by approaching each topic in a new or unusual way. (4) And give yourself plenty of time. Quality research can't be rushed.

This chapter will help you initiate your research projects, from selecting interesting topics to conducting effective research.

Learning Outcomes

LO1 Understand academic research.

LO2&3 Initiate the process and develop a plan.

LO4 Explore possible resources and sites.

LO5&6 Conduct searches and evaluate sources.

LO7 Create a working bibliography.

LO8 Review note taking.

LO9 Summarize, paraphrase, and quote source material.

What do you think?

I give myself plenty of time to complete research projects.

1   2   3   4   5

strongly agree   strongly disagree

joie de vivre
French for "joy of life," a quality in people who live life to its fullest

LO1 Understand academic research.

Take ownership of each research project by exploring a topic or an angle that truly interests you and compels you to get started. Your main goal is to become thoroughly knowledgeable about your topic and share your findings in a thoughtful way. The traditional **research paper** is a fairly long essay (5 to 15 pages), complete with a thesis statement, supporting evidence, integrated sources, and documentation. Research can also be presented in a field report, on a Web site, or in a multimedia presentation.

Your instructors, peers, and the academic community in general will be your main audience. However, you may also have a more specific audience in mind—smokers, Floridians, fellow immigrants, and so on. The expected voice in most research projects is formal or semiformal. Always try to maintain a thoughtful, confident tone throughout your writing. Generally, you should avoid the pronouns "I" and "you" in an effort to remain objective and academic. Unfortunately though, avoiding "I" and "you" can result in the overuse of the pronoun "one," so watch for that problem as well.

fyi Some instructors encourage students to connect research with personal experience, meaning that you can, at times, use the pronouns "I" and "you." But be careful to keep the focus where it belongs—on the topic. The best research writing always centers on compelling information about the topic.

RESEARCH INVOLVES MANY STEPS.

The research process involves getting started, planning, conducting research, and developing the results. While research generally follows these steps, you should understand that the process is dynamic, meaning that it can be full of twists and turns, detours and side trips. For example, during your research, you may discover information that will change your mind about the topic or about the thesis statement you developed earlier. The flowchart that follows in the next column shows you the different tasks related to research.

research paper
a fairly long essay (5–15 pages), complete with thesis statement, supporting evidence, integrated sources, and careful documentation

A Research Flowchart

Getting Started
- Review the assignment.
- Consider your resources.
- Choose a subject.

| List or cluster your current ideas and opinions. | Talk with others to learn opposing opinions. | Conduct preliminary research in reference works. |

Planning Your Research
Narrow the topic, form a research question or working thesis, develop a research plan, and select keyword searching terms.

Conducting Research

Conduct Primary Research	Take Careful Notes	Conduct Secondary Research
Observe, interview, survey, or experiment.	Reflect in your research journal.	Check books, articles, and Web sites.
Analyze primary documents and artifacts.	Create and add to a working bibliography.	Search catalogs, indexes, databases, and the Internet.

- Evaluate and take notes from sources.
- Summarize, paraphrase, and quote.

Organizing and Drafting
- Answer your research question or refine your thesis.
- Develop an outline.
- Write the research paper, integrating and documenting sources.

LO2 Initiate the process.

To get started, you need to do four things: (1) understand the assignment, (2) select a topic, (3) build research questions, and (4) develop a working thesis. Your research project will only be as good as the planning that you put into it, so attend to each step with care.

UNDERSTAND THE ASSIGNMENT.

The first important step in a research project is to thoroughly review the assignment. Take some initial notes about it; record key words, options, restrictions, and requirements. Finally, write down any questions you still have about the project, find answers, and proceed.

SELECT A TOPIC.

Author Joyce Carol Oates says, "As soon as you connect with your true subject, you will write." Your goal at the outset of a research project is to find your "true subject," an appropriate topic you sincerely want to write about.

Making It Manageable

In most cases, your instructor will establish a general subject area to get you started. Your job is to select a specific, manageable topic related to that subject. A topic is "manageable" when you can learn about it in a reasonable amount of time. (You may have to carry out some cursory research in order to select a topic.)

General Subject	Area of Interest	Manageable Topic
urban social problems	the homeless	increase in homeless families
World War II legislation & initiatives	the Marshall Plan	the Plan's impact on the new world order
alternative energy	new generation of vehicles	hybrid-electric vehicles

BUILD RESEARCH QUESTIONS.

Generating research questions helps you find meaningful information and ideas about your topic. These questions sharpen your research goal, and the answers become the focus of your writing. Create questions by following the guidelines below.

Needing to Know

List questions about your topic—both simple and complex—to discover what you need to know about it. Keep listing until you land on the **main question** you want to answer—the main issue you need to address. Then brainstorm **supporting questions** that you must research in order to adequately answer the main question.

Main Question:
Should consumers embrace hybrid-electric vehicles?

Supporting Questions (Who? What? When? Where? Why? How?):
Who has developed hybrid-electric cars?
What is a hybrid-electric car?
When were they developed?
Where are they currently in use?
Why are hybrids is use?
How do they work?

Main Question Checklist

_____ Is the question too narrow, too broad, or just about right for a research paper?

_____ Is the question too easy or too hard to answer?

_____ Am I committed to answering this question? Does it interest me?

_____ Will I be able to find enough information about it within a reasonable amount of time?

_____ Will the question and answers interest the reader?

DEVELOP A WORKING THESIS.

A **working thesis** offers a preliminary answer to your main research question. An effective working thesis keeps you focused during your research, helping you decide whether to read a particular book or just skim it, fully explore a Web site or quickly surf through it. When forming your working thesis, don't settle for a simple statement of fact about your topic; instead, form a statement that demands to be proved or that requires thoughtful explanation. The quick guide on the next page includes a formula for writing this statement.

working thesis
a preliminary answer to your main research question, the focus of your research

Formula:

a limited topic + a tentative claim, statement, or hypothesis = a working thesis

Samples:

Hybrid-electric cars offer consumers a reasonable alternative to gas-only cars.

The sharp increase in homeless families will force city planners to rethink their social service policies.

The Marshall Plan benefited Europe and the United States in three significant ways.

Use the following checklist to evaluate your working thesis.

Working Thesis Checklist

_____ Does my working thesis focus on a single, limited topic?

_____ Is it stated clearly and directly?

_____ Does it provide a preliminary answer to my main research question?

_____ Do I have access to information that supports it?

_____ Does my working thesis meet the requirements of the assignment?

Library of Congress classification
a system of classification used in most academic and research libraries

artifact
any object made or modified by a human culture and later discovered

fyi Remember that your working thesis is set in sand, not stone. Your thinking on it might change as you research the topic because different sources may push you in new directions. Such changes show that you are truly engaged in your research.

LO3 Develop a research plan.

As you develop your research plan, consider what you already know about your topic. You can find this out by freewriting, clustering, or talking about your topic. (See pages 24–25.) Push yourself to gather as many of your own thoughts and feelings about the topic as you can before you conduct any "outside" research. Once you determine what you already know, then you can decide what you still need to find out. You should also figure out what resources can help you develop your research questions and working thesis.

CHOOSE RESEARCH METHODS.

Do you need more background information? Is primary research a possibility? What other types of research are you interested in? The following information will answer your questions about planning your research.

Background Research

Take these steps to find information about central concepts and key terms related to your topic.

- Use the **Library of Congress** subject headings to find keywords for searching the library catalog, periodical databases, and the Internet (page 229).
- Conduct a preliminary search of the library catalog, journal databases, and the Internet to confirm that strong resources on your topic exist.
- Use specialized reference works to find background information, definitions, facts, and statistics (page 231).

Primary Research

If at all possible, conduct primary research about your topic. Primary research is firsthand research in which you carry out interviews, observe the topic in action, and so on.

- Use interviews (pages 118–119) and surveys (pages 225–226) to get key information from experts and others.
- Conduct observations or experiments (pages 122–123) to obtain hard data.
- Analyze original documents or **artifacts**.

Library Research

Search for important library resources with the help of a librarian or research specialist. As you probably know, the library contains a wide variety of useful materials.

- Use scholarly books to get in-depth, reliable material (pages 230–231).
- Refer to periodical articles (print or electronic) to get current, reliable information (pages 232–233). Select from news sources, popular magazines, scholarly journals, and trade journals.
- Consider other resources, such as recorded interviews, pamphlets, marketing studies, or various government publications.

Internet Research

The Internet serves as an incredible resource that you can access at your fingertips. Use the following information to help you plan effective Internet searches.

- Use tools, such as search engines and subject guides, that will lead you to quality resources (pages 234–239).
- Select reputable Web sites that librarians, instructors, or other experts recommend (pages 236–239).
- Test Web sites for reliability (pages 215).

fyi Sketch out tentative deadlines for completing each phase of your work: getting started, conducting research, drafting, and so on. Generally, you should spend about half your time on research and planning and half on writing. For some projects, you may have to formalize your planning in the form of a proposal, which shows your instructor that your plan is workable within the constraints of the assignment.

LO4 Explore possible resources and sites.

When researching your topic, be sure to use a wide range of quality resources, as opposed to relying exclusively on information, substantial or not, from a few Web sites. (Your instructor may establish guidelines for the number and type of resources you should consult.) As you review your researching options, consider which resources will give you the best information about your topic. A sociology paper on airport behavior may require personal, direct research; a business paper on the evolution of subprime mortgage loans may best be researched in business publications, government reports, journals, newspapers, and so on.

CONSIDER INFORMATION RESOURCES.

The sources of information available to you are almost unlimited, from interviewing someone to referring to bibliographies, from reviewing journal articles to studying graphics. Listed here are the common sources of information.

Type of Resource	Examples
Personal, primary resources	Memories, diaries, journals, logs, experiments, tests, observations, interviews, surveys
Reference works (print and electronic)	Dictionaries, thesauruses, encyclopedias, almanacs, yearbooks, atlases, directories, guides, handbooks, indexes, abstracts, catalogs, bibliographies
Books (print and electronic)	Nonfiction, how-to, biographies, fiction, trade books, scholarly and scientific studies
Periodicals and news sources	Print newspapers, magazines, and journals; broadcast news and news magazines; online magazines, news sources, and discussion groups
Audiovisual, digital, and multimedia resources	Graphics (tables, graphs, charts, maps, drawings, photos), audiotapes, CD's, videos, DVD's, Web pages, online databases
Government publications	Guides, programs, forms, legislation, regulations, reports, records, statistics
Business and nonprofit publications	Correspondence, reports, newsletters, pamphlets, brochures, ads, catalogs, instructions, handbooks, manuals, policies and procedures, seminar and training materials

CONSIDER INFORMATION SITES.

Where do you go to find the resources that you need? Consider the information sites listed below, remembering that many resources may be available in different forms in different locations. For example, a journal article may be available in a library or in an electronic database.

Information Location	Specific Sites
People	Experts (knowledge area, skill, occupation)
	Population segments or individuals (with representative or unusual experiences)
Libraries	General: public, college, online
	Specialized: legal, medical, government, business
Computer resources	Computers: software, CD-ROM's
	Networks: Internet and other online services (e-mail, limited-access databases, discussion groups, MUDs, chat rooms, Web sites, blogs, YouTube, image banks, wikis); intranets
Mass media	Radio (AM and FM), television (network, public, cable, satellite), print (newspapers, magazines, journals)
Testing, training, meeting, and observation sites	Plants, facilities, field sites, laboratories, research centers, universities, think tanks, conventions, conferences, seminars, museums, galleries, historical sites
Municipal, state, and federal government offices	Elected officials, representatives, offices and agencies, Government Printing Office, and Web sites (GPO, www.gpoaccess.gov)
Business and nonprofit publications	Computer databases, company files, desktop reference materials, bulletin boards (physical and electronic), company and department Web sites, departments and offices, associations, professional organizations, consulting, training, and business information services

LO5 Conduct keyword searches.

Keyword searching can help you find solid information in electronic library catalogs, online databases that index periodical articles (LexisNexis, EBSCOhost), print indexes to periodical publications, Internet resources, print books, and e-books. If you need additional help, consult with an information specialist in your library.

NAVIGATING THE SEARCH

Keywords give you compass points for navigating the vast sea of information ahead of you. To plot the best course, choose the best keywords.

Begin brainstorming a list of possible keywords—topics, titles, and names—based on your current knowledge and background reading. **Then consult the Library of Congress subject headings** to find the keywords librarians use when classifying materials. Topic entries like the one below contain keywords to use, along with narrower, related, and/or broader terms. When you are conducting subject searches of catalogs and databases, these are the terms that will get the best results.

Library of Congress Excerpt

Topic	**Immigrants** (*May Subd Geog*)
Tips	Here are entered works on foreign-born persons who enter a country intending to become permanent residents or citizens. This heading may be locally subdivided by names of places where immigrants settle. For works discussing emigrants from a particular place, an additional heading is assigned to designate the nationality of origin of the emigrant group and the place to which they have immigrated, e.g., Chinese—United States: American—Foreign countries.
"Used for"	UF Emigrants / Foreign-born population / Foreign population
"Broader term"	BT Persons
"Related term"	RT Aliens
"Narrower term"	NT Children of immigrants / Social work with immigrants / Teenage immigrants / Women immigrants
Subtopic	— Employment / USE Alien labor
Recommended keywords	— Housing (*May Subd Geog*) / — — Great Britain / — Legal status, laws, etc. / USE Emigration and immigration law

Employing Keyword Search Strategies

The goal of a keyword search is to find quality sources of information. To realize the best sources, employ these strategies:

Keyword Strategy

- **Get to know the database.** Look for answers to these questions: What material does the database contain? What time frames? What are you searching—authors, titles, subjects, full text? What are the search rules? How can you narrow the search?

- **Use a shotgun approach.** Start with the most likely keyword. If you have no "hits," choose a related term. Once you get some hits, check the citations for clues regarding which words to use as you continue searching.

- **Use Boolean operators to refine your search.** When you combine keywords with **Boolean operators**—such as those in the next column— you will obtain better results.

© Used under license from Shutterstock.com

Narrowing a Search ▶ and, +, not, –

Use when one term gives you too many hits, especially irrelevant ones.

buffalo **and** bison *or* buffalo + bison	Searches for citations containing both keywords
buffalo **not** water *or* buffalo -water	Searches for "buffalo" but not "water," so that you eliminate material on water buffalo

Expanding a Search ▶ or

Combine a term providing few hits with a related word

buffalo **or** bison	Searches for citations containing either term

Specifying a Phrase ▶ quotation marks

Indicate that you wish to search for the exact phrase enclosed

"reclamation project"	Searches for the exact phrase "reclamation project"

Sequencing Operations ▶ parentheses

Indicate that the operation should be performed before other operations in the search string

(buffalo or bison) and ranching	Searches first for citations containing either "buffalo" or "bison" before checking the resulting citations for "ranching"

Finding Variations ▶ wild card symbols

Depending on the database, symbols such as $, ?, or # can find variations of a word

ethic# ethic$	Searches for terms like *ethics* and *ethical*

Boolean operators
words or symbols used when searching research databases and that describe the relationship between various words or phrases in a search

LO6 Evaluate your sources.

Sources of information can be rated for depth and reliability based on their authorship, length, topic treatment, documentation, method of publication, distance from primary sources, and so on. Remember that credible sources boost your own credibility; sources that are not credible, destroy it.

RATE SOURCES.

Don't automatically use sources simply because they support your opinion; conversely, don't reject sources simply because they disagree with your perspective. Instead, base your selection of information on reliable, thoughtful criteria.

From Good to Bad

Use this table to target sources that fit your project's goals, to assess the quality of the sources, and to build a strong bibliography. The table is organized according to the depth and reliability of different sources, with "10" being the most reliable, and "0" being the most unreliable.

10 Scholarly Books and Articles: largely based on careful research; written by experts for experts; address topics in depth; involve peer review and careful editing; offer stable discussion of topic

9 Trade Books and Journal Articles: largely based on careful research; written by experts for educated general audience; sample periodicals: *Atlantic Monthly, Scientific American, Nature, Orion*

8 Government Resources: books, reports, Web pages, guides, statistics developed by experts at government agencies; provided as service to citizens; relatively objective; sample source: *Statistical Abstract of the United States*

7 Reviewed Official Online Documents: Internet resources posted by legitimate institutions—colleges and universities, research institutes, service organizations; although offering a particular perspective, sources tend to be balanced

6 Reference Works and Textbooks: provide general and specialized information; carefully researched, reviewed, and edited; lack depth for focused research (e.g., general encyclopedia entry)

5 News and Topical Stories from Quality Sources: provide current-affairs coverage (print and online), introduction-level articles of interest to general public; may lack depth and length; sample sources: the *Washington Post*, the *New York Times*; *Time, Psychology Today*; NPR's *All Things Considered*

4 Popular Magazine Stories: short, introductory articles often distant from primary sources and without documentation; heavy advertising; sample sources: *Glamour, Seventeen, Reader's Digest*

3 Business and Nonprofit Publications: pamphlets, reports, news releases, brochures, manuals; range from informative to sales-focused

2 List Server Discussions, Usenet Postings, Blog Articles, Talk Radio Discussions: highly open, fluid, undocumented, untested exchanges and publications; unstable resource

1 Unregulated Web Material: personal sites, joke sites, chat rooms, special-interest sites, advertising and junk e-mail (spam); no review process, little accountability, biased presentation

0 Tabloid Articles (print and Web): contain exaggerated and untrue stories written to titillate and exploit; sample source: the *National Enquirer*, the *Weekly World News*

TEST PRINT AND ONLINE SOURCE RELIABILITY.

When assessing the credibility of a source, consider the author and his or her perspective (or bias), and consider the source's timeliness and accuracy. The benchmarks in the quick guide on the next page apply to both print and online sources; note, however, the additional tests or discussions concerning sources on the Web.

Credible Author

Is the author an expert on this topic? What are her or his credentials, and can you confirm them? For example, an automotive engineer would be an expert on hybrid-vehicle technology, whereas a celebrity in a commercial would not.

> **Web test:** Is an author indicated? If so, are the author's credentials noted and contact information offered (for example, an e-mail address)?

Reliable Publication

Has the source been published by a scholarly press, a peer-reviewed professional journal, a quality trade-book publisher, or a trusted news source? Did you find this resource through a reliable search tool?

> **Web test:** Which individual or group posted this page? Is the site rated by a subject directory or library organization? How stable is the site—has it been around for a while and is the material current, well-documented, and readily accessible? Check the site's home page, and read "About Us" pages and mission statements.

Unbiased Discussion

While all sources come from a specific perspective and represent specific commitments, a biased source may be pushing an agenda in an unfair, unbalanced, incomplete manner. Watch for bias toward a certain region, country, political party, industry, gender, race, ethnic group, or religion. Be alert to connections among authors, financial backers, and the points of view shared. For example, if an author has functioned as a consultant to or a lobbyist for a particular industry or group (oil, animal rights), his or her allegiances may lead to a biased presentation of an issue.

> **Web test:** Is the online document one-sided? Is the site nonprofit (.org), government (.gov), commercial (.com), educational (.edu), business (.biz), informational (.info), network-related (.net), or military (.mil)? Is the site U.S. or international? Is this organization pushing a cause, product, service, or belief? How do advertising or special interests affect the site? You might suspect, for example, the scientific claims of a site sponsored by a pro-smoking organization.

Current Information

A five-year-old book on computers may be outdated, but a forty-year-old book on Abraham Lincoln could still be the best source. Given what you need, is this source's discussion up-to-date?

> **Web test:** When was the material originally posted and last updated? Are links live or dead?

Accurate Information

Bad research design, poor reporting, and sloppy documentation can lead to inaccurate information. Check the source for factual errors, statistical flaws, and conclusions that don't add up.

> **Web test:** Is the site information-rich or -poor—filled with helpful, factual materials or fluffy with thin, unsubstantiated opinions? Can you trace and confirm sources by following links or conducting your own search?

Full, Logical Support

Is the discussion of the topic reasonable, balanced, and complete? Are claims backed up with quality evidence? Does the source avoid faulty assumptions, twisted statistical analysis, logical fallacies, and unfair persuasion tactics? (See pages 138–141 for help.)

> **Web test:** Does the Web page offer well-supported claims and helpful links to additional information?

Quality Writing and Design

Is the source well written? Is it free of sarcasm, derogatory terms, cliches, catch phrases, mindless slogans, grammar slips, and spelling errors?

> **Web test:** Are words neutral ("conservative perspective") or emotionally charged ("fascist agenda")? Are pages well designed—with clear rather than flashy, distracting multimedia elements? Is the site easy to navigate?

Positive Relationship with Other Sources

Does the source disagree with other sources? If yes, is the disagreement about the facts themselves or about how to interpret the facts? Which source seems more credible?

> **Web test:** Is the site's information logically consistent with print sources? Do other reputable sites offer links to this site?

To evaluate visual resources, ask yourself the following types of questions: Is the graphic informative or merely decorative? Is the graphic manipulative in any way? What does it include or exclude? Is it well designed? And is it the product of a reliable source?

LO7 Create a working bibliography.

A working bibliography lists sources that you have used and/or intend to use. Compiling this list helps you track your research, develop your final bibliography, and avoid plagiarism.

BUILDING A BIBLIOGRAPHY

Use note cards (see below), a small, spiral-bound notebook, or a computer for your work. Research software such as TakeNote, EndNote, or Bookends Pro may prove helpful.

Include identifying information.

The explanations that follow tell you which details to include for each type of source you use. You may find it helpful later to record bibliographic details in the format of the documentation system you are expected to use—MLA or APA (pages 251–271). Also give each source a code number or letter.

Sample Working Bibliography Entries

Books: author, title and subtitle, publication details (place, publisher, date), call number

> #2
>
> Howells, Coral Ann. Alice Munro.
>
> Contemporary World Writers. Manchester and New York: Manchester UP, 1998.
>
> PS 8576.U57 Z7 1998
>
> Book provides good introduction to Alice Munro's fiction, chapters arranged by Munro's works; contains intro, conclusion, and bibliography; 1998 date means author doesn't cover Munro's recent fiction

working bibliography
a list of sources that you have read and/or intend to use in your research

Periodicals: author, article title, journal name, publication information (volume, number, date), page numbers, method of access (stacks, current periodical, database)

> #5
>
> Valdes, Marcela. "Some Stories Have to Be Told by Me: A Literary History of Alice Munro." Virginia Quarterly Review 82.3 (Summer 2006): 82-90.
>
> EBSCOhost Academic Search Premier http://web.ebscohost.com
>
> Article offers good introduction to Munro's life, her roots in Ontario, her writing career, and the key features of her stories

Online sources: author (if available), document title, site sponsor, database name, publication or posting date, access date, other publication information, URL

> #3
>
> "Alice Munro." Athabasca University Centre for Language and Literature: Canadian Writers. Updated 31 January 2008. Accessed 17 April 2008.
>
> http://www.athabascau.ca/writers/munro.html
>
> Site offers good introduction to Munro's writing, along with links to bibliography and other resources

Primary or field research: date conducted, name and/or descriptive title of person interviewed, place observed, survey conducted, document analyzed

> #4
>
> Thacker, Robert. E-mail interview. 7 March 2008.
>
> rthacker@mdu.edu
>
> Author of critical biography on Munro, Alice Munro: Writing Her Lives, offered really helpful insights into her creative process, especially useful for story "Carried Away"

LO8 Review note taking.

Accurate, thoughtful notes serve as the foundation for your research writing. A good note-taking system should help you (1) work efficiently, (2) glean key information from sources, (3) engage sources critically and reflectively, and (4) record quotations and paraphrases. Effective notes separate source material from your own ideas, which, in turn, helps you to avoid unintentional plagiarism.

SELECT A SYSTEM.

When taking notes, think carefully about the information that you record. Each idea should clearly relate to or enhance your understanding of the topic. What you shouldn't do is simply collect quotations to plunk in your paper, gather a lot of disconnected facts and details, or create extensive notes for every source.

Four note-taking systems are outlined in this section. Choose the system that works best for your project, or combine elements to develop your own system. Be aware that one note-taking style may work better than another, depending on the discipline. For example, in a literature class, the copy-and-annotating method works especially well.

System 1: Paper or electronic note cards . . .

Using paper note cards is the traditional method of note taking; however, note-taking software is now available with most word-processing programs and with programs like TakeNote, EndNote Plus, and Bookends Pro. Here's how a note-card system works:

1. Establish one set of cards (3 × 5 inches, if paper) for your bibliography.

2. On a second set of cards (4 × 6 inches, if paper), take notes on sources:

- Record one point from one source per card.
- Clarify the source: List the author's last name, a shortened title, or a code from the matching bibliography card. Include a page number.
- Provide a topic or heading: Called a slug, the topic helps you categorize and order information.
- Label the note as a summary, paraphrase, or quotation of the original.
- Distinguish between the source's information and your own thoughts.

Slug ▶ PROBLEMS WITH INTERNAL-COMBUSTION CARS

Quotation ▶ "In one year, the average gas-powered car produces five tons of carbon dioxide, which as it slowly builds up in the atmosphere

Page Number ▶ causes global warming." (p. 43)

— helpful fact about the extent of pollution caused by the traditional i-c engine

Comments ▶ — How does this number compare with what a hybrid produces?

Source ▶ #7

© Used under license from Shutterstock.com

Pros & Cons: Although note cards can be initially tedious and time consuming, they are very helpful for categorizing and organizing material for an outline and a first draft.

System 2: Copy (or save) and annotate . . .

The copy-and-**annotate** method involves working with photocopies, print versions, or digital texts of sources:

1. Selectively photocopy, print, or save important sources. Copy carefully, making sure you have full pages, including the page numbers.

2. As needed, add identifying information on the copy—author, publication details, and date. Each page should be easy to identify and trace. When working with books, simply copy the title and copyright pages and keep them with the rest of your notes.

3. As you read, mark up the copy and highlight key statements. In the margins or digital file, record your ideas:

- Ask questions. Insert a "?" in the margin, or write out the question.
- Make connections. Draw arrows to link ideas, or make notes like "see page 36."

annotate
underline or highlight important passages in a text and make notes in the margins

- Add asides. Record what you think and feel while reading.
- Define terms. Note important words that you need to understand.
- Create a marginal index. Write key words to identify themes and main parts.

Pros & Cons: Even though organizing the various pages for drafting can be inconvenient, copying, printing, or saving gives you an accurate record of your sources. And annotating, when approached with more care than mere skimming and highlighting, encourages critical thinking.

System 3: The computer notebook or research log . . .

The computer notebook or research log method involves taking notes on a computer or on sheets of paper. Here's how it works:

1. Establish a central location for your notes—a notebook, a file folder, a binder, or an electronic folder.

2. Take notes one source at a time, making sure to identify the source fully. Number your note pages.

3. Using your initials or some other symbol, distinguish your own thoughts from source material.

4. Use codes in your notes to identify which information in the notes relates to which topic in your outline. Then, under each topic in the outline, write the page number in your notes where that information is recorded. With a notebook or log, you may be able to rearrange your notes into an outline by using copy and paste—but don't lose source information in the process!

Pros & Cons: Taking notes in this way feels natural, although using them to outline and draft may require some time-consuming paper shuffling.

System 4: The double-entry notebook . . .

The double-entry notebook involves parallel note taking—notes from sources beside your own brainstorming, reaction, and reflection. Using a notebook or the columns feature of your word-processing program, do the following:

1. Divide pages vertically.

2. In the left column, record bibliographic information and take notes on sources.

3. In the right column, write your responses. Think about what the source is saying, why the point is important, whether you agree with it, and how the point relates to other ideas and other sources.

Pros & Cons: Although organizing the double-entry notes for drafting may be challenging, this method creates accurate source records and directly engages the researcher with the material.

Bibliographic Info and Notes	Responses
Cudworth, Erika. Environment and Society. Routledge Introductions to Environment Series. London and New York: Routledge, 2003.	*I've actually had a fair bit of personal experience with animals—the horses, ducks, dogs, and cats on our hobby farm. Will this chapter make trouble for my thinking?*
Ch. 6 "Society, Culture and Nature—Human Relations with Animals" Chapter looks at how social scientists have understood, historically, the relationship between people and animals (158).	*Yes, what really are the connections and differences between people and animals? Is it a different level of intelligence? Is there something more basic or fundamental? Are we afraid to see ourselves as animals, as creatures?*
The word "animal" is itself a problem when we remember that people too are animals, but the distinction is often sharply made by people themselves (159)	
"In everyday life, people interact with animals continually" (159). Author gives many common examples.	*Many examples—pets, food, TV programs, zoos—apply to me. Hadn't thought about how much my life is integrated with animal life! What does that integration look like? What does it mean for me, for the animals?*

LO9 Summarize, paraphrase, and quote.

© Used under license from Shutterstock.com

As you work with sources, decide what to put in your notes and how to record it—as a summary, a paraphrase, or a quotation. The passage below comes from an article on GM's development of fuel-cell technology. On the following pages, note how the researchers **summarize**, **paraphrase**, and **quote** material. Then practice the same strategies in your own source notes.

Source Passage

From Burns, L. D., McCormick, J. B., and Borroni-Bird, C. E. "Vehicle of Change." *Scientific American* 287:4 (October 2002): 10 pp.

When Karl Benz rolled his Patent Motorcar out of the barn in 1886, he literally set the wheels of change in motion. The advent of the automobile led to dramatic alterations in people's way of life as well as the global economy—transformations that no one expected at the time. The ever increasing availability of economical personal transportation remade the world into a more accessible place while spawning a complex industrial infrastructure that shaped modern society.

Now another revolution could be sparked by automotive technology: one fueled by hydrogen rather than petroleum. Fuel cells—which cleave hydrogen atoms into protons and electrons that drive electric motors while emitting nothing worse than water vapor—could make the automobile much more environmentally friendly. Not only could cars become cleaner, they could also become safer, more comfortable, more personalized—and even perhaps less expensive. Further, these fuel-cell vehicles could be instrumental in motivating a shift toward a "greener" energy economy based on hydrogen. As that occurs, energy use and production could change significantly. Thus, hydrogen fuel-cell cars and trucks could help ensure a future in which personal mobility—the freedom to travel independently—could be sustained indefinitely, without compromising the environment or depleting the earth's natural resources.

A confluence of factors makes the big change seem increasingly likely. For one, the petroleum-fueled internal-combustion engine (ICE), as highly refined, reliable, and economical as it is, is finally reaching its limits. Despite steady improvements, today's ICE vehicles are only 20 to 25 percent efficient in converting the energy content of fuels into drive-wheel power. And although the U.S. auto industry has cut exhaust emissions substantially since the unregulated 1960s—hydrocarbons dropped by 99 percent, carbon monoxide by 96 percent, and nitrogen oxides by 95 percent—the continued production of carbon dioxide causes concern because of its potential to change the planet's climate.

> **summarize**
> to condense in your own words the main points in a passage
>
> **paraphrase**
> to put a whole passage in your own words
>
> **quotation**
> a word-for-word statement or passage from an original source

SUMMARIZE.

Summarizing condenses in your own words the main points in a passage. Summarize when the source provides relevant ideas and information on your topic.

1. Reread the passage, jotting down a few key words.

2. State the main point in your own words. Add key supporting points, leaving out examples, details, and long explanations. Be objective: Don't mix your reactions with the summary.

3. Check your summary against the original, making sure that you use quotation marks around any exact phrases you borrow.

Sample Summary:

While the introduction of the car in the late nineteenth century has led to dramatic changes in society and world economics, another dramatic change is now taking place in the shift from gas engines to hydrogen technologies. Fuel cells may make the car "greener," and perhaps even safer, cheaper, and more comfortable. These automotive changes will affect the energy industry by making it more environmentally friendly; as a result, people will continue to enjoy mobility while transportation moves to renewable energy. One factor leading to this technological shift is that the internal-combustion engine has reached the limits of its efficiency, potential, and development—while remaining problematic with respect to emissions, climate change, and health.

fyi For instruction on effectively integrating quotations, paraphrases, and summaries into your writing, see pages 245–247.

PARAPHRASE.

Paraphrasing puts a whole passage in your own words. Paraphrase passages that present key points, explanations, or arguments that are useful to your project. Follow these steps:

1. Quickly review the entire passage for a sense of the whole, and then reread it sentence by sentence.
- State the ideas in your own words.
- Edit for clarity, but don't change the meaning.
- Put directly borrowed phrases in quotation marks.

2. Check your paraphrase against the original for accurate tone and meaning.

Sample Paraphrase:

Automobile technology may be delivering another radical economic and social change through the shift from gasoline to hydrogen fuel. By breaking hydrogen into protons and electrons so that the electrons run an electric motor with water vapor as the only the by-product, fuel cells could make the car a "green" machine. But this technology could also increase the automobile's safety, comfort, personal tailoring, and affordability. Moreover, this shift to fuel-cell engines in automobiles could lead to dramatic environmentally friendly changes in the broader energy industry, an industry that will be tied to hydrogen rather than to fossil fuels. The result of this shift will be radical changes in the way we use and produce energy. In other words, the shift to clean technology and hydrogen-powered vehicles could maintain society's valued mobility while preserving the environment and earth's natural resources.

QUOTE.

Quoting records statements or phrases from an original source word for word. Quote nuggets only—statements that are well phrased or authoritative:

1. Note the quotation's context—how it fits in the author's discussion.

2. Copy the passage word for word, enclosing it in quotation marks and checking its accuracy.

3. If you omit words, note that omission with an ellipsis. If you change any word for grammatical reasons, enclose it in brackets. (See page 247).

Sample Quotations:

This sentence captures the authors' main claim about the benefits and future of fuel-cell technology.

"[H]ydrogen fuel-cell cars and trucks could help ensure a future in which personal mobility . . . could be sustained indefinitely, without compromising the environment or depleting the earth's natural resources."

This quotation offers a well-phrased statement about the essential problem.

"[T]he petroleum-fueled internal-combustion engine (ICE), as highly refined, reliable, and economical as it is, is finally reaching its limits."

INSIGHT Careful note taking helps prevent unintentional plagiarism. Plagiarism—using source material without giving credit—is treated more fully elsewhere (pages 242-244). But at the planning stage, you can prevent this problem by (1) maintaining an accurate working bibliography, (2) distinguishing source material from your own ideas in your notes, (3) paraphrasing, summarizing, and quoting source material selectively and accurately, and (4) clearly identifying the source of the information, including material gleaned from the Internet.

"**Basic research is what**
I am doing when I don't know what I am doing."
—Wernher von Braun

19

Researching

Merriam-Webster's Collegiate Dictionary thinks it's pretty clever. A person who consults it to find the origin of the word *research* learns that it comes from the Middle French *recercher*, which means "to go about seeking"—after which *Webster's* promises "more at SEARCH."

In looking up *search*, one learns that the word comes from the Late Latin *circare*, which means "to go about" and which comes from the Latin *circum*, which means "round about." Then *Webster's* indicates there is "more at CIRCUM-."

Circum-, it turns out, comes from the Latin *circus*, which means "circle," and, yes, there's "more at CIRCLE." *Circle* comes from *circus*, of course, but it is also from (or akin to) the Greek *krikos*, which means "ring" and which is akin to the Old English *hring*, and—you guessed it—there's "more at RING."

So, you see, the clever editors of *Merriam-Webster's Collegiate Dictionary* are not content simply to provide you the etymology of *research*. They want you to research *research*. They want you "to go about seeking," to go "round about" in "circles" that feel like "circuses" and are all about "rings." They don't just define *research* for you—they give you a quick sampler of doing it.

In this chapter, you'll learn how research is about searching and re-searching and going about in circles—or to paraphrase Wernher von Braun—it is what you are doing when you don't know what you are doing. That's fine. Don't fret. Enjoy the process.

Learning Outcomes

LO1 Understand sources.

LO2 Conduct primary research.

LO3 Use the library.

LO4 Use books.

LO5 Find periodical articles.

LO6 Understand the Internet.

LO7 Find reliable information.

What do you think?

Research often *does* feel like a circus.

1	2	3	4	5
strongly agree			strongly disagree	

LO1 Understand sources.

Information sources for your research project can be either primary or secondary. Depending on your assignment, you may be required to use one or both kinds of sources.

THE SOURCES

Primary sources are original sources, which means they give firsthand information on a topic. These sources (such as diaries, people, or events) inform you directly about the topic, rather than through other people's explanations or interpretations. The most common forms of primary research are observations, interviews, surveys, experiments, and analyses of original documents and artifacts.

Secondary sources present secondhand information on your topic—information at least once removed from the original. This information has been compiled, summarized, analyzed, synthesized, interpreted, or evaluated by someone studying primary sources. Journal articles, encyclopedia entries, documentaries, and nonfiction books are typical examples of such secondary sources.

Tertiary sources present thirdhand information on your topic. They are essentially reports of reports of research and, therefore, are distant from the original information. Examples of tertiary sources would include some articles in popular magazines and entries in Wikipedia. Aside from giving you ideas for focusing your topic, tertiary sources should generally not be used in college research projects and should not appear in works-cited or reference lists.

The following are possible primary and secondary sources for a research project exploring hybrid car technology and its viability. **Note:** Whether a source is primary or secondary depends on what you are studying. For example, if you were studying U.S. *attitudes* toward hybrid cars, a newspaper editorial or a TV roundtable discussion would be a primary source. However, if you were studying hybrid technology itself, the same newspaper editorial or TV roundtable would be a secondary source.

Hybrid Car Technology

Primary Sources

- E-mail interview with automotive engineer
- Fuel-efficiency legislation
- Test-drive of a car at a dealership
- Published statistics about hybrid car sales

Secondary Sources

- Journal article discussing the development of hybrid car technology
- Newspaper editorial on fossil fuels
- TV news roundtable discussion of hybrid car advantages and disadvantages
- Promotional literature for a specific hybrid car

primary sources
original sources that give firsthand information about a topic

secondary sources
sources that are at least once removed from the original; sources that provide secondhand information

tertiary sources
sources that provide third-hand information, such as wikis; discouraged for college research projects

LO2 Conduct primary research.

When published sources can't give you the information that you need, consider conducting primary research. Primary research gives you direct, hands-on access to your topic, providing information precisely tailored to your needs. Such research takes time, however. It also requires special skills like designing surveys or analyzing statistics and original documents. The following quick guide is an overview of research methods. Choose those that best suit your project.

Quick Guide · Primary Research Methods

Surveys • **Surveys** and **questionnaires** gather written responses you can review, tabulate, and analyze. These research tools pull together varied information—from simple facts to personal opinions and attitudes.

Interviews • Interviews involve consulting two types of people. First, you can interview experts for their insights on your topic. Second, you can interview people whose direct experiences with the topic give you their personal insights. (See pages 118-121 for more about interviews.)

Observations • **Observations, inspections,** and **field research** require you to examine and analyze people, places, events, and so on. Whether you rely simply on your five senses or use scientific techniques, observing provides insights into the present state of your subject. (See pages 122-128 for more on field reports.)

Experiments • Experiments test hypotheses—predictions about why things do what they do—to arrive at conclusions that can be accepted and acted upon. Such testing often explores cause/effect relationships. (See pages 122-124 for more on lab reports.)

Analysis • Analysis of documents and artifacts involves studying original reports, statistics, legislation, literature, artwork, and historical records. Such analysis provides unique, close-up interpretations of your topic.

GUIDELINES

CONDUCTING SURVEYS

Your goal is to create a survey or questionnaire that collects facts and opinions from a target audience about your topic. To get valid information, follow these guidelines:

1. Find a focus. Define the writing situation. What is your specific topic? What is the purpose of your survey (what do you want to find out)? Who is the audience for your survey?

2. Create effective questions. Phrase questions so that they can be easily understood. Use neutral language to avoid skewing results. Use **closed questions** (e.g., rating, multiple choice, yes/no) to generate data that can be charted and quantified. Use **open-ended questions** (e.g., fill-in-the-blank, write-in answers) to bring in a wider variety of complex data.

survey/questionnaire
a set of questions created for the purpose of gathering information from respondents about a specific topic

observation
noting information received in person through the senses

inspection
the purposeful analysis of a site or situation in order to understand it

field research
an on-site scientific study conducted for the purpose of attaining raw data

closed questions
questions that can be answered with a simple fact or with a *yes* or a *no*

open-ended questions
questions that require elaborate answers

3. Draft your survey. Whether you present your survey on paper or online, organize it so that it's easy to complete.

> **Opening:** State who you are and why you need the information. Explain how to complete the survey and when and where to return it.
>
> **Middle:** Provide the questions. Guide the reader with numbers, instructions, and headings. Begin with basic, closed questions and progress to complex, open-ended questions. Move in a logical order from topic to topic.
>
> **Ending:** Thank the respondent for taking the survey and remind the person when and where to return it.

4. Revise your survey. Ask a friend or classmate to take your survey and help you revise it, if necessary, before publishing it. Take the survey yourself. Note questions that should be added or reworded or removed, parts that should be reorganized, places in which the voice should be more neutral, and instructions that should be clearer. After revising, try out your survey with a small test group, and revise again.

5. Edit your survey. Check sentences, words, letters, and each punctuation mark. Make certain your survey is error free before publishing it.

6. Conduct your survey. Distribute the survey to a clearly defined group that won't prejudice the sample (random or cross section). Encourage the target group to respond, aiming for 10 percent response if at all possible. Tabulate responses carefully and objectively. To develop statistically valid results, you may need expert help. Check with your instructor.

Student Model

Student writer Cho Lang created the following paper survey to determine how many athletes at her college used training supplements, how, and why. She also created a Web-based version of the survey, asking athletes to sign on anonymously to complete it.

Confidential Survey

My name is Cho Lang, and I'm conducting research about the use of training supplements. I'd like to hear from you, Alfred University's athletes. Please answer the questions below by circling or writing out your responses. Return your survey to me, care of the Dept. of Psychology, through campus mail by Friday, April 5. Your responses will remain confidential. (A)

1. Circle your gender. (B)

   Male   Female

2. Circle your year.

   Freshman   Sophomore   Junior   Senior

3. List the sports that you play.

4. Are you presently using a training supplement?

   Yes   No

   Note: If you circled "no," you may turn in your survey at this point.

5. Describe your supplement use (type, amount, and frequency). (C)

6. Who supervises your use of this training supplement?

   Coach   Trainer   Self   Others

7. How long have you used it?

   Less than 1 month   1–12 months   12+ months

8. How many pounds have you gained while using this supplement? (D)

9. How much has your athletic performance improved?

   None   1   2   3   4   5   Greatly

10. Circle any side effects you've experienced.

    Dehydration   Nausea   Diarrhea

Thank you for taking the time to complete this confidential survey. Please return it by Friday, April 5, to Cho Lang, care of the Dept. of Psychology, through campus mail.

> (A) The introduction includes the essential information about the survey.
> (B) The survey begins with clear, basic questions.
> (C) The survey asks an open-ended question.
> (D) The survey covers the topic thoroughly.

ANALYZING DOCUMENTS AND ARTIFACTS

An **original document** or record is one that relates directly to the event, issue, object, or phenomenon you are researching. Examining original documents and artifacts can involve studying letters, e-mail exchanges, case notes, literary texts, sales records, legislation, and material objects such as tools, sculptures, buildings, and tombs. As you analyze such documents and records, you examine evidence in an effort to understand a topic, arrive at a coherent conclusion about it, and support that judgment. How do you work with such diverse documents, records, and artifacts? Here are some guidelines:

Choose evidence close to your topic. Which texts, documents, records, and artifacts originated from or grew out of the topic you are researching? The closer to the topic, the more primary the source. Select materials that are directly related to your research questions or working thesis.

Topic: English labor riots of the 1830s

Evidence:

✓ copies of speeches given at demonstrations (to understand what rioters were demanding)

✓ names from police reports or union membership lists (to know who the rioters were)

✓ political speeches or legislation (to learn the political response to the riots)

✓ newspaper reports, works of art, or novels from the period (to discern the attitudes of people from that time)

✓ personal letters, diaries, family albums, gravestones, and funeral eulogies (to find people's personal stories and private opinions related to the riots)

Frame your examination with questions. To make sense of the text, document, record, or artifact, understand what you are looking for and why. List the secondary questions related to the main question behind your research project.

Topic: Development of cleaner vehicles (Legislative pressure?)

Documents: Clean Air Act of 1990, *The Plain English Guide to the Clean Air Act*

Ask:

✓ What are the requirements of the Clean Air Act?

✓ How do those requirements affect automotive technology?

✓ Are schedules for change or deadlines written into the Clean Air Act?

Put the document or artifact in context. So that the material takes on meaning, clarify its external and internal natures. First, consider its external nature—the five W's and H: What exactly is it? Who made it, when, where, why, and how? Second, consider its internal nature—what the document means: What does the language mean or refer to? What is its main message? What do the artifact's composition and style imply?

Topic: Historical perspective of Mary Wollstonecraft's *A Vindication of the Rights of Woman*

Contextualize:

• **External Context:** (5 W's and H) Discover *who* Mary Wollstonecraft was; *when, why,* and *where* she wrote this piece; *who* her audience was and *how* they responded; *what* type of document it is.

• **Internal Context:** (Meaning) Consider Wollstonecraft's essential argument and evidence, the nature of her views, their relationship to her times, and their relevance today.

> **original document**
> a record that relates directly to an event, an issue, an object, or a phenomenon

Draw coherent conclusions about meaning. Make sense of the source in relation to your research questions. What connections does the source reveal? What important changes or developments? What cause/effect relationships? What themes?

Topic: Clean Air Act

Conclusion:

This environmental legislation has encouraged the development of hybrid technology. The United States must produce cleaner cars if it hopes to improve its air quality.

Think about your discipline. Studying primary documents and artifacts is central to many disciplines—history, literature, theology, philosophy, political studies, and archaeology, for example. Good analysis depends on asking research questions appropriate for the discipline. Using the English labor riots of the 1830s again as an example, here's what three disciplines might ask:

Topic: English labor riots of the 1830s

Discipline response:

Political science: What role did political theories, structures, and processes play in the riots—both in causing and in responding to them?

Art: How were the concerns of the rioters embodied in the new "realist" style of the mid-1800s? Did artists sympathize with and address an alienated working-class audience? How did art comment on the social structures of the time?

Sociology: What type and quality of education did most workers have in the 1830s? How did that education affect their economic status and employment opportunities? Did issues related to the riots prompt changes in the English educational system? What changes and why?

collections
the materials housed within a library

subscription databases
online services that, for a fee, provide access to hundreds of thousands of articles

With these examples in mind, consider your own major: What questions would your discipline ask about the English labor riots, about Mary Wollstonecraft's *A Vindication of the Rights of Woman,* or about the Clean Air Act of 1990?

LO3 Use the library.

The library door is your gateway to information. Inside, the college library holds a wide range of research resources, from books to periodicals, from reference librarians to electronic databases.

MAKING THE LIBRARY WORK

To improve your ability to succeed at all your research assignments, become familiar with your college library system. Take advantage of tours and orientation sessions to learn its physical layout, resources, and services. Check your library's Web site for policies, tutorials, and research tools.

Knowing Where to Go

The college library offers four basic resources for your research projects.

Librarians are information experts who manage the library's materials and guide you to resources. They also can help you perform online searches.

Collections are the materials housed within the library, including books and electronic materials, periodicals, reference materials, and special collections.

Research tools are the systems and services to help you find what you need. They include online catalogs, print indexes and **subscription databases**, and Internet access to other libraries and online references.

Special services are additional options to help you complete research, including interlibrary loan, "hold" and "reserve" services, the reference desk, photocopies, CD burners, scanners, and presentation software.

CATALOG SEARCHES

Library materials are cataloged so they are easy to find. In most college libraries, books, videos, and other holdings are cataloged in an electronic database. To find material, use book titles, author names, and related keyword searching. (See pages 212–213.)

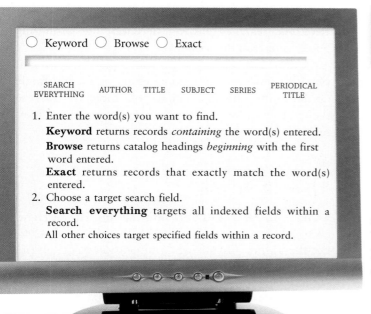

○ Keyword ○ Browse ○ Exact

| SEARCH EVERYTHING | AUTHOR | TITLE | SUBJECT | SERIES | PERIODICAL TITLE |

1. Enter the word(s) you want to find.
   Keyword returns records *containing* the word(s) entered.
   Browse returns catalog headings *beginning* with the first word entered.
   Exact returns records that exactly match the word(s) entered.
2. Choose a target search field.
   Search everything targets all indexed fields within a record.
   All other choices target specified fields within a record.

When you find a citation for a book or other resource (see below), the result will likely provide the author or editor's name, the title and subtitle, publisher and copyright date, descriptive information, subject headings (crucial list of topics), call number, and location. Use that information to determine whether the resource is worth exploring further and to figure out other avenues of research. *Note:* A number of items appearing in blue underlined type provide links to related books and other resources in the catalog.

Cudworth, Erika, 1966–

Title: Environment and Society

Publisher: London; New York: Routledge, 2003.

Physical descript.: xii, 232 p.: ill.; 24 cm.

Subjects: Human ecology [65 rec.]
Nature—Effect of human being on [15 rec.]
Environmental protection [25 rec.]

Call number: GF 41 .C83 2003

Location: Available—on shelf

Locating by Call Numbers

Library of Congress (LC) **call numbers** combine letters and numbers to specify a resource's broad subject area, topic, and authorship or title. Finding a book, DVD, or other item involves combining both the alphabetical and the numerical order.

Arctic Refuge: A Vanishing Wilderness?:
VIDEO QH84.1.A72 1990

subject area **(QH)**
topic number **(84)**
subtopic number **(1)**
cutter number **(A72)**

To find the example resource in the library, first note the tab VIDEO. Although not part of the call number, this locator will send you to a specific area of the library. Once there, follow the parts of the call number one at a time:

1. Find the section on natural history containing videos with the "QH" designation.

2. Follow the numbers until you reach "84."

3. Within the "84" items, find those with the subtopic "1."

4. Use the cutter number "A72" to locate the resource alphabetically with "A" and numerically with "72."

Note: In the LC system, pay careful attention to the arrangement of subject area letters, topic numbers, and subtopic numbers: Q98 comes before QH84; QH84 before QH8245; QH84.A72 before QH84.1.A72.

Library of Congress call numbers
a set of numbers and letters specifying the subject area, topic, and authorship or title of a book

Classification Systems

The **LC classification system** combines letters and numbers. The **Dewey decimal system**, which is used in some libraries, uses numbers only. Here is a list of the subject classes for both the LC and Dewey systems.

Category	LC	Dewey Decimal
General Works	A	000–999
Philosophy	B	100–199
Psychology		150–159
Religion		200–299
History: Auxiliary Sciences	C	910–929
History: General and Old World	D	930–999
History: American	E–F	970–979
Geography	G	910–919
Anthropology		571–573
Recreation		700–799
Social Sciences	H	300–399
Political Science	J	320–329
Law	K	340–349
Education	L	370–379
Music	M	780–789
Fine Arts	N	700–799
Language	P	800–899
Literature		400–499
Science	Q	500–599
Medicine	R	610–619
Agriculture	S	630–639
Technology	T	600–699
Military Science	U	355–359, 623
Naval Science	V	359, 623
Bibliography and Library Science	Z	010–019
		020–029

appendixes
sections (in a book) that provide additional or background information

glossaries
lists of important terms and their definitions

bibliographies
lists of works that cover a particular subject

LO4 Use books.

Your college library contains a range of books, from scholarly studies and reference works to trade books and biographies.

When you find a helpful book, browse nearby shelves for more books. If your library subscribes to an e-book service such as NetLibrary, you can conduct electronic searches, browse or check out promising books, and read them online.

Unfortunately, for most research projects, you simply don't have time to read an entire book, and rarely do the entire contents relate to your topic. Instead, use the strategy outlined below to refine your research effort.

Research Strategy

• **Check out front and back information.** The title and copyright pages give the book's full title and subtitle; the author's name; and publication information, including publication date and Library of Congress subject headings. The back may contain a note on the author's credentials and other publications.

• **Scan the table of contents.** Examine the contents page to see what the book covers and how it is organized. Ask yourself which chapters are relevant to your project.

• **Using key words, search the index.** Check the index for coverage and page locations of the topics most closely related to your project. Are there plenty of pages, or just a few? Are these pages concentrated or scattered throughout the book?

• **Skim the foreword, preface, or introduction.** Skimming the opening materials will often indicate the book's perspective, explain its origin, and preview its contents.

• **Check appendixes, glossaries, or bibliographies.** These special sections may be good sources of tables, graphics, definitions, statistics, and clues for further research.

• **Carefully read appropriate chapters and sections.** Think through the material you've read and take good notes. (See pages 217-218.) Follow references to authors and other works to do further research on the topic. Study footnotes and endnotes for insights and leads.

Informational Resources

Encyclopedias supply facts and overviews for topics arranged alphabetically. General encyclopedias, such as *Encyclopedia Britannica* or *Collier's Encyclopedia,* cover many fields of knowledge. Specialized encyclopedias, such as *McGraw-Hill Encyclopedia of Science and Technology* and the *Encyclopedia of American Film Comedy,* focus on a single topic.

Almanacs, yearbooks, and statistical resources, normally published annually, contain diverse facts. *The World Almanac and Book of Facts* presents information on politics, history, religion, business, social programs, education, and sports. *Statistical Abstract of the United States* provides data on population, geography, politics, employment, business, science, and industry.

Vocabulary resources supply information on languages. General dictionaries, such as *The American Heritage College Dictionary,* supply definitions and histories for a whole range of words. Specialized dictionaries, such as the *Dictionary of Engineering* or *The New Harvard Dictionary of Music,* define words common to a field, topic, or group. Bilingual dictionaries translate words from one language to another.

Biographical resources supply information about people. General biographies, such as *Who's Who in America,* cover a broad range of people. Other biographies, such as the *Dictionary of Scientific Biography* or *World Artists 1980-1990,* focus on people from a specific group.

Directories supply contact information for people, groups, and organizations: *The National Directory of Addresses and Telephone Numbers, USPS ZIP Code Lookup and Address Information* (online), *Official Congressional Directory.*

Research Tools

Guides and handbooks help readers explore specific topics: *The Handbook of North American Indians, A Guide to Prairie Fauna.*

Indexes point you to useful resources. Some indexes are general, such as *Readers' Guide to Periodical Literature;* others are more specific, such as *Environment Index* or *Business Periodicals Index.* (Many are now available online in databases your library subscribes to.)

Bibliographies list resources on a specific topic. A good current bibliography can be used as an example when you compile your own bibliography on a topic.

Abstracts, like indexes, direct you to articles on a particular topic. But abstracts also summarize those materials so you learn whether a resource is relevant before you invest time in locating and reading it. Abstracts are usually organized into subject areas: Computer Abstracts, Environmental Abstracts, Social Work Abstracts. They are incorporated in many online subscription databases.

encyclopedias
reference works filled with articles written about a variety of topics

almanacs/yearbooks
regularly published references that chronicle the major events of a specific time period

directories
references that provide contact information for people, groups, and organizations

indexes
searchable lists of resources on various topics

abstracts
summaries of resources; a collection of summaries in a specific subject area

LO5 Find periodical articles.

Periodicals are publications or broadcasts produced at regular intervals (daily, weekly, monthly, quarterly). Although some periodicals are broad in their subject matter and audience, as a rule they focus on a narrow range of topics geared toward a particular audience.

There are basically three forms of periodical publications. **Daily newspapers and newscasts** provide up-to-date information on current events, opinions, and trends—from politics to natural disasters (*Wall Street Journal, USA Today, The NewsHour*). **Weekly and monthly magazines and newscasts** generally provide more in-depth information on a wide range of topics (*Time, Newsweek, 60 Minutes*). Finally, **journals,** generally published quarterly, provide specialized scholarly information for a narrowly focused audience (*English Journal*).

ONLINE DATABASES

If your library subscribes to EBSCOhost, Lexis-Nexis, or another database service, use keyword searching (see pages 212–213) to find citations on your topic. You might start with the general version of such databases, such as EBSCOhost's Academic Search Elite, which provides access to more than 4,100 scholarly publications covering all disciplines.

Basic Search

The example **(Sample 1 on next page)** shows an EBSCOhost search screen for a search on hybrid electric cars. Notice how limiters, expanders, and other advanced features help you find the highest-quality materials.

periodicals
publications or broadcasts produced at regular intervals (daily, weekly, monthly, quarterly)

magazines
weekly, monthly, or semimonthly publications providing information to a broadly focused audience

journals
generally quarterly publications providing specialized scholarly information for a narrowly focused audience

MAKING THE ADVANCED SEARCH

A more focused research strategy involves turning to specialized databases, which are available for virtually every discipline and are often an option within search services such as EBSCOhost (for example, Business Source Elite, PsycINFO, ERIC) and Lexis-Nexis (for example, Legal, Medical, and Business databases). If a basic search turns up little, turn to specialized databases, seeking help from a librarian if necessary.

Citation Lists

Your database search should generate lists of citations, brief descriptions of articles that were flagged through keywords in titles, subject terms, abstracts, and so on. For example, a search focused on hybrid electric cars leads to the results shown **(Sample 2 on the next page)**. At this point, study the results and do the following:

- Refine the search by narrowing or expanding it.
- Mark specific citations for "capture" or further study.
- Re-sort the results.
- Follow links in a specific citation to further information.

Identifying Information

By studying citations (especially abstracts), you can determine if the article is relevant to your research, is available in an electronic version, and is available as a periodical. To develop your working bibliography (see page 216), you should also "capture" the article's identifying details by using the save, print, or e-mail function, or by recording the periodical's title, the issue and date, and the article's title and page numbers.

Full-Text Articles

When citations indicate that you have promising articles, access those articles efficiently, preferably through a direct link in the citation to an electronic copy. From

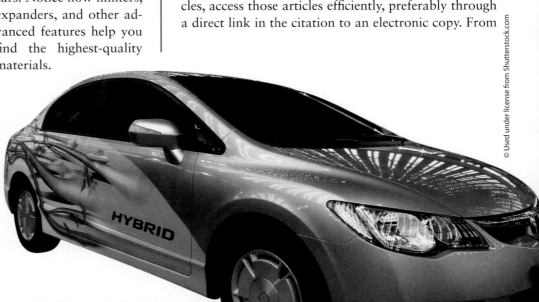

there you can print, save, or e-mail the article. If the article is not available electronically, track down a print version:

Check the online citation to see if your library has the article. If necessary, check your library's inventory of periodicals held; this list should be available online and/or in print. Examine especially closely the issues and dates available, the form (print or microfilm), and the location (bound or current shelves).

To get the article, follow your library's procedure. You may have to submit a request slip so that a librarian can get the periodical, or you may be able to get it yourself in the current, bound, or microfilm collection. If the article is not available online or in your library, use interlibrary loan.

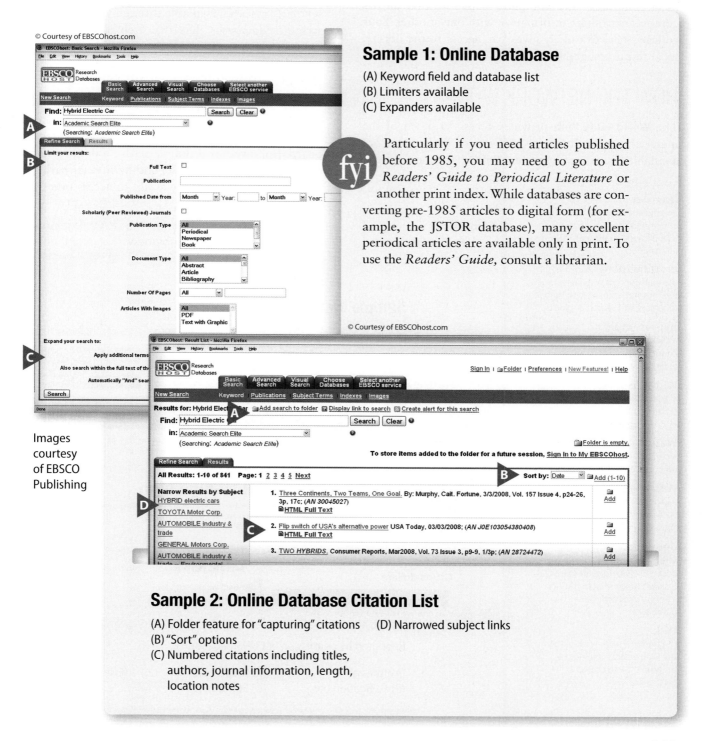

Images courtesy of EBSCO Publishing

Sample 1: Online Database

(A) Keyword field and database list
(B) Limiters available
(C) Expanders available

fyi Particularly if you need articles published before 1985, you may need to go to the *Readers' Guide to Periodical Literature* or another print index. While databases are converting pre-1985 articles to digital form (for example, the JSTOR database), many excellent periodical articles are available only in print. To use the *Readers' Guide,* consult a librarian.

Sample 2: Online Database Citation List

(A) Folder feature for "capturing" citations
(B) "Sort" options
(C) Numbered citations including titles, authors, journal information, length, location notes
(D) Narrowed subject links

LO6 Understand the Internet.

If you're familiar with the **Internet**, you already understand the basics of searching this medium. However, the following information may help you do quality research on the Net.

The Internet is a worldwide network of connected local computers and computer networks that allows computers to share information with one another. Your college's network likely gives you access to the library, local resources, and the Internet.

HOW THE NETWORK WORKS

The **World Wide Web** provides access to much of the material on the Internet. Millions of Web pages are available because of **hypertext links** that connect them. These links appear as clickable icons or highlighted Web addresses. A **Web site** is a group of related **Web pages** posted by the same sponsor or organization. A **home page** is a Web site's "entry" page. A **Web browser** such as Safari, Internet Explorer, or Firefox gives you access to Web resources through a variety of tools, such as directories and search engines. (Directories and **search engines** are special Web sites that provide a searchable listing of many services on the Web.)

Distinguish between the **deep Web** and the free Web. The deep Web includes material not generally accessible with popular search engines, such as all the scholarly research available through your library's subscription databases. The free Web offers less reliable information.

Understanding Internet Addresses

An Internet address is called a uniform resource locator (**URL**). The address includes the protocol indicating how the computer file should be accessed—often *http:* or *ftp:* (followed by a double slash); a domain name—often beginning with *www*; and additional path information (following a single slash) to access other pages within a site.

http://www.nrcs.usda.gov/news/

Internet
a worldwide network of connected computers that allows a sharing of information

World Wide Web
the collection of Web sites on the Internet accessible to Web browsers and search engines

hypertext link
a clickable bit of text that connects the user to another location on the Web

Web site
a group of related Web pages posted by the same sponsor or organization

Web page
a page viewable as a single unit on a Web site

Web browser
a program that provides access to Web resources through a variety of tools

deep Web
Internet materials not accessible via popular search engines but available through a library's subscription databases

URL
the uniform resource locator; the Web address telling the browser how to access a certain file

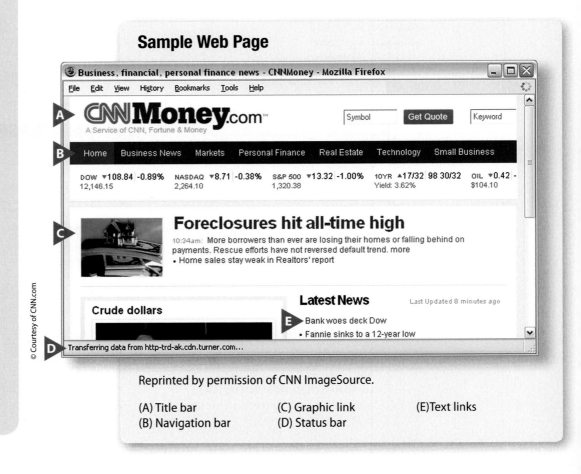

© Courtesy of CNN.com

Sample Web Page

Reprinted by permission of CNN ImageSource.

(A) Title bar (C) Graphic link (E) Text links
(B) Navigation bar (D) Status bar

The **domain name** is a key part of the address because it indicates what type of organization created the site and gives you clues about its goal or purpose—to educate, inform, persuade, sell, and/or entertain. Most sites combine a primary purpose with secondary ones.

Sample Domain Names

.com a commercial organization or business

.gov a government organization—federal, state, or local

.edu an educational institution

.org a nonprofit organization

.net an organization that is part of the Internet's infrastructure

.mil a military site

.biz a business site

.info any site primarily providing information

International addresses generally include national abbreviations (for example, Canada = .ca). This clue helps you determine the origin of the information and communicate more sensitively on the Internet.

Saving Internet Information

Accurately saving Internet addresses and material is an essential part of good research. Moreover, you may want to revisit sites and embed URLs in your research writing. Save Internet information through these methods:

Bookmark: Your browser can save a site's address through a "bookmark" or "favorites" function on your menu bar.

Printout: If a document looks promising, print a hard copy of it. Remember to write down all details needed for citing the source. (Although many details will automatically print with the document, some could be missing.)

Save or download: To keep an electronic copy of material, save the document to a specific drive on your computer. Beware of large files with many graphics: They take up a lot of space. To save just the text, highlight it, copy it, and then paste it into a word-processing program.

E-mail: If you're not at your own computer, you can e-mail the document's URL to your e-mail address through copy and paste.

© Used under license from Shutterstock.com

LO7 Find reliable information.

Because the Internet contains so much information of varying reliability, you need to become familiar with search tools that locate information you can trust. The key is knowing which search tool to use in which research situation. It's also important to proceed with caution.

Adhere to your assignment's restrictions on using Web sites (number and type). In fact, some instructors may not allow Web resources for specific projects, limiting you to print sources and scholarly articles available in subscription databases.

When you are using Web resources, make sure the sites are sponsored by legitimate, recognizable organizations: government agencies, nonprofit groups, and educational institutions. For most projects, avoid relying on personal, commercial, and special-interest sites, as well as chat rooms, blogs, and news groups. Test the quality and reliability of online information by using the benchmarks outlined on page 215.

Avoid developing your paper by simply copying and pasting together chunks of Web pages. By doing so, you not only fail to engage your sources meaningfully, but you also commit plagiarism. For more on plagiarism, see pages 242–244.

domain name
the name of a site, including the extension after the dot (.), which indicates what type of organization created the site

bookmark
a digital tag that allows the user to easily return to a favorite site

RELIABLE WEB SITES

Your library may sponsor a Web site that gives you access to quality Internet resources. For example, it may provide tutorials on using the Internet, guides to Internet resources in different disciplines, links to online document collections (Project Gutenberg, Etext Archives, New Bartleby Digital Library, and so on), or connections to other virtual resources (virtual libraries, subscription databases, search engines, directories, government documents, and online reference works). If your library provides access to the global catalog WorldCat, click on the "Internet" limiter to search for information recommended by librarians.

Finding other useful Web sites can be as easy as typing in a URL. If you don't have the exact URL, sometimes you can guess it, especially for an organization (company, government agency, or nonprofit group). Of course, you can also search for the Web site, checking the URLs that are presented to make sure you select the actual site you seek, not a copycat.

You can also find useful sites by following links provided on other useful sites. If you come across a helpful link (often highlighted in blue), click on the link to visit that new page. Note that the link may take you to another site.

Your browser keeps a record of the pages you visit. Click the back arrow to go back one page or the forward arrow to move ahead again. Clicking the right mouse button on these arrows shows a list of recently visited pages.

SUBJECT TREES

A **subject tree**, sometimes called a subject guide or directory, lists Web sites that have been organized into categories by experts who have reviewed those sites. Use subject trees or directories if you need to narrow down a broad topic or if you want sites that have been evaluated (quality over quantity).

How does a subject tree work? Essentially, it allows you to select from a broad range of subjects or "branches." With each topic choice, you narrow down your selection until you arrive at a list of Web sites, or you can keyword-search a limited number of Web sites.

Check whether your library subscribes to a service such as NetFirst, a database in which subject experts have cataloged

subject tree
a listing of Web sites, arranged by experts

Internet resources by topic. Here are some other common subject directories that you can likely access at your library:

WWW Virtual Library • http://vlib.org/Overview.html
Argus • http://www.clearinghouse.net
Librarians' Internet Index • http://www.lii.org
Google Directory • http://www.google.com/dirhp
LookSmart • http://looksmart.com

TIP

To get the best results from your search, avoid these problems: misspelling keywords; using vague or broad keywords (*education* or *business*); incorrectly combining Boolean operators; or shortening keywords too much.

Examine the subject-tree search explained below and on the next page. Afterward, conduct your own search using a subject tree available through your library.

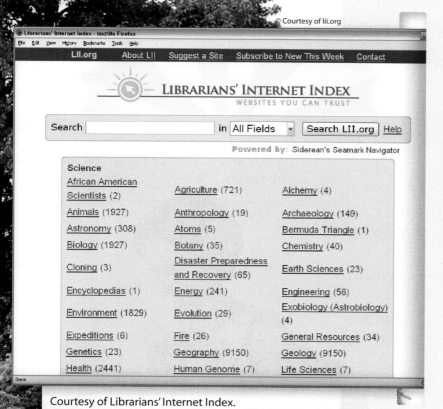

© Courtesy of lii.org

Courtesy of Librarians' Internet Index.

Courtesy of Librarians' Internet Index.

Subject-Tree Search
(Hybrid Electric Cars)

Step 1: Select an appropriate broad category. Study the subject tree to the left provided by the Librarians' Internet Index (Lii). To find reviewed Web sites containing information on hybrid electric cars, you could select from this start page a range of categories, depending on the angle you want to explore: Arts and Humanities, Business, Computers, Science, and so on. Each of these starting points will lead to a different listing of relevant sites. Another option would be to use the keyword search feature shown.

Step 2: Choose a fitting subcategory. If you chose Science, the subcategories shown here would appear. At this point, you would again have several choices: (1) to select Environment, (2) to follow Transportation, or (3) to do a keyword search of this now more limited grouping of Web sites. Each choice might lead to a distinct set of Web sites. In fact, your research may benefit by trying all three options.

Courtesy of Librarians'
Internet Index.

Step 3: Work toward a listing of Web sites. As you work down through narrower branches of the tree, you will arrive at a listing of relevant Web sites. Such sites, remember, have all been reviewed in terms of quality, though you still need to evaluate what you find. In the citation for a site, study the site title, the description of information available, site sponsorship, and the Web address (particularly the domain name). Use that information to determine the site's relevance to your research. At this point, you can save the results and/or click on the site's Web address and proceed to research the site.

(A) Site title
(B) Site description, types of content, members and sponsors
(C) Web address (link)

Visiting, Exploring, and Evaluating

Look through the listing of recommended sites. Once you have identified a promising site, follow the links provided. Study and evaluate the site by asking questions such as these:

1. Who authored or sponsored the site? What is the author's or sponsor's perspective on the topic? Why did the author post these pages? What can you find out about the author through a broader Internet search?

2. What content does the site offer? What depth of information is available?

3. Does the Web site function as a primary, secondary, or tertiary source?

4. What external links does the site offer? Might these links take you to additional resources that are relevant and reliable?

Insight: Careful investigation and evaluation of Web sites is even more important when you use search engines like those discussed on the next page. Use the resource evaluation guidelines on page 215 for Web pages that you find through either subject directories or search engines. Always proceed with caution, making sure that your research writing does not rely on unstable, shallow Web pages.

SEARCH AND METASEARCH

Unlike a subject directory, which provides a list crafted with human input, a search engine provides a list generated automatically by scouring millions of Web sites. Not all search engines are the same. Some search citations of Internet materials, whereas others conduct full-text searches. Choose a search engine that covers a large portion of the Internet, offers quality indexing, and provides high-powered search capabilities.

Basic search engines search millions of Web pages, and they include engines such as Alta Vista, AllTheWeb, Google, HotBot, Vivisimo, and Yahoo. (The URL for each of these is the engine name, without spaces, followed by <.com>.)

Metasearch tools search several basic search engines at once, and they include sites such as Ask, Dog Pile, Ixquick, and Northern Light. (The URL for each of these is the engine name, without spaces, followed by <.com>.)

fyi Deep-Web tools check Internet databases and other sources not accessible to basic search engines. One excellent deep-Web tool is Complete Planet at www.completeplanet.com.

Basic Web Search
(Toyota Hybrid Electric Cars)

© Courtesy of Google.com

Reprinted by permission of Google.

Step 1: Begin the search with precise terms. Using Boolean operators and quotation marks, you might begin with the search terms "Toyota" and "hybrid electric cars." The more precise your terms are, the better your results will be.

Step 2: Study the results and refine your search. The results of the initial search appear here. At this point, you can click one of the resulting Web links, click a sponsored link, follow links on the right to related topics, or narrow or broaden your search. For example, you might choose to check Toyota's pages on the Prius, view a history of hybrid cars from another commercial site, or view a *Popular Mechanics* article on hybrid vehicles.

Refinement through search questions with drop-down lists

(A) Results: sponsored sites (primarily advertising)

(B) Results: other Web pages

(C) Revising search and advanced search option

search engines
sites that search other Web sites using key words

metasearch tools
sites that search other search engines

"**Facts are stubborn things;**
and whatever may be our wishes, our inclinations, or the dictates
of our passion, they cannot alter the state of facts and evidence."
—John Adams

20

Research Paper

In 1960, the famed **paleontologist** Louis Leakey sent his young secretary on a four-month expedition to Tanzania to observe chimpanzees in the wild. Jane Goodall was not a trained scientist, but she was a keen observer, patient and meticulous and gentle. She did something naturalists had never thought of doing. She sat still and let the animals come to her. The first chimpanzee who approached she named David Greybeard— not Specimen TZ196001. And she took extensive notes, created detailed drawings, and learned more about wild chimpanzees in four months than humanity had learned since the dawn of time.

Then Jane came back to civilization. She had so much to report, but no one would listen to a twenty-something woman with no scientific degree who lived with chimps in the wild. At Leakey's request, Jane enrolled at Cambridge and by 1965 received her Ph.D. She did her paper chase and became Dr. Jane Goodall and wrote up her findings and changed the world.

The point is this: You can do all the research you want, but until you put it into a documented form that others in your field can read and respond to, your discoveries make no impact. You have to do the paper chase. You have to document.

Writing your research paper is the culmination of your discovery process. It's the chance for you to share your discoveries and change minds. This chapter will guide you through the process.

Learning Outcomes

LO1 Avoid plagiarism.

LO2 Avoid other source abuses.

LO3 Use sources well.

LO4 Write your research paper.

What do you think?

I'd love to spend four months in a remote place studying something in my field.

1	2	3	4	5
strongly agree				strongly disagree

paleontologist
a scientist who studies life forms that lived in past geologic time

LO1 Avoid plagiarism.

The road to **plagiarism** may be paved with the best intentions—or the worst. Either way, the result is a serious academic offense. As you write your research paper, do everything you can to stay off that road! Start by studying your school's and your instructor's guidelines on plagiarism and other academic offenses. Then study the following pages.

WHAT IS PLAGIARISM?

Plagiarism is using someone else's words, ideas, or images (what's called intellectual property) so they appear to be your own. When you plagiarize, you use source material—whether published in print or online—without acknowledging the source. In this sense, plagiarism refers to a range of thefts: submitting a paper you didn't write (even if you bought it), pasting source material into your paper and passing it off as your own, using exact quotations without quotation marks and documentation, and summarizing and paraphrasing material without **documentation**. And plagiarism is more than "word theft." The rules also apply to images, tables, graphs, charts, maps, music, videos, and so on.

What makes it wrong?

Plagiarism is stealing, and colleges punish it as such. It may result in a failing grade for the assignment or course, a note on your **academic transcript** (often seen by potential employers), and possibly even expulsion.

Aside from the punitive aspects, plagiarism short-circuits dialogue within a discipline. It discounts the work of other thinkers, disrespects writers and readers, insults instructors, and damages the reputation of colleges.

Also consider what plagiarism does to you. It prevents you from learning the skills you need to have as a scholar. It also demonstrates to others around you that you are not a serious thinker, that you aren't to be trusted, relied upon, or listened to. In short, it damages your reputation, a key component to your success academically and professionally.

plagiarism
presenting someone else's work or ideas as one's own

documentation
crediting sources of information through in-text citations or references and a list of works cited or references

academic transcript
the permanent record of educational achievement and activity

What does it look like?

Plagiarism can take on a number of forms. Read the passage below and then review the four types of plagiarism that follow, noting how each misuses the source.

> What makes Munro's characters so enthralling is their inconsistency; like real people, at one moment they declare they will cover the house in new siding, at the next, they vomit on their way to the hospital. They fight against and seek refuge in the people they love. The technique that Munro has forged to get at such contradictions is a sort of pointillism, the setting of one bright scene against another, with little regard for chronology.

Excerpt taken from page 87 of "Some Stories Have to Be Told by Me: A Literary History of Alice Munro," by Marcela Valdes, published in the *Virginia Quarterly Review* 82.3 (Summer 2006).

1. Submitting another writer's paper is the most blatant form of plagiarism. Whether the paper was written by another student, was downloaded and reformatted from the Internet, or was purchased from a "paper mill," the result is still plagiarism. Remember that though it may seem easy to plagiarize material from the Internet, it's equally easy for professors to use Internet tools to discover plagiarism.

2. Pasting material into your paper and passing it off as your own is another form of plagiarism. In the example below, the **boldface** material is plagiarized from the original article, masquerading as the writer's own idea.

> Life typically unfolds mysteriously for Munro's characters, with unexplained events and choices. **Like real people, at one moment they declare they will cover the house in new siding, at the next, they vomit on their way to the hospital.**

3. Using material without quotation marks and citation is another form of plagiarism. Whether you use a paragraph or a phrase, if you use the exact wording of a source, you must enclose the material in quotation marks and provide a source citation. The lack of quotation marks makes the **boldface** material plagiarized.

> What makes Munro's characters so typically human is that **they fight against and seek refuge in the people they love** (Valdes 87).

4. Failing to cite a source for summarized or para-phrased ideas is another form of plagiarism. Even if borrowed information has been reworded, the source must be acknowledged. In the following example, the writer correctly summarizes the passage's ideas but offers no citation.

> For the reader, the characters in Munro's stories are interesting because they are so changeable. Munro shows these changes by using a method of placing scenes side by side for contrast, without worrying about the chronological connections.

How do I avoid it?

Of course, some types of plagiarism may happen by accident, perhaps through sloppy note taking or inexpert use of punctuation. Plagiarism is like speeding—regardless of whether the infraction was purposeful or accidental, it carries the same consequences.

Preventing plagiarism begins the moment you get an assignment. Essentially, prevention requires commitment and diligence throughout the process. Begin, of course, by pledging never to plagiarize, no matter how easy the Internet may make it. Also follow the rules established by your college and your professor.

Avoiding Plagiarism Strategy

- **As you research,** take orderly notes and maintain an accurate **working bibliography**. (See page 216.) Make sure to carefully summarize, paraphrase, and quote material.

- **As you write,** carefully credit all material that is quoted, summarized, or paraphrased from another source. For quoted material, use quotation marks. For summaries and paraphrases, signal where borrowed material begins by using a phrase like "*As Valdes* notes, many of Munro's characters exhibit . . ."; then signal where the material ends by providing the source citation.

- **After you write,** compile a complete, accurate works-cited or reference list with full source information for all borrowed material in your writing.

LO2 Avoid other source abuses.

Plagiarism, though the most serious offense, is not the only source abuse to avoid when writing a paper with documented research. The information that follows covers source abuses that are subtly deceptive.

EIGHT TO ELIMINATE

Avoid these eight documentation pitfalls in your writing. The examples reference the excerpt on the previous page.

1. Using sources inaccurately: When you get a quotation wrong, botch a summary, paraphrase poorly, or misstate a statistic, you misrepresent the original. *Example:* In this quotation, the writer carelessly uses several wrong words that change the meaning, and also adds two words that are not in the original.

> As Marcela Valdes explains, "[w]hat makes Munro's characters so **appalling** is their **consistency**....They fight against and seek **refuse** in the people **they say** they love" (87).

2. Using source material out of context: By ripping a statement out of its **context** and forcing it into yours, you can make a source seem to say something that it didn't really say. *Example:* This writer uses part of a statement to say the opposite of the original.

> According to Marcela Valdes, while Munro's characters are interesting, Munro's weakness as a fiction writer is that she shows "little regard for chronology" (87).

CAUTION
PLAGIARISM AHEAD

working bibliography
list of the sources that you have used and/or intend to use in your research

context
the set of circumstances in which a statement is made; the text and other factors that surround a specific statement and are crucial to understanding it

3. Overusing source material: When your paper reads like a string of references, especially quotations, your own thinking disappears. *Example:* The writer takes the source passage, chops it up, and splices it together.

> Anyone who has read her stories knows that "[w]hat makes Munro's characters so enthralling is their inconsistency." That is to say, "like real people, at one moment they declare they will cover the house in new siding, at the next, they vomit on their way to the hospital." Moreover, "[t]hey fight against and seek refuge in the people they love." This method "that Munro has forged to get at such contradictions is a sort of pointillism," meaning "the setting of one bright scene against another, with little regard for chronology" (Valdes 87).

4. "Plunking" quotations: You "plunk" quotations into your paper by failing both to introduce them to the reader and to provide a follow-up. The discussion becomes choppy and disconnected. *Example:* The writer interrupts the flow of ideas with a quotation "out of the blue." In addition, the quotation hangs at the end of a paragraph with no follow-up.

> Typically, characters such as Del Jordan, Louisa Doud, and Almeda Roth experience a crisis through contact with particular men. "They fight against and seek refuge in the people they love" (Valdes 87).

5. Using "blanket" citations: Blanket citations make the reader guess where borrowed material begins and ends. For example, if you place a parenthetical citation at the end of a paragraph, does that citation cover the whole paragraph or just the final sentence?

6. Relying heavily on one source: If your writing is dominated by one source, the reader may doubt the depth and integrity of your research. Instead, your writing should show your reliance on a balanced diversity of sources.

fair use
rules governing the use of small (not large) portions of text, for noncommercial purposes

public domain
materials provided by the government, provided as part of the "copy left" movement, or, generally speaking, materials older than 75 years old

7. Failing to match in-text citations to bibliographic entries: All in-text citations must clearly refer to accurate entries in the works-cited, reference, or endnote pages. Mismatching occurs when (a) an in-text citation refers to a source not listed in the bibliography or (b) a bibliographic entry is never referenced in the paper itself.

8. Violating copyrights: When you copy, distribute, and/or post in whole or in part any intellectual property without permission from or payment to the copyright holder, you commit a copyright infringement, especially when you profit from this use. To avoid copyright violations in your research projects, do the following:

Avoiding Copyright Violations Strategy

- **Observe fair use guidelines:** Quote small portions of a document for limited purposes, such as education or research. Avoid copying large portions for your own gain.

- **Understand what's in the public domain:** You need not obtain permission to copy and use public domain materials—primarily documents created by the government, but also some material posted on the Internet as part of the "copy left" movement.

- **Observe intellectual property and copyright laws:** First, know your college's policies on copying documents. Second, realize that copyright protects the expression of ideas in a range of materials—writings, videos, songs, photographs, drawings, computer software, and so on. Always obtain permission to copy and distribute copyrighted materials.

- **Avoid changing a source** (e.g., a photo) without permission of the creator or copyright holder.

fyi Beyond plagiarism and related source abuses, there are other academic offenses to avoid. When you submit one paper in two different classes without permission from both instructors, you are "double dipping," taking double credit for one work. Also, when you submit another student's work as your own, or allow another student to submit your work as her or his own, you are guilty of a particular type of plagiarism called "Falstaffing."

LO3 Use sources well.

After you've found good sources and taken good notes on them, you want to use that research effectively in your writing. Specifically, you want to show (1) what information you are borrowing and (2) where you got it. By doing so, you create credibility. This section shows you how to develop credibility by integrating and documenting sources so as to avoid plagiarism and other abuses. (Note: For a full treatment of documentation, see pages 251-271.)

INTEGRATE SOURCES.

Source material—whether summary, paraphrase, or quotation—should be integrated smoothly into your discussion. To do so, you should focus on what you want to say, not on all the sources you've collected. Use sources to deepen and develop your point, provide evidence for your argument, give authority to your position, illustrate your point, or address a counterargument.

Managing Your Sources

Failure to manage your sources will result in those sources determining the course and character of your work. Here's a pattern you can follow to make sure you control your sources, rather than letting them control you:

Source Management Pattern

1. State and explain your idea, creating context for the source.

2. Identify and introduce the source, linking it to your discussion.

3. Summarize, paraphrase, or quote the source

4. Provide a citation in an appropriate spot.

5. Comment on the source by explaining, expanding on, or refuting it.

6. When appropriate, refer again to a source to further develop the ideas it contains.

(Review the keyed model that follows.)

Keyed Model:

> The motivation and urgency to create and improve hybrid-electric technology comes from a range of complex forces. Some of these forces are economic, others environmental, and still others social. In "Societal Lifestyle Costs of Cars with Alternative Fuels/Engines," Joan Ogden, Robert Williams, and Eric Larson argue that "[c]ontinued reliance on current transportation fuels and technologies poses serious oil supply insecurity, climate change, and urban air pollution risks" (7). Because of the nonrenewable nature of fossil fuels as well as their negative side effects, the transportation industry is confronted with making the most radical changes since the introduction of the internal-combustion automobile more than 100 years ago. Hybrid-electric vehicles are one response to this pressure.
>
> *1*
> *2*
> *3*
> *4*
> *5*
> *6*

Incorporating Quotations

Be especially careful with quotations, which can overwhelm your own thinking and create a choppy flow. Use restraint. Include only quotations that are key statements by authorities, well-phrased claims and conclusions, or passages that require word-by-word analysis and interpretation. Quotations—especially long ones—need to pull their weight, so generally paraphrase or summarize source material instead.

When you do use quotations, work them into your writing as smoothly as possible, paying attention to style, punctuation, and syntax. Use enough of the quotation to make your point without changing the meaning of the original. Place quotation marks around key phrases taken from the source.

> Ogden, Williams, and Larson also conclude that the hydrogen fuel-cell vehicle is "a strong candidate for becoming the Car of the Future," given the trend toward "tighter environmental constraints" and the "intense efforts underway" by automakers to develop commercially viable versions of such vehicles (25).

DOCUMENT SOURCES.

Just as you need to integrate source material carefully into your writing, so you must also carefully document where that source material comes from. The reader should recognize which material is yours and which is not.

Identifying the Start

Sources need to be introduced. It's the introduction that signals an encounter with ideas and facts from someone other than you, the writer.

First Reference: For the first reference to a source, use an attributive statement that indicates some of the following: author's name and credentials, title of the source, nature of the study or research, and helpful background.

> **Joan Ogden, Robert Williams, and Eric Larson, members of the Princeton Environmental Institute, explain** that modest improvements in energy efficiency and emissions reductions will not be enough over the next century because of anticipated transportation increases (7).

Subsequent References: For subsequent references to a source, use a simplified **attributive phrase**, such as the author's last name or a shortened version of the title.

> **Ogden, Williams, and Larson go on to argue** that "effectively addressing environmental and oil supply concerns will probably require radical changes in automotive engine/fuel technologies" (7).

Other References: In some situations, such as quoting straightforward facts, simply skip the attributive phrase. The parenthetical citation supplies sufficient attribution.

> Various types of transportation are by far the main consumers of oil (three-fourths of world oil imports); moreover, these same technologies are responsible for one-fourth of all greenhouse gas sources (Ogden, Williams, and Larson 7).

attributive phrase
a group of words that indicates the source of an idea or a quotation

The verb you use to introduce source material is key. Use fitting verbs, such as those in the table below. Normally, use the present tense. (Use the past tense only to stress the previous time frame of a source.)

> In their 2004 study, "Societal Lifecycle Costs of Cars with Alternative Fuels/Engines," Ogden, Williams, and Larson present a method for comparing and contrasting alternatives to internal-combustion engines. Earlier, these authors made preliminary steps …

Quick Guide — Introductory Verbs

accepts	declares	points out
acknowledges	defends	praises
adds	denies	proposes
affirms	describes	refutes
argues	disagrees	rejects
asserts	discusses	reminds
believes	emphasizes	responds
cautions	enumerates	shares
claims	explains	shows
compares	highlights	states
concludes	identifies	stresses
confirms	insists	suggests
considers	interprets	supports
contradicts	lists	urges
contrasts	maintains	verifies
criticizes	outlines	warns

Identifying the End

Quotations and Ideas: Closing quotation marks and a citation, as shown in the following example, indicate the end of a source quotation. Generally, place the citation immediately after any quotation, paraphrase, or summary. However, you may also place the citation early in the sentence or at the end if the parenthetical note is obviously obtrusive. When you discuss several details from a page in a source, use an attributive phrase at the beginning of your discussion and a single citation at the end.

> As the "Lifestyle Costs" study concludes, when greenhouse gases, air pollution, and oil insecurity are factored into the analysis, alternative-fuel vehicles "offer lower LCCs than typical new cars" (Ogden, Williams, and Larson 25).

Longer Quotations: If a quotation is longer than four typed lines, set it off from the main text. Generally, introduce the quotation with a complete sentence and a colon. Indent the quotation one inch (10 spaces) and double-space it, but don't put quotation marks around it. Put the citation outside the final punctuation mark.

> Toward the end of the study, Ogden, Williams, and Larson argue that changes to the fuel delivery system must be factored into planning:
>
> > In charting a course to the Car of the Future, societal LCC comparisons should be complemented by considerations of fuel infrastructure requirements. Because fuel infrastructure changes are costly, the number of major changes made over time should be minimized. The bifurcated strategy advanced here—of focusing on the H2FCV for the long term and advanced liquid hydrocarbon-fueled ICEVs and ICE/HEVs for the near term—would reduce the number of such infrastructure changes to one (an eventual shift to H2). (25)

Altering Quotations

Changing Quotations: You may shorten or change a quotation so that it fits more smoothly into your sentence—but don't alter the original meaning. Use an ellipsis within square brackets [. . .] to indicate that you have omitted words from the original. An **ellipsis** is three periods with spaces between them.

> In their projections of where fuel-cell vehicles are heading, Ogden, Williams, and Larson discuss GM's AUTOnomy vehicle, with its "radical redesign of the entire car. [. . .] In these cars, steering, braking, and other vehicle systems are controlled electronically rather than mechanically" (24).

Using Brackets: Use square brackets to indicate a clarification, to change a pronoun or verb tense, or to switch around uppercase and lowercase.

> As Ogden, Williams, and Larson explain, "[e]ven if such barriers [the high cost of fuel cells and the lack of an H2 fuel infrastructure] can be overcome, decades would be required before this embryonic technology could make major contributions in reducing the major externalities that characterize today's cars" (25).

ellipsis
a set of three periods with one space preceding and following each period; a punctuation mark that indicates deletion of material

LO4 Write your research paper.

Your research may generate a mass of notes, printouts, photocopies, electronic files, and more. Your goal is to move from this mass to a coherent structure for the paper you need to write. If you have systematically taken good notes, you are well on the way. Follow the guidelines below to move toward order.

1. Review your research materials. Is the information complete or at least sufficient for the project? Is the information reliable and accurate? How do different pieces of evidence connect to each other? What patterns do you see? By reviewing your research once, twice, and even three times, you'll begin to see your research paper taking shape before you.

2. Revisit your research questions and working thesis. Has research changed your perspective and position? Revise your thesis accordingly. A solid thesis gives you a roadmap for writing your paper.

3. Organize your work effectively. Reread the assignment, which may suggest a pattern of organization, such as comparison-contrast. If not, use a pattern of organization suggested by your thesis and support. Turn key ideas into main headings and arrange support and evidence under each. After categorizing information, decide on the best sequence for your ideas. The following quick guide explains some common organizational patterns available to you.

Quick Guide   Organizational Patterns

Argumentation asserts and supports a claim, counters opposition, and reasserts the claim.

Cause-effect explores the factors that lead to an event and the consequences that result from it.

Chronological order puts items in a time sequence.

Classification groups details based on common traits or qualities.

Comparison-contrast shows similarities and differences between two subjects.

Description orders details in terms of spatial relationships.

Explanation clarifies how something works by breaking the object or phenomenon into parts or phases and showing how they work together.

Order of importance arranges items from most to least or least to most important.

Problem-solution states a problem, explores its causes and effects, and presents solutions.

Question-answer moves back and forth from questions to answers in a sequence that logically clarifies a topic.

4. Develop your first draft. As you write your paper, your main goal is to develop and support your ideas, referring to sources but not being dominated by them. Your second goal is to respect sources by integrating them naturally and accurately, with correct documentation. (Review pages 246–247 to understand how to use source material.) Make sure to indicate the source of all borrowed ideas and quotations as you develop the following parts:

Opening. Start by saying something interesting or surprising to gain your reader's attention. Then establish common ground with your reader and the topic, and identify a specific issue or challenge. Finally, offer your thesis.

Middle. Develop your thesis by presenting each main point, expanding upon the points logically, including evidence such as facts and examples, and analyzing each issue. Think of each main point as a conversation you are having with your reader, in which you share the most interesting, amazing, and salient aspects of each point. Don't try to cram everything you have learned into the draft.

Closing. Review or tie together important points in your paper, reinforce your thesis, and draw a conclusion. In closing, expand the scope of your text by connecting the topic of the paper to the reader's experience or to life in general.

5. Revise your first draft. Ask a peer to read your first draft and indicate any parts that could be improved. Reread your draft as well, and use the following questions to help you revise it.

Revising Checklist

_____ Is my thesis clear?

_____ Do I support the thesis with strong main points?

_____ Do I support the main points with evidence and analysis?

_____ Have I used an organizational plan that fits the assignment, my topic, and purpose?

_____ Do the main points appear in the best order?

_____ Are the paragraphs (and the sentences within them) in the best order?

_____ Is my writing voice objective and scholarly, focused on the topic?

_____ Is my writing voice knowledgeable and engaging?

_____ Have I selected strong words and correctly used topic-specific terms?

_____ Do my sentences read smoothly?

6. Edit your paper. Once you have finished making large-scale improvements to your paper, it's time to edit your work and create a works-cited or reference section. Use the following questions to help you edit your work.

Editing Checklist

_____ Have I correctly punctuated sentences and abbreviations?

_____ Have I used correct capitalization with proper nouns?

_____ Have I double-checked the spelling of all specialized words, authors' names, and titles?

_____ Have I watched for easily confused words (_there, their, they're_)?

_____ Have I carefully checked the format of each in-text citation or reference? (See pages 254–260.)

_____ Have I carefully checked the format of each entry in my works-cited or reference section? (See pages 260–266.)

7. Design your paper. The two major documentation styles (MLA and APA) have strict requirements for the final presentation of a research report. Make certain that your paper follows the appropriate style and abides by any guidelines your instructor may have provided.

 For samples from MLA and APA papers—as well as help with documentation—see the following chapter, pages 251–271.)

"**The palest ink is better**
than the best memory."

—Chinese Proverb

21

MLA and APA Styles

To read these words, your eyes had to begin at the upper left corner of the page. As you continue, your eyes slide right to the end of each line, then down and left to the beginning of the next, and so on, until you reach the bottom right corner of the page. At that point, you will turn to the next page and continue. These are the basic conventions of reading in a language like English.

This book also uses a few common typesetting conventions, such as a hierarchy of heading sizes, a two-column format, featured material in separate boxes, and so on. You'll note a page number at the bottom of each page, along with running feet.

Adherence to these conventions makes it easier for you, the reader, to grasp the information in this book. Imagine if every book made up its own rules instead: some expecting you to begin at the back and work forward; some placing words in an outward spiral on the page; others zigzagging sentences back and forth. The result would be confusion and frustration.

So we use typographical conventions to make things easier. Similarly, publishers of scholarly essays add a few conventions of their own to ensure that the reader can easily grasp and locate sources. The two research styles most frequently used in college have been developed by the Modern Language Association (MLA) and the American Psychological Association (APA).

In this chapter, we provide you with instructions for using those two styles to format your research paper pages and to document your sources within the text of your paper and at its end. To best illuminate the rationale of each style, we compare them side by side throughout the chapter. In those few cases where one style calls for an item not covered by the other (as in MLA's standard for short verse citations, a source not likely to be used in APA), we have called out that information in a separate box.

As anyone who has studied a foreign tongue can attest, one's native language is revealed in a brand-new way by comparison. Contrast makes things clear. That has been our goal in presenting MLA and APA styles side by side in this chapter.

Learning Outcomes

LO1 Learn the basics of MLA & APA styles.

LO2 Understand in-text citations.

LO3 List books and other nonperiodical documents.

LO4 List print periodical articles.

LO5 List online sources.

LO6 List other sources.

What do you think?

Documentation makes an argument more convincing.

1	2	3	4	5
strongly agree			strongly disagree	

LO1 Learn the basics of MLA & APA styles.

MLA Style

Is a separate title page required?

MLA **No** (unless your instructor requires one). On the first page of a research paper, type your name, your instructor's name, the course name and number, and the date, one below the other. The title comes next, centered. Then simply begin the text on the next line.

Is an abstract required?

MLA **No.** An abstract (a summary of your research paper) is not an MLA requirement.

Is the research paper double-spaced?

MLA **Yes.** Double-space everything, even tables, captions, long quotations, or works-cited entries.

Are page numbers required?

MLA **Yes.** Pages should be numbered consecutively in the upper right corner, one-half inch from the top and flush with the right margin (one inch). Your last name should precede the page number.

What about longer quotations?

MLA Do not use quotation marks. (1) Indent verse quotations of more than three lines one inch (ten spaces). Each line of a poem or play begins a new line of the quotation. (2) When quoting prose that needs more than four typed lines, indent each line one inch (ten spaces) from the left margin. (3) To quote two or more paragraphs, further indent the first line of each paragraph a quarter-inch (three spaces). However, if the first sentence quoted does not begin a paragraph, do not indent it; use the additional indent only on the first lines of the successive paragraphs.

APA Style

APA **Yes.** Include your paper's title, your name, and the name of your school on three separate lines, double-spaced, centered, and beginning approximately one-third of the way down from the top of the page. Place the running head (an abbreviated title) in the upper left corner, and the page number 1 in the upper right.

APA **Usually.** An APA-style abstract is a paragraph summarizing your research paper. It is 150 to 250 words long. (See page 269.) Place your abstract on a new page and label it "Abstract" (centered); place the running head in the upper left corner, and the page number 2 in the upper right.

APA **Yes.** Double-space all text lines, titles, headings, quotations, captions, and references.

APA **Yes.** Page numbers appear at the top right margin, above the first line of text; but do not include your name. Instead, place the running head in the upper left corner.

APA Type quotations of 40 or more words in block style (all lines flush left) one-half inch (five spaces) in from the left margin. Indent the first lines of any additional paragraphs in the long quotation one-half inch (five spaces) in from the margin set for the quotation.

Is an appendix required?

MLA **No.** In MLA style, tables and illustrations are placed as close as possible to the related text.

APA **Maybe.** While tables and figures already appear on separate pages, one or more appendices may also be used to supplement the text of the paper.

How wide should the margins be?

MLA Top, bottom, left, and right margins should be one inch (except for page numbering). Do not justify lines, but rather leave the right margin ragged with no word breaks at the ends of lines.

APA Leave a margin of at least one inch on all four sides. Do not justify lines, but rather leave the right margin ragged with no word breaks at the ends of lines.

Are references placed in the text?

MLA **Yes.** Indicate only page numbers parenthetically if you identify the author in your text. Give the author's last name in a parenthetical reference if it is not mentioned in the text.

Example, author identified in the text:
Galuszka notes that minorities have limited opportunities for training in this field (9).

Example, author cited in parentheses:
Minorities currently have limited opportunities for training in this field (Galuszka 9).

APA **Yes.** Include the author's last name and the year, separated by a comma; for quotations, add the page number after a comma and "p."

Example without quotation:
Game-design training opportunities are limited for minorities (Galuszka, 2009).

Example with quotation:
"Few historically Black colleges and universities offer much in the way of computer gaming" (Galuszka, 2009, p. 9).

Is a list of sources used in the paper required?

MLA **Yes.** Full citations for all sources used (e.g., books, periodicals) are placed in an alphabetized list labeled "Works Cited" at the end of the paper, providing full publication details for each work cited in the report. Hanging indentation is required for the entries in this works-cited list.

Example:
Galuszka, Peter. "Getting into the Game." *Diverse: Issues in Higher Education* 19 Mar. 2009: 9–10. Print.

APA **Yes.** Full citations for all sources used (books, periodicals, and so on) are placed in an alphabetized list labeled "References" at the end of the paper, providing full publication details for each work referenced in the report. Hanging indentation is the standard format.

Example:
Galuszka, P. (2009, March 19). Getting into the game. *Diverse: Issues in Higher Education, 26*(3), 9-10.

What about headings?

MLA MLA style does not specify a particular format for headings within the text; normally, headings are used only for separate sections of the paper ("Works Cited" or "Notes," for example).

APA Headings, like an outline, show the organization of your APA paper and the importance of each topic. All topics of equal importance should have headings of the same level, or style. Below are the various levels of headings used in APA papers.

Level 1: **Centered, Boldface, Uppercase and Lowercase Heading**

Level 2: **Flush Left, Boldface, Uppercase and Lowercase Heading**

Level 3: **Indented, boldface, lowercase paragraph heading ending with a period.**

Level 4: ***Indented, boldface, italicized, lowercase paragraph heading ending with a period.***

Are reference markers needed if I submit my paper electronically?

MLA **Yes.** Number (in brackets) each paragraph at its beginning, followed by a space before starting the text.

APA **No.** APA style does not call for reference markers, but double-check with your instructor or publisher about acceptable file formats for any tables or figures.

Are there any other special instructions?

Always ask whether your school, department, or instructor has special requirements that may take precedence over the guidelines listed here.

LO2 Understand in-text citations.

As a general rule, keep citations brief and integrate them smoothly into your writing. When paraphrasing or summarizing, make it clear where your borrowing begins and ends. Use stylistic cues to distinguish the source's thoughts ("Kalmbach points out . . . ," "Some critics argue . . . ") from your own ("I believe . . . ," "It seems obvious, however . . ."). See pages 246–247 for more on integrating sources. Make sure each in-text citation clearly points to an entry in your list of sources. The identifying information (usually the author's last name) must be the word or words by which the entry is alphabetized in that list. When using a shortened title of a work, begin with the word by which the work is alphabetized in your list of sources (e.g., "Egyptian, Classical," for "Egyptian, Classical, and Middle Eastern Art"). When including a parenthetical citation at the end of a sentence, place it before the end punctuation. (See page 253.)

MLA NOTE

When citing inclusive page numbers larger than ninety-nine, MLA calls for giving only the two digits of the second number (*Augustyn* 113–14; not *Augustyn* 113–114).

One Author: A Complete Work

MLA   You do not need an in-text citation if you identify the author in your text. (This is the preferred way of citing a complete work.) Do not offer page numbers when citing complete works, articles in alphabetized encyclopedias, one-page articles, and unpaginated sources.

> In *No Need for Hunger*, Robert Spitzer recommends that the U.S. government develop a new foreign policy to help Third World countries overcome poverty and hunger.

However, you must give the author's last name in an in-text citation if it is not mentioned in the text.

> *No Need for Hunger* recommends that the U.S. government develop a new foreign policy to help Third World countries overcome poverty and hunger (Spitzer).

When a source is listed in your works-cited page with an editor, a translator, a speaker, or an artist, instead of the author, use that person's name in your citation.

APA   The correct form for a parenthetical reference to a single source by a single author is parenthesis, last name, comma, space, year of publication, parenthesis.

> … in this way, the public began to connect certain childhood vaccinations with an autism epidemic (Baker, 2008).

If the author is identified in your text, include the year in parentheses immediately after.

> Dohman (2009) argues that parents of affected children …

One Author: Part of a Work

MLA   List the necessary page numbers in parentheses if you borrow words or ideas from a particular source. Leave a space between the author's last name and the page reference. No abbreviation or punctuation is needed. (The first example below identifies the author in text, the second in parentheses.)

> Bullough writes that genetic engineering was dubbed "eugenics" by a cousin of Darwin's, Sir Francis Galton, in 1885 (5).

> Genetic engineering was dubbed "eugenics" by a cousin of Darwin's, Sir Francis Galton, in 1885 (Bullough 5).

APA   When you cite a specific part of a source, give the page, paragraph, or chapter, using the appropriate abbreviation (p. or pp., para.) or word (chapter). Always give the page number for a direct quotation.

> …while a variety of political and scientific forces were at work in the developing crisis, it was parents who pressed the case "that autism had become epidemic and that vaccines were its cause" (Baker, 2008, p. 251).

Two or More Works by the Same Author(s)

MLA   In addition to the author's last name(s) and page number(s), include a shortened version of the work's title when you cite two or more works by the same author(s).

> Wallerstein and Blakeslee claim that divorce creates an enduring identity for children of the marriage (*Unexpected Legacy* 62).

> They are intensely lonely despite active social lives (Wallerstein and Blakeslee, *Second Chances* 51).

APA   If the same author has published two or more articles in the same year, avoid confusion by placing a small letter *a* after the year for the first work listed in the reference list, *b* after the year for the next one, and so on. Alphabetize by title.

Parenthetical Citation:

> Reefs harbor life forms heretofore unknown (Milius, 2001a, 2001b).

References:

> Milius, D. (2001a). Another world hides inside coral reefs. *Science News, 160*(16), 244.

> Milius, D. (2001b). Unknown squids—with elbows— tease science. *Science News, 160*(24), 390.

Works by Authors with the Same Last Name

MLA   When citing different sources by authors with the same last name, it is best to use the authors' full names in the text to avoid confusion. If circumstances call for parenthetical references, add each author's first initial. If first initials are the same, use each author's full name.

Some critics think *Titus Andronicus* too abysmally melodramatic to be a work of Shakespeare (A. Parker 73). Others suggest that Shakespeare meant it as black comedy (D. Parker 486).

APA When citing different sources by authors with the same last name, add the authors' initials to avoid confusion, even if the publication dates are different.

While J. D. Wallace (2005) argued that privatizing social security would benefit only the wealthiest citizens, others such as E. S. Wallace (2006) supported greater control for individuals.

Works by Multiple Authors

MLA When citing a work by **two or three authors**, give the last names of every author in the same order that they appear in the works-cited section. (The correct order of the authors' names can be found on the title page of the book.)

Students learned more than a full year's Spanish in ten days using the complete supermemory method (Ostrander and Schroeder 51).

When citing a work by **four or more authors**, give the first author's last name as it appears in the works-cited section, followed by "et al." (meaning "and others").

Communication on the job is more than talking; it is "inseparable from your total behavior" (Culligan et al. 111).

APA When citing from **two to five authors**, all must be mentioned in the first text citation. The last two authors' names are always separated by a comma and an ampersand (&) when enclosed in parentheses.

Love changes not just who we are, but who we can become, as well (Lewis, Amini, & Lannon, 2000).

Subsequently, for works with **two authors**, *list both in every citation*. For works with **three to five authors**, *list all only the first time*; after that, use only the name of the first author followed by "et al.," like this:

These discoveries lead to the hypothesis that love actually alters the brain's structure (Lewis et al., 2000).

If your source has **six or more authors**, refer to the work by the first author's name followed by "et al.," both for the first reference in the text and all references after that. However, be sure to list all the authors (up to seven) in your references list.

According to a recent study, post-traumatic stress disorder (PTSD) continues to dominate the lives of Vietnam veterans, though in modified forms (Trembley et al., 2008).

A Work Authored by an Agency, a Committee, or an Organization

MLA If a book or other work was written by an organization such as an agency, a committee, or a task force, it is said to have a corporate author. If the corporate name is long, include it in the text (rather than in parentheses) to avoid disrupting the flow of your writing. After the full name has been used at least once, use a shortened form of the name (common abbreviations are acceptable) in subsequent references. For example, *Task Force* may be used for *Task Force on Education for Economic Growth*.

The thesis of the Task Force's report is that economic success depends on our ability to improve large-scale education and training as quickly as possible (113–14).

APA Treat the name of the group as if it were the last name of the author. If the name is long and easily abbreviated, provide the abbreviation in square brackets.

A problem for many veterans continues to be heightened sensitivity to noise (National Institute of Mental Health [NIMH], 2005).

Use the abbreviation without brackets in subsequent references.

In addition, veterans suffering from PTSD continue to have difficulty discussing their experiences (NIMH, 2005).

A Work with No Author Indicated

MLA When there is no author listed, give the title or a shortened version of the title as it appears in the works-cited section.

Statistics indicate that drinking water can make up 20 percent of a person's total exposure to lead (*Information* 572).

APA If your source lists no author, treat the first few words of the title (capitalized normally) as you would an author's last name. A title of an article or a chapter belongs in quotation marks; the titles of books or reports should be italicized.

…including a guide to low-stress postures ("How to Do It," 2001).

Two or More Works Included in One Citation

To cite multiple works within a single parenthetical reference, separate the references with a semicolon.

MLA The following example refers to a work by Albala and another by Lewis.

> In Medieval Europe, Latin translations of the works of Rhazes, a Persian scholar, were a primary source of medical knowledge (Albala 22; Lewis 266).

APA Remember to include the year of publication. Place the citations in alphabetical order, just as they would be ordered in the reference list:

> Others report near-death experiences (Rommer, 2000; Sabom, 1998).

MLA: A Series of Citations from a Single Work

If no confusion is possible, it is not necessary to name a source repeatedly when making multiple parenthetical references to that source in a single paragraph. If all references are to the same page, identify that page in a parenthetical note after the last reference. If the references are to different pages within the same work, you need identify the work only once, and then use a parenthetical note with page number alone for the subsequent references.

> Domesticating science meant not only spreading scientific knowledge, but also promoting it as a topic of public conversation (Heilbron 2). One way to enhance its charm was by depicting cherubic putti as "angelic research assistants" in book illustrations (5).

A Work Referred to in Another Work

MLA If you must cite an indirect source—that is, information from a source that is quoted from another source—use the abbreviation *qtd. in* (quoted in) before the indirect source in your reference.

> Paton improved the conditions in Diepkloof (a prison) by "removing all the more obvious aids to detention. The dormitories [were] open at night: the great barred gate [was] gone" (qtd. in Callan xviii).

APA If you need to cite a source that you have found referred to in another source (a "secondary" source), mention the original source in your text. Then, in your parenthetical citation, cite the secondary source, using the words "as cited in."

> …theorem given by Ullman (as cited in Hoffman, 1998).

A Work in an Anthology or a Collection

MLA When citing an entire work that is part of an anthology or a collection, a work identified by author in your list of works cited, treat the citation as you would for any other complete work.

> In "The Canadian Postmodern," Linda Hutcheon offers a clear analysis of the self-reflexive nature of contemporary Canadian fiction.

Similarly, if you are citing particular pages of such a work, follow the directions for citing part of a work.

> According to Hutcheon, "postmodernism seems to designate cultural practices that are fundamentally self-reflexive, in other words, art that is self-consciously artifice" (18).

An entry from a **reference work** such as an encyclopedia or a dictionary should be cited similarly to a work from an anthology or a collection. For a dictionary definition, include the abbreviation *def.* followed by the particular entry designation.

> This message becomes a juggernaut in the truest sense, a belief that "elicits blind devotion or sacrifice" ("Juggernaut," def. 1).

While many such entries are identified only by title (as above), some reference works include an author's name for each entry (as below). Others may identify the entry author by initials, with a list of full names elsewhere in the work.

> The decisions of the International Court of Justice are "based on principles of international law and cannot be appealed" (Pranger).

See pages 260–266 for guidelines on formatting these entries in your works-cited list.

APA When citing an article or a chapter in an anthology or a collection, use the authors' names for the specific article, not the names of the anthology's editors. (Similarly, the article should be listed by its authors' names in the reference section.)

Phonological changes can be understood from a variationist perspective (Guy, 2005).

A Sacred Text or Famous Literary Work

Sacred texts and famous literary works are published in many different editions. For that reason, when you are referring to specific sections of the work, it is best to

> ### MLA: Quoting Verse
>
> Do not use page numbers when referencing classic verse plays and poems. Instead, cite them by division (act, scene, canto, book, part) and line, using Arabic numerals for the various divisions unless your instructor prefers Roman numerals. Use periods to separate the various numbers.
>
> > In the first act, Hamlet comments, "How weary, stale, flat and unprofitable, / Seem to me all the uses of this world" (1.2.133-34).
>
> A slash, with a space on each side, shows where each new line of verse begins. If you are citing lines only, use the word *line* or *lines* in your first reference and numbers only in additional references.
>
> > At the beginning of the sestet in Robert Frost's "Design," the speaker asks this pointed question: "What had that flower to do with being white, / The wayside blue and innocent heal-all?" (lines 9–10).
>
> See page 252 for instructions for verse quotations of more than three lines.

identify parts, chapters, or other divisions instead of (or in addition to) your version's page numbers. Note that books of the Bible and other well-known literary works may be abbreviated, if no confusion is possible.

MLA If using page numbers, list them first, followed by an abbreviation for the type of division and the division number.

The more important a person's role in society—the more apparent power an individual has—the more that person is a slave to the forces of history (Tolstoy 690; bk. 9, ch. 1).

As Shakespeare's famous Danish prince observes, "One may smile, and smile, and be a villain" (*Ham.* 1.5.104).

APA The original date of publication may be unavailable or not pertinent. In such cases, use your edition's year of translation (for example, *trans. 2003*) or indicate your edition's year of publication (*2003 version*).

An interesting literary case of such dysfunctional family behavior can be found in Franz Kafka's *The Metamorphosis,* where it becomes the commandment of family duty for Gregor's parents and sister to swallow their disgust and endure him (trans. 1972, part 3).

"Generations come and generations go, but the earth remains forever" (*The New International Version Study Bible,* 1985 version, Eccles. 1.4).

Citing Internet Sources

MLA The current (seventh edition) *MLA Handbook* discourages use of Internet addresses, or URLs, as they can so easily change with time. Ideally, you should refer to an entire Web site by its title, or to a specific article on a site by its author; then, include full reference information in your works-cited list. A URL should be listed in your document or in your works-cited list only when the reader probably cannot locate the source without it, or if your instructor requires it. If that is the case, enclose the address in brackets:

<www.thecollegewriter.com/3e>

APA As with print sources, cite an electronic source by the author (or by shortened title if the author is unknown) and the publication date (not the date you accessed the source). If citing a specific part of the source, use an appropriate abbreviation: *p.* for page and *para.* for paragraph.

One study compared and contrasted the use of Web and touch screen transaction log files in a hospital setting (Nicholas, Huntington, & Williams, 2001).

Whenever possible, cite a Web site by its author and posting date. In addition, refer to a specific page or document rather than to a home page or a menu page. If you are referring to a specific part of a Web page that does not have page numbers, direct your reader, if possible, with a section heading and a paragraph number.

According to the National Multiple Sclerosis Society (2003, "Complexities" section, para. 2), understanding of MS could not begin until scientists began to research nerve transmission in the 1920s.

APA: Personal Communications

If for APA papers you do the kind of personal research recommended elsewhere in *Write*, you may have to cite personal communications that have provided you with some of your knowledge. Personal communications may include personal letters, phone calls, memos, and so forth. Because they are not published in a permanent form, APA style does not place them among the citations in your reference list. Instead, cite them only in the text of your paper in parentheses, like this:

…according to M. T. Cann (personal communication, April 1, 2009).

…by today (M. T. Cann, personal communication, April 1, 2009).

Quick Guide — MLA Works Cited

The works-cited section lists only the sources you have cited in your text. Begin your list on the page after the text and continue numbering each page. Format your works-cited pages using these guidelines and page 268.

1. Type the page number in the upper right corner, one-half inch from the top of the page, with your last name before it.

2. Center the title *Works Cited* (not in italics or underlined) one inch from the top; then double-space before the first entry.

3. Begin each entry flush with the left margin. If the entry runs more than one line, indent additional lines one-half inch (five spaces) or use the hanging indent function on your computer.

4. End each element of the entry with a period. (Elements are separated by periods in most cases unless only a space is sufficient.) Use a single space after all punctuation.

5. Double-space lines within each entry and between entries.

6. List each entry alphabetically by the author's last name. If there is no author, use the first word of the title (disregard *A, An,* or *The* as the first word). If there are multiple authors, alphabetize them according to which author is listed first in the publication.

7. The *MLA Handbook*, Seventh Edition, requires that each source be identified as *Print, Web,* or other (such as *Television* or *DVD*). For print sources, this information is included after the publisher and date. For Web publications, include *Web.* after the date of publication or updating of the site, and before the date you accessed the site.

8. A basic entry for a book follows:

   Black, Naomi. *Virginia Woolf as Feminist*. Ithaca: Cornell UP, 2004. Print.

9. A basic entry for a journal or magazine follows:

   Stelmach, Kathryn. "From Text to Tableau: Ekphrastic Enchantment in *Mrs. Dalloway* and *To the Lighthouse.*" *Studies in the Novel* 38.3 (Fall 2006): 304-26. Print.

10. A basic entry for an online source is given below. Note that the URL is included only if the reader probably cannot locate the source without it, or when your instructor requires it.

    Clarke, S. N. "Virginia Woolf (1882-1941): A Short Biography." *Virginia Woolf Society of Great Britain*. 2000. Web. 12 Mar. 2008.

The reference section lists all the sources you have cited in your text (with the exception of personal communications such as phone calls and e-mails). Begin your reference list on a new page after the last page of your paper. Number each reference page, continuing the numbering from the text. Then format your reference list by following the guidelines below.

1. Type the running head in the upper left corner and the page number in the upper right corner, approximately one-half inch from the top of the page.

2. Center the title, *References,* approximately one inch from the top; then double-space before the first entry.

3. Begin each entry flush with the left margin. If the entry runs more than one line, indent additional lines approximately one-half inch (five to seven spaces), using a hanging indent.

4. Adhere to the following conventions about spacing, capitalization, and italics:
   • Double-space between all lines on the reference page.
   • Use one space following each word and punctuation mark.

• With book and article titles, capitalize only the first letter of the title (and subtitle) and proper nouns.
   Example: *The impact of the cold war on Asia.*
   (Note that this capitalization practice differs from the presentation of titles in the body of the essay.)

• Use italics for titles of books and periodicals, not underlining.

5. List each entry alphabetically by the last name of the author, or, if no author is given, by the title (disregarding *A, An,* or *The*). For works with multiple authors, use the first author listed in the publication.

6. Follow these conventions with respect to abbreviations:
   • With authors' names, generally shorten first and middle names to initials, leaving a space after the period. For a work with more than one author, use an ampersand (&) before the last author's name.
   • For publisher locations, use the full city name plus the two-letter U.S. Postal Service abbreviation for the state. For international publishers, include a spelled-out province and country name.
   • Spell out "Press" or "Books" in full, but omit unnecessary terms like "Publishers," "Company," or "Inc."

LO3 List books and other nonperiodical documents.

MLA In MLA style, a works-cited entry for a book or similar document follows this general form.

> Author's last name, first name. *Title.* Place of publication, publisher, year published. Medium ("Print").

Publishers' Names: Publishers' names should be shortened by omitting articles *(A, An, The),* business abbreviations *(Co., Inc.),* and descriptive words *(Books, Press).* For publishing houses that consist of the names of more than one person, cite only the first of the surnames. Abbreviate University Press as UP. Also use standard abbreviations whenever possible (Assn., Acad.). In addition, use the following abbreviations in place of any information you cannot supply:

n.p.	*No place of publication given*
n.p.	*No publisher given*
n.d.	*No date of publication given*
n. pag.	*No pagination given*

APA In APA style, a reference-list entry for a book or similar document follows this general form.

> Author, A. (year). *Title.* Location: Publisher.

A Book by One Author

MLA The example below demonstrates the most basic book entry.

> Green, Christopher. *Picasso: Architecture and Vertigo.* New Haven: Yale UP, 2005. Print.

APA Capitalize only the first word of the title and the first word of any subtitle, along with proper nouns and initialisms.

> Kuriansky, J. (2007). *Beyond bullets and bombs: Grassroots peacebuilding between Israelis and Palestinians.* Westport, CT: Praeger Press.

Two or More Books by the Same Author

MLA List the books alphabetically according to title. After the first entry, substitute three hyphens for the author's name.

> Dershowitz, Alan M. *Rights from Wrongs.* New York: Basic, 2005. Print.

> - - - . *Supreme Injustice: How the High Court Hijacked Election 2000.* Oxford: Oxford UP, 2001. Print.

APA Arrange multiple works by the same author in chronological order, earliest first.

> Sacks, O. (1995). *An Anthropologist on Mars: Seven paradoxical tales.* New York, NY: Alfred A. Knopf.

> Sacks, O. (2007). *Musicophilia: Tales of music and the brain.* New York, NY: Alfred A. Knopf.

A Work by Two or More Authors

MLA For **two or three authors**, list them all, in title-page order, reversing only the first author's name.

> Bystydzienski, Jill M., and Estelle P. Resnik. *Women in Cross-Cultural Transitions.* Bloomington: Phi Delta Kappa Educational Foundation, 1994. Print.

For **four or more authors,** list only the first, followed by "et al."

> Schulte-Peevers, Andrea, et al. *Germany.* Victoria: Lonely Planet, 2000. Print.

APA List **up to seven authors** by last name and first initial, separating them by commas, with an ampersand (&) before the last.

> Hooyman, N., & Kramer, B. (2006). *Living through loss: Interventions across the life span.* New York, NY: Columbia University Press.

For **eight or more authors,** list the first six followed by an ellipsis, and then the last.

A Work Authored by an Agency, a Committee, or an Organization

MLA & **APA** Treat the organization as the author.

An Anonymous Book

MLA If no author or editor is listed, begin the entry with the title.

> *Chase's Calendar of Events 2002.* Chicago: Contemporary, 2002. Print.

APA If an author is listed as "Anonymous," treat it as the author's name. Otherwise, put the title in the author's spot.

> *Publication manual of the American Psychological Association* (5th ed.). (2001). Washington, DC: American Psychological Association.

A Single Work from an Anthology

MLA Place the title of the single work in quotation marks before the title of the complete work. (*Note:* Some large single works, such as complete plays, may call for italics instead.)

> Mitchell, Joseph. "The Bottom of the Harbor." *American Sea Writing.* Ed. Peter Neill. New York: Lib. of America, 2000. 584-608. Print.

APA Start with information about the individual work, followed by details about the collection in which it appears, including the page span. When editors' names come in the middle of an entry, follow the usual order: initial first, surname last. Note the placement of *Eds.* in parentheses in the following example.

> Guy, G. R. (2005). Variationist approaches to phonological change. In B. D. Joseph & R. D. Janda (Eds.), *The handbook of historical linguistics* (pp. 369-400). Malden, MA: Blackwell.

One Volume of a Multivolume Work

MLA Include the volume number after the title of the complete work.

> Cooke, Jacob Ernest, and Milton M. Klein, eds. *North America in Colonial Times.* Vol. 2. New York: Scribner's, 1998. Print.

If you cite two or more volumes of a multivolume work, give the total number of volumes in the work. Offer specific references to volume and page numbers in the parenthetical reference in your text, like this: (8: 112–114).

> Salzman, Jack, David Lionel Smith, and Cornel West. *Encyclopedia of African-American Culture and History.* 5 vols. New York: Simon, 1996. Print.

APA Indicate the volume in parentheses after the work's title.

> Salzman, J., Smith, D. L., & West, C. (Eds.). (1996). *Encyclopedia of African-American culture and history* (Vol. 4). New York, NY: Simon & Schuster Macmillan.

When a work is part of a larger series or collection, make a two-part title with the series and the particular volume you are citing.

> The Associated Press. (1995). *Twentieth-century America: Vol. 8. The crisis of national confidence: 1974-1980.* Danbury, CT: Grolier Educational Corp.

MLA: Citing Multiple Works or a Complete Anthology

To avoid unnecessary repetition when citing two or more entries from a larger collection, you may cite the collection once with complete publication information (see Rothfield, below). The individual entries (see Becker and Cuno, below) can then be cross-referenced by listing the author, title of the piece, editor of the collection, and page numbers.

> Becker, Carol. "The Brooklyn Controversy: A View from the Bridge." Rothfield 15-21.
>
> Cuno, James. "Sensation and the Ethics of Funding Exhibitions." Rothfield 162-170.
>
> Rothfield, Lawrence, ed. *Unsettling Sensation: Arts-Policy Lessons from the Brooklyn Museum of Art Controversy.* New Brunswick: Rutgers UP, 2001. Print. Rutgers Series on the Public Life of the Arts.

If you cite a **complete anthology**, begin the entry with the editor(s).

> Neill, Peter, ed. *American Sea Writing.* New York: Lib. of America, 2000. Print.
>
> Smith, Rochelle, and Sharon L. Jones, eds. *The Prentice Hall Anthology of African American Literature.* Upper Saddle River: Prentice, 2000. Print.

A Chapter, an Introduction, a Preface, a Foreword, or an Afterword

MLA To cite a chapter from a book, list the chapter title in quotation marks after the author's name. For an introduction, preface, foreword, or afterword, identify the part by type, with no quotation marks or underlining. Next, identify the author of the work, us-

ing the word "by." (If the book's author and the part's author are the same person, give just the last name after "by.") For a book that gives cover credit to an editor instead of an author, identify the editor as usual. Finally, list any page numbers for the part cited.

> Proulx, Annie. Introduction. *Dance of the Happy Shades.* By Alice Munro. Toronto: Penguin Canada, 2005. Print.

APA List the chapter title after the date of publication, followed by a period or appropriate end punctuation. Use *In* before the book title, and follow the book title with the inclusive page numbers of the chapter.

> Tattersall, I. (2002). How did we achieve humanity? In *The monkey in the mirror* (pp. 138-168). New York, NY: Harcourt.

A Group Author as Publisher

MLA List the unabbreviated group name as author, omitting any inital article *(A, An, The)*, then again as publisher, abbreviated as usual.

> Amnesty International. *Maze of Injustice: The Failure to Protect Indigenous Women from Sexual Violence in the USA.* London: Amnesty Intl., 2007. Print.

APA When the author is also the publisher, simply put *Author* in the spot where you would list the publisher's name.

> Amnesty International. (2007). *Maze of injustice: The failure to protect indigenous women from sexual violence in the USA.* London England: Author.

If the publication is a brochure, identify it as such in brackets after the title.

LO4 List print periodical articles.

MLA The general form for a periodical entry in MLA format follows.

> Author's last name, first name. "Article Title." *Periodical Title* Series number or name. Volume.issue. [separated by period but no space]. Publication date: page numbers. Medium (Print).

APA The general form for a periodical entry in APA format follows. If the periodical does not use volume and issue numbers, include some other designation with the year, such as the month and day, the month, or a season.

Author, A. (year). Article title. *Periodical Title, volume number* (issue number if paginated by issue), page numbers.

An Article in a Magazine or Scholarly Journal

MLA List the volume number immediately after the journal title, followed by a period and the issue number, and then the date of publication (in parentheses). End with the page numbers of the article followed by the medium of publication *(Print)*.

Sanchez, Melissa E. "Seduction and Service in *The Tempest.*" *Studies in Philology* 105.1 (Winter 2008): 50-82. Print.

"Feeding the Hungry." *Economist* 371.8374 (2004): 74. Print.

Note: If no volume number exists, list the issue number alone.

APA List author and year as for a book reference. (For a magazine, also include other date elements, as the month and day or the season.) In the article's title, lowercase all but the first word, proper nouns, acronyms, initialisms, and the first word of any subtitle. Capitalize the journal's title normally and italicize it. Italicize the volume number and place the issue number in parentheses, without italics. Provide inclusive page numbers.

Weintraub, B. (2007, October). Unusual suspects. *Psychology Today, 40*(5), 80-87.

Tomatoes target toughest cancer. (2002, February). *Prevention, 54*(2), 53.

Benson, P., Karlof, K. L., & Siperstein, G. N. (2008). Maternal involvement in the education of young children with autism spectrum disorders. *Autism: The International Journal of Research & Practice, 12*(1), 47-63.

A Newspaper Article

MLA Cite the edition of a major daily newspaper (if given) after the date (1 May 1995, Midwest ed.: 1). If a local paper's name does not include the city of publication, add it in brackets (not italicized) after the name.

Segal, Jeff, and Lauren Silva. "Case of Art Imitating Life?" *Wall Street Journal* 3 March 2008, Eastern ed.: C9. Print.

Swiech, Paul. "Human Service Agencies: 'It's Going to Take a Miracle.'" *Pantagraph* [Bloomington, IL] 30 June 2009: B7. Print.

To cite an article in a lettered section of the newspaper, list the section and the page number. (For example, A4 would refer to page 4 in section A of the newspaper.) If the sections are numbered, however, use a comma after the year (or the edition); then indicate the section and follow it with a colon, the page number (sec. 1:20), and the medium of publication you used. An unsigned newspaper article follows the same format:

"Bombs—Real and Threatened—Keep Northern Ireland Edgy." *Chicago Tribune* 6 Dec. 2001, sec. 1: 20. Print.

If an article is an unsigned editorial, put *Editorial* (no italics) and a period after the title.

"Hospital Power." Editorial. *Bangor Daily News* 14 Sept. 2004: A6. Print.

To identify a letter to the editor, put *Letter* (no italics) and a period after the author's name.

Sory, Forrest. Letter. *Discover* July 2001: 10. Print.

APA For newspaper articles, include the full publication date, year first followed by a comma, the month (spelled out) and the day. Identify the article's location in the newspaper using page numbers and section letters, as appropriate. If the article is a letter to the editor, identify it as such in brackets following the title. For newspapers, use *p.* or *pp.* before the page numbers; if the article is not on continuous pages, give all the page numbers, separated by commas.

Schmitt, E., & Shanker, T. (2008, March 18). U.S. adapts cold-war idea to fight terrorists. *The New York Times,* pp. 1A, 14A-15A.

Benderoff, E. (2008, March 14). Facebook sites face scrutiny for March Madness pools. *Chicago Tribune,* pp. 2C-3C.

An Abstract

An abstract is a summary of a work.

MLA To cite an abstract, first give the publication information for the original work (if any); then list the publication information for the abstract itself. Add the term *Abstract* and a period between these if the journal title does not include that word. If the journal identifies abstracts by item number, include the word *item* followed by the number. (Add the section identifier [A, B, or C] for those volumes of *Dissertation Abstracts [DA]* and *Dissertation Abstracts International [DAI]* that have one.) If no item number exists, list the page number(s).

Faber, A. J. "Examining Remarried Couples Through a Bowenian Family System Lens." *Journal of Divorce and Remarriage* 40.4 (2004): 121-33. *Social Work Abstracts* 40 (2004): item 1298. Print.

APA When referencing an abstract published separately from an article, provide publication details of the article followed by information about where the abstract was published.

Shlipak, M. G., Simon, J. A., Grady, O., Lin, F., Wenger, N. K., & Furberg, C. D. (2001, September). Renal insufficiency and cardiovascular events in postmenopausal women with coronary heart disease. *Journal of the American College of Cardiology, 38,* 705-711. Abstract retrieved from *Geriatrics,* 2001, *56*(12), Abstract No. 5645351.

LO5 List online sources.

The general form for an online entry in MLA style is given below.

MLA Start with the same elements given for a print source.

Author's last name, first name. Title of Work (in italics or quotation marks). *Web Site Title* (if different from title of work). Version or edition used. Publisher or sponsor (or N.p. if none identified). Publication date (or N.d.). Medium (Web). Date of access.

Include a URL only if your reader needs it to locate the source (or if your instructor requires it). See "Using URLs" below for instructions.

APA Whenever possible, use the final, archival version of an electronic resource (often called the version of record), as opposed to a prepublished version. In the reference entry for an electronic source, start with the same elements in the same order given for a print or other fixed-media resource (author, title, and so on). Then add the most reliable electronic retrieval information that will (a) clarify what version of the source you used and (b) help your reader find the source.

DOI: If possible, use the electronic document's digital object identifier (DOI). The DOI will usually be published at the beginning of the article or be available in the article's citation.

Author, A. A. (year). Title of article. *Title of Periodical, volume number* (issue number), pages. doi: code

URL: If a DOI is not available, give the URL (without a period at the end). Use the home or menu-page URL for subscription-only databases and online reference works.

Author, A. A. (year). Title of article. *Title of Periodical, volume number* (issue number), pages. Retrieved from URL

Retrieval Date: If the content of the document is stable (e.g., archival copy or copy of record with DOI), do not include a retrieval date in your reference entry. However, if the content is likely to change or be updated, then offer a retrieval date.

Author, A. A. (year). *Title of document.* Retrieved date from website: URL

Using URLs

MLA and APA documentation styles differ slightly in how they treat URLs (Internet addresses).

MLA If you need to include a URL, place it immediately following the date of access, a period, and a space. The URL should be enclosed in angle brackets and end with a period. Give the complete address, including *http,* for the work you are citing.

MacLeod, Donald. "Shake-Up for Academic Publishing." *Guardian Unlimited.* Guardian News and Media Ltd., 10 Nov. 2008. Web. 6 Jan. 2009. <http://www.guardian.co.uk/Archive/>.

"Fort Frederica." *National Parks Service.* U.S. Department of the Interior, n.d. Web. 27 Feb. 2009. <http://home.nps.gov/fofr/forteachers/curriculummaterials.htm>.

If the URL must be divided between two lines, break it only **after** a **single** or **double slash**. Do not add a hyphen.

APA When necessary, break a URL **before** a **slash** or **other punctuation mark**. Do not underline or italicize the URL, place it in angle brackets, or end it with a period.

An Undated Online Item

MLA List "n.d" in place of the missing date.

Booth, Philip. "Robert Frost's Prime Directive." *Poets.org.* Academy of American Poets, n.d. Web. 1 Oct. 2009.

APA List "(n.d.)" in place of the missing date.

National Institute of Allergy and Infectious Diseases. (n.d.). *Antimicrobial (drug) resistance.* Retrieved June 19, 2008, from http://www3.niaid.nih.gov/topics/AntimicrobialResistance/default.htm

A Home Page

MLA If a nonperiodical publication has no title, identify it with a descriptor such as *Home page, Introduction,* or *Online posting* (using no italics or quotation marks). You may add the name of the publication's creator or editor after the overall site title, if appropriate.

Wheaton, Wil. Home page. *Wil Wheaton dot Net.* N.p., 31 May 2006. Web. 19 Mar. 2009.

APA Whenever possible, cite a Web site by its author and posting date. In addition, refer to a specific page or document rather than to a home page or a menu page.

An Entry in an Online Reference Work

Unless the author of the entry is identified, begin with the entry name.

MLA Place the entry name in quotation marks.

"Eakins, Thomas." *Britannica Online Encyclopedia.* Encyclopedia Britannica, 2008. Web. 26 Sept. 2008.

APA Use the word "In" to identify the larger source.

Agonism. (2008). In *Encyclopaedia Britannica.* Retrieved March 18, 2008, from http://search.eb.com

An Electronic Book

MLA Include publication information for the original print version if available. Follow the date of publication with the electronic information.

Simon, Julian L. *The Ultimate Resource II: People, Materials, and Environment.* College Park: U of Maryland, 1996. U of Maryland Libraries. Web. 9 Apr. 2009.

APA Provide the DOI (see page 264) if one exists. Otherwise, use the phrase "Retrieved from" to introduce the URL.

Bittlestone, R. (2005). *Odysseus unbound.* doi: 10.2277/0521853575

Kafka, F. (2002). *Metamorphosis.* D. Wylie (Trans.). Retrieved from http://www.gutenberg.org/etext/5200

MLA: Online Multimedia

For online postings of photographs, videos, sound recordings, works of art, and so on, follow the examples on pages 264–265. In place of the original medium of publication, however, include the title of the database or Web site (italicized), followed by the medium (Web) and the date of access, as for other online entries.

Brumfield, William Craft. *Church of Saint Nicholas Mokryi.* 1996. Prints and Photographs Div., Lib. of Cong. *Brumfield Photograph Collection.* Web. 9 May 2009.

Sita Sings the Blues. Prod. Nina Paley. 2008. *Internet Archive.* Web. 5 June 2008.

LO6 List other sources.

A Television or Radio Program

MLA Include the medium (Television or Radio) at the end of the citation, followed by a period.

"U.S. Health Care Gets Boost from Charity." *60 Minutes.* CBS. WBBM, Chicago. 28 Feb. 2008. Television.

APA Indicate the episode by writers, if possible. Then follow with the airing date, the episode title, and the type of series in brackets. Add the producer(s) as you would the editors(s) of a print medium, and complete the entry with details about the series itself.

Berger, Cynthia. (Writer). (2001, December 19). Feederwatch [Radio series program]. In D. Byrd & J. Block (Producers), *Earth & Sky.* Austin, TX: The Production Block.

A Motion Picture or Performance

MLA The director, distributor, and year of release follow the title. Other information may be included if pertinent. End with the medium, in this case *Film*, followed by a period.

Atonement. Dir. Joe Wright. Perf. James McAvoy, Keira Knightley. Universal Pictures, 2007. Film.

Treat a **performance** as you would a film, but add its location and date.

Chanticleer: An Orchestra of Voices. Young Auditorium, Whitewater, WI. 23 Feb. 2003. Performance.

APA Give the name and function of the director, producer, or both.

Cohn, J., & Cohn, E. (Directors). (2007). *No country for old men* [Motion picture]. United States: Miramax Films.

A Video Recording or an Audio Recording

MLA Cite a filmstrip, slide program, videocassette, or DVD as you do a film; include the medium of publication last, followed by a period.

Monet: Shadow & Light. Devine Productions, 1999. Videocassette.

If you are citing a specific song on a musical recording, place its title in quotation marks before the title of the recording.

Bernstein, Leonard. "Maria." *West Side Story.* Columbia, 1995. CD.

APA Begin the entry with the speaker's or writer's name, not the producer. Indicate the type of recording in brackets.

Kim, E. (Author, speaker). (2000). *Ten thousand sorrows* [CD]. New York, NY: Random House.

For a **music recording**, give the name and function of the originators or primary contributors. Indicate the recording medium in brackets immediately following the title.

ARS Femina Ensemble. (1998). *Musica de la puebla de Los Angeles: Music by women of baroque Mexico, Cuba, & Europe* [CD]. Louisville, KY: Nannerl Recordings.

A Lecture, Speech, Reading, or Dissertation

MLA Provide the speaker's name, the title of the presentation (if known) in quotation marks, the meeting and the sponsoring organization, the location, and the date. End with an appropriate descriptive label such as *Address, Lecture,* or *Reading.*

Annan, Kofi. "Acceptance of Nobel Peace Prize." Oslo City Hall, Oslo, Norw. 10 Dec. 2001. Speech.

APA For an unpublished paper presented at a meeting, indicate when the paper was presented, at what meeting, in what location.

Lycan, W. (2002, June). *The plurality of consciousness.* Paper presented at the meeting of the Society for Philosophy and Psychology, New York, NY.

For an unpublished doctoral dissertation, place the dissertation's title in italics, even though the work is unpublished. Indicate the school at which the writer completed the dissertation.

Roberts, W. (2001). *Crime amidst suburban wealth* (Unpublished doctoral dissertation). Bowling Green State University, Bowling Green, OH.

The heading supplies identifying details.

The title (centered) indicates the paper's topic and theme.

The writer uses suggestive metaphors to create an engaging opening.

The essential problem or issue is introduced.

The introduction lists key questions that grow out of the writer's research and drive the paper forward.

Katie Hughey
Professor E. K. Trump
Political Science 350
17 April 2008

An American Hybrid:

The Art Museum as Public-Private Institution

The American art museum suffers from a multiple personality disorder. It is a strange hybrid, both public and private in nature, and beholden to a constituency so varied in its interests that the function of the museum has become increasingly difficult to discern. Much of the confusion surrounding the nature and proper function of the art museum in the United States has to do with the unique form that arts patronage has taken in this country. There is a primary difficulty facing funding of the arts in America—namely, the fact that the benefits of art and art museums are not easily stated in the simple utilitarian terms that justify expenditures on things like roads and a police force. For this reason, cultural patronage has largely been a private venture. The first American museums were born of the private collections of robber barons, organized as not-for-profit corporations, and placed under the control of private boards of trustees. Only subsequently were municipal governments asked to contribute by way of funding construction costs for new buildings and providing maintenance expenses.

The involvement of the government in the funding of art museums raises several questions that serve to highlight the confusing hybrid nature of this uniquely American cultural institution. First, why do governments fund museums at all? The short answer involves the educational benefits conferred on the public by art museums. But once a municipality has taken on the task of paying for a public service that happens to be provided by an autonomous private institution, the real question becomes one of control. Who exactly "owns" the museum? If the stated goal of the museum enterprise is public in nature, while the works hanging on the walls and the programs offered by the museum are supported mainly by private funds, to whom is the museum accountable? Is it appropriate, for example, for a museum . . .

The list of works cited begins on a separate page and includes the title, header, and page number.

Sources are listed in alphabetical order by author (or by title if no author is given).

Titles are properly italicized or placed in quotation marks.

Correct abbreviations are used throughout.

Items are double-spaced throughout. Second and subsequent lines are indented (hanging indent).

Works Cited

Becker, Carol. "The Brooklyn Controversy: A View from the Bridge." Rothfield 15-21.

Bowie, David. *BowieNet*. Davidbowie.com, n.d. Web. 5 April 2008.

Cuno, James. "Sensation and the Ethics of Funding Exhibitions." Rothfield 162-70.

Edelson, Gilbert. "Some Sensational Reflections." Rothfield 171-80.

Edelstein, Teri. "Sensational or Status Quo: Museums and Public Perception." Rothfield 104-14.

Fraser, Andrea. "A Sensation Chronicle." *Social Text* 19.2 (2001): 127-56. Print.

Halle, David, et al. "The Attitude of the Audience for 'Sensation' and of the General Public Toward Controversial Works of Art." Rothfield 134-52.

Levine, Peter. "Lessons from the Brooklyn Museum Controversy." *Philosophy and Public Policy Quarterly* 20.2-3 (2000): n. pag. Web. 7 April 2008.

Meyer, Karl. *The Art Museum: Power, Money, Ethics*. New York: Morrow, 1979. Print.

Presser, Stephen. "Reasons We Shouldn't Be Here: Things We Cannot Say." Rothfield 52-71.

Ross, David. "An All-Too-Predictable Sensation." Rothfield 96-103.

Rothfield, Lawrence, ed. *Unsettling Sensation: Arts-Policy Lessons from the Brooklyn Museum of Art Controversy*. New Brunswick: Rutgers UP, 2001. Print. Rutgers Ser. on the Public Life of the Arts.

Schuster, J. Mark. "Who Should Pay (for the Arts and Culture)? Who Should Decide? And What Difference Should It Make?" Rothfield 72-89.

Smolensky, Eugene. "Municipal Financing of the U.S. Fine Arts Museum: A Historical Rationale." *Journal of Economic History* 46.3 (1986): 757-68. Print.

Stántó, András. "Don't Shoot the Messenger: Why the Art World and the Press Don't Get Along." Rothfield 181-98.

Steinfels, Margaret. "Virgins No More." *Commonweal* 19 May 2000: 23-24. Print.

Strauss, David. "The False Promise of Free Speech." Rothfield 44-51.

APA Title Page

Type running head (abbreviated title in uppercase letters) top left and page number top right throughout paper.

Full title, author(s), and school name are centered on the page, typed in uppercase and lowercase.

Our Roots Go Back to Roanoke:

Investigating the Link between

the Lost Colony and the Lumbee People of North Carolina

Renee Danielle Singh

University of California Davis

APA Abstract

The abstract summarizes the paper's central issue, its main conclusion, the key reasoning and evidence presented, and the study's significance.

Abstract

While remaining something of a mystery, the disappearance in the late sixteenth century of a group of colonists from Roanoke Island off North Carolina is likely related to the mystery of the ancestry of the North Carolina's Native American Lumbee tribe. Using evidence from the parallel example of the Catawba Indians, as well as evidence related to baldcypress tree rings, historical analysis, immunology, genetic studies, and linguistic patterns, one can tentatively conclude that the lost colonists were perhaps captured by, intermarried with, and were absorbed by the sixteenth-century ancestors of the Lumbee. This conclusion points to the need for further study, as the Lumbee People's status as Native American is currently contested and needs to be resolved for them to be recognized by the federal government.

Running head: OUR ROOTS GO BACK TO ROANOKE   3

Our Roots Go Back to Roanoke:

Investigating the Link between the Lost Colony

and the Lumbee People of North Carolina

Introduction: Something is Terribly Wrong

Consider the following narrative, which features historical information from Kupperman (1984, 1985), Miller (2002), Oberg (1994), and Quinn (1985):

Imagine yourself sailing across the warm waters of the Atlantic. It is a time before airplanes and automobiles, and our nation, which someday will lie just a few miles ahead of you, is still called the "New World." You are on your way to an island off the coast of what will one day be called North Carolina, and you are anxious to see what a small group of colonists has accomplished since their arrival there three years ago. Yes, this is the age of colonization. This is the beginning of a nation.

As you draw closer to land, however, you get a strange feeling that something is terribly wrong. No fires are burning on the island, no greeters waving. Instead, an eerie silence fills the air. At once, you cast your anchor and row ashore, hoping that perhaps you've reached the wrong island by mistake. Surely, this is not the island destined to be the first true settlement in the New World. Surely, this is not Roanoke.

As you step ashore, your worst fears are confirmed. Pots and other artifacts lay unused on the ground, and the shelters show signs of neglect. Footprints and other marks are scattered about as well, but their makers are nowhere in sight. The colonists of Roanoke have vanished.

For over four hundred years, the fate of the lost colonists of Roanoke has remained a mystery. While there are many theories to date concerning what became of them, the most prevalent and well-supported theory argues that the colonists were assimilated into the indigenous tribes of . . .

Partial Reference List

All works referred to in the paper appear in the reference list, alphabetized by author (or title).

Each entry follows APA guidelines for listing authors, dates, titles, and publishing information.

Capitalization, punctuation, and hanging indentation are consistent with APA format.

References

Beltrane, T., & McQueen, D. V. (1979). Urban and rural Indian drinking patterns: The special case of the Lumbee. *International Journal of the Addictions, 14*(4), 533-548.

Blu, K. I. (1980). *The Lumbee problem: The making of an American Indian people.* Cambridge: Cambridge University Press.

Bryant, A., Goins, R. T., Bell, R., Herrell, R., Manson, S. M., & Buchwald, D. (2004). Health differences among Lumbee Indians using public and private sources of care. *Journal of Rural Health, 20*(3), 231-236.

Bryant, A., & LaFromboise, T. D. (2005). The racial identity and cultural orientation of Lumbee American Indian high school students. *Cultural Diversity & Ethnic Minority Psychology, 11*(1), 82-89.

Grier, J. O., Ruderman, R. J., & Johnson, A. H. (1979). HLA profile in the Lumbee Indians of North Carolina. *Transplant Proceedings, 11*(4), 1767-1769.

Humphrey, J. A., & Kupper, H. J. (1982). Homicide and suicide among the Cherokee and Lumbee Indians of North Carolina. *International Journal of Social Psychiatry, 28*(2), 121-128. doi: 10.1177/002076408202800210

Kupperman, K. O. (1984). *Roanoke, the abandoned colony.* Totowa, NJ: Rowman & Allanheld.

Kupperman, K. O. (1985). Roanoke lost. *American Heritage, 36*(5), 81-96.

Miller, L. (2002). *Roanoke: Solving the mystery of the lost colony.* New York, NY: Penguin.

Mires, P. B. (1994). Contact and contagion: The Roanoke colony and influenza. *Historical Archaeology, 28*(3), 30-38.

Molnar, S. (2002). *Human variation: Races, types, and ethnic groups.* Englewood Cliffs, NJ: Prentice Hall.

Oberg, M. L. (1994). Indians and Englishmen at the first Roanoke colony: A note on Pemisapan's conspiracy, 1585-86. *American Indian Culture & Research Journal, 18*(2), 75-89.

22

Punctuation

LO1 Period

PERIODS ARE USED . . .

The following principles will guide the conventional use of periods in your writing.

Learning Outcomes

LO1 Period

LO2 Ellipsis

LO3 Comma

LO4 Semicolon

LO5 Colon

LO6 Hyphen

LO7 Dash

LO8 Question Mark

LO9 Quotation Marks

LO10 Italics (Underlining)

LO11 Parentheses

LO12 Diagonal

LO13 Brackets

LO14 Exclamation Point

LO15 Apostrophe

What do you think?

Punctuation is the most challenging convention of English.

1	2	3	4	5
strongly agree				strongly disagree

After Sentences

Use a period to end a sentence that makes a statement, requests something, gives a mild command, or presents an indirect question.

Statement:	By 2005, women made up 56 percent of undergraduate students and 59 percent of graduate students.
Request:	Please read the instructions carefully.
Mild command:	If your topic sentence isn't clear, rewrite it.
Indirect question:	The professor asked if we had completed the test.

<u>Note:</u> It is *not* necessary to place a period after a statement that has parentheses around it and is part of another sentence.

Think about joining a club (**the student affairs office has a list of organizations**) for fun and for leadership experience.

After Initials and Abbreviations

Use a period after an initial and with some abbreviations.

Mr.	Mrs.	B.C.E.	Ph.D.	Sen. Russ Feingold
Jr.	Sr.	D.D.S.	U.S.	Booker T. Washington
Dr.	M.A.	p.m.	B.A.	A. A. Milne

Note: Some abbreviations (such as *pm*) can be written without periods. Use no spacing in abbreviations, but do insert a space between a person's initials.

When an abbreviation is the last word in a sentence, use only one period at the end of the sentence.

Mikhail eyed each door until he found the name Rosa Lopez, Ph.D.

As Decimal Points

Use a period as a decimal point.

The government spends approximately **$15.5** million each year just to process student-loan forms.

LO2 Ellipsis

ELLIPSES ARE USED . . .

The following principles will guide the conventional use of ellipses in your writing.

To Show Omitted Words

Use an ellipsis (three periods) to show that one or more words have been omitted from a sentence in a quotation. When typing, leave one space before and after each period.

(Original) We the people of the United States, in order to form a more perfect Union, establish justice, insure domestic tranquility, provide for the common defense, promote the general welfare, and secure the blessings of liberty to ourselves and our posterity, do ordain and establish this Constitution for the United States of America.

—Preamble, U.S. Constitution

(Quotation) "We the people . . . in order to form a more perfect Union . . . establish this Constitution for the United States of America."

Note: Omit internal punctuation (a comma, a semicolon, a colon, or a dash) on either side of an ellipsis, unless the punctuation is needed for clarity.

To Show Omissions After Sentences

If words are omitted at the end of a sentence in a quotation, place the ellipsis after the period or other end punctuation.

(Quotation) "Five score years ago, a great American, in whose symbolic shadow we stand, signed the Emancipation Proclamation. . . . But one hundred years later, we must face the tragic fact that the Negro is still not free."

—Martin Luther King, Jr., "I Have a Dream"

The first word of a sentence following a period and an ellipsis may be capitalized, even though it was not capitalized in the original.

(Quotation) "Five score years ago, a great American . . . signed the Emancipation Proclamation. . . . One hundred years later, . . . the Negro is still not free."

Note: If the quoted material forms a complete sentence (even if it was not in the original), use a period, then an ellipsis.

(Original) I am tired; my heart is sick and sad. From where the sun now stands I will fight no more forever.

—Chief Joseph of the Nez Percé

(Quotation) "I am tired. . . . I will fight no more forever."

To Show Pauses

Use an ellipsis to indicate a pause or to show unfinished thoughts.

Listen . . . did you hear that?

I can't figure out . . . this number doesn't . . . just how do I apply the equation in this case?

L○3 Comma

COMMAS ARE USED . . .

The following principles will guide the conventional use of commas in your writing.

Between Independent Clauses

Use a comma between independent clauses that are joined by a coordinating conjunction (*and, but, or, nor, for, yet, so*).

> Heath Ledger completed his brilliant portrayal as the Joker in *The Dark Knight*, **but** he died before the film was released.
>
> > *Note:* Do not confuse a compound verb with a compound sentence.
>
> Ledger's Joker became instantly iconic and won him the Oscar for best supporting actor.
> (compound verb)
>
> His death resulted from the abuse of prescription drugs, but it was ruled an accident.
> (compound sentence)

Between Items in a Series

Use commas to separate individual words, phrases, or clauses in a series. (A series contains at least three items.)

> Many college students must balance studying with **taking care of a family, working a job, getting exercise, and finding time to relax.**
>
> > *Note:* Do not use commas when all the items in a series are connected with *or*, *nor*, or *and*.
>
> Hmm . . . should I study or do laundry or go out?

To Separate Adjectives

Use commas to separate adjectives that *equally* modify the same noun. Notice in the examples below that no comma separates the last adjective from the noun.

> You should exercise regularly and follow a **sensible, healthful** diet.
>
> A good diet is one that includes lots of **high-protein, low-fat** foods.

To Determine Equal Modifiers

To determine whether adjectives modify a noun *equally*, use these two tests.

1. Reverse the order of the adjectives; if the sentence is clear, the adjectives modify equally. (In the example below, *hot* and *crowded* can be reversed, and the sentence is still clear; *short* and *coffee* cannot be reversed.)

> Matt was tired of working in the **hot, crowded** lab and decided to take a **short coffee** break.

2. Insert *and* between the adjectives; if the sentence reads well, use a comma when *and* is omitted. (The word *and* can be inserted between *hot* and *crowded*, but *and* does not make sense between *short* and *coffee*.)

To Set Off Nonrestrictive Appositives

A specific kind of explanatory word or phrase called an **appositive** identifies or renames a preceding noun or pronoun.

> Albert Einstein**, the famous mathematician and physicist,** developed the theory of relativity.
>
> > *Note:* Do not use commas with restrictive appositives. A restrictive appositive is essential to the basic meaning of the sentence.
>
> The famous physicist Albert Einstein developed the theory of relativity.

To Set Off Adverb Dependent Clauses

Use a comma after most introductory dependent clauses functioning as adverbs.

> **Although Charlemagne was a great patron of learning,** he never learned to write properly. (adverb dependent clause)

When the adverb dependent clause follows the independent clause and it is not essential to the meaning of the sentence, use a comma. This comma use generally applies to adverb clauses beginning with *even though*, *although*, *while*, or some other conjunction expressing a contrast.

> Charlemagne never learned to write properly, **even though he continued to practice.**

Note: A comma is *not* used if the dependent clause following the independent clause is needed to complete the meaning of the sentence.

> Maybe Charlemagne didn't learn **because he had an empire to run.**

After Introductory Phrases

Use a comma after introductory phrases.

> **In spite of his practicing,** Charlemagne's handwriting remained poor.

> *Note:* A comma is usually omitted if the phrase follows an independent clause.

> Charlemagne's handwriting remained poor **in spite of his practicing.**

> *Note:* You may omit the comma after a short (four or fewer words) introductory phrase unless it is needed to ensure clarity.

> **At 6:00 a.m.** he would rise and practice his penmanship.

A Closer Look
at Nonrestrictive and Restrictive Clauses and Phrases

Use Commas with Nonrestrictive Clauses and Phrases

Use commas to enclose nonrestrictive (unnecessary) phrases or dependent (adjective) clauses. A nonrestrictive phrase or dependent clause adds information that is not necessary to the basic meaning of the sentence. For example, if the clause or phrase (in **boldface**) were left out of the two examples below, the meaning of the sentences would remain clear. Therefore, commas are used to set off the nonrestrictive information.

> The locker rooms in Swain Hall, **which were painted and updated last summer,** give professors a place to shower.
> (nonrestrictive clause)

> Work-study programs, **offered on many campuses,** give students the opportunity to earn tuition money.
> (nonrestrictive phrase)

Don't Use Commas with Restrictive Clauses and Phrases

Do *not* use commas to set off restrictive (necessary) adjective clauses and phrases. A restrictive clause or phrase adds information that the reader needs to understand the sentence. For example, if the adjective clause and phrase (in **boldface**) were dropped from the examples below, the meaning would be unclear.

> Only the professors **who run at noon** use the locker rooms in Swain Hall to shower.
> (restrictive clause)

> Using tuition money **earned through work-study programs** is the only way some students can afford to go to college.
> (restrictive phrase)

Using "That" or "Which"

Use *that* to introduce restrictive (necessary) adjective clauses; use *which* to introduce nonrestrictive (unnecessary) adjective clauses. When the two words are used in this way, the reader can quickly distinguish the necessary information from the unnecessary.

> Campus jobs **that are funded by the university** are awarded to students only.
> (restrictive)

> The cafeteria, **which is run by an independent contractor,** can hire nonstudents.
> (nonrestrictive)

Note: Clauses beginning with *who* can be either restrictive or nonrestrictive.

> Students **who pay for their own education** are highly motivated.
> (restrictive)

> The admissions counselor, **who has studied student records,** said that many returning students earn high GPAs in spite of demanding family obligations.
> (nonrestrictive)

To Set Off Transitional Expressions

Use a comma to set off conjunctive adverbs and transitional phrases. (See page 278.)

> Handwriting is not, **as a matter of fact,** easy to improve upon later in life; **however,** it can be done if you are determined enough.

> *Note:* If a transitional expression blends smoothly with the rest of the sentence, it does not need to be set off.
>
> *Example:* If you are in fact coming, I'll see you there.

To Set Off Items in Addresses and Dates

Use commas to set off items in an address and the year in a date.

> Send your letter to **1600 Pennsylvania Avenue, Washington, DC 20006, before January 1, 2009,** or send an e-mail to president@whitehouse.gov.
>
> *Note:* No comma is placed between the state and ZIP code. Also, *no* comma separates the items if only the month and year are given: January 2009.

To Set Off Dialogue

Use commas to set off the words of the speaker from the rest of the sentence.

> **"Never be afraid to ask for help,"** advised Ms. Kane.
>
> **"With the evidence that we now have,"** Professor Thom said, **"many scientists believe there is life on Mars."**

To Separate Nouns of Direct Address

Use a comma to separate a noun of direct address from the rest of the sentence.

> **Jamie,** would you please stop whistling while I'm trying to work?

To Separate Interjections

Use a comma to separate a mild interjection from the rest of the sentence.

> **Okay,** so now what do I do?
>
> *Note:* Exclamation points are used after strong interjections: Wow! You're kidding!

To Set Off Interruptions

Use commas to set off a word, phrase, or clause that interrupts the movement of a sentence. Such expressions can be identified through these two tests: They may be (1) omitted or (2) placed nearly anywhere, both without changing the meaning of the sentence.

> For me, **well,** it was just a good job gone!
> —Langston Hughes, "A Good Job Gone"
>
> Lela, **as a general rule,** always comes to class ready for a pop quiz.

To Separate Numbers

Use commas to separate a series of numbers to distinguish hundreds, thousands, millions, and so on.

> Do you know how to write **$2,025** on a check?
>
> **25,000**   **973,240**   **18,620,197**

To Enclose Explanatory Words

Use commas to enclose an explanatory word or phrase.

> Time management, **according to many professionals,** is an important skill that should be taught in college.

To Separate Contrasted Elements

Use commas to separate contrasted elements.

> We work to become, **not to acquire.**
> —Eugene Delacroix
>
> Where all think alike, **no one thinks very much.**
> —Walter Lippmann

Before Tags

Use a comma before tags, which are short statements or questions at the ends of sentences.

> You studied for the test, **right?**

To Enclose Titles or Initials

Use commas to enclose a title or initials and given names that follow a surname.

> Until Martin, **Sr.,** was 15, he never had more than three months of schooling in any one year.
> —Ed Clayton, *Martin Luther King: The Peaceful Warrior*
>
> The genealogical files included the names Sanders, **L. H.,** and Sanders, **Lucy Hale.**
>
> *Note:* Some style manuals no longer require commas around titles such as Sr. or Jr.

Avoid Overusing Commas

CAUTION

The commas (in red) below are used incorrectly. Do *not* use a comma between the subject and its verb or the verb and its object.

Current periodicals on the subject of psychology, are available at nearly all bookstores.

I think she should read, *Psychology Today*.

Do *not* use a comma before an indirect quotation.

My roommate said, that she doesn't understand the notes I took.

For Clarity or Emphasis

Use a comma for clarity or for emphasis. There will be times when none of the traditional rules call for a comma, but one will be needed to prevent misreading or to emphasize an important idea.

What she does, does matter to us. (clarity)

It may be those who do most, dream most. (emphasis)
—Stephen Leacock

LO4 Semicolon

SEMICOLONS ARE USED . . .

The following principles will guide the conventional use of semicolons in your writing.

To Join Two Independent Clauses

Use a semicolon to join two or more closely related independent clauses that are not connected with a coordinating conjunction. In other words, each of the clauses could stand alone as a separate sentence.

I was thrown out of college for cheating on the metaphysics exam; I looked into the soul of the boy next to me.
—Woody Allen

Before Conjunctive Adverbs

Use a semicolon before a conjunctive adverb when the word clarifies the relationship between two indepen-

dent clauses in a compound sentence. A comma often follows the conjunctive adverb. Common conjunctive adverbs include *also*, *besides*, *however*, *instead*, *meanwhile*, *then*, and *therefore*.

Many college freshmen are on their own for the first time; **however,** others are already independent and may even have families.

Before Transitional Phrases

Use a semicolon before a transitional phrase when the phrase clarifies the relationship between two independent clauses in a compound sentence. A comma usually follows the transitional phrase.

Pablo was born in the Andes; **as a result,** he loves mountains.

Transitional Phrases

after all	in addition
as a matter of fact	in conclusion
as a result	in fact
at any rate	in other words
at the same time	in the first place
even so	on the contrary
for example	on the other hand
for instance	

To Separate Independent Clauses Containing Commas

Use a semicolon to separate independent clauses that contain internal commas, even when the independent clauses are connected by a coordinating conjunction.

Your MP3 player, computer, bike, and other valuables are expensive to replace; so include these items in your homeowner's insurance policy and remember to use the locks on your door, bike, and storage area.

To Separate Items in a Series That Contain Commas

Use a semicolon to separate items in a series when one or more of the items already contain commas.

My favorite foods are pizza with pepperoni, onions, and olives; peanut butter and banana sandwiches; and liver with bacon, peppers, and onions.

LO5 Colon

COLONS ARE USED . . .

The following principles will guide the conventional use of colons in your writing.

After Salutations

Use a colon after the salutation of a business letter.

> Dear Mr. Spielberg: | Dear Professor Higgins:
> Dear Members:

Between Numbers Indicating Time or Ratios

Use a colon between the hours, minutes, and seconds of a number indicating time.

> 8:30 p.m. | 9:45 a.m. | 10:24:55

Use a colon between two numbers in a ratio.

> The ratio of computers to students is 1:20.
>   (one to twenty)

For Emphasis

Use a colon to emphasize a word, a phrase, a clause, or a sentence that explains or adds impact to the main clause.

> I have one goal for myself: **to become the first person in my family to graduate from college.**

To Distinguish Parts of Publications

Use a colon between a title and a subtitle, volume and page, and chapter and verse.

> *Ron Brown: An Uncommon Life*
> *Britannica* 4:211
> Psalm 23:1–6

To Introduce Quotations

Use a colon to introduce a quotation following a complete sentence.

> **John Locke is credited with this prescription for a good life:** "A sound mind in a sound body."

> **Lou Gottlieb, however, offered this version:** "A sound mind or a sound body—take your pick."

To Introduce a List

Use a colon to introduce a list following a complete sentence.

> **A college student needs a number of things to succeed:** basic skills, creativity, and determination.

Avoid Colon Errors

CAUTION

Do *not* use a colon between a verb and its object or complement.

> Dave likes: comfortable space and time to think. (Incorrect)
>
> Dave likes two things: comfortable space and time to think. (Correct)

LO6 Hyphen

HYPHENS ARE USED . . .

The following principles will guide the conventional use of hyphens in your writing.

In Compound Words

Use a hyphen to make some compound words.

> great-great-grandfather (noun)
> starry-eyed (adjective)
> mother-in-law (noun)
> three-year-old (adjective and noun)

Writers sometimes combine words in new and unexpected ways. Such combinations are usually hyphenated.

> And they pried pieces of **baked-too-fast** sunshine cake from the roofs of their mouths and looked once more into the boy's eyes.
> —Toni Morrison, *Song of Solomon*

> <u>Note</u>: Consult a dictionary for compound words. Some compound words (*living room*) use an open spelling, with no hyphen. Others use a closed spelling (*bedroom*). Some do not use a hyphen when the word is a noun (*ice cream, ice skate*) but do use a hyphen when it is an adjective or a verb (*ice-cream sundae, ice-skate for hours*).

To Join Letters and Words

Use a hyphen to join a capital letter or a lowercase letter to a noun or a participle.

| T-shirt | U-turn | V-shaped | x-ray |

To Join Words in Compound Numbers

Use a hyphen to join the words in compound numbers from *twenty-one* to *ninety-nine* when it is necessary to write them out.

Forty-two people found seats in the cramped classroom.

Between Numbers in Fractions

Use a hyphen between the numerator and the denominator of a fraction, but not when one or both of these elements are already hyphenated.

| four-tenths | five-sixteenths |
| seven thirty-seconds (7/32) |

In a Special Series

Use a hyphen when two or more words have a common element that is omitted in all but the last term.

We have cedar posts in **four-**, **six-**, and **eight-**inch widths.

To Create New Words

Use a hyphen to form new words beginning with the prefixes *self, ex, all,* and *half.* Also use a hyphen to join any prefix to a proper noun, a proper adjective, or the official name of an office.

| post-Depression | mid-May | ex-mayor |

To Prevent Confusion

Use a hyphen with prefixes or suffixes to avoid confusion or awkward spelling.

re-cover (not *recover*) the sofa

shell-like (not *shelllike*) shape

To Join Numbers

Use a hyphen to join numbers indicating a range, a score, or a vote.

Students study **30-40** hours a week.

The final score was **84-82**.

To Divide Words

Use a hyphen to divide a word between syllables at the end of a line of print.

Quick Guide   Word Division

1. Leave enough of the word at the end of the line to identify the word.

2. Never divide a one-syllable word: | **rained, skills, through.**

3. Avoid dividing any word of five or fewer letters: | **paper, study, July.**

4. Never divide a one-letter syllable from the rest of the word: | **omit-ted,** not **o-mitted.**

5. Always divide a compound word between its basic units: | **sister-in-law,** not **sis-ter-in-law.**

6. Never divide abbreviations or contractions: | **shouldn't,** not **should-n't**

7. When a vowel is a syllable by itself, divide the word after the vowel: | **epi-sode,** not **ep-isode**

8. Avoid dividing a numeral: | **1,000,000,** not **1,000,-000**

9. Avoid dividing the last word in a paragraph.

10. Never divide the last word in more than two lines in a row.

11. Check a dictionary for acceptable word divisions.

To Form Adjectives

Use a hyphen to join two or more words that serve as a single-thought adjective before a noun.

> In real life I am a large, **big-boned** woman with rough, **man-working** hands.
> —Alice Walker, "Everyday Use"

Most single-thought adjectives are not hyphenated when they come after the noun.

> In real life, I am large and **big boned**.

> *Note:* When the first of these words is an adverb ending in *ly*, do *not* use a hyphen. Also, do *not* use a hyphen when a number or a letter is the final element in a single-thought adjective.

> fresh**ly** painted barn

> grade **A** milk
> *(letter is the final element)*

L○7 Dash

DASHES ARE USED . . .

The following principles will guide the conventional use of dashes in your writing.

To Set Off Nonessential Elements

Use a dash to set off nonessential elements—explanations, examples, or definitions—when you want to emphasize them.

> Near the semester's end—**and this is not always due to poor planning**—some students may find themselves in academic trouble.

> The term *caveat emptor*—**let the buyer beware**—is especially appropriate to Internet shopping.

To Set Off an Introductory Series

Use a dash to set off an introductory series from the clause that explains the series.

> **Cereal, coffee, and a newspaper**—without these I can't get going in the morning.

To Show Missing Text

Use a dash to show that words or letters are missing.

> **Mr.**—won't let us marry.
> —Alice Walker, *The Color Purple*

To Show Interrupted Speech

Use a dash (or an ellipsis) to show interrupted or faltering speech in dialogue. (Also see page 274.)

> Well, **I—ah—had** this terrible case of the flu, **and—then—ah—the** library closed because of that flash flood, **and—well—the** high humidity jammed my printer. —Excuse No. 101

> "If you think you can—"
> "I know I can—"
> "Don't interrupt!"

For Emphasis

Use a dash in place of a colon to introduce or to emphasize a word, a series, a phrase, or a clause.

> **Jogging**—that's what he lives for.

> **Life is like a grindstone**—whether it grinds you down or polishes you up depends on what you're made of.

> **This is how the world moves**—not like an arrow, but a boomerang.
> —Ralph Ellison

L○8 Question Mark

QUESTION MARKS ARE USED . . .

The following principles will guide the conventional use of question marks in your writing.

After Direct Questions

Use a question mark at the end of a direct question.

> What can I know? What ought I to do? What may I hope?
> —Immanuel Kant

> Since when do you have to agree with people to defend them from injustice? —Lillian Hellman

Note: No question mark is used after an indirect question.

> After listening to Edgar sing, Mr. Noteworthy asked him if he had ever had formal voice training.

Also Note: When a single-word question like *how, when,* or *why* is woven into the flow of a sentence, capitalization and special punctuation are not usually required.

> The questions we need to address at our next board meeting are not why or whether, but how and when.

After Quotations That Are Questions

When a question ends with a quotation that is also a question, use only one question mark and place it within the quotation marks.

> Do you often ask yourself, "What should I be?"

To Show Uncertainty

Use a question mark within parentheses to show uncertainty about a word or phrase within a sentence.

> This July will be the 42nd **(?)** anniversary of the first moon walk.

Note: Do *not* use a question mark in this manner for formal writing.

For Questions in Parentheses or Dashes

A question within parentheses—or a question set off by dashes—is punctuated with a question mark unless the sentence ends with a question mark.

> You must consult your handbook **(what choice do you have?)** when you need to know a punctuation rule.

> Should I use your charge card (you have one, don't you), or should I pay cash?

> Maybe somewhere in the pasts of these humbled people, there were cases of bad mothering or absent fathering or emotional neglect—**what family surviving the '50s was exempt?**—but I couldn't believe these human errors brought the physical changes in Frank.
> —Mary Kay Blakely, *Wake Me When It's Over*

LO9 Quotation Marks

QUOTATION MARKS ARE USED . . .

The following principles will guide the conventional use of quotation marks in your writing.

To Punctuate Titles of Works Within Other Works

Use quotation marks to punctuate some titles.

> "Two Friends" (short story)
> "New Car Designs" (newspaper article)
> "Desperado" (song)
> "Multiculturalism and the Language Battle" (lecture title)
> "The New Admissions Game" (magazine article)
> "Reflections on Advertising" (chapter in a book)
> "Blink" (television episode from *Doctor Who*)
> "Annabel Lee" (short poem)

For Special Words

Use quotation marks (1) to show that a word is being discussed as a word, (2) to indicate that a word or phrase is directly quoted, (3) to indicate that a word is slang, or (4) to point out that a word is being used in a humorous or ironic way.

> 1. A commentary on the times is that the word **"honesty"** is now preceded by **"old-fashioned."**
>
> 2. She said she was **"incensed."**
>
> 3. I drank a Dixie and ate bar peanuts and asked the bartender where I could hear **"chanky-chank,"** as Cajuns call their music.
>   —William Least Heat-Moon, *Blue Highways*
>
> 4. In an attempt to be popular, he works very hard at being **"cute."**

Note: A word being discussed as a word can also be set off with italics.

With Periods or Commas

Always place periods and commas inside quotation marks.

> "Dr. Slaughter wants you to have liquids, Will," Mama said anxiously. "He said not to give you any solid food tonight."
>
> —Olive Ann Burns, *Cold Sassy Tree*

With Exclamation Points or Question Marks

Place an exclamation point or a question mark inside quotation marks when it punctuates both the main sentence and the quotation *or* just the quotation; place it outside when it punctuates the main sentence.

> Do you often ask yourself, "What should I be?"

> I almost croaked when he asked, "That won't be a problem, will it?"

> Did he really say, "Finish this by tomorrow"?

A Closer Look
at Marking Quoted Material

For Direct Quotations

Use quotation marks before and after a direct quotation—a person's exact words.

> Sitting in my one-room apartment, I remember Mom saying, **"Don't go to the party with him."**

Note: Do *not* use quotation marks for *indirect* quotations.

> I remember Mom saying **that I should not date him.** (These are not the speaker's exact words.)

For Quoting Quotations

Use single quotation marks to punctuate quoted material within a quotation.

> "I was lucky," said Jane. "The proctor announced, **'Put your pencils down,'** just as I was filling in the last answer."

For Quoted Passages

Use quotation marks before and after a quoted passage. Any word that is not part of the original quotation must be placed inside brackets.

> **(Original)** First of all, it must accept responsibility for providing shelter for the homeless.

> **(Quotation)** "First of all, it **[the federal government]** must accept responsibility for providing shelter for the homeless."

Note: If you quote only part of the original passage, be sure to construct a sentence that is both accurate and grammatically correct.

> The report goes on to say that the federal government **"must accept responsibility for providing shelter for the homeless."**

For Long Quotations

If more than one paragraph is quoted, quotation marks are placed before each paragraph and at the end of the last paragraph (**Example A**). Quotations that are five or more lines (MLA style) or forty words or more (APA style) are usually set off from the text by indenting ten spaces from the left margin (a style called "block form"). Do not use quotation marks before or after a block-form quotation (**Example B**), except in cases where quotation marks appear in the original passage (**Example C**).

Example A

Example B

Example C

With Semicolons or Colons

Always place semicolons or colons outside quotation marks.

> I just read "Computers and Creativity"; I now have some different ideas about the role of computers in the arts.

LO10 Italics (Underlining)

ITALICS ARE USED . . .

The following principles will guide the conventional use of italics in your writing.

In Handwritten and Printed Material

Italics is a printer's term for a style of type that is slightly slanted. In this sentence, the word *happiness* is printed in italics. In material that is handwritten or typed on a machine that cannot print in italics, underline each word or letter that should be in italics.

> In The Road to Memphis, racism is a contagious disease.
>   (typed or handwritten)
>
> Mildred Taylor's *The Road to Memphis* exposes racism.
>   (printed)

For Titles

Use italics to indicate the titles of magazines, newspapers, books, pamphlets, full-length plays, films, videos, radio and television programs, book-length poems, ballets, operas, lengthy musical compositions, CDs, paintings and sculptures, legal cases, Web sites, and the names of ships and aircraft. (Also see page 196.)

> | | |
> |---|---|
> | *Newsweek* (magazine) | *The Nutcracker* (ballet) |
> | *New York Times* (newspaper) | *Up* (film) |
> | *Sister Carrie* (book) | *The Thinker* (sculpture) |
> | *Othello* (play) | *GeoCities* (Web site) |
> | *Enola Gay* (airplane) | *College Loans* (pamphlet) |
> | *Icky Thump* (CD) | *Nightline* (television program) |
> | *ACLU v. State of Ohio* (legal case) | |

When one title appears within another title, punctuate as follows:

> I wrote a paper entitled **"Of Fathers and *Dreams from My Father*."**
>
> He wants to watch **Inside the "New York Times"** on PBS tonight.
>   (title of newspaper in title of TV program)

For Key Terms

Italics are often used for a key term in a discussion or for a technical term, especially when it is accompanied by its definition. Italicize the term the first time it is used. Thereafter, put the term in Roman type.

> This flower has a ***zygomorphic*** (bilaterally symmetric) structure.

For Foreign Words and Scientific Names

Use italics for foreign words that have not been adopted into the English language; italics are also used to denote scientific names.

> Say ***arrivederci*** to your fears and try new activities.
>   (foreign word)
>
> The voyageurs discovered the shy ***Castor canadensis***, or North American beaver.
>   (scientific name)

LO11 Parentheses

PARENTHESES ARE USED . . .

The following principles will guide the conventional use of parentheses in your writing.

To Enclose Explanatory or Supplementary Material

Use parentheses to enclose explanatory or supplementary material that interrupts the normal sentence structure.

> The RA **(resident assistant)** became my best friend.

To Set Off Numbers in a List

Use parentheses to set off numbers used with a series of words or phrases.

> Dr. Beck told us (1) plan ahead, (2) stay flexible, and (3) follow through.

For Parenthetical Sentences

When using a full sentence within another sentence, do not capitalize it or use a period inside the parentheses.

> Your friend doesn't have the assignment **(he was just thinking about calling you)**, so you'll have to make a few more calls.

© Image copyright KULISH VIKTORIIA 2009/Used under license from Shutterstock.com

When the parenthetical sentence comes after the main sentence, capitalize and punctuate it the same way you would any other complete sentence.

> But Mom doesn't say boo to Dad; she's always sweet to him. **(Actually she's sort of sweet to everybody.)**
> —Norma Fox Mazer, *Up on Fong Mountain*

To Set Off References

Use parentheses to set off references to authors, titles, pages, and years.

> The statistics are alarming **(see page 9)** and demand action.

> *Note:* For unavoidable parentheses within parentheses (. . . [. . .] . . .), use brackets. Avoid overuse of parentheses by using commas instead.

LO12 Diagonal

DIAGONALS ARE USED . . .

The following principles will guide the conventional use of diagonals in your writing.

To Form Fractions or Show Choices

Use a diagonal (also called a *slash*) to form a fraction. Also place a diagonal between two words to indicate that either is acceptable.

> **My walking/running** shoe size is **5 1/2;** my dress shoes are **6 1/2.**

When Quoting Poetry

When quoting poetry, use a diagonal (with one space before and after) to show where each line ends in the actual poem.

> A dryness is upon the house / My father loved and tended. / Beyond his firm and sculptured door / His light and lease have ended.
> —Gwendolyn Brooks
> "In Honor of David Anderson Brooks, My Father"

LO13 Brackets

BRACKETS ARE USED . . .

The following principles will guide the conventional use of brackets in your writing.

With Words That Clarify

Use brackets before and after words that are added to clarify what another person has said or written.

> "They'd **[the sweat bees]** get into your mouth, ears, eyes, nose. You'd feel them all over you."
> —Marilyn Johnson and Sasha Nyary
> "Roosevelts in the Amazon"

> *Note:* The brackets indicate that the words *the sweat bees* are not part of the original quotation but were added for clarification.

Around Comments by Someone Other Than the Author

Place brackets around comments that have been added by someone other than the author or speaker.

> "In conclusion, *docendo discimus*. Let the school year begin!" **[Huh?]**

Around Editorial Corrections

Place brackets around an editorial correction or addition.

> "Brooklyn alone has 8 percent of lead poisoning **[victims]** nationwide," said Marjorie Moore.
> —Donna Actie, student writer

Around the Word *Sic*

Brackets should be placed around the word *sic* (Latin for "so" or "thus") in quoted material; the word indicates that an error appearing in the quoted material was made by the original speaker or writer.

> "There is a higher principal *[sic]* at stake here: Is the school administration aware of the situation?"

LO14 Exclamation Point

EXCLAMATION POINTS ARE USED . . .

The following principle will guide the conventional use of exclamation points in your writing.

To Express Strong Feeling

Use an exclamation point to express strong feeling. It may be placed at the end of a sentence (or an elliptical expression that stands for a sentence). Use exclamation points sparingly.

> "That's not the point," said Wangero. "These are all pieces of dresses Grandma used to wear. She did all this stitching by hand. **Imagine!**"
> —Alice Walker, "Everyday Use"

> Su-su-something's crawling up the back of my neck!
> —Mark Twain, *Roughing It*

> She was on tiptoe, stretching for an orange, when they heard, "**HEY YOU!**"
> —Beverley Naidoo, *Journey to Jo'burg*

LO15 Apostrophe

APOSTROPHES ARE USED . . .

The following principles will guide the conventional use of apostrophes in your writing.

In Contractions

Use an apostrophe to show that one or more letters have been left out of two words joined to form a contraction.

> **don't** . . . . o is left out
> **she'd** . . . . **woul** is left out
> **it's** . . . . i is left out

Note: An apostrophe is also used to show that one or more numerals or letters have been left out of numbers or words.

> class of **'02** . . . . **20** is left out
> good **mornin'** . . . . . . **g** is left out

To Form Plurals

Use an apostrophe and an *s* to form the plural of a letter, a number, a sign, or a word discussed as a word.

> A . . . . . . **A's**   8 . . . . . . **8's**   + ... **+'s**
> You use too many *and*'s in your writing.

> *Note:* If two apostrophes are called for in the same word, omit the second one.

> Follow closely the do's and **don'ts** (not **don't's**) on the checklist.

To Form Singular Possessives

The possessive form of singular nouns is usually made by adding an apostrophe and an *s*.

> **Spock's** ears   my **computer's** memory

> *Note:* When a singular noun of more than one syllable ends with an *s* or a *z* sound, the possessive may be formed by adding just an apostrophe—or an apostrophe and an *s*. When the singular noun is a one-syllable word, however, the possessive is usually formed by adding both an apostrophe and an *s*.

Dallas' sports teams or **Dallas's** sports teams
(two-syllable word)

Kiss's last concert   my **boss's** generosity
(one-syllable words)

To Form Plural Possessives

The possessive form of plural nouns ending in *s* is made by adding just an apostrophe.

the **Joneses'** great-grandfather

bosses' offices

Note: For plural nouns not ending in *s*, add an apostrophe and *s*.

women's health issues   **children's** program

To Determine Ownership

You will punctuate possessives correctly if you remember that the word that comes immediately before the apostrophe is the owner.

girl's guitar (*girl* is the owner)
girls' guitar (*girls* are the owners)

boss's office (*boss* is the owner)
bosses' office (*bosses* are the owners)

To Show Shared Possession

When possession is shared by more than one noun, use the possessive form for the last noun in the series.

Jason, Kamil, and **Elana's** sound system
(All three own the same system.)

Jason's, Kamil's, and **Elana's** sound systems
(Each owns a separate system.)

In Compound Nouns

The possessive of a compound noun is formed by placing the possessive ending after the last word.

his **mother-in-law's** name (singular)
the **secretary of state's** career (singular)

their **mothers-in-law's** names (plural)
the **secretaries of state's** careers (plural)

With Indefinite Pronouns

The possessive form of an indefinite pronoun is made by adding an apostrophe and an *s* to the pronoun.

everybody's grades

no one's mistake

one's choice

In expressions using *else*, add the apostrophe and *s* after the last word.

anyone else's lunch order

somebody else's desk

To Show Time or Amount

Use an apostrophe and an *s* with an adjective that is part of an expression indicating time or amount.

yesterday's news

a day's wage

a month's pay

Punctuation Marks

´ (é)	**Accent, acute**		.....	**Leaders**
` (è)	**Accent, grave**		¶	**Paragraph**
< >	**Angle brackets**		( )	**Parentheses**
'	**Apostrophe**		.	**Period**
*	**Asterisk**		?	**Question mark**
{ }	**Braces**		" "	**Quotation marks**
[ ]	**Brackets**		§	**Section**
∧	**Caret**		;	**Semicolon**
ç	**Cedilla**		˜ (ñ)	**Tilde**
^ (â)	**Circumflex**		____	**Underscore**
:	**Colon**			
,	**Comma**			
†	**Dagger**			
—	**Dash**			
/	**Diagonal/slash**			
¨ (ä)	**Dieresis**			
. . .	**Ellipsis**			
!	**Exclamation point**			
-	**Hyphen**			

23

Mechanics

LO1 Capitalization

USING CAPITAL LETTERS . . .

The following principles will guide the conventional use of capital letters in your writing. Throughout this section, examples demonstrate correct capitalization and serve as a handy reference during editing and proofreading.

Proper Nouns and Adjectives

Capitalize all proper nouns and all proper adjectives (adjectives derived from proper nouns). The chart below provides a quick overview of capitalization rules. The pages following explain specific or special uses of capitalization.

Learning Outcomes

LO1 Capitalization

LO2 Plurals

LO3 Numbers

LO4 Abbreviations

LO5 Acronyms and Initialisms

LO6 Basic Spelling Rules

LO7 Commonly Misspelled Words

What do you think?

I'm able to recognize mechanical errors.

1	2	3	4	5
strongly agree				strongly disagree

Quick Guide — Capitalization at a Glance

Days of the week . . . . **Sunday, Monday, Tuesday**
Months . . . . **June, July, August**
Holidays, holy days . . . . **Thanksgiving, Easter, Hanukkah**
Periods, events in history . . . . **Middle Ages, World War I**
Special events . . . . **Tate Memorial Dedication Ceremony**
Political parties . . . . **Republican Party, Socialist Party**
Official documents . . . . **the Declaration of Independence**
Trade names . . . . **Oscar Mayer hot dogs, Toyota Prius**
Formal epithets . . . . **Alexander the Great**
Official titles . . . . **Mayor John Spitzer, Senator Feinstein**
Official state nicknames . . . **the Badger State, the Aloha State**

Geographical Names

Planets, heavenly bodies	**Earth, Jupiter, the Milky Way**
Continents	**Australia, South America**
Countries	**Ireland, Grenada, Sri Lanka**
States, provinces	**Ohio, Utah, Nova Scotia**
Cities, towns, villages	**El Paso, Burlington, Wonewoc**
Streets, roads, highways . . .	**Park Avenue, Route 66, Interstate 90**
Sections of the United States and the world	**the Southwest, the Far East**
Landforms	**the Rocky Mountains, the Kalahari Desert**
Bodies of water	**the Nile River, Lake Superior, Bee Creek**
Public areas	**Central Park, Yellowstone National Park**

First Words

Capitalize the first word in every sentence and the first word in a full-sentence direct quotation. (Also see "For Direct Quotations" on page 283.)

Attending the orientation for new students is a good idea.

Max suggested, "**Let's** take the guided tour of the campus first."

Sentences in Parentheses

Capitalize the first word in a sentence that is enclosed in parentheses if that sentence is not contained within another complete sentence.

The bookstore has the software. (**Now** all I need is the computer.)

Note: Do *not* capitalize a sentence that is enclosed in parentheses and is located in the middle of another sentence. (Also see "For Parenthetical Sentences" on page 285.)

Your college will probably offer everything (this includes general access to a computer) that you'll need for a successful year.

Sentences Following Colons

Capitalize a complete sentence that follows a colon when that sentence is a formal statement, a quotation, or a sentence that you want to emphasize. (Also see "To Introduce Quotations" on page 279.)

Sydney Harris had this to say about computers: "**The** real danger is not that computers will begin to think like people, but that people will begin to think like computers."

Salutation and Complimentary Closing

In a letter, capitalize the first and all major words of the salutation. Capitalize only the first word of the complimentary closing.

Dear Personnel Director: **Sincerely** yours,

Sections of the Country

Words that indicate sections of the country are proper nouns and should be capitalized; words that simply indicate direction are not proper nouns.

Many businesses move to the **South**.
    (section of the country)

They move **south** to cut fuel costs and other expenses.
    (direction)

Languages, Ethnic Groups, Nationalities, and Religions

Capitalize languages, ethnic groups, nationalities, and religions.

African	American	Latino
Navajo	French	Islam

Nouns that refer to the Supreme Being and holy books are capitalized.

God	Allah	Jehovah
the Koran	Exodus	the Bible

Titles

Capitalize the first word of a title, the last word, and every word in between except articles (*a, an, the*), short prepositions, *to* in an infinitive, and coordinating conjunctions. Follow this rule for titles of books, newspapers, magazines, poems, plays, songs, articles, films, works of art, and stories.

Going to Meet the Man	*Chicago Tribune*
"Nothing Gold Can Stay"	"Jobs in the Cyber Arena"
A Midsummer Night's Dream	*The War of the Roses*

Note: When citing titles in a bibliography, check the style manual you've been asked to follow. For example, in APA style, only the first word and any proper nouns in a title are capitalized.

Organizations

Capitalize the name of an organization or a team and its members.

American Indian Movement	Democratic Party
Tampa Bay Buccaneers	Seattle Sounders

Abbreviations

Capitalize abbreviations of titles and organizations. (Some other abbreviations are also capitalized. See pages 294–297. Also see "After Initials and Abbreviations" on page 274.)

M.D.	Ph.D.	NAACP	C.E.	B.C.E.	GPA

Letters

Capitalize letters used to indicate a form or shape.

U-turn	I-beam	S-curve	V-shaped	T-shirt

Words Used as Names

Capitalize words like *father, mother, uncle, senator,* and *professor* only when they are parts of titles that include a personal name or when they are substituted for proper nouns (especially in direct address). (See "To Separate Nouns of Direct Address" on page 277.)

Hello, **Senator** Feingold. (*Senator* is part of the name.)
Our **senator** is an environmentalist.

Who was your chemistry **professor** last quarter?
I had **Professor** Williams for Chemistry 101.

Note: To test whether a word is being substituted for a proper noun, simply read the sentence with a proper noun in place of the word. If the proper noun fits in the sentence, the word being tested should be capitalized. Usually the word is not capitalized if it follows a possessive—*my, his, our, your,* and so on.

Did **Dad (Brad)** pack the stereo in the trailer?
(*Brad* works in this sentence.)

Did your **dad (Brad)** pack the stereo in the trailer?
(*Brad* does not work in this sentence; the word *dad* follows the possessive *your*.)

Titles of Courses

Words such as *technology, history,* and *science* are proper nouns when they are included in the titles of specific courses; they are common nouns when they name a field of study.

Who teaches **Art History 202?**
(title of a specific course)

Professor Bunker loves teaching **history.**
(a field of study)

Note: The words *freshman, sophomore, junior,* and *senior* are not capitalized unless they are part of an official title.

The seniors who maintained high GPAs were honored at the Mount Mary Senior Honors Banquet.

Internet and E-Mail

The words *Internet* and *World Wide Web* are always capitalized because they are considered proper nouns. When your writing includes a Web address (URL), capitalize any letters that the site's owner does (on printed materials or on the site itself). Not only is it respectful to reprint a Web address exactly as it appears elsewhere, but, in fact, some Web addresses are case sensitive and must be entered into a browser's address bar exactly as presented.

When doing research on the **Internet**, be sure to record each site's **Web** address (**URL**) and each contact's **e-mail** address.

Note: Some people include capital letters in their e-mail addresses to make certain features evident. Although e-mail addresses are not case sensitive, duplicate an address letter for letter, just as its owner uses it.

Avoid Capitalization Errors

Do not capitalize any of the following:

- A prefix attached to a proper noun
- Seasons of the year
- Words used to indicate direction or position
- Common nouns and titles that appear near, but are not part of, a proper noun

© AJE, 2009 / Used under license from Shutterstock.com

Capitalize	Do Not Capitalize
American	un-American
January, February	winter, spring
The South is quite conservative.	Turn south at the stop sign.
Duluth City College	a Duluth college
Chancellor John Bohm	John Bohm, our chancellor
President Obama	the president of the United States
Earth (the planet)	earthmover
Internet	e-mail

L○2 Plurals

FORMING PLURALS . . .

The following principles will guide the conventional spelling of plural words in your writing.

Nouns Ending in a Consonant

Some nouns remain unchanged when used as plurals (*species, moose, halibut,* and so on), but the plurals of most nouns are formed by adding an *s* to the singular form.

dorm—dorms
credit—credits
midterm—midterms

The plurals of nouns ending in *sh, ch, x, s,* and *z* are made by adding *es* to the singular form.

lunch—lunches
wish—wishes
class—classes

Nouns Ending in y

The plurals of common nouns that end in *y* (preceded by a consonant) are formed by changing the *y* to *i* and adding *es*.

dormitory—dormitories
sorority—sororities
duty—duties

The plurals of common nouns that end in *y* (preceded by a vowel) are formed by adding only an *s*

attorney—attorneys
monkey—monkeys
toy—toys

The plurals of all proper nouns ending in *y* (whether preceded by a consonant or a vowel) are formed by adding an *s*.

the three Kathys
the five Faheys

Nouns Ending in *o*

The plurals of words ending in *o* (preceded by a vowel) are formed by adding an *s*.

radio—radios
cameo—cameos
studio—studios

The plurals of most nouns ending in *o* (preceded by a consonant) are formed by adding *es*.

echo—echoes
hero—heroes
tomato—tomatoes

Musical terms always form plurals by adding an *s;* check a dictionary for other words of this type.

alto—altos
banjo—banjos
solo—solos
piano—pianos

Nouns Ending in *f* or *fe*

The plurals of nouns that end in *f* or *fe* are formed in one of two ways: If the final *f* sound is still heard in the plural form of the word, simply add *s;* if the final sound is a *v* sound, change the *f* to *ve* and add an *s.*

Note: The plurals of some nouns that end in *f* can be formed by either adding *s* or changing the *f* to *ve* and adding an *s.*

Plural ends with *f* sound:
  roof—roofs
  chief—chiefs

Plural ends with *v* sound:
  wife—wives
  loaf—loaves

Plural ends with either sound:
  hoof—hoofs, hooves
  scarf—scarfs, scarves

Irregular Spelling

Many foreign words (as well as some of English origin) form a plural by taking on an irregular spelling; others are now acceptable with the commonly used *s* or *es* ending. Take time to check a dictionary.

child—children
alumnus—alumni
goose—geese
syllabus—syllabi, syllabuses
datum—data
radius—radii, radiuses

Words Discussed as Words

The plurals of symbols, letters, figures, and words discussed as words are formed by adding an apostrophe and an *s*.

Note: You can choose to omit the apostrophe when the omission does not cause confusion.

Many colleges have now added A/B's and B/C's as standard grades.

YMCA's or YMCAs
CD's or CDs

Nouns Ending in *ful*

The plurals of nouns that end with *ful* are formed by adding an *s* at the end of the word.

three teaspoonfuls
two tankfuls
four bagfuls

Compound Nouns

The plurals of compound nouns are usually formed by adding an *s* or an *es* to the important word in the compound. (Also see "In Compound Words" on page 279.)

brothers-in-law
maids of honor
secretaries of state

Collective Nouns

Collective nouns do not change in form when they are used as plurals.

Because the spelling of the collective noun does not change, it is often the pronoun used in place of the collective noun that indicates whether the noun is singular or plural. Use a singular pronoun (**its**) to show that the collective noun is singular. Use a plural pronoun (**their**) to show that the collective noun is plural.

class (a unit—singular form)

class (individual members—plural form)

The class needs to change its motto. (The writer is thinking of the group as a unit.)

The class brainstormed with their professor. (The writer is thinking of the group as individuals.)

ESL Note: To determine whether a plural noun requires the article *the*, you must first determine whether it is a specific or a nonspecific noun. Specific plural nouns use *the*, whereas nonspecific plural nouns do not require a preceding article.

LO3 Numbers

USING NUMBERS VS. WORDS . . .

The following principles will guide the conventional use of numbers in your writing.

Numerals or Words

Numbers from one to one hundred are usually written as words; numbers 101 and greater are usually written as numerals. (APA style uses numerals for numbers 10 and higher.) Hyphenate the written numbers *twenty-one* to *ninety-nine*.

| two | seven | ten | twenty-five | 106 | 1,079 |

The same rule applies to the use of ordinal numbers.

| second | tenth | twenty-fifth | ninety-eighth |
| 106th | 333rd | | |

If numbers greater than 101 are used infrequently in a piece of writing, you may spell out those that can be written in one or two words.

> **two hundred**   **fifty thousand**   **six billion**

You may use a combination of numerals and words for very large numbers.

> **1.5 million**   **3 billion to 3.2 billion**   **6 trillion**

Numbers being compared or contrasted should be kept in the same style.

> **eight** to **eleven** years old *or* **8** to **11** years old

Particular decades may be spelled out or written as numerals.

> the **eighties** and **nineties** *or* the **'80s** and **'90s**

Numerals Only

Use numerals for the following forms: decimals, percentages, pages, chapters (and other parts of a book), addresses, dates, telephone numbers, identification numbers, and statistics.

26.2	**398-55-0000**	pages **287–289**
Chapter **7**	May **8, 2007**	**(212) 555–1234**
Highway **36**	**8** percent	a vote of **23** to **4**

> *Note:* Abbreviations and symbols are often used in charts, graphs, footnotes, and so forth, but typically they are not used in texts:
>
> He is **five feet one inch** tall and **ten years old**.
>
> She walked **three and one-half miles** to work through **twelve inches** of snow.

However, abbreviations and symbols may be used in scientific, mathematical, statistical, and technical texts (APA style):

> Between **20%** and **23%** of the cultures yielded positive results.
>
> Your **245B** model requires **220V**.

Always use numerals with abbreviations and symbols.

> **5'4"**   **8%**   **10** in.   **3** tbsp.   **6** lb. **8** oz.   **90°F**

Use numerals after the names of local branches of labor unions.

> The Office and Professional Employees International Union, Local **8**

Hyphenated Numbers

Hyphens are used to form compound modifiers indicating measurement. They are also used for inclusive numbers and written-out fractions.

a **three-mile** trip	the **2009–2013** presidential term
a **2,500-mile** road trip	**one-sixth** of the pie
a **thirteen-foot** clearance	**three-eighths** of the book

Time and Money

If time is expressed with an abbreviation, use numerals; if it is expressed in words, spell out the number.

> **4:00** a.m. or **four** o'clock (not 4 o'clock)
>
> the **5:15** p.m. train
>
> a **seven o'clock** wake-up call

If money is expressed with a symbol, use numerals; if the currency is expressed in words, spell out the number.

> **$20** or **twenty** dollars (not 20 dollars)

Abbreviations of time and of money may be used in text.

> The concert begins at **7:00** p.m., and tickets cost **$30**.

Words Only

Use words to express numbers that begin a sentence.

> **Fourteen** students "forgot" their assignments.
>
> **Three hundred** contest entries were received.
>
> *Note:* Change the sentence structure if this rule creates a clumsy construction.

> **Six hundred thirty-nine** students are new to the campus this fall. (Clumsy)
>
> This fall, **639** students are new to the campus. (Better)

Use words for numbers that precede a compound modifier that includes a numeral. (If the compound modifier uses a spelled-out number, use numerals in front of it.)

> She sold **twenty 35-millimeter** cameras in one day.
>
> The chef prepared **24 eight-ounce** filets.

Use words for the names of numbered streets of one hundred or less.

> **Ninth** Avenue   **123 Forty-fourth** Street

Use words for the names of buildings if that name is also its address.

> **One Thousand State Street**
>
> **Two Fifty Park Avenue**

Use words for references to particular centuries.

> **the twenty-first century**
>
> **the fourth century B.C.E.**

LO4 Abbreviations

An **abbreviation** is the shortened form of a word or a phrase. These abbreviations are always acceptable in both formal and informal writing:

> **Mr.   Mrs.   Ms.   Dr.   Jr.   a.m. (A.M.)   p.m. (P.M.)**

Note: In formal writing, do not abbreviate the names of states, countries, months, days, units of measure, or courses of study. Do not abbreviate the words *Street, Road, Avenue, Company,* and similar words when they are part of a proper name. Also, do not use signs or symbols (%, &, #, @) in place of words. (The dollar sign, however, is appropriate when numerals are used to express an amount of money. See "Time and Money" on page 293.)

Also Note: When abbreviations are called for (in charts, lists, bibliographies, notes, and indexes, for example), standard abbreviations are preferred. Reserve the postal abbreviations for ZIP code addresses.

Correspondence Abbreviations

States/Territories

	Standard	Postal
Alabama	Ala.	AL
Alaska	Alaska	AK
Arizona	Ariz.	AZ
Arkansas	Ark.	AR
California	Cal.	CA
Colorado	Colo.	CO
Connecticut	Conn.	CT
Delaware	Del.	DE
District of Columbia	D.C.	DC
Florida	Fla.	FL
Georgia	Ga.	GA
Guam	Guam	GU
Hawaii	Hawaii	HI
Idaho	Idaho	ID
Illinois	Ill.	IL
Indiana	Ind.	IN
Iowa	Ia.	IA
Kansas	Kans.	KS
Kentucky	Ky.	KY
Louisiana	La.	LA
Maine	Me.	ME
Maryland	Md.	MD
Massachusetts	Mass.	MA
Michigan	Mich.	MI
Minnesota	Minn.	MN
Mississippi	Miss.	MS
Missouri	Mo.	MO
Montana	Mont.	MT
Nebraska	Neb.	NE
Nevada	Nev.	NV
New Hampshire	N.H.	NH
New Jersey	N.J.	NJ
New Mexico	N. Mex.	NM
New York	N.Y.	NY
North Carolina	N.C.	NC
North Dakota	N. Dak.	ND
Ohio	Ohio	OH

	Standard	Postal
Oklahoma	Okla.	OK
Oregon	Ore.	OR
Pennsylvania	Pa.	PA
Puerto Rico	P.R.	PR
Rhode Island	R.I.	RI
South Carolina	S.C.	SC
South Dakota	S. Dak.	SD
Tennessee	Tenn.	TN
Texas	Tex.	TX
Utah	Utah	UT
Vermont	Vt.	VT
Virginia	Va.	VA
Virgin Islands	V.I.	VI
Washington	Wash.	WA
West Virginia	W. Va.	WV
Wisconsin	Wis.	WI
Wyoming	Wyo.	WY

Canadian Provinces

	Standard	Postal
Alberta	Alta.	AB
British Columbia	B.C.	BC
Labrador	Lab.	NL
Manitoba	Man.	MB
New Brunswick	N.B.	NB
Newfoundland	N.F.	NL
Northwest Territories	N.W.T.	NT
Nova Scotia	N.S.	NS
Nunavut		NU
Ontario	Ont.	ON
Prince Edward Island	P.E.I.	PE
Quebec	Que.	PQ
Saskatchewan	Sask.	SK
Yukon Territory	Y.T.	YT

Address Abbreviations

	Standard	Postal
Apartment	Apt.	APT
Avenue	Ave.	AVE
Boulevard	Blvd.	BLVD

	Standard	Postal
Circle	Cir.	CIR
Court	Ct.	CT
Drive	Dr.	DR
East	E.	E
Expressway	Expy.	EXPY
Freeway	Frwy.	FWY
Heights	Hts.	HTS
Highway	Hwy.	HWY
Hospital	Hosp.	HOSP
Junction	Junc.	JCT
Lake	L.	LK
Lakes	Ls.	LKS
Lane	Ln.	LN
Meadows	Mdws.	MDWS
North	N.	N
Palms	Palms	PLMS
Park	Pk.	PK
Parkway	Pky.	PKY
Place	Pl.	PL
Plaza	Plaza	PLZ
Post Office Box	P.O. Box	PO BOX
Ridge	Rdg.	RDG
River	R.	RV
Road	Rd.	RD
Room	Rm.	RM
Rural	R.	R
Rural Route	R.R.	RR
Shore	Sh.	SH
South	S.	S
Square	Sq.	SQ
Station	Sta.	STA
Street	St.	ST
Suite	Ste.	STE
Terrace	Ter.	TER
Turnpike	Tpke.	TPKE
Union	Un.	UN
View	View	VW
Village	Vil.	VLG
West	W.	W

© Larry Dale Gordon/zefa Value/Corbis

© Theo Allofs/zefa Value/Corbis

© Darko Kovacevic, 2009/ Used under license from Shutterstock.com

Common Abbreviations

abr. abridged, abridgment

AC, ac alternating current, air-conditioning

ack. acknowledgment

AM amplitude modulation

A.M., a.m. before noon (Latin *ante meridiem*)

AP advanced placement

ASAP as soon as possible

avg., av. average

B.A. bachelor of arts degree

BBB Better Business Bureau

B.C.E. before common era

bibliog. bibliography

biog. biographer, biographical, biography

B.S. bachelor of science degree

C 1. Celsius 2. centigrade 3. coulomb

c. 1. *circa* (about) 2. cup(s)

cc 1. cubic centimeter 2. carbon copy 3. community college

CDT, C.D.T. central daylight time

C.E. common era

CEEB College Entrance Examination Board

chap. chapter(s)

cm centimeter(s)

c/o care of

COD, c.o.d. 1. cash on delivery 2. collect on delivery

co-op cooperative

CST, C.S.T. central standard time

cu 1. cubic 2. cumulative

D.A. district attorney

d.b.a., d/b/a doing business as

DC, dc direct current

dec. deceased

dept. department

disc. discount

DST, D.S.T. daylight saving time

dup. duplicate

ed. edition, editor

e.g. for example (Latin *exempli gratia*)

EST, E.S.T. eastern standard time

etc. and so forth (Latin *et cetera*)

F Fahrenheit, French, Friday

FM frequency modulation

F.O.B., f.o.b. free on board

FYI for your information

g 1. gravity 2. gram(s)

gal. gallon(s)

gds. goods

gloss. glossary

GNP gross national product

GPA grade point average

hdqrs. headquarters

HIV human immunodeficiency virus

hp horsepower

Hz hertz

ibid. in the same place (Latin *ibidem*)

id. the same (Latin *idem*)

i.e. that is (Latin *id est*)

illus. illustration

inc. incorporated

IQ, I.Q. intelligence quotient

IRS Internal Revenue Service

ISBN International Standard Book Number

JP, J.P. justice of the peace

K 1. kelvin (temperature unit) 2. Kelvin (temperature scale)

kc kilocycle(s)

kg kilogram(s)

km kilometer(s)

kn knot(s)

kw kilowatt(s)

l liter(s), lake

lat. latitude

l.c. lowercase

lit. literary, literature

log logarithm, logic

long. longitude

Ltd., ltd. limited

m meter(s)

M.A. master of arts degree

man. manual

Mc, mc megacycle

MC master of ceremonies

M.D. doctor of medicine (Latin *medicinae doctor*)

mdse. merchandise

mfg. manufacture, manufacturing

mg milligram(s)

mi. 1. mile(s) 2. mill(s) (monetary unit)

misc. miscellaneous

ml milliliter(s)

mm millimeter(s)

mpg, m.p.g. miles per gallon

mph, m.p.h. miles per hour

MS 1. manuscript 2. multiple sclerosis

Ms. title of courtesy for a woman

M.S. master of science degree

MST, M.S.T. mountain standard time

NE northeast

neg. negative

N.S.F., n.s.f. not sufficient funds

NW northwest

oz, oz. ounce(s)

PA public-address system

pct. percent

pd. paid

PDT, P.D.T. Pacific daylight time

PFC, Pfc. private first class

pg., p. page

Ph.D. doctor of philosophy

P.M., p.m. after noon (Latin *post meridiem*)

POW, P.O.W. prisoner of war

pp. pages

ppd. 1. postpaid 2. prepaid

PR, P.R. public relations

PSAT Preliminary Scholastic Aptitude Test

psi, p.s.i. pounds per square inch

PST, P.S.T. Pacific standard time

PTA, P.T.A. Parent-Teacher Association

R.A. residence assistant

RF radio frequency

R.P.M., rpm revolutions per minute

R.S.V.P., r.s.v.p. please reply (French *répondez s'il vous plaît*)

SAT Scholastic Aptitude Test

SE southeast

SOS 1. international distress signal 2. any call for help

Sr. 1. senior (after surname) 2. sister (religious)

SRO, S.R.O. standing room only

std. standard

SW southwest

syn. synonymous, synonym

tbs., tbsp. tablespoon(s)

TM trademark

UHF, uhf ultrahigh frequency

v 1. physics: velocity 2. volume

V electricity: volt

VA Veterans Administration

VHF, vhf very high frequency

VIP informal: very important person

vol. 1. volume 2. volunteer

vs. versus, verse

W 1. electricity: watt(s) 2. physics: (also **w**) work 3. west

whse., whs. warehouse

whsle. wholesale

wkly. weekly

w/o without

wt. weight

www World Wide Web

LO5 Acronyms and Initialisms

USING OTHER ABBREVIATIONS . . .

The following information explains two other common types of abbreviations.

Acronyms

An acronym is a word formed from the first (or first few) letters of words in a set phrase. Even though acronyms are abbreviations, they require no periods.

radar	radio detecting and ranging
CARE	Cooperative for Assistance and Relief Everywhere
NASA	National Aeronautics and Space Administration
VISTA	Volunteers in Service to America
FICA	Federal Insurance Contributions Act

Initialisms

An initialism is similar to an acronym except that the initials used to form this abbreviation are pronounced individually.

CIA	Central Intelligence Agency
FBI	Federal Bureau of Investigation
FHA	Federal Housing Administration

Common Acronyms and Initialisms

AIDS	acquired immune deficiency syndrome
APR	annual percentage rate
CAD	computer-aided design
CAM	computer-aided manufacturing
CETA	Comprehensive Employment and Training Act
FAA	Federal Aviation Administration
FCC	Federal Communications Commission
FDA	Food and Drug Administration
FDIC	Federal Deposit Insurance Corporation
FEMA	Federal Emergency Management Agency
FHA	Federal Housing Administration
FTC	Federal Trade Commission
IRS	Internal Revenue Service
MADD	Mothers Against Drunk Driving
NAFTA	North American Free Trade Agreement
NATO	North Atlantic Treaty Organization
OEO	Office of Economic Opportunity
ORV	off-road vehicle
OSHA	Occupational Safety and Health Administration
PAC	political action committee
PIN	personal identification number
POP	point of purchase
PSA	public service announcement
REA	Rural Electrification Administration
RICO	Racketeer Influenced and Corrupt Organizations (Act)
ROTC	Reserve Officers' Training Corps
SADD	Students Against Destructive Decisions
SASE	self-addressed stamped envelope
SPOT	satellite positioning and tracking
SSA	Social Security Administration
SUV	sport-utility vehicle
SWAT	Special Weapons and Tactics
TDD	telecommunications device for the deaf
TMJ	temporomandibular joint
TVA	Tennessee Valley Authority
VA	Veterans Administration
WHO	World Health Organization

LO6 Basic Spelling Rules

CHECKING YOUR SPELLING . . .

The following common formulas will help you spell words correctly.

Write *i* Before *e*

Write *i* before *e* except after *c*, or when sounded like *a* as in *neighbor* and *weigh*.

believe	relief	receive	eight

Note: This sentence contains eight exceptions:

Neither sheik dared **leisurely seize either weird species** of **financiers.**

Words with Consonant Endings

When a one-syllable word (*bat*) ends in a consonant (*t*) preceded by one vowel (*a*), double the final consonant before adding a suffix that begins with a vowel (*batting*).

sum ⋯⋯ **summary**   god ⋯⋯ **goddess**

Note: When a multisyllable word (*control*) ends in a consonant (*l*) preceded by one vowel (*o*), the accent is on the last syllable (con *trol ʹ*), and the suffix begins with a vowel (*ing*)—the same rule holds true: Double the final consonant (*controlling*).

prefer ⋯⋯ **preferred**   begin ⋯⋯ **beginning**
forget ⋯⋯ **forgettable**   admit ⋯⋯ **admittance**

Words with a Final Silent *e*

If a word ends with a silent *e*, drop the *e* before adding a suffix that begins with a vowel. Do *not* drop the *e* when the suffix begins with a consonant.

state	stating	statement
like	liking	likeness
use	using	useful
nine	ninety	nineteen

Note: Exceptions are **judgment, truly, argument, ninth.**

Words Ending in *y*

When *y* is the last letter in a word and the *y* is preceded by a consonant, change the *y* to *i* before adding any suffix except those beginning with *i*.

fry ⋯⋯ **fries, frying**	hurry ⋯⋯ **hurried, hurrying**
lady ⋯⋯ **ladies**	ply ⋯⋯ **pliable**
happy ⋯⋯ **happiness**	beauty ⋯⋯ **beautiful**

Note: When forming the plural of a word that ends with a *y* that is preceded by a vowel, add *s*.

| toy ⋯⋯ **toys** | play ⋯⋯ **plays** |
| monkey ⋯⋯ **monkeys** | |

TIP

Never trust your spelling to even the best spell-checker. Carefully proofread and use a dictionary for words you know your spell-checker does not cover.

LO7 Becoming a Better Speller

Becoming a better speller is a worthwhile endeavor. Better spelling promotes better and more effective writing. Consider using the strategy that follows to improve your spelling. Then use the list of commonly misspelled words to double-check your spelling throughout a writing project.

Becoming-a-Better-Speller Strategy

- **Be patient.** Becoming a good speller takes time.

- **Check the correct pronunciation of each word you are attempting to spell.** Knowing the correct pronunciation of each word can help you to remember its spelling.

- **Note the meaning and history of each word as you are checking the dictionary for the pronunciation.** Knowing the meaning and history of a word provides you with a better notion of how the word is properly used, and it can help you remember the word's spelling.

- **Before you close the dictionary, practice spelling the word.** You can do so by looking away from the page and trying to "see" the word in your "mind's eye." Write the word on a piece of paper. Check the spelling in the dictionary and repeat the process until you are able to spell the word correctly.

- **Learn some spelling rules.** The rules in this handbook (page 298) are four of the most useful—although there are others.

- **Make a list of the words that you misspell.** Select the first ten words and practice spelling them.

  First: Read each word carefully; then write it on a piece of paper. Look at the written word to see that it's spelled correctly. Repeat the process for those words that you misspelled.

  Then: Ask someone to read the words to you so you can write them again. Then check for misspellings. Repeat both steps with your next ten words.

- **Write often.** As noted educator Frank Smith said,

  "There is little point in learning to spell if you have little intention of writing."

Commonly Misspelled Words

The commonly misspelled words that follow are hyphenated to show where they would logically be broken at the end of a line.

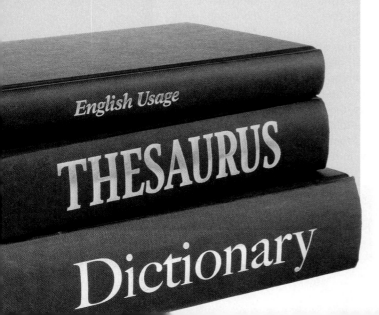

English Usage

THESAURUS

Dictionary

A

ab-bre-vi-ate	a-gainst	ap-prais-al
a-brupt	ag-gra-vate	ap-pre-ci-ate
ab-scess	ag-gres-sion	ap-proach
ab-sence	a-gree-able	ap-pro-pri-ate
ab-so-lute (-ly)	a-gree-ment	ap-prov-al
ab-sorb-ent	aisle	ap-prox-i-mate-ly
ab-surd	al-co-hol	ap-ti-tude
a-bun-dance	a-lign-ment	ar-chi-tect
ac-a-dem-ic	al-ley	arc-tic
ac-cede	al-lot-ted	ar-gu-ment
ac-cel-er-ate	al-low-ance	a-rith-me-tic
ac-cept (-ance)	all right	a-rouse
ac-ces-si-ble	al-most	ar-range-ment
ac-ces-so-ry	al-ready	ar-riv-al
ac-ci-den-tal-ly	al-though	ar-ti-cle
ac-com-mo-date	al-to-geth-er	ar-ti-fi-cial
ac-com-pa-ny	a-lu-mi-num	as-cend
ac-com-plice	al-um-nus	as-cer-tain
ac-com-plish	al-ways	as-i-nine
ac-cor-dance	am-a-teur	as-sas-sin
ac-cord-ing	a-mend-ment	as-sess (-ment)
ac-count	a-mong	as-sign-ment
ac-crued	a-mount	as-sist-ance
ac-cu-mu-late	a-nal-y-sis	as-so-ci-ate
ac-cu-rate	an-a-lyze	as-so-ci-a-tion
ac-cus-tom (ed)	an-cient	as-sume
ache	an-ec-dote	as-sur-ance
a-chieve (-ment)	an-es-thet-ic	as-ter-isk
ac-knowl-edge	an-gle	ath-lete
ac-quaint-ance	an-ni-hi-late	ath-let-ic
ac-qui-esce	an-ni-ver-sa-ry	at-tach
ac-quired	an-nounce	at-tack (ed)
ac-tu-al	an-noy-ance	at-tempt
a-dapt	an-nu-al	at-tend-ance
ad-di-tion (-al)	a-noint	at-ten-tion
ad-dress	a-non-y-mous	at-ti-tude
ad-e-quate	an-swer	at-tor-ney
ad-journed	ant-arc-tic	at-trac-tive
ad-just-ment	an-tic-i-pate	au-di-ble
ad-mi-ra-ble	anx-i-ety	au-di-ence
ad-mis-si-ble	anx-ious	au-dit
ad-mit-tance	a-part-ment	au-thor-i-ty
ad-van-ta-geous	a-pol-o-gize	au-to-mo-bile
ad-ver-tise-ment	ap-pa-ra-tus	au-tumn
ad-ver-tis-ing	ap-par-ent (-ly)	aux-il-ia-ry
ad-vice (n.)	ap-peal	a-vail-a-ble
ad-vis-able	ap-pear-ance	av-er-age
ad-vise (v.)	ap-pe-tite	aw-ful
ad-vis-er	ap-pli-ance	aw-ful-ly
ae-ri-al	ap-pli-ca-ble	awk-ward
af-fect	ap-pli-ca-tion	
af-fi-da-vit	ap-point-ment	

B

bac-ca-lau-re-ate
bach-e-lor
bag-gage
bal-ance
bal-loon
bal-lot
ba-nan-a
ban-dage
bank-rupt
bar-gain
bar-rel
base-ment
ba-sis
bat-tery
beau-ti-ful
beau-ty
be-com-ing
beg-gar
be-gin-ning
be-hav-ior
be-ing
be-lief
be-lieve
ben-e-fi-cial
ben-e-fit (-ed)
be-tween
bi-cy-cle
bis-cuit
bliz-zard
book-keep-er
bought
bouil-lon
bound-a-ry
break-fast
breath (n.)
breathe (v.)
brief
bril-liant
Brit-ain
bro-chure
brought
bruise
bud-get
bul-le-tin
buoy-ant
bu-reau
bur-glar
bury
busi-ness
busy

C

caf-e-te-ria
caf-feine
cal-en-dar
cam-paign
can-celed
can-di-date
can-is-ter
ca-noe
ca-pac-i-ty
cap-i-tal
cap-i-tol
cap-tain
car-bu-ret-or
ca-reer
car-i-ca-ture
car-riage
cash-ier
cas-se-role
cas-u-al-ty
cat-a-log
ca-tas-tro-phe
caught
cav-al-ry
cel-e-bra-tion
cem-e-ter-y
cen-sus
cen-tu-ry
cer-tain
cer-tif-i-cate
ces-sa-tion
chal-lenge
chan-cel-lor
change-a-ble
char-ac-ter (-is-tic)
chauf-feur
chief
chim-ney
choc-o-late
choice
choose
Chris-tian
cir-cuit
cir-cu-lar
cir-cum-stance
civ-i-li-za-tion
cli-en-tele
cli-mate
climb
clothes
coach
co-coa
co-er-cion

col-lar
col-lat-er-al
col-lege
col-le-giate
col-lo-qui-al
colo-nel
col-or
co-los-sal
col-umn
com-e-dy
com-ing
com-mence
com-mer-cial
com-mis-sion
com-mit
com-mit-ment
com-mit-ted
com-mit-tee
com-mu-ni-cate
com-mu-ni-ty
com-par-a-tive
com-par-i-son
com-pel
com-pe-tent
com-pe-ti-tion
com-pet-i-tive-ly
com-plain
com-ple-ment
com-plete-ly
com-plex-ion
com-pli-ment
com-pro-mise
con-cede
con-ceive
con-cern-ing
con-cert
con-ces-sion
con-clude
con-crete
con-curred
con-cur-rence
con-demn
con-de-scend
con-di-tion
con-fer-ence
con-ferred
con-fi-dence
con-fi-den-tial
con-grat-u-late
con-science
con-sci-en-tious
con-scious

con-sen-sus
con-se-quence
con-ser-va-tive
con-sid-er-ably
con-sign-ment
con-sis-tent
con-sti-tu-tion
con-tempt-ible
con-tin-u-al-ly
con-tin-ue
con-tin-u-ous
con-trol
con-tro-ver-sy
con-ven-ience
con-vince
cool-ly
co-op-er-ate
cor-dial
cor-po-ra-tion
cor-re-late
cor-re-spond
cor-re-spond-ence
cor-rob-o-rate
cough
coun-cil
coun-sel
coun-ter-feit
coun-try
cour-age
cou-ra-geous
cour-te-ous
cour-te-sy
cous-in
cov-er-age
cred-i-tor
cri-sis
crit-i-cism
crit-i-cize
cru-el
cu-ri-os-i-ty
cu-ri-ous
cur-rent
cur-ric-u-lum
cus-tom
cus-tom-ary
cus-tom-er
cyl-in-der

D

dai-ly
dair-y
dealt
debt-or
de-ceased
de-ceit-ful
de-ceive
de-cid-ed
de-ci-sion
dec-la-ra-tion
dec-o-rate
de-duct-i-ble
de-fend-ant
de-fense
de-ferred
def-i-cit
def-i-nite (-ly)
def-i-ni-tion
del-e-gate
de-li-cious
de-pend-ent
de-pos-i-tor
de-pot
de-scend
de-scribe
de-scrip-tion
de-sert
de-serve
de-sign
de-sir-able
de-sir-ous
de-spair
des-per-ate
de-spise
des-sert
de-te-ri-o-rate
de-ter-mine
de-vel-op
de-vel-op-ment
de-vice
de-vise
di-a-mond
di-a-phragm
di-ar-rhe-a
dic-tio-nary
dif-fer-ence
dif-fer-ent
dif-fi-cul-ty
di-lap-i-dat-ed
di-lem-ma
din-ing
di-plo-ma

di-rec-tor
dis-agree-able
dis-ap-pear
dis-ap-point
dis-ap-prove
dis-as-trous
dis-ci-pline
dis-cov-er
dis-crep-an-cy
dis-cuss
dis-cus-sion
dis-ease
dis-sat-is-fied
dis-si-pate
dis-tin-guish
dis-trib-ute
di-vide
di-vis-i-ble
di-vi-sion
doc-tor
doesn't
dom-i-nant
dor-mi-to-ry
doubt
drudg-ery
du-pli-cate
dye-ing
dy-ing

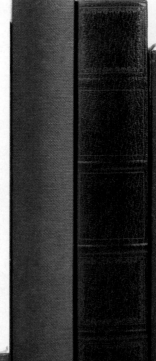

E

ea-ger-ly
ear-nest
eco-nom-i-cal
econ-o-my
ec-sta-sy
e-di-tion
ef-fer-ves-cent
ef-fi-ca-cy
ef-fi-cien-cy
eighth
ei-ther
e-lab-o-rate
e-lec-tric-i-ty
el-e-phant
el-i-gi-ble
e-lim-i-nate
el-lipse
em-bar-rass
e-mer-gen-cy
em-i-nent
em-pha-size
em-ploy-ee
em-ploy-ment
e-mul-sion
en-close
en-cour-age
en-deav-or
en-dorse-ment
en-gi-neer
En-glish
e-nor-mous
e-nough
en-ter-prise
en-ter-tain
en-thu-si-as-tic
en-tire-ly
en-trance
en-vel-op (v.)
en-ve-lope (n.)
en-vi-ron-ment
equip-ment
equipped
e-quiv-a-lent
es-pe-cial-ly
es-sen-tial
es-tab-lish
es-teemed
et-i-quette
ev-i-dence
ex-ag-ger-ate
ex-ceed
ex-cel-lent

ex-cept
ex-cep-tion-al-ly
ex-ces-sive
ex-cite
ex-ec-u-tive
ex-er-cise
ex-haust (-ed)
ex-hi-bi-tion
ex-hil-a-ra-tion
ex-is-tence
ex-or-bi-tant
ex-pect
ex-pe-di-tion
ex-pend-i-ture
ex-pen-sive
ex-pe-ri-ence
ex-plain
ex-pla-na-tion
ex-pres-sion
ex-qui-site
ex-ten-sion
ex-tinct
ex-traor-di-nar-y
ex-treme-ly

F

fa-cil-i-ties
fal-la-cy
fa-mil-iar
fa-mous
fas-ci-nate
fash-ion
fa-tigue (d)
fau-cet
fa-vor-ite
fea-si-ble
fea-ture
Feb-ru-ar-y
fed-er-al
fem-i-nine
fer-tile
fic-ti-tious
field
fierce
fi-ery
fi-nal-ly
fi-nan-cial-ly
fo-li-age
for-ci-ble
for-eign
for-feit
for-go
for-mal-ly
for-mer-ly
for-tu-nate
for-ty
for-ward
foun-tain
fourth
frag-ile
fran-ti-cal-ly
freight
friend
ful-fill
fun-da-men-tal
fur-ther-more
fu-tile

G

gad-get
gan-grene
ga-rage
gas-o-line
gauge
ge-ne-al-o-gy
gen-er-al-ly
gen-er-ous
ge-nius
gen-u-ine
ge-og-ra-phy
ghet-to
ghost
glo-ri-ous
gnaw
go-ril-la
gov-ern-ment
gov-er-nor
gra-cious
grad-u-a-tion
gram-mar
grate-ful
grat-i-tude
grease
grief
griev-ous
gro-cery
grudge
grue-some
guar-an-tee
guard
guard-i-an
guer-ril-la
guess
guid-ance
guide
guilty
gym-na-si-um
gyp-sy
gy-ro-scope

H

hab-i-tat
ham-mer
hand-ker-chief
han-dle (d)
hand-some
hap-haz-ard
hap-pen
hap-pi-ness
ha-rass
har-bor
hast-i-ly
hav-ing
haz-ard-ous
height
hem-or-rhage
hes-i-tate
hin-drance
his-to-ry
hoarse
hol-i-day
hon-or
hop-ing
hop-ping
horde
hor-ri-ble
hos-pi-tal
hu-mor-ous
hur-ried-ly
hy-drau-lic
hy-giene

I

i-am-bic
i-ci-cle
i-den-ti-cal
id-io-syn-cra-sy
il-leg-i-ble
il-lit-er-ate
il-lus-trate
im-ag-i-nary
im-ag-i-na-tive
im-ag-ine
im-i-ta-tion
im-me-di-ate-ly
im-mense
im-mi-grant
im-mor-tal
im-pa-tient
im-per-a-tive
im-por-tance
im-pos-si-ble
im-promp-tu
im-prove-ment
in-al-ien-able
in-ci-den-tal-ly
in-con-ve-nience
in-cred-i-ble
in-curred
in-def-i-nite-ly
in-del-i-ble
in-de-pend-ence
in-de-pend-ent
in-dict-ment
in-dis-pens-able
in-di-vid-u-al
in-duce-ment
in-dus-tri-al
in-dus-tri-ous
in-ev-i-ta-ble
in-fe-ri-or
in-ferred
in-fi-nite
in-flam-ma-ble
in-flu-en-tial
in-ge-nious
in-gen-u-ous
in-im-i-ta-ble
in-i-tial
ini-ti-a-tion
in-no-cence
in-no-cent
in-oc-u-la-tion
in-quir-y
in-stal-la-tion

I (cont)

in-stance
in-stead
in-sti-tute
in-struc-tor
in-sur-ance
in-tel-lec-tu-al
in-tel-li-gence
in-ten-tion
in-ter-cede
in-ter-est-ing
in-ter-fere
in-ter-mit-tent
in-ter-pret (-ed)
in-ter-rupt
in-ter-view
in-ti-mate
in-va-lid (n.)
in-ves-ti-gate
in-ves-tor
in-vi-ta-tion
ir-i-des-cent
ir-rel-e-vant
ir-re-sis-ti-ble
ir-rev-er-ent
ir-ri-gate
is-land
is-sue
i-tem-ized
i-tin-er-ar-y

J

jan-i-tor
jeal-ous (-y)
jeop-ar-dize
jew-el-ry
jour-nal
jour-ney
judg-ment
jus-tice
jus-ti-fi-able

K

kitch-en
knowl-edge
knuck-le

L

la-bel
lab-o-ra-to-ry
lac-quer
lan-guage
laugh
laun-dry
law-yer
league
lec-ture
le-gal
leg-i-ble
leg-is-la-ture
le-git-i-mate
lei-sure
length
let-ter-head
li-a-bil-i-ty
li-a-ble
li-ai-son
lib-er-al
li-brar-y
li-cense
lieu-ten-ant
light-ning
lik-able
like-ly
lin-eage
liq-ue-fy
liq-uid
lis-ten
lit-er-ary
lit-er-a-ture
live-li-hood
log-a-rithm
lone-li-ness
loose
lose
los-ing
lov-able
love-ly
lun-cheon
lux-u-ry

M

ma-chine
mag-a-zine
mag-nif-i-cent
main-tain
main-te-nance
ma-jor-i-ty
mak-ing
man-age-ment
ma-neu-ver
man-u-al
man-u-fac-ture
man-u-script
mar-riage
mar-shal
ma-te-ri-al
math-e-mat-ics
max-i-mum
may-or
mean-ness
meant
mea-sure
med-i-cine
me-di-eval
me-di-o-cre
me-di-um
mem-o-ran-dum
men-us
mer-chan-dise
mer-it
mes-sage
mile-age
mil-lion-aire
min-i-a-ture
min-i-mum
min-ute
mir-ror
mis-cel-la-neous
mis-chief
mis-chie-vous
mis-er-a-ble
mis-ery
mis-sile
mis-sion-ary
mis-spell
mois-ture
mol-e-cule
mo-men-tous
mo-not-o-nous
mon-u-ment
mort-gage
mu-nic-i-pal
mus-cle

N

mu-si-cian
mus-tache
mys-te-ri-ous
na-ive
nat-u-ral-ly
nec-es-sary
ne-ces-si-ty
neg-li-gi-ble
ne-go-ti-ate
neigh-bor-hood
nev-er-the-less
nick-el
niece
nine-teenth
nine-ty
no-tice-able
no-to-ri-ety
nu-cle-ar
nui-sance

O

o-be-di-ence
o-bey
o-blige
ob-sta-cle
oc-ca-sion
oc-ca-sion-al-ly
oc-cu-pant
oc-cur
oc-curred
oc-cur-rence
of-fense
of-fi-cial
of-ten
o-mis-sion
o-mit-ted
op-er-ate
o-pin-ion
op-po-nent
op-por-tu-ni-ty
op-po-site
op-ti-mism
or-di-nance
or-di-nar-i-ly
orig-i-nal
out-ra-geous

P

pag-eant
pam-phlet
par-a-dise
para-graph
par-al-lel
par-a-lyze
pa-ren-the-ses
pa-ren-the-sis
par-lia-ment
par-tial
par-tic-i-pant
par-tic-i-pate
par-tic-u-lar-ly
pas-time
pa-tience
pa-tron-age
pe-cu-liar
per-ceive
per-haps
per-il
per-ma-nent
per-mis-si-ble
per-pen-dic-u-lar
per-se-ver-ance
per-sis-tent
per-son-al (-ly)
per-son-nel
per-spi-ra-tion
per-suade
phase
phe-nom-e-non
phi-los-o-phy
phy-si-cian
piece
planned
pla-teau
plau-si-ble
play-wright
pleas-ant
plea-sure
pneu-mo-nia
pol-i-ti-cian
pos-sess
pos-ses-sion
pos-si-ble
prac-ti-cal-ly
prai-rie
pre-cede
pre-ce-dence
pre-ced-ing
pre-cious
pre-cise-ly

pre-ci-sion
pre-de-ces-sor
pref-er-a-ble
pref-er-ence
pre-ferred
prej-u-dice
pre-lim-i-nar-y
pre-mi-um
prep-a-ra-tion
pres-ence
prev-a-lent
pre-vi-ous
prim-i-tive
prin-ci-pal
prin-ci-ple
pri-or-i-ty
pris-on-er
priv-i-lege
prob-a-bly
pro-ce-dure
pro-ceed
pro-fes-sor
prom-i-nent
pro-nounce
pro-nun-ci-a-tion
pro-pa-gan-da
pros-e-cute
pro-tein
psy-chol-o-gy
pub-lic-ly
pump-kin
pur-chase
pur-sue
pur-su-ing
pur-suit

Q

qual-i-fied
qual-i-ty
quan-ti-ty
quar-ter
ques-tion-naire
quite
quo-tient

R

raise
rap-port
re-al-ize
re-al-ly
re-cede
re-ceipt
re-ceive
re-ceived
rec-i-pe
re-cip-i-ent
rec-og-ni-tion
rec-og-nize
rec-om-mend
re-cur-rence
ref-er-ence
re-ferred
reg-is-tra-tion
re-hearse
reign
re-im-burse
rel-e-vant
re-lieve
re-li-gious
re-mem-ber
re-mem-brance
rem-i-nisce
ren-dez-vous
re-new-al
rep-e-ti-tion
rep-re-sen-ta-tive
req-ui-si-tion
res-er-voir
re-sis-tance
re-spect-a-bly
re-spect-ful-ly
re-spec-tive-ly
re-spon-si-bil-i-ty
res-tau-rant
rheu-ma-tism
rhyme
rhythm
ri-dic-u-lous
route

S

sac-ri-le-gious
safe-ty
sal-a-ry
sand-wich
sat-is-fac-to-ry
Sat-ur-day
scarce-ly
scene
scen-er-y
sched-ule
schol-ar-ship
sci-ence
scis-sors
sec-re-tary
seize
sen-si-ble
sen-tence
sen-ti-nel
sep-a-rate
ser-geant
sev-er-al
se-vere-ly
shep-herd
sher-iff
shin-ing
siege
sig-nif-i-cance
sim-i-lar
si-mul-ta-ne-ous
since
sin-cere-ly
ski-ing
sol-dier
sol-emn
so-phis-ti-cat-ed
soph-o-more
so-ror-i-ty
source
sou-ve-nir
spa-ghet-ti
spe-cif-ic
spec-i-men
speech
sphere
spon-sor
spon-ta-ne-ous
sta-tion-ary
sta-tion-ery
sta-tis-tic
stat-ue
stat-ure
stat-ute

stom-ach
stopped
straight
strat-e-gy
strength
stretched
study-ing
sub-si-dize
sub-stan-tial
sub-sti-tute
sub-tle
suc-ceed
suc-cess
suf-fi-cient
sum-ma-rize
su-per-fi-cial
su-per-in-ten-dent
su-pe-ri-or-i-ty
su-per-sede
sup-ple-ment
sup-pose
sure-ly
sur-prise
sur-veil-lance
sur-vey
sus-cep-ti-ble
sus-pi-cious
sus-te-nance
syl-la-ble
sym-met-ri-cal
sym-pa-thy
sym-pho-ny
symp-tom
syn-chro-nous

T

tar-iff
tech-nique
tele-gram
tem-per-a-ment
tem-per-a-ture
tem-po-rary
ten-den-cy
ten-ta-tive
ter-res-tri-al
ter-ri-ble
ter-ri-to-ry
the-ater
their
there-fore
thief
thor-ough (-ly)
though
through-out
tired
to-bac-co
to-geth-er
to-mor-row
tongue
to-night
touch
tour-na-ment
tour-ni-quet
to-ward
trag-e-dy
trai-tor
tran-quil-iz-er
trans-ferred
trea-sur-er
tru-ly
Tues-day
tu-i-tion
typ-i-cal
typ-ing

U

unan-i-mous
un-con-scious
un-doubt-ed-ly
un-for-tu-nate-ly
unique
u-ni-son
uni-ver-si-ty
un-nec-es-sary
un-prec-e-dent-ed
un-til
up-per
ur-gent
us-able
use-ful
using
usu-al-ly
u-ten-sil
u-til-ize

V

va-can-cies
va-ca-tion
vac-u-um
vague
valu-able
va-ri-ety
var-i-ous
veg-e-ta-ble
ve-hi-cle
veil
ve-loc-i-ty
ven-geance
vi-cin-i-ty
view
vig-i-lance
vil-lain
vi-o-lence
vis-i-bil-i-ty
vis-i-ble
vis-i-tor
voice
vol-ume
vol-un-tary
vol-un-teer

W

wan-der
war-rant
weath-er
Wednes-day
weird
wel-come
wel-fare
where
wheth-er
which
whole
whol-ly
whose
width
wom-en
worth-while
wor-thy
wreck-age
wres-tler
writ-ing
writ-ten
wrought

Y

yel-low
yes-ter-day
yield

24

Grammar

Grammar is the study of the structure and features of the language, consisting of rules and standards that are to be followed to produce acceptable writing and speaking. **Parts of speech** refers to the eight different categories that indicate how words are used in the English language—as *nouns, pronouns, verbs, adjectives, adverbs, prepositions, conjunctions,* or *interjections.*

Learning Outcomes

Understand the parts of speech:

LO1 Noun   **LO5** Adverb

LO2 Pronoun   **LO6** Preposition

LO3 Verb   **LO7** Conjunction

LO4 Adjective   **LO8** Interjection

What do you think?

Nouns and verbs are the heart and soul of writing.

1	2	3	4	5
strongly agree				strongly disagree

LO1 Noun

A noun is a word that names something: a person, a place, a thing, or an idea.

Toni Morrison/author	*Lone Star*/film
Renaissance/era	UC-Davis/university
A Congress of Wonders/book	

CLASSES OF NOUNS

All nouns are either *proper nouns* or *common nouns.* Nouns may also be classified as *individual* or *collective,* or *concrete* or *abstract.*

Proper Nouns

A proper noun, which is always capitalized, names a specific person, place, thing, or idea.

Rembrandt, Bertrand Russell (people)

Stratford-upon-Avon, Tower of London (places)

The Night Watch, Rosetta stone (things)

New Deal, Christianity (ideas)

Common Nouns

A common noun is a general name for a person, a place, a thing, or an idea. Common nouns are not capitalized.

optimist, instructor (people)	cafeteria, park (places)
computer, chair (things)	freedom, love (ideas)

Collective Nouns

A collective noun names a group or a unit.

family	audience	crowd
committee	team	class

Concrete Nouns

A concrete noun names a thing that is tangible (can be seen, touched, heard, smelled, or tasted).

child	the White Stripes	gym
village	microwave oven	pizza

Abstract Nouns

An abstract noun names an idea, a condition, or a feeling—in other words, something that cannot be seen, touched, heard, smelled, or tasted.

beauty	Jungian psychology	anxiety
agoraphobia	trust	

FORMS OF NOUNS

Nouns are grouped according to their *number, gender,* and *case.*

Number of Nouns

Number indicates whether a noun is singular or plural.

A singular noun refers to one person, place, thing, or idea.

student	laboratory	lecture
note	grade	result

A plural noun refers to more than one person, place, thing, or idea.

students	laboratories	lectures
notes	grades	results

Gender of Nouns

Gender indicates whether a noun is masculine, feminine, neuter, or indefinite.

Masculine ··········	father king brother men colt rooster
Feminine ··········	mother queen sister women filly hen
Neuter (without gender) ··············	notebook monitor car printer
Indefinite (masculine or feminine) ··········	professor customer children doctor people

Case of Nouns

The case of a noun tells what role the noun plays in a sentence. There are three cases: *nominative, possessive,* and *objective.*

A noun in the **nominative case** is used as a subject. The subject of a sentence tells who or what the sentence is about.

> **Dean Henning** manages the College of Arts and Communication.
>
> *Note:* A noun is also in the nominative case when it is used as a predicate noun (or predicate nominative). A predicate noun follows a linking verb, usually a form of the *be* verb (such as *am, is, are, was, were, be, being, been*), and repeats or renames the subject.
>
> Ms. Yokum is the **person** to talk to about the college's impact in our community.

A noun in the **possessive case** shows possession or ownership. In this form, it acts as an adjective.

> Our **president's** willingness to discuss concerns with students has boosted campus morale.

© Image Source/Corbis

A noun in the **objective case** serves as an object of the preposition, a direct object, an indirect object, or an object complement.

> To survive, institutions of higher **learning** sometimes cut **budgets** in spite of **protests** from **students** and **instructors**.
> (*Learning* is the object of the preposition *of*, *protests* is the object of the preposition *in spite of*, *budgets* is the direct object of the verb *cut*, and *students* and *instructors* are the objects of the preposition *from*.)

A Closer Look
at Direct and Indirect Objects

A **direct object** is a noun (or pronoun) that identifies what or who receives the action of the verb.

> Budget cutbacks reduced class **choices**. (*Choices* is the direct object of the active verb *reduced*.)

An **indirect object** is a noun (or pronoun) that identifies the person *to whom* or *for whom* something is done, or the thing *to which* or *for which* something is done. An indirect object is always accompanied by a direct object.

> Recent budget cuts have given **students** fewer class choices. (*Choices* is the direct object of *have given*; *students* is the indirect object.)

ESL Note: Not every transitive verb is followed by both a direct object and an indirect object. Both can, however, follow *give, send, show, tell, teach, find, sell, ask, offer, pay, pass,* and *hand*.

LO2 Pronoun

 pronoun is a word that is used in place of a noun.

> Roger was the most interesting 10-year-old **I** ever taught. **He** was a good thinker and thus a good writer. **I** remember **his** paragraph about the cowboy hat **he** received from **his** grandparents. **It** was "too new looking." The brim was not rolled properly. But the hat's imperfections were not the main idea in Roger's writing. No, the main idea was how **he** was fixing the hat **himself** by wearing **it** when **he** showered.

Antecedents

An antecedent is the noun or pronoun that the pronoun refers to or replaces. Most pronouns have antecedents, but not all do. (See "Indefinite Pronouns" on page 307.)

> As the wellness **counselor** checked *her* chart, several **students** *who* were waiting *their* turns shifted uncomfortably.
> (*Counselor* is the antecedent of *her*; *students* is the antecedent of *who* and *their*.)

Note: Each pronoun must agree with its antecedent in number, person, and gender. (See pages 308–309.)

CLASSES OF PRONOUNS

There are several classes of pronouns: *personal, reflexive* and *intensive, relative, indefinite, interrogative, demonstrative,* and *reciprocal.*

Quick Guide	**Classes of Pronouns**
Personal	I, me, my, mine / we, us, our, ours / you, your, yours / they, them, their, theirs / he, him, his, she, her, hers, it, its
Reflexive and Intensive	myself, yourself, himself, herself, itself, ourselves, yourselves, themselves
Relative	who, whose, whom, which, that
Indefinite	all, another, any, anybody, anyone, anything, both, each, each one, either, everybody, everyone, everything, few, many, most, much, neither, nobody, none, no one, nothing, one, other, several, some, somebody, someone, something, such
Interrogative	who, whose, whom, which, what
Demonstrative	this, that, these, those
Reciprocal	each other, one another

Personal Pronouns

A personal pronoun refers to a specific person or thing.

> *Marge* started **her** car; **she** drove the antique convertible to *Monterey,* where **she** hoped to sell **it** at an auction.

© Image copyright Alexander Kalina 2009/Used under license from Shutterstock.com
© Graffizone/iStockphoto.com

Reflexive and Intensive Pronouns

A **reflexive pronoun** is formed by adding *-self* or *-selves* to a personal pronoun. A reflexive pronoun can act as a direct object or an indirect object of a verb, an object of a preposition, or a predicate nominative.

> Charles loves **himself**.
> (direct object of *loves*)
>
> Charles gives **himself** A's for fashion sense
> (indirect object of *gives*)
>
> Charles smiles at **himself** in store windows.
> (object of preposition *at*)
>
> Charles can be **himself** anywhere.
> (predicate nominative)

An **intensive pronoun** intensifies, or emphasizes, the noun or pronoun it refers to.

> Leo **himself** taught his children to invest their lives in others.
>
> The lesson was sometimes painful—but they learned it **themselves**.

Relative Pronouns

A relative pronoun relates an adjective dependent (relative) clause to the noun or pronoun it modifies. (The noun is italicized in each example below; the relative pronoun is in bold.)

> *Freshmen* **who** believe they have a lot to learn are absolutely right.
>
> Just navigating this *campus,* **which** is huge, can be challenging.

Indefinite Pronouns

An indefinite pronoun refers to unnamed or unknown people, places, or things.

> **Everyone** seemed amused when I was searching for my classroom in the student center.
> (The antecedent of *everyone* is unnamed.)
>
> **Nothing** is more unnerving than rushing at the last minute into the wrong room for the wrong class.
> (The antecedent of *nothing* is unknown.)

Most indefinite pronouns are singular, so when they are used as subjects, they should have singular verbs. (See pages 325–328.)

Interrogative Pronouns

An interrogative pronoun asks a question.

> So **which** will it be—highlighting and attaching a campus map to the inside of your backpack, or being lost and late for the first two weeks?
>
> *Note:* When an interrogative pronoun modifies a noun, it functions as an adjective.

Demonstrative Pronouns

A demonstrative pronoun points out people, places, or things.

> We advise **this**: Bring along as many maps and schedules as you need.
>
> **Those** are useful tools. **That** is the solution.
>
> *Note:* When a demonstrative pronoun modifies a noun, it functions as an adjective.

FORMS OF PERSONAL PRONOUNS

The **form** of a personal pronoun indicates its *number* (singular or plural), its *person* (first, second, or third), its *case* (nominative, possessive, or objective), and its *gender* (masculine, feminine, neuter, or indefinite).

Number of Pronouns

A personal pronoun is either singular (*I, you, he, she, it*) or plural (*we, you, they*).

> **He** should have a budget and stick to it. (singular)
>
> **We** can help new students learn about budgeting. (plural)

Person of Pronouns

The person of a pronoun indicates whether the person is speaking (first person), is spoken to (second person), or is spoken about (third person).

First person is used to name the speaker(s).

> I know I need to handle **my** stress in a healthful way, especially during exam week; **my** usual chips-and-doughnuts binge isn't helping. (singular)
>
> **We** all decided to bike to the tennis court. (plural)

Second person is used to name the person(s) spoken to.

> Maria, **you** grab the rackets, okay? (singular)
>
> John and Tanya, can **you** find the water bottles? (plural)

Third person is used to name the person(s) or thing(s) spoken about.

> Today's students are interested in wellness issues. **They** are concerned about **their** health, fitness, and nutrition. (plural)
>
> Maria practices yoga and feels **she** is calmer for **her** choice. (singular)
>
> One of the advantages of regular exercise is that **it** raises one's energy level. (singular)

Case of Pronouns

The case of each pronoun tells what role it plays in a sentence. There are three cases: *nominative, possessive,* and *objective*.

A pronoun in the **nominative case** is used as a subject. The following are nominative forms: *I, you, he, she, it, we, they*.

> **He** found an old map in the trunk.
>
> My friend and **I** went biking. (not *me*)

A pronoun is also in the nominative case when it is used as a predicate nominative, following a linking verb (*am, is, are, was, were, seems*) and renaming the subject.

> It was **he** who discovered electricity. (not *him*)

A pronoun in the **possessive case** shows possession or ownership: *my, mine, our, ours, his, her, hers, their, theirs, its, your, yours*. A possessive pronoun before a noun acts as an adjective: *your coat*.

> That coat is **hers**. | This coat is **mine**. | **Your** coat is lost.

A pronoun in the **objective case** can be used as the direct object, indirect object, object of a preposition, or object complement: *me, you, him, her, it, us, them*.

> Professor Adler hired **her**.
> (*Her* is the direct object of the verb *hired*.)
>
> He showed Mary and **me** the language lab.
> (*Me* is the indirect object of the verb *showed*.)
>
> He introduced the three of **us**—Mary, Shavonn, and **me**—to the faculty.
> (*Us* is the object of the preposition *of*; *me* is part of the appositive renaming *us*.)

Gender of Pronouns

The gender of a pronoun indicates whether the pronoun is masculine, feminine, neuter, or indefinite.

Masculine	he, him, his
Feminine	she, her, hers
Neuter (without gender)	it, its
Indefinite (masculine or feminine)	they, them, their

Quick Guide — Number, Person, and Case of Personal Pronouns

	Nominative Case	Possessive Case	Objective Case
First Person Singular	I	my, mine	me
Second Person Singular	you	your, yours	you
Third Person Singular	he, she, it	his, her, hers, its	him, her, it
First Person Plural	we	our, ours	us
Second Person Plural	you	your, yours	you
Third Person Plural	they	their, theirs	them

LO3 Verb

A verb shows action (*pondered, grins*), links words (*is, seemed*), or accompanies another action verb as an auxiliary or helping verb (*can, does*).

Harry **honked** the horn. (shows action)

Harry **is** impatient. (links words)

Harry **was** honking the truck's horn. (accompanies the verb *honking*)

CLASSES OF VERBS

Verbs are classified as action, auxiliary (helping), or linking (state of being).

Action Verbs: Transitive and Intransitive

As its name implies, an action verb shows action. Some action verbs are *transitive*; others are *intransitive*. (The term *action* does not always refer to a physical activity.)

Rain **splashed** the windshield. (transitive verb)

Josie **drove** off the road. (intransitive verb)

Transitive verbs have direct objects that receive the action. (See "A Closer Look" on page 306.)

> The health-care industry **employs** more than 7 million **workers** in the United States.
> (*Workers* is the direct object of the action verb *employs*.)

Intransitive verbs communicate action that is complete in itself. They do not need an object to receive the action.

> My new college roommate **smiles** and **laughs** a lot.

> *Note:* Some verbs can be either transitive or intransitive.

> Ms. Hull **teaches** physiology and microbiology.
> (transitive)

> She **teaches** well.
> (intransitive)

Auxiliary (Helping) Verbs

Auxiliary verbs (helping verbs) help to form some of the *tenses*, the *mood*, and the *voice* of the main verb. (See pages 311–312.) In the following example, the auxiliary verbs are in **bold,** and the main verbs are in *italics.*

Auxiliary Verbs			
is	being	shall	has
am	been	should	had
are	can	may	do
was	could	might	does
were	will	must	did
be	would	have	

> I believe, I **have** always *believed,* and I **will** always *believe* in private enterprise as the backbone of economic well-being in America.
>
> —Franklin D. Roosevelt

> *ESL Note:* "Be" auxiliary verbs are always followed by either a verb ending in *ing* or a past participle.

Linking (State of Being) Verbs

A linking verb is a special form of intransitive verb that links the subject of a sentence to a noun, a pronoun, or an adjective in the predicate. (See the chart in the next column.)

> The streets **are** flooded. (adjective)

> The streets **are** rivers! (noun)

Common Linking Verbs	am	become	is
	are	been	was
	be	being	were
Additional Linking Verbs	appear	seem	remain
	feel	sound	smell
	look	grow	taste

> *Note:* The verbs listed as "additional linking verbs" above function as linking verbs when they do not show actual action. An adjective usually follows these linking verbs.

> The sky **looked** ominous.
> (adjective)

> My little brother **grew** frightened.
> (adjective)

> *Note:* When these same words are used as action verbs, an adverb or a direct object may follow them.

> I **looked** carefully at him.
> (adverb)

> My little brother **grew** corn for a science project.
> (direct object)

FORMS OF VERBS

A verb's form differs depending on its *number* (singular, plural), *person* (first, second, third), *tense* (present, past, future, present perfect, past perfect, future perfect), *voice* (active, passive), and *mood* (indicative, imperative, subjunctive).

Number of a Verb

Number indicates whether a verb is singular or plural. The verb and its subject both must be singular, or they both must be plural. (See "Subject-Verb Agreement," pages 325–328.)

> My college **enrolls** high schoolers in summer programs. (singular)

> Many colleges **enroll** high schoolers in summer courses. (plural)

Person of a Verb

Person indicates whether the subject of the verb is *first, second,* or *third person.* The verb and its subject must be in the same person. Verbs usually have a different form only in **third person singular of the present tense.**

	1ˢᵗ Person	2ⁿᵈ Person	3ʳᵈ Person
Singular	I think	you think	he/she/it thinks
Plural	we think	you think	they think

Tense of a Verb

Tense indicates the time of an action or state of being. There are three basic *tenses* (past, present, and future) and three verbal *aspects* (progressive, perfect, and perfect progressive).

Present Tense

Present tense expresses action happening at the present time or regularly.

> In the United States, more than 75 percent of workers **hold** service jobs.

Present progressive tense also expresses action that is happening continually, in an ongoing fashion at the present time, but it is formed by combining *am, are,* or *is* and the present participle (ending in *ing*) of the main verb.

> More women than ever before **are working** outside the home.

Present perfect tense expresses action that began in the past and has recently been completed or that continues up to the present time.

> My sister **has taken** four years of swimming lessons.

Present perfect progressive tense also expresses an action that began in the past but stresses the continuing nature of the action. Like the present progressive tense, it is formed by combining auxiliary verbs (*have been* or *has been*) and present participles.

> She **has been taking** them since she was six years old.

Past Tense

Past tense expresses action that was completed at a particular time in the past.

> A hundred years ago, more than 75 percent of laborers **worked** in agriculture.

Past progressive tense expresses past action that continued over time. It is formed by combining *was* or *were* with the present participle of the main verb.

> In 1900, my great-grandparents **were farming**.

Past perfect tense expresses an action in the past that was completed at a specific time before another past action occurred.

> By the time we sat down for dinner, my cousins **had eaten** all the olives.

Past perfect progressive tense expresses a past action but stresses the continuing nature of the action. It is formed by using *had been* along with the present participle.

> They **had been eating** the olives all afternoon.

Future Tense

Future tense expresses action that will take place in the future.

> Next summer I **will work** as a lifeguard.

Future progressive tense expresses an action that will be continuous in the future.

> I **will be working** for the park district at North Beach.

Future perfect tense expresses future action that will be completed by a specific time.

> By 10:00 p.m., I **will have completed** my research project.

Future perfect progressive tense also expresses future action that will be completed by a specific time but (as with other perfect progressive tenses) stresses the action's continuous nature. It is formed using *will have been* along with the present participle.

> I **will have been researching** the project for three weeks by the time it's due.

Voice of a Verb

Voice indicates whether the subject is acting or being acted upon.

Active voice indicates that the subject of the verb is performing the action.

People **update** their résumés on a regular basis.
(The subject, *people*, is acting; *résumés* is the direct object.)

Passive voice indicates that the subject of the verb is being acted upon or is receiving the action. A passive verb is formed by combining a *be* verb with a past participle.

Your résumé **should be updated** on a regular basis.
(The subject, *résumé*, is receiving the action.)

Using Active Voice

Generally, use active voice rather than passive voice for more direct, energetic writing. To change your passive sentences to active ones, do the following: First, find the noun that is doing the action and make it the subject. Then find the word that had been the subject and use it as the direct object.

Passive: The winning goal **was scored** by Eva.
(The subject, *goal*, is not acting.)

Active: Eva **scored** the winning goal.
(The subject, *Eva*, is acting.)

Note: When you want to emphasize the receiver more than the doer—or when the doer is unknown—use the passive voice. (Much technical and scientific writing regularly uses the passive voice.)

Mood of a Verb

The mood of a verb indicates the tone or attitude with which a statement is made.

Indicative mood, the most common, is used to state a fact or to ask a question.

Can any theme **capture** the essence of the complex 1960s culture? President John F. Kennedy's directive [to the right] **represents** one ideal popular during that decade.

Imperative mood is used to give a command. (The subject of an imperative sentence is *you*, which is usually understood and not stated in the sentence.)

Ask not what your country can do for you—**ask** what you can do for your country.

—John F. Kennedy

© Bettmann/Corbis

Subjunctive mood is used to express a wish, an impossibility or unlikely condition, or a necessity. The subjunctive mood is often used with *if* or *that*. The verb forms below create an atypical subject-verb agreement, forming the subjunctive mood.

If I **were** rich, I would travel for the rest of my life.
(a wish)

If each of your brain cells **were** one person, there would be enough people to populate 25 planets.
(an impossibility)

The English Department requires that every student **pass** a proficiency test.
(a necessity)

Verbals

A verbal is a word that is made from a verb, but it functions as a noun, an adjective, or an adverb. There are three types of verbals: *gerunds, infinitives,* and *participles.*

Gerunds

A **gerund** ends in *ing* and is used as a noun.

Waking each morning is the first challenge.
(subject)

I start **moving** at about seven o'clock.
(direct object)

I work at **jump-starting** my weary system.
(object of the preposition)

As Woody Allen once said, "Eighty percent of life is **showing up.**"
(predicate nominative)

Infinitives

An **infinitive** is *to* and the base form of the verb. The infinitive may be used as a noun, an adjective, or an adverb.

> **To succeed** is not easy. (noun)
>
> That is the most important thing **to remember**. (adjective)
>
> Students are wise **to work** hard. (adverb)

> *ESL Note:* It can be difficult to know whether a gerund or an infinitive should follow a verb. It's helpful to become familiar with lists of specific verbs that can be followed by one but not the other.

Participles

A **present participle** ends in *ing* and functions as an adjective. A **past participle** ends in *ed* (or another past tense form) and also functions as an adjective.

> The **studying** students were annoyed by the **partying** ones.
>
> The students **playing** loud music were **annoying**. (These participles function as adjectives: *studying, partying, playing,* and *annoying* students. Notice, however, that *playing* has a direct object: *music.* All three types of verbals may have direct objects. See "Verbal Phrase" on page 321.)

Using Verbals

Make sure that you use verbals correctly; look carefully at the examples below.

> **Verbal:** **Diving** is a popular Olympic sport.
> (*Diving* is a gerund used as a subject.)
>
> **Diving** gracefully, the Olympian hoped to get high marks.
> (*Diving* is a participle modifying *Olympian.*)
>
> **Verb:** The next competitor was **diving** in the practice pool.
> (Here, *diving* is a verb, not a verbal.)

IRREGULAR VERBS

Irregular verbs can often be confusing. That's because the past tense and past participle of irregular verbs are formed by changing the word itself, not merely by adding *d* or *ed*. The following list contains the most troublesome irregular verbs.

Common Irregular Verbs and Their Principal Parts

Present Tense	Past Tense	Past Participle	Present Tense	Past Tense	Past Participle
am, be	was, were	been	leave	left	left
arise	arose	arisen	lend	lent	lent
awake	awoke, awaked	awoken, awaked	let	let	let
			lie (deceive)	lied	lied
beat	beat	beaten	lie (recline)	lay	lain
become	became	become	make	made	made
begin	began	begun	mean	meant	meant
bite	bit	bitten, bit	meet	met	met
blow	blew	blown	pay	paid	paid
break	broke	broken	prove	proved	proved, proven
bring	brought	brought			
build	built	built	put	put	put
burn	burnt, burned	burnt, burned	read	read	read
			ride	rode	ridden
burst	burst	burst	ring	rang	rung
buy	bought	bought	rise	rose	risen
catch	caught	caught	run	ran	run
choose	chose	chosen	see	saw	seen
come	came	come	set	set	set
cost	cost	cost	shake	shook	shaken
cut	cut	cut	shine (light)	shone	shone
dig	dug	dug	shine (polish)	shined	shined
dive	dived, dove	dived	show	showed	shown
do	did	done	shrink	shrank	shrunk
draw	drew	drawn	sing	sang	sung
dream	dreamed, dreamt	dreamed, dreamt	sink	sank	sunk
			sit	sat	sat
drink	drank	drunk	sleep	slept	slept
drive	drove	driven	speak	spoke	spoken
eat	ate	eaten	spend	spent	spent
fall	fell	fallen	spring	sprang	sprung
feel	felt	felt	stand	stood	stood
fight	fought	fought	steal	stole	stolen
find	found	found	strike	struck	struck, stricken
flee	fled	fled			
fly	flew	flown	strive	strove	striven
forget	forgot	forgotten, forgot	swear	swore	sworn
			swim	swam	swum
freeze	froze	frozen	swing	swung	swung
get	got	gotten	take	took	taken
give	gave	given	teach	taught	taught
go	went	gone	tear	tore	torn
grow	grew	grown	tell	told	told
hang (execute)	hanged	hanged	think	thought	thought
hang (suspend)	hung	hung	throw	threw	thrown
have	had	had	wake	woke, waked	woken, waked
hear	heard	heard			
hide	hid	hidden	wear	wore	worn
hit	hit	hit	weave	wove	woven
keep	kept	kept	wind	wound	wound
know	knew	known	wring	wrung	wrung
lay	laid	laid	write	wrote	written
lead	led	led			

LO4 Adjective

An adjective describes or modifies a noun or pronoun. The articles *a*, *an*, and *the* are adjectives.

> Advertising is **a big** and **powerful** industry.
> (*A*, *big*, and *powerful* modify the noun *industry*.)

> *Note:* Many demonstrative, indefinite, and interrogative forms may be used as either adjectives or pronouns (*that*, *these*, *many*, *some*, *whose*, and so on). These words are adjectives if they come before a noun and modify it; they are pronouns if they stand alone.

> **Some** advertisements are less than truthful.
> (*Some* modifies *advertisements* and is an adjective.)

> **Many** cause us to chuckle at their outrageous claims.
> (*Many* stands alone; it is a pronoun and replaces the noun *advertisements*.)

Proper Adjectives

Proper adjectives are created from proper nouns and are capitalized.

> **English** has been influenced by advertising slogans.
> (proper noun)

> The **English** language is constantly changing.
> (proper adjective)

Predicate Adjectives

A predicate adjective follows a form of the *be* verb (or other linking verb) and describes the subject. (See "Linking (State of Being) Verbs" on page 310.)

> At its best, advertising is **useful**; at its worst, **deceptive**.
> (*Useful* and *deceptive* modify the noun *advertising*.)

Forms of Adjectives

Adjectives have three forms: *positive*, *comparative*, and *superlative*.

The **positive form** is the adjective in its regular form. It describes a noun or a pronoun without comparing it to anyone or anything else.

> Joysport walking shoes are **strong** and **comfortable**.

The **comparative form** (*-er*, *more*, or *less*) compares two things. (*More* and *less* are used generally with adjectives of two or more syllables.)

> Air soles make Mile Eaters **stronger** and **more comfortable** than Joysports.

The **superlative form** (*-est*, *most*, or *least*) compares three or more things. (*Most* and *least* are used most often with adjectives of two or more syllables.)

> My old Canvas Wonders are the **strongest, most comfortable** shoes of all!

> *ESL Note:* Two or more adjectives before a noun should have a certain order when they do not modify the noun equally. (See "To Determine Equal Modifiers" on page 275.)

LO5 Adverb

An adverb describes or modifies a verb, an adjective, another adverb, or a whole sentence. An adverb answers questions such as *how, when, where, why, how often,* or *how much*.

> The temperature fell **sharply**.
> (*Sharply* modifies the verb *fell*.)

> The temperature was **quite** low.
> (*Quite* modifies the adjective *low*.)

> The temperature dropped **very quickly**.
> (*Very* modifies the adverb *quickly*, which modifies the verb *dropped*.)

> **Unfortunately,** the temperature stayed cool.
> (*Unfortunately* modifies the whole sentence.)

Types of Adverbs

Adverbs can be grouped in four ways: *time, place, manner,* and *degree*.

Time: These adverbs tell *when, how often,* and *how long*.

| today, yesterday | daily, weekly | briefly, eternally |

Place: These adverbs tell *where, to where,* and *from where*.

| here, there | nearby, beyond | backward, forward |

Manner: These adverbs often end in *ly* and tell *how* something is done.

| precisely | regularly | regally | well |

Degree: These adverbs tell *how much* or *how little*.

| substantially | greatly | entirely | partly | too |

Forms of Adverbs

Adverbs have three forms: *positive, comparative,* and *superlative*.

The **positive form** is the adverb in its regular form. It describes a verb, an adjective, or another adverb without comparing it to anyone or anything else.

> With Joysport shoes, you'll walk **fast**. They support your feet **well**.

The **comparative form** (*-er, more,* or *less*) compares two things. (*More* and *less* are used generally with adverbs of two or more syllables.)

> Wear Jockos instead of Joysports, and you'll walk **faster**. Jockos' special soles support your feet **better** than the Joysports do.

The **superlative form** (*-est, most,* or *least*) compares three or more things. (*Most* and *least* are used most often with adverbs of two or more syllables.)

> Really, I walk **fastest** wearing my old Canvas Wonders. They seem to support my feet, my knees, and my pocketbook **best** of all.

Regular Adverbs

positive	comparative	superlative
fast	faster	fastest
effectively	more effectively	most effectively

Irregular Adverbs

positive	comparative	superlative
well	better	best
badly	worse	worst

LO6 Preposition

A preposition is a word (or group of words) that shows the relationship between its object (a noun or pronoun following the preposition) and another word in the sentence.

> **Regarding** your reasons **for** going **to** college, do they all hinge **on** getting a good job **after** graduation?
> (In this sentence, *reasons, going, college, getting,* and *graduation* are objects of their preceding prepositions *regarding, for, to, on,* and *after*.)

Prepositional Phrases

A prepositional phrase includes the preposition, the object of the preposition, and the modifiers of the object. A prepositional phrase may function as an adverb or an adjective.

> A broader knowledge **of the world** is one benefit **of higher education**.
> (The two phrases function as adjectives modifying the nouns *knowledge* and *benefit* respectively.)

> He placed the flower **in the window**.
> (The phrase functions as an adverb modifying the verb *placed*.)

Prepositions

aboard	despite	out
about	down	out of
above	down from	outside
according to	during	outside of
across	except	over
across from	except for	over to
after	excepting	owing to
against	for	past
along	from	prior to
alongside	from among	regarding
alongside of	from between	round
along with	from under	save
amid	in	since
among	in addition to	subsequent to
apart from	in behalf of	through
around	in front of	throughout
as far as	in place of	till
aside from	in regard to	to
at	inside	together with
away from	inside of	toward
back of	in spite of	under
because of	instead of	underneath
before	into	until
behind	like	unto
below	near	up
beneath	near to	upon
beside	notwithstanding	up to
besides	of	with
between	off	within
beyond	on	without
but	on account of	
by	on behalf of	
by means of	onto	
concerning	on top of	
considering	opposite	

ESL Note: Prepositions often pair up with a verb and become part of an idiom, a slang expression, or a two-word verb.

 LO7 Conjunction

A conjunction connects individual words or groups of words.

When we came back to Paris, it was clear **and** cold **and** lovely.
—Ernest Hemingway

Coordinating Conjunctions

Coordinating conjunctions usually connect a word to a word, a phrase to a phrase, or a clause to a clause. The words, phrases, or clauses joined by a coordinating conjunction are equal in importance or are of the same type.

Civilization is a race between education **and** catastrophe.
—H. G. Wells

Correlative Conjunctions

Correlative conjunctions are a type of coordinating conjunction used in pairs.

There are two inadvisable ways to think: **either** believe everything **or** doubt everything.

Subordinating Conjunctions

Subordinating conjunctions connect two clauses that are not equally important. A subordinating conjunction connects a dependent clause to an independent clause. The conjunction is part of the dependent clause.

Experience is the worst teacher; it gives the test **before** it presents the lesson.
(The clause *before it presents the lesson* is dependent. It connects to the independent clause *it gives the test*.)

<u>Note:</u> Relative pronouns can also connect clauses. (See "Relative Pronouns" on page 221.)

Conjunctions

Coordinating .... and, but, or, nor, for, so, yet

Correlative .... either, or; neither, nor; not only, but (but also); both, and; whether, or

Subordinating ..... after, although, as, as if, as long as, because, before, even though, if, in order that, provided that, since, so that, than, that, though, unless, until, when, whenever, where, while

LO8 Interjection

An interjection communicates strong emotion or surprise (*oh, ouch, hey,* and so on). Punctuation (often a comma or an exclamation point) is used to set off an interjection.

> **Hey! Wait! Well,** so much for catching the bus.

A Closer Look
at the Parts of Speech

Noun

A noun is a word that names something: a person, a place, a thing, or an idea.

Toni Morrison/author	*Lone Star*/film
UC–Davis/university	Renaissance/era
A Congress of Wonders/book	

Pronoun

A pronoun is a word used in place of a noun.

I	my	that	themselves	which
it	ours	they	everybody	you

Verb

A verb is a word that expresses action, links words, or acts as an auxiliary verb to the main verb.

are	break	drag	fly	run	sit	was
bite	catch	eat	is	see	tear	were

Adjective

An adjective describes or modifies a noun or pronoun. (The articles *a, an,* and *the* are adjectives.)

> **The carbonated** drink went down easy on **that hot, dry** day. (*The* and *carbonated* modify *drink; that, hot,* and *dry* modify *day.*)

Adverb

An adverb describes or modifies a verb, an adjective, another adverb, or a whole sentence. An adverb generally answers questions such as *how, when, where, how often,* or *how much.*

greatly	precisely	regularly	there
here	today	partly	quickly
slowly	yesterday	nearly	loudly

Preposition

A preposition is a word (or group of words) that shows the relationship between its object (a noun or pronoun that follows the preposition) and another word in the sentence. Prepositions introduce prepositional phrases, which are modifiers.

across	for	with	out	to	of

Conjunction

A conjunction connects individual words or groups of words.

and	because	but	for	or	since	so	yet

Interjection

An interjection is a word that communicates strong emotion or surprise. Punctuation (often a comma or an exclamation point) is used to set off an interjection from the rest of the sentence.

> **Stop! No! What,** am I invisible?

25
Sentences

A sentence is made up of at least a subject (sometimes understood) and a verb and expresses a complete thought. Sentences can make statements, ask questions, give commands, or express strong feeling. The following sentence makes a statement:

> The Web delivers the universe in a box.

LO1 Using Subjects and Predicates

Sentences have two main parts: a subject and a predicate.

> **Technology frustrates many people.**

In the sentence above, **technology** is the subject—the sentence talks about technology. **Frustrates many people** is the complete predicate—it tells what the subject is doing.

THE SUBJECT

The subject names the person or thing either performing the action, receiving the action, or being described or renamed. The subject is most often a noun or a pronoun.

> **Technology** is an integral part of almost every business.
>
> **Manufacturers** need technology to compete in the world market.
>
> **They** could not go far without it.

A verbal phrase or a noun dependent clause may also function as a subject.

> **To survive without technology** is difficult.
> (infinitive phrase)
>
> **Downloading information from the Web** is easy.
> (gerund phrase)
>
> **That the information age would arrive** was inevitable. (noun dependent clause)
>
> > _Note:_ To determine the subject of a sentence, ask yourself _who_ or _what_ performs or receives the action or is described.

In most sentences, the subject comes before the verb; however, in many questions and in some other instances, that order is reversed.

Simple Subject

A simple subject is the subject without the words that describe or modify it.

> Thirty years ago, reasonably well-trained **mechanics** could fix any car on the road.

Complete Subject

A complete subject is the simple subject and the words that describe or modify it.

> Thirty years ago, **reasonably well-trained mechanics** could fix any car on the road.

Compound Subject

A compound subject is composed of two or more simple subjects joined by a conjunction and sharing the same predicate(s).

> Today, **mechanics** and **technicians** would need to master a half million manual pages to fix every car on the road.
>
> **Dealerships** and their service **departments** must sometimes explain that situation to the customers.

Understood Subject

Sometimes a subject is understood. This means it is not stated in the sentence, but a reader clearly understands what the subject is. An understood subject occurs in a command (imperative sentence). The subject You is understood in the following two sentences.

> You | Park on this side of the street.
> You | Put the CD player in the trunk.

Delayed Subject

In sentences that begin with _There is, There was,_ or _Here is,_ the subject follows the verb.

> There are 70,000 **fans** in the stadium.
> (_Fans_ is subject; _are_ is the verb. _There_ is an expletive, an empty word.)
>
> Here is a **problem** for stadium security.
> (_Problem_ is the subject. _Here_ is an adverb.)
>
> > _Note:_ The subject is also delayed in questions.
>
> Where was the **event**?
> (_Event_ is the subject.)
>
> Was **Dave Matthews** playing?
> (_Dave Matthews_ is the subject.)

THE PREDICATE (VERB)

The predicate, which contains the verb, is the part of the sentence that either tells what the subject is doing, tells what is being done to the subject, or describes or renames the subject.

> Students **need technical skills as well as basic academic skills.**

Simple Predicate

A simple predicate is the complete verb without the words that describe or modify it. (The complete verb is the main verb plus any helping verbs.)

> Today's workplace **requires** employees to have a range of skills.

Complete Predicate

A complete predicate is the verb, all the words that modify or explain it, and any objects or complements.

> Today's workplace **requires employees to have a range of skills.**

Compound Predicate

A compound predicate is composed of two or more simple predicates joined by a conjunction and sharing the same subject.

> Engineers **analyze** problems and **calculate** solutions.

Direct Object

A direct object is the part of the predicate that receives the action of an active transitive verb. A direct object makes the meaning of the verb complete.

> Marcos visited several **campuses.**
> (The direct object *campuses* receives the action of the verb *visited* by answering the question "Marcos visited what?")
>
> _Note:_ A direct object may be compound.
>
> A counselor explained the academic **programs** and the application **process.**

Indirect Object

An indirect object is the part of the predicate that tells *to whom/to what* or *for whom/for what* something is done. A sentence with an indirect object must also have a direct object.

> (Example) I showed our **children** my new school.
>
> To find an indirect object ask . . .
> • What is the verb? **showed**
> • Showed what? **school** (direct object)
> • Showed school to whom? **children** (indirect object)
>
> _Note:_ An indirect object may be compound.
>
> I gave the **instructor** and a few **classmates** my e-mail address.

LO2 Using Phrases

A phrase is a group of related words that functions as a single part of speech. A phrase lacks a subject, a predicate, or both. There are three phrases in the following sentence:

> Examples **of technology can be found in ancient civilizations.**

> **of technology** ····· (prepositional phrase that functions as an adjective; no subject or predicate)
>
> **can be found** ······ (verb phrase—the main verb plus helping verbs; no subject)
>
> **in ancient civilizations** ·········· (prepositional phrase that functions as an adverb; no subject or predicate)

TYPES OF PHRASES

There are several types of phrases: *verb, verbal, prepositional, appositive,* and *absolute.*

Verb Phrase

A **verb phrase** consists of a main verb and its helping verbs.

> Students, worried about exams, **have camped** at the library all week.

Verbal Phrase

A verbal phrase is a phrase that expands on one of the three types of verbals: *gerund, infinitive,* or *participle.* A **gerund phrase** consists of a gerund and its modifiers and objects. The whole phrase functions as a noun.

> **Becoming a marine biologist** is Rashanda's dream.
> (The gerund phrase is used as the subject of the sentence.)
>
> She has acquainted herself with the various methods for **collecting sea-life samples**.
> (The gerund phrase is used as the object of the preposition *for.*)

An **infinitive phrase** consists of an infinitive and its modifiers and objects. The whole phrase functions as a noun, an adjective, or an adverb.

> **To dream** is the first step in any endeavor.
> (The infinitive phrase functions as a noun and is used as the subject.)
>
> Remember **to make a plan to realize your dream**.
> (The infinitive phrase *to make a plan* functions as a noun and is used as a direct object; *to realize your dream* functions as an adjective modifying *plan.*)
>
> Finally, apply all of your talents and skills **to achieve your goals**.
> (The infinitive phrase functions as an adverb modifying *apply.*)

A **participial phrase** consists of a present or past participle (a verb form ending in *ing* or *ed*) and its modifiers. The phrase functions as an adjective.

> **Doing poorly in biology,** Theo signed up for a tutor.
> (The participial phrase modifies the noun *Theo.*)
>
> Some students **frustrated by difficult course work** don't seek help.
> (The participial phrase modifies the noun *students.*)

Functions of Verbal Phrases

	Noun	Adjective	Adverb
Gerund	✓		
Infinitive	✓	✓	✓
Participial		✓	

Prepositional Phrase

A prepositional phrase is a group of words beginning with a preposition and ending with its object, a noun or a pronoun. Prepositional phrases are used mainly as adjectives and adverbs.

> Denying the existence **of exam week** hasn't worked **for anyone** yet.
> (The prepositional phrase *of exam week* is used as an adjective modifying the noun *existence; for anyone* is used as an adverb modifying the verb *has worked.*)
>
> Test days still dawn, and GPAs still plummet **for the unprepared student**.
> (The prepositional phrase *for the unprepared student* is used as an adverb modifying the verbs *dawn* and *plummet.*)
>
> <u>Note:</u> Do not mistake the following adverbs for nouns and incorrectly use them as objects of prepositions: *here, there, everywhere.*

Appositive Phrase

An appositive phrase, which follows a noun or a pronoun and renames it, consists of a noun and its modifiers. An appositive adds new information about the noun or pronoun it follows.

> The Olympic-size pool, **a prized addition to the physical education building,** gets plenty of use.
> (The appositive phrase renames *pool.*)

Absolute Phrase

An absolute phrase consists of a noun and a participle (plus the participle's object, if there is one, and any modifiers). It usually modifies the entire sentence.

> **Their enthusiasm sometimes waning,** the students who cannot swim are required to take lessons.
> (The noun *enthusiasm* is modified by the present participle *waning;* the entire phrase modifies *students.*)

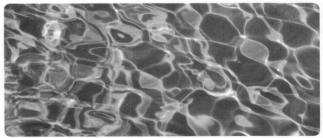

© Marino , 2009 / Used under license from Shutterstock.com

LO3 Using Clauses

A clause is a group of related words that has both a subject and a verb. A clause can be either independent or dependent. An independent clause contains at least one subject and one verb, presents a complete thought, and can stand alone as a sentence; a dependent clause (also called a subordinate clause) does not present a complete thought and cannot stand alone (make sense) as a sentence.

> Though airplanes are twentieth-century inventions (dependent clause), people have always dreamed of flying (independent clause).

TYPES OF CLAUSES

There are three basic types of dependent, or subordinate, clauses: *adverb, adjective,* and *noun.* These dependent clauses are combined with independent clauses to form complex and compound-complex sentences.

Adverb Clause

An adverb clause is used like an adverb to modify a verb, an adjective, or an adverb. All adverb clauses begin with subordinating conjunctions.

> **Because Orville won a coin toss,** he got to fly the power-driven air machine first.
> (The adverb clause modifies the verb *got.*)

Adjective Clause

An adjective clause is used like an adjective to modify a noun or a pronoun. Adjective clauses begin with relative pronouns *(which, that, who).*

> The men **who invented the first airplane** were brothers, Orville and Wilbur Wright.
> (The adjective clause modifies the noun *men.* *Who* is the subject of the adjective clause.)

> The first flight, **which took place December 17, 1903,** was made by Orville.
> (The adjective clause modifies the noun *flight.* *Which* is the subject of the adjective clause.)

Noun Clause

A noun clause is used in place of a noun. Noun clauses can appear as subjects, as direct or indirect objects, as predicate nominatives, or as objects of prepositions. They are introduced by subordinating words such as *what, that, when, why, how, whatever, who, whom, whoever,* and *whomever.*

> He wants to know **what made modern aviation possible.**
> (The noun clause functions as the object of the infinitive.)

> **Whoever invents an airplane with vertical takeoff ability** will be a hero.
> (The noun clause functions as the subject.)

> <u>Note:</u> If you can replace a whole clause with the pronoun *something* or *someone,* it is a noun clause.

LO4 Using Sentence Variety

sentence can be classified according to the kind of statement it makes and according to the way it is constructed.

KINDS OF SENTENCES

Sentences can make five basic kinds of statements: *declarative*, *interrogative*, *imperative*, *exclamatory*, or *conditional*.

Declarative Sentence

Declarative sentences make statements. They tell us something about a person, a place, a thing, or an idea.

> In 1955, Rosa Parks refused to follow segregation rules on a bus in Montgomery, Alabama.

Interrogative Sentence

Interrogative sentences ask questions.

> Do you think Ms. Parks knew she was making history?
>
> Would you have had the courage to do what she did?

Imperative Sentence

Imperative sentences give commands. They often contain an understood subject (you).

> Read chapters 6 through 10 for tomorrow.
>
> *Note:* Imperative sentences with the understood subject (you) are the only sentences in which it is acceptable to omit a stated subject.

Exclamatory Sentence

Exclamatory sentences communicate strong emotion or surprise. They are punctuated with exclamation points.

> I simply can't keep up with these long reading assignments!
>
> Oh my gosh, you scared me!

Conditional Sentence

Conditional sentences express two circumstances. One of the circumstances depends on the other circumstance. The words *if*, *when*, or *unless* are often used in the dependent clause in conditional sentences.

> **If** you practice a few study-reading techniques, college reading loads will be manageable.
>
> **When** I manage my time, it seems I have more of it.
>
> Don't ask me to help you **unless** you are willing to do the reading first.

STRUCTURE OF SENTENCES

A sentence may be *simple*, *compound*, *complex*, or *compound-complex*, depending on how the independent and dependent clauses are combined.

Simple Sentence

A simple sentence contains one independent clause. The independent clause may have compound subjects and verbs, and it may also contain phrases.

My **back aches.**	(single subject: *back*; single verb: *aches*)
My **teeth** and my **eyes hurt**.	(compound subject: *teeth* and *eyes*; single verb: *hurt*)
My **memory** and my **logic come** and **go**.	(compound subject: *memory* and *logic*; compound verb: *come* and *go*)
I **must need** a vacation...	(single subject: *I*; single verb: *must need*; direct object: *vacation*)

Compound Sentence

A compound sentence consists of two independent clauses. The clauses must be joined by a semicolon, by a comma and a coordinating conjunction (*and, but, or, nor, so, for, yet*), or by a semicolon followed by a conjunctive adverb (*besides, however, instead, meanwhile, then, therefore*) and a comma.

I had eight hours of sleep, **so** why am I so exhausted?

I eat the right foods; I drink plenty of water.

I take good care of myself; **however,** I may need more exercise.

Complex Sentence

A complex sentence contains one **independent clause** (in bold) and one or more dependent clauses (underlined).

When I can, **I get eight hours of sleep.**

I always get to sleep by eleven if I have an early class or a test the next morning.

When I get up on time, and if someone hasn't used up all the milk, **I eat breakfast.**

Note: When the dependent clause comes before the independent clause, use a comma.

Compound-Complex Sentence

A compound-complex sentence contains two or more **independent clauses** (in bold) and one or more dependent clauses (underlined).

If I'm not in a hurry, **I take leisurely walks,** and **I try to spot some wildlife.**

I saw a hawk when I was walking, and **other smaller birds were chasing it.**

Once I surprised a red fox, and **we both stopped for a moment, studying each other,** before it bolted.

© Steve Byland , 2009 / Used under license from Shutterstock.com

© Media Union ,2009 / Used under license from Shutterstock.com

26

Sentence Errors

LO1 Subject-Verb Agreement

The subject and verb of any clause must agree in both *person* and *number*. Person indicates whether the subject of the verb is *first, second,* or *third person. Number* indicates whether the subject and verb are *singular* or *plural*.

	Singular	Plural
First Person	I am	we are
Second Person	you are	you are
Third Person	he is	they are

AGREEMENT IN NUMBER . . .

A verb must agree in number (singular or plural) with its subject.

The **student was** rewarded for her hard work.
Both the subject *student* and the verb *was* are singular; they agree in number.

Note: Do not be confused by phrases that come between the subject and the verb. Such phrases may begin with words like *in addition to, as well as,* or *together with*.

The **instructor**, as well as the students, **is** expected to attend the orientation.
(In this sentence, *instructor* is the subject, so the verb must be singular *[is]*. The word *students* is the object of the preposition *as well as,* so it has no effect on the number of the verb.)

Learning Outcomes

LO1 Subject-Verb Agreement

LO2 Pronoun-Antecedent Agreement

LO3 Shifts in Sentence Construction

LO4 Fragments, Comma Splices, and Run-Ons

LO5 Misplaced and Dangling Modifiers

LO6 Ambiguous Wording

LO7 Nonstandard Language

What do you think?

I'm able to recognize the errors listed above.

1	2	3	4	5
strongly agree				strongly disagree

Compound Subjects

Compound subjects connected with *and* usually require a plural verb.

Dedication and creativity are trademarks of successful students.

Note: If a compound subject joined by *and* is thought of as a unit, use a singular verb.

Macaroni and cheese is always available in the cafeteria.

Delayed Subjects

Delayed subjects occur when the verb comes *before* the subject in a sentence. In these inverted sentences, the true (delayed) subject must still agree with the verb.

There **are** many nontraditional **students** on our campus.

Here **is** the **syllabus** you need.
(*Students* and *syllabus* are the subjects of the two sentences above, not the adverbs *there* and *here*.)

Note: Using an inverted sentence, on occasion, will lend variety to your writing style. Simply remember to make the delayed subjects agree with the verbs.

However, included among the list's topmost items **was "revise research paper."**
(Because the true subject here is singular—one item—the singular verb *was* is correct.)

Titles as Subjects

When the subject of a sentence is the title of a work of art, literature, or music, the verb should be singular. This is also true of a word (or phrase) being used as a word (or phrase).

Lyrical Ballads **was** published in 1798 by two of England's greatest poets, Wordsworth and Coleridge.
(Even though the title of the book, *Lyrical Ballads*, is plural in form, it is still a single title being used as the subject, correctly taking the singular verb *was*.)

"Over-the-counter drugs" is a phrase that means nonprescription medications.
(Even though the phrase is plural in form, it is still a single phrase being used as the subject, correctly taking the singular verb *is*.)

Singular Subjects with *Or* or *Nor*

Singular subjects joined by *or* or *nor* take a singular verb.

Neither a **textbook** nor a **notebook is required** for this class.

Note: When the subject nearer a present-tense verb is the singular pronoun *I* or *you*, the correct singular verb does not end in *s*.

Neither **Marcus** nor **I feel** (not *feels*) right about this.

Either **Rosa** or **you have** (not *has*) to take notes for me.

Either **you** or **Rosa has** to take notes for me.

Singular/Plural Subjects

When one of the subjects joined by *or* or *nor* is singular and one is plural, the verb must agree with the subject nearer the verb.

Neither the **professor** nor her **students were** in the lab.
(The plural subject *students* is nearer the verb; therefore, the plural verb *were* agrees with *students*.)

Neither the **students** nor the **professor was** in the lab.
(The singular subject *professor* is nearer the verb; therefore, the singular verb *was* is used to agree with *professor*.)

Collective Nouns

Generally, collective nouns (*faculty, pair, crew, assembly, congress, species, crowd, army, team, committee,* and so on) take a singular verb. However, if you want to emphasize differences among individuals in the group or are referring to the group as individuals, you can use a plural verb.

My lab **team takes** its work very seriously.
(*Team* refers to the group as a unit; it requires a singular verb, *takes*.)

The **team assume** separate responsibilities for each study they undertake.
(In this example, *team* refers to individuals within the group; it requires a plural verb, *assume*.)

Note: Collective nouns such as (the) *police, poor, elderly,* and *young* use plural verbs.

The **police direct** traffic here between 7:00 and 9:00 a.m.

Plural Nouns with Singular Meaning

Some nouns that are plural in form but singular in meaning take a singular verb: *mumps, measles, news, mathematics, economics, robotics,* and so on.

> **Economics is** sometimes called "the dismal science."
>
> ---
>
> The economic **news is** not very good.
>
> *Note:* The most common exceptions are *scissors, trousers, glasses,* and *pliers.*
>
> The **scissors are** missing again.
>
> ---
>
> **Are** these **trousers** prewashed?

With Linking Verbs

When a sentence contains a linking verb (usually a form of *be*)—and a noun or pronoun comes before and after that verb—the verb must agree with the subject, not the predicate nominative (the noun or pronoun coming after the verb).

> The **cause** of his problem **was** poor study **habits.**
> (*Cause* requires a singular verb, even though the predicate nominative, *habits,* is plural.)
>
> ---
>
> His poor study **habits were** the **cause** of his problem.
> (*Habits* requires a plural verb, even though the predicate nominative, *cause,* is singular.)

Nouns Showing Measurement, Time, and Money

Mathematical phrases and phrases that name a period of time, a unit of measurement, or an amount of money take a singular verb.

> Three and three **is** six.
>
> ---
>
> Eight pages **is** a long paper on this topic.
>
> ---
>
> In my opinion, two dollars **is** a high price for a cup of coffee.

Relative Pronouns

When a relative pronoun (*who, which, that*) is used as the subject of a dependent clause, the number of the verb is determined by that pronoun's antecedent. (The *antecedent* is the word to which the pronoun refers.)

> This is one of the **books that are** required for English class.
> (The relative pronoun *that* requires the plural verb *are* because its antecedent is *books,* not the word *one.* To test this type of sentence for agreement, read the *of* phrase first: *Of the books that are* . . .)
>
> *Note:* Generally, the antecedent is the nearest noun or pronoun to the relative pronoun and is often the object of a preposition. Sometimes, however, the antecedent is not the nearest noun or pronoun, especially in sentences with the phrase "the only one of":
>
> Dr. Graciosa wondered why Claire was the only **one** of her students **who was** not attending lectures regularly.
> (In this case, the addition of the modifiers *the only* changes the meaning of the sentence. The antecedent of *who* is *one,* not *students.* Only one student was not attending.)

Indefinite Pronoun with Singular Verb

Many indefinite pronouns (*someone, somebody, something; anyone, anybody, anything; no one, nobody, nothing; everyone, everybody, everything; each, either, neither, one, this*) serving as subjects require a singular verb.

> **Everybody is** welcome to attend the chancellor's reception.
>
> ---
>
> **No one was** sent an invitation.
>
> *Note:* Although it may seem to indicate more than one, *each* is a singular pronoun and requires a singular verb. Do not be confused by words or phrases that come between the indefinite pronoun and the verb.
>
> **Each** of the new students **is** (not *are*) encouraged to attend the reception.

Indefinite Pronoun with Plural Verb

Some indefinite pronouns (*both, few, many, most,* and *several*) are plural; they require a plural verb.

Few are offered the opportunity to study abroad.

Most take advantage of opportunities closer to home.

Indefinite Pronoun or Quantity Word with Singular/Plural Verb

Some indefinite pronouns or quantity words (*all, any, most, part, half, none,* and *some*) may be either singular or plural, depending on the nouns they refer to. Look inside the prepositional phrase to see what the antecedent is.

Some of the students **were** missing.
(*Students*, the noun that *some* refers to, is plural; therefore, the pronoun *some* is considered plural, and the plural verb *were* is used to agree with it.)

Most of the lecture **was** over by the time we arrived. (Because *lecture* is singular, *most* is also singular, requiring the singular verb *was*.)

LO2 Pronoun–Antecedent Agreement

pronoun must agree in number, person, and gender (sex) with its *antecedent*. The antecedent is the word to which the pronoun refers.

Yoshi brought **his** laptop computer and e-book to school.
(The pronoun *his* refers to the antecedent *Yoshi*. Both the pronoun and its antecedent are singular, third person, and masculine; therefore, the pronoun is said to agree with its antecedent.)

AGREEMENT IN NUMBER . . .

The following principles will guide you in making sure pronouns and antecedents agree in number.

Singular Pronoun

Use a singular pronoun to refer to such antecedents as *each, either, neither, one, anyone, anybody, everyone,*

everybody, somebody, another, nobody, and *a person*.

Each of the maintenance vehicles has **their** doors locked at night. (Incorrect)

Each of the maintenance vehicles has **its** doors locked at night.
(Correct: Both *each* and *its* are singular.)

Somebody left **his or her** (not *their*) vehicle unlocked. (Correct)

Plural Pronoun

When a plural pronoun *(they, their)* is mistakenly used with a singular indefinite pronoun (such as *everyone* or *everybody*), you may correct the sentence by replacing *their* or *they* with optional pronouns (*her or his* or *he or she*) or by making the antecedent plural.

Everyone must learn to wait **their** turn. (Incorrect)

Everyone must learn to wait **her or his** turn. (Correct: Optional pronouns *her or his* are used.)

People must learn to wait **their** turns. (Correct: The singular antecedent *everyone* has been changed to the plural antecedent *people*.)

Two or More Antecedents

When two or more antecedents are joined by *and*, they are considered plural.

Tomas and **Jamal** are finishing **their** assignments.

When two or more singular antecedents are joined by *or* or *nor*, they are considered singular.

Connie or **Shavonn** left **her** headset in the library.

Note: If one of the antecedents is masculine and one feminine, the pronouns should likewise be masculine and feminine.

Is **Ahmad** or **Phyllis** bringing **his or her** laptop computer?

Note: If one of the antecedents joined by *or* or *nor* is singular and one is plural, the pronoun is made to agree with the nearer antecedent.

Neither **Ravi** nor his **friends** want to spend **their** time studying.

Neither his **friends** nor **Ravi** wants to spend **his** time studying.

LO3 Shifts in Sentence Construction

A shift is an improper change in structure midway through a sentence.

FOUR TYPES OF SHIFT . . .

When constructing sentences, avoid shifts in person, tense, or voice as well as unparallel constructions.

Shift in Person

Shift in person is mixing first, second, or third person within a sentence.

> **Shift:** **One** may get spring fever unless **you** live in California or Florida. (The sentence shifts from third person, *one*, to second person, *you*.)
>
> **Corrected:** **You** may get spring fever unless **you** live in California or Florida. (Both pronouns are second person.)
>
> **Corrected:** **People** may get spring fever unless **they** live in California or Florida. (Both the noun *people* and the pronoun *they* are third person.)

© Fotolistic , 2009 / Used under license from Shutterstock.com

Shift in Tense

Shift in tense is using more than one tense in a sentence when only one is needed.

> **Shift:** Sheila **looked** at nine apartments in one weekend before she **had chosen** one. (Tense shifts from past to past perfect for no reason.)
>
> **Corrected:** Sheila **looked** at nine apartments in one weekend before she **chose** one. (Both verbs are past tense.)

Shift in Voice

Shift in voice is mixing active with passive voice. Usually, a sentence beginning in active voice should remain so to the end.

> **Shift:** As you **look** (active voice) for just the right place, many interesting apartments **will** probably **be seen**. (passive voice)
>
> **Corrected:** As you **look** (active voice) for just the right place, you **will** probably **see** (active voice) many interesting apartments.

Unparallel Construction

Unparallel construction occurs when the writer shifts from using one kind of word or phrase to another in the middle of a sentence.

> **Shift:** In my hometown, people pass the time **shooting pool, pitching horseshoes,** and **at softball games**. (The writer shifts from using gerund phrases, *shooting pool* and *pitching horseshoes*, to using a prepositional phrase, *at softball games*.)
>
> **Parallel:** In my hometown, people pass the time **shooting pool, pitching horseshoes,** and **playing softball**. (Now all three activities are expressed in a parallel way, as gerund phrases.)

LO4 Fragments, Comma Splices, and Run-Ons

Except in a few special situations, you should use complete sentences when you write. By definition, a complete sentence expresses a complete thought. Sometimes a sentence may contain several ideas, and it is important to have those ideas work together to form a clear, interesting thought that expresses your exact meaning. Sentence errors can derail meaning.

SENTENCE ERRORS . . .

Among the most common sentence errors that writers make are fragments, comma splices, and run-ons.

Fragments

A fragment is a phrase or dependent clause used as a sentence. It is not a sentence, however, because a phrase lacks a subject, a verb, or some other essential part, and a dependent clause must be connected to an independent clause to complete its meaning.

Fragment:	Pete gunned the engine. **Forgetting that the boat was hooked to the dock.** (This is a sentence followed by a fragment. This error can be corrected by combining the fragment with the sentence.)
Corrected:	Pete gunned the engine, forgetting that the boat was hooked to the dock.
Fragment:	**Even though my best friend had a little boy last year.** (This clause does not convey a complete thought. We need to know what is happening despite the birth of the little boy.)
Corrected:	Even though my best friend had a little boy last year, I do not comprehend the full meaning of "motherhood."

Comma Splices

A comma splice is a mistake made when two independent clauses are connected ("spliced") with only a comma. The comma is not enough: A period, semicolon, or conjunction is needed.

Splice:	People say that being a stay-at-home mom or dad is an important job, their actions tell a different story.
Corrected:	People say that being a stay-at-home mom or dad is an important job, **but** their actions tell a different story. (The coordinating conjunction *but*, added after the comma, corrects the splice.)
Corrected:	People say that being a stay-at-home mom or dad is an important job; their actions tell a different story. (A semicolon replaces the comma to make the sentence correct.)
Corrected:	People say that being a stay-at-home mom or dad is an important job. **Their** actions tell a different story. (A period creates two sentences and corrects the splice.)

Run-Ons

A run-on sentence is actually two sentences (two independent clauses) joined without adequate punctuation or a connecting word.

Run-On:	The Alamo holds a special place in American history it was the site of an important battle between the United States and Mexico.
Corrected:	The Alamo holds a special place in American history **because** it was the site of an important battle between the United States and Mexico. (A subordinating conjunction is added to fix the run-on by making the second clause dependent.)

Run-Ons: Antonio de Santa Anna, the president of Mexico who once held a funeral for his amputated leg, is the same Santa Anna who stormed the Alamo he led his troops to victory over the Texan rebels defending that fort. Two famous American frontiersmen were killed in the battle they were James Bowie and Davy Crockett. Santa Anna enjoyed fame, power, and respect among his followers. He died in 1876 he was poor, blind, and ignored.

Corrected: Antonio de Santa Anna, the president of Mexico who once held a funeral for his amputated leg, is the same Santa Anna who stormed the Alamo. He led his troops to victory over the Texan rebels defending that fort. Two famous American frontiersmen were killed in the battle; they were James Bowie and Davy Crockett. Santa Anna enjoyed fame, power, and respect among his followers. When he died in 1876, he was poor, blind, and ignored.

The writer corrected the run-on sentences in the paragraph above by adding punctuation, and by using a subordinating conjunction to form a dependent clause. In the following paragraph, the writer has made further improvements by revising and combining sentences, creating a more fluent style.

Improved: Antonio de Santa Anna, the president of Mexico who once held a funeral for his amputated leg, is the same Santa Anna who stormed the Alamo. He led his troops to victory over Texan rebels defending that fort. Two famous American frontiersmen, **James Bowie and Davy Crockett, were killed in the battle**. Santa Anna enjoyed fame, power, and respect among his followers; **but when** he died in 1876, he was poor, blind, and ignored.

fyi After making a correction, you may see an opportunity to add, cut, or improve something else. Correcting and editing sentences can result in a clearer message and an improved writing style—outcomes that are worth the effort.

LO5 Misplaced and Dangling Modifiers

Writing is thinking. Before you can write clearly, you must think clearly. Nothing is more frustrating for the reader than having to reread something just to understand its basic meaning. Misplaced and dangling modifiers muddle the meaning of sentences.

PLACING MODIFIERS . . .

The following principles will help you ensure that modifiers are placed correctly.

Misplaced Modifiers

Misplaced modifiers are descriptive words or phrases so separated from what they are describing that the reader is confused.

Misplaced: The neighbor's dog has **nearly** been **barking** nonstop for two hours. (*Nearly* been barking?)

Corrected: The neighbor's dog has been barking nonstop for **nearly two hours**. (Watch your placement of *only, just, nearly, barely,* and so on.)

Misplaced: The commercial advertised an assortment of combs for active **people** with **unbreakable teeth**. (*People* with unbreakable teeth?)

Corrected: The commercial advertised an assortment of **combs with unbreakable teeth** for active people. (*Combs* with unbreakable teeth)

Misplaced: The pool staff gave large beach towels to the **students marked with chlorine-resistant ID numbers**. (*Students* marked with chlorine-resistant ID numbers?)

Corrected: The pool staff gave large beach **towels marked with chlorine-resistant ID numbers** to the students. (*Towels* marked with chlorine-resistant ID numbers)

Dangling Modifiers

Dangling modifiers are descriptive phrases that tell about a subject that isn't stated in the sentence. Participial phrases, containing *ing* or *ed* words, are often used in this incorrect way.

Dangling:	After standing in line all afternoon, the manager said that all the tickets had been sold. (It sounds as if the manager has been *standing in line all afternoon.*)
Corrected:	**After we had stood in line all afternoon,** the manager informed us that all the tickets had been sold.
Dangling:	After living in the house for one month, the electrician recommended updating all the wiring. (It sounds as if the electrician has been *living in the house.*)
Corrected:	After living in the house for one month, **we hired an electrician, who recommended that we update all the wiring.**

LO6 Ambiguous Wording

Ambiguous wording makes writing unclear—mixing up pronouns, leaving comparisons incomplete, or resulting in two possible meanings.

AVOIDING AMBIGUITY . . .

As you write, revise, and edit, check for indefinite pronoun references, incomplete comparisons, and unclear wording.

Indefinite Pronoun References

An indefinite reference is a problem caused by careless use of pronouns. There must always be a word or phrase nearby (its antecedent) that a pronoun clearly replaces.

Indefinite:	When Tonya attempted to put her dictionary on the shelf, it fell to the floor. (The pronoun *it* could refer to either the dictionary or the shelf since both are singular nouns.)
Corrected:	When Tonya attempted to put her dictionary on the shelf, **the shelf** fell to the floor.
Indefinite:	Juanita reminded Kerri that she needed to photocopy her résumé before going to her interview. (Who *needed to photocopy her résumé*—Juanita or Kerri?)
Corrected:	Juanita reminded Kerri **to photocopy her résumé before going to her interview.**

Incomplete Comparisons

Incomplete comparisons—leaving out words that show exactly what is being compared to what—can confuse the reader.

Incomplete:	After completing our lab experiment, we concluded that helium is lighter. (*Lighter* than what?)
Corrected:	After completing our lab experiment, we concluded that helium is **lighter than oxygen.**

Unclear Wording

One type of ambiguous wording results in two or more possible meanings due to an unclear reference to something elsewhere in the sentence.

Unclear:	I couldn't believe that my sister bought a cat with all those allergy problems. (Who has the *allergy problems*—the cat or the sister?)
Corrected:	I couldn't believe that my sister, **who has allergies, bought a cat.**
Unclear:	Dao intended to wash the car when he finished his homework, but he never did. (It is unclear which he *never did*—wash the car or finish his homework.)
Corrected:	Dao intended to wash the car when he finished his homework, **but he never did manage to wash the car.**

LO7 Nonstandard Language

Nonstandard language is language that does not conform to the standards set by schools, media, and public institutions. It is often acceptable in everyday conversation and in fictional writing, but it is seldom used in formal speech or other forms of writing.

STANDARDIZING LANGUAGE . . .

As you write, revise, and edit, avoid colloquial language, double prepositions, substitutions, double negatives, and slang.

Colloquial Language

Colloquial language is used in informal conversation but is unacceptable in formal writing.

| **Colloquial:** | Hey, wait up! Cal wants to go with. |
| **Standard:** | **Hey, wait!** Cal wants to go **with us.** |

Double Preposition

The use of certain double prepositions—*off of, off to, from off*—is unacceptable.

| **Double Preposition:** | Pick up the dirty clothes from off the floor. |
| **Standard:** | Pick up the dirty clothes **from the floor.** |

Substitution

Avoid substituting *and* for *to*.

| **Substitution:** | Try and get to class on time. |
| **Standard:** | **Try to** get to class on time. |

Avoid substituting *of* for *have* when combining with *could, would, should,* or *might*.

| **Substitution:** | I should of studied for that exam. |
| **Standard:** | **I should have** studied for that exam. |

Double Negative

A double negative is the use of two negative words to express a single negative idea. Double negatives are unacceptable in academic writing.

| **Double Negative:** | After paying for essentials, I haven't got no money left. |
| **Standard:** | **I haven't got any** money left. **I have no** money left. |

Slang

Avoid the use of slang or any "in" words in formal writing.

| **Slang:** | The way the stadium roof opened was way cool. |
| **Standard:** | The way the stadium roof opened **was remarkable.** |

Quick Guide — Avoiding Sentence Problems

1. Use subjects and verbs that agree.
2. Use pronouns and antecedents that agree.
3. Watch for inappropriate shifts.
4. Use complete sentences.
5. Use correctly placed modifiers and clear wording.
6. Use standard, acceptable language.

27

Multilingual and ESL Guidelines

English may be your second, third, or fifth language. As a multilingual learner, you bring to your writing a unique cultural experience and knowledge base. This broader perspective can enhance and benefit all of your writing tasks. Whether you are an international student or someone who has lived in North America a long time and is now learning more about English, this chapter provides you with important information about writing in English.

Learning Outcomes

LO1 Five of the Parts of Speech

LO2 Understanding Sentence Basics

LO3 Sentence Problems

LO4 Numbers, Word Parts, and Idioms

What do you think?

Nouns and verbs are the heart and soul of writing.

1	2	3	4	5
strongly agree				strongly disagree

LO1 Five of the Parts of Speech

NOUN

Nouns are words that name people, places, and things. This information tells how to use nouns correctly.

Count Nouns

Count nouns refer to things that can be counted. They can have *a*, *an*, *the*, or *one* in front of them. One or more adjectives can come between the articles *a*, *an*, *the*, or *one* and the singular count noun.

an apple, one orange, a plum, a purple plum

Count nouns can be singular, as in the examples above, or they can be plural as shown here.

plums, apples, oranges

Note: When count nouns are plural, they can have the article *the,* a number, or a demonstrative adjective in front of them. (See "Usage Strategy" on page 336.)

> I used the plums to make a pie.
>
> He placed five apples on my desk.
>
> These oranges are so juicy!

The *number* of a noun refers to whether it names a single thing *(book),* in which case its number is *singular,* or whether it names more than one thing *(books),* in which case its number is *plural.*

Note: There are different ways in which the plural forms of nouns are created. For more information, see pages 291–292.

Noncount Nouns

Noncount nouns refer to things that cannot be counted. Do not use *a, an,* or *one* in front of them. They have no plural form, so they always take a singular verb. Some nouns that end in *s* are not plural; they are noncount nouns.

> fruit, furniture, rain, thunder, advice, mathematics, news

Abstract nouns name ideas or conditions instead of people, places, or objects. Many abstract nouns are noncount nouns.

> The students had fun at the party. Good health is a wonderful gift.

Collective nouns name a whole category or group and can be noncount nouns.

> homework, furniture, money

Note: The parts or components of a group or category named by a noncount noun are often count nouns. For example, *report* and *assignment* are count nouns that are parts of the collective, noncount noun *homework.*

Two-Way Nouns

Some nouns can be used as either count or noncount nouns, depending on what they refer to.

> I would like a glass of water. (count noun)
>
> Glass is used to make windows. (noncount noun)

© moodboard/Corbis

Articles, Adjectives, and Quantifiers as Noun Markers

Use articles and other noun markers or modifiers to give more information about nouns.

Specific Article: The specific (or *definite*) article *the* is used to refer to a specific noun.

> I found the book I misplaced yesterday.

Indefinite Articles: Use the indefinite article *a* or *an* to refer to a nonspecific noun. Use *an* before singular nouns beginning with the vowels *a, e, i, o,* and *u.* Use *a* before nouns beginning with all other letters of the alphabet, the consonants. Exceptions do occur: *a* unit; *a* university.

> I always take an apple to work.
>
> It is good to have a book with you when you travel.

Indefinite Adjectives: Indefinite adjectives can also mark nonspecific nouns—*all, any, each, either, every, few, many, more, most, neither, several, some* (for singular and plural count nouns); *all, any, more, most, much, some* (for noncount nouns).

> Every student is encouraged to register early.
>
> Most classes fill quickly.
>
> More rain is forecast.

Usage Strategy: Articles

Listed below are a number of guidelines to help you determine whether to use an article and which one to use.

Use a or **an** with <u>singular</u> count nouns that do not refer to one specific item.	**A** <u>zebra</u> has black and white stripes. **An** <u>apple</u> is good for you.
Do not use a or **an** with <u>plural</u> count nouns.	<u>Zebras</u> have black and white stripes. <u>Apples</u> are good for you.
Do not use a or **an** with <u>noncount</u> nouns.	<u>Homework</u> needs to be done promptly.
Use the with <u>singular</u> count nouns that refer to one specific item.	**The** <u>apple</u> you gave me was delicious.
Use the with <u>plural</u> count nouns.	**The** <u>zebras</u> at Brookfield Zoo were healthy.
Use the with <u>noncount</u> nouns.	**The** <u>money</u> from my uncle is a gift.
Do not use the with most <u>singular proper</u>, nouns. *Note:* There are many exceptions (the Sahara Desert, the Sears Tower, the Fourth of July).	Mother Theresa loved the poor and downcast.
Use the with <u>plural proper</u> nouns.	**the** <u>Joneses</u> (both Mr. and Mrs. Jones), **the** <u>Rocky Mountains</u>, **the** <u>United States</u>

Possessive Adjectives: The possessive case of nouns and pronouns can be used as adjectives to mark nouns.

> **possessive nouns:** *Tanya's, father's, store's*
> This is <u>Tanya's</u> car, not her <u>father's</u> car.

> **possessive pronouns:** *my, your, his, her, its, our*
> <u>My</u> hat is purple, and <u>your</u> hat is red.

Demonstrative Adjectives: Demonstrative pronouns can be used as adjectives to mark nouns. Use *this, that, these,* or *those* for singular and plural count nouns; use *this* or *that* for noncount nouns.

> <u>Those</u> chairs are lovely. Where did you buy <u>that</u> furniture?

Quantifiers: Quantifers are expressions of quantity and measure used with nouns. The following expressions of quantity can be used with count nouns: *each, every, both, a couple of, a few, several, many, a number of.*

> We enjoyed <u>both</u> concerts we attended. <u>A couple of</u> songs performed were familiar to us.

You may use a number to indicate a specific quantity of a count noun.

> I saw <u>fifteen</u> cardinals in the park.

You may use *a + quantity* (such as *bag, bottle, bowl, carton, glass,* or *piece*) + *of + noun* to indicate a specific quantity of a noncount noun.

> I bought <u>a carton of milk</u>, <u>a head of lettuce</u>, <u>a piece of cheese</u>, and <u>a bag of flour</u> at the grocery store.

You may use the following expressions with noncount nouns: *a little, much, a great deal of.*

> We had <u>much</u> wind and <u>a little</u> rain as the storm passed through yesterday.

You may use the following expressions of quantity with both count and noncount nouns: *no/not any, some, a lot of, lots of, plenty of, most, all.*

> I would like <u>some</u> apples *(count noun)* and <u>some</u> rice *(noncount noun)*, please.

VERB

Verbs convey much of a sentence's meaning. Using verb tenses and forms correctly ensures that your reader will understand the intended meaning of your sentences. For a more thorough review of verbs, see pages 309–313.

Progressive (Continuous) Tenses

Progressive or continuous tense verbs express action in progress (see page 311).

To form the present progressive tense, use the helping verb *am, is,* or *are* with the *ing* form of the main verb.

> He is washing the car right now.
> Kent and Chen are studying for a test.

To form the past progressive tense, use the helping verb *was* or *were* with the *ing* form of the main verb.

> Yesterday he was working in the garden all day.
> Julia and Juan were watching a movie.

To form the future progressive tense, use *will* or a phrase that indicates the future, the helping verb *be,* and the *ing* form of the main verb.

> Next week he will be painting the house.
> He plans to be painting the house soon.

Note that some verbs, such as those discussed below, are generally not used in the progressive tenses.

- Verbs that express thoughts, attitudes, and desires: *know, understand, want, prefer*

  > Correct: Kala knows how to ride a motorcycle.
  >
  > Incorrect: Kala is knowing how to ride a motorcycle.

- Verbs that describe appearances: *seem, resemble*
- Verbs that indicate possession: *belong, have, own, possess*
- Verbs that signify inclusion: *contain, hold*

Objects and Complements of Verbs

Active transitive verbs take objects. These can be direct objects, indirect objects, or object complements. Linking verbs take subject complements—predicate nominatives or predicate adjectives—that rename or describe the subject.

Infinitives as Objects: Infinitives can follow many verbs, including these: *agree, appear, attempt, consent, decide, demand, deserve, endeavor, fail, hesitate, hope, intend, need, offer, plan, prepare, promise, refuse, seem, tend, volunteer, wish.* (See page 313 for more on infinitives.)

> He promised to bring some samples.

The following verbs are among those that can be followed by a noun or pronoun plus the infinitive: *ask, beg, choose, expect, intend, need, prepare, promise, want.*

> I expect you to be there on time.

NOTE

Except in the passive voice, the following verbs must have a noun or pronoun before the infinitive: *advise, allow, appoint, authorize, cause, challenge, command, convince, encourage, forbid, force, hire, instruct, invite, order, permit, remind, require, select, teach, tell, tempt, trust.*

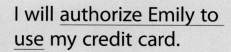

I will authorize Emily to use my credit card.

Unmarked infinitives (no *to*) can follow these verbs: *have, help, let, make.*

> These glasses help me see the board.

Gerunds as Objects: Gerunds can follow these verbs: *admit, avoid, consider, deny, discuss, dislike, enjoy, finish, imagine, miss, postpone, quit, recall, recommend, regret.*

> I recommended hiring Ian for the job.

Here *hiring* is the direct object of the active verb *recommended*, and *Ian* is the object of the gerund.

Infinitives or Gerunds as Objects: Either gerunds or infinitives can follow these verbs: *begin, continue, hate, like, love, prefer, remember, start, stop, try.*

> I hate having cold feet. I hate to have cold feet. (In either form, the verbal phrase is the direct object of the verb *hate*.)

Note: Sometimes the meaning of a sentence will change depending on whether you use a gerund or an infinitive.

> I stopped to smoke. (I stopped weeding the garden to smoke a cigarette.)
> I stopped smoking. (I no longer smoke.)

© Grafissimo/istockphoto.com

Common Modal Auxiliary Verbs

Modal auxiliary verbs are a kind of auxiliary verb. They help the main verb express meaning. Modals are sometimes grouped with other helping or auxiliary verbs.

Modal verbs must be followed by the base form of a verb without *to* (not by a gerund or an infinitive). Also, modal verbs do not change form; they are always used as they appear in the following chart.

Modal	Expresses	Sample Sentence
can	ability	I **can** program a VCR.
could	ability	I **could** babysit Tuesday.
	possibility	He **could** be sick.
might	possibility	I **might** be early.
may, might	possibility	I **may** sleep late Saturday.
	request	**May** I be excused?
must	strong need	I **must** study more.
have to	strong need	I **have to** (have got to) exercise.
ought to	feeling of duty	I **ought to** (should) help Dad.
should	advisability	She **should** retire.
	expectation	I **should** have caught that train.
shall	intent	**Shall** I stay longer?
will	intent	I **will** visit my grandma soon.
would	intent	I **would** live to regret my offer.
	repeated action	He **would** walk in the meadow.
would + you	polite request	**Would you** help me?
could + you	polite request	**Could you** type this letter?
will + you	polite request	**Will you** give me a ride?
can + you	polite request	**Can you** make supper tonight?

Common Two-Word Verbs

This chart lists some common verbs in which two words—a verb and a preposition—work together to express a specific action. A noun or pronoun is often inserted between the parts of the two-word verb when it is used in a sentence: break *it* down, call *it* off.

break down	to take apart or fall apart
call off	cancel
call up	make a phone call
clear out	leave a place quickly
cross out	draw a line through
do over	repeat
figure out	find a solution
fill in/out	complete a form or an application
fill up	fill a container or tank
* **find out**	discover
* **get in**	enter a vehicle or building
* **get out of**	leave a car, a house, or a situation
* **get over**	recover from a sickness or a problem
give back	return something
give in/up	surrender or quit
hand in	give homework to a teacher
hand out	give someone something
hang up	put down a phone receiver
leave out	omit or don't use
let in/out	allow someone or something to enter or go out
look up	find information
mix up	confuse
pay back	return money or a favor
pick out	choose
point out	call attention to
put away	return something to its proper place
put down	place something on a table, the floor, and so on.
put off	delay doing something
shut off	turn off a machine or light
* **take part**	participate
talk over	discuss
think over	consider carefully
try on	put on clothing to see if it fits
turn down	lower the volume
turn up	raise the volume
write down	write on a piece of paper

*These two-word verbs should not have a noun or pronoun inserted between their parts.

Spelling Guidelines for Verb Forms

The same spelling rules that apply when adding a suffix to other words apply to verbs as well. Most verbs need a suffix to indicate tense or form. The third-person singular form of a verb, for example, usually ends in *s*, but it can also end in *es*. Formation of *ing* and *ed* forms of verbs and verbals needs careful attention, too. Consult the rules below to determine how to spell the past tense of certain verbs. (For general spelling guidelines, see page 298.)

 There may be exceptions to these rules when forming the past tense of irregular verbs. The past tense of such verbs is formed by changing the word itself, not merely by adding *d* or *ed*. (See the chart of irregular verbs on page 313.)

Past Tense: Adding *ed*

Add *ed* ... when a verb ends with two consonants.	touch—touched ask—asked pass—passed
when a verb ends with a consonant preceded by two vowels.	heal—healed gain—gained
when a verb ends in *y* preceded by a vowel.	annoy—annoyed flay—flayed
when a multisyllable verb's last syllable is not stressed (even when the last syllable ends with a consonant preceded by a vowel).	budget—budgeted enter—entered
Change *y* to *i* and add *ed* when a verb ends in *y* preceded by a consonant.	liquefy—liquefied worry—worried
Double the final consonant and add *ed* ... when a verb has one syllable and ends with a consonant preceded by a vowel.	wrap—wrapped drop—dropped
when a multisyllable verb's last syllable is stressed and also ends with a consonant preceded by a vowel.	admit—admitted confer—conferred

Past Tense: Adding *d*

Add *d* ...

when a verb ends with *e*.

chime—chimed	
tape—taped	

when a verb ends with *ie*.

tie—tied	
die—died	
lie—lied	

Present Tense: Adding *ing*

Drop the *e* and add *ing* when the verb ends in *e*.

drive—driving	
rise—rising	

Double the final consonant and add *ing* ...

when a verb has one syllable and ends with a consonant preceded by a vowel.

wrap—wrapping	
sit—sitting	

when a multisyllable verb's last syllable is stressed and also ends in a consonant preceded by a vowel.

forget—forgetting	
begin—beginning	

Change *ie* to *y* and add *ing* when a verb ends with *ie*.

tie—tying	
die—dying	
lie—lying	

Add *ing* ...

when a verb ends with two consonants.

touch—touching	
ask—asking	
pass—passing	

when a verb ends with a consonant preceded by two vowels.

heal—healing	
gain—gaining	

when a verb ends in *y*.

buy—buying	
study—studying	
cry—crying	

when a multisyllable verb's last syllable is not stressed (even when the last syllable ends with a consonant preceded by a vowel).

budget—budgeting	
enter—entering	

Present Tense: Adding *s* or *es*

Add *es* ...

when a verb ends in *ch, sh, s, x,* or *z*.

watch—watches	
fix—fixes	

to *do* and *go*.

do—does	
go—goes	

Change *y* to *i* and add *es* when the verb ends in *y* preceded by a consonant.

liquefy—liquefies	
quantify—quantifies	

Add *s* to most other verbs, including those already ending in *e* and those that end in *y* prededed by a vowel.

write—writes	
buy—buys	

NOTE

Never trust your spelling to even the best computer spell-checker. Carefully proofread, and use a dictionary for questionable words your spell-checker may miss.

© IuSh ,2009 / Used under license from Shutterstock.com

© Sebastian Crocker ,2009 / Used under license from Shutterstock.com

ADJECTIVE

Placing Adjectives

An adjective often comes before the noun it modifies. When several adjectives are used in a row, it is important to arrange them, in the well-established sequence used in English writing and speaking. The following list shows the usual order of adjectives. Consider the following guidelines for placing adjectives correctly.

First, place . . .

(1) articles,	a, an, the
demonstrative adjectives, or	that, those
possessives	my, her, Misha's

Then place words that . . .

(2) indicate time	first, next, final
(3) tell how many	one, few, some
(4) evaluate	beautiful, dignified, graceful
(5) tell what size	big, small, short, tall
(6) tell what shape	round, square
(7) describe a condition	messy, clean, dark
(8) tell what age	old, young, new, antique
(9) tell what color	blue, red, yellow
(10) tell what nationality	English, Chinese, Mexican
(11) tell what religion	Buddhist, Jewish, Protestant
(12) tell what material	satin, velvet, wooden

Finally, place nouns . . .

(13) nouns used as adjectives	computer monitor, spice rack

Examples:

my second try (1 + 2 + noun)

gorgeous young white swans (4 + 8 + 9 + noun)

Present and Past Participles as Adjectives

Both the present participle (*ing* form) and the past participle (*ed* form) can be used as adjectives. The following chart offers several pairs of participles to consider.

annoying/annoyed	exciting/excited
boring/bored	exhausting/exhausted
confusing/confused	fascinating/fascinated
depressing/depressed	surprising/surprised

Note: Exercise care in choosing whether to use the present participle or the past participle in your writing.

Each has slightly different meaning, as the following examples show.

A **present participle** should be used to describe a person or thing that causes a feeling or situation.

His annoying comments made me angry.

A **past participle** should be used to describe a person or thing that experiences a feeling or situation.

He was annoyed because he had to wait so long.

Nouns as Adjectives

Nouns sometimes function as adjectives by modifying another noun. When a noun is used as an adjective, it is always singular.

Many European cities have rose gardens.

Marta recently joined a book club.

TIP:

Try to avoid using more than two nouns as adjectives for another noun. These "noun compounds" can get confusing. Prepositional phrases may get the meaning across better than long noun strings.

Clear: Omar is a crew member in a restaurant kitchen.

Confusing: Omar is a restaurant kitchen crew member.

ADVERB

Consider the following guidelines for placing adverbs correctly.

Placing Adverbs

Place adverbs that tell how often (*frequently, seldom, never, always, sometimes*) after a helping (auxiliary) verb and before the main verb. In a sentence without a helping verb, adverbs that tell *how often* are placed before an action verb but after a linking verb.

The salesclerk will usually help me.

Place adverbs that tell when *(yesterday, now, at five o'clock)* at the end of a sentence.

> Auntie El came home <u>yesterday</u>.

Place adverbs that tell where *(upside down, around, downstairs)* after the verb they modify. Many prepositional phrases *(at the beach, under the stairs, below the water)* function as adverbs that tell where.

> We waited <u>on the porch</u>.

Place adverbs that tell how *(quickly, slowly, loudly)* either at the beginning, in the middle, or at the end of a sentence—but not between a verb and its direct object.

> <u>Softly</u> he called my name/He <u>softly</u> called my name. He called my name <u>softly</u>.

Place adverbs that modify adjectives directly before the adjective.

> That is a <u>most</u> unusual dress.

Place adverbs that modify clauses either in front of, within, or at the end of the clause.

> <u>Fortunately</u>, we were not involved in the accident. We were not involved, <u>fortunately</u>, in the accident. We were not involved in the accident, <u>fortunately</u>.

<u>Note</u>: Adverbs that are used with verbs that have direct objects must *not* be placed between the verb and its object.

> Correct: Luis <u>usually</u> catches the most fish.
>   <u>Usually</u> Luis catches the most fish.
> Incorrect: Luis catches <u>usually</u> the most fish.

PREPOSITION

A preposition is used with a noun to form a prepositional phrase, which acts as a modifier—either an adverb or an adjective. See pages 315–316 for a list of common prepositions and for more information about prepositions.

Using *in*, *on*, *at*, and *by*

In, *on*, *at*, and *by* are four common prepositions that refer to time and place. Here are some examples of how these prepositions are used in each case.

To show time . . .

On a specific day or date	<u>on</u> June 7, <u>on</u> Wednesday
In part of a day	<u>in</u> the afternoon
In a year or month	<u>in</u> 2008, <u>in</u> April
In a period of time	completed <u>in</u> an hour
By a specific time or date	<u>by</u> noon, <u>by</u> the fifth of May
At a specific time of day or night	<u>at</u> 3:30 this afternoon

To show place . . .

At a meeting place or location	<u>at</u> school, <u>at</u> the park
At the edge of something	standing <u>at</u> the bar
At the corner of something	turning <u>at</u> the intersection
At a target	throwing a dart <u>at</u> the bull's-eye
On a surface	left <u>on</u> the floor
On an electronic medium	<u>on</u> the Internet, <u>on</u> television
In an enclosed space	<u>in</u> the box, <u>in</u> the room
In a geographic location	<u>in</u> New York City, <u>in</u> Germany
In a print medium	<u>in</u> a journal
By a landmark	<u>by</u> the fountain

TIP:

Do not insert a preposition between a transitive verb and its direct object. Intransitive verbs, however, are often followed by a prepositional phrase (a phrase that begins with a preposition).

I <u>cooked</u> hot dogs on the grill. (transitive verb)

I <u>ate</u> in the park. (intransitive verb)

Phrasal Prepositions

Some prepositional phrases begin with more than one preposition. These phrasal prepositions are commonly used in both written and spoken communication. A list of common phrasal prepositions follows:

according to	by way of	instead of
across from	except for	on the side of
along with	in case of	up to
because of	in spite of	with respect to

LO2 Understanding Sentence Basics

BASIC PATTERNS

Simple sentences in the English language follow the five basic patterns shown below.

Subject + Verb

```
 ┌─S─┐ ┌─V─┐
 Naomie winked.
```

Some verbs like *winked* are intransitive. Intransitive verbs *do not* need a direct object to express a complete thought.

Subject + Verb + Direct Object

```
 ┌─S─┐ ┌─V─┐ ┌─DO─┐
 Harris grinds his teeth.
```

Some verbs like *grinds* are transitive. Transitive verbs *do* need a direct object to express a complete thought.

Subject + Verb + Indirect Object + Direct Object

```
 ┌─S─┐ ┌─V─┐ ┌─IO─┐ ┌──DO──┐
 Elena offered her friend an anchovy.
```

The direct object names who or what receives the action; the indirect object names to whom or for whom the action was done.

Subject + Verb + Direct Object + Object Complement

```
 ┌────S────┐ ┌─V─┐ ┌DO┐ ┌──────OC──────┐
 The chancellor named Ravi the outstanding
 student of 2010.
```

The object complement renames or describes the direct object.

Subject + Linking Verb + Predicate Nominative (or Predicate Adjective)

```
 ┌─S─┐ LV ┌────────PN────────┐
 Paula is a computer programmer.
```

```
 ┌─S─┐ L ┌──PA──┐
 Paula is very intelligent.
```

A linking verb connects the subject to the predicate noun or predicate adjective. The predicate noun renames the subject; the predicate adjective describes the subject.

Inverted Order: The Exception

In the preceding sentence patterns, the subject comes before the verb. Sometimes, though, the subject comes *after* the verb:

Linking Verb + Subject + Predicate Noun

```
 LV ┌─S─┐ ┌PN┐
 Is Lorisa a poet? (question)
```

Linking Verb + Subject

```
 LV ┌──S──┐
 There was a meeting.
```

LO3 Sentence Problems

AVOIDING TROUBLE

This section looks at potential trouble spots and sentence problems. For more information about English sentences, their parts, and how to construct them, see pages 318-324. Then see pages 325-333 for types of problems and errors found in English writing.

Double Negatives

When making a sentence negative, use *not* or another negative adverb (*never, rarely, hardly, seldom*, and so on), but do not use both, which results in a double negative (see page 333).

Subject–Verb Agreement

Be sure the subject and verb in every clause agree in person and number. (See pages 325–328.)

> The <u>student was</u> rewarded for her hard work.
>
> The <u>students were</u> rewarded for their hard work.
>
> The <u>instructor</u>, as well as the students, <u>is</u> expected to attend the orientation.
>
> The <u>students</u>, as well as the instructor, <u>are</u> expected to attend the orientation.

Omitted Words

Do not omit subjects or the expletives *there* or *here*. In all English clauses and sentences (except imperatives in which the subject *you* is understood), there must be a subject.

> Correct: Your mother was very quiet; <u>she</u> seemed to be upset.
>
> Incorrect: Your mother was very quiet; seemed to be upset.
>
> Correct: <u>There</u> is not much time left.
>
> Incorrect: Not much time left.

Repeated Words

Do not repeat the subject of a clause or sentence.

> Correct: The doctor prescribed an antibiotic.
>
> Incorrect: The doctor, <u>she</u> prescribed an antibiotic.

Do not repeat an object in an adjective dependent clause.

> Correct: I forgot the flowers that I intended to give to my hosts.
>
> Incorrect: I forgot the flowers that I intended to give <u>them</u> to my hosts.

NOTE

Sometimes the introductory relative pronoun in an adjective dependent clause is omitted but understood.

I forgot the flowers I intended to give to my hosts. (The relative pronoun *that* is omitted.)

Conditional Sentences

Conditional sentences express situations that require certain conditions to be met. Selecting the correct verb tenses for the two clauses of a conditional sentence can be problematic. The following information explains the three types of conditional sentences and the verb tenses that are needed to form them.

Factual conditionals: The conditional clause begins with *if*, *when*, *whenever*, or a similar expression; and the verbs in the conditional clause and the main clause are in the same tense.

> <u>Whenever</u> we <u>had</u> time, we <u>took</u> a break and <u>went</u> for a swim.

Predictive conditionals: These sentences express future conditions and possible results. The conditional clause begins with *if* or *unless* and has a present tense verb. The main clause uses a modal (*will, can, should, may, might*) plus the base form of the verb.

> <u>Unless</u> we <u>find</u> a better deal, we <u>will buy</u> this sound system.

Hypothetical past conditionals: These sentences describe a situation that is unlikely to happen or that is contrary to fact. To describe situations in the past, the verb in the conditional clause is in the past perfect tense, and the verb in the main clause is formed from *would have, could have*, or *might have* plus the past participle.

> If we <u>had started out</u> earlier, we <u>would have arrived</u> on time.

<u>Note:</u> If the hypothetical situation is a present or future one, the verb in the conditional clause is in the past tense, and the verb in the main clause is formed from *would, could*, or *might* plus the base form of the verb.

> If we <u>bought</u> groceries once a week, we <u>would</u> not <u>have</u> to go to the store so often.

Quoted and Reported Speech

Quoted speech is the use of exact words from another source in your own writing; you must enclose these words in quotation marks. It is also possible to report nearly exact words without quotation marks. This is called reported speech, or indirect quotation. (See pages 282–284 to review the correct use of quotation marks.)

> **Direct:** Felicia said, "Don't worry about tomorrow."
> **Indirect:** Felicia said that you don't have to worry about tomorrow.

In the case of a question, when a direct quotation is changed to an indirect quotation, the question mark is not needed.

> **Direct:** Ahmad asked, "Which of you will give me a hand?"
> **Indirect:** Ahmad asked which of us would give him a hand.

Notice how pronouns are often changed in indirect quotations.

> **Direct:** My friends said, "You're crazy."
> **Indirect:** My friends said that I was crazy.

Note: In academic writing, using someone else's spoken or written words in one's own writing without properly acknowledging the source is called plagiarism. Plagiarism is severely penalized in academic situations. (See pages 242–244.)

LO4 Numbers, Word Parts, and Idioms

NUMBERS

As a multilingual/ESL learner, you may be accustomed to writing numbers in a way that is different from the way it is done in North America. It is important to become familiar with the North American conventions for writing numbers. Pages 292–294 show you how numbers are written and punctuated in both word and numeral form.

Using Punctuation with Numerals

Note that the **period** is used to express percentages (5.5%, 75.9%) and the **comma** is used to organize large numbers into units (7,000; 23,100; 231,990,000). Commas are not used, however, in writing the year (2012).

Cardinal Numbers

Cardinal numbers are used when counting a number of parts or objects. Cardinal numbers can be used as nouns (she counted to **ten**), pronouns (I invited many guests, but only **three** came), or adjectives (there are **ten** boys here).

Write out in words the numbers one through one hundred. Numbers 101 and greater are usually written as numerals.

Ordinal Numbers

Ordinal numbers show place or succession in a series: the fourth row, the twenty-first century, the tenth time, and so on. Ordinal numbers are used to talk about the parts into which a whole can be divided, such as a fourth or a tenth, and as the denominator in fractions, such as one-fourth or three-fifths. Written fractions can also be used as nouns (I gave him **four-fifths**) or as adjectives (a **four-fifths** majority).

Note: See the list at right for the names and symbols of the first twenty-five ordinal numbers. Consult a college dictionary for a complete list of cardinal and ordinal numbers.

First	1st
Second	2nd
Third	3rd
Fourth	4th
Fifth	5th
Sixth	6th
Seventh	7th
Eighth	8th
Ninth	9th
Tenth	10th
Eleventh	11th
Twelfth	12th
Thirteenth	13th
Fourteenth	14th
Fifteenth	15th
Sixteenth	16th
Seventeenth	17th
Eighteenth	18th
Nineteenth	19th
Twentieth	20th
Twenty-first	21st
Twenty-second	22nd
Twenty-third	23rd
Twenty-fourth	24th
Twenty-fifth	25th

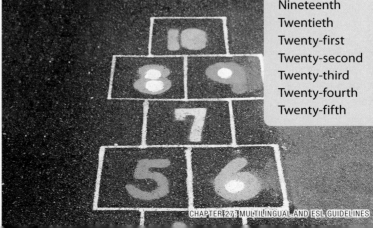

WORD PARTS

Following is a list of many common word parts and their meanings. Learning them can help you determine the meanings of unfamiliar words as you come across them in your reading. For instance, if you know that *hemi* means "half," you can conclude that *hemisphere* means "half of a sphere."

Quick Guide | Prefixes, Suffixes, and Roots

Prefixes	Meaning
a, an	not, without
anti, ant	against
co, con, com	together, with
di	two, twice
dis, dif	apart, away
ex, e, ec, ef	out
hemi, semi	half
il, ir, in, im	not
inter	between
intra	within
multi	many
non	not
ob, of, op, oc	toward, against
per	throughout
post	after
super, supr	above, more
trans, tra	across, beyond
tri	three
uni	one

Suffixes	Meaning
able, ible	able, can do
age	act of, state of
al	relating to
ate	cause, make
en	made of
ence, ency	action, quality
esis, osis	action, process
ice	condition, quality
ile	relating to
ish	resembling
ment	act of, state of
ology	study, theory
ous	full of, having
sion, tion	act of, state of
some	like, tending to
tude	state of
ward	in the direction of

Roots	Meaning
acu	sharp
am, amor	love, liking
anthrop	man
aster, astr	star
auto	self
biblio	book
bio	life
capit, capt	head
chron	time
cit	to call, start
cred	believe
dem	people
dict	say, speak
erg	work
fid, feder	faith, trust
fract, frag	break
graph, gram	write, written
ject	throw
log, ology	word, study, speech
man	hand
micro	small
mit, miss	send
nom	law, order
onym	name
path, pathy	feeling, suffering
rupt	break
scrib, script	write
spec, spect, spic	look
tele	far
tempo	time
tox	poison
vac	empty
ver, veri	true
zo	animal

IDIOMS

Idioms are phrases that are used in a special way. An idiom can't be understood just by knowing the meaning of each word in the phrase. It must be learned as a whole. For example, the idiom *to bury the hatchet* means "to settle an argument," even though the individual words in the phrase mean something much different. These pages list some of the common idioms in American English.

Idioms	Use and Meaning
a bad apple	One troublemaker on a team may be called a bad apple. (*a bad influence*)
an axe to grind	Mom has an axe to grind with the owners of the dog that dug up her flower garden. (*a problem to settle*)
as the crow flies	She lives only two miles from here as the crow flies. (*in a straight line*)
beat around the bush	Dad said, "Where were you? Don't beat around the bush." (*avoid getting to the point*)
benefit of the doubt	Ms. Hy gave Henri the benefit of the doubt when he explained why he fell asleep in class. (*another chance*)
beyond the shadow of a doubt	Salvatore won the 50-yard dash beyond the shadow of a doubt. (*for certain*)
blew my top	When my money got stolen, I blew my top. (*showed great anger*)
bone to pick	Nick had a bone to pick with Adrian when he learned they both liked the same girl. (*problem to settle*)
break the ice	Shanta was the first to break the ice in the room full of new students. (*start a conversation*)
burn the midnight oil	Carmen had to burn the midnight oil the day before the big test. (*work late into the night*)
chomping at the bit	Dwayne was chomping at the bit when it was his turn to bat. (*eager, excited*)
cold shoulder	Alicia always gives me the cold shoulder after our disagreements. (*ignores me*)

cry wolf	If you cry wolf too often, no one will come when you really need help. (*say you are in trouble when you aren't*)
drop in the bucket	My donation was a drop in the bucket. (*a small amount compared with what's needed*)
face the music	José had to face the music when he got caught cheating on the test. (*deal with the punishment*)
flew off the handle	Tramayne flew off the handle when he saw his little brother playing with matches. (*became very angry*)
floating on air	Teresa was floating on air when she read the letter. (*feeling very happy*)
food for thought	The coach gave us some food for thought when she said that winning isn't everything. (*something to think about*)
get down to business	In five minutes you need to get down to business on this assignment. (*start working*)
get the upper hand	The other team will get the upper hand if we don't play better in the second half. (*probably win*)
hit the ceiling	Rosa hit the ceiling when she saw her sister painting the television. (*was very angry*)
hit the hay	Patrice hit the hay early because she was tired. (*went to bed*)
in a nutshell	In a nutshell, Coach Roby told us to play our best. (*to summarize*)
in the nick of time	Zong grabbed his little brother's hand in the nick of time before he touched the hot pan. (*just in time*)
in the same boat	My friend and I are in the same boat when it comes to doing Saturday chores. (*have the same problem*)
iron out	Jamil and his brother were told to iron out their differences about cleaning their room. (*solve, work out*)
it stands to reason	It stands to reason that if you keep lifting weights, you will get stronger. (*it makes sense*)
knuckle down	Grandpa told me to knuckle down at school if I want to be a doctor. (*work hard*)

learn the ropes	Being new in school, I knew it would take some time to learn the ropes. (*get to know how things are done*)
let's face it	"Let's face it!" said Mr. Sills. "You're a better long distance runner than you are a sprinter." (*let's admit it*)
let the cat out of the bag	Tia let the cat out of the bag and got her sister in trouble. (*told a secret*)
lose face	If I strike out again, I will lose face. (*be embarrassed*)
nose to the grindstone	If I keep my nose to the grindstone, I will finish my homework in one hour. (*work hard*
on cloud nine	Walking home from the party, I was on cloud nine. (*feeling very happy*)
on pins and needles	I was on pins and needles as I waited to see the doctor. (*feeling nervous*)
over and above	Over and above the assigned reading, I read two library books. (*in addition to*)
put his foot in his mouth	Chivas put his foot in his mouth when he called his teacher by the wrong name. (*said something embarrassing*)
put your best foot forward	Grandpa said that whenever you do something, you should put your best foot forward. (*do the best that you can do*)
rock the boat	The coach said, "Don't rock the boat if you want to stay on the team." (*cause trouble*)
rude awakening	I had a rude awakening when I saw the letter F at the top of my Spanish quiz. (*sudden, unpleasant surprise*)
save face	Grant tried to save face when he said he was sorry for making fun of me in class. (*fix an embarrassing situation*)
see eye to eye	My sister and I finally see eye to eye about who gets to use the phone first after school. (*are in agreement*)
sight unseen	Grandma bought the television sight unseen. (*without seeing it first*)

take a dim view	My brother will take a dim view if I don't help him at the store. (*disapprove*)
take it with a grain of salt	If my sister tells you she has no homework, take it with a grain of salt. (*don't believe everything you're told*)
take the bull by the horns	This team needs to take the bull by the horns to win the game. (*take control*)
through thick and thin	Max and I will be friends through thick and thin. (*in good times and in bad times*)
time flies	When you're having fun, time flies. (*time passes quickly*)
time to kill	We had time to kill before the ballpark gates would open. (*extra time*)
to go overboard	The teacher told us not to go overboard with fancy lettering on our posters. (*to do too much*)
under the weather	I was feeling under the weather, so I didn't go to school. (*sick*)
word of mouth	We found out who the new teacher was by word of mouth. (*talking to other people*)

Note: Like idioms, collocations are groups of words that often appear together. They may help you identify different senses of a word; for example, *old* has a slightly different meaning in these collocations: *old man, old friends*. You will be able to say what you mean if you check for collocations.

GLOSSARY

A

abstracts
summaries of resources; a collection of summaries in a specific subject area

academic essay
carefully planned writing in which the writer analyzes, explains, interprets, or argues for or against a topic

academic transcript
the permanent record of educational achievement and activity

active sentences
sentences in which the subject performs the action

active voice
a subject-verb construction in which the subject performs the action

almanacs/yearbooks
regularly published references that chronicle the major events of a specific time period

anecdotes
brief stories or "slices of life" that help make a point

annotate
underline or highlight important passages in a text and make notes in the margins

appeal
an argument that connects to the reader's needs, such as achievement, belonging, or survival

appendixes
sections (in a book) that provide additional or background information

application essay
a reflective essay that focuses on experiences and qualities that suit the writer for a specific position or program

argument
a course of logical thinking intended to convince the reader to accept an idea or to take action

argumentative essay
writing that presents an argument about a timely, debatable topic

artifact
any object made or modified by a human culture

assessment
the way that writing will be evaluated

attributive phrase
a group of words that indicates the source of an idea or a quotation

audience
the intended reader or readers for your writing

authoritative
backed by research and expert analysis

B

basic listing
a brief, somewhat informal itemizing of main points

benefits
positive or helpful results

biased words
words that unfairly or disrespectfully depict individuals or groups

bibliographies
lists of works that cover a particular subject

blogs
online journals (short for "Weblog")

body language
the physical cues that indicate a person's level of comfort, interest, engagement, and so forth

bookmark
a digital tag that allows the user to easily return to a favorite site

Boolean operators
words or symbols used when searching research databases and that describe the relationship between various words or phrases in a search

C

camera-eye approach
sharing details as though through a camera lens moving across a subject

cause-effect analysis
a paper that examines the conditions or actions that lead to specific outcomes

chronological order
time order; relating details in the order that they occurred

cliches
overused words and phrases such as *piece of cake*

climax
the most exciting moment in a narrative; the moment at which the person succeeds, fails, or learns something

closed questions
questions that can be answered with a simple fact or with a *yes* or a *no*

clustering
a form of brainstorming by freely recording words and phrases around a nucleus word

coherence
strong connection between sentences in a paragraph, achieved through transition and repetition

collections
the materials housed within a library

comparison-contrast analysis
a paper that shows the similarities and differences between two topics

complimentary closing
the polite sign-off line of a letter, following the body and preceding the signature

concessions
recognizing valid arguments on the other side

conflict
the obstacles or adversaries confronted by people in narratives; person vs. person, person vs. society, person vs. the supernatural, person vs. nature, person vs. self, person vs. technology

connotation
the suggestion made by a word; a word's implied meaning

context
the set of circumstances in which a statement is made; the text and other factors that surround a specific statement and are crucial to understanding it

continuum of communication
a list of written communication options from informal to formal

controversies
issues about which there are two or more strongly opposing sides; highly debatable issues

conventions
the standard rules for spelling, punctuation, mechanics, usage, and grammar

cumulative sentence
a sentence that has modifying phrases and clauses before, after, or in the middle of the base clause

D

debatable topic
a topic that is not a mere fact but can be argued from at least two different angles

deductive reasoning
reasoning that works from general principles or ideas; through specific applications, support, and/or examples; to a conclusion

deep Web
Internet materials not accessible via popular search engines but available through a library's subscription databases

defensible position
a claim that is debatable but can be strongly supported by evidence; a claim that is neither a fact nor an unsupportable opinion

denotation
the dictionary definition of a word; a word's literal meaning

dialogue
the words spoken by people and set apart with quotation marks

directed writing
an exploration tactic using one of a set of thinking moves: describe, compare, associate, analyze, argue, or apply

directories
references that provide contact information for people, groups, and organizations

documentation
crediting sources of information, through in-text citations or references and a list of works cited or references

domain name
the name of a site, including the extension after the dot (.), which indicates what type of organization created the site

drafting
writing sentences and paragraphs to create an initial draft with an opening, a middle, and a closing

E

editing
refining a draft in terms of word choice and sentence style and checking it for conventions

ellipsis
a set of three periods with one space preceding and following each period; a punctuation mark that indicates deletion of material

encyclopedias
reference works filled with articles written about a variety of topics

etymology
the origin of a word

extended definition
a type of analytical writing that explores the meaning of a specific term, providing denotation, connotation, and a variety of perspectives on the term

extreme claims
claims that include words *(all, best, never, worst)* that are overly positive or negative

F

facts
statements that can be checked for accuracy

fair use
rules governing the use of small (not large) portions of text, for noncommercial purposes

fake writing voice
a writing voice that sounds overly academic, bland, or unnatural

feasible
doable; reasonable—given time, budgets, resources, and consequences

field research
an on-site scientific study conducted for the purpose of attaining raw data

first draft
the initial writing in which the writer connects facts and details about the topic

five W's
the questions *who? what? when? where?* and *why?* (and sometimes *how?*)

focus
the specific part of a subject to be covered in your writing

focused freewriting
freewriting that is approached from a specific angle or as a quick draft of a paper

form
the type of writing; for example, report, letter, proposal, editorial, essay, story, or poem

formal English
carefully worded language suitable for most academic writing

forms
questionnaires, surveys, suggestion boxes, and other features that allow visitors to Web sites to interact with the host

formulaic writing
writing that stiffly adheres to a traditional format and fails to make a strong impact

freewriting
a form of nonstop writing used during the early stages of the writing process to collect thoughts and ideas

G

glossaries
lists of important terms and their definitions

graphic organizer
a chart or diagram for arranging main points and essential details

H

hyperlinks
specially formatted text that enables readers to click to another spot on the Web

hypertext link
a clickable bit of text that connects the user to another location on the Web

I

implications
natural results, direct and indirect, whether good or bad

indexes
searchable lists of resources on various topics

inductive reasoning
reasoning that works from the particular details toward general conclusions

informal English
language characterized by a more relaxed, personal tone suitable for personal writing

inside address
the reader's name and address

inspection
the purposeful analysis of a site or situation in order to understand it

intensity
a writer's level of concern for the topic, as indicated by the writing voice

Internet
a worldwide network of connected computers that allows a sharing of information

interviewee
the person who is the focus of the interview and answers the interviewer's questions

J

jargon
highly technical terms not familiar to the general reader

joie de vivre
French for "joy of life," a quality in people who live life to its fullest

journal
a notebook used regularly for personal writing

journals
generally quarterly publications providing specialized scholarly information for a narrowly focused audience

L

"La Marseillaise"
the song of Marseille; the national anthem of France

level of language
the level of formality that a writer uses—informal, semiformal, or formal

Library of Congress call numbers
a set of numbers and letters specifying the subject area, topic, and authorship or title of a book

Library of Congress classification
a system of classification (and organization) used in most academic and research libraries

line diagram
a graphic organizer used to arrange ideas for expository writing

logical fallacies
false arguments based on bits of fuzzy, dishonest, or incomplete thinking

loose sentence
a sentence that provides a base clause near the beginning, followed by explanatory phrases and clauses

M

magazines
weekly, monthly, or semimonthly publications providing information to a broadly focused audience

main claim
a debatable statement, the thesis or key point in an argument

medium
the way that writing is delivered; for example, in a printed publication or online

menus
structured lists of links that operate like a Web site's table of contents

metaphor
a comparison that equates two dissimilar things without using *like* or *as;* saying that one thing is another

metasearch tools
sites that search other search engines

method of assessment
the way in which a piece of writing is evaluated, with a rubric, by peer review, or so on

mnemonics
memory techniques in which you associate new ideas with more recognizable or memorable words, images, or ideas

modifiers
words that limit or describe other words or groups of words; adjectives and adverbs

MUDs
text-based "worlds" that people can share

N

nominal constructions
noun forms of verbs such as *description, instructions, confirmation*

nucleus word
the central term in a cluster, connecting all other ideas

O

observation
noting information received in person through the senses

open-ended questions
questions that require elaborate answers

opinions
personally held attitudes or beliefs

options
choices provided within an assignment

order of importance
a pattern of organization often used in persuasive writing in which the writer begins or ends with the most convincing argument

order of location
organizing details according to their position; progressing from near to far, inside to outside, and so on

organizing pattern
the way that details are arranged in writing; for example, chronological order or cause/effect order

original document
a record that relates directly to an event, an issue, an object, or a phenomenon

orphan
a single line of a new paragraph at the bottom of a page

overall design
the pattern the writing takes to move the ideas along—time order, compare-contrast, and so on

OWLs
online writing labs where you can get answers to your writing problems

P

page design
the elements (typography, spacing, graphics) that create the look of a paper; readability is the focus of design for academic writing

paleontologist
a scientist who studies life forms that lived in past geologic time

parallelism
repeating phrases or sentence structures to show the relationship between ideas

paraphrase
to put a whole passage in your own words

passive sentences
sentences in which the subject is acted upon

passive voice
a subject-verb construction in which the subject is acted upon

PDF
portable document file; a file format that preserves a document according to its exact appearance and is readable using Adobe Reader software

periodicals
publications or broadcasts produced at regular intervals (daily, weekly, monthly, quarterly)

personal narrative
writing about a memorable experience; may include personal reflections and thoughts

pivotal points
moments in which an important change occurs; literally, a point at which a person changes direction

plagiarism
presenting someone else's work or ideas as one's own

planning
the thinking and organizing that go into establishing a direction and structure for writing

platitudes
stale or unoriginal remarks

point of view
the perspective from which the writer approaches the writing, including first-person, second-person, or third-person point of view

primary sources
original sources that give firsthand information about a topic

proofread
check a final copy for errors before submitting it

public domain
materials provided by the government, provided as part of the "copy left" movement, or, generally speaking, materials older than 75 years old

publishing
sharing your finished writing with your instructor and peers, and/or sending it out to a print or online publication

purpose
the goal of a piece of writing; for example, to inform, analyze, or persuade

Q

qualifiers
words or phrases that limit or refine a claim, making it more reasonable

quotation
a word-for-word statement or passage from an original source

R

rapport
personal connection, trust, and teamwork

rebuttal
a tactful argument aimed at weakening the opposing point of view

redirect
restate the main claim or argument

redundancy
words used together that mean nearly the same thing

refute
prove false, illogical, or undesirable

repetition
repeating words or synonyms where necessary to remind the reader of what has already been said

research paper
a fairly long essay (5–15 pages), complete with thesis statement, supporting evidence, integrated sources, and careful documentation

restrictions
limitations of choice within an assignment

résumé
a document that outlines a person's job objective, skills, experience, and education; a curriculum vitae (cv)

revising
improving a draft through large-scale changes such as adding, deleting, rearranging, and reworking

revision
the process of making changes or improvements to a first draft

rhetoric
the art of using language effectively

rhetorical situation
the dynamics—subject, audience, and purpose—that affect a writer's decisions about the initial selecting and research

RTF
rich text file; a file format that preserves basic formatting such as bolds, italics, and tabs but is readable by most word processors

S

salutation
the greeting in a letter; the line that begins *Dear*

sans serif type
type that does not have tails; may work well for headings and subheadings

search engines
sites that search other Web sites using key words

secondary sources
sources that are at least once removed from the original; sources that provide secondhand information

sensory details
sights, sounds, smells, tastes, textures, temperatures, and other details connected to the five senses—showing rather than telling about the subject

sentence combining
combining ideas in sentences to show relationships and make connections

sentence expanding
extending basic ideas with different types of phrases and clauses

sentence outline
a more formal method of arrangement in which you state each main point and essential detail as a complete sentence

sentence variety
varying the beginnings, lengths, and types of your sentences

serif type
type that has tails at the tops and the bottoms of the letters; works best for text copy

showcase portfolio
a collection of appropriate finished pieces of writing for evaluation

slang
words considered outside standard English because they are faddish, familiar to few people, and sometimes insulting

slanted questions
questions that presuppose a specific answer

spatial organization
a pattern of organization in which you logically order descriptive details from far to near, from left to right, from top to bottom, and so on

specific nouns
nouns, such as *Meryl Streep*, that are clear, exact, and strong

study group
a group of classmates working together to understand course material

style
the personal variety, originality, and clarity of your writing

subject
the general area covered by a writing assignment

subject tree
a listing of Web sites, arranged by experts

subscription databases
online services that, for a fee, provide access to hundreds of thousands of articles

summarize
to condense in your own words the main points in a passage

summary
a shortened version of a piece of writing, giving all the main points but no supporting details

surface changes
the edited (corrected) words, phrases, and sentences in your writing

survey/questionnaire
a set of questions created for the purpose of gathering information from respondents about a specific topic

T

tableau
a dramatic scene or setting; a striking picture

tactful
being sensitive to the feelings of others; avoiding unnecessary offense

taxonomy
a system of classification of items—plants, animals, ideas, movements, and so on

telepathy
communicating thoughts over distance

tertiary sources
sources that provide thirdhand information, such as wikis; discouraged for college research projects

thesis statement
a sentence or set of sentences that sums up the central idea of a piece of writing

thought details
impressions, emotions, predictions, and reflections; details that reveal perceptions rather than sensations

tombstone
a heading or a subheading sitting alone at the bottom of a page

tone
the overall feeling or effect created by a writer's thoughts and use of words

topic outline
a less formal method of arrangement in which you state each main point and essential detail as a word or a phrase

transitions
words and phrases that help tie ideas together

typography
the size and style of type that is used

U

uninspiring draft
a draft in which a writer fails to engage the reader and make a lasting impression

unity
oneness in a paragraph achieved through focus on a single idea

URL
the uniform resource locator; the Web address telling the browser how to access a certain file

V

vivid verbs
specific action verbs, such as *lunge,* that help create clear images

voice
the tone of the writing, often affected by the personality of the writer

W

Web browser
a program that provides access to Web resources through a variety of tools

Web page
a page viewable as a single unit on a Web site

Web site
a group of related Web pages posted by the same sponsor or organization

widow
a single word or a short line carried over to the top of a page

working bibliography
a list of sources that you have read and/or intend to use in your research

working portfolio
a collection of documents at various stages of development

working thesis
a preliminary answer to your main research question; the focus of your research

World Wide Web
the collection of Web sites on the Internet accessible to Web browsers and search engines

worn-out topic
an essay topic that is dull or unoriginal

writing portfolio
a collection of your writing

writing process
the steps that a writer should follow to develop a thoughtful and thorough piece of writing

CREDITS

This page constitutes an extension of the copyright page. We have made every effort to trace the ownership of all copyrighted material and to secure permission from copyright holders. In the event of any question arising as to the use of any material, we will be pleased to make the necessary corrections in future printings. Thanks are due to the following authors, publishers, and agents for permission to use the material indicated.

Chapter 4
page 46: From *Of Human Bondage* by W. Somerset Maugham

Chapter 9
page 105: Instructions by Verne Meyer/John Van Rys from "Downloading Photographs from the MC-150 Digital Camera," from Van Rys/Meyer/Sebranek, *The Business Writer,* 1st edition. Copyright © 2006 by Houghton Mifflin Company.

Chapter 10
page 114: "Two Views of the River" by Mark Twain from his 1883 memoir, *Life on the Mississippi.*

Chapter 12
page 132: "Uncle Sam and Aunt Samantha" by Anna Quindlen from *Newsweek,* November 5, 2001. Reprinted by permission of International Creative Management, Inc. Copyright © 2001 by Anna Quindlen.

page 137: "I Have a Dream" excerpt by Martin Luther King, Jr. By arrangement with the Estate of Martin Luther King, Jr., c/o Writer's House as agent for the proprietor, New York, NY. Copyright © 1963 Martin Luther King, Jr. Copyright renewed 1991 Coretta Scott King.

page 137: From "Soul of a Citizen" by Paul Rogat Loeb. Copyright © 1999A by the author and reprinted by permission of St. Martins Press, LLC.

Chapter 14
page 164: Jane Kenyon, "Let Evening Come" from *Collected Poems.* Copyright © 2005 by The Estate of Jane Kenyon. Reprinted with the permission of Graywolf Press, Minneapolis, Minnesota. www.graywolfpress.org.

Chapter 18
page 219: "Vehicle of Change" by L.D. Burns, J.B. McCormick, C.E. Borroni-Bird from *Scientific American* 287:4 (October 2002) 10.

Chapter 20
page 242: Excerpt taken from page 87 of "Some Stories Have to Be Told by Me: A Literary History of Alice Munro," by Marcela Valdes, published in the *Virginia Quarterly Review* 82.3 (Summer 2006).

Chapter 21
page 270: "Our Roots Go Back to Roanoake: Investigating the Link Between the Lost Colony and the Lumbee People of North Carolina" by Renee Danielle Singh. From *Prized Writing* 2005-2006. The University Writing Program of the University of California at Davis, © The Regents of the University of California.

Student Models

The authors and editors of *COMP: Write* gratefully acknowledge the many students who gave us permission to reprint their fine writing.

INDEX

A

A/an, 335
Abbreviations, 294–297
  Acronyms and
      initialisms, 297
  Capitalization, 288, 291
  Common, 296
  Correspondence, 294
  Internet, 235
  State, 294–295
Absolute phrase, 69, 321
Abstract noun, 96, 305, 335
Abstracts, 11, 122, 211, 231, 232,
    252, 264, 269
  APA, 252, 264, 269
  As research tools, 11, 211, 214,
    231, 232
  Citation of, 264
  Writing, 15, 122, 252, 269
Academic style, 52, 56, 208
  Active or passive voice, 12, 58,
    73, 74, 123, 125, 310, 312,
    329, 337
Accent mark, 287
Accept/except, 77
Acronyms, 199, 263, 297
  As memory guides, 199
Acrostics, 199
Action verb, 73, 74, 309, 310, 341
Active voice, 58, 312, 329
  Active or passive, 12, 58, 73,
    74, 123, 125, 310, 312,
    329, 337
Address, 75, 175, 177, 178, 179,
    183, 297
  Abbreviations, 295
  Direct, 277, 290
  E-mail, 175, 176, 192
  Internet, 187, 234, 235, 238,
    258, 264
  Punctuation of, 277, 293, 294

Adjective,
  Clause, 276, 322
  Comparative, 314
  Compound, 279, 280, 293, 294
  Demonstrative, 314, 334, 336,
    341
  Forms of, 314
  Hyphenated, 279, 280, 281,
    293
  Infinitive phrase, acting as, 321
  Nouns as, 280, 286, 287, 288,
    305, 314, 336, 341, 342
  Participial phrase, acting as, 321
  Participles as, 313, 321, 341
  Placing, 341
  Positive, 314
  Possessive, 290, 336, 341
  Predicate, 314, 337, 343
  Prepositional phrase,
    acting as, 315, 320, 321
  Proper, 280, 288, 314
  Quantifiers, 336
  Separating with
    commas, 275, 276
  Superlative, 314
  To show time or amount, 287

Adverb,
  Clause, 275, 322
  Comparative, 315
  Conjunctive, 70, 72, 277, 278
  Forms of, 315
  Infinitive phrase,
    acting as, 321
  Placing, 341–342
  Positive, 315
  Superlative, 315
  Types of, 315
Agreement,
  Pronoun-antecedent, 327, 328
  Subject-verb, 310, 312, 325,
    343
Aids, visual, 5, 21, 137, 151, 154,
    189, 192, 211, 216
Alliteration, 164, 165, 170
Allusion, 167
Almanac, 211, 231
Ambiguous wording, 123, 140,
    325, 332
Analogies, 44, 62, 104, 105, 137,
    140, 150, 154, 167
  Paragraph, 44

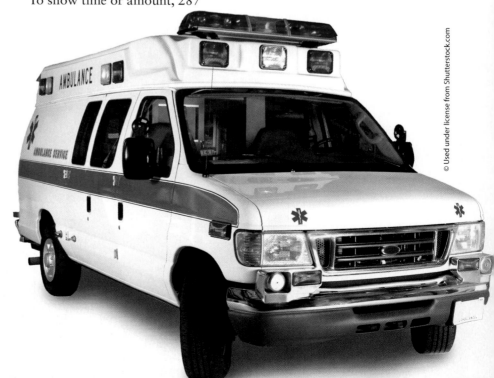

© Used under license from Shutterstock.com

B

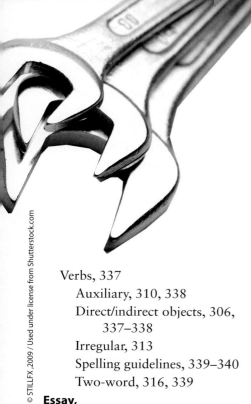

Plurals of, 292
Use of, 334, 345
Film review, 166
First draft, 3, 7–8, 20, 38–49, 51,
    52–53, 84–85, 87–88, 91,
    96–97, 100, 111, 147, 150,
    160–161, 174, 181, 183, 249
First words,
    Capitalizing, 77, 289
    Numbers, 293
Five W's, 5, 26, 118, 227
Focus, 6, 20, 29, 30, 31, 34, 40, 41,
    53, 54, 60, 64, 84, 85, 87, 88,
    97, 118, 136, 147, 150, 154,
    160, 161, 181, 209, 210, 245,
    249
Foot, 170
Foreign words, italics, 284
Form, 21
Formatting,
    APA style, 251, 252–266,
      267–268
    MLA style, 251, 252–266,
      269–271
Forms of address, 75, 177, 290
Forms of writing, 5, 82–271
    Abstract, 122, 231, 252, 264,
      269
    Analysis, literary, 34, 35, 100–
      102, 112–113, 158–170
    Analytical, 37, 94–115, 137,
      225
    Application, letter of, 179
    Business letters, 177–180, 279
    College, 56–57
    Descriptive, 82–93
    E-mail, 173–175, 183, 185
    Essay. *See* Essay.
    Expository. *See* Expository
      writing.
    Internet, 186–195
    Memo, 174, 176
    Narrative, 29, 32, 42, 82–93,
      169
    Persuasive, 33, 37, 144–157
    Report. *See* Report writing.
    Résumé, 183–185
    Review. *See* Review.
Fraction, punctuation, 280, 285,

293, 345
Fragment, sentence, 325, 330
Freewriting, 5, 24, 26, 52
Future perfect tense, 310, 311
Future tense, 310, 311

G

Gender, 75
    Noun, 305
    Pronoun, 306, 308, 309, 328
Gender references, 75–76, 177
Generalization, 139
Genre, 34, 35, 161, 168
Gerund, 312, 313, 319, 321, 329,
    338
Gerund phrase, 319, 321, 329
Grammar, 77, 272, 304–317
Graphic organizers, 6, 35, 36–37
    Cause/effect, 36
    Classification, 37, 99
    Cluster, 4, 24
    Comparison, 36
    Comparison/contrast, 36
    Definition, 37
    Line Diagram, 35
    Persuasion, 37
    Problem/solution web, 6, 36
    Process analysis, 37
    Sensory details, 84
    Thought details, 84
    Venn diagram, 36
Groups, study, 198
Guidelines for writing,
    About literature and the
      arts, 160–161
    Analysis of a process, 102–103
    Application essay, 181
    Cause-effect essay, 108–109
      Thesis, 32
    Classification essay, 99–100

Thesis, 33
Comparison-contrast essay,
    111–112
    Thesis, 32–33
Correspondence, 174
Definition essay, 96–97
    Thesis, 33
Description essay, 84–85
    Thesis, 32
Description and reflection essay,
    91–93
    Thesis, 32
Editing, 13–14
Freewriting, 24
Interview report, 118–119
Lab reports. *See* Lab, experi-
    ment, and field reports.
Letter, 177
Literary analysis, 160–161
Narration essay, 87–88
    Thesis, 32
Paraphrases, 219, 221

J

Jargon, 57, 68, 75, 150
Job application, 179–185
Journal writing, 23
Justify, key word, 200

K

Key terms, italic, 284
Key words, in essay tests, 200–201
Keyword searching, 213

L

Lab, experiment, and field reports, 117, 122–128
    Guidelines, 122–123
Lab reports. *See* Lab, experiment, and field reports.
    Model, 123–124
Language,
    Addressing,
        Age, 77
        Disability, 75
        Ethnicity, 76
        Gender, 75, 76
        Occupation, 76
    Body, 119
    Capitalizing, 289
    Cliches, 75
    Constructing sentences, 329
    Heightened, 168
    Jargon, 57, 68, 75, 150
    Level of, 30
    Misusing, 140–141
    Nonstandard, 71, 325, 333
    Parts of speech, 304, 317, 334–343
    Slanted, 141
    Usage, 77
    Using fair language, 75–77
Leaders, 287
Letter,
    Joined to a word, 280
    Plural, 286
Letters,
    Application, 179
    Business, 177–180
    Recommendation request, 180
Library, 211, 223, 228–230, 236
    Catalog searches, 212, 229–230
    Classification systems,
        Dewey decimal, 230
        Library of Congress, 230
    Readers' Guide, 233
    Reference works, 208, 214
Limiting the subject, 23
Linking verb, 310, 314, 327, 343
Links, 189, 190, 191, 234, 238, 239
List, colon before, 179
List server, 195, 214
Listing, 25, 34
    Brainstorming, 25
    Colon before, 179
Literary analyses, 158–165
    Guidelines, 160–161
Literary terms, 167–169
Location, arrangement by, 6, 84–85

Logic,

    Fallacies of, 53, 131, 138–141
    Inductive/deductive patterns, 41, 134

M

Mailing lists, Internet, 195
Masculine gender, 305, 308, 309, 328
Matching test, 204
Measurement nouns, 327
Mechanics of writing, 77, 123, 272, 288–303
Memory techniques, 199
Memos, writing, 176
Message boards, 195
Messages, e-mail, 174, 175, 235
Metaphor, 87, 168
Metasearch tools, Internet, 239
Methods of organization.
    See Development.
Metonymy, 168
Misplaced modifier, 71, 331
Missing text, 281
MLA documentation style, 250–268
    Guidelines, 252–254
    Parenthetical references, 255–258
    Sample research paper, 267–268
    Works-cited quick guide, 259
    Works-cited references, 260–266, 268

Questions,
    Interview, 118
    Prewriting, 10
    Surveys, 225–226
Quick guides,
    Boolean operators, 213
    Essay test, taking, 204
    Freewriting, 24
    Informational resources, 231
    Introductory verbs, 246
    Key words, 22, 200
    Organizational patterns, 248
    Reference list,
        APA, 260
        MLA, 259
    Reliability test, 215
    Research paper, 225
    Sentence problems, avoiding, 333
    Thesis, 42, 210
    Transitions, 61
    Works cited, 259–260
    Writing center, 65
Quintet, 170
Quotation marks, 213, 282–284, 287
Quotations, 282–284
    Dialogue, 277, 285
    Indirect, 283, 344–345
    Introductions to, 279
    Poetry, 285
    Research writing, 217, 219, 242–243, 245, 252

Quotation within a quotation, 283
Quoted questions, 282

R

Ratio, punctuation of, 279
Readers' Guide, 231, 232
Reading,
    Memory techniques, 199
    Periodical articles, 232–233
Reasoning,
    Develop a line of, 146
    Inductive and deductive, 134
Reciprocal pronoun, 307
Recommendation request letter, 180
Redundancy, 68
Reference books, 230, 231
Reference entries, APA, 251–271
References, parenthetical, 285
    APA, 251–271
    MLA, 251–271
Reflective writing, 91–93
    Essays of, 92–93
    Guidelines, 91–92
Reflexive pronoun, 307
Refrain, 170
Relative pronoun, 307, 327
Religions, capitalizing, 289

Report writing, 116–128
    Lab, experiment, and field reports. *See* Lab, experiment, and field reports.
    Interview, 118–121
    Summary, 219–220
Request letter, for a recommendation, 180
Request, punctuation of, 273
Research,
    Conducting primary, 225
    Methods, 210–211
Research paper, 206–249
    Abstract, APA, 554
    Bibliography, working, 216
    Checklist and Activities, 64, 209, 210, 249
    Conducting, 225
        Interviews, 118–119
        Key word searches, 212–213
        Surveys, 225–226
    Developing a plan, 34–35, 210–211
    Documenting sources. *See* Sources, 254–258
    Drafting, 38–39, 249
    Editing and proofreading, 249
    Flowchart, 208
    Guidelines,
        APA, 251–271
        MLA, 251–271
    Information resources/sites, 211–212
    Keyword searches, 212–213
    Note-taking, 217–218
    Other source abuses, 243–244
    Paraphrasing sources, 219–221
    Plagiarism, avoiding, 242–243
    Planning and conducting research, 206–271
        Note-taking systems, 217–218
        Organizing, 6, 248
        Primary Research, 223–238
        Process, a flowchart, 208
        Quoting, summarizing, and paraphrasing, 219–221

© Nagy Melinda, 2009 / Used under license from Shutterstock.com

> To help you succeed, we have designed an "In Review" card for each chapter.

Chapter Summary

Introduction

The best way to develop a piece of writing is t[...] end product. Using the **writing process** allo[...] and develop it more thoroughly and thoughtfully. This means that you can't rush writing if you want to do your best work. In this chapter, you learn how one student writer, Angela Franco, uses the writing process to develop an essay for her Environmental Policies class.

> This column provides an overview of the major concepts in the chapter, with helpful graphics.

LO1 Angela initiated the process.

To get started, Angela did three things: (1) gained a clear understanding of the assignment, including purpose, audience, and **method of assessment**, (2) selected a suitable writing topic, and (3) collected information about it. Without doing these tasks, she would not be able to do any planning or writing. To identify a topic, she first narrowed her focus to water pollution. Then by **clustering** and **freewriting** she was able to identify a topic that met the requirements of the assignment. To research her topic, she did another freewriting and then referred to other sources of information.

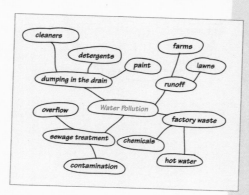

LO2 Angela planned her writing.

During her **planning**, Angela (1) formed a **thesis statement**, (2) selected an appropriate method of organization for her essay, and (3) organized her research for writing. Angela's thesis statement stated a claim about her topic, and she decided to use problem-solution as her method of organization.

LO3 Angela wrote her first draft.

Writing a **first draft** gave Angela an opportunity to connect all of her ideas about [...] topic. She realized, however, that this was only a first look at a developing writing i[...] made sure to include a beginning, a middle, and an ending in the draft.

LO4 Angela completed her first revision.

Before Angela began revising, she set her first draft aside for awhile. The time away [...] her "see" her writing more clearly. Angela focused on three key traits during the **re**[...] step: ideas, organization, and **voice**. These traits are critical because they carry her [...] message. At this point, her changes are intended to add clarity, coherency, and dep[...] her writing.

Glossary Terms

writing process
the steps that a writer should follow to develop a thoughtful and thorough piece of writing

method of assessment
the way in which a piece of writing is evaluated, with a rubric, by peer review, or s[...]

> This column provides glossary terms in the order that they appear in the chapter.

clu[...]
a fo[...]
rec[...]
nuc[...]

nucleus word
the central term in a cluster, connecting all other ideas

freewriting
a form of nonstop writing used during the early stages of the writing process to collect thoughts and ideas

planning
the thinking and organizing that go into establishing a direction and structure for writing

thesis statement
a sentence or set of sentences that sums up the central idea of a piece of writing

revising
improving a draft through large-scale changes such as adding, deleting, rearranging, and reworking

voice
the tone of the writing, often affected by the personality of the writer

How to Use This Card

1. **Preview the card before reading the chapter.**
2. **Read the chapter carefully.**
3. **Go to class (and pay attention).**
4. **Review the card to make sure you understand.**
5. **Use the card as a handy guide to the writing process.**

editing
refining a draft in terms of word choice and sentence style and checking it for conventions

conventions
the standard rules for spelling, punctuation, mechanics, usage, and grammar

proofread
check a final copy for errors before submitting it

LO5 Angela completed her second revision.

Angela asked a writing peer to review her work. She carefully reviewed the peer comments and made changes accordingly. The comments were extremely helpful because they provided specific suggestions rather than general comments such as "Your opening needs work." (It's important to remember that each reviewer's comments are only suggestions; a writer should act on only those with which she truly agrees.)

LO6 Angela edited her writing for style.

Once Angela had made all of the necessary revisions, she **edited** a clean copy of her writing for style and readability. To do so, she focused on line-by-line issues such as word choice and sentence fluency. Her goal was to make her writing as clear and engaging as possible.

LO7 Angela edited her writing for correctness.

As Angela edited for correctness, she focused on one **convention** (spelling, grammar, and so on) at a time to be more thorough. She referred to the handbook section in *COMP: Write* for help (pages 272-348), and she used the spell-checker and grammar-checker on her computer. She also asked a trusted peer to edit her work for conventions.

LO8 Angela completed her essay.

While formatting her edited essay, Angel added a head and page numbers. She also added more documentation and a reference page at the end, following APA style. She then **proofread** her final copy before submitting it.

Effective Writing Checklist

Check your finished work using these traits or standards as a guide.

Stimulating Ideas The writing

> Checklists and quick-reference guides help you get the most out of each chapter.

_____ presents interesting and i

_____ maintains a clear focus or ___ eme, concern, or question.

_____ develops the focus through a line of thought or reasoning elaborated with sufficient details or evidence.

_____ holds the reader's attention (and answers her or his questions).

Logical Organization

_____ includes a clear beginning, middle, and ending.

_____ contains specific details, arranged in an order that builds understanding with readers.

_____ uses transitions to link sentences and paragraphs.

Engaging Voice

_____ speaks in a sincere, natural way that fits the writing situation.

_____ shows that the writer really cares about the subject.

Appropriate Word Choice

_____ contains specific, clear words.

_____ uses a level of language appropriate for the type of writing and the audience.

Overall Fluency

_____ flows smoothly from sentence to sentence.

_____ displays varied sentence beginnings and lengths.

_____ follows a style that fits the situation (e.g., familiar versus academic).

Correct, Accurate Copy

_____ adheres to the rules of grammar, spelling, and punctuation.

_____ follows established documentation guidelines.

Reader-Friendly Design

_____ exhibits a polished, professional design in terms of overall format, page layout, and typographical choices.

_____ makes the document attractive and easy to read.

_____ is formatted correctly in MLA or APA style.

Chapter Summary

Introduction

The best way to develop a piece of writing is to think of it as a process rather than as an end product. Using the **writing process** allows a writer to stay with the writing longer and develop it more thoroughly and thoughtfully. This means that you can't rush writing if you want to do your best work. In this chapter, you learn how one student writer, Angela Franco, uses the writing process to develop an essay for her Environmental Policies class.

LO1 Angela initiated the process.

To get started, Angela did three things: (1) gained a clear understanding of the assignment, including purpose, audience, and **method of assessment**, (2) selected a suitable writing topic, and (3) collected information about it. Without doing these tasks, she would not be able to do any planning or writing. To identify a topic, she first narrowed her focus to water pollution. Then by **clustering** and **freewriting** she was able to identify a topic that met the requirements of the assignment. To research her topic, she did another freewriting and then referred to other sources of information.

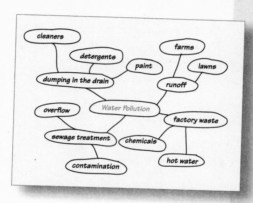

LO2 Angela planned her writing.

During her **planning**, Angela (1) formed a **thesis statement**, (2) selected an appropriate method of organization for her essay, and (3) organized her research for writing. Angela's thesis statement stated a claim about her topic, and she decided to use problem-solution as her method of organization.

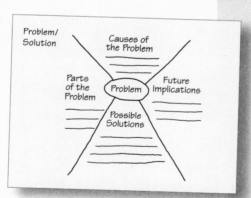

LO3 Angela wrote her first draft.

Writing a **first draft** gave Angela an opportunity to connect all of her ideas about her topic. She realized, however, that this was only a first look at a developing writing idea. She made sure to include a beginning, a middle, and an ending in the draft.

LO4 Angela completed her first revision.

Before Angela began revising, she set her first draft aside for awhile. The time away helped her "see" her writing more clearly. Angela focused on three key traits during the **revision** step: ideas, organization, and **voice**. These traits are critical because they carry her message. At this point, her changes are intended to add clarity, coherence, and depth to her writing.

Glossary Terms

writing process
the steps that a writer should follow to develop a thoughtful and thorough piece of writing

method of assessment
the way in which a piece of writing is evaluated, with a rubric, by peer review, or so on

clustering
a form of brainstorming by freely recording words and phrases around a nucleus word

nucleus word
the central term in a cluster, connecting all other ideas

freewriting
a form of nonstop writing used during the early stages of the writing process to collect thoughts and ideas

planning
the thinking and organizing that go into establishing a direction and structure for writing

thesis statement
a sentence or set of sentences that sums up the central idea of a piece of writing

revising
improving a draft through large-scale changes such as adding, deleting, rearranging, and reworking

voice
the tone of the writing, often affected by the personality of the writer

editing
refining a draft in terms of word choice and sentence style and checking it for conventions

conventions
the standard rules for spelling, punctuation, mechanics, usage, and grammar

proofread
check a final copy for errors before submitting it

L○5 Angela completed her second revision.

Angela asked a writing peer to review her work. She carefully reviewed the peer comments and made changes accordingly. The comments were extremely helpful because they provided specific suggestions rather than general comments such as "Your opening needs work." (It's important to remember that each reviewer's comments are only suggestions; a writer should act on only those with which she truly agrees.)

L○6 Angela edited her writing for style.

Once Angela had made all of the necessary revisions, she **edited** a clean copy of her writing for style and readability. To do so, she focused on line-by-line issues such as word choice and sentence fluency. Her goal was to make her writing as clear and engaging as possible.

L○7 Angela edited her writing for correctness.

As Angela edited for correctness, she focused on one **convention** (spelling, grammar, and so on) at a time to be more thorough. She referred to the handbook section in *COMP: Write* for help (pages 272-348), and she used the spell-checker and grammar-checker on her computer. She also asked a trusted peer to edit her work for conventions.

L○8 Angela completed her essay.

While formatting her edited essay, Angel added a head and page numbers. She also added more documentation and a reference page at the end, following APA style. She then **proofread** her final copy before submitting it.

Effective Writing Checklist

Check your finished work using these traits or standards as a guide.

Stimulating Ideas The writing . . .

_____ presents interesting and important information.

_____ maintains a clear focus or purpose—centered on a thesis, theme, concern, or question.

_____ develops the focus through a line of thought or reasoning elaborated with sufficient details or evidence.

_____ holds the reader's attention (and answers her or his questions).

Logical Organization

_____ includes a clear beginning, middle, and ending.

_____ contains specific details, arranged in an order that builds understanding with readers.

_____ uses transitions to link sentences and paragraphs.

Engaging Voice

_____ speaks in a sincere, natural way that fits the writing situation.

_____ shows that the writer really cares about the subject.

Appropriate Word Choice

_____ contains specific, clear words.

_____ uses a level of language appropriate for the type of writing and the audience.

Overall Fluency

_____ flows smoothly from sentence to sentence.

_____ displays varied sentence beginnings and lengths.

_____ follows a style that fits the situation (e.g., familiar versus academic).

Correct, Accurate Copy

_____ adheres to the rules of grammar, spelling, and punctuation.

_____ follows established documentation guidelines.

Reader-Friendly Design

_____ exhibits a polished, professional design in terms of overall format, page layout, and typographical choices.

_____ makes the document attractive and easy to read.

_____ is formatted correctly in MLA or APA style.

Chapter Summary

LO1 Discover your process.

Every writer works differently to complete a piece of writing. The key is discovering a process you are comfortable with. To get started writing, keep in mind the six basic steps in the writing process: getting started, **planning, drafting**, **revising**, **editing**, and submitting. This process is flexible, not rigid. A writer may adapt the process to his or her situation and assignment. To do so, consider the following ideas:

- Writing does not follow a straight path.
- Each assignment presents distinct challenges.
- Writing can involve collaboration.
- Each writer works differently.
- Good writing can't be rushed.
- Different steps focus on different issues.

Remember, there's no right or wrong writing process—what matters is the end result.

LO2 Analyze the situation.

Rhetoric is the art of using language effectively. Language is effective when all aspects of the message fit the **subject**, address the needs of the **audience**, and fulfill the writer's **purpose.** All three elements of the **rhetorical situation**—subject, audience, and purpose—should be considered during each stage in the writing process. The rhetorical situation impacts writing decisions, including **form** (such as an essay or a report), **medium** (such as paper or electronic), and **organizational strategy** (such as cause/effect or chronological order).

LO3 Understand the assignment.

Most college writing assignments spell out the objective, the task, the formal requirements, and suggested approaches and topics. Before starting an assignment, read through the directions. Be aware of **key words**, such as *analyze, argue, define,* or *summarize*—these words explain the purpose or task of the assignment. Also note any **options** or **restrictions** on the assignment. After you read the assignment, think about the course goals and how they relate to the task at hand. Do you know the **assessment** criteria for your work? Then put the assignment in perspective. How does this assignment fit with others? Is it more or less important? Finally, see if you can make this assignment connect with your interests.

Glossary Terms

planning
the thinking and organizing that go into establishing a direction and structure for writing

thesis statement
a sentence or set of sentences that sums up the central idea of a piece of writing

drafting
writing sentences and paragraphs to create an initial draft with an opening, a middle, and a closing

revising
improving a draft through large-scale changes such as adding, deleting, rearranging, and reworking

editing
refining a draft in terms of word choice and sentence style and checking it for conventions

rhetoric
the art of using language effectively

subject
the general area covered by a writing assignment

audience
the intended reader or readers for your writing

purpose
the goal of a piece of writing; for example, to inform, analyze, or persuade

rhetorical situation
the dynamics—subject, audience, and purpose—that affect a writer's decisions about the initial selecting and research

form
the type of writing; for example, report, letter, proposal, editorial, essay, story, or poem

medium
the way that writing is delivered; for example, in a printed publication or online

organizing pattern
the way that details are arranged in writing; for example, chronological order or cause/effect order

options
choices provided within an assignment

restrictions
limitations of choice within an assignment

assessment
the way that writing will be evaluated

journal
a notebook used regularly for personal writing

freewriting
a form of nonstop writing used during the early stages of the writing process to collect thoughts and ideas

clustering
a form of brainstorming by freely recording words and phrases around a nucleus word

focused freewriting
freewriting that is approached from a specific angle or as a quick draft of a paper

five W's
the questions *who? what? when? where?* and *why?* (and sometimes *how?*)

directed writing
an exploration tactic using one of a set of thinking moves: describe, compare, associate, analyze, argue, or apply

LO4 Select a topic.

A successful writing topic fulfills four objectives.

1. It meets the requirements of the assignment.
2. It is limited in scope.
3. It is familiar to the writer or can be researched.
4. It genuinely interests the writer.

You can find writing topics in class notes, handouts, search engines, or databases. Prewriting strategies such as **journal** writing, **freewriting**, **clustering**, and listing are also effective topic generators. For ideas, see the chart below.

	What is it?	How does it benefit the writer?	How can it help find writing topics?
Journaling	Periodic personal writing in a journal or notebook	Helps writer reflect on feelings, develop new thoughts, and record the happenings of the day	Writers can review journals, underlining ideas that could be explored in writing assignments.
Freewriting	The act of writing nonstop for 10 minutes or longer to think through ideas	Helps the writer get thoughts down on paper and develop and organize those thoughts	Freewriting reveals potential writing ideas that otherwise may never come to mind.
Clustering	A prewriting strategy in which a key word or phrase is circled and surrounded by associated words	Helps connect related ideas	The web of interconnected ideas provides writing topics to explore.
Listing	Writing down ideas as they come to mind, beginning with a key concept	Helps get ideas down on paper	A quick scan of a list can be a starting point for finding a writing topic.

LO5 Gather details.

Before a writer can develop a thoughtful piece of writing, he or she must carry out the necessary reading, reflecting, and researching. Writers begin gathering details by uncovering what they already know. Some gathering strategies include **focused freewriting**, answering the **5 W's**, and **directed writing**. Another way writers gather details is by asking questions about their topic. These questions address problems, policies, and concepts. Finding a variety of meaningful sources of information is another crucial step in gathering details. In addition to books and Web sites, consider primary sources such as interviews, observations, and surveys.

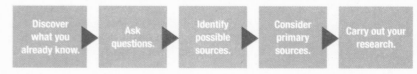

Discover what you already know. ▶ Ask questions. ▶ Identify possible sources. ▶ Consider primary sources. ▶ Carry out your research.

Chapter Summary

Introduction

Planning consists primarily of (1) establishing a thesis or focus for writing and (2) organizing the supporting information. Far less planning is required for **personal narratives** than for **academic essays**. The main goal of planning is to establish the structure of a writing project.

LO1 Take inventory of your thoughts.

Review the **rhetorical situation** to see how well you match up with your topic. You can do this by asking yourself questions about the **subject, audience,** and **purpose** of your writing. After you assess the situation, decide if you need to pick a different topic, carry out more research, or move ahead with your planning.

- **Subject:** How much do I already know about the subject? Do I need to know more? Is additional information available?
- **Audience:** How much does my audience know about the subject? How can I get them interested in my ideas?
- **Purpose:** What are the requirements of the assignment? Do I have enough time to do a good job with this topic?

LO2 Form your thesis statement.

Once you develop a more focused interest in your topic, you're ready to form a **thesis statement** for your essay. A thesis states what you want to explore or explain in your essay. An effective thesis statement sets the **tone** and the direction for your writing. It usually identifies your topic plus a claim you want to make about it. This formula will help you write thesis statements:

> **A manageable or limited topic** (wind power)
> + **a specific claim** (provides a viable energy source in the plains states)
> = **an effective thesis statement.**

> **Thesis Statement:** Wind power provides a viable energy source in the plains states.

LO3 Select a method of development.

An effective thesis statement will often suggest an **organizing pattern** for your essay. In this way, a thesis statement provides direction and shape for your writing. Common organizing patterns include the following:

- chronological
- **spatial**
- cause-effect
- comparison
- classification
- process
- definition
- problem-solution
- **order of importance**

Glossary Terms

planning
the thinking and organizing that go into establishing a direction and structure for writing

personal narrative
writing about a memorable experience; may include personal reflections and thoughts

academic essay
carefully planned writing in which the writer analyzes, explains, interprets, or argues for or against a topic

rhetorical situation
the dynamics—subject, audience, and purpose—that affect a writer's decisions about the initial selecting and research

level of language
the level of formality that a writer uses—informal, semiformal, or formal

thesis statement
a sentence or set of sentences that sums up the central idea of a piece of writing

tone
the overall feeling, or effect created by a writer's thoughts and use of words

organizing pattern
the way that details are arranged in writing; for example, chronological order or cause/effect order

spatial organization
a pattern of organization in which you logically order descriptive details from far to near, from left to right, from top to bottom, and so on

etymology
the origin of a word

order of importance
a pattern of organization often used in persuasive writing in which the writer begins or ends with the most convincing argument

basic listing
a brief, somewhat informal itemizing of main points

topic outline
a less formal method of arrangement in which you state each main point and essential detail as a word or a phrase

sentence outline
a more formal method of arrangement in which you state each main point and essential detail as a complete sentence

graphic organizer
a chart or diagram for arranging main points and essential details

line diagram
a graphic organizer used to arrange ideas for expository writing

L○4 Develop a plan or an outline.

Once you have established a thesis and an organizing pattern for your essay, you are ready to arrange the supporting information you have collected. A **basic listing** of main points may work for some writing. However, for more complex pieces, use a **topic or sentence outline** or a **graphic organizer**, like the **line diagram** below, to arrange your information. (There is a graphic organizer that coordinates with almost every pattern of organization.)

Outline Format

I.
  A.
  B.
    1.
    2.
      a.
      b.
        (1)
        (2)
          (a)
          (b)

Sample Graphic Organizer

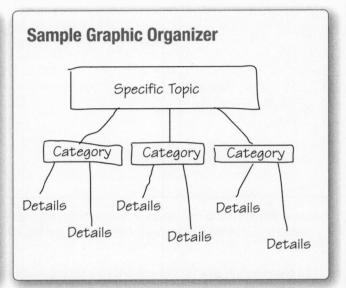

Note: When outlining, do not start a new subdivision unless it will contain at least two points. This means that each *1* must have a *2* and each *a* must have a *b*.

Review Checklist

Use this checklist as a guide to help you plan your writing.

Thesis I have . . .

_____ reviewed the information I've collected up to this point.

_____ identified a specific focus or feature of my topic to develop.

_____ stated a focus in a working thesis statement.

_____ adjusted or changed the thesis as needed to make it supportable.

Development I have . . .

_____ identified a pattern of organization for my essay.

_____ arranged my main points and supporting ideas in a list, an outline, or a graphic organizer.

Chapter Summary

LO1 Review the writing situation.

The first draft of your writing should be like wet clay, taking a basic shape that you will work into its final form. Before writing, think again about your audience, purpose, and subject.

Reconsider your audience.

- What is their knowledge of your subject?
- What is their attitude toward it?
- Write in a person-to-person style.

Reconsider your purpose. Ask . . .

- What do I want my writing to do? (its task)
- What do I want to say? (your thesis)
- How do I want to say it? (your idea list or outline)

Focus on your subject.

- Write in a natural voice to avoid hesitation.
- Use your plan as a guide, but don't feel bound by it.
- Develop your main points, noting new ones as they come, but without losing track of your thesis.
- Include as much detail as possible.
- Quote sources accurately.
- Continue until you reach a natural stopping point.
- Write the draft in one or two sittings, if possible.

LO2 Open with interest.

The common view of an opening is a funnel that draws the reader in and then narrows its focus to the main point or thesis statement. Don't let this structure constrict you, however. Try whatever seems to work, and just relax and write. You can always revise the opening later, and many writers do, after they've finished the middle of the piece. When you write the opening, it should . . .

Engage the reader.

- Mention little-known facts.
- Ask a challenging question.
- Provide a thought-provoking quotation.
- Offer a brief story.
- Or introduce the topic straightaway, if it is unique.

Establish your direction.

- Identify the topic—perhaps a problem, a need, or an opportunity.
- Put the topic in perspective by connecting it to others and showing its importance.
- Acknowledge other views about the topic.

Introduce your main point. (Use one of these strategies.)

- Narrow your **focus** to identify what interests you about the topic.
- Raise a question and build toward the answer (inductive thinking).
- Craft a sentence that states your **thesis**, or central claim (deductive thinking).

Glossary Terms

audience
the intended reader or readers for your writing

purpose
the goal of a piece of writing; for example, to inform, analyze, or persuade

focus
the specific part of a subject to be covered in your writing

thesis statement
a sentence or set of sentences that sums up the central idea of a piece of writing

implications
natural results, direct and indirect,
whether good or bad

benefits
positive or helpful results

summary
a shortened version of a piece of
writing, giving all the main points
but no supporting details

paraphrase
to put a whole passage in your
own words

quotation
a word-for-word statement or passage
from an original source

Quick Guide   **Advancing Your Thesis**

You can support your main points with . . .

- an **explanation** that provides important facts, details, and examples.

- **narration** that shares a brief story or
re-creates an experience to illustrate an
idea.

- **description** that tells in detail how
someone or something looks or works.

- a **definition** that identifies or clarifies
the meaning of a term or an idea.

- **analysis** that examines the parts of
something to better understand the
whole.

- a **comparison** that provides examples
to show how two things are alike or
different.

- an **argument** that uses logic or evidence to prove that something is true.

- **reflection** that expresses your thoughts
or feelings about something.

- **expert evidence** that adds the analysis
or commentary of an authority.

L◯3 Develop the middle.

The "heavy lifting" of your essay occurs in the middle. This is where you develop
the main points that support your thesis statement. Include effective details to
illustrate and support these points. As you draft the middle, new ideas may arise.
Use "scratch outlines" to explore where these ideas may take you, but don't wander
too far from your main thesis. In your middle, be sure to . . .

- **Advance your thesis, using supporting strategies:** Explain,
narrate, describe, define, analyze, compare, argue, reflect, and/or cite
authorities. (See the quick guide.)
- **Test your ideas:** Anticipate your reader's questions, consider alternatives,
and answer objections a skeptical reader might pose.
- **Build a coherent structure:** Telegraph your organizational style early,
and use transitions to move smoothly from one idea to the next.
- **Arrange supporting details with the appropriate
organizational strategies:** analogy, cause and effect, chronological
order, classification, compare and contrast, climax, definition, illustration,
narration, or process.

L◯4 End with purpose.

The closing of your writing is a chance to tie up loose ends, clarify key points, and
leave the reader with food for thought. It is a good idea to try out different endings
and choose the one that works best for your essay. As you close . . .

- **Reassert the main point:** Remind the reader what you set out to do,
check off key points you've covered, answer any unanswered questions, and
rephrase the thesis in the light of your most important support.
- **Urge the reader:** Show **implications** raised by your thesis, predict
future problems or solutions, or list the **benefits** of accepting or applying
your ideas.
- **Complete and unify your message:** Refocus, unify, and otherwise
reinforce your thesis.

L◯5 Use sources effectively.

Writing often involves presenting your own thoughts in relation to ideas from
research. Use *creativity* to make your own connections concerning those ideas and
take *care* to respect and cite the sources. Use outside sources only to add context
and authority for your own ideas.

Think rhetorically. Use sources that aid your purpose. Remain focused on your
role as an independent thinker and writer.

Practice drafting strategies: Keep your sources handy (to integrate them
without disrupting the flow of your drafting); consider starting your draft with
a strong source reference; advance and deepen your thesis with sources (but
don't overwhelm your draft with source material); and save the best **summary**,
paraphrase, **quotation**, or detail for last, if that helps clinch your main point.

Cross-Curricular Connections

Not all disciplines use the same documentation style. Be
sure to use the appropriate one for your essay.

Chapter Summary

LO1 Address whole-paper issues.

Revising involves improving the overall quality of the ideas, organization, and voice in a piece of writing. When revising, first look at the big picture, or rhetorical situation. Think about the subject, purpose, and audience of your writing. Does your draft fulfill its purpose and connect with your reader? Does it address the topic fully and clearly?

LO2 Revise your first draft.

Revising takes time and effort. Ideally, you should set your first draft aside for a few days to help you look at it more objectively and make the needed changes. When you are ready to begin revising, think globally. Focus on the overall strength of the ideas, organization, and voice.

- **Ideas:** Check your thesis, focus, or theme. Have you answered your reader's most pressing questions? Is your support fair and logical?
- **Organization:** Do the ideas move smoothly and logically from one point to the next?
- **Voice:** Are the tone and attitude appropriate? Does the voice match the paper's purpose?

LO3 Revise for ideas and organization.

As you review your draft for content, make sure the ideas are fully developed and the organization is clear. To revise for ideas, make sure your writing answers the reader's basic questions and supports a clear thesis. A clear **thesis** centers on one main issue or theme. After you revise your ideas, look at your organization. The best organization leads the reader logically and clearly from one point to the next. Revising for organization means checking the overall plan, opening ideas, flow of ideas, and closing ideas (see below).

Glossary Terms

revising
improving a draft through large-scale changes such as adding, deleting, rearranging, and reworking

worn-out topic
an essay topic that is dull or unoriginal

fake writing voice
a writing voice that sounds overly academic, bland, or unnatural

uninspiring draft
a draft in which a writer fails to engage the reader and make a lasting impression

formulaic writing
writing that stiffly adheres to a traditional format and fails to make a strong impact

overall design
the pattern the writing takes to move the ideas along—time order, compare-contrast, and so on

logical fallacies
false arguments based on bits of fuzzy, dishonest, or incomplete thinking

appeal
an argument that connects to the reader's needs, such as achievement, belonging, or survival

intensity
a writer's level of concern for the topic, as indicated by the writing voice

formal English
carefully worded language suitable for most academic writing

Overall Plan	Opening Ideas	Flow of Ideas	Closing Ideas
Does the sequence of ideas advance the thesis?	Does the opening engage the reader, establish a direction, and express the thesis?	Are the thoughts connected clearly with strong transitions?	Does the ending reassert the main point in a fresh way and provide the reader with food for thought?

slang
words considered outside standard English because they are faddish, familiar to few people, and sometimes insulting

informal English
language characterized by a more relaxed, personal tone suitable for personal writing

qualifiers
words or phrases that limit or refine a claim, making it more reasonable

passive voice
a subject-verb construction in which the subject is acted upon

active voice
a subject-verb construction in which the subject performs the action

unity
oneness in a paragraph achieved through focus on a single idea

coherence
strong connection between sentences in a paragraph, achieved through transition and repetition

repetition
repeating words or synonyms where necessary to remind the reader of what has already been said

parallelism
repeating phrases or sentence structures to show the relationship between ideas

transitions
words and phrases that help tie ideas together

sensory details
sights, sounds, smells, tastes, textures, temperatures, and other details connected to the five senses—showing rather than telling about the subject

anecdotes
brief stories or "slices of life" that help make a point

LO4 Revise for voice.

A writer's interest in the topic and reader is reflected in the voice. When revising for voice, check the level of commitment and intensity in your writing. In terms of style, college writing requires an academic approach. Academic style uses language that facilitates a thoughtful, engaged discussion on the topic. Features to watch for when revising for style include the use of personal pronouns, jargon, the level of formality, and the use of qualifiers. Also review your writing for active and passive verbs.

Weaknesses of Passive Voice: The passive voice tends to be wordy, sluggish, and impersonal. In most instances, active verbs should replace passive ones.

Strengths of Passive Voice: The passive voice has some important uses: (1) when you need to be tactful (say, in a bad-news letter), (2) if you wish to stress the object or person acted upon, and (3) if the actual actor is understood, unknown, or unimportant.

LO5 Address paragraph issues.

Paragraphs that are loosely held together, poorly developed, or unclear should be revised for focus, unity, and coherence. **Unity** is achieved when all the details help to develop a single main topic or achieve a single main effect. When revising for unity, be sure the writing has a clear, well-focused topic sentence, and that the sentences in the body of the paragraph support the topic sentence. **Coherence**, on the other hand, is achieved when a paragraph flows smoothly. **Repetition** and **transitions** (see chart) can improve coherence. Finally, revise for completeness by strengthening your main point. To do this, add specific supporting details. Consider adding facts, statistics, anecdotes, comparisons, and quotations.

Transitions
Location: across, beyond, throughout
Time: before, first, later, next, then
Compare: also, similarly, likewise
Contrast: although, however, yet
Add: along with, another, finally

LO6 Revise collaboratively.

Every writer can benefit from feedback from an interested audience. If you are asked to review a peer's work, the OAQS method can help you give clear, helpful, and complete feedback. OAQS stands for *observe, appreciate, question,* and *suggest* (see below).

Observe	Appreciate	Question	Suggest
Discover and comment on the writer's purpose.	Praise something in the writing that you like.	Ask whatever you want to know after you're done reading.	Give helpful advice about possible changes.

LO7 Use the writing center.

A college writing center or lab is a place where a trained adviser will help you develop and strengthen a piece of writing. When you go to a writing center, be open to change, but don't expect the adviser to write, edit, or proofread your paper for you. The adviser can help you choose a topic, generate ideas, and identify problems; it's your job to use the information to improve your paper.

Chapter Summary

Introduction

Editing and proofreading deal with the line-by-line changes that you make to improve the readability and accuracy of your writing. When you **edit**, you make sure that your words, phrases, and sentences are clear and correct. When you **proofread**, you check your final copy for errors. Always have the proper editing tool on hand before you begin your work, including *COMP: Write* and a dictionary. Also make sure to have a trusted writing peer help you edit your work.

LO1 Review the overall style of your writing.

Editing is the process of making **surface changes** in your writing, as opposed to revising, which is the process of making deep changes in the content. Follow this general plan whenever you edit for style:

- **Read your revised writing aloud.** Or better yet, have a writing peer read it aloud to you.
- **Be sure that your style fits the rhetorical situation.** Does your writing sound as if you have a clear aim or goal in mind? Is the tone honest and sincere? Do the words and phrases sound like you.
- **Study your sentences for style and clarity.** Your sentences work if they clearly and effectively communicate worthy ideas.
- **Consider your word choice.** Use strong nouns and verbs, use **modifiers** selectively, and avoid **redundancy** and **jargon**.

LO2 Write effective sentences.

The goal is to use a variety of sentences lengths and types to emphasize certain ideas, to create a particular rhythm, to speed things up or slow them down. **Expanding sentences** is the process of extending basic ideas with different types of phrases and clauses. A **loose sentence** provides a base clause followed by explanatory phrases and clauses. A **cumulative sentence** can have modifying details before, after, and in the middle of the base clause.

> **Loose sentence: Julie was studying** at the kitchen table, completely focused, memorizing a list of vocabulary words.

> **Cumulative sentence:** With his hands in his face, **Tony was laughing** half-heartedly, looking puzzled and embarrassed.

There are many ways to expand a main idea or base clause. (See page 69.) **Sentence combining** helps you show relationships and make connections between ideas. It can also make your writing more readable. (See page 70 for ways to combine basic ideas.)

LO3 Check your sentences for style and correctness.

The best sentences are the ones that do not draw undue attention to themselves. They are smooth reading and engaging, effectively carrying the reader along from one main point to the next. If the sentences in your writing seem too predictable or sound too much alike, edit them for **sentence variety**. Use this strategy to check your sentences for variety:

Glossary Terms

editing
refining a draft in terms of word choice and sentence style and checking it for conventions

proofreading
checking a final copy for errors before submitting it

surface changes
the edited (corrected) words, phrases, and sentences in your writing

style
the personal variety, originality, and clarity of your writing

modifiers
words that limit or describe other words or groups of words; adjectives and adverbs

redundancy
words used together that mean nearly the same thing: *repeat again*

jargon
highly technical terms not familiar to the general reader

sentence expanding
extending basic ideas with different types of phrases and clauses

loose sentence
a sentence that provides a base clause near the beginning, followed by explanatory phrases and clauses

cumulative sentence
a sentence that can have modifying phrases and clauses before, after, or in the middle of the base clause

sentence combining
combining ideas in sentences to show relationships and make connections

sentence variety
varying the beginnings, lengths, and types of your sentences

parallelism
repeating phrases or sentence structures to show the relationship between ideas

active voice
a subject-verb construction in which the subject performs the action

passive voice
a subject-verb construction in which the subject is acted upon

nominal constructions
noun forms of verbs such as *description, instructions, confirmation*

specific nouns
nouns, such as *Meryl Streep,* that are clear, exact, and strong

vivid verbs
specific action verbs, such as *lunge,* that help create clear images

cliches
overused words and phrases such as *piece of cake*

biased words
words that unfairly or disrespectfully depict individuals or groups

conventions
the standard rules for spelling, mechanics, usage, and grammar

Sentence Variety Strategy

- In one column on a piece of paper, list the opening words in each of your sentences. Then decide if you need to vary some of your sentence beginnings.
- In another column, identify the number of words in each sentence. Then decide if you need to change the lengths of some of your sentences.
- In a third column, list the kinds of sentences used (exclamatory, declarative, interrogative, and so on). Then, based on your analysis, use the instructions on pages 71–72 to edit your sentences as needed.

Use **parallel structures** to clarify relationships between ideas and/or to give your writing rhythm. In addition, write **active voice** verbs instead of **passive voice** verbs to give your writing energy and forward motion.

- **Active voice verbs:** Children *require* plenty of calories for growth.
- **Passive voice verbs:** A surplus of calories are required for growth in children.

Also avoid sentences that sound sluggish because they start with "it is" or "there is," contain too many negative words (*no, not, neither/nor*), or include too many **nominal constructions**, or noun forms of verbs, such as *discussion, description,* or *confirmation.*

LO4 Avoid imprecise, misleading, and biased words.

The best words are the ones that effectively contribute to the overall meaning, feeling, and sound in a piece of writing. Whenever possible, use **specific nouns** and **vivid verbs**, and avoid using jargon and **cliches**. Also avoid using **biased words**—words that unfairly depict individuals or groups.

Occupational Issues

NOT RECOMMENDED	PREFERRED
chairman	**chair, presiding officer, moderator**
salesman	**sales representative, salesperson**
mailman	**mail carrier, postal worker, letter carrier**
fireman	**firefighter**
businessman	**executive, manager, businessperson**
congressman	**member of Congress, representative, senator**
steward, stewardess	**flight attendant**
policeman, policewoman	**police officer**

LO5 Edit and proofread for conventions.

To complete your editing, check your revised writing for **conventions**. Refer to the guidelines on page 77 to make sure that you don't miss anything. Use these same guidelines to help you proofread your final copy as well. For additional help, refer to the Handbook in this book. (See pages 273–348.)

- Review punctuation and mechanics.
- Look for usage and grammar errors.
- Check for spelling errors.
- Check your writing for form and presentation.

Chapter Summary

Introduction

Publishing makes all of your planning, drafting, and revising for a particular piece worth the effort, and it should help you do your best work. The most immediate, and perhaps the most helpful, form of submitting is sharing a finished piece with your instructor and writing peers. How they react to your writing helps you identify ways to improve your composing skills. You can also submit your writing to various print and online sources, as well as include it in your writing portfolio. Each potential publisher will have specific guidelines to follow for submissions.

LO1 Format your writing.

Make readability your goal when it comes to **page design**. Keep your design clear and uncluttered and follow the designated documentation style: MLA (pages 251-268) or APA (pages 251-271). Use an easy-to-read **serif font** for your main text, but consider a **sans serif font**, like this, for headings and subheadings. Avoid **widows**, **orphans**, and **tombstones** at the bottom or top of each page. And consider using lists or graphics to present information, but use them selectively.

MLA Paper

Hughey 1

Katie Hughey
Professor E. K. Trump
Political Science 350
17 April 2008

An American Hybrid:

The Art Museum as Public–Private Institution

The American art museum suffers from a multiple personality disorder. It is a strange hybrid, both public and private in nature, and beholden to a constituency so varied in its interests that the function of the museum has become increasingly difficult to discern. Much of the confusion surrounding the nature and proper function of the art museum in the United States has to do with the unique form that arts patronage has taken in this country. There is a primary difficulty facing funding of the arts in America—namely, the fact that the benefits of art and art museums are not easily stated in the simple utilitarian terms that justify expenditures on things like roads and a police force. For this reason, cultural patronage has largely been a private venture. The first American museums were born of the private collections of robber barons, organized as not-for-profit corporations, and placed under the control of private boards of trustees. Only subsequently were municipal governments asked to contribute by way of funding construction costs for new buildings and providing maintenance expenses.

The involvement of the government in the funding of art museums raises several questions that serve to highlight the confusing hybrid

APA Paper

Our Roots 3

Our Roots Go Back to Roanoke:
Investigating the Link between the Lost Colony
and the Lumbee People of North Carolina

Introduction: Something Is Terribly Wrong

Consider the following narrative, which features historical information from Kupperman (1984, 1985), Miller (2002), Oberg (1994), and Quinn (1985):

Imagine yourself sailing across the warm waters of the Atlantic. It is a time before airplanes and automobiles, and our nation, which someday will lie just a few miles ahead of you, is still called the "New World." You are on your way to an island off the coast of what will one day be called North Carolina, and you are anxious to see what a small group of colonists has accomplished since their arrival there three years ago. Yes, this is the age of colonization. This is the beginning of a nation.

As you draw closer to land, however, you get a strange feeling that something is terribly wrong. No fires are burning on the island, no greeters waving. Instead, an eerie silence fills the air. At once, you cast your anchor and row ashore, hoping that perhaps you've reached the wrong island by mistake. Surely, this is not the island destined to be the first true settlement in the New World? Surely, this is not Roanoke?

Glossary Terms

publishing
sharing your finished writing with your instructor and peers, and/or sending it out to a print or online publication

page design
the elements (typography, spacing, graphics) that create the look of a paper; readability is the focus of design for academic writing

typography
the size and style of type that is used

serif type
type that has tails at the tops and the bottoms of the letters; works best for text copy

sans serif type
type that does not have tails; may work well for headings and subheadings

widow
a single word or a short line carried over to the top of a page

orphan
a single line of a new paragraph at the bottom of a page

tombstone
a heading or a subheading sitting alone at the bottom of a page

writing portfolio
a collection of your writing

working portfolio
a collection of documents at various stages of development

showcase portfolio
a collection of appropriate finished pieces of writing for evaluation

LO2 Create a writing portfolio.

A **writing portfolio** is a collection of your writing, usually demonstrating your skills as a writer. While a **working portfolio** stores writing in various stages of development, a **showcase portfolio** includes appropriate finished pieces for evaluation. Think of compiling a showcase portfolio as a semester-long project—not something you can do at the last minute. Make sure to follow your instructor's requirements for your portfolio. A showcase portfolio usually contains the following documents:

- A table of contents listing the pieces included in your portfolio
- An opening essay or letter detailing the story behind your portfolio (how and why you compiled these particular pieces)
- A specified number of—and different types of—finished pieces
- A cover sheet attached to each piece of writing, discussing the reason for its selection, the amount of work that went into it, and so on
- Evaluation sheets or checklists charting your writing progress and skills mastery

Submissions and Portfolio Checklist

_____ The publishing method (such as an essay given to an instructor or posted on a Web site) is appropriate for my assignment, program, and career goals.

_____ The publishing process tests and develops my skills as a writer and scholar.

_____ The document's format (e.g., parts, headings, layout, margins, typography, and documentation) conforms to all of the instructor's guidelines.

_____ My portfolio documents address the topics and show the level of research and scholarship expected by my readers.

_____ The voice and style of my portfolio documents are appropriate for the kinds of writing done in the program or job for which I am applying.

_____ The portfolio includes an engaging essay or cover letter that clearly explains the portfolio's design, purpose, and focus.

Chapter Summary

LO1 **Describe a person, place, or thing.**

When you write to describe a person, place, or thing, follow these guidelines:

1. **Select a topic,** focusing on a person, place, or thing that you know well and can describe in numerous ways.
2. **Gather details** using a sensory chart or thought chart, as below.

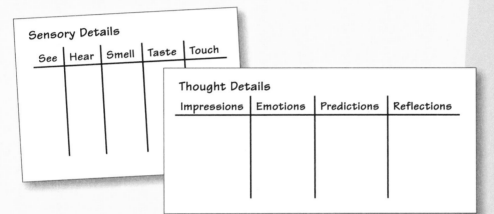

Sensory Details

See	Hear	Smell	Taste	Touch

Thought Details

Impressions	Emotions	Predictions	Reflections

3. **Write your first draft,** with the following parts:
   * **Opening:** Capture your reader's attention and introduce your topic.
   * **Middle:** Develop your description by organizing sensory and thought details using **order of location** or the **camera-eye approach.**
   * **Closing:** Include an especially memorable image and reflect on your topic.
4. **Share your description** with a reader and ask the person for suggestions for revision.
5. **Revise your description,** making sure the writing focuses well on your topic, using sensory and thought details, and organizing them in the best way.
6. **Edit and proofread** your work and **prepare your final copy.**

Description	**Narration**	**Reflection**
Beyond the End of the Road	**Mzee Owitti**	**The Stream in the Ravine**
David Bani describes a journey over rough roads to a remote Mayan village to repair a well and share a film.	Jacqui Nyangi Owitti narrates her journey to an African village to take part in the funeral observances for her grandfather.	Nicole Suurdt reflects on a stream she discovered as a child and uses the stream as a symbol of a vanished past.

Glossary Terms

telepathy
communicating thoughts over distance

tableau
a dramatic scene or setting; a striking picture

sensory details
sights, sounds, smells, tastes, textures, temperatures, and other details connected to the five senses—showing rather than telling about the subject

thought details
impressions, emotions, predictions, and reflections; details that reveal perceptions rather than sensations

camera-eye approach
sharing details as though through a camera lens moving across a subject

order of location
organizing details according to their position; progressing from near to far, inside to outside, and so on

climax
the most exciting moment in a narrative; the moment at which the person succeeds, fails, or learns something

metaphor
a comparison that equates two dissimilar things without using *like* or *as;* saying that one thing is another

dialogue
the words spoken by people and set apart with quotation marks

conflict
the obstacles or adversaries confronted by people in narratives; person vs. person, person vs. society, person vs. the supernatural, person vs. nature, person vs. self, person vs. technology

pivotal points
moments in which an important change occurs; literally, a point at which a person changes direction

chronological order
time order; relating details in the order that they occurred

point of view
the perspective from which the writer approaches the writing, including first-person, second-person, or third-person point of view

L○2 Narrate an event.

When you write to narrate an event, use these quick guidelines:

1. **Select a topic,** focusing on a story that you would like to share with others.
2. **Narrow your focus** by thinking about a specific moment or outcome. Think about the key moment, or climax of the story, what was really going on, and what you learned.
3. **Determine your purpose and audience,** reflecting on why you are telling the story (to entertain, remind, celebrate, warn, and so on).
4. **Gather details,** sorting through photo albums, videos, e-mails, or journal entries or interviewing someone who was there.
5. **Collaborate** by telling someone your story and asking for comments.
6. **Write your first draft** by setting the stage and using dialogue and action to build the plot to a climax. Reflect on what the event meant to you.
7. **Share your story** and get feedback from your listener/reader.
8. **Revise your writing,** making sure your narrative clearly re-creates the event for your reader.
9. **Edit and proofread** your narrative and **prepare your final copy.**

L○3 Reflect on life.

When you create a reflection, use the following quick guidelines:

1. **Select a topic,** thinking of an experience that influenced you in some important way.
2. **Get the big picture** by reviewing photos or videos and talking with someone who shared the experience. Reflect on the meaning of the experience and how it changed you.
3. **Get organized** by creating a brief outline that shows how the key information fits in chronological order.
4. **Write your first draft,** recording the events as guided by your outline and reflecting on the meaning of the events.
5. **Review and revise** your reflection, making sure it says what you want it to say, without gaps or weak spots.
6. **Test your reflection,** considering the voice and point of view.
7. **Get feedback,** asking a classmate to read and respond to the reflection.
8. **Edit and proofread your essay** for style and conventions.
9. **Publish your writing** by sharing it with friends and those involved.

Chapter Summary

Introduction

An analysis looks at a topic from many different perspectives. Basic analyses include extended definitions, classification essays, and process essays.

LO1 Create an extended definition.

When you write an extended definition, follow these quick guidelines:

1. **Select a topic,** focusing on words that are abstract or complex. Also consider adjectives connected to personal experience.
2. **Identify what you know** about the word by freewriting about it.
3. **Gather information** about the word by consulting a general or specialized dictionary, interviewing experts, checking reference works, researching etymology, doing a Web search, and listing synonyms.
4. **Compress what you know,** using this formula: term = general class + specific characteristics.

> **Term = general class + specific characteristics**

5. **Organize the information,** using a definition diagram (see right).
6. **Draft the essay,** creating these three parts:
   - **Opening:** Get the reader's attention and introduce the term.
   - **Middle:** Show your reader precisely what the word does or does not mean, extending the definition with etymology, connotation, current usage, and so on.
   - **Closing:** Review your main point and close your essay.
7. **Get feedback** from a classmate or someone in your college's writing center.
8. **Revise and edit the essay,** using the feedback to make major improvements, refine style, and correct conventions.
9. **Publish the essay,** sharing it with friends, family, and classmates.

Glossary Terms

denotation
the dictionary definition of a word; a word's literal meaning

connotation
the suggestion made by a word; a word's implied meaning

taxonomy
a system of classification of items—plants, animals, ideas, movements, and so on

extended definition
a type of analytical writing that explores the meaning of a specific term, providing denotation, connotation, and a variety of perspectives on the term

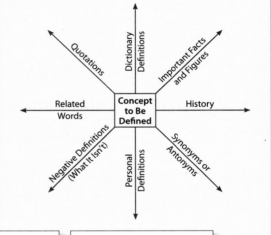

Economic Disparities Fuel Human Trafficking

Shon Bogar defines the term "human trafficking" as the illegal movement of humans across national boundaries by use of force, coercion, fraud, or deception and for the purpose of exploitation.

Four Ways to Talk About Literature

John Van Rys discusses four approaches to literary analysis—text centered, audience centered, author centered, and ideological.

Wayward Cells

Kerri Mertz writes about the process of cancer's formation and spread, comparing it to breakdown in a factory.

Downloading Photographs from the MC-150 Digital Camera

This set of instructions provides step-by-step guidance for downloading photos.

	Classification criteria	Details of each approach
Subgroup 1	Text-centered approach	Trait 1 Trait 2 Trait 3
Subgroup 2	Audience-centered approach	Trait 1 Trait 2 Trait 3
Subgroup 3	Author-centered approach	Trait 1 Trait 2 Trait 3
Subgroup 4	Ideas outside literature	Trait 1 Trait 2 Trait 3

Revising and Editing Checklist

The writing has . . .

____ Subgroups that are consistent, exclusive, and complete

____ Organization that helps the reader understand the subject

____ Appropriate examples that clarify the nature and function of each subgroup

____ A unifying conclusion

____ An informed, reader-friendly voice

____ Clear, complete sentences

____ Unified paragraphs linked with appropriate transitions

____ Correct usage, grammar, punctuation, and spelling

Editing Checklist

____ Word choice appropriate for your least-informed reader

____ Clear transitions between steps

____ Consistent verb tense in all steps

____ For *instructions*—verbs that give clear commands (imperative mood)

____ Correct, consistent terminology

____ Informed, respectful voice

____ Proper format (particularly for *instructions*—adequate white space)

L○2 Write a classification essay.

When you create a classification essay, follow these quick guidelines:

1. **Select a topic** by writing five or six general subject areas and recording specific topics next to each.
2. **Look at the big picture** by researching your topic and reviewing your purpose. Then divide the subject into distinct, understandable subgroups.
3. **Choose and test your criteria,** making sure subgroups are consistent, exclusive, and complete.
4. **Gather and organize information,** using a classification grid (see left).
5. **Draft a working thesis** that states your topic and main point.
6. **Draft the essay,** creating the following parts:
   - **Opening:** Get your reader's attention and present your thesis.
   - **Middle:** Develop the thesis by discussing each subgroup, explaining its traits, and showing how it is distinct.
   - **Closing:** Bring the components and subgroups back together.
7. **Get feedback** from a classmate or someone from the writing center.
8. **Revise and edit** your draft, using the checklist on the left, and publish it.

L○3 Explain a process.

When you write to explain a process, follow these quick guidelines:

1. **Select a topic,** considering processes that have multiple steps carried out over time.
2. **Review the process,** filling out a process organizer (see right).
3. **Research to find information** about the process and the steps required.
4. **Organize the information** in chronological order.
5. **Draft the document,** creating an opening, a middle, and a closing that match the type of classification you are doing:
   - **Describing a process:** Introduce the process and thesis, describe the step-by-step progression, and sum up the process.
   - **Writing instructions:** Name the process, present each step separately, number it, and explain any follow-up.
   - **Explaining a process:** Introduce the topic, explain how to do each step, and explain any follow-up.
6. **Revise the writing and test it** to make sure it is clear and complete.
7. **Get feedback** from a classmate or someone in the writing center.
8. **Edit your draft** using the checklist to the left and publish the essay.

Process Organizer

Subject
- Step 1
- Step 2
- Step 3

Outcome

Chapter Summary

LO1 Understand special strategies.

Cause-effect and **comparison-contrast** papers provide special analyses of their subjects.

LO2 Create a cause-effect essay.

The goal of a cause-effect essay is to analyze and explain the causes, effects, or both the causes and the effects of some phenomenon (fact, occurrence, or circumstance.)

Guidelines

1. **Select a topic.** Choose a topic and prove its causes, its effects, or both.
2. **Narrow and research the topic.** Brainstorm a list of related causes and effects in two columns. Next, do preliminary research to expand the list and distinguish primary causes and effects from secondary ones.
3. **Draft and test your thesis.** Draft a working thesis that introduces the topic, along with the causes and/or effects you intend to discuss.
4. **Gather and analyze information.** Research your topic, looking for clear evidence that links specific causes to specific effects.
5. **Get organized.** Develop an outline that lays out your thesis and argument in a clear pattern. Under each main point asserting a cause-effect connection, list details from your research that support the connection.
6. **Use your outline to draft the essay.** Show how each specific cause leads to each specific effect, citing examples as needed.
7. **Revise the essay.** Check especially the organization of your material, using the checklist in *COMP: Write*.
8. **Get feedback.** Ask a peer or someone from your college's writing center to read your essay.
9. **Edit the essay for clarity and correctness.** Check for the following: precise, appropriate word choice; complete, smooth sentences; clear transitions between paragraphs; correct names, dates, and supporting details; correct mechanics, usage, and grammar.
10. **Publish your essay.** Share your writing with others.

Cause-Effect Essay

Adrenaline Junkies

Student Sarah Hanley uses both research and her military experience to identify the causes and effects of adrenaline highs.

Comparison-Contrast Essays

Beyond Control

Janae Sebranek compares the fate of two tragic literary characters, Bigger in *Native Son* and Alan in *Equus*.

Two Views of the River

Author Mark Twain contrasts his mindset as an apprentice with his perspective as a steamboat pilot on the Mississippi River.

Glossary Terms

cause-effect analysis
a paper that examines the conditions or actions that lead to specific outcomes

comparison-contrast analysis
a paper that shows the similarities and differences between two topics

L◯2 Write a comparison-contrast essay.

The goal of writing a comparison-contrast essay is to set two or more subjects side by side, show the reader how they are similar and/or different, and draw conclusions or make some point based on what you have shown.

Guidelines

1. **Select a topic.** Choose two subjects whose comparison and/or contrast gives the reader some insight into who or what they are.
2. **Get the big picture.** Using a computer or a paper and pen, create three columns as show below. Brainstorm a list of traits under each heading.
   Subject 1 Traits   *Shared Traits*   *Subject 2 Traits*
3. **Gather information.** Research the subjects, using hands-on analysis when possible.
4. **Draft a working thesis.** Write a sentence stating the core of what you learned about the subjects and whether you are comparing, contrasting, or both.
5. **Get organized.** Decide how to organize your essay—subject by subject or trait by trait.
6. **Draft the essay.**
   - **Subject by subject.** *Opening*—get readers' attention and introduce the subject and thesis. *Middle*—describe one subject completely before describing the other; organize traits in a parallel way. *Conclusion*—point out similarities and differences, note their significance, and restate your main point
   - **Trait by trait** *Opening*—get readers' attention and introduce the subjects and thesis. *Middle*—compare and/or contrast one trait for both subjects before moving on to the next trait, and so on. *Conclusion*—summarize the key relationships, note their significance, and restate your main point.
7. **Revise the essay.** Check the essay for the ideas, organization, and voice.
8. **Get feedback.** Ask for feedback from a peer or writing tutor.
9. **Edit your essay.** Correct spelling, punctuation, usage, and grammar errors. Also, pay attention to transitions and correct quotations.
10. **Publish your essay.** Share your writing with others.

Reports

Chapter Summary

LO1 Understand report writing.

An interview report describes, clarifies, and relays the **interviewee's** ideas, experiences, and personality. Lab, experiment, and field reports share new discoveries and findings about important subjects.

LO2 Write an interview report.

The goal of an interview report is to gain insights by interviewing someone and then sharing the revelations you discover with readers.

Guidelines:

1. **Choose a person to interview.** Choose from the expert (an authority on your topic), the experienced (a person who has had unique, direct experiences with your topic), or the unique (when your purpose is to focus on a person rather than a topic).

2. **Plan the interview.** Determine your **goal**. Choose a **recording method** and a **medium**. Then do some research on the interview subject. After this, contact the subject and politely request an interview. Schedule a time and place convenient for the interviewee. Gather and test the **tools and equipment** you will use.

3. **Prepare questions.** See the "Interview Questions Checklist" below.

4. **Conduct the interview.** (1) Arrive on time. (2) Introduce yourself. (3) With permission, set up interview equipment. (4) Take notes on key facts and quotations. (5) Be flexible and **tactful**. (6) Give the interviewee a chance to add any final thoughts.

5. **Follow up.** Review your notes and fill in blanks. By phone or in writing, clarify points and thank the interviewee.

6. **Organize and draft the report.** Begin your report with background and a point that grabs the reader's interest. Summarize and paraphrase material from the interview. Use quotations selectively to give insight or stress a point. If appropriate, you may weave your thoughts and reflections into the report.

7. **Get feedback and revise the report.** Ask someone to read over your report.

8. **Edit and proofread.** Review your report for precise word choice, smooth sentences, and correct grammar.

9. **Prepare a final copy.** Submit a clean copy to your instructor, but also look for ways to publish your report.

Glossary Terms

interviewee
the person who is the focus of the interview and answers the interviewer's questions

closed questions
questions that can be answered with a simple fact or with a *yes* or a *no*

open-ended questions
questions that require elaborate answers

slanted questions
questions that presuppose a specific answer

rapport
personal connection, trust, and teamwork

body language
the physical cues that indicate a person's level of comfort, interest, engagement, and so forth

tactful
being sensitive to the feelings of others; avoiding unnecessary offense

Interview Questions Checklist

5 W's + H

_____ Consider using some or all of the journalistic questions (*who, what, when, where, why,* and *how*).

Dynamics

_____ Understand the difference between open and closed questions.

Cautions

_____ Avoid slanted questions.

Focus

_____ Think about specific topics to cover and write questions for each one. Start with a simple question. Then ask targeted questions—ones that you must ask to get the information you need.

Preparedness

_____ Rehearse your questions, visualizing how the interview should go.

The Dead Business

In this interview report, student writer Benjamin Meyer tours a funeral home and interviews the director.

Working with Hydrochloric Acid

In this lab report, Cody Williams describes a chemical compound and informs readers about its nature.

The Effects of Temperature and Inhibitors on the Fermentation Process for Ethanol

In this lab report, student writer Andrea Pizano shares the results of an experiment she completed to explore how different factors affect fermentation.

Sommerville Development Corporation

In this field report, a team of writers investigates the causes and effects of cockroach infestation in an apartment complex.

LO3 Write a lab, experiment, or field report.

Your goal is to accurately record and thoughtfully interpret the results of a scientific study or experiment.

Guidelines:

1. **Review the assignment.** Begin by reviewing the lab manual and any handouts. Read background information on the topic in textbooks and other sources.

2. **Establish a field or lab notebook.** Use the notebook to plan research, record what you do, collect data, make drawings, and reflect on results.

3. **Plan and complete your study or experiment.** Develop key research questions. State your hypotheses and design procedures for testing them. Gather tools, and conduct the test.

4. **Draft the report.**
   - *Methods:* Start by explaining what you did to study your topic or test the hypothesis. Supply essential details, factors, and explanations.
   - *Results:* Share your data in a graphical form. Then draw attention to the major observations and key trends available in the data.
   - *Discussion:* Interpret the results by relating the data to your original questions and hypotheses, offering conclusions and supporting each conclusion with details.
   - *Introduction:* Explain why you undertook the study, provide background information and any needed definitions, and raise your key questions and/or hypotheses.
   - *Summary or abstract:* An abstract is a one-paragraph summary that allows the reader to (1) get the report in a nutshell and (2) determine whether or not to read the study.
   - *Title:* Develop a precise title that captures the "story" of your study.
   - *Front and end matter:* If so required, add a title page, a reference page, and appendixes.

5. **Share and revise the draft.**

6. **Edit and proofread.** Check for the conventions of science writing (measured use of the passive voice, past and present tenses of verbs, objectivity, mechanics).

7. **Prepare and share your report.** Submit a polished report to your instructor.

Chapter Summary

LO1 Understand an argument.

An **argument** consists of at least one claim and the support for it. One way to understand an argument is to employ the SQ3R strategy when reading it:

Survey: Think about who the author is and what the subject, purpose, and audience are.

Question: Ask yourself, What is the main argument? What supports this argument?

Read: Read carefully and look for answers to the questions.

Recite: Summarize the main point and supports.

Review: Reread as needed to clarify your thinking.

> ### Uncle Sam and Aunt Samantha
>
> Anna Quindlen argues that the responsibility of military service should fall equally on the shoulders of men and women.

LO2 Recognize an argument's organization.

Some arguments are organized using **inductive reasoning,** working from particular details toward a general conclusion. Other arguments use **deductive reasoning,** starting with a general principal and following it with the specific supports and examples.

Arguments also follow two main patterns: the first focuses on the main argument before addressing any counterarguments; the second treats each argument and corresponding counterargument point-by-point throughout the process.

LO3 Understand what makes a strong claim.

The **main claim** of an argument should be a debatable statement, not a fact (which can be checked) or an **opinion** (a personal belief). An **extreme claim** is hard to support because it leaves no room for exceptions and is easy to attack. Qualifiers help limit claims and make them easier to support.

LO4 Identify claims of truth, value, and policy.

There are three basic types of claims:

- **Claims of truth** state that something is or is not the case.
- **Claims of value** state that something does or does not have worth.
- **Claims of policy** state that something should or shouldn't be done.

LO5 Assess the quality of the support.

A strong claim needs equally strong support, which can come in various forms:

- **Observations and anecdotes** share what people have experienced.
- **Statistics** offer concrete numbers about a topic.
- **Tests and experiments** provide hard data developed scientifically.
- **Graphics** provide information in visual form.
- **Analogies** compare two things, creating clarity.

Glossary Terms

argumentative essay
writing that presents an argument about a timely, debatable topic

argument
a course of logical thinking intended to convince the reader to accept an idea or to take action

inductive reasoning
reasoning that works from the particular details toward general conclusions

deductive reasoning
reasoning that works from general principles or ideas; through specific applications, support, and/or examples; to a conclusion

main claim
a debatable statement, the thesis or key point in an argument

facts
statements that can be checked for accuracy

opinions
personally held attitudes or beliefs

extreme claims
claims that include words *(all, best, never, worst)* that are overly positive or negative

qualifiers
words or phrases that limit or restrict a claim, making it more reasonable

authoritative
backed by research and expert analysis

concessions
recognizing valid arguments on the other side

rebuttal
a tactful argument aimed at weakening the opposing point of view

redirect
restate the main claim or argument

- **Expert testimony** offers insights from an authority on the topic.
- **Illustrations, examples, and demonstrations** provide specific instances.
- **Analyses** examine parts of a topic, breaking them down, comparing, contrasting, classifying, and so on.
- **Predictions** offer insights into possible outcomes or consequences.

When thinking through an argument, consider warrants—the unspoken thinking used to build the argument.

LO6 Recognize logical fallacies.

Logical fallacies are shortcuts in thinking that weaken arguments. There are five main ways that fallacies arise:

- **Distorting the Issue:** These fallacies unfairly represent the situation (e.g., bare assertion, begging the question, oversimplification, either/or thinking, complex question, straw man).
- **Sabotaging the Argument:** These fallacies unfairly disrupt the discussion (e.g., red herring, misuse of humor, appeal to pity, use of threats, bandwagon mentality, appeal to popular sentiment).
- **Drawing Faulty Conclusions from the Evidence:** These fallacies make unfair assumptions (e.g., appeal to ignorance, hasty or broad generalization, false cause, slippery slope).
- **Misusing Evidence:** These fallacies unfairly deal with the facts of the issue (e.g., impressing with numbers, half-truths, unreliable testimonial, attack against the person, hypothesis contrary to fact, false analogy).
- **Misusing Language:** These fallacies create confusion through language abuse (e.g., obfuscation, ambiguity, slanted language).

LO7 Learn about additional strategies.

The following strategies help writers create strong arguments.

- **Making concessions** means acknowledging the limits of one's own argument and recognizing some value in a counterargument.
- **Offering rebuttals** means pointing out weaknesses in a counterargument.
- **Redirecting claims** means restating the main argument after concessions and rebuttals.
- **Making appeals** means demonstrating credibility, using sound logic, and addressing the reader's needs.

Chapter Summary

LO1 Understand persuasion.

When you write to persuade, your writing must appeal to your reader's interests, wants, or needs. Do so by identifying the topic and purpose, and then presenting your support in a way that appeals to your reader.

LO2 Take a position.

The goal of position papers is to take a stand on a controversial issue. Aim to explain what you believe and why you believe it.

Guidelines for position papers:

1. **Select a topic.** Through reading, viewing, or surfing the Internet, explore current issues that reasonable people disagree upon.
2. **Take stock.** What is your current position on the topic? Why? What evidence do you have?
3. **Get inside the issue.** (1) Investigate all possible positions on the issue. (2) Consider doing firsthand research that will help you speak with authority and passion. (3) Develop a line of reasoning supporting your position.
4. **Refine your position.** Before you organize and draft your essay, clarify your position. If it helps, use this formula: *I believe this to be true about _____.*
5. **Organize your development and support.** Consider these organizational patterns: traditional pattern, blatant confession, delayed gratification, changed mind, and winning over.
6. **Write your first draft.** *Opening:* Seize the reader's imagination. Supply background information. *Development:* Support your position statement, using solid logic and reliable support. *Closing:* End on a lively, thoughtful note that stresses your commitment to the issue.
7. **Share your position.** Ask a peer to read your position and give you feedback.
8. **Revise your writing.** Consider your reviewer's comments and review the draft yourself.
9. **Edit and proofread.** Check especially that your writing is free of slogans, cliches, platitudes, insults, and jargon.
10. **Prepare and publish your final essay.** Submit your essay for publication.

LO3 Persuade readers to act.

The goal of a persuasive essay is to urge individual readers to change their behavior or to take action on an issue.

Guidelines for persuasive essays:

1. **Select a topic.** List issues about which you feel passionately, issues in which you see a need for change.
2. **Choose and analyze your audience.** Think about who your readers are.
3. **Narrow your focus and determine your purpose.** Consider what you can achieve within the assignment's constraints.

Glossary Terms

controversies
issues about which there are two or more strongly opposed sides; highly debatable issues

defensible position
a claim that is debatable but can be strongly supported by evidence; a claim that is neither a fact nor an unsupportable opinion

refute
prove false, illogical, or undesirable

cliches
overused words and phrases such as *piece of cake*

debatable topic
a topic that is not a mere fact but can be argued from at least two different angles

tone
the overall feeling or effect created by a writer's thoughts and use of words

jargon
highly technical terms not familiar to the general reader

feasible
doable; reasonable—given time, budgets, resources, and consequences

Persuading Readers to Act Outline

Introduction: claim
- Support: point 1
- Support: point 2
- Support: point 3

Conclusion: call to action

4. **Generate ideas and support.** Consider opposing viewpoints.

5. **Organize your thinking.** Consider the "Persuading Readers to Act Outline" to the left.

6. **Write your first draft.** *Opening:* Gain the readers' attention, raise the issue, help the readers care about it, and state your claim. *Development:* Decide where to play your most persuasive supporting arguments. Anticipate readers' questions. *Closing:* Consider restating your claim, summarizing your support, or encouraging your readers to take action.

7. **Share your essay.** Try out your thinking and persuasive appeals with a reader.

8. **Revise your writing.** Think about your reviewer's comments, and then revise your essay.

9. **Edit and proofread.** Avoid cliches and **jargon**.

10. **Prepare and publish your final essay.** Submit your essay for publication.

An Apology for the Life of Ms. Barbie D. Doll

In this position paper, Rita Isakson argues that Barbie is being scapegoated for complex social problems facing girls.

To Drill or Not to Drill

In this persuasive essay, Rebecca Pasok persuades readers to support lifestyle choices and energy policies that do not require drilling.

Preparing for Agroterror

In this problem-solution essay, Brian Ley defines agroterrorism, predicts that it could become a serious problem, and proposes a multifaceted solution.

L○4 Propose a solution.

The goal of a problem-solution essay is to argue for a positive change, convincing readers to accept and contribute to that change.

Guidelines for problem-solution essays:

1. **Select and narrow a topic.**

2. **Identify and analyze your audience.** You could have three audiences: decision makers, people affected by the problem, and a public that needs to learn about the problem and get behind a solution.

3. **Probe the problem.** (1) Define the problem; (2) determine the problem's seriousness; (3) analyze causes; (4) explore context; and (5) think creatively.

4. **Brainstorm possible solutions.** List all imaginable solutions—both modest and radical fixes. Then evaluate the alternatives.

5. **Choose the best solution and map out support.** State a workable plan that attacks causes and treats effects. Then identify support for your solution.

6. **Outline your proposal and complete a first draft.** A proposal's structure is quite simple: Describe the problem, offer a solution, and defend the solution.

7. **Get feedback and revise the draft.** Share your draft with a peer or tutor.

8. **Edit and proofread.** Check for accurate word choice; smooth, energetic sentences; and correct grammar, spelling, and format.

9. **Prepare and share your final essay.** Submit your essay for publication.

Chapter Summary

LO1 Understand the arts.

The arts include forms of aesthetic expression such as literature, poetry, music, dance, painting, sculpture, architecture, and film. Art always reflects and sometimes embodies the time and place of its creation.

LO2 Write about the arts.

Follow the guidelines below to write an analysis of an artwork.

1. **Select a topic.** Choose a poem, short story, novel, painting, film, concert, play, or other art form to analyze.
2. **Understand the work.** Experience the artwork thoughtfully, looking carefully at content, form, and overall effect.
3. **Gather information.** Take careful notes, annotate copies of texts, and freewrite to explore your response.
4. **Organize your thoughts.** Review your notes, form a thesis, and use an outline to organize support.
5. **Write the first draft.** Create a strong opening that grabs the reader's attention, introduces the artwork, and states your thesis. Develop a middle that analyzes the artwork and provides support for your thesis. Create a conclusion that ties up the analysis.
6. **Review and revise.** Reread your analysis, making sure the thesis and support are strong, that you thoroughly understand the art, and that you have analyzed formal aspects of it.
7. **Get feedback.** Have a classmate or someone from the writing center respond to your essay.
8. **Edit and proofread.** Check to correct punctuation, capitalization, spelling, and grammar.
9. **Publish your essay.**

LO3 Understand literary terms.

Consult the terms listed on the front and back of this card.

Literary Terms

allusion
reference to a person, a place, or an event in history or literature

analogy
comparison of two or more similar objects, suggesting parallels

anecdote
short summary of an interesting or humorous incident or event

antagonist
person or thing actively working against the protagonist

climax
the turning point; an intense moment characterized by a key event

conflict
the problem or struggle in a story, triggering the action

denouement
the outcome of a play or story

diction
an author's choice of words based on correctness or effectiveness

exposition
the introductory section of a story or play

falling action
the action that follows the climax of a play or story

figure of speech
a literary device used to create a special effect

"Good Country People": Broken Body, Broken Soul

Anya Terekhina analyzes Flannery O'Connor's short story, "Good Country People," showing how Hulga's physical impairments symbolize her character flaws, and how Manley exploits both.

"Let Evening Come": An Invitation to the Inevitable

Sherry Van Edgom analyzes Jane Kenyon's poem "Let Evening Come," showing how Kenyon depicts death through the symbol of evening settling across a farm.

Terror on the Silver Screen: Who Are the Aliens?

David Schaap analyzes Stephen Spielberg's film *War of the Worlds,* arguing that though the imagery evokes 9/11, the aliens aren't terrorists but "Spielberg's universal stand-in for whatever strikes fear into viewers' hearts."

Sigur Ros, *Agaetis Byrjun*

Annie Moore reviews a performance of an experimental Icelandic rock band, comparing the music to a gathering and bursting storm and predicting that the band would change the world of music.

genre
a category or type of literature

imagery
words used to appeal to the senses

irony
a deliberate discrepancy in meaning or in the way something is understood

mood
the feeling that a piece of literature arouses in the reader

paradox
a statement that seems contradictory but may be true

plot
the action or sequence of events in a story

point of view
the vantage point from which the story unfolds

protagonist
the main character or hero of the story

resolution
the portion of the play in which the problem is solved

rising action
the series of conflicts that builds toward the climax

satire
literary tone used to ridicule human vice or weakness

setting
time and place in which the action of a literary work occurs

structure
the organization a writer uses for a work

style
how the author uses words, phrases, and sentences

symbol
one thing used to represent another

theme
a work's statement about life

tone
the overall feeling or effect created by a writer's use of words

LO4 Understand poetic terms.

Learn and use the poetic terms listed below.

alliteration
the repetition of initial consonant sounds

assonance
the repetition of vowel sounds

blank verse
a poem with meter but without rhyme

consonance
the repetition of consonant sounds

foot
the smallest repeated pattern of stressed and unstressed syllables

onomatopoeia
use of words that sound like their meaning

refrain
the repetition of a line or phrase at intervals

rhythm
the ordered or free occurrences of sound in poetry

stanza
a division of poetry named for the number of lines it contains

verse
a metric line of poetry

Chapter Summary

LO1 Create correspondence.

The goal of correspondence is to effectively and appropriately communicate an idea, whether via text message, e-mail, memo, blog, or letter. When corresponding in the workplace, follow these steps:

1. **Understand the writing situation**—subject, purpose, and audience.
2. **Select an appropriate form.** Consider the **continuum of communication** and choose the form that best fits the writing situation.
3. **Write your main point.** In one or two sentences, write the main thing you want your reader to know.
4. **Gather details.** For more formal and complex messages, gather details that support your main point.
5. **Write a first draft.** Organize your details based on the reader's likely response. Use different approaches for different messages: good/neutral news *(state main point and provide supporting details),* bad news *(provide buffer statement),* and persuasion *(hook reader and build interest before making main point).*
6. **Revise and edit your writing.**

E-mails and memos are two main forms of workplace communication.

- **Effective e-mail creation.** Stick to the facts; provide a clear subject line; select readers carefully; use short paragraphs and lists; carefully revise and edit your message before clicking "send"; err on the side of caution; provide appropriate attachments.
- **Effective memo creation.** Use memos when e-mail won't serve; use clear organization.

LO2 Correctly format a letter.

Formal business letters follow a precise format that includes the following features:

1. **Heading** gives the writer's complete address, either in letterhead or typed out, followed by the date.
2. **Inside address** gives the reader's name and address.
3. **Salutation** begins with Dear and ends with a colon, not a comma.
4. **Body** consists of singled-spaced paragraphs with double-spacing between paragraphs.
5. **Complimentary closing** uses *Sincerely, Yours sincerely,* or *Yours truly* followed by a comma; uses *Best wishes* if you know the person well.
6. **Signature** includes the writer's name both handwritten and keyed.
7. **Initials** when someone keys the letter for the writer, that person's initials appear (in lowercase) after the writer's (in capitals) and a colon.
8. **Enclosure** if a document (brochure, form, copy) is enclosed with the letter, the word *Enclosure* or *Encl.* appears below the initials.
9. **Copies** if a copy of the letter is sent elsewhere, type *cc:* beneath the enclosure line, followed by the person's or department's name.

Glossary Terms

"La Marseillaise"
the song of Marseille; the national anthem of France

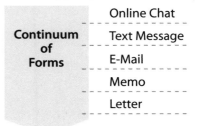

Continuum of Communication

Informal (Quick)

Continuum of Forms

- Online Chat
- Text Message
- E-Mail
- Memo
- Letter

Formal (Deliberate)

continuum of communication
a list of written communication options from informal to formal

inside address
the reader's name and address

salutation
the greeting in a letter; the line that begins *Dear*

complimentary closing
the polite sign-off line of a letter, following the body and preceding the signature

application essay

a reflective essay that focuses on experiences and qualities that suit the writer for a specific position or program

résumé

a document that outlines a person's job objective, skills, experience, and education; a curriculum vitae (cv)

RTF

rich text file; a file format that preserves basic formatting such as bolds, italics, and tabs but is readable by most word processors

PDF

portable document file; a file format that preserves a document according to its exact appearance and is readable using Adobe Reader software

Application Essay: *Gathering details*

- What **topic** should the essay focus on?
- What **position** are you applying for?
- What **qualities** would an ideal candidate have?
- What **qualities** do you have?
- What is your **education**?
- What **experience** do you have?
- What **special skills** do you have?
- What **factor** sets you apart from other applicants?

LO3 Write an application essay.

The goal of an application essay is to convince the reader to accept your application. Follow these guidelines:

1. **Analyze the situation.** Read any instructions about writing the essay. Then think about the subject, purpose, and audience.
2. **Gather details.** See "Application Essay" feature below.
3. **Write your first draft.**
   - An **opening** with a fresh, interesting starting statement, and a clear focus or theme.
   - A **middle** that develops the focus or theme clearly and concisely—with some details and examples—in a way appropriate to the instructions.
   - A **closing** that stresses a positive point and looks forward to participating in the program, internship, organization, or position.
4. **Revise your essay.** Pay special attention to the ideas, organization, voice, and word choice.
5. **Edit and submit your essay.** Check the essay for errors in punctuation, capitalization, spelling, and grammar.

LO4 Prepare a résumé.

The goal of a **résumé** is to present a vivid word picture of your skills, knowledge, and past responsibilities. Follow these guidelines:

1. **Consider the writing situation.** What job is it? What company or organization is it? Who will read the résumé? What qualities are needed for the position? What qualities do you have?
2. **Gather details.** Summarize skills that you have that relate to the job you are applying for.
3. **Create a first draft.** Include the following information:
   - *Personal data:* name, address, phone number, e-mail address
   - *Job objective:* the type of position you want and the type of organization for which you want to work
   - *Skills summary:* the key qualities and skills you bring to a position, listed with supporting details
   - *Experience:* positions you've held, and your specific duties and your accomplishments
   - *Education:* degrees, courses, and special projects
   - *Other experiences:* volunteer work, awards, achievements, tutoring jobs, extra-curricular activities, licenses, and certifications
4. **Revise your first draft.** Pay special attention to the ideas, organization, voice, and word choice.
5. **Edit and submit your résumé.** Edit for any factual errors as well as errors in punctuation, capitalization, spelling, and grammar.

Electronic Résumés

For a résumé pasted into a job search engine, remove special coding and feature search terms drawn from the job announcement.

Chapter Summary

LO1 Understand page elements.

Web pages use the same elements as printed pages, but, unlike printed pages, Web pages are fluid, and they can include both elements and functions.

The basic page elements found on a Web page include headings, body text, preformatted text, lists, images, background, and tables.

Web-page functions set electronic pages apart from printed pages, because readers can interact with Web pages. Web-page functions include **hyperlinks**, **menus**, and **forms**.

Tips for Web design

- **Simple is best.** Simple pages display quickly and have the least chance of breaking.
- **Different computers display things differently.** Not every computer has the same font styles installed, and colors look different on different monitors. Always check your work on many different systems.
- **The user is king (or queen).** No matter which font style and size you choose, the reader can change how things are displayed on her or his screen. Focus on useful content and clear organization rather than elaborate design.

LO2 Develop a Web site.

When developing a Web site, follow these guidelines:

1. **Get focused.** Create an overview of the project—the subject, the purpose, and the audience. What is the site's central subject? What is the primary purpose of the site? Who is the site's audience?
2. **Establish your central message.** Develop a mission statement for your Web site.
3. **Create a site map.** A map for a simple site might include only four items—a home page, page "A," page "B," and page "C." Here are four principles to keep in mind: (1) No one will read your entire site. (2) Your site will have many small audiences. (3) Web sites are not linear. (4) You may need to build the site in phases.
4. **Study similar sites.** Check out different sites for ideas, *organization, voice, words, sentences, correctness,* and *design.*
5. **Gather and prioritize content.** Brainstorm and research the actual content, with the goal of creating an outline for your site.
6. **Think about support materials.** List the documents (brochures, artworks, instructions, poems, reports) that will be presented on your site.
   Note: Steps 7 and 8 are on the reverse side of the review card.
7. **Design and develop pages.** Consider design principles such as grids, balance, and page variety. Also consider these drafting principles:
   - Identify the site. Write a brief introduction informing visitors about the site's purpose.
   - Provide clear links. Create links for your pages, using clear descriptors.
   - Introduce each page. Give each page a brief introduction that clearly identifies it.
   - Title each page. Give each page a descriptive title.

Glossary Terms

hyperlinks
specially formatted text that enables readers to click to another spot on the Web

menus
structured lists of links that operate like a Web site's table of contents

forms
questionnaires, surveys, suggestion boxes, and other features that allow visitors to Web sites to interact with the host

OWLs
online writing labs where you can get answers to your writing problems

MUDs
multi-user dimension; text-based "worlds" that people can share

blogs
online journals (short for "Weblog")

- Keep pages uncluttered. Use short paragraphs, separated by headings and visuals.
- Save the page as HTML. To be viewed in a Web browser, your pages must be formatted in Hypertext Markup Language (HTML).

8. **Test, refine, and post your site.**
   - Check the site yourself. Does the site make sense? Is it easily navigated?
   - Get peer review. Ask an outsider to review your site for usability.
   - Check the text. Trim wherever possible; check spelling and punctuation.
   - Check the graphics. Do images load properly? Do they load quickly?
   - Provide a feedback link. Provide an e-mail address.
   - Post the site. Upload the site to your hosting site.
   - Check for universality. View the site on several different types of computers, using different browsers.
   - Announce the site. Advertise your site in e-mails. Submit it to search sites.
   - Monitor the site. Pay attention to traffic, feedback from users, and any use of resources or services.
   - Make adjustments and updates. Update site with fresh content regularly.

L◯3 Consider sample sites.

Study other student and academic Web sites for insights about what makes for strong Web content and design.

L◯4 Understand other writing venues.

Consider other writing opportunities available on the Internet, such as those listed below.

- **OWLs**
- **MUDs**
- Message boards
- Mailing lists
- Chat servers
- **Blogs** (Weblogs)
- Instant messaging (IM)

Chapter Summary

Introduction

Exam-panic dreams are a common experience for those in college. They are unpleasant, but they reflect your desire to succeed on exams and other challenges, as well as your concern about being prepared. This chapter helps you prepare.

LO1 Prepare for exams.

Proper preparation is the key to doing well on exams. Reviewing material while it is still fresh in your mind can move it from short-term to long-term memory. Also, spending about one hour per week reviewing material can pay dividends when exam time comes.

A **study group** can keep you interested in a subject, impel you to keep up with class work, and increase your retention of important material. Here are some tips for creating a study group:

- **Ask five to six people,** especially motivated, collaborative ones.
- **Consider a chat room,** whether hosted through your school or through Yahoo, Google, or a similar service.
- **Arrange a time and place** for a first session and designate someone to keep the group on task.
- **Set realistic goals** that everyone can agree on, including polite use of people skills.
- **Evaluate after the first session** and set up another session for anyone who wants to continue meeting.

Mnemonics and other memory aids can help you remember material:

- **Acronyms** use the first letter in each word of a sentence to form a new word.
- **Acrostics** form a phrase or silly sentence in which the first letter of each word helps you remember the items in a series.
- **Categories** organize information for easier recall.
- **Peg words** create a chain of associations with objects in a room, a sequence of events, or a familiar pattern.
- **Rhymes** help connect ideas.

LO2 Respond to essay questions.

When planning and writing a response to a specific question, you're working against the clock, so use your time wisely. For example, if you have 45 minutes, reserve the first 5 to 10 minutes for planning, Then use the next 30 minutes for the actual writing, and use the final 5 minutes to review your response.

Follow these guidelines:

1. **Reread the question several times,** watching for key words.
2. **Rephrase the question** into a thesis statement (or topic sentence) with a clear point.
3. **Outline the main points** you plan to cover in your answer.
4. **Write your essay (or paragraph),** including your thesis statement (or topic sentence) and following your outline.
5. **Review your response** for missing information, wrong words, confusing phrases, errors in spelling and punctuation, and so on.

Glossary Terms

study group
a group of classmates working together to understand course material

mnemonics
memory techniques in which you associate new ideas with more recognizable or memorable words, images, or ideas

Key Words

analyze
to break down a larger problem or situation into separate parts or relationships

classify
to place persons or things together in a group because they share similar characteristics

compare
to use examples to show how things are similar and different, placing the greater emphasis on similarities

contrast
to use examples to show how things are different

compare and contrast
to use examples that show the similarities and differences between two things

define
to give the meaning for a term

describe
to give a detailed sketch or impression of a topic

diagram
to explain with lines or pictures

discuss
to review an issue from all sides

evaluate
to make a value judgment by giving the pluses and minuses

explain
to make clear through analysis

justify
to tell why a position or point of view is good or right

outline
to organize a set of facts or ideas by listing main points and subpoints

prove
to bring out the truth by giving evidence

review
to reexamine or summarize key characteristics or points.

state
to present a concise statement of a position, fact, or point of view

summarize
to present the main points of an issue in a shortened form

trace
to present a series of related facts in a step-by-step sequence

L○3 Understand objective questions.

Here are tips for success when responding to standard types of objective questions:

True/False

- Read the entire question. If any part is false, the answer is false.
- Pay attention to words, numbers, names, and dates.
- Note that most statements with *all, every, always,* and *never* are false.
- Don't be confused by double negatives.

Matching

- Read both lists first, noting similar descriptions.
- When matching words, match the part of speech: noun to noun, verb to verb, and so on.
- When matching words to phrases, start with the phrase and go to the word.
- Cross out each answer as it is used, unless answers can be used more than once.
- If you need to write individual letters, use capital letters, which are more distinct than lowercase.

Multiple-Choice

- Read the directions and note whether you need the correct answer, the best answer, or all correct answers.
- Watch for negative words like *not, never, except,* and *unless.*
- Think of the answer before looking at the choices.
- Read all choices before selecting an answer.

Chapter Summary

LO1 Understand academic research.

Think of a **research paper** as a long essay (5 to 15 pages) with a thesis statement, supporting evidence, integrated sources, and documentation. It should have a formal or semiformal voice. (Check with your instructor to find out if "I" or "you" voice is allowed.) Research involves getting started, planning, conducting research, and organizing and drafting.

LO2 Initiate the process.

Getting started includes four tasks:

1. **Understand the assignment,** noting options and restrictions.
2. **Select a manageable topic,** narrowing from a general subject area to a specific topic.
3. **Brainstorm research questions,** including simple and complex questions and main and secondary questions.
4. **Develop a working thesis,** offering a preliminary answer to the main research question.

LO3 Develop a research plan.

Begin by determining what you already know, and plan on doing four types of research:

- **Background research** helps you determine what resources are available to you.
- **Primary research** provides firsthand information through interviews, observations, experiments, original documents, and artifacts.
- **Library research** grounds your paper in scholarly books and articles.
- **Internet research** puts free Web and deep Web resources at your fingertips.

LO4 Explore possible resources and sites.

Consider the wide variety of resources available to you:

- Primary resources
- Reference works and books
- Articles
- Audiovisual, digital, and multimedia sources
- Government and business publications

Consider the information sites available as well.

- People and primary research
- Libraries
- Computer resources
- Mass media
- Government and business sites

Glossary Terms

joie de vivre
French for "joy of life," a quality in people who live life to its fullest

research paper
a fairly long essay (5–15 pages), complete with thesis statement, supporting evidence, integrated sources, and careful documentation

working thesis
a preliminary answer to your main research question, the focus of your research

Library of Congress classification
a system of classification (and organization) used in most academic and research libraries

artifact
any object made or modified by a human culture

Boolean operators
words or symbols used when searching research databases and that describe the relationship between various words or phrases in a search

working bibliography
a list of sources that you have read and/or intend to use in your research

annotate
underline or highlight important passages in a text and make notes in the margins

summarize
to condense in your own words the main points in a passage

paraphrase
to put a whole passage in your own words

quotation
a word-for-word statement or passage from an original source

L◯5 Conduct keyword searches.

Keyword searching can help you find solid information in electronic library catalogs, online databases, print indexes, Internet resources, print books, and e-books. Follow these tips:

- **Choose keywords carefully,** brainstorming a list and consulting the **Library of Congress** subject headings.
- **Use keyword strategies,** getting to know the database, modifying your keywords to broaden or narrow the search, and using **Boolean operators** (and, +, not, -, or, and so on).

L◯6 Evaluate sources.

Not all sources are created equal. To make certain you end up with quality information, you need to evaluate sources.

- **Use** scholarly sources, trade books, government publications, reference works, textbooks, and news reports from reputable outlets.
- **Avoid** sales material, blog articles, talk radio discussions, unregulated Web material, and tabloid articles.

As you evaluate the reliability of a source, look for credible authors, reliable publications, unbiased discussion, current and accurate information, logical support, quality writing and design, and a positive relationship with other sources.

L◯7 Create a working bibliography.

As you research, create a working bibliography that tracks the source material you are using. See the chapter for sample working bibliography entries for books, periodicals, online sources, and primary or field research.

L◯8 Review note taking.

Use a note-taking system that lets you efficiently glean information, engage sources, and note quotations and paraphrases. Consider these systems:

1. **Paper or electronic note cards** let you record one point per card and note the source.
2. **Copy (or save) and annotate** lets you selectively photocopy, print, or save important sources, adding identifying information.
3. **A computer notebook or research log** lets you take notes on sources, using initials to distinguish your thinking from source material.
4. **A double-entry notebook** lets you record material from sources in one column and your thinking or reflections in a second column.

L◯9 Summarize, paraphrase, and quote source material.

As you take notes, use these three strategies:

- **Summarize useful passages,** capturing the main point in a few words.
- **Paraphrase key passages,** putting a whole passage in your own words.
- **Quote specific sentences,** when the original source makes an important point in a concise and powerful way.

Chapter Summary

LO1 Understand sources.

Research projects generally include primary sources (providing firsthand information) and secondary sources (providing secondhand information) but should avoid tertiary sources (third-hand information).

LO2 Conduct primary research.

Primary research includes surveys, questionnaires, interviews, observations, inspections, field research, experiments, documents, and artifacts. (See the chapter for guidelines and a model of a survey.)

When working with documents and artifacts, do the following:

- Choose evidence close to your topic.
- Frame your examination with questions.
- Put the document or artifact in context.
- Draw coherent conclusions about meaning.
- Think about your discipline

LO3 Use the library.

The library offers numerous aids to help with your research, including librarians, collections, research tools, subscription databases, and special services.

A catalog search will produce a list of materials that may assist your research, and indicates where the materials can be found in the library. Many libraries use **Library of Congress** call numbers to organize their materials, but other libraries use the Dewey decimal system.

LO4 Use books.

To get the most out of books, follow these steps:

- Check out front and back information.
- Scan the table of contents.
- Using key words, search the index.
- Skim the foreword, preface, or introduction.
- Check **appendices, glossaries**, or **bibliographies**.
- Carefully read appropriate chapters and sections.

Consider special informational resources, such as **encyclopedias, almanacs, yearbooks,** statistical resources, vocabulary resources, biographical resources, **directories**, guides, handbooks, **indexes**, bibliographies, and **abstracts**.

Glossary Terms

primary sources
original sources that give firsthand information about a topic

secondary sources
sources that are at least once removed from the original; sources that provide secondhand information

tertiary sources
sources that provide thirdhand information, such as wikis; discouraged for college research projects

survey/questionnaire
a set of questions created for the purpose of gathering information from respondents about a specific topic

observation
noting information received in person through the senses

inspection
the purposeful analysis of a site or situation in order to understand it

field research
an on-site scientific study conducted for the purpose of attaining raw data

closed questions
questions that can be answered with a simple fact or with a *yes* or a *no*

open-ended questions
questions that require elaborate answers

original document
a record that relates directly to an event, an issue, an object, or a phenomenon

collections
the materials housed within a library

subscription database
an online service that, for a fee, provides access to hundreds of thousands of articles

Library of Congress call numbers
a set of numbers and letters specifying the subject area, topic, and authorship or title of a book

appendixes
sections (in a book) that provide additional or background information

glossaries
lists of important terms and their definitions

bibliographies
lists of works that cover a particular subject

encyclopedias
reference works filled with articles written about a variety of topics

almanacs/yearbooks
regularly published references that chronicle the major events of a specific time period

directories
references that provide contact information for people, groups, and organizations

indexes
searchable lists of resources on various topics

abstracts
summaries of resources; a collection of summaries in a specific subject area

periodicals
publications or broadcasts produced at regular intervals (daily, weekly, monthly, quarterly)

magazines
weekly, monthly, or semimonthly publications providing information to a broadly focused audience

journals
generally quarterly publications providing specialized scholarly information for a narrowly focused audience

Internet
a worldwide network of connected computers that allows a sharing of information

World Wide Web
the collection of Web sites on the Internet accessible to Web browsers and search engines

hypertext link
a clickable bit of text that connects the user to another location on the Web

Web site
a group of related Web pages posted by the same sponsor or organization

Web page
a page viewable as a single unit on a Web site

Web browser
a program that provides access to Web resources through a variety of tools

LO5 Find periodical articles.

Periodicals includes newspapers, newscasts, magazines, and journals. Often, the best way to access periodical articles is through an online database such as EBSCOhost. Through a basic or advanced search, you will receive a citation list with identifying information. Select a promising article, and access the full-text version of it.

LO6 Understand the Internet.

The **Internet** allows computers to access files on many different computers in many different locations. Each file has a unique Internet address called a **URL,** which includes a **domain name** identifying the site and type of organization that created it. When you find information you wish to access again, you can **bookmark** it, print it out, save or download it, or e-mail it to yourself.

LO7 Find reliable information.

Much information on the Internet is valuable and accurate, but much is not. That's why you need to make certain you select reliable sites. Make sure your sources are sponsored by legitimate, recognizable organizations, such as government agencies, nonprofit groups, and educational institutions. Avoid relying on personal, commercial, and special interest sites.

Use **search engines** to find information online, as well as **metasearch tools,** which search basic search engines. Also remember to use deep-Web tools to discover sources not accessible to basic search engines. For searches, follow these steps:

1. **Begin the search with precise terms.** Use quotation marks around exact phrases.
2. **Study the results and refine your search.** Narrow or broaden your search as needed, and click through to find promising materials.

deep Web
Internet materials not accessible via popular search engines but available through a library's subscription databases

URL
the uniform resource locator; the Web address telling the browser how to access a certain file

domain name
the name of a site, including the extension after the dot (.), which indicates what type of organization created the site

bookmark
a digital tag that allows the user to easily return to a favorite site

subject tree
a listing of Web sites, arranged by experts

search engines
sites that search other Web sites using key words

metasearch tools
sites that search other search engines

Chapter Summary

LO1 Avoid plagiarism.

Plagiarism is using someone else's words, ideas, or images so they appear to be your own. Plagiarism is stealing, and colleges punish it as such. It may result in a failing grade for the assignment or course, a note on your academic transcript, and possibly even expulsion.

Plagiarism comes in many forms:

- Submitting another writer's paper as your own.
- Pasting material into your paper and passing it off as your own.
- Using material without quotation marks and citation.
- Failing to cite a source for summarized or paraphrased ideas.

To avoid plagiarism, do the following:

- **As you research,** take orderly notes and maintain an accurate **working bibliography**.
- **As you write,** carefully credit all material that is quoted, summarized, or paraphrased from another source.
- **After you write,** compile a complete, accurate works-cited or references list with full source information for all borrowed material.

LO2 Avoid other source abuses.

Sources should be treated carefully in a research paper. Avoid these other source abuses:

- **Using sources inaccurately,** so that the original is misrepresented
- **Using source material out of** context, so that the original meaning is distorted
- **Overusing source material,** so that your own thinking disappears
- **"Plunking" quotations,** by using them with no lead-up or follow up
- **Using blanket citations**, so that it is difficult to determine where source material begins and ends
- **Relying heavily on one source,** so that your research lacks depth and breadth
- **Failing to match in-text citations to bibliographic entries** by including sources in one place but not the other
- **Double-dipping** by turning in an assignment in two different classes without first getting permission from instructors
- **Falstaffing** by writing a paper for someone else or having the person write a paper for you.
- **Violating copyright** by copying, distributing, or posting intellectual property without permission of the holder.

LO3 Use sources well.

When you use sources in your writing, integrate them carefully. First, state and explain your idea, creating context for the source. Then identify and introduce the source, and summarize, paraphrase, or quote it. Provide a citation and comment on the source by explaining, expanding on, or refuting it.

Remember, you should clearly identify the start and end of material that is borrowed.

Glossary Terms

paleontologist
a scientist who studies life forms that lived in past geologic time

plagiarism
presenting someone else's work or ideas as one's own

documentation
crediting sources of information through in-text citations or references and a list of works cited or references

academic transcript
the permanent record of educational achievement and activity

working bibliography
list of the sources that you have used and/or intend to use in your research

context
the set of circumstances in which a statement is made; the text and other factors that surround a specific statement and are crucial to understanding it

fair use
rules governing the use of small (not large) portions of text, for noncommercial purposes

public domain
materials provided by the government, provided as part of the "copy left" movement, or generally speaking, materials older than 75 years old

attributive phrase
a group of words that indicates the source of an idea or a quotation

ellipsis
a set of three periods with one space preceding and following each period; a punctuation mark that indicates deletion of material

LO4 Write your research paper.

As you write your research paper, use these quick guidelines:

1. **Review your research materials,** making sure they are complete, reliable, and accurate.
2. **Revisit your research questions and working thesis** and revise accordingly.
3. **Organize your work** using an appropriate pattern, such as cause-effect organization, chronological order, or question-and-answer organization.
4. **Develop your first draft** with the following parts:
   - **Opening:** Gain your reader's attention, establish common ground, and offer your thesis.
   - **Middle:** Develop your thesis by presenting each main point and expanding on it with a variety of details.
   - **Closing:** Reinforce your thesis and draw a conclusion.
5. **Revise and edit your work** using the checklists below.

Revising Checklist

_____ Is my thesis clear?

_____ Do I have strong main points to support it?

_____ Are the main points supported with evidence and analysis?

_____ Have I used an organizational plan that fits the assignment, my topic, and purpose?

_____ Do the main points appear in the best order?

_____ Are the paragraphs in the best order? The sentences within the paragraphs?

_____ Is my writing voice objective and scholarly, focused on the topic?

_____ Is my writing voice knowledgeable and engaging?

_____ Have I selected strong words and correctly used topic-specific terms?

_____ Do my sentences read smoothly?

Editing Checklist

_____ Have I correctly punctuated sentences and abbreviations?

_____ Have I used correct capitalization with proper nouns?

_____ Have I double-checked the spelling of all specialized words, author names, and titles?

_____ Have I watched for easily confused words (*there, their, they're*)?

_____ Have I carefully checked each in-text citation or reference for correct format? (See pages 254–260.)

_____ Have I carefully checked each entry in my works-cited or references section, making sure that the entries follow the correct format? (See pages 260–266.)

Chapter Summary

LO1 Learn the basics of MLA & APA styles.

Here is a quick rundown of the similarities and differences between **MLA** and **APA** styles:

	MLA	APA
• Is a separate title page required?	No	Yes
• Is an abstract required?	No	Usually
• Is the research paper double-spaced?	Yes	Yes
• Are page numbers required?	Yes	Yes
• Is an appendix required?	No	Maybe
• Are references placed in the text?	Yes	Yes
• Is a list of sources required?	Yes	Yes

Each style has special rules about setting margins, using headings, and displaying longer quotations. (See page 254.)

LO2 Understand in-text citations.

An in-text citation indicates the beginning and ending of material that is summarized, paraphrased, or quoted and identifies the original source. When creating an in-text citation, whether in MLA or APA format, do the following:

- Keep citations brief and integrate them smoothly into your writing.
- Clearly indicate the beginning and ending of borrowed material.
- Make sure citations clearly point to entries in the list of sources.
- When using a shortened title, begin with the first important word.
- Place parenthetical citations before the end punctuation.

Parenthetical Citations	MLA	APA
One author, complete work:	(Baker)	(Baker, 2008)
One author, part of work:	(Baker 5)	(Baker, 2008, p. 5)
Multiple authors:	(Rand and Baker 51)	(Rand & Baker, 2010, p. 51)

Note: In MLA, if the author and title are given in text, the parenthetical citation can provide just the page number:

> In *On the Lam,* Rand and Baker indicate that the rise in homelessness coincided with "least restrictive environment" legislation (51).

LO3 List books and other nonperiodical documents.

LO4 List print periodical articles.

LO5 List online sources.

LO6 List other sources: primary, personal, and multimedia.

See reverse side for MLA and APA Quick Guides.

Research Terms

MLA
the Modern Language Association; the professional organization that sets style decisions for English and humanities disciplines

APA
the American Psychological Association; the professional organization that sets style decisions for psychology, sociology, and other related disciplines

in-text citation
references within the text of a research report, indicating the origin of summarized, paraphrased, or quoted materials

works-cited list
in an MLA paper, a list of all sources cited within the paper, arranged alphabetically by author's last name

references section
in an APA paper, a list of all sources referred to within the paper, arranged alphabetically by author's last name

Quick Guide — MLA Works Cited

The works-cited section lists only the sources you have cited in your text. Begin your list on the page after the text and continue numbering each page. Format your works-cited pages using these guidelines and page 268.

1. Type the page number in the upper right corner, one-half inch from the top of the page, with your last name before it.

2. Center the title *Works Cited* (not in italics or underlined) one inch from the top; then double-space before the first entry.

3. Begin each entry flush with the left margin. If the entry runs more than one line, indent additional lines one-half inch (five spaces) or use the hanging indent function on your computer.

4. End each element of the entry with a period. (Elements are separated by periods in most cases unless only a space is sufficient.) Use a single space after all punctuation.

5. Double-space lines within each entry and between entries.

6. List each entry alphabetically by the author's last name. If there is no author, use the first word of the title (disregard *A, An,* or *The* as the first word). If there are multiple authors, alphabetize them according to which author is listed first in the publication.

7. The *MLA Handbook*, Seventh Edition, requires that each source be identified as *Print, Web,* or other (such as *Television* or *DVD*). For print sources, this information is included after the publisher and date. For Web publications, include *Web.* after the date of publication or updating of the site, and before the date you accessed the site.

8. A basic entry for a book follows:

> Black, Naomi. *Virginia Woolf as Feminist.* Ithaca: Cornell UP, 2004. Print.

9. A basic entry for a journal or magazine follows:

> Stelmach, Kathryn. "From Text to Tableau: Ekphrastic Enchantment in *Mrs. Dalloway* and *To the Lighthouse.*" *Studies in the Novel* 38.3 (Fall 2006): 304-26. Print.

10. A basic entry for an online source is given below. Note that the URL is included only if the reader probably cannot locate the source without it, or when your instructor requires it.

> Clarke, S. N. "Virginia Woolf (1882-1941): A Short Biography." *Virginia Woolf Society of Great Britain.* 2000. Web. 12 Mar. 2008.

Quick Guide — APA References

The reference section lists all the sources you have cited in your text (with the exception of personal communications such as phone calls and e-mails). Begin your reference list on a new page after the last page of your paper. Number each reference page, continuing the numbering from the text. Then format your reference list by following the guidelines below.

1. Type the running head in the upper left corner and the page number in the upper right corner, approximately one-half inch from the top of the page.

2. Center the title, *References,* approximately one inch from the top; then double-space before the first entry.

3. Begin each entry flush with the left margin. If the entry runs more than one line, indent additional lines approximately one-half inch (five to seven spaces), using a hanging indent.

4. Adhere to the following conventions about spacing, capitalization, and italics:

   • Double-space between all lines on the reference page.

   • Use one space following each word and punctuation mark.

   • With book and article titles, capitalize only the first letter of the title (and subtitle) and proper nouns.

   Example: *The impact of the cold war on Asia.*

(Note that this capitalization practice differs from the presentation of titles in the body of the essay.)

   • Use italics for titles of books and periodicals, not underlining.

5. List each entry alphabetically by the last name of the author, or, if no author is given, by the title (disregarding *A, An,* or *The*). For works with multiple authors, use the first author listed in the publication.

6. Follow these conventions with respect to abbreviations:

   • With authors' names, generally shorten first and middle names to initials, leaving a space after the period. For a work with more than one author, use an ampersand (&) before the last author's name.

   • For publisher locations, use the full city name plus the two-letter U.S. Postal Service abbreviation for the state. For international publishers, include a spelled-out province and country name.

   • Spell out "Press" or "Books" in full, but omit unnecessary terms like "Publishers," "Company," or "Inc."

Chapter Summary

LO1 Period

Use a period . . .

- after sentences other than questions or strong commands.
- after initials and abbreviations and as decimal points in numbers.

LO2 Ellipsis

Use an **ellipsis** to show omitted words and to show pauses.

LO3 Comma

Use commas . . .

- between **independent clauses** along with a coordinating conjunction.
- between items in a **series**, including the second-to-last item.
- to separate **equal adjectives**.
- to set off **nonrestrictive appositives**.
- to set off **adverb dependent clauses** that begin a sentence or are nonessential.
- after introductory phrases.
- to set of transitional expressions.
- to set off items in addresses and dates (July 2, 2010).
- to set off dialogue.
- to separate nouns of **direct address**.
- to separate interjections from the rest of the sentence.
- to set off interruptions from the rest of the sentence.
- to separate numbers into hundreds, thousands, millions, and so forth.
- to enclose explanatory words.
- to separate contrasted elements.
- before **tags**.
- to enclose titles or initials.
- for clarity or emphasis.

LO4 Semicolon

Use a semicolon . . .

- to join two closely related independent clauses.
- before **conjunctive adverbs** used in a compound sentence.
- before transitional phrases in a compound sentence.
- to separate independent clauses containing commas.
- to separate items in a series that contains commas.

LO5 Colon

Use a colon . . .

- after **salutations** in business letters.
- between numbers indicating time or ratios.
- for emphasis.
- to distinguish parts of publications.
- to introduce quotations or a list (with a complete sentence before it).

Punctuation Terms

ellipsis
a set of three periods with one space preceding and following each period; a punctuation mark that indicates deletion of material

independent clause
a group of words that includes a subject and predicate and expresses a complete thought

series
a sequence of words, phrases, or clauses

equal adjectives
two or more adjectives that modify a word equally (they can be placed in any order)

nonrestrictive appositive
a group of words that renames or modifies the word it follows but does not provide essential information

adverb dependent clauses
subordinate clauses that answer one of the adverb questions: *how, when, where, why, to what degree, how often*

direct address
use of a name or title to speak directly to someone

tags
short statements or questions at the ends of sentences

conjunctive adverb
words such as *also, besides, however, instead, meanwhile then,* and *therefore*

salutation
the *Dear* line in a business letter

indirect question
a question embedded within a statement
(he asked if we were going)

L◯6 Hyphen

Use a hyphen . . .

- to make compound words.
- to join letters to words *(T-shirt, U-turn)*.
- in numbers *twenty-one* to *ninety-nine*.
- to prevent confusion *(re-create)*.
- to join numbers indicating a range.
- to divide words at the end of lines.

L◯7 Dash

Use a dash . . .

- to set off nonessential elements.
- to set off an introductory series.
- for missing text—interrupted speech.
- for emphasis.

L◯8 Question Mark

Use a question mark . . .

- after direct questions, (but not after **indirect questions**).
- after questions in quotations, parentheses, or brackets.

L◯9 Quotation Marks

Use quotation marks . . .

- for direct quotations.
- around titles of short works.
- for words discussed as words.
- for slang and ironic usages.

L◯10 Italics (Underlining)

Use italics (in print) or underlining (in handwriting) . . .

- for titles of long works.
- for key terms and foreign words.

L◯11 Parentheses

Use parentheses . . .

- to enclose explanatory material.
- to set off numbers in a list.
- for parenthetical sentences.
- to set off references.

L◯12 Diagonal

Use a diagonal (slash) to form fractions, show choices, or show line breaks in quoted poetry.

L◯13 Brackets

Use brackets to add clarifications or comments to quoted material.

L◯14 Exclamation Point

Use an exclamation point to express strong feeling or to set off interjections.

L◯15 Apostrophe

Use an apostrophe . . .

- in contractions to replace the missing letters.
- to form possessives *(Joan's, the Jones's)*.
- in plurals of letters, numbers, signs, and words used as words *(A's, 2's, +'s, and's)*.

Chapter Summary

LO1 Capitalization

- **Proper Nouns and Adjectives** Capitalize all proper nouns and adjectives.
- **First Words** Capitalize the first word in a full-sentence direct quotation.
- **Sentences in Parentheses** Capitalize the first word in a sentence that is enclosed in parentheses if that sentence is not contained within another complete sentence.
- **Sentences Following Colons** Capitalize a complete sentence that follows a colon when that sentence is a formal statement, a quotation, or a sentence that you want to emphasize.
- **Salutation and Complimentary Closing** Capitalize the first and all major words of the salutation in a letter; capitalize the first word of a complimentary closing.
- **Sections of the Country** Words that indicate sections of the country should be capitalized; words that simply indicate direction should not be capitalized.
- **Languages, Ethnic Groups, Nationalities, and Religions** Capitalize all words relating to the preceding list.

- **Titles** Capitalize the first word of a title, the last word, and every word in between except articles (*a, an, the*), short prepositions, *to* in an infinitive, and coordinating conjunctions.
- **Organizations** Capitalize the name of an organization or a team and its members.
- **Abbreviations** Capitalize abbreviations of titles and organizations.
- **Words Used as Names** Capitalize words like *mother* and *senator* when they are parts of titles that include a personal name or when they are substituted for proper nouns.
- **Titles of Courses** Words such as *technology, history,* and *science* are capitalized as proper nouns when they are included in the titles of specific courses.
- **Internet and E-Mail** The words *Internet* and *World Wide Web* are always capitalized because they are considered proper nouns.

LO2 Plurals

- **Nouns Ending in a Consonant** Plurals of most nouns are formed by adding an *s* to the singular form. The plurals of nouns ending in *sh, ch, x, s,* and *z* are made by adding *es* to the singular form.
- **Nouns Ending in y**
  - The plurals of common nouns that end in *y* (preceded by a consonant) are formed by changing the *y* to *i* and adding *es*.
  - The plurals of common nouns that end in *y* (preceded by a vowel) are formed by adding only an *s*.
- The plurals of all proper nouns ending in *y* (whether preceded by a consonant or a vowel) are formed by adding an *s*.
- **Nouns Ending in o**
  - The plurals of words ending in *o* (preceded by a vowel) are formed by adding an *s*.
  - The plurals of most nouns ending in *o* (preceded by a consonant) are formed by adding *es*.

- **Nouns Ending in f or fe** The plurals of nouns that end in *f* or *fe* are formed in one of two ways: If the final *f* sound is still heard in the plural form of the word, simply add *s;* if the final sound is a *v* sound, change the *f* to *ve* and add an *s*.
- **Words Discussed as Words** The plurals of symbols, letters, figures, and words discussed as words are formed by adding an apostrophe and an *s*.
- **Nouns Ending in ful** The plurals of nouns that end with *ful* are formed by adding an *s* at the end of the word.
- **Compound Nouns** The plurals of compound nouns are usually formed by adding an *s* or an *es* to the important word in the compound.
- **Collective Nouns** Collective nouns do not change in form when they are used as plurals. Use a singular pronoun *(its)* to show that the collective noun is singular. Use a plural pronoun *(their)* to show that the collective noun is plural.

L◯3 Numbers

- **Numerals or Words** Numbers from one to one hundred are usually written as words; numbers 101 and greater are usually written as numerals. (APA style uses numerals for numbers 10 and higher.)
- **Numerals Only** Use numerals for the following forms: decimals, percentages, pages, chapters (and other parts of a book), addresses, dates, telephone numbers, identification numbers, and statistics.
- **Hyphenated Numbers** Hyphens are used to form compound modifiers indicating measurement. They are also used for inclusive numbers and written-out fractions.

- **Time and Money** If time is expressed with an abbreviation, use numerals; if it is expressed in words, spell out the number. If money is expressed with a symbol, use numerals; if the currency is expressed in words, spell out the number.
- **Words Only** Use words to express numbers that begin a sentence. Use words for numbers that precede a compound modifier that includes a numeral. Use words for the names of numbered streets of one hundred or less. Use words for the names of buildings if that name is also its address. Use words for references to particular centuries.

L◯4 Abbreviations

- An abbreviation is the shortened form of a word or a phrase. These abbreviations are always acceptable in both formal and informal writing: *Mr. Mrs. Dr. Jr. a.m. (A.M.).*

- When abbreviations are called for (in charts, lists, bibliographies, notes, and indexes, for example), standard abbreviations are preferred. Reserve the postal abbreviations for zip code addresses.

L◯5 Acronyms and Initialisms

- An acronym is a word formed from the first (or first few) letters of words in a set phrase. Even though acronyms are abbreviations, they require no periods.
  - Example: **NASA** National Aeronautics and Space Administration

- An initialism is similar to an acronym except that the initials used to form this abbreviation are pronounced individually.
  - **CIA** Central Intelligence Agency

L◯6 Basic Spelling Rules

- **Write *i* Before *e*** Write *i* before *e* except after *c,* or when sounded like *a* as in *neighbor* and *weigh.*
  - Examples: *believe, relief, eight*
- **Words with Consonant Endings** When a one-syllable word *(bat)* ends in a consonant *(t)* preceded by one vowel *(a),* double the final consonant before adding a suffix that beings with a vowel *(batting).*
  - Examples: sum—**summary,** god—**goddess**

- **Words with a Final Silent *e*** If a word ends with a silent *e,* drop the *e* before adding a suffix that begins with a vowel. Do *not* drop the *e* when the suffix begins with a consonant.
- **Words Ending in *y*** When *y* is the last letter in a word and the *y* is preceded by a consonant, change the *y* to *i* before adding any suffix except those beginning with *i.*

L◯7 Commonly Misspelled Words

Steps to Becoming a Better Speller:

1. Be patient.
2. Check the correct pronunciation of each word you are attempting to spell.
3. Note the meaning and history of each word as you are checking the dictionary for the pronunciation.
4. Before you close a dictionary, practice spelling the word.
5. Learn some spelling rules.
6. Make a list of the words that you misspell.
7. Write often.

Chapter Summary

LO1 Noun

A **noun** names a person, a place, a thing, or an idea.

Classes of Nouns

common woman	or	**proper** Katie Couric
individual journalist	or	**collective** team
concrete desk	or	**abstract** integrity

Nouns also have three forms:

- **number** (singular or plural)
- **gender** (masculine, feminine, neuter, or indefinite)
- **case** (nominative, possessive, objective)

LO2 Pronoun

A **pronoun** is used in place of a noun. An antecedent is the word the pronoun replaces. Pronouns have seven classes:

- **personal** (I, me, you, she, it)
- **reflexive and intensive** (myself, yourself, himself)
- **relative** (who, which, that)
- **indefinite** (all, another, few)
- **interrogative** (who, whose)
- **demonstrative** (this, that)
- **reciprocal** (each other, one another)

Pronouns have **number**, **gender**, and **case** and designate **person**.

LO3 Verb

A **verb** shows action, helps a main verb, or links words to the subject.

An **action verb** can be **transitive** (with a direct object) or **intransitive** (no direct object).

An **auxiliary verb** helps another verb form **tense**, **mood**, and **voice**.

Grammar Terms

noun
a word that names a person, a place, a thing, or an idea

common noun
a general name of a person, a place, a thing, or an idea

proper noun
a capitalized noun that names a specific person, place, thing, or idea

collective noun
a noun that names a group or a unit

abstract noun
a noun that names an idea, a condition, or a feeling

number
singular or plural

gender
masculine, feminine, neuter, or indefinite

case
nominative, possessive, or objective

nominative
a word used as a subject or predicate nominative

possessive
a word showing ownership

objective
a word used as an object

pronoun
a word used in place of a noun

antecedent
the word replaced by a pronoun

personal pronoun
a pronoun referring to a specific person or thing

reflexive pronoun
a personal pronoun ending in –self or –selves

relative pronoun
a pronoun that relates an adjective dependent clause to the noun or pronoun it modifies

indefinite pronoun
a pronoun that refers to unnamed or unknown people, places, or things

interrogative pronoun
a pronoun that asks a question

demonstrative pronoun
a pronoun that points out people, places, and things

person
whether the person is speaking, spoken to, or spoken about (first, second, or third person)

verb
a word that shows action, links words, or accompanies another verb

action verb
a verb that shows action

transitive verb
a verb that takes a direct object

intransitive verb
a verb that does not take a direct object

auxiliary verb
a verb that joins with another verb to form tense, mood, and voice

Glossary Terms

linking verb
an intransitive verb followed by a predicate nominative or adjective

tense
the time of an action or a state of being (past, present, future)

past tense
action happening previously

present tense
action happening now or regularly

future tense
action that will take place later

progressive tense
action continued over time

perfect tense
action completed at one time

voice of a verb
whether the subject is acting or being acted upon

active voice
a voice that indicates the subject is doing the action

passive voice
a voice indicating that the subject is being acted upon

mood of a verb
the tone or attitude with which a statement is made

indicative mood
the mood used to state a fact or ask a question

subjunctive mood
the mood used to express a wish, an impossible or unlikely condition, or a necessity

verbal
a word made from a verb but functioning as a noun, an adjective, or an adverb

gerund
a verbal ending in *ing* and functioning as a noun

infinitive
a verbal formed from *to* and the base form of the verb and used as a noun, an adjective, or an adverb

participle
a verbal ending in *ing* or *ed* and functioning as an adjective

irregular verbs
verbs that form the past tense and past participle by changing the word itself, not merely by adding *d* or *ed*

adjective
a word that describes or modifies a noun or pronoun

proper adjective
a capitalized adjective formed from a proper noun

predicate adjective
an adjective that follows a linking verb and describes the subject

positive form
an adjective or adverb in its regular form, describing a word without comparing it

comparative form
an adjective or adverb that compares two things (using -*er*, *more*, or *less*)

superlative form
an adjective or adverb that compares three or more things (using –*est*, *most*, or *least*)

adverb
a word that describes or modifies a verb, an adjective, another adverb, or a whole sentence

preposition
a word or group of words that shows a relationship between its object and another word in the sentence

prepositional phrase
a phrase formed from a preposition, the object of the preposition, and the modifiers of the object

conjunction
a word that connects individual words or groups

coordinating conjunction
a conjunction that shows an equal relationship between things it connects

correlative conjunction
conjunctions that come in pairs (such as *either/or*)

subordinating conjunction
a conjunction connecting clauses and showing an unequal relationship

interjection
a word or group of words that communicates emotion or surprise

A **linking verb** connects the subject to a noun, a pronoun, or an adjective.

Verbs have **number, person,** and **tense** (past, present, future). **Active voice** means the subject is acting, and **passive voice** that it is acted upon.

Verbals include **gerunds, infinitives,** and **participles**.

LO4 Adjective

An **adjective** describes a noun or pronoun. A **proper adjective** is formed from a proper noun and is capitalized.

Adjectives have **positive, comparative,** and **superlative** forms.

LO5 Adverb

An **adverb** describes a verb, an adjective, an adverb, or a whole sentence. Adverbs describe *time, place, manner,* and *degree.* They have **positive, comparative,** and **superlative** forms.

LO6 Preposition

A **preposition** relates a noun or pronoun to another word. A **prepositional phrase** functions as an adjective or adverb.

LO7 Conjunction

A **conjunction** connects words. **Coordinating conjunctions** connect them equally, and **subordinating conjunctions** connect clauses unequally. A **correlative conjunction** has two parts *(both/and)*.

LO8 Interjection

An **interjection** expresses emotion and is set off by a comma or an exclamation point.

Chapter Summary

LO1 Using Subjects and Predicates

A **sentence** is made up of a subject (sometimes understood) and a predicate.

The subject names the person or thing either performing the action, receiving the action, or being described or renamed. There are five types of subjects to think about: (1) **simple subject**, (2) **complete subject**, (3) **compound subject**, (4) **understood subject**, and (5) **delayed subject**.

The predicate, which contains the verb, is the part of the sentence that either tells what the subject is doing, tells what is being done to the subject, or describes or renames the subject. There are five types of subjects to think about: (1) **simple predicate**, (2) **complete predicate**, (3) **compound predicate**, (4) **direct object**, and (5) **indirect object**.

LO2 Using Phrases

A phrase is a group of related words that functions as a single part of speech. A phrase lacks a subject, a predicate, or both.

There are several types of phrases: *verb, verbal, prepositional, appositive,* and absolute.

- **Verb phrase:** a main verb and its helping verbs.
  Example: Students, worried about exams, **have camped** at the library all week.
- **Verbal phrase:** a phrase that expands on one of the three types of verbals: *gerund, infinitive,* or *participle.*
  - A **gerund phrase** consists of a gerund and its modifiers and objects. The whole phrase functions as a noun.
    Example: **Becoming a marine biologist** is Rashanda's dream.
  - An **infinitive phrase** consists of an infinitive and its modifiers and objects. The phrase functions as a noun, an adjective, or an adverb.
    Example: **To dream** is the first step in any endeavor.
  - A **participial phrase** consists of a present or past participle (a verb form ending in *ing* or *ed*) and its modifiers. The phrase functions as an adjective.
    Example: **Doing poorly in biology,** Theo signed up for a tutor.
- **Prepositional phrase:** a phrase beginning with a preposition and ending with an object, a noun or a pronoun; the phrase functions as an adjective or adverb.
  Example: Denying the existence **of exam week** hasn't worked **for anyone** yet.
- **Appositive phrase:** a phrase consisting of a noun and its modifiers and renaming a noun or pronoun that it follows.
  Example: The Olympic-size pool, **a prized addition to the physical education building,** gets plenty of use.
- **Absolute phrase:** a phrase consisting of a noun and a participle (plus the participle's object, if there is one, and any modifiers) and modifying the whole sentence.
  Example: **Their enthusiasm sometimes waning,** the students who cannot swim are required to take lessons.

Sentence Terms

sentence
a group of words that includes at least a subject (sometimes understood) and a verb and expresses a complete thought

simple subject
the subject without the words that describe or modify it

complete subject
the simple subject and the words that describe or modify it

compound subject
two or more simple subjects joined by a conjunction and sharing the same predicate(s)

understood subject
subject that is not stated in the sentence, but the reader clearly understands what the subject is

delayed subject
a subject that follows the verb, in sentences that begin with *There is, There was,* or *Here is*

simple predict
the complete verb without the words that describe or modify it

complete predicate
the verb, all the words that modify or explain it, and any objects or complements

compound predicate
two or more verbs joined by a conjunction, all the words that modify or explain them, and any objects or complements

direct object
the part of the predicate that receives the action of an active transitive verb

indirect object
the part of the predicate that tells to whom/to what or for whom/for what something is done

adverb clause
a clause that modifies a verb, an adjective, or an adverb

adjective clause
a clause that modifies a noun or a pronoun

noun clause
a clause used in place of a noun (subject, direct or indirect object, predicate nominative, or object of preposition)

declarative sentence
a statement

interrogative sentence
a question

imperative sentence
a command

exclamatory sentence
an expression of emotion, punctuated with an exclamation point (or comma)

conditional sentence
a sentence in which one clause depends on another

simple sentence
one independent clause that provides a complete thought

compound sentence
two independent clauses joined by a semicolon or a coordinating conjunction preceded by a comma

complex sentence
an independent clause joined with one or more dependent clauses

compound-complex sentence
a compound sentence joined with one or more dependent clauses

LO3 Using clauses.

A **clause** is a group of related words that has a subject and a verb. An **independent clause** contains at least one subject and one verb, presents a complete thought, and can stand alone as a sentence; a **dependent clause** (also called a subordinate clause) does not present a complete thought and cannot stand alone (make sense) as a sentence.

> Though airplanes are twentieth-century inventions (dependent clause), people have always dreamed of flying (independent clause).

Types of Dependent Clauses
There are three basic types of dependent clauses.

1. **Adverb clause**
   Example: **Because Orville won a coin toss,** he got to fly the power-driven air machine first.
2. **Adjective clause**
   Example: The men **who invented the first airplane** were brothers, Orville and Wilbur Wright.
3. **Noun clause**
   Example: He wants to know **what made modern aviation possible.** (The noun clause functions as the object of the infinitive.)

LO4 Using sentence variety.

Kinds of Sentences

- **Declarative sentence**
  Example: In 1955, Rosa Parks refused to follow segregation rules on a bus in Montgomery, Alabama.
- **Interrogative sentence**
  Example: Do you think Ms. Parks knew she was making history?
- **Imperative sentence**
  Example: Turn your cell phones off.
- **Exclamatory sentence**
  Example: I can't believe your hilarious ring tone!
- **Conditional sentence**
  Example: When I manage my time, it seems I have more of it.

Structure of Sentences

- **Simple sentence**
  Example: My **back aches**. (single subject: *back;* single verb: *aches*)
- **Compound sentence**
  Example: I eat the right foods, and I drink plenty of water.
- **Complex sentence**
  Example: When I can, **I get eight hours of sleep. (**dependent clause, **independent clause**)
- **Compound-complex sentence**
  Example: **I saw a hawk** when I was walking, and **other smaller birds were chasing it. (independent clauses,** dependent clause)

Chapter Summary

LO1 Subject-Verb Agreement

The subject and verb of any clause must agree in both *person* (first, second, or third person) and *number* (singular or plural).

Subject-Verb Agreement Rules:

- **Compound subjects** are connected with and usually require a plural verb.
- **Delayed subjects** must agree with the verb.
- When the subject of a sentence is the title of a work of art, literature, or music, the verb should be singular.
- Singular subjects joined by *or* or *nor* take a singular verb.
- When one of the subjects joined by *or* or *nor* is singular and one is plural, the verb must agree with the subject nearer the verb.
- Generally, **collective nouns** (*faculty, pair, crew, assembly*) take a singular verb. However, when emphasizing differences among individuals in the group or referring to the group as individuals, use a plural verb.
- Some nouns that are plural in form but singular in meaning take a singular verb: *mumps, measles, news, mathematics,* and so on.
- Mathematical phrases and phrases that name a period of time, a unit of measurement, or an amount of money take a singular verb.
- When a **relative pronoun** is used as the subject of a dependent clause, that pronoun's antecedent determines the number of the verb.
- Many indefinite pronouns (*someone, anybody, everything, neither*) serving as subjects require a singular verb.
- Some indefinite pronouns (*both, few, many, most,* and *several*) are plural; they require a plural verb.

LO2 Pronoun-Antecedent Agreement

A pronoun must agree in number, person, and gender with its **antecedent**.

Pronoun-Antecedent Agreement Rules:

- Use a singular pronoun to refer to such antecedents as *each, one, everyone, another,* and so on. *Incorrect:* Each of the maintenance vehicles has **their** doors locked at night. *Correct:* Each of the maintenance vehicles has **its** doors locked at night.
- Do not use a plural pronoun (*they, their*) with a singular noun or an indefinite pronoun (such as *everyone* or *everybody*). *Incorrect:* Everyone should place *their* exam paper in the basket. *Correct:* Everyone should place *her or his* exam paper in the basket. **or** Students should place *their* exam papers in the basket.
- When two or more antecedents are joined by *and,* they are considered plural. *Incorrect:* Revising and editing *is* important in the writing process. *Correct:* Revising and editing are important in the writing process.

LO3 Shifts in Sentence Construction

A shift is an improper change in structure midway through a sentence.

- **Shift in person** *Incorrect:* **One** may get spring fever unless **you** live in California

Sentence Terms

compound subject
two or more simple subjects joined by a conjunction and sharing the same predicate(s)

delayed subject
a subject that follows the verb, in sentences that begin with *There is, There was,* or *Here is*

collective noun
a noun that names a group or unit

relative pronoun
the words *who, which,* and *that,* which relate an adjective clause to the noun or pronoun it modifies

antecedent
the noun that the pronoun refers to or replaces

shift in person
mixing first, second, or third person within a sentence

shift in tense
using more than one tense in a sentence when only one is needed

shift in voice
mixing active with passive voice

unparallel construction
mixing different grammatical forms in elements that are used in pairs or series

fragment
a phrase or dependent clause used as a sentence

comma splice
a mistake made when two independent clauses are connected with only a comma

run-on sentence
two independent clauses joined without adequate punctuation or a connecting word

misplaced modifiers
descriptive words or phrases separated from what they are describing

dangling modifiers
words or phrases that describe something that isn't stated in the sentence

indefinite reference
pronoun that would refer to more than one antecedent

incomplete comparison
the result of leaving out a word or words that are necessary to show exactly what is being compared to what

unclear wording
ambiguous wording resulting in two or more possible meanings

colloquial language
speech suitable for ordinary, everyday conversation but not for formal speech or writing

double negative
two negative words used to express a single negative idea

slang
informal words or phrases used by a particular group of people.

or Florida. *Correct:* **You** may get spring fever unless **you** live in California or Florida.

- **Shift in tense** *Incorrect:* Sheila **looked** at nine apartments before she **had chosen** one. *Correct:* Sheila **looked** at nine apartments before she **chose** one.
- **Shift in voice** *Incorrect:* As you **look** (active) for just the right place, many interesting apartments **will** probably **be seen** (passive). *Correct:* As you **look** (active) for just the right place, you **will** probably see (active) many interesting apartments.
- **Unparallel construction** *Incorrect:* In my hometown, people pass the time **shooting pool, pitching horseshoes,** and **at softball games.** *Correct:* In my hometown, people pass the time **shooting pool, pitching horseshoes,** and **playing softball.**

L◯4 Fragments, Comma Splices, and Run-Ons

- **Fragment** *Incorrect:* Pete gunned the engine. Forgetting that the boat was hooked to the dock. *Correct:* Pete gunned the engine, forgetting that the boat was hooked to the dock.
- **Comma splice** *Incorrect:* People say that being a stay-at-home mom or dad is important, their actions tell a different story. *Correct:* People say that being a stay-at-home mom or dad is important, **but** their actions tell a different story.
- **Run-Ons** *Incorrect:* The Alamo holds a special place in American history it was the site of an important battle. *Correct:* The Alamo holds a special place in American history. It was the site of an important battle.

L◯5 Misplaced and Dangling Modifiers

- **Misplaced modifiers** *Incorrect:* The neighbor's dog has nearly been barking nonstop for two hours. *Correct:* The neighbor's dog has been barking nonstop for **nearly two hours.**
- **Dangling modifiers** *Incorrect:* After standing in line all afternoon, the manager informed us that all the tickets had been sold. *Correct:* **After we had stood in line all afternoon,** we found out that all the tickets had been sold.

L◯6 Ambiguous Wording

- **Indefinite reference** *Incorrect:* When Tonya attempted to put her dictionary on the shelf, it fell to the floor. *Correct:* When Tonya attempted to put her dictionary on the shelf, **the shelf** fell to the floor.
- **Incomplete comparison** *Incorrect:* After completing our lab experiment, we concluded that helium is lighter. *Correct:* After completing our lab experiment, we concluded that helium is **lighter than oxygen.**
- **Unclear wording** *Incorrect:* I couldn't believe that my sister bought a cat with all those allergy problems. *Correct:* I couldn't believe that my sister, **who has allergies,** bought a cat.

L◯7 Nonstandard Language

Nonstandard language is language that does not conform to the standards set by schools, media, and public institutions. Such language is often acceptable in everyday conversation, but not formal writing. Examples: **colloquial language,** double preposition, substitution, **double negative,** and **slang.**